W9-BYK-786

The Regions of Great Britain

See the map opposite and on the Inside covers.

Palace of Westminster and Big Ben from the River Thames, London
© IDREAMSTOCK / age fotostock

THE**GREEN**GUIDE
Great Britain

MICHELIN

How to...

Planning
Your Trip

Introducing
Great Britain

Discovering
Great Britain

Green Guides - Discover the Destination

Main sections

PLANNING YOUR TRIP
The blue-tabbed section gives you **ideas for your trip** and **practical information.**

INTRODUCTION
The orange-tabbed section explores **Nature, History, Art and Culture** and the **Region Today.**

DISCOVERING
The green-tabbed section features Principal Sights by region, **Sights, Walking Tours, Excursions,** and **Driving Tours.**

Region intros

At the start of each region in the Discovering section is a brief introduction. Accompanied by the region maps, these provide an overview of the main tourism areas and their background.

Region maps

Star ratings

Michelin has given star ratings for more than 100 years. If you're pressed for time, we recommend you visit the three or two star sights first:

★★★ Highly recommended

★★ Recommended

★ Interesting

Tours

We've selected driving and walking tours that show you the best of each town or region. Step by step directions are accompanied by detailed maps with marked routes. If you are short on time, you can follow the star ratings to decide where to stop. Selected addresses give you options for accommodation and dining en route.

Addresses

We've selected some of the best hotels, restaurants, cafés, shops, nightlife and entertainment to fit all budgets. See the Legend on the cover flap for an explanation of the price categories. See the back of the guide for an index of where to find hotels and restaurants.

Other reading

- Michelin Guide Great Britain & Ireland
- Eating Out in Pubs
- Green Guide London
- Green Guide Scotland
- Must Sees London
- Road Atlas - Great Britain & Ireland
- Regional Maps 501, 502, 503, 504

Welcome to Great Britain

Three unique countries and many different landscapes make up Great Britain and its surrounding isles. England, Scotland and Wales have been inhabited by Man (*Homo sapiens*) for tens of thousands of years, but have been politically unified only since 1707, so it is little wonder that they boast different cultures, even different languages in some parts. Until quite recently London's fashions and styles held sway over the UK, but with a gradual decentralisation of not only politics, but attitudes and even lifestyles, today cultural diversity is celebrated throughout the land with many regions, towns and villages, refining, reviving and reinventing their own respective identities. Eat local, drink local, shop local and explore local are the new mantras, and have made Britain a much more rewarding place for both overseas and domestic visitors. Moreover, only a century or so ago, Britain ruled a quarter of the world and this influence can also be found throughout the land. Whereas Britain once exported its way of life to the world, now it is a net importer. If you are in search of traditional Britain with all its heritage, history, pomp and high culture however, have no fear – this still plays a vital role, but, as you will discover, nothing stands still for long.

Grassmarket, Edinburgh during Edinburgh Festival Fringe
© Findlay Rankin / age fotostock

Planning Your Trip

Introducing Great Britain

Discovering Great Britain

Prehistoric stones, Avebury, Wiltshire
© stockcam / iStockPhoto.com

Regions of Great Britain

London (pp150-191)

The capital is one of the most cosmopolitan, dynamic, fashionable and cultural cities on Earth, home not only to such iconic images as Big Ben, Tower Bridge, red double-decker buses, and bear-skinned guards, but also thriving Bengali markets, speedboat rides through the Docklands and stunning new views of the city atop the very best of 21C architecture. For a crash course in the whole of British history and culture, it is also an essential first stop.

Surrey, Kent, Sussex (pp192-217)

These three leafy southern counties provide the main gateways to Britain by air, rail and sea. In summer, bohemian Brighton ('London-by-the-Sea'), and year-round, historic Canterbury are the major attractions, but the small towns and rolling downs of Sussex should not be overlooked.

Cliveden, Upper Thames Valley, Oxfordshire
© Ellen Rooney / age fotostock

Hampshire, Dorset, Wiltshire (pp218-253)

These counties form the old heartland of Wessex, in the 11C, the last English kingdom to be invaded by the Danes. Wiltshire is world renowned for Stonehenge, but Avebury is equally enthralling, while Dorset houses mysteries of its own, some of England's loveliest villages and is the home of modern palaeontology with its prehistoric fossils at Lyme Regis. The capital of Hampshire, Winchester, was King Alfred's seat, and capital of England. It is still a fascinating city. Elsewhere, Hampshire is home to ancient 'forest' land and, at Portsmouth, England's naval heritage. It is a rich mix where the distant past is never far away

Chilterns, Oxfordshire, Cotswolds (pp254-279)

The rolling Cotswolds hills are a draw for visitors in search of classic British rural scenery, populated with archetypal English villages, where little has changed in decades. Oxford easily justifies its reputation as one of Britain's top attractions; its university and town is a wealth of culture, history and architectural wonder with a thriving student life. The county is also home to great country houses, notably Blenheim Palace. The Chiltern Hills region is much less explored, but a wonderful place for walking with idyllic villages and scenery of its own.

Bristol, Bath, Somerset (pp280-301)

Cultured Bath, with its Roman springs (open for public bathing) and stunning Regency architecture, is England's finest 18C city, invigorated by first-class independent shopping and pubs. Built upon maritime and engineering trades, buzzing Bristol has a rich dockside heritage and Georgian beauty too. Somerset boasts the picturesque Cheddar Gorge and mythical Glastonbury.

Devon and Cornwall (pp302-337)

England's holiday playground enjoys beaches and crags, historic towns and cities, picture-postcard villages and fishing harbours, unspoiled moors and national parks, stately homes and even statelier gardens, and a fascinating industrial heritage.

East Anglia (pp338-359)

Bucolic East Anglia was a favourite of Constable. Its canvas remains abundantly green, devoid of relief, but blessed by traditional seaside resorts, preserved medieval towns and villages, extensive waterways and the historic university city of Cambridge.

East Midlands (pp360-375)

Nottingham's Robin Hood is the region's star name, and even if there is little evidence of the outlaw, the city has more than just a legend to sustain visitor interest. On the lonely east coast, Lincoln is an historic gem of a city with a remarkable cathedral as the main attraction. En route make sure to stop at Stamford, one of England's best preserved late-medieval stone towns.

West Midlands and the Peak (pp376-407)

The Industrial Revolution began here in Ironbridge amid the idyllic rolling hills and gorges of Shropshire. Today, a series of museums and a re-created village make up Britain's finest industrial heritage complex. A short distance away, in England's second city, Birmingham, you can follow the progress of this revolution via more museums and heritage attractions through to the post Industrial stage of a modern vibrant city now designed for leisure breaks. Its countryside is home to unspoilt shires, magnificent country houses and the world-famous cultural pilgrimage of Shakespeare's birthplace, Stratford-upon-Avon. The caves, dales and hills of the Peak District are among England's earliest tourist destinations.

Ludlow Castle, Shropshire
© Chris Warren / age fotostock

The North West (pp408-429)

The two great cities of Liverpool and Manchester dominate this region. Neither are intrinsically attractive, but amid the jumble of both city centres lie magnificent Victorian buildings, dockland developments and city institutions (including magnificent libraries), while behind the façades are a number of Britain's finest and most fascinating museum collections. Fans of football, music and nightlife should head this way. The walled town of Chester is rich in Roman history, while Blackpool is a long-established and archetypal British seaside resort.

Cumbria and the Lakes (pp430-443)

The Lake District is regarded by many visitors as England's most beautiful countryside. It has inspired poets and writers for over 200 years and is still, justifiably, one of the most popular holiday regions in Britain with attractions as diverse as Beatrix Potter's house and a white-knuckle Via Ferrata. Once regarded as the 'Odd Corner of England', the Lake District, which in 2017 became Britain's newest World Heritage Site, never disappoints.

Yorkshire (pp444-473)

Britain's largest county has arguably more variety than any other. The city of York, with its magnificent minster, outstanding railway museum and rich Roman past, is unmissable. The great outdoors of the dales and moors beckons walkers, while more genteel tourists enjoy the towns of Harrogate and Richmond. Metro types flock to Leeds for shopping, nightlife and museums, while in summer the unspoilt resorts of Scarborough and Whitby are seaside favourites.

The North East (pp474-493)

The dynamic focus of the North East is Newcastle-upon-Tyne. Its famous and distinctive River Tyne 'bridgescape' has been revitalised with iconic 21C riverside arts centres that complement its lively nightlife. Nearby, the small but perfectly formed cathedral city of Durham is one of the jewels of England. On Hadrian's Wall you can walk in the footsteps of the Romans, while at much-loved Alnwick Castle and Garden fans can follow the adventures of Harry Potter.

Goathland Moor, North York Moors National Park
© daverhead / iStockphoto.com

Scotland (pp494-559)

In Scotland, you'll not only find the traditional icons of kilts and tartans, shortbread and whisky, bagpipes, castles and golf, but also a modern country re-inventing itself. A visit to Edinburgh is the perfect introduction to Scotland and a must for its magnificent setting, its peerless Georgian architecture, great museums and art galleries, and its rich history which reflects the story of much of the country. Edinburgh Festival is a wonderful experience if you can avoid sensory overload! Glasgow makes an excellent foil to the capital, not as pretty, but more 'Scottish' in character, with a superb shopping and nightlife scene, and also home to some of the UK's finest museums and galleries.

South of Edinburgh and Glasgow, the Borders are a gentle introduction to the country in terms of scenery and culture, while to the north Loch Lomond and the Trossachs are picture-book touring country. Beyond Perthshire lie some of the most remote parts of Britain. Among the Highland and Islands, expect breathtaking landscapes, revelationary prehistory, and, away from the population centres, a way of life little-changed in decades. Bring warm clothing and a sense of adventure.

Wales (pp560-589)

Like Scotland, Wales offers dramatic mountain scenery and a very different historical and cultural perspective. Wales is the least densely populated country in Britain, and across much of the Principality, particularly in mid-Wales, sheep far outnumber people. Its spectacular castles are a reminder of a violent history with the English.

Cardiff is an excellent introduction to the country, with revitalised docklands, superb museums and many cultural attractions that explore and illustrate the mining and iron-and-steel industries on which modern Wales is founded. Nearby, the Gower peninsula is one of Britain's loveliest coastlines with arguably Wales' best beaches, a claim disputed by Pembrokeshire on the west coast, which is also famous as an extreme sports centre.

North Wales is dominated by Snowdon (Yr Wyddfa), as much an attraction for visitors who simply want to take the train to the summit as it is for serious walkers and rock climbers. The North Wales coastline is home to many beautiful beaches and the famed fantasy village of Portmeirion.

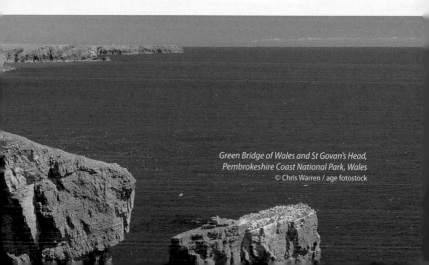

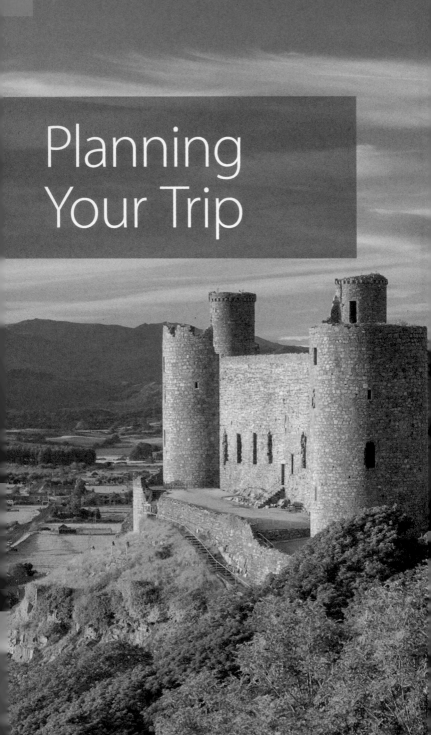

Planning
Your Trip

Harlech Castle, North Wales
© Chris Warren/age fotostock

Planning
Your Trip

Bedruthan Steps, North Cornwall Coast
© Mark Bauer/age fotostock

Inspiration

WHAT'S HOT

– In 2017, **the English Lake District** was awarded Unesco World Heritage status.

– In 2016, **Stratford-upon-Avon** commemorated 400 years since the death of William Shakespeare with a range of new exhibitions.

– The same year, was the 300th anniversary of **'Capability' Brown**, a prominent landscape gardener who created more than 170 gardens in Britain, many of which are still open to the public. His work was commemorated in 2016, which was promoted as the 'Year of the GREAT English Garden'.

– The **National Museums of Scotland** opened 10 new galleries in 2016, displaying internationally important collections of Science and Technology, and Art and Design.

– At **Llantrisant** in South Wales, the Royal Mint, which has been producing coins and medals for numerous countries worldwide for more than 1 100 years, opened a new, purpose-built visitor centre in 2016.

– In 2017, **Kingston-upon-Hull** (see p467) became the UK's Capital of Culture. In 2021, the honour will fall to Coventry.

Grand Gallery, National Museum of Scotland, Edinburgh © Patrice Hauser/hemis.fr

Britain's Cities

The great thing about British cities is their individuality and local character. Each of those mentioned below is recommended not only for its historic sights, vernacular architecture and cultural treasure houses, but for the insight it gives into the character of the nation. Between city and city, town and town, there are long-standing regional and local identities that characterise each and coalesce their idiosyncrasies to generate a synergy of the harmonious relationships, and occasional differences, that exemplify Britain today.

BATH ⓑSee p288

England's most complete and most beautiful Georgian metropolis is also its most elegant small city. Enjoying a picturesque natural setting, it houses the country's best-preserved Roman baths and a superb new thermo-mineral spa. But it is the lovely 18C golden stone crescents and terraces so beloved of Jane Austen, and its individuality (of housing, shopping…) that leave a lasting impression.

BRISTOL ⓑSee p280

Bristol made its fortune from maritime mercantile trade and with the redevelopment of its docks once again looks to the sea. The city also boasts a potent mix of Georgian beauty, as exemplified by the suburb of Clifton (also boasting Britain's most breathtaking bridge), and a vibrant Bohemian contemporary art and music and art scene; its best known son being Banksy.

BIRMINGHAM ⓑSee p390

Britain's second city – in numbers, if not visitor importance – is today a hotbed of shopping and is fast becoming an important European business and cultural centre. By night the world-class Royal Ballet and City Symphony Orchestra entertain, while by day there are some of Britain's finest contemporary and historic buildings, galleries and industrial heritage attractions to enjoy.

CAMBRIDGE ⓑSee p330

England's archetypal small University town, with the magnificent Gothic 15C King's College chapel at its heart, Cambridge is smaller and more intimate than Oxford but shares the same icons of students on bicycles, and punting on the river. Its venerable colleges and libraries (open to the public) are remarkable as much for their architecture and appearance, as for the priceless treasures they guard.

CARDIFF ⓒSee p560

Once the busiest port in the world, Cardiff grew rich on the country's legendary coal and iron industries. But, during the 20C, as these declined, so did Cardiff, and its docks – one of the largest systems in the world became moribund. Today, the port is busy again (albeit a shadow of its glory days), and in a remarkable revival the waterfront has been turned to leisure use and government purposes with some striking buildings.

EDINBURGH ⓒSee p502

The perfect introduction to Scotland, Edinburgh is arguably the most beautiful city in the UK. It enjoys not only a wonderful natural setting, but offers a picture-book history lesson from medieval Old Town to Georgian New Town, best taken in from a series of spectacular vantage points, such as Arthur's Seat and Salisbury Crags, that no other city can equal.

GLASGOW ⓒSee p513

Edinburgh may be Scotland's picture-postcard city, but in terms of arts and culture, world-class museums, stylish places to eat and stay, and some of the best shopping in the UK, Glasgow is every bit the equal, a rough diamond in comparison, but many would say it was more authentic. And for sheer down-to-earth 'Scottishness', it is the nation's number one, a quality epitomised in the name of its official guide: 'People make Glasgow'.

LIVERPOOL ⓒSee p415

This once-great Victorian city and port grew dizzy with 'Beatlemania' and the 'Mersey Beat' in the 1960s, but by the 1980s had plummeted into an economic and civil abyss. Reinvestment in its waterfront and a massive cultural boost paid dividends in the 1990s, and the city became European Capital of Culture in 2008. Its most priceless asset however is its people, whose humorous self-effacing, yet proud outlook, lives long in visitors' memories.

TOURIST OFFICES

Visit Britain (www.visitbritain. com), formerly known as the British Tourist Authority provides assistance in planning a trip to Great Britain and an excellent range of brochures and maps. It works in cooperation with the three National Tourist Boards (for England, Wales and Scotland), the Regional Tourist Boards and other tourist organisations. The official national websites are also very useful:
www.visitengland.com
www.visitscotland.com
www.visitwales.com
www.edinburgh.org

TOURIST INFORMATION

There are **tourist information centres** in all parts of the country with information on sightseeing, accommodation, places to eat, transport, entertainment, sports and local events. They are usually well signposted, but some are open only during the summer season; the address and telephone number of the local tourist office can be found in sidebars throughout this guide.

LONDON ⓒSee p148

Britain's most iconic city is laden with landmarks, imagery and culture, instantly recognisable all over the world. Begin your great British odyssey here, and allow at least three days just to scratch the surface of its myriad attractions and vibrant all-encompassing entertainment scene. Like most major capitals, it is always fascinating, often frantic and largely atypical of the country in general. To experience the 'real' atmosphere of Britain, you'll need to explore far outside its boundaries.

Kelvingrove Art Gallery and Museum, Glasgow

MANCHESTER ⚤See p108

One of England's great mercantile Georgian and Victorian cities, and capital of the North, Manchester's fame is largely thanks to football. Its music and nightlife scene is also highly rated and it is a measure of the city's present cultural significance that the Imperial War Museum North opened here in 2002, and in 2012 the BBC relocated en masse to Manchester, or more precisely to its buzzing new docklands area, Salford Quays, the former site of Manchester Docks.

NEWCASTLE ⚤See p478

Britain's best-loved sculpture, *Angel of the North,* welcomes visitors to Newcastle-upon-Tyne and its dramatic riverside site. Rich history and the distinctive dialect spoken by its population of 'Geordies' give this undisputed capital of the north-east of England an exceptionally strong identity. Despite recent decline, the city retains great vigour as a commercial, educational, entertainment, shopping and cultural centre. As the Guggenheim is to Bilbao, the BALTIC Centre for Contemporary Arts and The Sage music venue are powerful symbols of the city's new cultural ambitions.

OXFORD ⚤See p200

The city of Oxford is famed as the home of England's oldest university. Its romantic townscape of 'dreaming spires' and mellow ancient golden Cotswold stone buildings, buzzes with students on bicycles or punting on the river. For decades it has been the perfect setting for English fiction and television drama. Like Cambridge, its venerable colleges and libraries (open to the public) are remarkable as much for their architecture and appearance, as for the priceless treasures they hold. So diverse is the heritage of Oxford that its buildings alone demonstrate examples of every architectural period since the times of the Saxons.

YORK ⚤See p458

Tourist capital of the north, York is famous for its Minster – arguably the finest building in England. It also boasts the world's finest railway museum (one of the best visitor attractions in the country). But it is the very fabric of this walled city, with its important Roman remains and hundreds of well preserved medieval and Georgian houses, squeezed into tiny lanes and narrow, cobbled alleyways, that draw so many visitors to this characterful city.

25

Historic Properties

B ritain is blessed with more historic properties – castles, palaces, mansions, stately homes and gardens – that are open to the public, than any other country in the world. Moreover the standard of interpretation and what's on offer these days is higher than ever before. Hushed reverential visits standing behind red ropes are a thing of the past; today you are more likely to chat with a colourful costumed character from the property's past, or be able to rent a room and live like a duke and duchess for a night.

CASTLES

Britain's castles are among the finest in the world, with intact fortresses spanning over 800 years, from Windsor Castle (c 1080) to Castle Drogo (begun 1910). Many ruins go back much further. The apogee of castle building was the late 13C and the finest examples are in Wales; in Scotland, travel to the Grampians.

1. Caernarfon Castle (see p575) – was constructed not only as a military stronghold but also as a seat of government and a royal palace, with a striking riverside location.
2. Leeds Castle (see p195) – 'The loveliest castle in the world' lives up to its hype with a picture-book setting on two islands in a lake, sumptuous interiors and glorious grounds.
3. Stirling Castle (see p521) – Similar to Edinburgh Castle in style and location, but without the crowds, it boasts magnificent Renaissance decoration and beautifully refurbished royal apartments.
4. Warwick Castle (see p380) – Built in 1068 on a bend in the River Avon by William the Conqueror, Britain's favourite medieval castle has beautiful grounds and is busy all year round with lavish interpretations of its colourful past.
5. Windsor Castle (see p180) – A castle fit for Royalty, which it has been for over 900 years, with magnificent apartments, chapel and a 'Changing of the Guard', without the crowds that gather around Buckingham Palace in London.

CATHEDRALS

Britain's cathedrals are not only amazing architectural achievements and repositories of centuries of local and national history, but retain their original function as spiritual retreats. Moving with the times however, many now feature visitor centres, refectory cafés, exhibitions, and cathedral tours.

1. Canterbury Cathedral (see p196) – Britain's most famous medieval shrine still attracts hundreds of thousands of visitors each year. Don't miss the atmospheric crypt.
2. Durham Cathedral (see p474) – The great sandstone mass of the Norman cathedral rising above the deep wooded gorge of the River Wear is a sublime fusion of architecture and landscape.
3. St Paul's Cathedral (see p166) – Wren's masterpiece and last resting place is the apogee of English Baroque church architecture. The views from the Whispering Galleries are breathtaking.
4. Westminster Abbey (see p157) – The coronation hall and national pantheon of royalty, statesmen, poets, writers and other heroes, features magnificent monuments and stunning architecture.
5. York Minster (see p458) – The largest Gothic church north of the Alps is world famous for its stained glass; watch the glaziers restoring it and also climb the tower. The minster is the seat of the Archbishop of York, and has been the site of Christian presence since the 4C.

Leeds Castle

ANCIENT BRITAIN

Britain's oldest monuments predate the Pyramids of Egypt. In England, Wiltshire boasts Stonehenge and Avebury, in Scotland the Orkneys and Shetlands are rich in prehistoric remains, and almost anywhere off the beaten track in Wales, Scotland and Cornwall you stumble upon dolmens and standing stones.

1. Avebury (see p242) – Here you can go right up to the giant standing stones (up to 40 tons), and there's a pretty village around them too.

2. Callanish *(Calanais)* **Standing Stones** (see p548) – 'Scotland's Stonehenge', is contemporary with the English monument and scores high on atmosphere thanks to its remote location and lack of crowds

3. Jorvik (see p462) – Step into a 'Time Capsule' to travel back to October 948 and learn all about the Vikings in York, or Jorvik ('Yor-vik') as they called this important trading base.

4. Mousa broch (see p550) – Dating from the 1st or 2nd century AD, and still standing over 13m, this is the finest surviving Iron Age broch (fortified farm) tower in Britain.

5. Stonehenge (see p241) – Most famous of all, the meaning of Stonehege may never be deciphered, but this ring of ancient stones provides fascination for everyone.

STATELY HOMES

The houses of the British aristocracy, complete with reminders of the old class system and 'Upstairs–Downstairs' lifestyle, feed the UK TV schedules and the imaginations of visitors. The finest are comparable to – or even grander than – Britain's royal palaces.

1. Blenheim Palace (see p265) – Vanbrugh's dramatic innovative palatial Baroque masterpiece is matched by Capability Brown's sublime landscaping achievement.

2. Castle Howard (see p464) – Made famous by *Brideshead Revisited*, this is another Vanbrugh triumph of architecture and landscaping.

3. Chatsworth House (see p398) – 'The second Versailles', set in glorious grounds, amid magnificent countryside, not only features one of Europe's outstanding private art collections, but is also one of Northern England's best family days out.

4. Longleat House (see p238) – One of Britain's best examples of High Elizabethan architecture, surrounded by an African safari park, Britain's best mazes and more.

5. Waddesdon Manor (see p254) – The perfect French Renaissance chateau in lush parkland, complete with its world-class Rothschild art, furniture, porcelain and carpets collections.

Llechwedd Slate Caverns

INDUSTRIAL HERITAGE

The world's Industrial Revolution began in the dark Satanic mills of Ironbridge and was refined in the rest of Britain. See not only how things were made (or mined), but also who made them, and how they toiled under often extreme conditions.

1. Big Pit (see p563) and the **National Coal Mining Museum for England** – Go underground at both sites to understand the history and sacrifices of British miners.

2. Black Country Living Museum (see p395) – Costumed actors present the everyday life of a typical mid-19C Black Country coal-mining village, with some 50 reconstructed building and a pit head.

3. Ironbridge (see p386) – The most comprehensive complex of its kind in the world, this fascinating World Heritage site explores early heavy industries, as well as artisan crafts, in sylvan Shropshire surroundings.

4. Llechwedd Slate Caverns (see p581) – Dive into the Welsh hillside aboard a small train, see skilled slate splitters at work and get a taste of early-20C village life.

5. Geevor Tin Mine (see p331) – Still in commercial use until 1990, this is the largest preserved mining site in the UK, with a guided underground tour through 18C and 19C workings.

ROMAN BRITAIN

What did the Romans ever do for us? Although little survives of most major public projects, enough remains to paint a vivid picture of life in this Northern outpost of Empire, which began in 55 BCE with the arrival of Julius Caesar and ended c. AD 410 with the departure of the legions.

1. Chedworth Roman Villa (see p270) – One of the largest Romano-British villas in the country, with fine examples of mosaics and bathhouses.

2. Fishbourne Roman Palace (see p210) – The largest Roman home in Britain, boasting the biggest collection of mosaics still in situ in the UK.

3. Hadrian's Wall (see p482) – Several museums and interpretations of camps and settlements still located on the wall tell us what military and civilian life was like on Rome's physical northwest frontier, separating Caledonia (Scotland) from the rest of Britannia.

4. Roman Baths, Bath (see p286) – A fascinating lesson in how the Romans brought their bathing traditions to Britain, brilliantly told, in spectacular surroundings.

5. Yorkshire Museum (see p463) – many of the country's finest Roman artefacts illustrate the grandeur of life in the Roman capital of Eboracum (York).

VILLAGE LIFE

The quintessential English village features a green – ideally with a duck pond – surrounded by pub, post office, church and a mix of thatched and timbered houses. Even in 21C England many villages are still like this. There are however many other fascinating variations on the theme.

1. Bibury (see p269) – A Cotswolds picture postcard of river, stone bridges, weavers' cottages, Bibury Court and a wooded background.

2. Chipping Campden (see p272) – A perfectly harmonious mellow limestone High Street, late medieval houses and a monumental 'wool church'.

3. Clovelly (see p318) – This striking Mediterranean-style white village, where donkeys and mules are still the only form of transport, tumbles steeply down to the sea.

4. Lacock (see p244) – The National Trust own this four-street stone-and-brick village, which has provided a film set for numerous period TV dramas and movies, including two *Harry Potter* films.

5. Portmeirion (see p582) – 'The Village' is a fantasy Italianate ensemble in a glorious seaside setting, made famous by the cult TV series *The Prisoner*.

ROYAL REALM

Love them or leave them, and most visitors to the UK fall firmly into the former category, there's a never-ending fascination as to how the Royal Family – past and present – go (or went) about their daily and ceremonial lives.

1. Buckingham Palace (see p159) – Step inside the most famous address in Britain and gaze upon the treasures and trappings of its foremost family.

2. Hampton Court Palace & Gardens (see p178) – An evocative insight into the world of Henry VIII (among other monarchs) at Britain's top Tudor palace, with superb interpretation and magnificent grounds.

3. Osborne House (see p226) – This was the favourite home of Queen Victoria for her family holidays and combines royal grandeur with domestic normality.

4. Royal Yacht Britannia (see p510) – Explore every detail of the surprisingly homely ship, which carried Queen Elizabeth II and her family around the world for 44 years on nearly one thousand official engagements.

5. Royal Pavilion Brighton (see p206) – This eye-popping Anglo-Indian confection is like no other royal palace you'll ever see outside the sub-Continent.

Lacock, Wiltshire

© C. Ochterbeck/MICHELIN

Natural World

B ritain is as famous for its well-watered green and pleasant land as its love of horticulture, from classically landscaped parklands with grand vistas and curious follies, to intimate flower-filled gardens.

PARKS AND GARDENS

1. Abbey House Gardens (see p247) – If you think the gardens, in a picture-postcard setting beside Malmesbury abbey, are stunning, wait until you see the Naked Gardeners, who tend them!

2. Eden Project (see p324) – This spectacular family-friendly 21C take on the old botanic garden is one of the world's top eco attractions.

3. Glendurgan Garden (see p328) – Richly planted Cornish garden with subtropical trees and shrubs in a spectacular ravine location dropping down to the waterside.

4. Hidcote (see p274) – A labyrinth of 'garden rooms', some with unusual contents, creates an Alice-in-Wonderland effect at these much-loved Cotswold gardens.

5. Inverewe (see p548) – In a magnificent coastal setting, these Gulf-Stream blessed gardens are in colour almost all year despite sharing the same latitude as St Petersburg.

6. Royal Botanic Gardens, Kew (see p180) – The most famous gardens in Britain feature flowers and plants from every corner of the globe, many in stunning glasshouses.

7. Powis Castle Garden (see p576) – Laid out under the influence of Italian and French styles, this magnificent terraced garden steps down from a picturesque castle.

8. Stourhead (see p239) – A supreme example of English landscape style including a Palladian mansion, fine examples of garden architecture and rare planting.

9. Stowe Landsaped Gardens (see p257) – Stroll back into the 18C through a series of classic bucolic vistas dotted with lakes, bridges, monuments and grand follies.

10. Tresco Abbey gardens (see p335) – Subtropical gardens in the Scilly Isles, which even at the winter equinox have over 300 plants in flower.

Eden Project, Cornwall

© Tamsyn Williams/Eden Project

NATIONAL PARKS

While Britain's many formal parks and garden attractions will suit visitors who enjoy a stroll but still want their creature comforts to hand, hardier types who want to 'get away from it all' and be a bit more energetic, don't need to go far either.

The first National Park, the Peak District, was declared in 1951, the most recent in 2011. In total there are now 15 parks, encompassing protected areas of mountains, meadows, moorlands, woods and wetlands that anyone can visit, and where people live, work and still shape the landscape. Today, millions of visitors use the parks for walking, climbing, cycling, horse riding, canoeing and many other outdoor activities. All parks have visitor centres to advise on a range of activities, from extreme sports (including local places to buy/hire equipment, local experts/guides, etc.) to 'soft adventures' and activities for all the family.

NORTHERN ENGLAND

Northumberland (see p487)

This is England's most tranquil and least visited National Park, where hills and valleys stretch from Hadrian's Wall to the Scottish border. A long-distance walk in the footsteps of the Roman legionaires is a popular activity, while the forest park of Kielder is a great delight and splendidly remote.

Lake District (see p432)

The largest, most picturesque and most eulogised of England's national parks. now enjoying World Heritage Site status, is crowded at peak times in 'honeypot' locations, but there are many quieter areas to be found. Glacial action has created England's highest mountain (Scafell Pike) and its deepest lake (Wastwater), while many charming villages have developed over the centuries to service this walkers' paradise. But there is only one named 'lake', Bassenthwaite; all the rest are 'tarns', 'meres' or 'waters'.

Yorkshire Dales (see p453)

Famed for its walking and long-distance paths, approximately half of the Yorkshire Dales National Park is comprised of farmland. The other half is a dramatic landscape featuring limestone scenery with crags, caves, peaks, and swallow holes.

North York Moors (see p469)

Wilder and harsher in climate and terrain – which varies from high moorland to spectacular coast – than the Dales, the North York Moors park is also known for its walking trails.

The Peak (see p398)

Britain's first national park is the starting point for the 268-mile long Pennine Way. As well as long-distance walking, the park is famous for its many caves, with several showcaves open to visitors, while others are the preserve of speleologists.

SOUTHERN ENGLAND

Exmoor (see p321)

Moorland, where wild red deer and Exmoor ponies roam, woodland, valleys and farmland, all make up this diverse landscape, which culminates in high cliffs that plunge into the Bristol Channel. Horseriding and mountain biking are popular.

Dartmoor (see p314)

Walking, cycling and horseriding are the top activities on this moorland, famous for its many ancient stones and Dartmoor ponies. Letterboxing, the forerunner of geocaching, was first introduced on Dartmoor.

New Forest (see p232)

Despite the name, much of the central New Forest is open heather-covered heath, punctuated by attractive, historic villages, though there are also spectacular ancient and ornamental woodlands. Cycling and horse riding are the favourite activities with watersports on the river Beaulieu and at the coast.

Pen-y-Fan, Brecon Beacons

© tirc83/iStockphoto.com

South Downs (see p209)

This national park in south-east England is unique in that it includes towns and villages within its boundaries. Much of it is gentle rolling countryside is easily explored by walking, cycling or horse riding.

The [Norfolk and Suffolk] Broads (see p352)

Formed from lakes, marshes and flooded peat workings which offer 125mi (200km) of lock-free tidal rivers the main activity on the Broads is, naturally, boating.

SCOTLAND

Cairngorms (see p540)

This Scottish fastness is Britain's last true wilderness. It includes its second highest mountain range: its biggest native forests; sparkling rivers and lochs; and remote moorland and farmland. The UK's premier ski resort, Aviemore, is the winter focus of activities. During the summer, climbing, mountain biking and walking take over.

Loch Lomond & the Trossachs (see p526)

The bonnie banks of Loch Lomond and the picture-postcard Trossachs countryside are perfect for walking, cycling (mountain biking is very popular) and watersports.

WALES

Snowdonia (see p583)

Snowdon is the highest mountain in England and Wales and presides over the most spectacular scenery south of Scotland. However, while anyone of reasonable fitness can ascend Snowdon, there are many possibilities for rock climbers, too (Sir Edmund Hillary trained on Snowdon prior to being the first man to conquer Everest), and the Park is also renowned for mountain biking.

Pembrokeshire Coast (see p571)

The Pembrokeshire Coast National Park may be one of the smallest by area, but it has a coast made up of some of Britain's best beaches, and is remarkable for its high cliffs, rock formations and indented bays. The small offshore islands are a paradise for birdwatchers. Surfing, windsurfing, diving and RIB rides are very popular and coasteering was invented here.

Brecon Beacons (see p569)

This sparsely populated upland area with its eastern extremity on the Welsh border, offers a broad range of activities. The southern belt of limestone cliffs, riddled with sinkholes and caves, is spectacular. But the terrain is tough and often demanding, and used as a training ground for Britain's elite military forces.

USEFUL WEBSITES

TOURIST OFFICES

www.visitbritain.com
www.visitengland.com
www.visitscotland.com
www.visitwales.com
www.visitlondon.com
www.edinburgh.org
www.visitcardiff.com

TRAVEL PLANNING

www.viamichelin.com
Plan your trip with Michelin's online
route planner via the best places
to see, dine and stay. Explore
further with Michelin's online
magazines for tourists, motorists
and gastronomists. You can even
upload details of your own journeys
and discover other users' favourite
journeys to download onto your
Michelin GPS

Digital Guides

http://travel.michelin.com
Useful visitor-oriented and cultural
information on over 85 countries
and more than 30 000 tourist
attractions. You can book hotels
thought the site at attractive
rates without fees (subject to
hotel terms) and there is also a
customisable travel book to
prepare for your next trip.

www.scotland-info.co.uk
The 80 000-word Guide to Scotland
is a personal labour of love by
a Scottish author, largely based
on her personal travels. A very
professional site with excellent
suggestions on accommodation.

www.aboutscotland.com
Well-designed good looking site,
with clickable maps, good pictures,
personally tested accommodation
and lively features and articles
about visiting Scotland.

London

www.londontown.com
www.timeout.com/london
www.tourist-information-uk.com

News

www.bbc.co.uk/news
The BBC front page with breaking
news, magazine stories and links to
the rest of the **BBC website.**

HISTORY & NATURE

♦ **National Trust**
   www.nationaltrust.org.uk
   One of the largest landowners
   in the United Kingdom. Owns
   and protects many heritage
   properties and natural
   beauty spots.

♦ **National Trust for Scotland**
   www.nts.org.uk
   NTS Scotland is concerned with
   preservation and conservation
   of natural and human heritage
   in Scotland.

♦ **English Heritage**
   www.english-heritage.org.uk
   Exists to protect and promote
   England's historic environment
   and over 400 properties (many
   of which are ruins).

♦ **Cadw (Welsh Historic
   Monuments)**
   http://cadw.gov.wales
   Responsible for historic
   monuments in Wales, including
   many famous castles among its
   125 properties.

♦ **Historic Environment Scotland**
   www.historicenvironment.scot
   Responsible for over 300
   historic monuments; formerly
   Historic Scotland.

The Great Outdoors

The temperate climate of Great Britain has helped to make it the home of many outdoor sports and games. There are few days in the year when outdoor activities are impossible and the long coastline, the rivers and lakes, the mountains and lowlands provide opportunities for all kinds of sports. The mild and moist climate has fostered the development of many games played on a flat grass surface – the national pastimes being football (both "soccer" and rugby) in winter, and cricket in summer. Every weekend (weather permitting) from May to September, cricket matches are played on club fields and village green.

CYCLING

Britain is fast becoming a much more cycle-friendly country, in spite of often heavy traffic conditions. Having British riders winning the Tour de France in recent years has certainly helped. Most local tourist information centres will give advice on cycle hire and routes, including traffic-free alternatives. The **National Cycle Network** (www. sustrans.org.uk) comprises around 10 000 miles/16 100km of signposted cycle routes, around a third of which are traffic-free. Just click on their 'Map' link to find routes close to where you're staying. The national association, the Cyclists'Touring Club (CTC) can also help with itineraries and maps.

Cyclists' Touring Club
📞0844 736 8451. www.ctc.org.uk.

FISHING

There are over 6 million fishermen in Britain (2010: freshwater and sea fishing). The season for coarse fishing/ angling (which applies to freshwater fish, other than trout, salmon and char) runs from 15 March to 15 June; permits and advice on local waters can be obtained from any tackle shop. The waters around Britain provide ample opportunity for anglers to test their skills. Salmon and trout fishing, for which licences are required, is found in Scotland, England and Wales. Sea-angling is popular, particularly along the south-western and Northumbrian coastlines. Sea angling festivals are regular features.

Angling Trust
www.anglingtrust.net
Salmon and Trout Association
www.fishpal.com/SalmonAndTrout.

GOLF

Great Britain is the spiritual home of the game and very well supplied with golf courses, ranging from links courses on the coast to inland park courses. Most are privately owned but are happy to accept visitors. Municipal courses are usually very heavily used, with long queues at the first tee at weekends. In Scotland, green fees are less expensive and queues are rare. **Michelin** Maps 501 to 504 and the annual red-cover *Michelin Guide Great Britain & Ireland* give information about golf courses. For more choices visit www.uk-golfguide.com.

GAME SHOOTING

Game shooting takes place all over Britain but the more famous grouse moors are In Scotland, and the shooting season opens on 12 August.

WALKING AND CLIMBING

Throughout the country there are many thousands of miles of bridleways and official footpaths, including way marked **Long Distance Footpaths**, which give access to superb hill and coastal scenery. Some of the very best walking is provided by the national parks. Large sections of the English and Welsh countryside are now designated as 'Access Land', where walkers can roam freely. Under different legislation, this is much the same situation in Scotland, subject to certain restrictions in all countries. For hill walkers and mountaineers, the Lake District, Wales and Scotland provide the most challenging ascents. All walkers and climbers should be aware of the potential dangers and be properly equipped. Rock climbers are also advised to inform the police, or someone else responsible, of their plans before hazardous climbs.

The Ramblers Association
www.ramblers.org.uk is the national body.

Climbers, hill walkers and mountaineers should visit **www.thebmc.co.uk.**

HORSE RIDING

The British have a longstanding love affair with horses and there are professionally run horse riding centres all over the country (even central London), catering to all levels. There is no central UK organisation so ask at the nearest tourist information centre.

BOATING, SAILING AND CRUISING

Britain has many miles of coastline, estuaries, rivers, lakes and canals, all of which offer facilities for enjoying the water. There are all kinds of opportunities for amateur and professional sailors – a cabin cruiser on the Norfolk Broads, a narrowboat on the canal network, a punt or a rowing boat on the river.

On the rivers, lakes and reservoirs there are marinas and moorings for cruisers, yachts and sailing boats; along the coast there are facilities for ocean-going yachts.

Most of the **canal network** has now been rescued from dereliction, and as well as being in use by locals also offers angling, towpath walks and cruises and holidays on narrowboats.

Norfolk Broads
www.enjoythebroads.com.

British Waterways
http://canalrivertrust.org.uk.

Walking over the Packhorse Bridge, Watendlath, Lake District

© Tim Graham/age fotostock

SKIING

Only Scotland has ski resorts – at Lochaber, Glenshee, Lecht and Aviemore in the Cairngorms; Glen Coe, and the Nevis Range near Fort William. All have ski schools and Aviemore is the most fully developed resort. Forest trails have been opened up for cross-country skiing. The best snow conditions are usually found in March and April, but up-to-the minute snow reports are available from **Ski Scotland;** http://ski.visitscotland.com. There are several dry ski slopes all over Britain.

WINDSURFING AND WATERSKIING

Schools and changing facilities for windsurfers are available on many inland waters and at popular places along the coast. Newquay is the UK's surfing capital and the English Surf School is the best source of information; try also www.surfing-waves.com. If you wish to waterski or wakeboard, some clubs offer a day membership system.

English Surf School
www.englishsurfschool.com.

British Water Ski & Wakeboard
www.bwsw.org.uk.

Activities for Kids

B ritain in the 21C is an excellent place for families with children, with a whole host of increasingly sophisticated interactive attractions competing for your attention (beware it can get expensive!).

THINGS TO DO

In this guide, sights of *particular interest* to children are indicated with a KIDS symbol (👪), though rare these days is the visitor attraction that does not cater in some way for young ones. All attractions offer discounts for children and /or discounted family tickets for two or more children. Here are a few highlights:

London & Windsor
– South Kensington Museums
  (see p175)
– Covent Garden (see p164)
– London Zoo (see p168)
– Legoland (see p185)

Surrey, Kent and Sussex
– Thorpe Park (see p194)
– Chessington Adventures (see p194),
– Howletts (see p203)

Hampshire, Dorset, Wiltshire
– Portsmouth Historic Dockyard
  (see p218)
– Dinosaur Isle (see p227)
– Beaulieu Motor Museum (see p232)
– Longleat Safari Park (see p240)

Chilterns, Oxfordshire, Cotswolds
– Woburn Safari Park (see p260)
– Bourton-on-the-Water (see p272)

Bristol, Bath and Somerset
– At-Bristol Science Centre (see p283)
– Bristol Zoo (see p285)
– Wookey Hole (see p294)
– Cheddar Gorge & Caves (see p294)

Devon and Cornwall
– Kents Cavern (see p307)
– Paignton Zoo (see p308)
– National Marine Aquarium (see p311)
– Land's End (see p332)

East Anglia
– Nene Valley Railway (see p357)
– Old Gaol House, King's Lynn
  (see p352)
– Norwich Castle (see p349)

East Midlands
– National Justice Museum (see p362)
  National Space Centre (see p364)

West Midlands and the Peak
– Warwick Castle (see p382)
– Alton Towers (see p405)
– Enginuity/Blists Hill (see p389)
– Cadbury World (see p397)
– Black Country Living Museum
  (see p395)

North West
– Museum of Science and Industry,
  Manchester (see p411)
– Manchester United Museum and
  Stadium Tour (see p413)
– Blackpool (see p425)

Cumbria and the Lakes
– Hill Top (see p433)
– The Lakes Aquarium (see p433)
– Pencil Museum (see p437)

Yorkshire
– Magna Science Adventure Centre
  (see p446)
– Royal Armouries Museum (see p447)
– National Science and Media Museum
  (see p450)
– Mother Shipton's Cave (see p460)
– Jorvik (see p464)
– National Railway Museum (see p465)
– Lightwater Valley (see p458)

North East
– Alnwick Castle & Garden (see p488)
– Beamish (see p478)
– Life Science Centre (see p483)

Scotland
– Edinburgh Zoo (see p512)
– Our Dynamic Earth (see p509)
– Glasgow Science Centre (see p519)
– Riverside Museum (see p519)
– Cairngorm Reindeer (see 538)
– Loch Ness Exhibition (see p546)

Wales
– National Museum Cardiff (see p562)
– Big Pit (see p565)
– Techniquest (see p564)
– National Showcaves (see p570)

What to Buy & Where to Shop

Britain is one of the great shop windows of the world, famed in so many spheres of production and with so many acclaimed designers over the years from Hardy Amies through Mary Quant and Vivienne Westwood to Alexander McQueen.

WHAT TO BUY

For many visitors clothing is top of the shopping list. There is a huge choice of woollen articles in cashmere or lambswool, particularly in Scotland. Classic styles are sold by well-known names such as Jaeger, Burberry, Marks and Spencer, John Lewis, Debenhams and House of Fraser. The very best made-to-measure (bespoke) clothing for men is traditionally available in London in Savile Row (tailors) and Jermyn Street (shirt-makers), though these days many of the larger provincial cities (Birmingham, Manchester, Leeds, and of course the capitals of Edinburgh and Cardiff) boast outlets that are equally fashionable.

The best makes of traditional porcelain – Wedgwood, Royal Worcester, Royal Doulton – are available in London and elsewhere while very acceptable 'seconds' can be bought at the factory or in 'reject shops'. Britain is equally well known for its modern wares. Antique shops and markets abound in Britain and although it is becoming increasingly difficult to find bargains in mainstream outlets, lovers of historical bric-a-brac and smaller, less valuable items will find plenty to divert them.

Traditional foodie souvenirs include Scotch whisky, smoked salmon (try flaky smoked salmon), tea and marmalade, though these days it might well be artisan cheeses or even a do-it-yourself molecular gastronomy kit!

WHERE TO SHOP

London literally has it all: the greatest department stores, the biggest brand-name outlets, quirky specialists, the liveliest and most fascinating street markets, the poshest antique and jewellery stores. It also has crowds and higher prices.

The capital no longer has the monopoly on famous names however: Selfridges famously occupies Birmingham's most iconic new building, Harvey Nichols have opened in Edinburgh, Leeds, Bristol, Birmingham, Manchester and Edinburgh, and other big London retail names have realised there are profits to be made in the provinces. It is of course no coincidence that these cities, alongside Glasgow and Cardiff, offer the most comprehensive shopping options outside London.

Bicester Village, near Oxford, is the UK's leading outlet shopping centre with 130 designer boutiques at discounted prices. Or you might like to visit small towns or (real) villages, which have gained a reputation for their wares. Ludlow for food; Hay-on-Wye for books, Rye for antiques…

The good news for shoppers who prefer little to large is that independent shops have become more prevalent everywhere, even in the big cities; notably in Cardiff and Edinburgh while Bath, Brighton and Norwich are renowned for the quality and quantity of their one-off shops. There are vibrant markets in Oxford, Glasgow (The Barras), Cardiff and Birmingham (Rag Market) where local crafts and upmarket foodstuffs are sold to visitors alongside everyday fruit 'n' veg to locals. Almost every modest-sized town has a weekly market selling local produce.

And don't forget the much-maligned attraction gift shop, particularly in London, where the major museums and sights have excellent ranges. Most visitor attractions have some kind of souvenir shop attached, not all of which is tat.

Festivals & Events

The British have always been excellent when it comes to staging pomp and ceremony, even if (compared to revellers in Europe) many of our other celebrations have some way to go to match continental passions. In recent years music and literary festivals have come strongly to the fore.

ENGLAND AND WALES

For a full programme of events by themes, regions and/or dates, visit www.visitbritain.com.

SPRING

MARCH
Wales – St David's Day (1 Mar). Welsh patriots wear a leek or a daffodil (two national emblems) on their lapels to mark their patron saint's national day.

APRIL
The Thames (London) – Oxford-Cambridge Boat Race. The world's most famous rowing race. www.theboatrace.org.

EASTER
Isle of Man: Easter Festival of Running. A 3-day running extravaganza. www.easterfestival.info.

MAY
Helston – Flora Day Furry Dance. Spectacular processional dances (early May). www.helstonfloraday.org.uk.

SUMMER MUSIC FESTIVALS

Britain is well served with music festivals. The biggest is Glastonbury. Other festivals that attract big name acts are Reading Festival; Leeds Festival; O2 Wireless Festival, Hyde Park, London; V Festival, Weston Park, Staffs; Isle of Wight Festival. Popular crossover music and world music festivals include Bestival (Isle of Wight) and WOMAD (Charlton Park, Wilts). Visit www.efestivals.co.uk.

Blair Castle – Last weekend in May. **Atholl Highlanders Annual Parade, Highland Games**. www.blair-castle.co.uk.
London (Royal Hospital, Chelsea) – *Chelsea Flower Show.* Internationally famous flower show. www.rhs.org.uk.
Brighton – Brighton Festival. The largest arts festival in England: music, theatre, dance, circus, art, film, literature, debate, outdoor and family events. http://brightonfestival.org.
Glyndebourne, East Sussex – Glyndebourne Festival Opera (May–Aug). Britain's most prestigious opera programme, culminating in a traditional picnic. http://glyndebourne.com.

SUMMER

Blackpool – September–October. **Blackpool Illuminations**. www.blackpool-illuminations.net.
Peak District – May-September. **Well Dressing**: in Peak villages inc. Eyam, Monyash, Warksworth, Youlgreave.
Isle of Man TT – Late May–early June. **World-famous motorcycle road racing**. www.iomtt.com.
London – Mid-July–mid-September. **Henry Wood Promenade Concerts (BBC Proms)**: Royal Albert Hall. www.royalalberthall.com; www.bbc.co.uk/proms.

JUNE
Aldeburgh Festival – Classical music festival. www.aldeburgh.co.uk.
Ascot – Royal Ascot (the highlight of the British horse-racing calendar). www.ascot.co.uk.
London – Trooping the Colour: the Queen's official birthday parade on Horse Guards Parade. www.householddivision.org.uk/trooping-the-colour.

JULY: Harbour Festival, Britstol

© Patrick J Hanrahan/iStockphoto.com

Hay-on-Wye – Hay-on-Wye (late May–early Jun) **Hay Festival of Literature and the Arts** ('Hay Book Festival') interviews/talks by famous writers from Britain and abroad. www.hayfestival.com.

Wimbledon – last week Jun–1st week Jul. **Lawn Tennis Championships**. www.wimbledon.com.

Henley Royal Regatta – late June–early July. The world's premier amateur regatta. www.hrr.co.uk.

JULY

Llangollen – **International Eisteddfod.** International Musical Competitions. http://international-eisteddfod.co.uk.

Cambridge – **Cambridge Folk Festival**. The most important folk festival in the UK (and beyond). www.cambridgefolkfestival.co.uk.

King's Lynn – **Festival of Music (classical and jazz) and the Arts**. www.kingslynnfestival.org.uk.

Bristol – **Harbour Festival**. Live music, dance and street performers. www.bristolharbourfestival.co.uk.

Gloucester, Hereford, Worcester – **Three Choirs Festival** (end July–early August). Choral concerts which alternate between the three cities. http://3choirs.org.

River Thames – **Swan-Upping**: Marking of swans on the Thames. www.royalswan.co.uk.

AUGUST

Jersey – **Battle of Flowers**: floral-inspired carnival. www.battleofflowers.com.

Portsmouth – **International Kite Festival**. www.portsmouthkite festival.org.uk.

Liverpool – **Liverpool International Music Festival**. Europe's biggest annual free city centre music festival. www.limfestival.com.

London – **Notting Hill Carnival**. www.thelondonnottinghillcarnival.com.

AUGUST–SEPTEMBER

Isle of Man – **Festival of Motorcycling**, a unique action-packed 2 weeks of events. www.iomfom.com.

Isle of Man – **End-to-End Mountain Bike Challenge**. Get to see the whole island on two wheels. www.manxe2e.org.

AUTUMN

OCTOBER

Canterbury – **Canterbury Festival**. www.canterburyfestival.co.uk.

Nottingham – **Goose Fair**. Europe's largest funfair. www.nottinghamcity.gov.uk.

Nationwide – 31 Oct. **Halloween** festivities.

NOVEMBER

London to Brighton – First Sun. **Veteran Car Run**.
www.veterancarrun.com.

Nationwide – 5 Nov. Fireworks and bonfires commemorate Guy Fawkes and the Gunpowder Plot.

City of London – 2nd Sat November. Lord Mayor's Show. Grand street parade plus fireworks.
www.lordmayorsshow.org.

London – Late November–early December. State Opening of Parliament. www.parliament.uk.

WINTER

DECEMBER

London – Christmas highlights in London include Midnight Mass at St Paul's Cathedral; lights and dressed shop windows on Regent Street and Oxford Street; and the enormous Trafalgar Square Christmas tree.

SCOTLAND

For a full programme of events visit www.scotland.org/experience-scotland.

DECEMBER:
Trafalgar Square
Christmas tree,
London

© Pawel Libera/London and Partners

SPRING

MARCH

Aberdeen – Aberdeen Jazz Festival. www.aberdeenjazzfestival.com.

APRIL

Ayr – Scottish Grand National. The premier Scottish horseracing event. www.ayr-racecourse.co.uk.

Melrose – Melrose Sevens. Seven-a-side rugby tournament.

APRIL–MAY

Shetland – Shetland Folk Festival : www.shetlandfolkfestival.com.

Speyside – Spirit of Speyside Whisky Festival. www.spiritofspeyside.com.

MAY

Nationwide – Beginning of the Highland Games.

Ayrshire – Burns an 'a' that. www.visitscotland.com/about/robert-burns/festival.

Blair Castle – Atholl Highlanders Parade. www.blair-castle.co.uk.

MAY–JUNE

Angus – Glens Walking Festival. www.visitangus.com.

SUMMER

JUNE

Edinburgh – Edinburgh International Film Festival. www.edfilmfest.org.uk.

Fort William – UCI Mountain Bike World Cup.
http://fortwilliamworldcup.co.uk.

Glasgow – West End Festival. The city's largest cultural event. www.westendfestival.co.uk.

Kirkwall and Stromness (Orkney) – Classical music, drama, dance, literature and the visual arts. www.stmagnusfestival.com.

JUNE-JULY

Glasgow – Glasgow Jazz Festival. www.jazzfest.co.uk.

JULY

Edinburgh – Edinburgh International Jazz and Blues Festival. www.edinburghjazzfestival.com.

Fochabers – Traditional and Contemporary Celtic Music Festival. www.speyfest.com.

Glasgow – Merchant City Festival. Live music, dance, food and drink. www.merchantcityfestival.com.
Outer Hebrides – **Stornoway, also Lewis and Harris**) – Hebridean Celtic Festival. www.hebceltfest.com.
Aberdeen – International Youth Festival : dance, opera, drama, jazz, world music. www.aiyf.org.

AUGUST

Bellabeg, Strathdon – Games Day (4th Sat). March of the Lonach Highlanders plus Highland Games. www.lonach.org.
Edinburgh– Edinburgh International Festival (www.eif.co.uk); Fringe Festival (www.edfringe.com); Military Tattoo (www.edintattoo.co.uk); Edinburgh International Book Festival (www.edbookfest.co.uk).
Glasgow – Glasgow International Piping Festival, World Pipe Band Championship. www.pipinglive.co.uk.
Largs – Viking Festival (late Aug–first week Sept). Anniversary of Battle of Largs 1263, the last Viking invasion in the UK. www.largsvikingfestival.com.
Oban – Argyllshire Gathering. www.obangames.com.
Dunoon – Cowal Highland Gathering (last weekend Aug): biggest, most spectacular Highland games in the world. www.cowalgathering.com.
Dunkeld – Birnam Highland Games (last Sat Aug). www.birnamhighlandgames.com.
Inverness – Belladrum Tartan Heart Festival. Indie, rock, dance, Celtic, blues, roots and children's ents. www.tartanheartfestival.co.uk.

SEPTEMBER

Arran – Mountain Festival. Hill-walking and mountaineering festival. www.arranmountainfestival.co.uk.
Ayr – William Hill Ayr Gold Cup Festival. www.ayr-racecourse.co.uk.
Braemar – Braemar Highland Gathering (1st Sat). www.braemargathering.org.
Dunbar – Traditional Music Festival www.dunbarmusicfestival.co.uk.

AUGUST: Edinburgh Festival Fringe

Fort William – Ben Nevis Race. Up and down Britain's highest mountain, as fast as you can. www.bennevisrace.co.uk.
Highlands – Blas Festival: Celtic music festival. www.blas festival.com.
Borders – Walking Festival www.borderswalking.com.

WINTER

NOVEMBER

Nationwide – St Andrew's Day (30 Nov).

DECEMBER

Nationwide– Christmas festivities, Christmas Markets and Hogmanay (New Year's Eve) celebrations, particularly spectacular in **Edinburgh** (www.edinburghchristmas.com), **Glasgow** (www.glasgowloveschristmas.com) and **Stonehaven** where a Fireball Ceremony chases away evil spirits (www.stonehavenfireballs.co.uk).

JANUARY

Nationwide– Burns Night : Burns' Suppers (25 Jan) in honour of the national poet.
Glasgow – Celtic Connections. Music festival. www.celticconnections.com.
Shetland – Up Helly Aa. Europe's largest and most spectacular fire festival. www.uphellyaa.org.

FEBRUARY

Glasgow – Glasgow Film Festival. www.glasgowfilm.org/festival.

Practical Info

TOP TIPS

Best time to go: Early summer before the school holidays, or September–October.

Best way around: By train! Start in London, then pick a major city or two as a base for day trips.

Best for sightseeing: London, Edinburgh, York, Oxford, Liverpool.

Best accommodation: Luxury country inn or a boutique B&B.

Need to know: The British sense of humour!

Need to taste: Molecular gastronomy in a top restaurant; elsewhere try the country pubs for fish 'n' chips, steak 'n' kidney pie, Yorkshire Pudding, apple crumble and custard, sticky toffee pudding, local cheeses; real ale, locally brewed ales, British wine.

Before You Go

WHEN TO GO
SEASONS

There is no season of the year when it's too hot, too cold, too wet or too dry for you to enjoy the sights, but the changeable British climate lives up to its reputation. Many would say that the distinction between the seasons is increasingly blurred, and many excellent weather periods occur when least expected.
Spring and autumn are the best seasons for visiting parks and gardens, when the flowers are in bloom or the leaves are turning colour; most stately homes and other country sites are closed from October to Easter. In **spring** as the days grow longer and warmer, the light is glorious. **Summer** is unpredictable with moderate temperatures; in July and August there may be occasional heat waves in the southern areas, when the thermometer tops 30°C or the days may be cloudy and cool. **Autumn** can start dry and sunny, with clear skies and beautiful sunsets, while the air is crisp and invigorating. But as the days grow shorter, the temperature usually lowers. In **winter**, southern areas can remain fairly mild until Christmas. There may be cold snaps, but the temperature rarely drops below freezing. However, wind and dampness can make it feel very cold. Autumn and winter are the best time for visiting museums or for shopping, as places are less crowded, except in the weeks before Christmas.

CLIMATE

Chatting about the weather is a great British tradition, if only because it is so unpredictable and rain is often accompanied by brighter spells. The moist and breezy oceanic climate has many compensations. Stressful extremes of either heat or cold are rare, so that outdoor activity of some kind is almost always possible.
Although the western mountains receive the highest amount of precipitation, it is in the west that the tempering effects of the **Gulf Stream** are felt and where subtropical plants can flourish in sheltered locations. The drier, sunnier climate of the east and south is more continental in character, with colder winters and warmer summers.

GETTING THERE
BY AIR

Various national and other independent airlines operate services to the capital's five airports. Heathrow and Gatwick service the majority of flights:
London Heathrow (LHR)
London Gatwick (LGW)
London Luton (LTN)
London Stansted (STN)
London City (LCY)
Services also run to major regional airports (Aberdeen, Birmingham, Cardiff, Edinburgh, Glasgow, Inverness, Liverpool, Manchester, Newcastle, Prestwick).

PUBLIC HOLIDAYS	
1 January	New Year's Day
Good Friday	Friday before Easter Day
Easter Monday	Monday after Easter Day
First Monday in May	May Day
Last Monday in May	Spring Bank Holiday
Last Monday in August	Bank Holiday
25 December	Christmas Day
26 December	Boxing Day

BY SEA

There are numerous cross-Channel (passenger and car ferries, hovercraft) and other ferry or shipping services from the continent. For details apply to travel agencies or to the ferry companies.

Brittany Ferries 𝄯0330 159 7000.
www.brittanyferries.com
Irish Ferries 𝄯(353) 818 300 400.
www.irishferries.com
P&O Ferries 𝄯0800 130 0030
(General enquiries: 𝄯01304 863 000);
(Ireland (353) 1 686 9467).
www.poferries.com
Stena Line 𝄯08447 70 70 70.
www.stenaline.co.uk

BY TRAIN

The **Channel Tunnel** provides a direct Eurostar rail link from London St Pancras International to France and Belgium. Eurostar also runs from Ebbsfleet International and from Ashford International station (both in Kent). There is also a road/rail link between Folkestone and Calais.
Eurostar www.eurostar.com
𝄯03432 186 186 (ticket and bookings); 𝄯+44 1233 617 575 outside the UK.
BritRail and InterRail Passes are available to overseas visitors and are well worth considering if you intend to travel extensively in Britain by rail, particularly given the relatively high cost of rail travel if you buy tickets while in Britain. (Note that Eurail passes are *not* valid for train travel in Great Britain), European residents (including Brits) can use the InterRail Pass, but you can only buy a BritRail Pass if you are not a UK resident. BritRail Passes allow travel on consecutive days for various periods. ⊘ These concessions can be obtained only outside Britain and should be purchased from appointed agents before the beginning of the journey in question. For more details on BritRail passes, visit www.britrail.com; for details of InterRail passes visit www.interrail.eu.

BY CAR
Documents

EU nationals require a valid **national driving licence**; US nationals require a driving licence valid for 12 months – a permit is available from your local branch of the **American Automobile Association:** 𝄯www.aaa.com. Other nationals require an international driving licence.
If you intend bringing your own vehicle to the UK, you will need to have the **registration papers** (logbook) for the vehicle and a nationality plate of the approved size.

Insurance

Insurance cover is compulsory and although an **International Insurance Certificate** (Green Card) is no longer a legal requirement in Britain, it is the most effective proof of insurance cover and is internationally recognised by the police and other authorities. Certain UK motoring organisations offer accident insurance and breakdown service plans for members. The American Automobile Association (www.aaa.com) have special plans for their respective memberships.

ENTRY REQUIREMENTS

EU nationals should hold some means of identification, such as a **passport**. Non-EU nationals must be in possession of a valid national passport. Loss or theft should be reported to the appropriate embassy or consulate and to the local police. A visa to visit the United Kingdom is not required by nationals of the member states of the European Union and of the Commonwealth (including Australia, Canada, New Zealand and South Africa) and the USA. Nationals of other countries should check with the British Embassy and apply for a **visa** if necessary in good time.
The US Department of State provides useful information for US nationals on obtaining a passport, visa

requirements, customs regulations, medical care, etc. for international travel online at http://travel.state.gov.

CUSTOMS REGULATIONS

Tax-free allowances for various commodities are governed by EU legislation except in the Channel Islands and the Isle of Man, which have different regulations. Details of these allowances and restrictions are available at most ports of entry to Great Britain.

It is prohibited to import into the United Kingdom any drugs, firearms and ammunition, obscene material featuring children, counterfeit merchandise, unlicensed livestock (birds or animals), anything related to endangered species (furs, ivory, horn, leather) and certain plants (potatoes, bulbs, seeds, trees).

You can bring some goods from abroad without having to pay UK tax or 'duty' (customs charges), as long as they're for your own use.

If you're coming from a European Union (EU) country, you can bring in an unlimited amount of most goods; if from outside the EU you can only bring in a certain amount without paying duty or tax – up to your duty-free allowance. You must tell customs about ('declare') any other goods when you arrive at the UK border, as well as anything that's banned or restricted in the UK.

Further information on British customs regulations and "duty free" allowances are outlined on their website; visit www.hmrc.gov.uk (insert Customs Allowances in 'Search'). US allowances can be found at http://travel.state.gov.

HEALTH

Visitors to Britain are entitled to treatment at the Accident and Emergency (A&E) Departments of National Health Service hospitals. For an overnight or longer stay in hospital, payment will probably be required. It is therefore advisable to take out adequate insurance cover before leaving home. Visitors from EU countries should apply to their own National Social Security Offices for a **European Health Insurance Card** (EHIC) – the replacement for Form E111 – which entitles them to medical treatment under an EU Reciprocal Medical Treatment arrangement. Nationals of non-EU countries should take out comprehensive insurance. American Express offers a service, "Global Assist", for any medical, legal or personal emergency – visit www.americanexpress.com or call ☎01273 696 933.

♿ ACCESSIBILITY

Many of the sights described in this guide are accessible to less abled people; they are designated by the ♿ symbol in the Entry Times and Charges for the attractions. However, this symbol should not be taken to signify anything other than general accessibility (as specified by the attraction) and it is always advisable to call ahead.

The red-cover **Michelin Guide Great Britain & Ireland** indicates hotels with facilities suitable for disabled people; it is advisable to book in advance. **Tourism For All** is the national charity for UK residents: ☎0845 124 9971. www.tourismforall.org.uk. Their other site, www.openbritain.net, is a useful one-stop shop for accessible tourism in the UK, offering a simple way to find accessible destinations and places to stay.

On Arrival

GETTING AROUND
BY TRAIN
The UK has a large railway network and most populated places can be accessed via rail. Virgin Trains (www. virgintrains.co.uk) operate main line services from London up both the east coast and west coast, but there are many cross-country services, too. Rail tickets can be expensive, so make sure you buy in advance. Once you are in Great Britain, for information on rail services and on other concessionary tickets, including combined train and bus tickets, call ✆03457 48 49 50. www.nationalrail. co.uk. To buy train tickets, either go to the station, buy online in advance from the above website, at www.thetrainline.com, or from the individual train operators.

BY COACH/BUS
National Express, in association with other bus operators, runs express coach services covering the whole country. ✆0871 781 8181. www.nationalexpress.com. Cheap intercity bus companies include Megabus (https:// uk.megabus.com) while easyBus www.easybus.co.uk offers cheap airport transfer services to and from central London. For comprehensive public transport information in the UK, call ✆0871 200 22 33 or visit www.traveline.info.

BY CAR
Motoring Organisations
The major motoring organisations in Great Britain are the Automobile Association and the Royal Automobile Club. Each provides services for non-resident members of affiliated clubs.
Automobile Association
✆0800 085 2721. www.theaa.com
Royal Automobile Club
✆0330 159 1111. www.rac.co.uk

© Transport for London

CONGESTION CHARGING
At present London is the only city, in the UK with a congestion charge. This is payable by drivers entering the central part of the city Mon–Fri 7am–6pm. **Driving into London is not recommended for visitors at any time**, but if you must, then familiarise yourself with how to pay by visiting www.tfl.gov.uk/ roadusers/congestioncharging.

Road Regulations
The **minimum driving age** is 17 years old. Traffic drives **on the left** and overtakes on the right. Headlights must be used at night even in built-up areas and at other times when visibility is poor. There are severe penalties for driving after drinking more than the legal limit of alcohol. Important traffic signs are shown at the end of the red-cover *Michelin Guide Great Britain & Ireland.* Signage in the UK corresponds in general to international norms.

Seat Belts
It is compulsory for all passengers to wear seat belts in the UK.

Speed Limits
Maximum speeds are:
70mph/112kph, motorways or dual carriageways
60mph/96kph, other roads
30mph/48kph, in towns and cities.

Parking

Off-street parking is indicated by blue signs with white lettering (Parking or P); payment is made on leaving or in advance for a certain period. There are also parking meters, disc systems and paying parking zones; in the last case tickets must be obtained from ticket machines (small change necessary) and displayed inside the windscreen. There is an increasing number of locations where parking is 'Pay on Exit', and where payment can be made by credit card. Illegal parking is liable to fines and also in certain cases to the vehicle being clamped or towed away. The usual restrictions are as follows:

Double red line = no stopping at any time (freeway)
Double yellow line = no parking at any time
Single yellow line = no parking for set periods as indicated on panel
Broken yellow line = parking limited to certain times only.

Route Planning

The whole of Great Britain is covered by the **Michelin map series 501-504** (scale 1:400 000) and the **Michelin Road Atlas of Great Britain and Ireland** (scale 1: 300 000). In addition to the usual detailed road information, they indicate tourist features such as beaches or bathing areas, swimming pools, golf courses, racecourses, scenic routes, tourist sights, country parks, etc. These publications are an essential complement to the annual **Michelin Guide Great Britain & Ireland,** which offers an up-to-date selection of hotels and restaurants organised alphabetically by town, all inspected and graded by Michelin and marked on maps throughout. Traffic in and around towns is heavy during the rush hour (morning and evening). It is also very heavy on major roads at the weekend in summer, particularly bank holiday weekends.

Car Rental

There are car rental agencies at airports, railway stations and in all large towns throughout Great Britain. European cars usually have manual transmission but automatic cars are available on demand. An international driving licence is required for non-EU nationals. Most companies will not rent to drivers aged under 21 or 25. The following firms operate on a national basis:
Avis ℘0808 284 0014.
www.avis.co.uk
Budget ℘0808 284 4444.
www.budget.co.uk
National Car Rental ℘0800 121 8303.
www.nationalcar.co.uk
EasyCar ℘0800 640 7000.
www.easycar.com
Europcar ℘00871 384 9900.
www.europcar.co.uk
Hertz ℘0207 026 00 77.
www.hertz.co.uk

Petrol/Gas

In service stations dual-pumps are the rule. Unleaded pumps have green handles or a green stripe.

Tolls

Tolls are rare; they are levied only on the most recent bridges, the M6 Midland Expressway toll road (by-passes Birmingham traffic), a few minor country bridges as well as road tunnels (Dartford, Tyne).

Driving Conditions

In general, the closer you are to London and the South East, the more congested the roads become. If you intend making a major city (particularly London) the base for your trip, don't consider driving at all. In this case, using public transport for excursions out of town is a much better idea than car hire.
All major (and many minor) cities and towns in Britain suffer traffic problems and you should avoid rush hours (7.30am to 9.30am and 5pm to 6.30pm) wherever possible.
ⓐ Check out traffic delays on www.highways.gov.uk/traffic-information.

PLACES TO STAY
USEFUL WEBSITES

www.visitbritain.com The official Visit Britain site includes Britain's largest accommodation listing with over 37 000 places to stay.

www.viamichelin.com Plan your trip around some of Britain's finest places to see, dine and stay with Michelin's online route planner and magazine.

www.distinctlydifferent.co.uk Visit this site if you would like to stay in a former windmill, a lighthouse, a church, a gypsy caravan, dovecote…

Types of Accommodation

Accommodation in Britain runs the whole range from a room in a characterful historic pub to an anonymous but (usually) comfortable night in a chain hotel, from a cheap room in a B&B (bed and breakfast in a private house) to being pampered in some of the world's finest and most sophisticated hotels. That said, in the last few years a good number of top-end B&Bs have gone 'designer-boutique' and can cost more than a conventional hotel room with more facilities.

London is still the most expensive place to stay in the UK, though some top hotel rates in provincial cities are now on a par with London prices. If price is not a problem, you can find top-quality designer hotels, many offering spa facilities and wellness treatments, in many large British cities and all over the countryside.

At the other end of the price spectrum, there is also a proliferation of no-frills chain hotels offering very competitive deals.

Wherever you choose to stay, try to book in advance online for the best deals, but if you do simply turn up at the hotel desk, ask what is the best deal they can offer you (do not simply accept the published room rate) and be prepared to haggle – the later in the day it is, the better your chances of securing a cheaper room.

Reservation Services

Most tourist information centres will provide, free of charge, an information booklet listing all hotels, bed-and-breakfast and other accommodation. Many will arrange accommodation for a small fee. Room prices are normally just that – the price per room – however, even for a double room, they may be quoted per person. In London the **British Hotels Reservation Centre** can help. They have 14 outlets located at Heathrow airport, St Pancras and Victoria railway stations, Victoria Coach Station, Trafalgar Square and New Oxford Street. ☎020 7096 2620.

Budget Accommodation
Bed and Breakfast (B&B)

Many private individuals take in a limited number of guests. Prices include bed and breakfast, usually the cooked variety. A few offer an evening meal though the choice will of course be limited. Local tourist information centres usually have a list of the bed-and-breakfast establishments in the area and book if necessary for a fee. Many houses advertise with a 'B&B' sign.

Rural Accommodation

An interesting way of spending a holiday is to stay on one of the many different types of working farm – arable, livestock, hill or mixed – sometimes set in the heart of glorious countryside. For information apply for the booklet **Farm Stay UK** supplied by the company of the same name: ☎024 7669 6909. www.farmstayuk.co.uk.

Universities and Colleges

During summer holidays many universities offer low-cost accommodation in halls of residence. www.universityrooms.co.uk.

Youth Hostels

There are 250 youth hostels in Great Britain are open to members of the **Youth Hostel Association (England**

and Wales), or to those with an international membership card. ✆0800 0191 700 (reservations). www. yha.org.uk. For Scotland contact the **Scottish Youth Hostel Association** ✆0845 293 7373 (reservations). www.syha.org.uk.
International Youth Hostel Federation www.hihostels.com. There are also many **independent hostels** throughout Britain. ✆01629 580 427. http://independenthostels. co.uk.

Camping

Local tourist information centres supply lists of sites. Many more are available through **The Camping and Caravanning Club** ✆024 7647 5426. www.campingandcaravanningclub. co.uk. A three-month temporary membership includes special deals with up to 30 percent off overnight stops.

Self catering accommodation

If you are likely to stay in one place for a week or more, it is worth considering renting a self-catering property, which give you much greater freedom of movement. Ask at local tourist offices for information, or check the tourist websites in advance

WHERE TO EAT
USEFUL WEBSITES
www.viamichelin.com
A useful trip planner featuring some of Britain's finest places to stay and eat alongside a gastronomy, tourism and motoring magazine.
www.squaremeal.co.uk
Reviews of restaurants and bars in London and around the UK by food critics, alongside foodie event reviews.
www.london-eating.co.uk
This site is based on reader reviews and also features money-saving offers.

Restaurants
Dining out in the UK has undergone a revolution in the last two decades

and now ranks among the very best in the world. Thanks to its colonial past and its cosmopolitan nature, the UK offers authentic tastes from all over the world, often cooked by native chefs, or collected, magpie-like, by celebrity chefs from culinary tours of the world. Restaurants are becoming less and less formal with only the top hotel dining rooms and traditional establishments still stipulating dress codes. Hours too have become more flexible though many places still serve lunch from around 12 noon to around 2.30pm and dinner from around 7pm to 10pm, and close in between. Only in London and the more buzzing centres will you find a good selection of late dining restaurants. Prices tend to be high compared to many other parts of the world, though eating at lunchtime from set menus can save you a small fortune. Making a reservation for weekend nights and Sunday lunchtime is recommended and if you want to eat in Britain's top restaurants you may need to book weeks in advance (though it's always worth checking at the last minute for cancellations). A selection of places to eat can be found in the Address Books throughout this guide. The Legend at the back of the book explains the symbols used in the Address Books.

Bistros, brasseries and cafés
These European-style establishments, usually serving a variety of relatively simple, pan-European dishes, are the places for snacks, informal meals and drinks in trendy upbeat surroundings right throughout the day and night. The UK now has a profusion of US-style cafés on the high streets of most large towns. Less common these days is the traditional English café, sometimes called a "caff' or "greasy spoon". This is traditionally the place for a good old-fashioned fry-up (bacon, eggs, sausages, etc.), washed down with a mug of strong tea.

Pubs (Public Houses)
Gastropubs

Eating out in public houses ('pubs') has changed enormously in recent years, with more and more establishments putting the emphasis on serving food rather than merely serving drinks. This has led to the rise of the so-called "gastropub", originally only found in London and the Home Counties, but now spread to all parts of the country. The typical gastropub is a sort of British bistro; stylish, blending modern with traditional, and serving a relatively short menu of Modern European/Modern British food. Prices vary enormously and in many places you may spend as much as you would in a smart restaurant. Beware that the pub-food revolution also means that many pubs with no history of serving food have jumped onto the bandwagon, many with little expertise or knowledge, consequently serving poor-quality overpriced food. Steer clear of pubs offering long menus and complicated dishes, unless they have an established name. Equally, some 'pubs' are Michelin-starred.

Pub Hours and Regulations

Pubs' statutory maximum licensing hours were until quite recently: Monday–Saturday 11am–11pm, and Sunday 12.30pm–10.30pm, with many closing during the afternoon. In 2005, '24-hour drinking laws' came into operation allowing the country's pubs, clubs and bars to open, in theory, around the clock. In practice, relatively few premises applied for a licence to extend their hours. Pubs that serve meals (now the majority) normally allow children on the premises as long as they remain within the eating area and even more traditionally inclined pubs may allow children in before a certain time (say 8pm or 9pm). The best policy is to ask someone behind the bar before marching in with children.

MICHELIN GUIDE (RED COVER)

The annual **Michelin Guide Great Britain & Ireland** presents our selection of the best hotels and restaurants, based on regular on-the-spot visits and enquiries. Pleasant settings, attractive décor, quiet or secluded locations and a warm welcome are identified by special symbols. The guide not only celebrates the very best chefs and cuisine that Great Britain has to offer, but also reflects the trend towards informal eating with its Bib Gourmand award to restaurants and good food at moderate prices.

Michelin's **Eating Out in Pubs** guide selects the 500 best dining pubs.

You must be 18 to be served with alcohol and, if you look younger, you will almost certainly be asked for some form of age identification.

Global cuisine

In the major cities of the United Kingdom you can expect to find the cuisines of almost every country in the world. Increasingly modern Britain, unlike many of her European neighbours, has learned to embrace global cuisine and cooking, even at home. Every town in the UK has its share of Indian and Chinese establishments. In places where large Asian immigrant communities have settled (e.g. Bradford or Birmingham) restaurants from the Indian subcontinent are ubiquitous. After years of simply being the cheap option after the pubs closed, many ethnic restaurants have now moved upmarket to enjoy critical acclaim.

Practical A–Z

BUSINESS HOURS

Shops are open 10am–2pm, 5–8.30pm, although large stores and malls are often open through lunch. Most shops close Sundays, and some on Saturday afternoons. Traditional British shopping hours are Mondays to Saturdays from 9am/9.30am to 5.30pm/6pm. Many larger shops, particularly in out-of-town locations, also open Sundays from 10am or 11am to 4pm. There is late-night shopping (until 7pm/8pm) in most large cities on Wednesdays or Thursdays; supermarkets usually close later than other shops. Smaller individual shops may close during the lunch hour; on the other hand some stay open until very late. Many towns have an early closing day when shops are closed during the afternoon. Traditionally the winter sales before and after Christmas and New Year, and the summer sales in June and July have always been a popular time for shopping, as prices are reduced on a great range of goods. However, sales now appear on the High Street at other times of year too.

ENTRY TIMES

In the Discovering section of the guide the times we generally give are opening hours; for example, 10am–6pm means the site *closes* at 6pm. In practice many places have a last entry time of 30 minutes to an hour before closing time. If the last entry time is more than an hour before closing time (normally only larger attractions stipulate this) or the attraction specifically states last entry time (as opposed to closing time), we also state this. In general, however, it is always best to arrive at least 90 minutes before an attraction closes for the day, if only to get your money's worth and allow you time to see the site.

00 61	Australia
00 1	Canada
00 353	Republic of Ireland
00 64	New Zealand
00 44	United Kingdom
00 1	United States of America
155	International Operator

100	Operator
118 500	BT Directory Enquiries in the UK (cost £2.75 per call plus £2.75 per minute, or part thereof, from BT landlines)
999	Emergency number (free nationwide); ask for Fire, Police, Ambulance, Coastguard, Mountain Rescue or Cave Rescue

COMMUNICATIONS

If staying for longer than a few days, you may want to pick up a pay-as-you-go SIM card for your mobile phone. Rates vary enormously between operators and there are multiple tariffs and variations to choose from.

Some public telephones accept credit cards, but 'phone boxes' are few and far between these days.

International Calls

To make an international call dial ✆00 followed by the country code, followed by the area code (without the initial 0), followed by the subscriber's number.

ELECTRICITY

The electric current is 230 volts AC (50 HZ); 3-pin flat wall sockets are standard. An adaptor or multiple point plug is required for non-British appliances.

EMBASSIES AND CONSULATES

Australia
High Commission:
Australia House, The Strand,
London WC2B 4LA.
☎020 7379 4334.
www.uk.embassy.gov.au.

Canada
High Commission:
Canada House, Trafalgar Square,
London SW1Y 5BJ.
☎0207 004 6000.
www.canada.org.uk.
Consulates: Cardiff ☎02920 449635.
Edinburgh ☎07702 359 916.

Japan
Embassy and Consulate:
101-104 Piccadilly, London W1J 7JT.
☎020 7465 6500.
www.uk.emb-japan.go.jp.
Consulate Scotland:
2 Melville Crescent, Edinburgh
EH3 7HW. ☎0131 225 4777.
www. edinburgh.uk.emb-japan.go.jp.

New Zealand
High Commission:
New Zealand House,
80 Haymarket, London SW1Y 4TQ.
☎020 7930 8422.
www.nzembassy.com.
Honorary Consulate, Scotland:
☎0131 222 8109.

South Africa
High Commission:
South Africa House, Trafalgar Square,
London WC2N 5DP.
☎020 7451 7299.
http://southafricahouseuk.com.

USA
Embassy:
24 Grosvenor Square, London W1A
2LQ. ☎020 7499 9000.
https://uk.usembassy.gov.
Consulate Scotland:
3 Regent Terrace, Edinburgh
EH7 5BW. ☎0131 556 8315.
http://edinburgh.usconsulate.gov.

Welsh Affairs Office:
☎0229 2002 6419.
http://cardiff.usvpp.gov.

EMERGENCIES
Dial **999** and an operator will ask
you which service (Police, Fire or
Ambulance) you require. These calls
are free from any phone.
☎ Dial **101** for non-urgent calls to
local police.

MAIL/POST
Post offices are generally open
Mondays to Fridays, 9.30am to
5.30pm and Saturday mornings,
9.30am to 12.30pm.
Royal Mail pricing is now based
on the *size* of a letter as well as the
more traditional weight, for example
Postcard/standard small-letter first-
class rate: UK 63p (up to 100g that are
no more than 5mm thick and up to
C5 in size), international standard £1. If
you are unsure, you will need to go in
person to a post office or visit www.
royalmail.com/price-finder for details.
Stamps are available from post
offices, newsagents and tobacconists,
and some supermarkets.
Poste restante items are held for 14
days; proof of identity is required.
Airmail delivery usually takes 3 to
4 days in Europe and 4 to 7 days
elsewhere in the world.

MONEY
Banks
Banks are generally open from
Mondays to Fridays, 9.30am to
3.30pm; some banks offer a limited
service on Saturday mornings; all
banks are closed on Sundays and
bank holidays. Most banks have
cash dispensers (ATMs) that accept
international credit cards; most do not
charge a fee for cash withdrawals (be
sure to look for a notice to that effect).
Exchange facilities outside these
hours are available at airports,
currency exchange companies,
travel agencies, hotels and some
large supermarkets.

Some form of identification is necessary when cashing travellers' cheques in banks. Commission charges vary; hotels usually charge more than banks.

Credit Cards

The main credit cards (American Express, Access/Mastercard/Visa/Barclaycard) are widely accepted in shops, hotels, restaurants and petrol stations; Diners Club is less accepted. Most banks have cash dispensers which accept international credit cards.

Currency

The official currency in Great Britain is the pound sterling. The decimal system (100 pence = £1) is used throughout Great Britain; Scotland has different notes including £1 and £100 notes, which are legal tender outside Scotland, though you may occasionally have difficulty getting some shopkeepers in England to accept them.

The Channel Islands and Isle of Man have different notes and coins, which are not valid elsewhere.

The common currency – in descending order of value – is £50 (rare in general circulation), £20, £10 and £5 (notes); £2, £1, 50p, 20p, 10p, 5p (silver coins) and 2p and 1p (copper coins).

The Euro is accepted in several larger stores in London, but check the rate of exchange if planning to make large purchases.

PUBLIC HOLIDAYS

The table (*page 43*) gives the public (**bank**) holidays in England and Wales, when most shops and municipal museums are closed.

In addition to the usual school holidays in the spring and summer and at Christmas, there are half-term breaks in February, May and October.

SMOKING

It is illegal to smoke in **all** public places, including the great British pub and on public transport. Most, however, have some kind of outdoor area for smokers.

TAX
VAT

Many stores in London, Edinburgh and other tourist cities and towns participate in the Retail Export Scheme (look for the sign "Tax-Free Shopping"). This means that customers may be entitled to receive a refund of VAT paid on goods (currently 20 percent) exported to destinations outside the European Union. There is no statutory minimum sale value although retailers may set a minimum transaction value (normally around £75) below which they will not operate the scheme. Ask the sales assistant for the form for reclaiming the tax. Fill in the form, keep it safe and present it again at the point of exit from the UK for the refund to be passed on to you. Note that VAT refunds cannot be processed after you return home.

Gift Aid and donations

Gift Aid is a government scheme of tax relief on money donated to UK charities, which since 2007 may be applied at the entrance to visitor attractions with charitable status. The scheme is *only* for UK taxpayers and in most cases you will be asked for your postcode and name, which will then be verified instantly (electronically) by a machine at the site entrance in order to minimise waiting time. You will then be given the choice of buying a ticket with or without gift aid. The former is usually 10 percent higher, though (somewhat confusingly) you may also be offered the ticket at the same price with the option of free readmission for a year! This is a loophole which means that the site can still reclaim Gift Aid without asking their customers to pay any more for admission. Beware that in some cases you may be asked for the gift aid inclusive price straight

© omnimarketing / iStockphoto.com

away, thus putting the onus on you to ask for the cheaper ticket. If so, remember there is absolutely no obligation for you to pay the higher amount (and if you are an overseas visitor the scheme does not apply to you anyway).

In a few instances if you do choose to pay the higher price you may be given an incentive to pay the higher price in the form of a voucher redeemable in the shop, or against refreshments. If you spend the full amount of this voucher (which in most cases will only amount to the price of a coffee or less), then you will pay less overall but the charity/visitor attraction will still gain extra revenue. Beware also that regardless of Gift Aid some historical attractions lead with a price that includes a 'charitable donation'. Remember that you are under no obligation to pay this; simply ask for the standard price ticket instead.

☺Within this guidebook we have given entry prices *without* gift aid or charitable donations.

TIME

In winter, standard time throughout the British Isles is Greenwich Mean Time (GMT). In summer clocks are advanced by an hour to give British Summer Time (BST). The times change over a weekend in March and October.

TIPPING

Although Britain has not historically been a tip-conscious nation, it is generally accepted that 10 percent is the norm for most services (waiters, taxi drivers, guides…) with £1–£2 upwards to baggage porters etc. Many restaurants will add a service charge ('service included') of 10 per cent or even 12.5 per cent to the final bill. In this case, no further tip is necessary and you are completely within your legal rights to withhold all or part of this if the service has not been to your satisfaction.

If you want to make sure the staff (as opposed to the management) get the tip, give it in cash. Bar staff are not generally tipped, though if the service has been good and you have had several drinks over the course of an evening you may ask the bartender if they would like a drink (they may just take the cash equivalent) or you might tell them to keep the change.

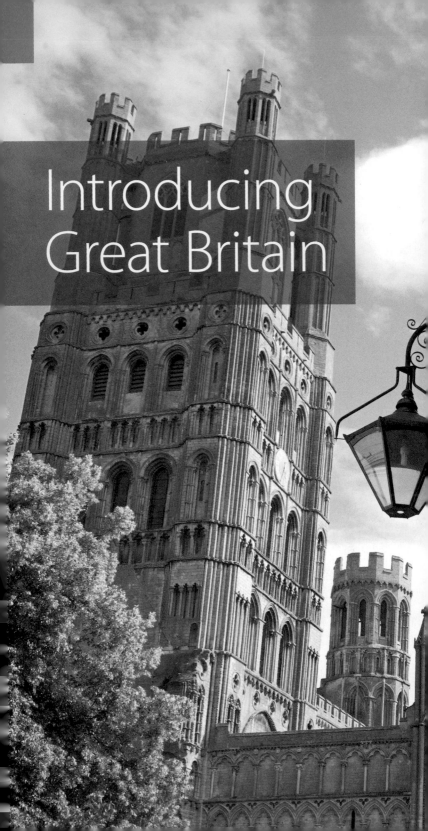

Introducing
Great Britain

MINSTER TAVERN

Ely Cathedral, Cambridgeshire
© Wilfried Krecichwost / Bridge / Photononstop

Features

594
e Approved

you can't walk by
without trying our
— Award Winning —
FISH
& chips...
...fresh line battered
COD
served with
mushy peas, petit pois,
chips &
tartare sauce

High Street, Stratford-upon-Avon, Warwickshire
© Ludovic Maisant/hemis.fr

Britain Today

Britain in 2018 is a place of continuing uncertainty. After years of austerity there are signs of economic recovery. The election of a government with a clear majority in 2015, removed the compromises of an uneasy coalition between the Conservative and the Liberal Democrats, but the 2016 decision to leave the European Union and the snap election in 2017, in which the government lost its overall majority, continues to generate uncertainty on many levels. In terms of the social and economic problems the country faces, Britain is no different from any of the western European countries, but has a more extensive cultural and ethnic mix.

From the visitors' point of view, Britain remains a fascinating and historically fortuitous country, with the some of finest architecture, monuments, theatres, entertainment and bizarre events in Europe. It is also a place that today rivals France for its culinary excellence with several restaurants now boasting at least one Michelin star.

Cathedral Yard, Manchester © George-Standen/iStockphoto.com

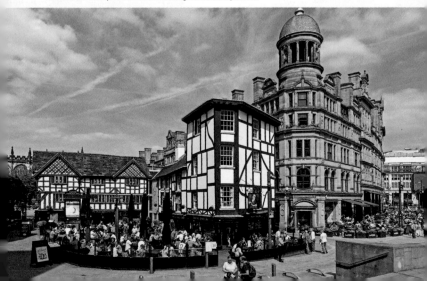

Way of Life

The Great British way of life is in a state of significant flux. Are Scotland (and Wales) about to go their own separate ways? Who now represents the working classes? Does anyone trust politicians or the financial institutions? And what does it mean to be British these days anyway?

PEOPLE

2016: 65.64 million

Great Britain has long been a cosmopolitan place, shaped by the cultures and peoples that have arrived through invasion, migration, empire and trade, ever since rising sea levels separated the island from mainland Europe. Much of the white population is a hodgepodge of pre-Celtic, Celtic, Roman, Viking, Anglo-Saxon and Norman ancestry. More recent arrivals follow in the shadow of the dwindling memory of the British Empire and the United Kingdom's continuing high profile in international affairs. Alongside increasing movement of citizens within the European Union, all of this ensures that Britain remains a place of change.

It is said that there are around 200 different languages spoken within these shores. Around 8–10 percent of the population is from ethnic minorities, but the concentration of immigrants varies enormously by region and by area. In wealthy rural and semi-rural parts of the country the population is overwhelmingly white, whereas many innercity suburbs of London and provincial cities such as Birmingham and Bradford have substantial communities of other ethnicity.

The United Kingdom has a long history of immigration, with large-scale **European influxes** in the 19C and early-20C. After the Second World War many **West Indians** were invited to help with the shortage of labour and they were followed around a decade later by immigrants from **India** and **Pakistan**. There has also been a steady stream of **Chinese**, most notably from the former colony of Hong Kong.

British society is far more integrated than it was 30 years ago, but it is still to some extent insular. Recent statistics indicate that social mobility is not as high as the government had previously hinted. However, the rigid class divisions of the past have relaxed considerably and equal opportunities continues to be a leading issue. This is perhaps best represented by the huge numbers of students of all classes and ethnicities that join the workforce each year from Britain's government subsidised-universities.

21ST CENTURY TRENDS

Since the relaxing of laws on labour movement and the expansion of the European Union, more Europeans (particularly from eastern Europe) have made Britain their home. **Poles** in particular have arrived in large numbers and have been among the most successful at assimilating into the community, largely as a result of their value in the skilled manual labour market and their readiness to learn to speak English. How the free movement of labour will be affected by Brexit remains to be seen.

The recent conflicts and degree of polarisation between the **Muslim** and Christian worlds has exacerbated tensions in some areas of Britain, and in some instances radical Muslim clerics have been arrested or expelled from the country. However, the moderate majority, who now account for over 3 percent of the population, flourish in the UK. **Multiculturalism** is an important political topic in modern Great Britain, with an ongoing debate that focuses on balancing the rights and responsibilities of immigrants. National polls regularly indicate that the favourite meal on the nation's tables is the British-Indian dish, chicken tikka masala. On the whole, Britain continues to be a very tolerant society and welcomes immigrants, although there is also a growing feeling among many people that the UK has become a "soft touch".

Has immigration over recent decades been good for both the economy and overall quality of life in Great Britain? The debate is far from clear. Independent research has proved inconclusive. The issue was rekindled in 2013 with the rise of UKIP, the UK Independence Party, who are the fourth most popular party in England, although they were not very successful in the 2015 and 2017 elections. They wish to sever all UK ties with the EU and would like much stricter controls on immigration. To some extent, the outcome of the Brexit referendum in June 2016 made the continuing relevance of UKIP unclear.

Britain continues to be a safe haven for **political refugees** and asylum seekers from several trouble spots of the world. While many residents would like to wash their hands of such problems, others point to the legacy of Empire and the leading role that Britain still plays in many parts of the world.

BEING BRITISH

By the time the Millennium drew to a close the concept of being British had become increasingly nebulous. The country is now home to immigrants from over 100 different ethnic backgrounds, and many are now second generation, some retaining the garb and traditions of their country but speaking in a broad English regional accent. Sport is the most obvious melting pot where English-born players of Indian fathers play cricket for England against India, while many top British athletes, particularly footballers, are of Afro-Caribbean extraction. Meanwhile, "being British" abroad has taken something of a battering as a result of football hooliganism and the continuing popularity of cheap, boozy holidays by the sea. With streamlined 21C communications, a growing interest in all things regional (from dialects to food, music and handicrafts), and with fashionable wealthy cities like Cardiff and Edinburgh to call their own, Scotland and Wales are no longer sleepy backwaters to be patronised by London. Of the three mainland British nations it is the English who have suffered the most with regard to their sense of identity. The regionalisation of power to Scotland and Wales (even if the really big decisions are still taken in Whitehall), large-scale immigration, and the demands and legislation of the European Union, have taken their toll on the English national psyche. Meanwhile the Scots and Welsh have grown in confidence.

LIFESTYLE

Over the last three decades British lifestyle has become increasingly Ameri-

THE CULT OF CELEBRITY

The current British fixation with celebrity really kicked off in the 1980s. It was fuelled by tabloid newspapers, such as The *Sun*, and magazines such as *Hello,* which quickly spawned a whole raft of cheap sensationalist "celeb"-spotting titles that now form a mind-boggling display on the racks in high-street newsagents. Now a ubiquitous medium, long after Big Brother's arrival on these shores in 2000, reality television has brought a cult of non-celebrity to the fore. Today, more people are famous for being famous than ever before. Open a 'celeb' section of a magazine and you may be hard-pressed to recognise anyone if you don't watch UK reality shows. It is common for fallen stars to use reality shows as a way back to the limelight, yet somehow their former successes are always tarnished in the process, particularly in a medium where characters are exposed and performances must be maintained full time. A-list celebrities clear a wide path.

canised with more time spent at work, less time spent on the family, a move from the city to the suburbs, shopping at out-of-town centres rather than in neighbourhood corner shops, and an increasing reliance on the motor car over public transport. Materialism and conspicuous consumption reached its zenith in the late-1980s and early-1990s as typified by 'yuppies' (young upwardly mobile professionals) flaunting expensive cars and massive salaries, at least until the recession of the early-90s. The new Millennium boom in London's financial services industry brought enormous City bonuses, while exacerbating a spendthrift consumer culture. All of this came to an abrupt stop in 2008 with the collapse of credit markets around the globe. Economic conditions have been, at best, cautious ever since. British society has shifted from the relatively tight knit community structure of the 1950s and 60s to a culture of the individual. While many people have benefited in material terms from the economic boom years, lifestyle changes have had serious implications on the country's physical infrastructure, behaviour and health. Topical debate is dominated by recurring issues of "binge (excessive) drinking", teenage pregnancies, poor childcare, increasing obesity, issues arising from poverty, and lack of moral leadership.

RELIGION

Sunday has long ceased to be the 'day of rest'. The main Sunday pastimes are now shopping and sport. Church attendances in the UK have plummeted and the UK is third from bottom in this respect in Europe. Fewer than 15 percent of Britons attend church at least once a month, and less than half of the population now identifies with the Christian faith, while 42% say they have no religion they identify with. Moreover, one in five British people identify themselves as atheist, 7% as agnostic and 3% as humanist. Of course, with the huge influx of immigration in the UK there are also many other religions now being practised here.

SPORT

The British have long been a sporting nation, popularising many international sports (football/soccer, golf, cricket, rugby, tennis). Football remains the most popular team game with the English Premier League acknowledged widely as the best (and certainly the richest) in the world. However, its make-up (over 55 percent of players are foreign) is one of the principal reasons for the over-hyped but under performing English national team, which has failed to win an international tournament since 1966.

MEDIA

British media varies from the sublime to the ridiculous, as represented by the tabloid (small-format) newspapers that specialise in deliberately outlandish features and celebrity gossip. Despite claims of dumbing down to retain its audience in the face of increasing multi-channel satellite and cable TV competition, the BBC retains its unique licence fee subsidy and maintains a strong presence in global media, underpinned by informative programming and a welcome absence of advertising.

The BBC dominates the airwaves with several national digital radio stations and many more local frequencies, while its investment in the online iPlayer has paid dividends in the longrun, with many users choosing to watch key events, such as Wimbledon tennis, online instead of on TV.

Of the newspapers, *The Daily Telegraph*, *The Times*, *The Guardian* and *The Independent* are all serious daily reads peppered with informed opinion leaning towards the left *(The Guardian)* and the right *(The Daily Telegraph)* with varying shades of politics in between. "Red-top" tabloid newspapers enjoy far wider circulation and run the gamut of entertainment from the ostentatious headlines of the *Mail on Sunday* to the best selling pages of *The Sun*. The *Daily Mirror*, *Daily Mail* and *Daily Express* are other populist newspapers, each enjoying large readerships nationwide.

Languages of Britain

The trend towards localisation and the current fascination with regional foods, crafts and community identity make this as good a time as any to be a Welsh or Gaelic speaker. Conversely, speaking English is still *de rigeur* and for immigrants a key indicator of integration into British society.

ENGLISH

The English language owes its rich vocabulary to the many peoples who have settled in Great Britain or with whom the British have come into contact through overseas exploration and conquest. Old English's origins are Anglo-Saxon and thus West Germanic, with a peppering of Old Norse (Viking). Middle English was Norman influenced, while Modern English continues to develop and adopt from other languages. In 1600, there were about 2 million native English-speakers. The number is now nearer 400 million, including not only the population of countries such as Australia and New Zealand, Canada and the United States of America, but also of those where English is the only common and thus official second language.

Old English, Anglo-Saxon and Norman French

Old English, a Germanic dialect spoken in the year 400 from Jutland to northern France, was established in Britain by 800 and by the 16C had taken on the syntax and grammar of modern English. Although Norman French was the official language after the Norman Conquest, Anglo-Saxon eventually gained precedence and Norman French survives principally in formal expressions used in law and royal protocol. It continued to be spoken in the Channel Islands long after it became obsolete in England.

Modern English

English is a very flexible language which has readily absorbed a considerable inheritance from Celtic, Roman, Anglo-Saxon, Viking and Norman-French origins. Although the spoken language owes most to Anglo-Saxon, the written language shows the influence of Latin, which for many centuries formed the major study of the educated classes. Immigration over the past hundred years or so has brought many other languages into everyday use by sizeable communities in Britain. Yiddish-speaking Jews came from Russia in the 19C and early-20C and their German-speaking co-religionists fled from Nazi persecution in the 1930, while the Windrush Generation arrived from the Caribbean after World War II.

Today, Indians and Pakistanis make up the largest immigrant communities. Generations born here are often bilingual, speaking the mother tongue of their community and English with the local accent, peppering both languages with borrowed words. Visit Bradford, Southall (Outer London), Slough (near Windsor) and various other Asian-dominated communities around the country and you will find that English is very much the second, or perhaps even third language (albeit widely spoken). In recent years, Poles have become the third largest foreign-born community after Irish- and Indian-born people in Britain, and the Polish language is now the second most spoken language in England. Polish will no doubt play a significant role in the English lexicon.

CELTIC

Celtic-speakers were pushed westward by the invading Anglo-Saxons and their language was relegated to 'second-class' status. Gaelic (pronounced gah-lic), as some of the various branches of the Celtic language are now known, is still spoken in parts of Scotland and Ireland. Scottish Gaelic declined in status in Lowland Scotland during the medieval period, while the Highland Clearances and teaching of English led to its decline in the Highlands in the 18C–19C.

Welsh

In the Statute of Rhuddlan in 1284, Edward I recognised Welsh as an official and legal language. After the Battle of Bosworth in 1485, Welsh nobles hopefully followed the Tudors to London but Henry VIII decreed that "no person shall hold office within the Realme, except they exercise the English speech". The tradition of poetry and literature in the Welsh language, guarded by the bards and *eisteddfodau*, dates from Taliesin in the 7C. In 1500, the Bible was published in Welsh by Bishop Morgan and it was largely the willingness of the Church in Wales to preach in Welsh which saved the language from extinction. Reading in Welsh was encouraged by the Sunday School Movement, begun in Bala in 1789. The University of Wales was established in 1893. Teaching in Welsh was introduced in primary schools in 1939 and in secondary schools in 1956. Since 1982, Channel S4C has broadcast television in the Welsh language. Recent legislation has enhanced, even enshrined the language's status in law, and the quality of its teaching has also improved enormously in recent years.

Scots Gaelic

In Scotland, the Gaelic-speaking area, the *Gàidhealtachd*, is mostly confined to the Western Isles. The language, which was the mother tongue of 50% of the population in the 16C, is now spoken by less than 2%. The Normanised Kings of Scotland, especially David I (1124–53), introduced the Anglo-Norman language and later contact with the English court led to English becoming the language of the aristocracy. After the Union of 1603, the Statute of Iona attempted to impose the teaching of English on the sons of the chiefs and in 1616 the Scottish Privy Council decreed – '*that the Inglishe tongue be universallie plantit and the Scots language, one of chief and principalle causis of the continewance of barbaritie and incivilitie amongst the inhabitantis of the Ilis and Heylandis, may be abolisheit and removeit*'.

In 1777, a Gaelic Society was formed in London, the first of many all over the world, which maintain and encourage Gaelic language and literature. The percentage of Gaelic-speakers in Scotland is increasing slowly, particularly in Lowland areas.

Cornish

This branch of the Celtic languages was the only language of the Cornish peninsula until towards the end of the reign of Henry VIII. Although Dolly Pentreath, who was born in Mousehole in 1686 and died in December 1777, is claimed to be the last speaker of Cornish, there were no doubt other Cornish speakers, none of whom would have outlived the 18C. Modern efforts to revive the language have had some success.

Manx

The language spoken in the Isle of Man was similar to the Gaelic of the Western Isles of Scotland, but there has been no significant Manx-speaking community since the 1940s.

NORN

This Viking language, akin to Icelandic, survived in Orkney and Shetland until the 18C. It was the dominant tongue in Orkney until the Scottish-speaking Sinclairs became Earls of Orkney in 1379 and it remained the language of Shetland until well after the pledging of the Northern Isles to James III of Scotland in 1468–69. Modern dialects of both Shetland and Orkney still contain a sizeable body of words of Norn origin – types of wind and weather, flowers, plants and animals, seasons and holidays. A high percentage of place names throughout the islands are Norn.

Government

The Mother of Parliaments, famous for exporting its brand of democracy all over the world, most notably during the days of Empire, has in essence changed little over decades. These days however, decision making is more transparent in higher places and easier to influence at a local level.

DIVIDING A NATION

Britain is composed of England, Wales and Scotland, and, along with Northern Ireland forms the United Kingdom. The Channel Islands and the Isle of Man have their own independently administered jurisdictions and are known as Crown dependencies, but form part of the British Isles.

MONARCHY

The United Kingdom is a **constitutional monarchy**, a form of government in which supreme power is nominally vested in the sovereign (the king or queen). The origins of monarchy lie in the seven English kingdoms of the 6C–9C – Northumbria, East Anglia, Mercia, Essex, Wessex, Sussex and Kent. Alfred the Great (871–899) began to establish effective rule, but it was Canute (Cnut), a Danish king, who achieved unification.

The **coronation** ceremony gave a priestly role to the anointed monarch, especially from the Norman Conquest (1066) onwards. The Wars of the Roses, which dominated the 15C, were about dynastic rivalry, while the Tudors gained much from their exploitation of the mystique of monarchy. Although the kingdoms of England and Scotland were united in 1603, the Parliaments were not united until the Act of Union in 1709. The stubborn character of the Stuarts and the insistence of Charles I on the divine right of kings was in part responsible for the Civil War and the king's execution, which was followed by the **Commonwealth** (1649–60) under Oliver Cromwell, the only period during which the country was not a monarchy. At the **Restoration** (1660), the monarch's powers were placed under considerable restraints which were increased at the Glorious Revolution (1688) and the accession of William of Orange. The last attempt made by the Stuarts to regain the crown was crushed in the Jacobite risings of 1715 and 1745. During the reign of Queen Victoria (1837–1901) the monarch's right in relation to ministers was defined as 'the right to be consulted, to encourage and

MONARCHY IN MODERNITY

In 1997, the death of Diana, Princess of Wales, in a car accident in Paris, was the culmination of a series of events (divorces, scandals, revelations) that had rocked the Royal Family and caused the British public to question their validity. However, by the time the Queen celebrated her Jubilee year in 2002, and in 2015 her Diamond Jubilee as well as becoming Britain's longest reigning monarch, much of Britain had regained a sense of loyalty to the institution. But the question of succession remains. Prince Charles treads a fine line between traditionalist and moderniser with a common touch, but his age, and marriage to former lover and divorcee Camilla Parker Bowles, makes many prefer his elder son, Prince William, whose popularity was endorsed by his marriage to Kate Middleton in 2011 and the birth of their son George in 2013, and daughter, Charlotte in 2015; a third child is expected in 2018.

to warn', although Victoria clung tena-
ciously to her supervision of the Empire.

UK PARLIAMENT

The United Kingdom has no written
constitution. The present situation has
been achieved by the enactment of
new laws at key points in history. The
document known as **Magna Carta** was
sealed by a reluctant King John at Run-
nymede (near Windsor) on 15 June 1215.
Clause 39 guarantees every free man
security from illegal interference in his
person or his property. Since the reign
of Henry VII (or perhaps even earlier)
Habeas Corpus has been used to protect people against arbitrary arrest by
requiring the appearance in court of the
accused within a specified period.

The supreme legislature in the United
Kingdom is Parliament, which consists
of the **House of Commons** and the
House of Lords. Medieval Parliaments
were mainly meetings between the
king and his lords. The Commons were
rarely summoned and had no regular
meeting place nor even the right of free
speech until the 16C. Between 1430 and
1832, the right to vote was restricted
to those possessing a freehold worth
40 shillings. The Reform Act of 1867
enfranchised all borough householders;
county householders were included in
1884. In 1918, the franchise was granted
to all men over 21 and women over
30; in 1928 the vote was extended to
women over 21. Today, all over the age
of 18 are entitled to vote provided they
have entered their names on the elec-
toral roll. Since 1949 the Parliamentary
constituencies have been organised on
the principle that each should contain
about 65 000 voters, which produces
650 Members of the House of Commons.
The member elected to represent a
constituency is the candidate who
receives the largest number of votes.
The government is formed by the
party that wins the greatest number
of seats. The **House of Lords** consists
of the **Lords Spiritual** (the senior bishops of the Church of England) and the
Lords Temporal (dukes, marquesses,
earls, viscounts and barons). Under the
crown, the country is governed by laws
which are enacted by the **Legislature**
– the two Houses of Parliament – and
enforced by the **Judiciary** – the courts
of the land.

DEVOLUTION

Each of the three smaller nations has
its own parliament or assembly. The
Northern Ireland Assembly was created in 1973 from the old Northern
Ireland Parliament (with its legislative
powers withdrawn); in 1997 Scotland
regained its Parliament, previously dissolved in 1707; in 2006 Wales set up its
own Senedd (Parliament). The latter two
can pass their own laws though matters related to national security, foreign
policy and economic policy are handled
by Westminster for the time being. The
largest and most powerful of the three
is Scotland, whose current government,
the Scottish Nationalist Party, aims to
detach itself from Westminster and
eventually break away from the UK completely. As a starting point for the latter,
a referendum was held in September
2014, when the pro-Independence Scottish government asked 'Should Scotland
be an independent country?'. The No
side won, with 55.3 percent of the vote.

REGIONAL GOVERNMENT

While legislation and matters of state
have always been the prerogative of
Westminster, between 1994 and 2011,
England was divided into 11 regions
(North East, North West, East Midlands,
etc) each with its own government.
With the abolition of these bodies the
political picture has become more complex and infinitely more fragmented
with an emphasis on localism. Each of
Greater London's 33 boroughs admin-
isters its own regulations, while matters
that affect London as a whole are dealt
with by the London Assembly, headed
by the Mayor. Outside of London, the
country is mostly divided into parishes
that elect councillors to a county council, district council or non-metropolitan
who are responsible for local education
and infrastructure services plus strategic planning within a county.

Economy

The worst of the 2008 Recession is hopefully now behind the UK, but analysts are still scratching their heads as to which sectors will lead the UK recovery, though it seems London's global status will inevitably drive the change.

AGRICULTURE AND FISHING

Until the 18C, the economy of Britain was largely agricultural. In the 18C a combination of social and economic conditions led to landowners devoting their wealth and attention to improving land and methods of cultivation, giving rise to the **Agricultural Revolution**. Rapid population growth made it necessary to increase domestic agricultural productivity, as this was before the days of extensive overseas trade of consumables. Land enclosure became increasingly widespread, with even common land being suppressed by Acts of Parliament, landowners arguing that the system of enclosure was better for raising livestock, a more profitable form of agriculture than arable farming. Landowners enlarged their estates by taking over land abandoned by people leaving the countryside for the town, or emigrating to the New World, and developed a system based on maximising profit by introducing many efficient new farming methods. Milestones in this evolution include the use of fertiliser, abandoning the practice of leaving land to lie fallow every three years, and the introduction of new crop varieties (root crops for fodder and cultivated pasture) which in turn fostered the development of stock raising and increasing selectivity.

Nowadays, the average size of an English farm is around 50ha, and in Wales and Northen Ireland 40ha; Scottish farms are much larger. Agriculture, mechanised as much as possible, employs only 2.3% of the workforce. The practice of mixed farming, combining stock raising and crop farming, means that modern Britain meets its domestic needs in milk, eggs and potatoes, and almost totally in meat (with a national flock of about 29 million head, the United Kingdom is

eighth in the world for farming sheep). The European Union's Common Agricultural Policy has hit British farmers hard, the imposition of quotas forcing them to cut production of milk and adopt less intensive farming methods.

The **fishing industry**, once a mainstay of the island's economy, has declined considerably mainly because of modifications to national fishing boundaries and their attendant fishing rights. Arrangements drawn up for the Anglo-Irish zone and the approved quotas mean the annual catch for UK vessels is around 630 000 tons, which has not succeeded in arresting the decline of once-great fishing ports such as Kingston-upon-Hull or Grimsby after the departure of the canning factories.

ENERGY SOURCES

Coal was mined well before the 18C (Newcastle was exporting 33 000 tons of coal per year as early as the mid-16C), but became a large-scale industry only after the invention of the steam engine. Since the industry's heyday in the early 20C, production has been dropping steadily, despite a brief revival in the 1950s. Nowadays, in the wake of sweeping pit closures, in which deposits were exhausted or where it was felt extraction was no longer profitable, production has dropped significantly. In 2014, total UK production was 12 million tons, mainly concentrated in Yorkshire and Nottinghamshire, an all-time low. Production figures have not been helped by the fact that the high cost of exploiting most mines means that Britain can import coal more cheaply from countries such as Australia, nor by competition from oil and gas. In the 1960s, prospecting in the **North Sea** gave rise to sufficiently promising results for the countries bordering the sea to reach an agreement, under the Continental Shelf Act of 1964, on zones for extracting **natural gas**. Thanks to deposits along the Norfolk and Lincolnshire coasts, Britain is the world's fifth-largest producer, however, domestic demand is so great that gas has to be imported from Norway. Further north, off Scotland and the Shetland Islands, oil deposits give Great Britain dwindling independence in the energy sector, with total crude oil production at 40 million tons in 2014, down from 133 million tons in 1998.

Like the majority of developed countries, the United Kingdom converts a large proportion of its primary energy sources into electricity. About 70 percent of the electricity currently produced is thermal in origin (the Drax power station in Yorkshire is the most powerful in Europe). **Hydroelectricity** is negligible, as the relatively flat relief makes it impossible to build any sizeable hydroelectric power stations (only existing stations are in Scotland and Wales).

Nuclear energy, which has evolved since the construction of the experimental reactor at Calder Hall inaugurated in 1956, is now produced by nine nuclear power stations, all of which are to be found on the coast so that they can be cooled adequately. More recently, the wind has been harnessed to produce energy with massive turbines appearing all over the country.

INDUSTRY

In the second half of the 18C, hot on the heels of the Agricultural Revolution, capital began to flow from the land into industry, with new industrialists using the money from their family's success as cultivators of the land to set up factories, mills and businesses.

The presence of iron ore in Yorkshire, the Midlands and Scotland gave rise to the **iron and steel industry** (*see Ironbridge Gorge Museum*) which at its peak in the 19C was one of the industries at the core of the country's economy. However, by the beginning of the 20C the mineral deposits were exhausted, and Britain found itself importing ore from abroad, effectively bringing about the decline of its own inland iron and steel regions (Durham, the Midlands) in favour of those located on the coast (Teesside) and in South Wales (Port Talbot, Newport). In 2013, UK steel production was 11.9 million tons per year, surprisingly an increase over the previous four years, but still much lower than in the 1970s. Metal processing industries have equally suffered gravely in the face of competition from abroad.

There are few remaining large UK **shipyards** operating in the commercial sector, although a large naval shipbuilding programme for the Royal Navy, replacing old aircraft carriers, promises some continuity for the naval yards of Portsmouth, Plymouth, the Clyde, Barrow and Rosyth.

Britain's **car industry** once led Europe, with production levels of 2.3 million vehicles in the mid-1960s. It included some prestigious national companies, such as Triumph, Rover, Jaguar, Bentley and Rolls-Royce. Industrial disputes gave rise to a management crisis, however, culminating in nationalisation (British Leyland in 1975) and privatisation. In 2012, the UK's automotive industry ranked fourteenth in the world by production quantity, reflecting the massive increase in car production in other countries like China, Japan, South Korea and India. Japanese firms like Honda, Nissan and Toyota have assembly plants in the UK. VW owns Bentley, Ford owns Aston Martin, while BMW holds a corral of largely defunct British brands, but does produce the Mini (Oxfordshire) and Rolls-Royce cars (Chichester). As of 2008, Tata, an Indian car manufacturer, owns Jaguar Land Rover.

Britain has contributed to the rapid evolution of the **electronics and computer industries**. Foreign companies such as Honeywell, Burroughs, IBM, Hewlett-Packard and Mitsubishi have set up business in Scotland, providing a much-needed economic impetus in place of the region's defunct traditional industries. In 2009, the govern-

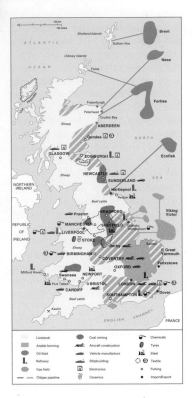

TRADE

Britain imports more primary materials than it exports. Services, particularly insurance, banking and business services, account for the largest proportion of GDP, while industry, particularly heavy industry, continues to decline in importance. A reduction in trade with North America has been offset by an increase in volume of trade with European Union member-states, now half of British exports.

Settlement markets, marine and air insurance brokers (Lloyd's, the world's leading marine risk insurers), life insurance, bank loans, deposits and other financial services combine to make the City of London the world's foremost **financial centre**. The huge profits generated by this business sector and the interest from investments abroad guarantee the United Kingdom's income.

COPING WITH CRISIS

Britain was the first European country to emerge from the economic crisis of the late-1980s/early-1990s; and during the second half of the decade and the early part of the Millennium continued to out-perform its neighbours and most other world economies in employment, inflation and other economic indicators. The credit freeze resulting from the debt crisis in 2007–08 placed the UK back in recession. In response, the government launched a controversial austerity programme, with large cutbacks in public spending, combined with quantitative easing (the creation, if not physical printing, of new money). The opposition claim that the strategy is not working, vindicated by the "double-dip recession" (when GDP shrank after a quarter or two of positive growth) and pointing out that the disposable income of most people has declined dramatically over the last few years. In 2013, the government at last had favourable figures to show, with the UK economy growing 0.8 percent in the third quarter, due largely to banking, telecoms, computing and government spending. In 2015, inflation fell to 0%, but by 2017 had risen to 2.9%, a four-year high.

ment placed much emphasis on Digital Britain as one of the pillars of the plan to beat the recession, with continuing investment in **communications** and bolstering of **creative industries**.

Britain developed a flourishing **textile industry**, thanks to its large numbers of resident sheep and the groundbreaking inventions of the Industrial Revolution, and maintained its position as world leader until the mid-20C. Yorkshire, with Bradford as capital, was home to 80 percent of wool production. Lancashire, with Manchester as its centre, specialised in cotton. However, this national industry has been overtaken by artificial fibres, illustrating the role that the **chemical industry** now plays in Britain's economy. Some of Britain's largest industrial groups are chemical based. The largest British chemicals firm is British Petroleum (BP), and two other giants in the field of petrochemicals are supported by an Anglo-Dutch financial association: Shell and Unilever.

Traditional Festivities

Many rural traditions have declined owing to population mobility, the building over of land once dedicated to festivals and the adoption of new farming methods. On the other hand the popularity of outdoor activities, particularly those connected with sport and horses, has led to many of them evolving into fashionable events in the social calendar.

MORRIS DANCING

The origins of Morris dancing are uncertain. According to some the word Morris derives from Moorish. The dancers are traditionally men, dressed in white shirts and trousers, with bells tied below the knee and sometimes colourful hats. Dancers knock stout sticks and wave handkerchiefs as they dance.

THE MAYPOLE

Until the 17C many parishes had permanent maypoles, pagan fertility symbols belonging to a spring festival, tacitly accepted and tamed by the Christian church. In 1644, however, under the Puritans, the Maypole was banned throughout England but returned at the Restoration (1660), marking both May Day and Oak Apple Day, anniversary of Charles II's entry into London.

PANCAKE DAY

Shrove Tuesday, the day preceding the first day of Lent, is the occasion for cooking, tossing and eating sweet pancakes, which are served with sugar and lemon juice. Pancake races are also held in which competitors toss a pancake while running.

CHEESE ROLLING

Cooper's Hill, Gloucestershire. A Whit Monday/Spring Bank Holiday festival. Officially banned in 2010, 8lb Double Gloucester cheeses are still rolled down a steep slope, with the youth of the village and assorted nutters allowed to chase after it at the count of three. Injury frequently occurs, but the tradition somehow survives in this generally risk-averse culture.

THE FURRY DANCE

Helston. The sole remaining example of a communal spring festival dance in Britain, this dance, a celebration of the passing of Winter, has taken place in Helston, Cornwall, for centuries, on 8 May, feast day of St Michael the Archangel, patron saint of the church.

WELL DRESSING

Christianity forbade the worship of water spirits but many wells were simply 'purged' and re-dedicated to the Blessed Virgin or one of the saints. In Derbyshire the custom of decking wells or springs with flowers still continues, under the auspices of the church. Large pictures are formed on boards covered with clay, the design being picked out in flowers, pebbles, shells or any natural object; manufactured materials are not used. It is said that the most famous well dressing, at Tissington, began in its present form either after a prolonged drought in 1615 when only the wells of Tissington continued to give water or in thanksgiving for deliverance from the Black Death (1348–49).

EISTEDDFODAU

Wales is famous for its international cultural festivals offering song, music and dance (Builth Wells, Llangollen). Many contestants perform in costumes.

HIGHLAND GAMES

The games, which originated in 11C contests in the arts of war, are held in Scotland between June and September. The heavy events include putting the shot, throwing the hammer and tossing the caber, complemented by pipe bands.

Gourmet Guide to Britain

Britain provides a cosmopolitan choice of food but also has a rich tradition of regional dishes, all using local fish, game, fruit and dairy products to best advantage. Some of the treats listed below can be hard to find and rarely appear on restaurant menus. You may need to enlist the services of local specialists, such as independent butchers, food shops or farmers' markets in order to track them down.

MODERN BRITISH CUISINE

Modern cuisine in the UK has never been in better health, fed by a revitalised respect for quality produce and cooking. Immigration and increased foreign travel has resulted in a broadening of general tastes, meaning that there are few cuisines that cannot be found in Britain these days. London boasts just about every style of kitchen in the world, and the big cities, while nowhere near as comprehensive, now offer an increasingly global choice of restaurants alongside the old favourites of French, Italian, 'Indian' (usually Bangladeshi), Thai and Chinese.

British taste buds have been tantalised for over five decades by TV chefs from Fanny Craddock in the 1960s to the likes of today's celebrity superchefs: Gordon Ramsay, Jamie Oliver and Heston Blumenthal. The latter generation, with their carefully contrived images

(respectively – swearing Scotsman on a rescue mission; pukka London lad saving the nation from school dinner horrors; and mad molecular gastronomic scientist) have helped to energise British cooking. Every year has a new hit TV series, from *Masterchef* to *The Great British Bake Off*. The latter ensures that eggs, baking powder and whatever other ingredients, the contestants prescribe, are greedily snapped up from the supermarket shelves the day after.

SURREY, KENT AND SUSSEX

See pp192–217.

Kent is known as 'The Garden of England', largely on account of its **orchards** and **hop** gardens. Hops are used to flavour beer and were traditionally dried in conical shaped oast houses on farms. Today most hops are dried industrially, but the oast houses remain a distinctive part of the Kent landscape. Not

Borough Market, Southwark, London

© Massimo Borchi / Sime / Photononstop

surprisingly Kent is famous for its brewing heritage and boasts Britain's oldest brewery, **Shepherd Neame**, located in Faversham. They have been rolling out the barrels since 1698 and are open to visitors for tours (*www.shepherd neame.co.uk/brewery*). Also at Faversham is Brogdale Farm (*www.brogdalecollections.co.uk*), home to the **National Fruit Collection**, including many varieties of apples and pears, plums and cherries, soft fruits, quinces, and more. Orchard tours (*Apr–Oct*) and regular food festivals are staged.

Biddenden vineyard is Kent's oldest commercial vineyard, est. 1969. In addition to still table wines and sparkling wines they also produce traditional Kentish ciders and farm-pressed apple juices (open for tours, *www.biddendenvine yards.com*). **Chapel Down**, at Tenterden (*www.chapeldown.com*) is one of England's leading premium wine producers; apparently Chapel Down was served at Buckingham Palace as part of the 2012 Royal Wedding celebration. They are open for guided tours, have a very good wine and food store (showcasing local suppliers), and a restaurant.

Whitstable is famous for its oysters. You can get them anywhere in town; the most famous restaurant and oyster bar is Wheelers, est. 1856. In late July the town stages its oyster festival www. whitstableoysterfestival.com.

In **Canterbury**, the Goods Shed (*http:// thegoodsshed.co.uk*), a beautifully converted Victorian warehouse next to Canterbury West train station, houses a daily Farmers Market (closed Mon), food hall, a small diner and an excellent restaurant. It includes a butcher, a 'bottle shop' (featuring the largest number of British bottled beers in the South East), a cheesemaker with around 40 artisanal varieties, and much more.

The county's major regional event is the **Kent Food & Drink Festival** (third weekend Sept, *www.canterbury.co.uk*) It's not often that you think about beer and Surrey at the same time, but a tour around the **Hog's Back Brewery** (*www. hogsback.co.uk*) set in 18C farm buildings between Guildford and Farnham,

may well change all that. Brewing since 1992 and supplying all over the county and beyond, the tours are humorous, informative and intoxicatingly generous with the sampling of their excellent ales (as well as an excellent cider and lager). **Denbies English vineyard** (open for tours, *www.denbies.co.uk*) in Dorking, Surrey is the UK's largest vineyard and produces sparkling and table wines. In Sussex, Lurgashall Winery (*www. lurgashall.co.uk*) enjoys a picturesque location and produces English liqueurs, meads and county wines. Its visitor centre and small museum is housed in 17C and 19C century farm buildings.

Surrey's largest farmer's market, at **Guildford**, attracts over 60 stallholders (*1st Tue month except Jan*). **Shoreham-by-Sea** (*2nd Sat of month*) is home to the largest Farmers' Market in Sussex, also with around 60 stallholders. Based in the heart of the fashionable North Laine district, **Brighton Farm Market** is open Tuesday to Saturday and every second and fourth Sunday, with around 25 to 30 food stalls each Saturday

One of Britain's most unusual food festivals, the **West Dean Chilli Fiesta**, is held in West Dean Gardens Sussex, (*Aug, www.westdean.org.uk/Events*) showcasing over 300 chillies and their multiple uses, from chilli beer and ice cream to some of the hottest sauces known to man. Beer and cider tents sooth overheated palates.

HAMPSHIRE, DORSET, WILTSHIRE
 See pp218–253

In Hampshire, the delightful Georgian town of **Alresford** ("Arlsford"), together with the beautiful adjacent village of Old Alreford, near Winchester, is known for it **watercress**, with the steam trains of the Mid-Hants Railway's famous Watercress Line (*www.watercressline. co.uk*) passing alongside beds where the green peppery salad plant is grown. There is an Annual Watercress Festival (*www.watercressfestival.org*) on the middle Sunday in May.

On the south coast between Southampton and Portsmouth, **Wickham**

Vineyards (open for tours, *www.wick hamvineyard.co.uk*) produces award-winning wines.

Winchester stages the largest – and also recently voted the best – farmers' market in the country (*second and last Sun of month, also some Sats, www.visit winchester.co.uk*) with around 95 local producers showcasing local Hampshire food and drink.

Dorset is the beginning of the West Country, famous for its **cider** (see Somerset, below). Dorset also puts its apples to good use in the delicious and ubiquitous **Dorset Apple Cake** (best served warm with cream). The county is also known for **Dorset Blue** cheese, and its close relative, **Blue Vinny**. Try the latter in Puddletown, near Dorchester, at The Blue Vinny Restaurant (*www.the bluevinny.co.uk*).

Hall & Woodhouse (*www.hall-wood-house.co.uk*), best known for their Badger beers, offers brewery tours from their visitor centre in Blandford St Mary, near Wimborne.

Wiltshire has a long history of pig-keeping and is famous for its high quality, traditionally cured pork and bacon, and particularly its ham. In fact its town, Swindon, derives its name from 'swine down' or 'pig hill' after the herds of pigs that used to graze there. The perfect accompaniment to Wiltshire ham is **Wiltshire Tracklements** (*www.trackle-ments.co.uk*), producing some of the country's finest mustards, chutneys, relishes and other meat accompaniments. Wash it down with a pint of the nationally acclaimed 6X Bitter from **Wadworth Brewery** (*www.wadworth. co.uk*) at Devizes. The brewery's giant shire horses still can be seen pulling the dray (traditional delivery wagon) around the streets of the old market town, and brewery tours from the visitor centre (*Mon–Sat*).

Lardy Cake is a well-known traditional Wiltshire confection, made of lard or butter, dough, sugar and dried fruit. It has a delicious toffee taste and is highly fattening.

Bacon Fraise is a 15C agricultural worker's breakfast dish, consisting of fried bacon, which is then covered with batter and then cooked in the oven. It's worth a try, if you can find it. More easy to track down, in traditional butcher's shops or at farmers' markets, is Devizes Pie, which contains pork accompanied by lamb, veal, tongue and vegetables. In the 18C, **Wiltshire cheese** was popular throughout the UK, but demand for milk in London led Wiltshire's dairy farmers to abandon production. Thankfully, North Wiltshire Cheese Loaf can now be bought at specialist shops and local farmers' markets.

The **Isle of Wight**'s most unusual foodstuffs come from The **Garlic Farm** at Newchurch (www.thegarlicfarm.co.uk). In addition to fresh bulbs, smoked garlic, garlic bread, pickles and relishes etc, they also do garlic beer and garlic ice cream. You can taste some of them at their own café-restaurant. The Isle of Wight Garlic Festival (mid/late Aug, *www.thegarlicfarm.co.uk*) attracts around 25 000 visitors each year.

CHILTERNS, OXFORDSHIRE, COTSWOLDS
♿ See pp254–279

Oxford's Victorian **Covered Market** (*www.oxford-coveredmarket.co.uk*), trading since 1774, is foodie heaven, chock-a-block with butchers, fresh fruit and vegetable stalls, fishmongers, cookie makers, chocolatiers and bakers, mixed with retail shops and small cafés, all under one roof. Pick up a jar of Frank Cooper's **Oxford marmalade** from here; made in Oxford between 1874 and 1967, it is supposedly a favourite of HM the Queen. Captain Scott took a jar to the Arctic on his fateful final mission in 1912 and it was found, perfectly preserved, along with the remains of the expedition, in 1980. Frank Cooper was a grocer and you can see the building where he came up with the recipe on the High Street in Oxford at number 83, although it has long since changed hands.

Oxford sausages, sometimes know as Oxford Skates, are traditionally skinless, semi-circular and made of a combination of veal and pork. Oxford's covered market is a good place to find them, as well as **Oxford Blue Cheese**, which was created in the 1990s and has won many awards. **Oxford sauce** would be a perfect accompaniment to Oxford sausages, being similar to Cumberland sauce, but it is no longer widely used. Oxford's butchers have long been associated with its colleges, and so there are some unique cuts of meat hewn here, including **Oxford John**, a lamb steak from the leg, and Oxford brawn, which is made from the meat of a pig's head. Lovers of traditional desserts should try a **Banbury Cake**, which is made from puff pastry, currants and rosewater. Oxford has a number of stodgy puddings to its name. **Oxford Pudding** is made of apricots, cream, eggs and puff pastry; **New College Pudding** is similar to a steamed pudding and is made of suet and currants; **Spiced Oxford Cake** is a type of fruitcake; while **Hollygog Pudding** is a mess of treacle and crumbly dough, best served with custard.

Hook Norton Brewery has been operating from the small village of Hook Norton (between Chipping Norton and Banbury) for over 150 years (*tours Mon–Sat; www.hooky.co.uk*). The brewery's shire horses can be seen delivering in the streets of Hook Norton village.

Brakspear beers have been brewed in Oxfordshire since the early 18C. When the original Henley Brewery closed in 2002 (now occupied by the Hotel du Vin), the **Wychwood** Brewery in Witney took over brewing the beers, and moved several large pieces of historic brewing kit to their home in Witney (*tours Sat–Sun afternoons, pre-booking advised; www.brakspear-beers.co.uk*).

Brightwell vineyard, beside the Thames, near Wallingford is the region's largest wine producer (*sales and tastings; Fri–Sun pm, tours by appointment; brightwellvineyard.co.uk*).

Gloucestershire is known for its semi-hard **Gloucester cheese**, made from the milk of Gloucestershire breed cows farmed within the county. It always comes in rounds – with Double Gloucester aged for a longer period. It can be found all over, but for a wide choice of traditional cheeses – both local and beyond – from an expert cheesemonger, visit the House of Cheese, Tetbury (*www.houseofcheese.co.uk*).

Gloucestershire Old Spots Pork, which comes from a black-spotted pedigree breed of pigs, has recently become a protected name under EU regulations and is prized for its tenderness and juiciness. Aylesbury has a long history of "ducking" and the free-range **Aylesbury duck** is famous for its taste.

BRISTOL, BATH AND SOMERSET
⌖See pp280–301

Bristol's association with chocolate goes back to 1847 when Joseph Fry invented eating **chocolate** as we know it today, moulding solid chocolate in his Bristol shop (until then chocolate was just a drink). The last chocolate maker in the city is Guilbert's (*www.guilbertschocolates.co.uk*), hand-making chocolates here since 1910. The Bristol Chocolate Festival (end Mar) at Harbourside celebrates the city's heritage.

The Victorian market buildings on **Corn Street** are the daily home of St Nicholas Market (*www.stnicholasmarketbristol.co.uk*), a bastion of both local and global cuisine. The emphasis is on local food every Wednesday at the Bristol Farmer's Market, and on the first Sunday of the month for the Slow Food Market.

Bath is famous for the **Bath Bun**, a rich egg-and-sugar brioche invented by Dr William Oliver (1695–1764). Try one at Sally Lunn's (*www.sallylunns.co.uk*). He also invented the **Bath Oliver** biscuit, usually eaten with cheese. In 1997 Bath hosted Britain first modern day farmers' market. It is still held at Green Park Station (*www.bathfarmersmarket.co.uk*).

Somerset is "where the cider apples grow". Good places to see and taste are Sheppy's Cider Farm, Shop and Museum (*www.sheppyscider.com*); Perry's Cider (*www.perryscider.co.uk*); The Somerset Distillery (*www.ciderbrandy.co.uk*); Pennard Organic Wines & Cider & Avalon Vineyard (*www.avalonvineyard.co.uk*). The term 'scrumpy' refers to the still (non-sparkling) stronger/more alcoholic types of cider.

Somerset is also the birthplace of **Cheddar cheese**. The Cheddar Gorge Cheese Company (*www.cheddaronline. co.uk*) are the only cheese makers left in Cheddar.

DEVON AND CORNWALL

♿ See pp302–338

Cornwall's most famous food is the ubiquitous **Cornish pasty**, a D-shaped shortcrust pastry case, traditionally enclosing potato, swede, onion and steak/beef. It is said that the top edge was crimped into a "handle" (which would be thrown away) so that tin miners could safely eat the pasty without touching it with their arsenic-tainted fingers. Highly rated traditional pasty shops include The Lizard Pasty Shop (*www.annspasties.co.uk*) at Helston. Pasties also feature in the new Cornish Pasty Museum at Cornucopia (*www. cornucopiacornwall.com*).

The **pilchard** (an adult sardine) was once the mainstay of the Cornish fishing industry, In 1871, nearly 16 000 tons were caught, but by the end of the 20C it had declined to a mere 6 tons per annum, and the image of pilchards was that of a tinned food of last resort. In 2003, however, the humble pilchard was reborn as the fashionable "Cornish sardine" and sales have come on recently in leaps and bounds. Cornwall's fish champion is TV chef Rick Stein (*www.rickstein. com*), who, along with Michelin-starred Paul Ainsworth, has elevated Padstow (♿ *see North Cornwall Coast, p329*) into a shrine for fish and seafood gourmets.

Mackerel, the main catch of St Ives, is widespread throughout Cornwall, and is also sold potted. You can hire a boat and line and catch your own, at several places, with no experience.

Clotted cream is associated with both Devon and Cornwall. Rich and thick, it is made by indirectly heating full-cream cow's milk (using steam or a water bath) and then leaving it to cool slowly. It is an indispensable part of a "cream tea" (scones, jam and cream, served with tea). Another sweet Cornish treat is the saffron cake or bun. Although traditionally associated with Easter, it is widely available all year.

Devon's rich milk is still being used to create a variety of Devon cheeses. **Devon Blue** comes from Totnes, while **Beenleigh Blue** is made from ewes milk from the River Dart area and **Harbourne Blue** is made from the milk of goats that graze on Dartmoor. Other Devon cheeses of note include Curworthy, Sharpham, Tyning and Belstone. The Victorian market in Barnstaple is a good place to pick up all of the above. Devon's pear orchards used to supply the fair in Barnstaple, hence the origins of the **Barnstaple Fair Pears** dessert.

Laverbread is a traditional Welsh baked good that has long been popular in North Devon; its key ingredient is seaweed, *laver*, collected from the beach. The traditional drink of Devon and Cornwall is **cider** (♿ *see also Somerset*). You can see how it is made at **Healey's Cornish Cyder Farm** (www. thecornishcyderfarm.co.uk) near Truro. Wine making also takes place in the Southwest. **Vineyards** open for tours include: **Yearlstone** (*www.yearlstone. co.uk*) at Bickleigh, Devon; Sharpham (*www.sharpham.com*) at Totnes, Devon, who also boast a creamery producing superb cheeses; Camel valley, near Bodmin, Cornwall (*www.camelvalley.com*), whose sparkling wines have won top international prizes in recent years.

South Devon is one of the best places in the West Country both for eating out in general and for local produce; **South Devon crab** is said to be one of the finest varieties of crab in the world. In a beautiful setting, the **Dartmouth Food Festival** (*late Oct; www.dartmouthfood-festival.com*) is a very high-quality major annual event.

The largest food festival in the region is **Flavourfest**, held in Plymouth, with 100 stalls attracting 150 000 people (*mid-Aug; www.plymouth.gov.uk*). Plymouth is famous for gin; its **Black Friars Distillery** is the oldest working gin distillery in England (*www.ply mouthgin.com*), making **Plymouth Gin** since 1793.

EAST ANGLIA

See pp338–359

Norfolk's most famous foods are Cromer crabs and Norfolk Black Turkeys. Less readily available is the local speciality of dumplings, mussels in cider and mustard. During the summer, samphire, 'poor man's asparagus', grows wild along the salt marshes and is eaten with melted butter.

Suffolk is known for its apple juice and cider, while on the coast they serve a spicy shrimp pie, cooked with wine, mace and cloves in a puff pastry case.

From Essex comes sausages and bacon, while Colchester is famous for its oysters (both native and Rock Oysters) and its more affordable cockles.

Local foodies beat a path to **3At3 Delicatessen and Café** (*www.3at3deli.com*), which takes its name not only from its address (3 Three Cups Walk), but also the three counties, Cambridgeshire, Suffolk and Norfolk, from which their produce is sourced. It is also ideally located opposite the cathedral.

In Essex, in the centre of Colchester, **Gunton's** (*www.guntons.co.uk*), founded 1936, is a delightful traditional grocer/deli selling hand roasted coffee, hand packed teas, well over 100 different cheeses, their own home cooked gammon, and much more.

Jimmy's Farm, near Ipswich (*http://jimmysfarm.com*) is not only a farm shop and restaurant but a family attraction with nature trails and regular events. Its butchers is one of the best in England; home to the Rare Breed Essex Pig, it has gained numerous awards for its sausages. Jimmy himself is something of a celebrity having starred in several TV programmes and has a range of (free range) food products to his name, also on sale in local supermarkets.

In summer, it's worth the diversion down to the farm (also near Ipswich) to sample the Fruit Cream Ices at **Alder Tree** (*www.alder-tree.co.uk*). A mix of the highest quality sorbet and full-bodied ice cream, their Damson flavour, or Tayberry and Toffee Apple may tempt.

EAST MIDLANDS

See pp360–375

The small market town of **Melton Mowbray** boasts the title of "UK Rural Capital of Food" and is synonymous with Melton Mowbray Pork Pies. These handmade pies are encased in a rich hot-water crust pastry, then traditionally baked without using a supporting tin or hoop, which gives the pie its classic bow-sided shape. Natural bone-stock jelly is added to the pie after baking to enhance the natural uncured (and slightly spiced) pork flavour. They are generally eaten cold as a snack. The oldest pork pie bakery in the country, Dickinson & Morris (*www.porkpie.co.uk*) have been baking at Ye Olde Pork Pie Shoppe in the centre of the town since 1851 (production has recently moved to an out-of-town factory).

Melton Mowbray is also home to one of the six producers of Stilton cheese (*www.stiltoncheese.com*), which by law can only be produced in the three counties of Derbyshire, Nottinghamshire and Leicestershire. Colston Bassett is another of the six accredited places, and its creamery has a small shop selling Colston Bassett Stilton, though it is not open to the public for tours. Another well known local cheese is **Red Leicester**, a hard cows' milk cheese made in a similar way as Cheddar, but with a moister, crumblier texture and a milder flavour. It is coloured with a vegetable dye called annatto, which gives the distinctive orange appearance.

The **Melton Mowbray Food Festival** showcases the food of the **East Midlands** (first weekend Oct, *http://meltonmowbrayfoodfestival.co.uk*).

Near Melton Mowbray, at Old Dalby, is the Belvoir (pronounced "beaver") Brewery (tours daily, *www.belvoirbrewery.co.uk*). Lincolnshire is historically associated with the **Lincolnshire sausage**, available nationwide, which has a distinctive sage flavour. The area's best artisan cheese is Lincolnshire Poacher (*www.lincolnshirepoachercheese.com*). You can find it in The Cheese Society Shop & Café (*www.thecheesesociety.co.uk*) in the city centre, and at The

Cheese Shop, at Louth (*www.thecheese shoplouth.co.uk*), east of Lincoln, which in 2011, won the *Daily Telegraph* "Best Small Food Shop in Britain" award.

Salt pork filled with herbs, otherwise known as **stuffed chine**, is a speciality of Lincolnshire. A chine is a square cut of meat cut from between the shoulder-blades. The county is also a producer of **haslet** (pronounced 'hacelet'). This traditional pork meat loaf is seasoned with sage.

Lincolnshire plum bread is made with dried fruit (sultanas and currants rather than plums) – it's worth finding a good baker for a better version than some sold in supermarkets.

Samphire is relatively widely available in Lincolnshire, where it grows on the marshland. **Grantham Gingerbread** is also well-known here, which has a hard crust, slightly gooey interior and strong ginger flavour.

Lincolnshire's best known brewery is **Bateman's** (*www.bateman.co.uk*, daily tours). Based in Wainfleet, south west of Skegness, they have been in business since 1874. IPA and Nut Brown are a couple of its well-known beers.

Held during the first week of October, **Nottingham Goose Fair** (*www.notting hamcity.gov.uk*) dates back to the 13C, making it perhaps the oldest in the country. Today, it is just a funfair, but nevertheless, roast goose remains a popular dish in Nottingham. Bramley cooking apples originate in Nottingham and there's no way better to eat them than baked in a **Nottingham Batter Pudding**.

WEST MIDLANDS AND THE PEAK DISTRICT
See pp376–407

The charming market town of **Ludlow**, in Shropshire, is known as the provincial food and drink capital of England, thanks to its abundance of high quality independent food specialists in all sectors of the market. There are too many good local food shops to mention here but Wall's butchers (*www.wallsbutchers. co.uk*), Price's bakery (*www.pricesthe-bakers.co.uk*); and the Mousetrap (*see below*) are particularly worth a visit. Just out of town the award-winning **Ludlow Food Centre** (*www.ludlow foodcentre.co.uk*) is a one-stop foodie heaven that brings together local farming, food production and retailing. You can watch much of the food preparation through large windows around the edge of the store as you shop. Its butchery sources meat from the Centre's own estate, its bakery uses local flour, it has a deli – which sells Shropshire Fidget Pie, made with gammon, cooking apples, onions and potatoes – plus a jam and pickle kitchen and a cafe/restaurant where you can sample their own home-made pasta and pastries.

The highlight of the food year is the **Ludlow Food Festival** (Sept; *www. foodfestival.co.uk*) featuring over 180 exhibitors and producers from Ludlow and the Marches (England–Wales border country). The **Ludlow Spring Festival** (May; *www.ludlowspringfestival. co.uk*) is a beery celebration including over 180 draught real ales and 60 food producers. A weekly Farmers' Market (*www.localtoludlow.org.uk*) takes place the second and fourth Thursday of each month.

Herefordshire has a proud, near 200-year old reputation for the quality of its **beef**, and the Hereford bull is a symbol of the town. The county is also renowned for **cider** making, and Weston's Cider (*www.westons-cider.co.uk*), in Much Marcle, offer daily tours. Visit too The Cider Museum in Hereford (*see p386*). Much less traditional is one of the county's more recent success stories, a premium vodka, made from potato and apple, at Chase Distillery (*www.chase distillery.co.uk*), near Ledbury. Voted best vodka in the world 2010, it is on sale nationwide; stockists include the Ludlow Food Centre (*see above*). Chase also produce liqueurs, gin, marmalade vodka and an apple vodka. Find out more on one of their tours.

You can watch **Little Herefordshire Cheese** being made at Pleck Farm, Monkland, west of Leominster (*www. monklandcheesedairy.co.uk*); its shop also stocks a range of other British farm cheeses, and has a rustic café too. Look Mousetrap Cheese (*www.mousetrapcheese.co.uk*) who have shops in Leominster, Ludlow and Hereford.

Bakewell, in Derbyshire, has given its name to the now ubiquitous commercially produced shortcrust pastry, jam and almond Bakewell Tart. Two shops in Bakewell offer what they both claim is the original recipe. The Bakewell Tart Shop & Coffee House (*www.bakewell-tartshop.co.uk*) sells a Bakewell Tart, while the (more historic) Old Original Bakewell Pudding Shop (*www.bakewellpuddingshop.co.uk*) – which has a café/restaurant attached – bakes and sells Bakewell Pudding.

Pork scratchings are a popular pub snack in this region. These salted, crisp pieces of cooked pig skin are sold in small plastic bags.

Coventry used to be known for its **Coventry Godcakes**, which have a tri-angular shape in reference to the Holy Trinity. Now revived, you can get them at Esquires Coffee House, at the city's Transport Museum.

Recently Birmingham has become famous for its many restaurants serving **Balti** cuisine (*www.balti-birmingham.co.uk*); the balti is the steel wok-like pan, traditionally heated over a gas flame. The cuisine may have originated from the Pakistani Kashmir but is frequently said to have been invented in Birmingham.

THE NORTH WEST

☞ See pp408–429

Liverpudlians are traditionally known as 'Scousers', a term that is thought to come from the food, **scouse** (derived from the German *Lebskaus*, or Scandinavian *lapskaus/lobscouse*), which was originally a thrifty leftovers stew of mutton/lamb and vegetables, sometimes served with a sharp vinegary beetroot or red cabbage. It's increasingly hard to find; try local pubs, Maggie May's Café on Bold Street, or the Malmaison Hotel. The best restaurants to find local specialities on the menu in **Liverpool** are The London Carriage Works (*www.thelondoncarriageworks.co.uk)* and Deli-

fonseca (*www.delifonseca.co.uk*). Malmaison Hotel (*www.malmaison.com*) is also good. The former is not only one of the city's finest places to eat, but a fierce champion of local producers. Delifonseca is more casual, though still serving seriously good food in its restaurants, each of which shares the same roof as the deli in its two city branches.

On the cheeseboard, look out for **Lancashire** (Mrs Kirkham's is a popular make; *www.mrskirkhamscheese.co.uk*) and **Cheshire** cheeses. Both offer blue mould varieties; Garstang Blue from Lancashire, and Blue Cheshire. Two of the best regional cheese shops are The Cheese Shop (116 Northgate Street; Chester: *www.chestercheeseshop.co.uk*) who stock over 150 different British cheeses, and the Liverpool Cheese Company Ltd (*www.liverpoolcheesecompany.co.uk*), based in an old Grade-II-listed dairy in picturesque Woolton Village, Liverpool.

On the **Wirral peninsula**, Claremont Farm (*www.claremontfarm.co.uk*) is famous for its asparagus (in season from late May to August) and is regarded as "the good food hub of the Wirral" with a farm shop, and food events staged year-round including the Wirral Food and Drink Festival (first weekend May; *www.wirralfoodfestival.co.uk*).

Liverpool city centre hosts five **farmers' markets** each month (*http://liverpool.gov.uk*). The Wirral Farmers' Market (*www.wirralfarmersmarket.co.uk*) in New Ferry is always popular with over 30 stalls. The biggest city event of the year is the Food and Drink Festival (early Sept; *www.liverpoolfoodanddrinkfestival.co.uk*).

Manchester hosts the biggest food festival in the North West, lasting 10 days (early–mid-Oct; *http://foodanddrinkfestival.com*). The city's best retail showcase for local produce is the Unicorn (*www.unicorn-grocery.co.uk*) deli-grocery at Chorlton, South Manchester, run on a co-operative basis.

For a **brewery tour** visit **Robinson's** in Stockport (*www.robinsonsvisitorscentre.co.uk*), who have been brewing in the area since 1838. Also just outside

Manchester is Eccles, birthplace of the famous raisin-filled puff pastry **Eccles Cake**, delicious eaten warm. The nearest version of the long-gone original is probably the **Real Lancashire brand** (*www.lancashireecclescakes.co.uk*).

Other **regional specialities** to look out for are: Lancashire hotpot, lamb/mutton, vegetables and onions, topped with sliced potatoes and slow-cooked in the oven; potted shrimps from Southport; Goosnargh corn-fed chicken and duck, from Goosenargh, near Preston. For the renowned **Bury Black Pudding** and much more, visit Bury Market (Wed, Fri and Sat, *www.burymarket.com*).

The **Hollies Farm Shops** (*www.thehollies farmshop.co.uk*), at Little Budworth, Tarporley, near Chester, and Lower Stretton, near Warrington (halfway between Chester and Manchester) have been described as the "Harrods Food Hall(s) of the North", crammed with locally sourced, traditionally produced foods. Both shops have café/restaurants which feature local produce. You can also dine very well at both locations.

CUMBRIA AND THE LAKES

See pp430–443

Two places that promote all things Cumbrian in their comprehensive **food halls**, and offer café-restaurants to taste there and then, are **Cranstons** (*www.cranstons.net*) in Penrith and the **Rheged Centre** (*www.rheged.com*), just outside the town. Cranstons is the larger of the two, has the greater pedigree (est. 1914), and are master butchers; Rheged has a range of other Lake District-themed attractions.

The region's most famous meat product is the traditional **Cumberland Sausage** (along with neighbouring Westmoreland, Cumberland was absorbed into Cumbria in 1974). This long, chunky, textured, peppery pork sausage is characterised by its formation into a rope-like coil, as opposed to being divided into "links". It can be found everywhere in the region and beyond, but for some of the very best try Cranstons (*see above*), and Higginson's butchers, Grange-over-Sands. To accompany your

Cumberland sausage, try **Cumberland sauce** (*see below*).

In restaurants look out for **Morecambe Salt Marsh Lamb** and **Cumbrian Mutton**, the latter championed by Prince Charles and taken up by many top chefs. In basic terms, mutton is meat from sheep that are older than lambs, though even its aficionados cannot agree on the exact definition.

Cumbria's fells and moors are well suited to **sheep farming**, with hardy breeds chosen to weather out the colder months.

On the coast look for **Solway Oysters**, cockles, scallops (the smaller flavourful '**Queenies**' from the Isle of Man are best) and potted shrimps in butter from **Morecambe Bay**. Manx **kippers** are another Isle of Man speciality. **Char** is a tasty lake fish from Coniston, Windermere and Wast Water.

Thornby Moor Dairy (*www.thornby moordairy.co.uk*) at Thursby make artisan cheese entirely by hand in open vats, including traditional, cloth-bound Cumberland Cheese. The cheesemaking room can be seen through a gallery window and the shop assistant will explain the process to visitors.

The perfect accompaniment to both local cheese and meats is the comprehensive range of traditional preserves, relishes, pickles and chutneys sold by The **Hawkshead Relish Company** (*www.hawksheadrelish.com*) from their shop in Hawkshead. These include Damson Ketchup, made from local Westmorland **damsons**, and old-fashioned **Cumberland Sauce**, once famous nationwide. This rich pungent pouring sauce is traditionally made with a mixture of redcurrants, damson wine, oranges and lemons, redcurrant jelly, Dijon mustard, port and ground ginger. Regional sweet treats include the widely available **Kendal Mintcake** and the much more exclusive **Grasmere Gingerbread**, sold only in Grasmere (*see p434*).

For something completely off-the-wall, seek out **Kendal Mint Cake Vodka** (*www.mintdrinks.co.uk*) in Kendal.

A relative newcomer to the local food scene is **Cartmel Sticky Toffee Pudding** (*www.cartmelvillageshop.co.uk*), hand baked in the kitchen of Cartmel Village Shop, but also available throughout the North West.

If you want to see how traditional Cumbrian real ale is brewed, **Jennings Brewery** (*www.jenningsbrewery.co.uk*) at Cockermouth, on its current site since 1874, is open for tours.

YORKSHIRE
See pp444–473

Yorkshire is synonymous with the famous **Yorkshire pudding** (batter), which originated here, and is the staple accompaniment to roast beef. Like the Yorkshire pudding, the term **York ham** is unprotected, and has been copied worldwide by vastly inferior products. You can try the real thing, however, from **Ye Olde Pie & Sausage Shoppe** in The Shambles.

From the Yorkshire Dales comes the county's most famous cheese, crumbly **Wensleydale** from Hawes. At the Wensleydale Creamery (*www.wensleydale. co.uk*) you can see how it is made and visit their museum, shop, café and restaurant. Artisan cheesemakers, **Shepherds Purse** (*www.shepherdspurse. co.uk*) produce a wide range of local cheeses including blue varieties.

Two excellent delicatessens in **York** that champion local producers are **The Hairy Fig Deli and Café** (*http://thehairyfig. co.uk*) in Fossgate, and **Henshelwoods Delicatessen** (*www.deliyork.co.uk*) on Newgate Market. Elsewhere, **Castle Howard** boasts the award-winning Farm Shop.

Sweet local treats such as **Yorkshire parkin**, a rich, dark loaf made with black treacle, oatmeal and ground ginger; **fat rascals**, which are fruit scones made with almonds, vine fruit, cherries and citrus peel; and **Yorkshire curd tart**, a sweet pastry base covered in a layer of lemon curd and filled with fresh curd cheese, nutmeg and currants; are all best sampled at **Betty's Tea Rooms** (*www.bettys.co.uk*). You can keep it local with a cup of Yorkshire tea by Taylor's

of Harrogate. Betty's is a Yorkshire food institution in its own right. Alongside their beautiful original café in Harrogate (est 1919) are two more café-tearooms in York and three other branches in the county.

Haver bread, sometimes known as clapbread, is made from fermented oatmeal and milk. **Old Peculiar Cake**, made with Yorkshire-brewed Theakston's Old Peculiar Ale (*see below*) is just one of the many rich fruit cakes baked in the area. They occasionally take their names from towns such as Ripon and Batley. If you are offered 'High Tea' at dinnertime in Yorkshire, this is not simply 'afternoon tea' but a meal, followed by cakes and tea!

Whitby is a picturesque resort that has retained its fishing fleet, and its Magpie Café (*www.magpiecafe.co.uk*) is reckoned by many to serve the best fish and chips (eat-in or take-away) in Britain. Its sit-down menu offers specialities such as **Lindisfarne oysters**, **Whitby crab** and **Whitby kippers**. The last can be bought exclusively from the rustic shop and smokehouse of **Fortune Kippers** (*www. fortuneskippers.co.uk*) who have been trading, nestled below Whitby abbey ruins, since 1872.

Fish and chips is a popular dish nationwide, but Yorkshire has many of the best fish and chip shops in the country, with the original **Harry Ramsden** shop and restaurant at Guisley often cited as the 'world's most famous'. It now trades as the **Wetherby Whaler**.

Yorkshire has a wide choice of beers. The perfect place to see them being made is the village of **Masham**, which has two small traditional breweries, **Theakston** (*www.theakstons.co.uk*) and the **Black Sheep Brewery** (*www.black sheepbrewery.com*), the latter started in 1992 by Paul Theakston. Both offer tours (*see p455*). For ale, tea, deli-and-dairy, fish-and-chips and Wensleydale trails visit *www.yorkshire.com/delicious*.

Bilberries grow in the wild in Yorkshire and you may find them served up in pies, crumbles and pancakes, among other desserts.

York Food and Drink Festival (*www.yorkfoodfestival.com*) takes places across the city in late September, with a smaller two-day event early June.

THE NORTH EAST
♿See pp474–493

Northumberland beef and lamb are renowned for their quality. In restaurants, look out for breeds of lamb such as **Hexham Blackface**, and **Cheviot**, and beef breeds such as **Gallaway**, and **Welsh Black**. **Alnwick Stew** is a traditional winter dish (not easy to find these days), of gammon or ham, with layers of sliced onion, and potatoes, flavoured with mustard and bay leaf.

Pan Haggerty, popular throughout Northumberland, is traditionally served from the pan, its thin sliced potato and onions cooked with a layer of cheese. Its name is perhaps derived from the French *hachis*, meaning sliced. **Celery cheese** is worth trying, as is **Whitley Goose**, which has nothing to do with any sort of bird; it's a dish of onions, cheddar, butter and cream. One of the most famous dishes of the region is **Pease Pudding**, which has its origins in medieval times. It's a boiled vegetable dish similar to mushy peas, consisting of split yellow peas, salt and spices, cooked with bacon or a ham joint.

The freshest fish in the region are landed at **North Shields Fish Quay**, and go, among other places, to **Colmans** of South Shields (*http://colmansfishandchips.com*), voted the best fish and chip shop in England in 2011. Family-owned and operated since 1926 you can eat here or take-away.

The small coastal village of Craster is famous for **Craster Kippers**. L.Robson & Sons (*www.kipper.co.uk*) prepare traditional oak-smoked kippers and salmon in their original 130-year old smokehouses. You can't see inside but you can buy direct or enjoy their products in the company's own Craster Seafood Restaurant on site. There is an even older smokehouse, dating back to 1843, at The Fishermans Kitchen in Seahouses. Now run by Swallowfish (*www.swallowfish.co.uk*) visitors can buy kippers and all kinds of fish and seafood, both fresh and smoked. Historic photos and objects are on display in the shop. Other seafood delicacies of the region include potted salmon and baked herrings.

The holy island of **Lindisfarne** has been famous for its **oysters**, tended by the monks, since around the 14C. The monks, long gone, also introduced mead, a sweet wine made with fermented grape juice, honey and herbs, and fortified with fine spirits. You can taste and buy at **St Aidan's Winery** (*http://lindisfarne-mead.co.uk*) who also make and sell Lindisfarne English fruit wines and liqueurs.

Honey lovers can also visit **Chain Bridge Honey Farm** (*www.chainbridgehoney.co.uk*) on the border in Berwick Upon Tweed. This is the largest natural producer of comb honey in the country, with a visitor centre and café (the latter inside a double-decker bus!).

The region's most famous drink is **Newcastle Brown Ale**; synonymous with the city it was brewed in from 1927 until 2010 when production moved to Tadcaster, Yorkshire. It has a sweet, nutty taste, somewhere between a bitter and a classic sweet brown ale. You'll find it in every bar.

EAT! NewcastleGateshead (late Aug–early Sept, *www.eatnewcastlegateshead.com*), is a quirky, imaginative food festival, which includes street-food markets, a beer and chilli festival and a huge range of events.

SCOTLAND
♿See pp494–559

Start the day with two Scottish icons, porridge (with salt or sugar) and rich dark **Dundee Maramalade** on hot buttered toast. The same city is also famous for its rich fruit **Dundee Cake**.

With thousands of miles of coastline, famous lochs and fishing rivers, there's never a shortage of seafood. **Scottish Salmon** is most famous, best fresh, but also excellent when smoked. Other smoked fish dishes include: **Cullan Skink** soup, made with smoked haddock; **Arbroath smokies** (smoked haddock); **kippers** (split, salted, smoked herring); the Scottish Indian former Raj curried breakfast treat of **kedgeree**, combining smoked haddock with rice and hard-boiled eggs. The East Neuk (Fife) shoreline is famous for its shell-fish and **Partan bree** is a tasty crab soup from north eastern Scotland.

Scottish beef, particularly **Aberdeen Angus**, and lamb are renowned year-round. In the game season look for venison and red grouse. Served all year round (though most famously on Burns' Night) **Haggis** is made from sheep's pluck (heart, liver and lungs), minced with onion, oatmeal, suet, spices, and salt, mixed with stock, and tradition-ally encased in the animal's stomach, though sausage skin is now the norm. It always comes with swede (the Scots refer to this as turnip or 'neeps') and is traditionally accompanied by a wee dram of whisky. Mutton (sheep) pies are made with hot water pastry.

Sweet treats inlude **Atholl Brose**, made with oatmeal, honey, cream and whis key; add some fresh Scottish raspber-ries and you have **Cranachan**. Oatmeal bannocks (flat breads) may be spread with local honey, and yes you really can get deep-fried Mars Bars, though not everywhere; if you have a super sweet tooth try the chip shops in Stonehaven or Glasgow. More wholesome is the ubiquitous Scottish **shortbread**.

Good delis to look out for are **Peckham's** (*www.peckhams.co.uk*) in Glasgow and Edinburgh while **Valvona & Crolla** (*www.valvonacrolla.co.uk*) is an Edin-burgh institution. **Gordon & MacPhail** in Elgin (*www.gordonandmacphail.com*) claims the world's most extensive range of whiskies, while **Royal Mile Whiskies** (*www.royalmilewhiskies.com*)in Edin-burgh is another of the world's great specialist whisky merchants. True disci-ples will want to follow the Malt Whisky Trail (*www.visitscotland.com*), taking in classic distilleries like Glenfiddich and Glenlivet.

WALES
♿ See pp559–587

Although not as famous as Scottish cuisine, Welsh food boasts some dis-tinctive dishes. Its most ubiquitous meat is **lamb**, traditionally roasted (or grilled in chops and steaks) and eaten with mint sauce or redcurrant jelly. **Welsh honey lamb** is a delicious dish, cooked in cider, with thyme and garlic, basted with honey. Recently there has been a resurgence of interest in mutton (produced from an older sheep) with a gamier taste than sweet young lamb, which is less than a year old.

Another tradition meat dish is **faggots**, rich balls of mixed meat and offal, bound with oatmeal, cooked in a rich gravy and traditionally served with mashed potatoes and mushy peas.

The humble leek, a member of the onion family, and an official emblem of Wales, appears in many dishes.

The Principality's most famous cheese is the light and crumbly **Caerphilly** – ideal for **Welsh Rarebit**, a snack of cheese mixed with beer (or milk) and mustard, cooked until creamy, poured on toast, then browned under a grill.

A speciality of the Gower is the local sea trout – **sewin** – perhaps stuffed with herbs before being cooked. It might be accompanied by **laverbread**, which is actually a type of seaweed. This is also a traditional breakfast accompaniment.

Bara brith (Welsh tea bread) is a rich cake bread, full of dried fruits and citrus peel. Another tea-time treat are **Welsh cakes**, a griddle scone flavoured with spice and dried fruit, baked on a flat iron, best served warm, with butter, and sprinkled with sugar.

For a list of some of the best places to try all these specialities, head to www. visitwales.com.

British Booze

With the decline, if not the demise, of the traditional British pub, drinkers are switching from quantity to quality. "Boutique breweries" have proliferated in recent years and have thrived. Wine is now a staple for many Brits, the majority imported, though British wine is excellent.

BEER

Beers in Britain can be divided into two principal types: ales and lagers which differ principally in their respective warm and cool fermentations. Beer is served in kegs or casks.

Keg beer is filtered, pasteurised and chilled and then packed into pressurised containers from which it gets its name.

Cask beer or 'real ale' is neither filtered, pasteurised nor chilled and is served from casks using simple pumps. It is considered to be a more flavoursome and natural beer.

Bitter is the traditional beer in England and Wales. Most are a ruddy brown colour with a slightly bitter taste imparted by hops. Some bitters are quite fruity in taste and the higher the alcoholic content the sweeter the brew.

Mild is normally only found in Wales, the West Midlands and the North West of England. The name refers to the hop character as it is a gentle, sweetish and full-flavoured beer. It is generally lower in alcohol and darker in colour than bitter, caused by the addition of caramel or by using dark malt.

Stout can be either dry, as brewed in Ireland (Guinness is the standard bearer) with a pronounced roast flavour with plenty of hoppy bitterness, or sweet. The latter, sweetened with sugar before being bottled, are now rare.

In addition there are **pale ales** (like bitter), brown ales (sweet, like mild) and old ales (sweet and strong) and barley wine, a very sweet, very strong beer.

In **Scotland**, draught beers are often sold as 60/- (shillings), 70/-, 80/- or even 90/-. This is a reference to the now-defunct shilling, which indicated the barrel tax in the late-1800s calculated on alcoholic strength. The 60/- and 90/- brews are now rare. Alternatively, the beers may be referred to as light, heavy or export which refers to the body and strength.

CIDER

Cider has been brewed from apples in Britain since Celtic times. Only bitter apples are used for "real" West Country cider, which is dry in taste, flat

Glenfiddich Distillery, Dufftown, Grampians, Scotland © Don Fuchs / Look / Photononstop

(non-sparkling) and high in alcoholic content. A sparkling cider is produced by a secondary fermentation.

WHISKY

The term whisky is derived from the Gaelic for 'water of life', *Uisge beatha*. **Scotch whisky** can only be produced in Scotland, by the distillation of malted and unmalted barley, maize, rye, and mixtures of two or more of these.

Malt whisky is produced only from malted barley traditionally dried over peat fires. A single malt whisky comes from one single distillery and has not been blended with whiskies from other distilleries. The whisky is matured in oak, ideally sherry casks, for at least three years, which affects both its colour and its flavour. All malts have a more distinctive aroma and more intense flavour than grain whiskies and each distillery will produce a completely individual whisky. There are approximately 100 malt whisky distilleries in Scotland. **Grain whisky** is made from a mixture of any malted or unmalted cereal such as maize or wheat and is distilled in the Coffey, or patent still, by a continuous process. It matures more quickly than malt whisky. Very little grain whisky is ever drunk unblended.

Blended whisky is a mix of more than one malt whisky or a mix of malt and grain whiskies to produce a soft, smooth and consistent drink. There are over 2 000 such blends, which form the vast majority of Scottish whisky production.

Deluxe whiskies are special because of the ages and qualities of the malts and grain whiskies used in them. They usually include a higher proportion of malts than in most blends.

Irish whiskey (note the spelling with an e) is traditionally made from cereals, distilled three times and matured for at least seven years.

WINE

Britain's wine industry has improved in leaps and bounds in recent years and there are now several high-quality small vineyards, mostly in the south of the country. The best are: Camel Valley, Cornwall; Three Choirs, Gloucestershire; Nyetimber, West Sussex; Ridgeview, East Sussex; Denbies, Surrey; and Chapel Down, Kent. Unfortunately, although the quality of these wines match their overseas competitors, the British climate and cost of land does not allow producers to reap economies of scale (total production represents only 1 per cent of British wine consumption), so they are always dearer than their foreign equivalents. However, Taittinger is to become the first French champagne house to produce sparkling wine in the UK after investing in a former Kent apple orchard (2015).

Only the more expensive restaurants tend to stock English wines and in pubs you will rarely see English wines from the grape (sweet English fruit wines are sometimes available).

British History

Britain's tangible ancient history goes back some 5 000 years, with relics such as Stonehenge (Wiltshire) and Skara Brae (Orkney) offering tantalising glimpses of the nation's prehistoric roots. The foundations for Modern Britain were laid from late-medieval times to the 20C, when it became a major player on the world stage in both European and World affairs, from wars and royal intermarriages to Victorian Empire. The fact that Britain has not been invaded for nearly 1 000 years happily means much of its ancient way of life, from customs and traditions, to the actual countryside and a significant number of buildings – from castles and palaces to villages and humble houses – are many centuries old. Moreover, many of its structures (in some case whole villages) are not just intact, but accessible to visitors. The conservation and heritage industry in the UK is one of the best in the world and does an excellent job of interpreting the country's long and colourful past.

Hadrian's Wall, Cuddy's Crags near Housesteads Roman Fort.
©Martyn Unsworth/iStockphoto.com

Origins, Celts and Romans

B ritain is positioned at the western edge of Europe, from which it has received successive waves of immigrants who have merged their cultures, languages, beliefs and energies to create an island race which has explored, traded with, dominated and settled other lands all over the world.

FIRST SETTLERS

Some 8 000 years ago, Britain, until then part of the greater European land mass, became detached from continental Europe by the rise in sea level caused by retreating glaciers. Around 5000 BCE, hunter-gatherers arrived, later turning to farming, which began to transform the landscape into the pattern much as we see today. Having satisfied their survival needs, between 4000 BCE and 1800 BCE they began grander, more spiritually inclined projects such as the construction of Stonehenge and other stone alignments. Around 700 BCE saw the arrival of the '**Beaker**' people, who brought a knowledge of metalworking and the Aryan roots of the English language – words such as father, mother, sister and brother.

CELTS

Also around 700 BCE Celtic settlers arrived. The **Celts** brought their language, their chariots, the use of coinage and a love of finery, gold and ornaments. Iron swords gave them an ascendancy in battle over the native Britons, estimated at around a million, who were pushed westwards. By 100 BCE, their lifestyle and customs were well established in Britain. However, the different groups of Celts had only a dialect in common and their lack of any idea of "nationhood" made them vulnerable to the might of Rome.

ROMANS

The **Romans** had no strategic interest in the offshore island of Britannia but the lure of corn, gold, iron, slaves and hunting dogs was enough to entice them to invade. By AD 70 much of the north and Wales had been subdued and 50 or more towns had been established, linked by a network of roads. Rome gave Britain its laws and extended the use of coinage into a recognised system, essential to trade in an "urban" society. In 313, Christianity was established as the official religion. The Roman conquest of Caledonia was never fully accomplished although there were two main periods of occupation. The initial one (c.80–c.100), which started with Julius Agricola's push northwards, is notable for the victory at Mons Graupius (somewhere in the North East). The second period followed the death in 138 of the Emperor Hadrian (builder of the wall). By the end of the 4C Roman power was waning.

55 BCE	Julius Caesar lands in Britain
CE 42	Roman invasion of Britain under the Emperor Claudius
61	Revolt of the Iceni under Queen **Boadicea**
122	Beginning of the construction of **Hadrian's Wall**
410	Roman legions withdraw from Britain

Early Medieval Britain

With the withdrawal of the Romans, Britain fell into disrepair but its Anglo-Saxon roots were already in place. The nation began to form from these Germanic tribes alongside Danes, Vikings, Celts and early Britons.

ANGLO-SAXONS AND VIKINGS

Saxons, in the form of Germanic mercenaries, had manned many of the shore forts of Britain before the final withdrawal of regular Roman troops in AD 410. As pay became scarce, the mercenaries seized tracts of good farming land and settled permanently. **Angle** (from Angeln, Germany), **Saxon** (lower Saxony) and **Jute** (lower Jutland) invasions cemented their position in the 5C. These warring tribes gradually formed cohesive kingdoms, gaining territories through wars with old **Briton** states, eventually claiming between them an area roughly equivalent to present-day England. These kingdoms traded as far afield as Russia and Constantinople and were constantly engaged in power struggles between themselves. When St Augustine arrived in Kent in 597, he found that Christianity was already established at the court of **King Ethelbert** of Kent, whose wife Queen Bertha was a Christian princess. Until the **Synod of Whitby** in 664 the practices of the Roman Church existed side by side with those of the Celtic Church, which had a different way of calculating the date of Easter and a strong and distinctive monastic tradition.

King of Wessex (West Saxons) in the south of Great Britain from 871, **Alfred the Great** became the dominant ruler in England. Of all the Anglo-Saxon kingdoms, that of Wessex was the only one able to repel invasion by the **Great Danish Army** (a united army of formerly uncoordinated bands of **Vikings**), which was defeated at the **Battle of Edington** in 878. However, the Vikings signed a treaty with Alfred that allowed them to retain control of their conquered lands – most of northern and eastern England. Alfred then set about establishing a navy, a standing army, a network of fortified towns known as *burhs*, and a system of taxation and conscription to supply them. **Edward the Elder** succeeded his father Alred the Great in 899, reclaiming control of all of Mercia, East Anglia and Essex from the Vikings. By 918, all of the Danes south of the Humber had submitted to him. His successor **Athelstan** conquered the last remaining Viking kingdom, York, making him the first Anglo-Saxon ruler of all of England. Athelstan also invaded Scotland in 934, forcing **King Constantine of Scotland** to submit to him. On Athelstan's death, **King Olaf Guthfrithson** of Dublin invaded Northumbria and occupied York, later moving on to the rest of the English kingdoms. Athelstan's successor, **Edmund I**, (ruled 939–946) eventually managed to reclaim vassalage over Mercia, the Five Boroughs of the Danelaw and the Danish Kingdom of East Anglia. Edmund established a policy of safe borders through treaties with **King Malcolm I of Scotland** and the **Norse-Gael Uí Ímair** dynasty, whose members from the mid-9th century ruled much of Northern England, the Irish Sea region, the Kingdom of Dublin and the western coast of Scotland.

449	First waves of Angles, Saxons and Jutes land in Britain; Hengist and Horsa land at Ebbsfleet in East Kent

Depiction of Augustine preaching before King Ethelbert

597	**Augustine**, sent by Pope Gregory to convert the British to Christianity, founds a Benedictine monastery in Canterbury
851	Viking raiders winter regularly in Britain and become settlers
871-99	Reign of **Alfred the Great**, King of Wessex, who contains the united Viking invasion in 878

THE ROAD TO 1066

Edmund I of England's successor, **Eadred**, ruled from 946–955, engaging in further attrition with Viking interests in Northumbria and York, notably with the former King of Norway, '**Eric Bloodaxe**', who had two short-lived terms as King of Northumbria. By 952, Eadred had finally removed the threat of a Northumbrian king, replacing him with earls. Eadred's successor, **Eadwig**, faced conflicts with his family, his thegns and the church, leading to the split of his kingdom, so that his brother Edgar ruled Northumbria and Mercia, while Eadwig retained Wessex. His short rule was followed by that of his brother, **Edgar I** (ruled 959–975), under whom the Kingdom of England was reunited and all the kings of Britain pledged their allegiance. However, from Edgar's death in 975 until the Norman Conquest, there was not a single succession to the throne that was not contested. It was the beginning of the end for the Anglo-Saxon kings.

King of England from 975–978, **Edward the Martyr**, oversaw a brief reign during which civil war almost broke out within his kingdom and his earls rose to greater political power, essentially ruling the kingdom for him. After his half-brother's murder, **Ethelred 'the Unready'** became king at just ten years old, granting further power to the earls. During Ethelred's disastrous reign (978–1013 and 1014–1016), England was attacked by the Danes. In 1013 **Swein**, King of Denmark, invaded and briefly became king while Ethelred fled to Normandy in 1013. He returned in 1014 on Swein's death to reclaim the throne. Ethelred's son and heir, **Edmund 'Ironside'**, resisted another Danish invasion in 1016 led by **Cnut the Great**. He fought five battles against the Danes, but lost the Battle of Assandun, after which Cnut eventually claimed the English throne, becoming King of England (1016–1035) and later, Denmark (1018–1035). On his death, the English throne passed to his son **Harold Harefoot** (ruled 1035–1040), while that

Depiction of Harold, son of Earl Godwin swearing an oath to Duke William of Normandy

of Denmark passed to **Harthacnut** (1035–1042) – though Harold's death once again reunited the crowns under his brother's rule (1040–1042).

On Harthacnut's death, **Edward the Confessor**, son of Ethelred and his Norman wife, Emma, became king of England, though **Magnus I of Norway** succeeded to the Danish throne and extended his claim over England. Edward, who spent much of his childhood in exile in Normandy, gave land and positions to Normans. Edward gained popular approval as a devout saintly character, but suffered from rebellious and powerful earls, in particular the Godwins of Wessex. To guard the southeast shoreline against invasion and pillage, Edward established the enduring maritime federation known as the **Cinque Ports** (Five Ports), in which Sandwich, Dover, Romney, Hythe and Hastings grouped together to supply ships and men for defence.

As part of his claim to the English throne, his great-nephew, **Duke William of Normandy**, is said to have made Harold, son of Earl Godwin, swear an oath to help William succeed on Edward's death. On 5 January 1066, days after the consecration of his abbey church at Westminster, Edward died, Harold took the throne and the stage was set for a Norman invasion, while the threat of Magnus I of Norway's claim, and that of his successor **Harold Hardrada**, still loomed large.

911	Kingdom of Normandy founded by Rollo, a Viking
1016-35	Reign of **Canute** (Cnut), first Danish King of England
1042-66	Reign of **Edward the Confessor**

EARLY MEDIEVAL SCOTLAND AND WALES

The Anglo-Saxon invasions forced the indigenous Britons to take refuge in the wilds of Cornwall, Wales, and beyond Hadrian's Wall in southwest **Scotland**. It was at Whithorn that the Romano-Briton St Ninian established the first Christian community in the late-4C. Over the next centuries, Christianity gained footing. In the 8C and 9C the first Norse raiders arrived. These were followed by peaceful settlers who occupied the Western Isles. The kingdoms of the Picts and Scots merged, under the Scot **Kenneth MacAlpine**, to form Alba, the territory north of the Forth and Clyde that later became known as Scotia, while the western fringes remained under Norse sway. Territorial conflicts with the English and the Norsemen marked the next two centuries.

The character of modern **Wales** was first formed by the Romans, who pushed the Britons west into the area now known as Wales. It was then a number of kingdoms, rarely united by any one ruler. Mercia (corresponding to today's Midlands) became the dominant Anglo-Saxon kingdom and built Offa's Dyke as the Welsh border.

Late Medieval Britain

The Norman Conquest solidified England's feudal system from 1066 onwards. In the following centuries, dynastic struggles were to plague Britain and the continent.

NORMANS

The **Normans** were descendants of Norsemen, Vikings, who had settled in northern France in 876. Following the death of Edward the Confessor, Duke William of Normandy, accompanied by some 5 000 knights and followers, invaded England and defeated Harold Godwinson at the **Battle of Hastings** on 14 October 1066, the last time the country was successfully invaded. Duke William, better known as William the Conqueror imposed a strong central authority on a group of kingdoms that ranked among the richest in western Europe. By the time of the **Domesday Survey** only a handful of English names feature amongst the list of 'tenants in chief', revealing a massive shift in ownership of land, and only one of 16 bishops was an Englishman. By 1200 almost every Anglo-Saxon cathedral and abbey, reminders for the vanquished English of their great past, had been demolished and replaced by Norman works. Forty years after the conquest, however, English soldiers fought for an English-born king, **Henry I**, in his French territories.

1066	Harold Godwinson repels the army of Harold Hardrada at the Battle of Stamford Bridge. He then marches south to confront the Norman invasion at the **Battle of Hastings** under Duke William of Normandy. Harold is killed and William is crowned on Christmas Day in Westminster abbey
1086	Domesday Survey made by William I to reassess the value of property throughout England for taxation purposes
1100-35	Reign of **Henry I**, whose marriage to Matilda of Scots unites the Norman and Saxon royal houses
1135-54	Reign of **Stephen**. Henry of Anjou acknowledged as heir to the throne by the Treaty of Winchester

PLANTAGENETS

Henry II, Count of Anjou, married Eleanor, whose dowry brought Aquitaine and Poitou to the English Crown. His dispute over the relative rights of Church and State with Thomas Becket, whom he himself had appointed as Archbishop of Canterbury, led to Becket's murder. Henry's reign deserves to be remembered for the restoration of order in a ravaged country, the institution of legal reforms, which included the establishment of the jury, the system of assize courts and coroners' courts, two reforms of the coinage and the granting of many town charters. He also encouraged the expansion of sheep farming as English wool was of high quality; the heavy duties levied on its export contributed to England's prosperity.

WELSH MARCHER CASTLES

Although the English kings and Welsh leaders had fought for centuries it was Edward I who led the first true conquest of Wales in 1277, securing the lands with his famous castles, at Harlech, Caernarfon, Conwy, Beaumaris and elsewhere. Between 1276 and 1296 17 castles were built or re-fortified by Edward I to consolidate English power in North Wales. The four best-preserved fortresses that once patrolled the North Welsh borders (or Marches) are Conwy, Caernarfon, Harlech and Beaumaris. They are among the most remarkable group of medieval monuments to be seen in Europe.

The four major castles were the work of the greatest military architect of the day, **Master James of St George**, brought by Edward from Savoy. Most were built to be supplied from the sea, as land travel in Snowdonia was impossible for Edward's forces. Square towers were replaced by round, which were less vulnerable to undermining; concentric defences, the inner overlooking outer, made their appearance. The garrisons of these massive stone fortifications were small – only some 30 men-at-arms plus a few cavalry and crossbowmen. Planned walled towns, similar to the "bastides" of southern France, housed the settlers, who helped hold the territory. Documents detailing the conscription of labour from all over England, the costs of timber, stone, transport, a wall, a turret, even a latrine, can still be read.

The despotic manner of ruling and of raising revenue adopted by Henry's son, **King John**, caused the barons to unite and force the king to sign **Magna Carta**, which guaranteed every man freedom from illegal interference with his person or property and the basis of much subsequent English legislation.

The ineffectual reign of John's son, **Henry III**, was marked by baronial opposition and internal strife. He was forced to call the first "parliament" in 1264.

His son, **Edward I**, a typical Plantagenet, fair haired, tall and energetic, was for much of his reign at war with France and Wales and Scotland; on the last two he imposed English administration and justice. During his reign, the constitutional importance of Parliament increased; his Model Parliament of 1295 included representatives from shire, city and borough.

His son, **Edward II**, cared for little other than his own pleasure and his reign saw the effective loss of all that his father had won. His wife, Isabel of France, humiliated by her husband's conduct, invaded and deposed Edward.

1154	Accession of **Henry II**, Count of Anjou (Plantagenet)
1170	Murder of Thomas Becket in Canterbury Cathedral
1189	Henry II defeated in battle by his son Richard
1189-99	Reign of **Richard I** (the **Lionheart**)
1199-1216	Reign of **King John**. Most of Normandy, Maine, Anjou and Brittany lost
1215	John forced to sign **Magna Carta** by the barons
1216-72	Reign of **Henry III**
1271-1307	Reign of **Edward I**
1296-98	North of England ravaged by Scots under **William Wallace**; defeated at Falkirk and executed in 1305
1307-27	Reign of **Edward II**
1314	Edward II defeated at Bannockburn by Robert I, King of Scotland

1327	Edward II murdered at Berkeley Castle
1327-77	Reign of **Edward III**
1328	Robert I recognised as king of an independent Scotland

HUNDRED YEARS WAR (1337–1453)

The son of Edward II, **Edward III**, sought reconciliation with the barons and pursued an enlightened trade policy. He reorganised the Navy and led England into the **Hundred Years War**, claiming not only Aquitaine but the throne of France. In 1348 the Black Death plague reached England and the labour force was reduced by one-third. The throne passed from Edward III to his grandson, **Richard II**, with his uncle, John of Gaunt, acting as regent. In time Richard quarrelled with the barons. John of Gaunt was exiled together with his son Henry Bolingbroke, who returned to recover his father's confiscated estates, deposed Richard and became king.

Henry IV was threatened with rebellion by the Welsh and the Percys, Earls of Northumberland, and with invasion from France.

Henry V resumed the Hundred Years War and English claims to the French throne. On his death his infant son was crowned **Henry VI** in 1429 in Westminster Abbey and in 1431 in Notre Dame in Paris.

1337	Beginning of the **Hundred Years War** with France
1348	The **Black Death**
1377-99	Reign of **Richard II**
1381	Peasants' Revolt, in part provoked by the government's attempt to control wages
1398	Richard II deposed by Henry Bolingbroke
1399-1413	Reign of **Henry IV**
1400	Death of Richard II
1413-22	Reign of **Henry V**
1415	English defeat French at Battle of Agincourt
1420	Treaty of Troyes makes Henry V heir to the French throne
1422-61	Reign of **Henry VI** with Duke of Gloucester and Duke of Lancaster as regents
1453	Hundred Years War ends

WARS OF THE ROSES

The regency created by the deposing of Edward II fostered the counter-claims of York and Lancaster to develop into the **Wars of the Roses**. The Lancastrians (**Henry IV**, **Henry V** and **Henry VI**), represented by the red rose of Lancaster, claimed the throne by direct male descent from John of Gaunt, fourth son of Edward III. The Yorkists (**Edward IV**, **Edward V** and **Richard III**), represented by the white rose of York, were descended from Lionel, Edward's third son, but in the female line. The dispute ended when Elizabeth of York married Henry Tudor, a Lancastrian.

Edward V and his younger brother, Richard, known as the **Little Princes in the Tower**, were imprisoned by their uncle Richard, Duke of Gloucester. Their claim to the throne was deemed illegitimate by Parliament. Gloucester was proclaimed **Richard III** and the princes were probably murdered at the Tower of London.

1455-87	**Wars of the Roses**, over 30 years of sporadic fighting and periods of armed peace, between the houses of Lancaster and York, rival claimants to the throne
1461-83	Reign of **Edward IV**
1465	Henry VI captured and imprisoned in the Tower of London
1470	Restoration of Henry VI by Warwick and flight of Edward
1471	Murder of Henry VI and Prince Edward by Edward IV following his victory at Tewkesbury
1483	Reign of **Edward V** ending in his and his brother's imprisonment in the Tower of London
1483-85	Reign of **Richard III**
1485	Battle of Bosworth Field: Richard defeated and killed by Henry Tudor

LATE MEDIEVAL SCOTLAND

Under the influence of **Queen Margaret**, and during the reigns of her sons – in particular Edgar, Alexander I and David I – the Celtic kingdom of Scotland took on a feudal character as towns grew and royal charters were granted. Monastic life flourished as religious communities from France set up sister houses throughout Scotland. In 1098, **King Edgar**, son of **Malcolm III** (Canmore), ceded the islands to Norway. **Alexander II** (1214–49) attempted to curb Norse rule but it was his son **Alexander III** (1249–86) who, following the Battle of Largs, returned the Western Isles to Scotland. Relations with England remained tense.

On the death in 1290 of Alexander III's granddaughter, the direct heir to the throne, Edward I installed **John Balliol** as king (and his vassal). However, following Balliol's 1295 treaty with the French, Edward set out for the north on the first of several "pacification" campaigns and thus started a long period of intermittent warfare.

The years of struggle for independence from English overlordship helped forge national identity and heroes. **William Wallace** led early resistance, achieving a famous victory at **Stirling Bridge** (1297). However, he was captured in 1305 and taken to London where he was executed. The next to rally opposition was **Robert the Bruce** (1274–1329), grandson of one of the original competitors and therefore with a legitimate claim to the throne. Following the killing of John Comyn, the son of another competitor, and the representative of the Balliol line, Bruce had himself crowned at Scone in 1306. Slowly he forced the submission of the varying fiefs and his victory at Bannockburn (1314) was crucial in achieving independence. Although now independent, royal authority in Scotland was undermined by feuds and intrigue as bloody power struggles broke out among the clan chiefs. The monarchy prevailed, however, and the powerful Albany and Douglas clans were subdued in the 15C. The Scots also supported France in its rivalry with England and the first of many "auld alliances" were forged. In 1424 **James I** took the reins of power. His son James II succeeded in 1437 following the assassination of his father at Perth. In 1460 **James II** was killed at the siege of Roxburgh Castle and **James III** became king.

Absolute Monarchy

The Renaissance period witnessed growing conflicts between royalty and other institutions (notably the Church and Parliament). The Tudors in the 16C and the Stuarts in the 17C were the embodiment of absolute monarchy. This period was also all about the struggle between the Catholic, Protestant and Anglican churches and communities.

TUDORS

Henry VII ruled shrewdly and his control of finances restored order and a healthy Treasury after the Wars of the Roses. His son, **Henry VIII**, was a "Renaissance Man", an accomplished musician, linguist, scholar and soldier. He was an autocratic monarch of capricious temper and elastic conscience, who achieved union with Ireland and Wales and greatly strengthened the Navy. Thomas Wolsey, appointed Chancellor in 1515, fell from favour for failing to obtain papal approval for Henry to divorce Catherine of Aragon; his palace at Hampton Court was confiscated by the king. The **Dissolution of the Monasteries** caused the greatest redistribution of land in England since the Norman Conquest. Wool, much of which had been exported raw in the previous century, was now nearly all made into cloth at home.

The popularity of **Mary**, daughter of Henry VIII and Catherine of Aragon, was undermined by her insistence on marrying Philip II of Spain, who was a Roman Catholic, the burning of 300 alleged heretics, and war with France, which resulted in the loss of Calais, England's last possession in continental Europe.

Elizabeth I, daughter of Henry VIII and Anne Boleyn, restored a moderate Anglicanism, though potential Roman Catholic conspiracies to supplant her were ruthlessly suppressed. She sought to avoid the needless expense of war by diplomacy and a network of informers controlled by her Secretaries, Cecil and Walsingham. Opposition to Elizabeth as queen focused on **Mary Queen of Scots** and looked to Spain for assistance. The long struggle against Spain, mostly fought out at sea, culminated in the launch of the Spanish Armada, the final and unsuccessful attempt by Spain to conquer England and re-establish

QUEEN OF SCOTS

In 1513 the accession of **James IV of Scotland** followed his father, James III's death at the Battle of Sauchieburn. James IV was also to die in war, at Flodden in 1513. His son, **James V**, died at Falkland Palace in 1542, leaving his queen, Mary of Guise, and their daughter Mary, who assumed the title Queen of Scots. However, when the Scots refused an alliance between the young Mary and Henry VIII's son, Edward, English troops invaded, in what was known as **The Rough Wooing**. Meanwhile a growing French influence at court was resented by the nobility and the Reformation, fired up by **John Knox**'s sermons, gained ground; monastic houses were destroyed and Catholicism was banned. During the short tragic reign (1561–67) of **Mary Queen of Scots**, conspiracies and violence were rife and personal scandal finally turned the populace to rebellion. Her flight to England, after her abdication in favour of her infant son, ended in imprisonment and execution by Elizabeth I.

the Roman Catholic faith; its defeat was the greatest military victory of Elizabeth I's reign. Elizabeth I presided over a period of exploration and enterprise, a flowering of national culture and the arts; most of **William Shakespeare**'s greatest plays were produced between 1592 and 1616.

1485-1509	Reign of **Henry VII**
1509-47	Reign of **Henry VIII**
1513	Defeat and death of James IV of Scotland at Flodden
1535	Execution of Sir Thomas More, Chancellor, for refusing to sign the Act of Supremacy, acknowledging Henry VIII as head of the Church in place of the Pope
1536-39	Dissolution of the Monasteries. Excommunication of Henry VIII
1547-53	Reign of **Edward VI**
1553-58	Reign of **Mary I**; Roman Catholicism re-established
1558-1603	Reign of **Elizabeth I**
1567-1625	Reign of James VI, King of the Scots
1580	Circumnavigation of the world by **Francis Drake**
1587	Execution of Mary Queen of Scots
1588	Defeat of the Spanish Armada

STUARTS

Elizabeth I was succeeded by **James I of England** (**and VI of Scotland**). The **Gunpowder Plot** was a conspiracy of Roman Catholics who attempted to assassinate James in Parliament, despite his willingness to extend to them a measure of toleration.

Charles I inherited his father's belief in an absolute monarchy – the "divine right of kings" – and attempted to rule without Parliament from 1626 to 1640. Moreover, his marriage to a Roman Catholic, Henrietta Maria of France, was unpopular with the people. When he was finally forced to recall Parliament, the Members of the House responded by condemning his adviser, the Earl of Strafford, to death for treason, refusing to grant the king money until he discussed their grievances, and they passed a Bill preventing any future dissolution of Parliament without their consent. When, in 1642, Charles I attempted to arrest five members of Parliament he sowed the final seeds for the coming conflict.

1603-25	Reign of **James I** (also James VI of Scotland)
1605	Gunpowder Plot intended to assassinate the king in Parliament
1620	Pilgrim Fathers set sail for America
1625-49	Reign of **Charles I**
1626	Dissolution of Parliament by the king

THE ENGLISH CIVIL WAR

The **English Civil War** broke out in August 1642. Charles I established his headquarters in Oxford, but the balance was tilted against him by Scots

THE COVENANTERS

James VI united the crowns of Scotland and England under one monarch, following the childless death of his cousin, Elizabeth I of England. In the 17C, James VI attempted to achieve control of the Church through bishops appointed by the crown. His son, Charles I, aroused further strong Presbyterian opposition in Scotland with the forced introduction of the **Scottish Prayer Book**. In 1638, the **National Covenant** was drawn up, which pledged Scottish defiance of the religious policy of Charles I. In 1644, led by Montrose, the Covenanters were victorious against England, but defeat came at the **Battle of Philiphaugh** (1645) and Montrose was forced into exile. After the death of Charles I, Cromwell finished off the Covenanters' army.

support for the Parliamentarians. The North was lost after the Battle of Marston Moor in 1644 and, following the formation of the **New Model Army** by **Cromwell** and **Fairfax** and its victory at Naseby in 1645, the Royalists surrendered at Oxford the following year. The king surrendered to the Scots who handed him over to Parliament in 1647. A compromise was attempted but Charles wavered. He played off one faction in Parliament against another and sought finance and troops from abroad. In 1648, the war resumed. The Scots to whom Charles promised a Presbyterian England in return for their help, invaded England but were defeated in August at Preston and Charles I was captured. The army demanded his death.

Under the **Commonwealth and Protectorate** the monarchy and the House of Lords were abolished and replaced by a Council of State of 40 members. Attempts by the "Rump" Parliament to turn itself into a permanent non-elected body caused Cromwell to dissolve it and form the Protectorate in 1653, in which he, as Lord Protector, ruled by decree. He was accepted by the majority of a war-weary population but, on his death in 1658, the lack of a competent successor provoked negotiations which led to the Restoration of the Monarchy.

1649	Trial and execution of the king
1649	Beginning of the **Commonwealth**. England is ruled not by a monarch but by Oliver Cromwell, a commoner
1651	Coronation at Scone of Charles II. He is defeated at the Battle of Worcester and flees to France.

THE RESTORATION

The **Restoration** in May 1660 ended 10 years of Puritan restriction and opened a period of optimism and a flourishing of theatre, painting and the arts. In the Declaration of Breda Charles II appeared to promise something for almost every political faction. The **Navigation Acts**, specifying that English goods must be carried in English ships, did much to develop commerce.

In 1685, just after the death of Charles II, his illegitimate son, the Duke of Monmouth, led a rebellion against James II that was brutally repressed. This and the introduction of pro-Catholic policies, two Declarations of Indulgence in 1687 and 1688, the trial and acquittal of the Seven Bishops and the birth of a son James, who became the "Old Pretender", all intensified fears of a Roman Catholic succession. Disaffected politicians approached William of Orange, married to Mary, James' daughter, and offered him the throne.

MONMOUTH REBELLION

The death of Charles II – and the prospect of a new line of openly Catholic monarchs with the accession of his brother James VII – inspired the ill-fated **Monmouth rebellion** in Scotland, led by Charles II's illegitimate son. In 1689, the Protestant **Mary and William** were invited to rule. Viscount Dundee rallied the **Jacobites** (those faithful to King James VII), but after an initial victory at Killiecrankie the Highland army was crushed at Dunkeld. In 1707, the Crowns of England and Scotland were joined together in the **Act of Union**.

1660-85	Reign of **Charles II**
1665	**Great Plague** kills more than 68,000 Londoners
1666	**Great Fire of London** destroys 80 percent of the city
1672	Declaration of Indulgence relaxing penal laws against Roman Catholics and other dissenters
1672-74	War against the Dutch
1673	Test Act excluding Roman Catholics and other non-conformists from civil office
1677	Marriage of Charles II's niece, Mary, to William of Orange
1679	Habeas Corpus Act reinforcing existing powers protecting individuals against arbitrary imprisonment
1685-88	Reign of **James II**
1685	Monmouth Rebellion – unsuccessful attempt to claim the throne by the Duke of Monmouth, illegitimate son of Charles II
1687	Dissolution of Parliament by James II

THE GLORIOUS REVOLUTION

William III landed in England in 1688. In 1689 he was crowned with his wife Mary as his queen. Jacobite supporters of the exiled James II were decisively defeated in both Ireland and Scotland and much of William's reign was devoted, with the Grand Alliance he formed with Austria, the Netherlands, Spain and the German states, to obstructing the territorial ambitions of Louis XIV of France.

Queen Anne, staunch Protestant and supporter of the Glorious Revolution (1688), which deposed her father, James II, also strove to reduce the power and influence of France in Europe and to ensure a Protestant succession to the throne. Marlborough's victory at Blenheim and his successes in the Low Countries achieved much of the first aim. After 18 pregnancies and the death of her last surviving child in 1701, Anne agreed to the **Act of Settlement** providing for the throne to pass to Sophia, Electress of Hanover, grand daughter of James I, or to her heirs.

The "**Whigs**" were the members of the political party which had invited William to take the throne. They formed powerful juntas during the reigns of William and Anne and ensured the Hanoverian succession. In the 1860s they became the Liberal Party. The **"Tories"** accepted the Glorious Revolution but became associated with Jacobite feelings and were out of favour until the new Tory party, under Pitt the Younger, took office in 1783. They developed into the Conservative Party under Peel in 1834.

Crown offered to William and Mary, engraved by H Bourne after EM Ward

The **Jacobites**, supporters of the Stuart claim to the throne, made two attempts to dethrone the Hanoverian George I. James II's son, the "Old Pretender", led the first Jacobite rising in 1715 and his eldest son, Charles Edward Stuart, "Bonnie Prince Charlie", the "Young Pretender", led a similar rising in 1745, which ended in 1746 at Culloden, the last battle fought on British soil. He died in exile in 1788 and his younger brother died childless in 1807.

1688	William of Orange invited to England Exile of James II to France
1689-94	Reign of **William III and Mary II**
1689	Defeat of Scottish Jacobites at Killiecrankie. Londonderry besieged by James II; Grand Alliance between England, Austria, the Netherlands and German states in war against France
1690	Battle of the Boyne and defeat of James II and the Irish Jacobites
1694-1702	Reign of **William III** following the death of Mary II
1694	Triennial Act sees Parliament meet at least once every three years and sit for a maximum three years
1694 & 1695	Bank of England founded, then Bank of Scotland
1702-14	Reign of **Queen Anne**

British Empire

With the battles between Parliament and the monarchy concluded, maritime supremacy established and industrial output exploding, Britain focused on international trade and colonisation.

HANOVERIANS

By the time **George I** ascended the throne in 1714, the United Kingdom was already a European economic and naval power which had played a major part in weakening the influence of France in Europe.

George II is notable for being the last monarch to command his forces personally in battle, at Dettingen in 1743 in the war of the Austrian Succession. He was succeeded by his grandson, the unfortunate **George III**, prone to bouts of apparent madness (possibly due to porphyria or arsenic poisoning). He was unable to reverse the trend towards constitutional monarchy, but he did try to exercise the right of a king to govern. This caused great unpopularity, and he was forced to acknowledge the reality of party politics. Foreign policy was dominated by the king's determination to suppress the American Revolution and the **Napoleonic Wars**, which arose from the threat posed by the Revolution in France to established European powers.

George IV had supported the Whig cause in opposition to his father's Tory advisers and was much influenced by the politician Charles James Fox.

William IV was 65 when he succeeded his unpopular brother. Dissatisfaction with Parliamentary representation was near to causing revolutionary radicals to join forces with the mob.

1704	English capture Gibraltar; victory at Blenheim
1707	Act of Union joins English and Scottish Parliament
1714-27	Reign of **George I**
1715	Jacobite rebellion, led by James Edward Stuart
1727-60	Reign of **George II**
1745	Jacobite rebellion led by Bonnie Prince Charlie, the Young Pretender, which ended at Culloden in 1746
1752	Gregorian Calendar adopted
1756	Beginning of the Seven Years War. Ministry formed by Pitt the Elder
1757	Recapture of Calcutta. Battle of Plassey won by Clive
1759	Defeat of the French army by General Wolfe on the Heights of Abraham, Quebec
1760-1820	Reign of **George III**
1760	Conquest of Canada
1763	Seven Years War ended in the Treaty of Paris
1773	**Boston Tea Party** protest against forced imports of East India Company tea into the American colonies
1776	American Declaration of Independence; *The Wealth of Nations* published by Adam Smith
1781	British surrender at Yorktown
1793	War against Revolutionary France
1799	First levy of income tax to finance the war
1805	Naval victory at Trafalgar and death of Nelson
1807	Abolition of the slave trade within the British Empire

HIGHLAND CLEARANCES

The Jacobite uprising of 1745 was led by Charles Edward Stuart, otherwise known as Bonnie Prince Charlie (1720–88). His Highland Army won an initial victory at Prestonpans, but he was defeated at Culloden in 1746 and fled into exile. The aftermath was tragic for the Highlands. Highlanders were disarmed, their national dress proscribed and chieftains deprived of their rights. Eviction and loss of the traditional way of life ensued; this period became known as the Highland Clearances and was complete by around 1860. Mass emigration followed for the many who faced abject poverty.

INDUSTRIAL REVOLUTION

Vast social changes occurred as the labour force moved from the land into town; overcrowding often bred unrest between worker and employer. The Napoleonic Wars both stimulated this industrialism and aggravated the unrest but by the mid-19C it was clear that in Britain industrial revolution would not be followed by political revolution.

From around 1790 onwards, **Scotland** was becoming one of the commercial and industrial powerhouses of the British Empire, with flourishing textile, coal mining, engineering, railway construction and steel industries. Most famously, Glasgow and the Clyde became a major shipbuilding centre and Glasgow became "Second City of the Empire" after London. Up until the First World War fishing was also a major economic activity.

In the late-18C the Industrial Revolution transformed **South Wales**. The presence of iron ore, limestone and large coal deposits in southeast Wales meant that this region was ideal for the establishment of iron and steel works and coal mines. By 1830, Britain was the largest iron producer in the world, and South Wales alone accounted for 40 percent of this output. Cardiff was soon among the most important coal ports in the world and Swansea among the most important steel ports. The iron and steel industry was not to last, however, as ore was exhausted and other countries took advantage of the new technologies. By the end of the 19C, iron production was in decline and coal was king in South Wales.

1731	Agriculture revolutionised by the invention of the horse hoe and seed drill by Jethro Tull
1733	Invention of the flying shuttle by John Kay
1769	Patents issued for Watt's steam engine and Arkwright's water frame
1781	Watt's steam engine for rotary motion patented
1787	Invention of the power loom by Cartwright
1825	Opening of the Stockton and Darlington railway. Completion of the Menai Bridge by Telford
1833	Factory Act abolishes child labour
1834	Tolpuddle Martyrs transported to Australia for forming an agriculture Trade Union
1851	Great Exhibition in the Crystal Palace in Hyde Park
1856	Invention of the Bessemer process of steel making in industrial quantities

THE VICTORIAN ERA

As William IV's two daughters had died as infants, he was succeeded on his death by his niece, Victoria. Queen **Victoria**, the last monarch of the House of Hanover, was only 18 when she came to the throne. She went on to give her name to an illustrious age, and become Britain's longest-reigning sovereign until that distinction was surpassed by Elizabeth II in 2015. Victoria's husband, the **Prince Consort, Albert of Saxe-Coburg**, was her closest adviser until his premature death in 1861. He persuaded her that the crown should not be aligned with any political party – a principle that has endured. He was the instigator of the **Great Exhibition**, which took place between May and October in 1851. It contained exhibits from all nations and was a proud declaration of the high point of the Industrial Revolution, celebrating the inventiveness, technical achievement and prosperity which are the hallmarks of the Victorian

Age. Victoria's son, **Edward VII**, who was excluded from royal duties and responsibilities until 1892, greatly increased the prestige of the monarchy by his own charm and by reviving royal public ceremonial.

1812-14	Anglo-American War ended by Treaty of Ghent
1815	Battle of Waterloo; defeat of Napoleon; Congress of Vienna
1820-30	Reign of **George IV**
1823	Reform of criminal law and prisons by Peel
1829	Catholic Emancipation Act. Formation of the Metropolitan Police
1830-37	Reign of **William IV**
1832	First Parliamentary Reform Act
1837-1901	Reign of **Queen Victoria**
1840	Marriage of Victoria to Prince Albert. Introduction of the world's first adhesive postage stamp
1842	Chartist movement campaigns for Parliamentaryreform
1846	Repeal of the Corn Laws
1848	Cholera epidemic. Public Health Act
1854-56	**Crimean War**, ends with the Treaty of Paris
1857	Indian Mutiny
1858	Government of India transferred from the East India Company to the Crown
1861	Death of Prince Albert
1863	Opening of the first underground railway in London, the Metropolitan Railway
1871	Bank holidays introduced
1876	Victoria made Empress of India. Elementary education made obligatory
1884	Invention of the steam turbine by Parsons
1888	Local Government Act establishing county councils and county boroughs
1895	First Motor Show in London
1899–1902	Boer War ends in the Peace of Vereeniging, leading to union of South Africa (1910)

20th to 21st Century

Following the two world wars Great Britain took its place at the top table of the free world. Today, Britain's military powers may have diminished, but its status remains and it is still a key player in world politics.

WORLD AT WAR

WORLD WAR I AND INTER-WAR YEARS

The assassination of Archduke Ferdinand at Sarajevo in 1914 plunged Europe (and beyond) into a futile stalemate war in which a million British troops died and many millions more lost their lives. Meanwhile in Ireland a desire for independence had also reached crisis point and in Easter 1916 an uprising in Dublin was ruthlessly put down by British troops.

A significant after-effect of the First World War in Great Britain was a loosening of **class structure**. The "lions led by donkeys" were now much less likely to follow orders in peacetime and the Labour Party made great strides, coming to power for the first time (albeit in a Liberal coalition) in 1923. Across the water in Ireland the independence movement was continuing and in 1921 an Irish Free State was created. It led to the Irish Civil War, which ended in 1923.

In Britain the **General Strike** of 1926 underlined the country's growing restlessness and this unrest worsened in the 1930s, as the worldwide economy slumped into the Great Depression.

1910-36	Reign of **George V**
1914-18	First World War
1914	Formation of Kitchener's "Volunteer Army"
1916	Easter Rising in Dublin
1917	Name of the Royal Family changed to Windsor by George V
1918	Women over 30 granted vote
1919	Treaty of Versailles
1921	Creation of the Irish Free State
1924	British Empire Exhibition
1926	General Strike
1928	Women over 21 granted vote
1931	**The Depression** – many people out of work
1936	Accession and abdication of **Edward VIII**
1936-52	Reign of **George VI**

WORLD WAR II

A policy of appeasement was taken towards the growing ambitions of Adolf Hitler, characterised by Prime Minister Neville Chamberlain in 1938, who returned from a meeting with the Führer and delivered the now-infamous words 'I believe it is peace in our time'. When it became clear, however, in 1939, with the invasion of Poland, that war was the only option for Britain, the country found itself seriously unprepared. By mid-1940 Britain was isolated and prepared to be invaded by Hitler's army from across the Channel.

The evacuation of troops at Dunkirk was the nadir. The tide, however, was about to turn. In May **Winston Churchill** became prime minister and the **Battle of Britain** had halted the Luftwaffe's ambitions. This led to the **Blitz** over London and other major cities, in the autumn and winter of 1940–41. In 1941 the **United States** entered the war and the Germans became disastrously entrenched on the **Eastern Front** in Russia. By 1944 the German armies were in retreat and the **Normandy (D-Day) Landings** spearheaded the liberation of Europe.

1900	Labour Party formed
1901-10	Reign of **Edward VII**
1903	Women's suffrage movement started by Mrs Pankhurst
1905	First motor buses in London

1939-45	**Second World War**
1940	**Winston Churchill** becomes prime minister
1940	Evacuation of Dunkirk; **Battle of Britain**
1944	**Normandy landings**

POST-WAR BRITAIN

The years following the Second World War marked the end of the British Empire. In most cases this was a peaceful transition. India achieved independence in 1947 and within the next 10 years virtually all of Britain's overseas dependencies followed suit, changing into the **British Commonwealth**, an informal non-political union which fosters economic cooperation and best practices between member nations.

After 1945 key industries were nationalised and the **Welfare State** was born with the National Health Service, improved pensions and benefits.

Elizabeth II, who succeeded to the throne in 1952, has done much to strengthen the role of monarchy both at home and abroad and even following the royalty's recent troubled years the Queen remains enormously popular within and outside Great Britain.

The austere 1950s were succeeded by the "**Swinging Sixties**", a period of cultural upheaval and optimism which saw the rise of youth culture, London become the epicentre of the fashion universe, and, of course, The Beatles.

The decade ended badly in Northern Ireland where violent disputes, known as **The Troubles**, flared up between Protestant and Catholic organisations. Despite the efforts of the British Army and the Royal Ulster Constabulary, over the next 29 years some 3,700 people were to lose their lives, many in indiscriminate bombings.

As traditional heavy industries went into decline or moved to other parts of the world, **Scotland**'s economy waned badly. However, in the late-1970s, the discovery and exploitation of North Sea oil and natural gas in the fields around the Shetland Isles proved a massive boon to Scotland in general and to the Highlands and Islands in particular. In the last three decades the Scottish economy has moved to a technology and service base, as the oil runs out. Today it is estimated that around 80 percent of all Scotland's employees work in services, a sector which enjoyed significant growth until 2008 and the slump of 2009.

1947	Independence and partition of India. Nationalisation of railways and road transport
1950–1953	Korean War
1952	Accession of **Elizabeth II**
1958	Treaty of Rome - European Economic Community/ EEC (now the European Union/EU)
1959	Discovery of North Sea oil
1965	Death of Sir Winston Churchill
1969	Beginning of '**The Troubles**' in Northern Ireland
1973	United Kingdom becomes a founding member of the EEC

THATCHER AND THE CONSERVATIVE YEARS

By contrast with the upbeat 1960s the 1970s was a decade of industrial slump and strife. Against this background, in 1979, **Margaret Thatcher**, Britain's first ever female party leader (of the Conservatives) also became Britain's first female prime minister. She went on to become the most charismatic leader since Winston Churchill but her ideology, which came to be known as **Thatcherism** – deeply in favour of individualism over collectivism and capitalism over social responsibility – polarised the country. The bitter year-long miners' strike of 1984–85 and subsequent pit closures and massive job losses were the most obvious sign of this. Yet while Britain's industrial base declined other sectors of the economy (mostly services) boomed. Thatcher went on to win three general elections and while she was reviled by many, some look back fondly on her strong style of leadership.

1979	**Margaret Thatcher** elected first woman Prime Minister (serves until 1991)
1982	Falklands War
1990–1991	Gulf War
1992–1995	Bosnian War

Cardiff Bay with the Pierhead building and the National Assembly, Wales

© Chris Hepburn/iStockphoto.com

CLOSURE OF THE PITS

The **coal industry** reached its zenith in the 1920s with over a quarter of a million miners working in over 600 coalfields providing one-third of the world's coal. Exhaustion of the seams, under-investment in the pits, and the recession of the 1930s meant that only half of these were still operating by the outbreak of the Second World War. Pit closures became an acrimonious political issue in the 1980s and resulted in the bitter and ultimately disastrous miners' strike of 1984–85. Today every pit of any reasonable size and every foundry has gone. Despite the gloom of the recent past, Wales in the 21C looks forward to a brighter future with its own Parliament, a renewed interest in the language, national identity and massive urban regeneration projects at Cardiff, Swansea, Llanelli and Ebbw Vale.

NEW LABOUR

Although Britain had joined the **European (Economic) Union** in 1973, European policy issues had remained mostly on the back burner. In the post-Thatcher years, however, these, alongside other issues like the immensely unpopular poll tax, led to the unravelling of the Conservatives. John Major gave the Tories another term after Thatcher stepped down, but by 1997 the reformed centrist media-savvy Labour party, reborn as New Labour under **Tony Blair**, had taken centre stage. His dynamic, reformist and optimistic brand of politics earned him a massive majority in Parliament, with policies that moved away from traditional labour values in favour of The City, big business and closer links with Europe. The creation of the Scottish Parliament and the Welsh Assembly, which were both ratified in 1997, marked a new stage in the relationships between the constituent parts of the United Kingdom though most of the real power has remained firmly rooted in Whitehall and Westminster.

The decade ended under a shadow as Tony Blair's reign gave way to the failure of Gordon Brown's premiership, dogged by the continuing wars in **Iraq** and **Afghanistan**, increasing crime, human rights and privacy issues, and the beginning of a serious recession.

1997	Election of a **Labour Government**, led by **Tony Blair**.
1998	Good Friday Agreement, referendum and meeting of Northern Ireland Assembly
1999	Opening of Scottish Parliament and Welsh Assembly
2001–present	Afghanistan War (Coalition forces withdrew in 2014)
2002	Queen's Golden Jubilee.
2003	Iraq War
2005	Terrorist bombs explode in London killing 52 people
2007	Gordon Brown becomes the new prime minister
2008	UK economy enters recession. Troops withdrawn from Iraq.
2009	Last surviving British soldier of WWI dies.

COALITION, DEVOLUTION & THE ROAD TO REFERENDUM

Although the Scottish Parliament was abolished in 1707 there had been calls for Scottish devolution, if not quite full independence, since the mid-18C. In 1999 the Scottish Parliament was reinstated, and in 2005 moved to their new permanent residence at the foot of the Royal Mile in Edinburgh. The Parliament has responsibility over wide areas of Scottish affairs, even though in theory at least, Westminster retains powers to amend or even abolish it. A referendum for full Scottish independence took place in September 2014, and failed to produce the majority required.

At election in 2010, the Labour government was routed but, with no clear majority for the other parties the first **coalition government** in the UK since the Second World War sees the Conservatives and Liberal Democats (Lib Dems) sharing power. Only a year later, cracks begin to appear in the Conservative-Lib Dem coalition. The thorny issue of Britain's EU involvement is reignited as PM **David Cameron** defies the European Union by refusing to enter a treaty to save the euro.

The City of London

2011	**Prince William**, marries Catherine Middleton; they are created the Duke and Duchess of Cambridge.
2012	Britain stages a hugely successful **Olympic Games**.
2013	**Prince George** is born to Prince William and Kate, Duchess of Cambridge.
2013	Replacing Southward Towers and opened to the public in February, the **Shard**, at 309.6m, is the tallest building in the European Union. It was designed by the Italian architect Renzo Piano.
2015	The **Conservative party** wins an outright majority, while the Scottish National Party (SNP) secure almost all Parliamentary seats in Scotland.
	PM David Cameron promises a referendum before the end of 2017 on Britain's continued membership of the European Union.
2015	Prince William and Kate, the Duchess of Cambridge have their second child, **Princess Charlotte**.
2015	**Queen Elizabeth II** celebrated 60 years as reigning monarch, and becomes Britain's longest-serving monarch.
2016	Britain holds a **referendum** to determine whether the country should leave the EU; a majority of 52%-48% voted to leave, and Britain began the long process of withdrawal. Because he supported continued membership of the EU, David Cameron, following the success of the leave vote, resigned as prime minister, and was succeeded by the former Home Secretary, Theresa May in an uncontested election.
2017	In March, **terrorist attack** took place in the vicinity of the Palace of Westminster, when an attacker drove a car into pedestrians along the south side of Westminster bridge. Six people, including the attacker, died as a result of the incident, and around 50 others were injured.
2017	In May, a lone attacker detonated a shrapnel-laden home-made bomb at Manchester Arena in Manchester, following a concert by American singer Ariana Grande. Twenty-three adults and children were killed, including the attacker, and 250 were injured.
2017	In a snap election, intended to bolster the slim Conservative majority in Parliament, the Conservative Party in fact lost its overall majority, and continued as a minority government, supported by a tenuous alliance with Northern Ireland's Democratic Unionist Party (DUP). The Scottish National Party lose 21 of the seats they held from 2015.
2017	Centenary of the **Battle of Passchendaele**, a campaign of the First World War, also known as the Third Battle of Ypres: there were 275 000 British casualties, and 220 000 German.
2017	**Prince Philip**, the Duke of Edinburgh, aged 96, retires from public office.

Scientific Progress

Between 1760 and 1850, the Industrial Revolution turned Britain into the world's first industrial nation. Power-driven machines replaced human muscle and factory production replaced cottage industry. New methods and new machines supplied expanding markets and growing demand.

POWER

In 1712 **Thomas Newcomen** designed the first practical piston and steam engine and his idea was later much improved by **James Watt**. Such engines were needed to pump water and to raise men and ore from mines and soon replaced waterwheels as the power source for the cotton factories which sprang up in Lancashire. Then **Richard Trevithick** (1771–1833), Cornish tin miner, designed a boiler with the fire box inside which he showed to **George Stephenson** (1781–1848) and his son, **Robert** (1803–59). This became the basis of the early "locomotives". Without abundant coal, however, sufficient iron could never have been produced for all the new machines. By 1880, 154 million tons of coal were being transported across Britain. Cast iron had been produced by Shropshire ironmaster **Abraham Darby** in Coalbrookdale in 1709 and was used for the cylinders of early steam engines and for bridges and aqueducts. Wrought iron with greater tensile strength was developed in the 1790s, allowing more accurate and stronger machine parts, railway lines and bridging materials. In 1856 **Sir Henry Bessemer** devised a system in which compressed air is blown through the molten metal, burning off impurities and producing a stronger steel.

TRANSPORT

Thomas Telford (1757–1834) built roads and bridges for the use of stagecoaches and broad-wheeled wagons transporting people and goods. However, these were often impassable in winter so cheap transport for bulk goods was also provided by over 4 000mi/6 400km of canals, pioneered by James Brindley (1716–72). Eventually heavy goods and long-distance passenger traffic passed to the railways. Engineered by George Stephenson (of in 1825, the Stockton and Darlington Railway was the first passenger-carrying public steam railway in the world, by 1835 the railway had become the vital element of the Industrial Revolution – swift, efficient and cheap transport for raw materials and finished goods. The success of Stephenson's Rocket proved the feasibility of locomotives. Isambard Kingdom Brunel (1806–59), Chief Engineer to the Great Western Railway, designed the Clifton Suspension Bridge and also the first successful trans-Atlantic steamship, the Great Western, in 1837.

William Henry Morris – Lord Nuffield, the most influential of British car manufacturers, began with bicycles and made his first car in 1913. He is probably best remembered for his 1959 "Mini". John Boyd Dunlop started with bicycles too. In 1888, this Scottish veterinary surgeon invented the first pneumatic tyre. It was **John Loudon McAdam**, an Ayrshire engineer, who devised the "Tarmacadam" surfacing for roads. More recently **Christopher Cockerell** patented a design for the first hovercraft in 1955.

AVIATION

The names of **Charles Rolls** and **Henry Royce** will always be associated with the grand cars they pioneered although their contribution to aviation is arguably even greater. A Rolls-Royce engine powered Sir Frank Whittle's Gloster E28/29, the first jet aircraft, and the De Havilland Comet, the world's first commercial passenger-carrying jet airliner, which made its maiden flight in 1949. British aerospace designers worked with their French counterparts in the development of Concorde, the world's first supersonic airliner.

SCIENCE

In 1660, Sir **Francis Bacon** (1561–1626) founded the Royal Society; it was granted a Charter by Charles II in 1662 "to promote discussion, particularly in the physical sciences". **Robert Boyle** and **Sir Christopher Wren** were founder members and Sir Isaac Newton was its president from 1703 to 1727. **Michael Faraday** was appointed assistant to Sir Humphrey Davy, inventor of the miners' Safety Lamp, in 1812. It was Faraday's work with electromagnetism which led to the development of the electric dynamo and motor. An early form of computer, the "difference engine" was invented by **Charles Babbage** in 1833 and can be seen in the library of King's College, Cambridge. **Edmond Halley**, friend of Newton, became Astronomer Royal in 1720. He is best remembered for the comet named after him, and for correctly predicting its 76-year cycle and return in 1758.

In 1925, a Scottish engineer, **John Logie Baird**, produced a live, moving, grey-scale television image from reflected light in his rooms in Soho, London. He went on to demonstrate the world's first colour transmission in July 1928 though it took nearly another four decades before most of the general public were able to watch colour TV.

During the 1930s, Robert Watson Watt (a descendant of James Watt) argued that radio waves could be bounced off an aircraft as it travelled, in order to determine its exact position. He proved the technology worked, and so RADAR was born. Immediately this played a vital part in the defence of the country during the Battle of Britain and later came to revolutionise travel.

The radio telescope at Jodrell Bank, set up by **Sir Bernard Lovell** in 1955, is still one of the largest in the world and contributes to our widening knowledge of our Universe. In 1968, **Antony Hewish**, a British astronomer at Cambridge, first discovered pulsars, cosmic sources of light or radio energy. In 1988, **Professor Stephen Hawking** studied black holes and wrote his seminal treatise, *A Brief History of Time*.

MEDICINE

It was **William Harvey**, physician to James I and Charles I, who discovered the circulation of the blood. More recent British achievements in medicine have been those of Dr Jacob Bell who, with Dr Simpson from Edinburgh, introduced chloroform anaesthesia, which met with public approval after Queen Victoria used it during the birth of Prince Leopold in 1853. **Sir Alexander Fleming** discovered the effects of penicillin in killing bacteria in 1928. The "double-helix" structure of DNA (de-oxy-ribo-

Portsmouth dockyard © Jean Brooks / age fotostock

nucleic acid) – the major component of chromosomes that carry genetic information and control inheritance of characteristics – was proposed by Francis Crick working at the Cavendish Laboratory in Cambridge, with his American colleague, James Watson, in 1953. The cloning of Dolly the sheep, in 1996, by the Roslin Institute in Scotland marked a new era in genetic engineering.

NATURAL HISTORY

John Tradescant and son were gardeners to Charles I and planted the first physic (medicinal plant) garden in 1628, leading to the remarkable Chelsea Physic Garden, founded in 1673, open to the public today. James Hutton (1726–97) wrote a treatise entitled A Theory of the Earth (1785), which forms the basis of modern geology.

Sir Joseph Banks (1743–1820), botanist and explorer, accompanied James Cook's expedition round the world in Endeavour (1768–71) and collected many previously unknown plants. Together with the biologist Thomas Huxley (1825–95), they supported the pioneering research of Charles Darwin (1809–1882), the father of the theory of evolution outlined in his famous work, On the Origin of Species, which had a great impact on the study of natural sciences.

EXPLORATION

Maritime exploration spurred on by the enquiring spirit of the 16C led to the discovery of new worlds. Following the voyages of Portuguese explorers, **John Cabot**, a Genoese settled in Bristol, discovered Nova Scotia and Newfoundland. Rivalry between England and Spain and other European nations in search of trade, as well as scientific advances in navigational aids and improvements in ship construction, led to an explosion of maritime exploration. English mariners included: John Hawkins (1532–95), who introduced tobacco and sweet potatoes to England; **Sir Francis Drake** (c1540–96), the first Englishman to circumnavigate the world; **Sir Walter Raleigh** (1552–1618), who discovered Virginia; Martin Frobisher, who explored the North Atlantic and discovered Baffin Island (1574). Hudson Bay in Canada is named after the explorer Henry Hudson (1610). Captain **James Cook** (1728–79) explored the Pacific, and charted the coasts of Australia and New Zealand and surveyed the Newfoundland coast.

Other famous explorers include **Mungo Park** (1771–1806), who explored West Africa and attempted to trace the course of the Niger River; **David Livingstone** (1813–73), a doctor and missionary who campaigned against the slave trade and was the first to cross the African mainland from east to west and discovered the Victoria Falls and Lake Nyasa (now Lake Malawi); Alexander Mackenzie (1755–1820), the first man to cross the American continent by land (1783); and John McDouall Stuart (1815–66), who explored the Australian desert.

Britain's Art and Culture

Britain's culture, art, architecture and fashions are famous throughout most of the world. The early settlers took a New England to the USA and at the height of Empire (in the 1920s), British culture would be exported to – and to some degree imposed on – almost a quarter of the Earth. Today, British architects and designers still play a very prominent role, in fields as far apart as fashion and construction, while the UK, invariably led by London, is a tolerant melting pot of so many different styles and ethnicities that it continues to innovate and export many of its best ideas and icons.

Millennium Bridge and St Paul's Cathedral, London © Jon Arnold/hemis.fr

Roman to Romanesque

The Romans were Britain's first great builders and innovators. Their style eventually gave way to the Romanesque, from around 1000 through to the 12C, characterised by heavy vaulted arched church architecture, still prevalent in many of Britain's cathedrals.

ROMAN

Pre-Roman, Iron Age architecture is best observed in impressive hillforts such as at Maidenhead and in Scottish brochs. The Roman invasion began in Kent; **Richborough Castle** was part of the Roman system of coastal defences, a series of forts in the southeast under the control of the "Count of the Saxon Shore". Their capital was St Albans, linked by military roads to other major settlements in Bath, Chester, Lincoln and York. London was a trading post near a river crossing on the Thames.

Examples of domestic Roman architecture in Britain are the theatre at St Albans and the ruined **villas** at Chedworth, Fishbourne, Bignor and Brading with their mosaics. Their greatest military enterprise was **Hadrian's Wall**, a defensive wall reinforced by military camps stretching from Wallsend on the Tyne to Bowness on the Solway Firth (73mi/117km) to guard the northern boundary of the Empire.

PRE-ROMANESQUE

Few buildings survive from this period, c.650 to the Norman Conquest. Much Saxon work, in timber, was destroyed in Viking raids. **All Saints, Brixworth** (c.680) in Northamptonshire makes use of Roman brick and the apse was surrounded by an external ring-crypt, a feature first found in St Peter's in Rome (c.590). **All Saints**, at **Earl's Barton** nearby, has a late Saxon tower. Saxon crypts survive at **Hexham**, **Repton** and **Ripon**.

ROMANESQUE (NORMAN)

These bold, massive buildings continued to be erected until after the death of Henry II in 1189 and nowhere else in Europe is there such a richness or variation of Norman work, nor such an abundance of surviving examples. In English cathedrals, the naves tend to be much longer than on the continent, for example **Ely** (13 bays) and **Norwich** (14); the eastern end was usually shorter. **Durham cathedral**, begun in 1093, where the whole interior is one Romanesque scheme, is a fine example of Norman work in Britain, though externally only the lower parts of the tower and nave and the choir show true Romanesque work. Its stone vaulting, completed in 1133, survives in its original form. **Southwell Minster** has a west front c.1130, with later Perpendicular windows. The eastern end of **Norwich cathedral** is triapsidal. Its spire and clerestory are later Gothic, but the remainder is Norman. **Rochester, Gloucester, Peterborough, Lincoln, Exeter, Hereford, St Albans**, and the abbey churches of **Tewkesbury** and **Waltham**, are all part of England's heritage of Norman work.

Every county has parish churches with a Norman nave or tower, west doorway, or south porch or chancel arch. **Iffley church**, Oxfordshire, west front (c.1170), **St Mary and St David, Kilpeck**, Herefordshire (c.1140) with Scandinavian influence in the carving, and **St Nicholas, Barfreston**, Kent, are just some of the hundreds well worth visiting.

Most secular buildings are fortified. The **White Tower**, the keep of the Tower of London, was the first work (1080) of William the Conqueror. **Rochester Castle** c.1130, though ruined, gives an impression of living conditions, while **Chepstow Castle** (1067) is one of the earliest secular stone buildings in Britain.

ECCLESIASTICAL ARCHITECTURE

Saxon towers

EARL'S BARTON, Northamptonshire – Late 10C

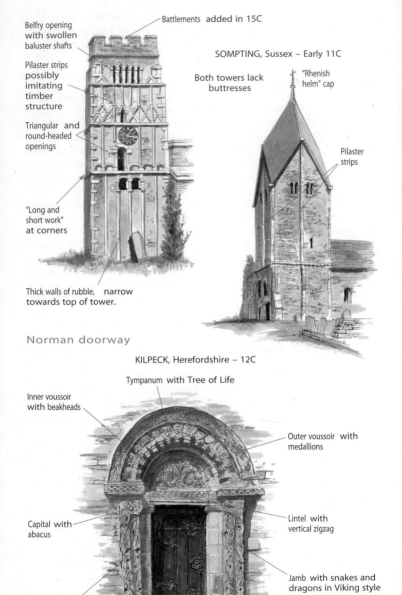

Battlements added in 15C

Belfry opening with swollen baluster shafts

Pilaster strips possibly imitating timber structure

Triangular and round-headed openings

"Long and short work" at corners

Thick walls of rubble, narrow towards top of tower.

SOMPTING, Sussex – Early 11C

Both towers lack buttresses

"Rhenish helm" cap

Pilaster strips

Norman doorway

KILPECK, Herefordshire – 12C

Tympanum with Tree of Life

Inner voussoir with beakheads

Outer voussoir with medallions

Capital with abacus

Lintel with vertical zigzag

Jamb with snakes and dragons in Viking style

Shaft with superimposed figures

R. Corbel/MICHELIN

Norman cathedral

Durham Cathedral was largely completed between 1095 and 1133. It exemplifies the grandeur and solidity of Norman architecture. The characteristic rounded arch prevails, but the pointed-rib vaults anticipate the structural achievements of Gothic architecture.

The side elevation of the nave is divided into: triforium/clerestory and arcade

Corbel

Rounded crossing arch

Diagonal ribs

Pointed-rib vault

Blind arcade

Round pier with incised chevrons

Compound pier

Pier with lozenge decoration

Cushion capital

Choir

Nave

19C rood screen

18C rose window

R. Corbel/MICHELIN

Gothic

The Gothic style evolved in northern France; the Abbey of St Denis outside Paris is the earliest example. Gothic designs resulted in larger and higher buildings, flooded with light. Heavy columns were replaced by slimmer clustered column shafts; towers became taller and more slender. In England Gothic architecture remained in use much longer than elsewhere in Europe, as it evolved through four phases and retained its distinctive character.

TRANSITIONAL (1145–89)

Transitional buildings have both pointed and round arches, especially in windows and vaults. **Ripon cathedral** (1181) is a good example but the most outstanding is the choir of **Canterbury cathedral**.

EARLY ENGLISH (C.1190–1307)

Distinctive features are the ribbed vaults, narrow pointed arches and lancet windows. **Salisbury cathedral**, built between 1220 and 1258, is the only English cathedral to have been built virtually in one operation, hence in a single style. See also **Wells**, the façades of **Peterborough** and **Ripon**, much of **Lichfield**, and the abbeys of **Tintern** and **Fountains**, and **Bolton Priory**.

DECORATED (C.1280–1377)

Ely cathedral, with its octagon and lantern (1323–30), was one of the early experiments in new spatial form and lighting. Other examples include the west façades of **Exeter** and **York**.

PERPENDICULAR

The last – and longest – phase of Gothic architecture in Britain is uniquely English in style. There is an emphasis on vertical lines but the principal features are panelled decoration all over the building, an increase in window area and the consequent development – very much later than in France – of the flying buttress. Fan-vault roofing, a peculiarly English design, can best be seen in **King's College Chapel**, Cambridge (1146–1515), **Eton College**

Salisbury Cathedral

© Jevgenija Pigozne/imageBROKER/age fotostock

Chapel (1441) and **St George's Chapel**, Windsor (1475–1509).

Contemporary with the fan vault, and equally English, was the development of the **timber roof**. Tie and collar designs from the 13C and 14C developed into more complex 15C and 16C **hammerbeam** roofs over churches and guildhalls, of which **Westminster Hall** (Hugh Herland, c.1395) is an example. Others are the Great Hall at **Hampton Court** (1535) and **Rufford Old Hall**, near Ormskirk, Lancashire (1505). England also has a wealth of medieval timber-framed houses, built in areas where stone was scarce – **Rufford Old Hall**, the **Guildhall** at Lavenham and the **Feathers Hotel** in Ludlow.

TUDOR–JACOBEAN

This period began with the accession of Henry VII in 1485 and covers the transition from Gothic to Classicism. Tudor Gothic, both ecclesiastical and secular, can be seen in **Bath Abbey** and the brick-built **Hampton Court Palace**. From 1550 to 1620 building was largely domestic, for a thriving middle class and a wealthy aristocracy. **Longleat House** (1550–80) in Wiltshire, **Montacute House** (1588–1601) in Somerset, and Bess of Hardwick's **Hardwick Hall** (1591–97) in Derbyshire are outstanding examples. The courtyard layout of medieval days was abandoned for the E or H-shaped plan, a central rectangular block with projecting wings. The **Long Gallery** – used for exercise on winter days – became a feature of all the great houses of the Elizabethan period.

Half-timbered houses were built in areas where stone was scarce – **Little Moreton Hall** (1559) in Cheshire and **Speke Hall**, near Liverpool, begun in 1490 and still being added to in 1612. The staircase began to assume an importance in the design of Elizabethan houses and by Jacobean times had become, in many houses, the focus of the whole interior – Ham, Hatfield, Knole and Audley End.

The architectural ideas of the **Renaissance** were brought to England by **Inigo Jones** (1573–1652). His two most

Knole House, Kent

© Peter Baker/age fotostock

outstanding public buildings are the **Banqueting Hall** (1619–22) in London and the **Queen's House** (1616–35) in Greenwich.

He also rebuilt part of **Wilton House** (1647–53) in Wiltshire, where his adherence to Classical proportions is evident in the "double cube" room. Architects in England who had never seen an ancient Classical building based their work on "Pattern Books" published by Renaissance designers.

TUDOR FORTS

In 1538, faced with the threat of invasion to re-establish the Pope's authority, Henry VIII began to construct a chain of forts and batteries to prevent an enemy invasion fleet from making use of the principal anchorages, landing places and ports.

The first forts built in 1539-40 – Deal, Walmer and Dover in Kent, Calshot and Hurst, overlooking Southampton Water and The Solent, and St Mawes and Pendennis in Cornwall – were squat with thick walls and rounded parapets. In most a central circular keep was surrounded by lower round bastions or enclosed by a circular curtain wall. They were designed to be defended by cannon mounted on carriages and sited on several tiers of platforms to compensate for the limited vertical traverse of each cannon. Lateral traverse was limited only by the splay of the gun ports.

Gothic

SALISBURY CATHEDRAL (1220-58)

Of great length and highly compartmentalised in layout like most English cathedrals, Salisbury is exceptional in having been completed in a single style –Early English – in a short space of time. The only major addition was the tall crossing tower and spire (404ft) built c 1334.

Close – A distinctive feature of many English cathedrals, a precinct with houses for cathedral officials. Grassed area formerly a graveyard.

Nave   Transept   Spire and crossing tower

Choir Transept

Chancel

Lady Chapel dedicated to the Virgin Mary

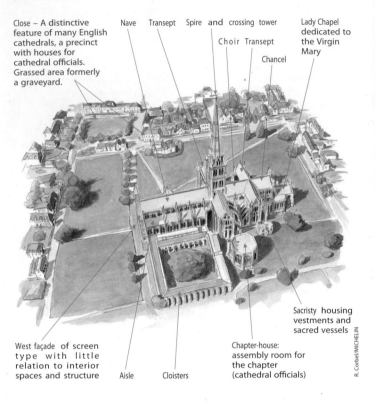

Sacristy housing vestments and sacred vessels

R. Corbel/MICHELIN

West façade of screen type with little relation to interior spaces and structure

Aisle   Cloisters

Chapter-house: assembly room for the chapter (cathedral officials)

WINDOWS

R. Corbel/MICHELIN

Simple 5-lancet Early English window c 1170, tall, narrow and with acutely-pointed arch

Space between lancets enlivened by addition of quatrefoil c 1270

Window in Decorated style with fully developed flowing tracery c 1350

Large window in Perpendicular style with 4-centred arch and horizontal emphasis through use of transoms

LITTLE MORETON HALL, Cheshire

A moated manor house built between the mid-15C and c 1580 with elaborate timber-framing and carved decoration characteristic of the Welsh Marches, Cheshire and Lancashire. Despite its date, this, and many other houses like it, is still medieval in character.

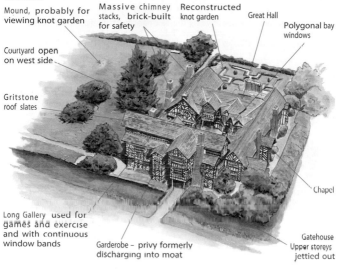

Mound, probably for viewing knot garden

Massive chimney stacks, brick-built for safety

Reconstructed knot garden

Great Hall

Polygonal bay windows

Courtyard open on west side

Gritstone roof slates

Chapel

Long Gallery used for games and exercise and with continuous window bands

Garderobe – privy formerly discharging into moat

Gatehouse Upper storeys jettied out

F. Corbel/MICHELIN

VAULTING

Boss   Ridge rib   Tierceron

Nave vault with liernes (linking ribs not joined to central boss or springer)
Canterbury Cathedral c 1390 - 1405

Fan vault with pendants: the ultimate development of this highly ornamental, non-structural vault
Henry VII's Chapel, Westminster 1503-12

R. Corbel/MICHELIN

Military Architecture

B ritain is famous for its variety and quantity of often superbly preserved castles, which pepper the landscape from Cornwall to northern Scotland, and so vividly mark the Conquest of Wales.

Norman motte and bailey

In the immediate post-Conquest years the Normans built timber castles, using an artificial or natural earthen mound ("motte"). A stockaded outer enclosure combined stables, storehouses etc ("bailey"). From c 1150 rebuilding took place in stone.

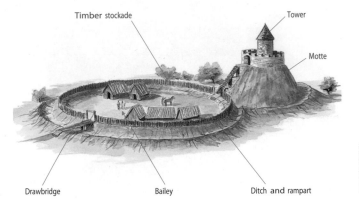

Timber stockade   Tower

Motte

Drawbridge   Bailey   Ditch and rampart

R. Corbel/MICHELIN

CAERPHILLY CASTLE, South Wales

A late 13C concentric castle which served as a model for Edward I's strongholds in North Wales

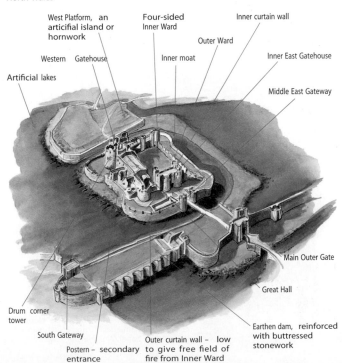

West Platform, an articifial island or hornwork

Four-sided Inner Ward

Inner curtain wall

Outer Ward

Western Gatehouse

Inner moat

Inner East Gatehouse

Middle East Gateway

Artificial lakes

Main Outer Gate

Great Hall

Drum corner tower

South Gateway

Postern – secondary entrance

Outer curtain wall – low to give free field of fire from Inner Ward

Earthen dam, reinforced with buttressed stonework

R. Corbel/MICHELIN

BODIAM CASTLE, Sussex

Based on French and southern Italian strongholds of the previous century, Bodiam (late 14C) is a perfectly symmetrical square castle, surrounded by a moat and with an array of well-preserved defensive features.

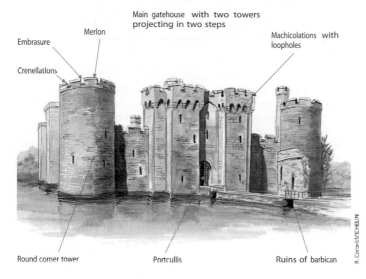

Main gatehouse with two towers projecting in two steps

Merlon

Embrasure

Machicolations with loopholes

Crenellations

Round corner tower

Portcullis

Ruins of barbican

R. Corbel/MICHELIN

CAERNARFON – A bastide town and castle of the late 13C, North Wales

English kings laid out numerous planned towns ("bastides") to attract settlers and control territory in areas like Gascony and Wales. Though the medieval houses of the English colonists have long since disappeared, Caernarfon retains its castle, its walls and its rectangular street layout.

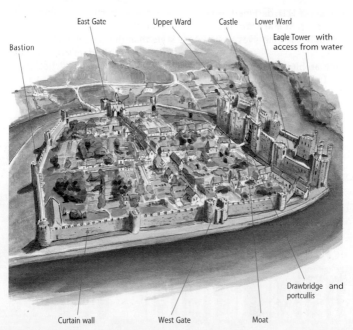

Bastion

East Gate

Upper Ward

Castle

Lower Ward

Eagle Tower with access from water

Curtain wall

West Gate

Moat

Drawbridge and portcullis

R. Corbel/MICHELIN

Classicism

Though Classicism was introduced by Inigo Jones, it was in the reign of Charles I (1625–49) that the style really began to make its mark on the English scene.

The dominant figure of Classicism was **Sir Christopher Wren** (1632–1723). After the Great Fire of London, he was responsible for 53 churches and the new **St Paul's Cathedral**, as well as the **Royal Naval College** at Greenwich and a new wing for **Hampton Court Palace**, which harmonises well with the Tudor brickwork. The **Sheldonian Theatre** (1669) at Oxford, and the **Library** of **Trinity College**, Cambridge (1676–84) are two of his best-known works outside London. **Sir John Vanbrugh** (1664–1726), soldier and playwright, who turned architect in 1699, was one of the chief exponents of the **Baroque** in England; his masterpieces, produced in collaboration with **Nicholas Hawksmoor** (1661–1736), are **Castle Howard**, **Blenheim Palace** and **Seaton Delaval**. Hawksmoor, under a commission of 1711, designed six London churches. **St Mary Woolnoth** in the City of London survives to shows his style.

Baroque architecture brought fantasy and movement to the Classical order but found little favour in England. It was replaced in the 1720s with **Palladianism**, also a foreign "implant" but one with a symmetry which was eagerly adapted by architects such as **Colen Campbell** (**Houghton Hall**) and **William Kent** (**Holkham Hall**). Palladian houses were set carefully in landscaped parks – many by **Lancelot "Capability" Brown** – a far cry from the formality of French and Italian gardens of the period. He designed over 170 parks, remodelling the great estate parks of the English gentry to resemble an ordered version of nature.

Robert Adam (1728–92), son of a Scottish architect, returned from the Grand Tour, having absorbed the principles of ancient architecture and learnt much neoclassical theory. He and his brothers set up in practice in London in 1758, introducing a lighter, more decorative style than the Palladian work then in vogue. Most of Adam's buildings are domestic and he also had great flair as an interior designer.

Old Royal Naval College, Greenwich   © James Brittain / View / Photononstop

English Baroque

ST PAUL'S CATHEDRAL, City of London, West façade

Built by Sir Christopher Wren between 1675 and 1710, the cathedral combines Renaissance and Baroque elements in a masterly way. The dome, inspired by St Peter's in Rome, is in three parts: the lightweight and beautifully shaped outer dome, an inner dome, and between them an (invisible) brick core carrying the heavy lantern which helps hold the outer dome in place.

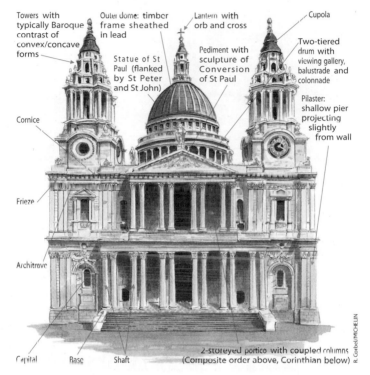

Towers with typically Baroque contrast of convex/concave forms

Outer dome: timber frame sheathed in lead

Lantern with orb and cross

Cupola

Statue of St Paul (flanked by St Peter and St John)

Pediment with sculpture of Conversion of St Paul

Two-tiered drum with viewing gallery, balustrade and colonnade

Pilaster: shallow pier projecting slightly from wall

Cornice

Frieze

Architrave

Capital

Base

Shaft

2-storeyed portico with coupled columns (Composite order above, Corinthian below)

R. Corbel/MICHELIN

GEORGIAN HOUSING AND PLANNING

In the 18C and early 19C, extensions to inland spas, and later to seaside towns saw a fusion of urban planning and landscape design. In Bath, John Wood the Elder and John Wood the Younger built the splendidly urbane sequence of Queen Square (1736), Gay Street (1734-60), The Circus (1754) and Royal Crescent, the latter a palace-like composition made up of relatively small terraced houses facing out to parkland.

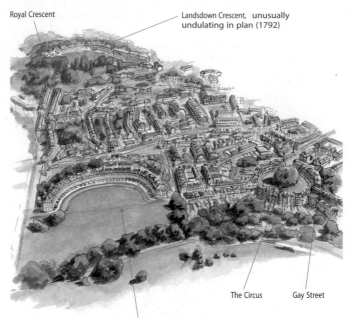

Royal Crescent

Landsdown Crescent, unusually undulating in plan (1792)

The Circus   Gay Street

Ha-ha sunken wall permitting uninterrupted view

R. Corbel/MICHELIN

In London, strict regulations governed the design of terraced houses which were rated 1-4 according to their size and value.

Sash-windows with thin wooden glazing bars help unify façades. Small or square windows of top floor act as visual stop. Classical appearance aided by low-pitched roofs (sometimes partly concealed by parapet) and lack of emphasis on chimneys. Tall windows emphasize importance of first floor reception rooms.

First-rate
house

Second-rate
house

Third-rate
house

Fourth-rate
house

R. Corbel/MICHELIN

19th to 20th Century

The 19C was predominantly an age of stylistic revivals. The Industrial Revolution and the movement of people into towns stimulated the construction of factories and mills and housing. Iron and glass played a part in the mass-production of these buildings. At first individual craftsmanship was evident in mouldings, decoration and furniture but by 1900 much of this had vanished.

John Nash (1752–1835), builder of many terraces round Regent's Park and down Regent Street in London, also designed the **Royal Pavilion** at Brighton. **Sir John Soane** (1753–1837), probably the last of the original designers, is represented by his house at Lincoln's Inn Fields, now the **Sir John Soane Museum**.

From 1840 the trend was towards the Gothic Revival which reached its height between 1855 and 1885. **Sir Charles Barry** (1795–1860) rebuilt the **Palace of Westminster** after the 1834 fire. Alfred Waterhouse (1830–1905) designed the Natural History Museum and built Manchester Town Hall.

The 19C was also the Railway Age. **Isambard Kingdom Brunel** (1806–59), Chief Engineer to the Great Western Railway in 1833, also designed the Clifton Suspension Bridge. **Thomas Telford** (1757–1834) built roads, bridges and canals throughout the country. He was responsible for the London–Holyhead road and for the bridge (1826), which carries it over the Menai Strait. In the 20C Art Nouveau had little influence on architecture but there was passing interest in interior decoration, fabrics and stained glass in the new style. Reinforced concrete was the main structural development. Between the wars, the outstanding figure was **Sir Edwin Lutyens** (1869–1944), who adapted Classicism to the needs of the day, in civic and housing design as well as ecclesiastical. His was the genius behind New Delhi in India and he also designed the **Cenotaph** in Whitehall and **Hampstead Garden Suburb** in London. **Sir Giles Gilbert Scott** (1880–1960), grandson of Sir George, the 19C architect, built the last great cathedral in the Gothic style, the red sandstone **Anglican Cathedral** of Liverpool. He also set the pattern for power stations with his 1929 design for **Battersea Power Station**.

"Urban planning" was not a 20C idea. Haussmann redesigned much of Paris in the 1860s and the Italian Renaissance painter Martini has left us his picture, painted in 1475, of The Ideal City. In Britain, **Welwyn Garden City**, built near St Albans in 1920, was one of the first New Towns, an extension of the Garden Suburb concept. The planned layout of streets, cul-de-sacs and closes, romantically named and lined with semi-detached and detached houses, was copied across the country after the 1939–45 war, in an attempt to check the "urban sprawl" in London, Lancashire, the Clyde Valley and South Wales. The 1946 New Towns Act provided for 28 such New Towns; **Harlow New Town** by Gibberd was built in 1947, **Cumbernauld**, near Glasgow, in the 1950s and **Milton Keynes** in rural Buckinghamshire in the 1970s. As costs escalated and concern grew over the decay of city centres, the building of new towns was halted. Pedestrian zones and the banishing of traffic have helped to conserve both the fabric and spirit of established town and city centres. **Poundbury** village in Dorchester, Dorset (1993–94), which stresses the importance of architecture on a human scale and is sponsored by the Prince of Wales, represents the latest trend in urban planning.

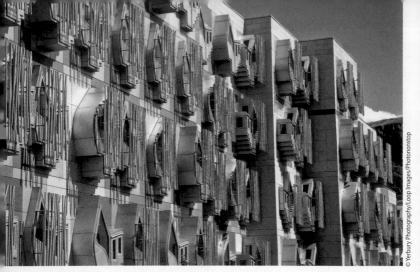

Exterior details, Scottish Parliament, Edinburgh

Outstanding among examples of 20C architecture is Sir Basil Spence's **Coventry Cathedral** (1956–62), remarkable in itself and in the way it blends with the older buildings around it. The imaginative circular design of **Liverpool Metropolitan Cathedral** (consecrated 1967) was the work of **Sir Frederick Gibberd**. In the secular sphere, education – established and new universities – and the arts provided good opportunities for pioneering work: Sainsbury Centre for Visual Arts, East Anglia, Norman Foster 1991; Downing College library, Cambridge, Quinlan Terry 1987; St John College Garden Quad, Oxford, 1993.

Custom-built galleries were designed for the Sainsbury Collection (1970s) at Norwich (Norman Foster), Burrell's donation in Glasgow (B Gasson) and the Tate Gallery at St Ives (1993, Evans and Shalev).

Other areas that have provided great scope for exciting modern architecture over the last few years are sports venues – the new **Wembley Stadium** and Lord's Cricket Ground stand (Michael Hopkins); opera houses – Glyndebourne and Covent Garden, **Royal Opera House** refurbishment and extension; London office developments – **Lloyd's Building**, Canary Wharf, Broadgate, The Ark, Swiss Re Tower ("**The Gherkin**") and City Hall. Major commissions (bridges, community and other projects) approved by the Millennium Commission heralded an explosion of original design for the turn of the century. Many of these are now popular visitor attractions: the **Eden Project**, Cornwall; Dynamic Earth, Edinburgh; the Great Glasshouse at the National Botanic Garden of Wales; in Manchester, The Lowry, The Imperial War Museum of the North and Urbis; in Glasgow, the Glasgow Science Centre and **The Armadillo**. All break new ground in structural and materials technology, as does **The Shard** in London.

The most controversial projects have been the reviled **Millennium Dome**, London, and the **Scottish Parliament building** in Edinburgh. The Parliament building was finally completed in 2004, three years late and ten times over-budget. The Dome was a commercial failure for many years and only recently (under its new guise as the O2 Arena) has found success as a concert venue.

The regeneration of derelict industrial sites and obsolete docks has met with considerable success in Liverpool, Cardiff and particularly the massive **London Dockland** scheme of the 1990s (still ongoing).

The conservation and reuse of existing industrial buildings is most apparent in two huge and stunning art galleries at opposite ends of the country: **Tate Modern**; in London (formerly a power station): the **Baltic Centre for Contemporary Art**, in Gateshead (formerly a flour mill).

VICTORIAN ARCHITECTURE

ST PANCRAS STATION, London

The Midland Hotel, completed in the Gothic Revival style in 1876 by Sir George Gilbert Scott, conceals the great train shed whose iron and glass arch was the widest (249ft) in the world at the time. Marrying Venetian, French, Flemish and English Gothic in a triumphal synthesis, Scott's building was also a functional masterpiece, housing the myriad activities of a railway terminus on a restricted, triangular site.

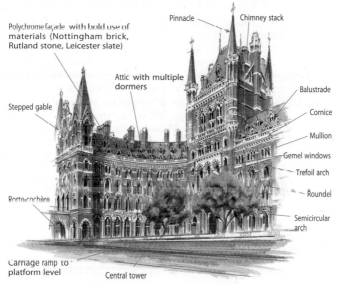

Polychrome façade with bold use of materials (Nottingham brick, Rutland stone, Leicester slate)

Pinnacle

Chimney stack

Attic with multiple dormers

Balustrade

Cornice

Stepped gable

Mullion

Gemel windows

Trefoil arch

Roundel

Porte-cochère

Semicircular arch

Carriage ramp to platform level

Central tower

EARLY MODERN ARCHITECTURE

GLASGOW SCHOOL OF ART

In touch with continental Art Nouveau and looking forward to 20C functionalism, Charles Rennie Mackintosh was also inspired by the robust forms of Scottish baronial architecture. Rising castle-like from its steeply sloping site, his Glasgow School of Art (1897-1909) combines strict utility of purpose with innovative, near-abstract forms and decorative Art Nouveau elements.

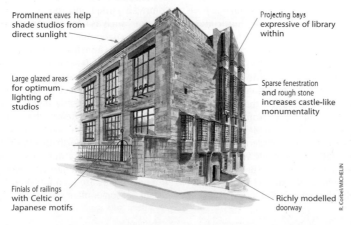

Prominent eaves help shade studios from direct sunlight

Projecting bays expressive of library within

Large glazed areas for optimum lighting of studios

Sparse fenestration and rough stone increases castle-like monumentality

Finials of railings with Celtic or Japanese motifs

Richly modelled doorway

R. Corbel/MICHELIN

Parks and Gardens

The British, and particularly the English are obsessed with their gardens, whether tending their own patch or visiting grander designs.

A keen appreciation of country life and the pleasures of nature goes back to the Middle Ages when Royal Forests covered much of the land and every person of consequence had a deer park. It was in the 18C, however, that the face of lowland Britain was transformed in pursuit of the aesthetic ideals of the country's "greatest original contribution to the arts", the **English Landscape Movement**. Ruthlessly sweeping away the grand avenues, parterres and topiary of the previous century, the grandees and lesser gentry of the Georgian age, aided by professionals like **Lancelot "Capability" Brown** (1716–83) and **Humphry Repton** (1752–1818), swept away the boundaries separating house, garden and surrounding countryside to make ambitious compositions fusing buildings and statuary, lawns and woodland, lakes and rivers into a picturesque vision of idealised nature. The movement embraced the Ideal Theory of Art, where everyday objects were seen as imperfect copies of universal ideas, for the artist to perfect. As well as their grander creations (**Blenheim**, **Stourhead**), there are many lesser achievements in landscaping that have bequeathed a passion for horticulture. Britain has a wonderful heritage of gardens, many of which are open to visitors. Owing to the vagaries of the climate, particularly the closeness of the Gulf Stream, conditions have proved favourable to many of the plant collections brought back from all over the world, particularly in the 18C and 19C. The chief name in garden design in the late-19C and early-20C was Gertrude Jekyll (Knebworth and Broughton Castle), who often worked in collaboration with the architect Sir Edwin Lutyens.

Plant trials and serious **horticultural study** are conducted at **Kew Gardens** in London, at **Wisley** in Surrey, the gardens of the Royal Horticultural Society, at Harlow Carr and the Botanic Gardens in Edinburgh (17C) and Glasgow. A few of the earliest **medicinal gardens** are still in existence, such as the Botanic Gardens (1621) in Oxford and the Chelsea Physic Garden (1673) in London.

A Museum of **Garden History** occupies Lambeth parish church and graveyard, where John Tradescant, gardener to King Charles I, is buried. Examples of the early knot garden have been created here and at Hampton Court. Formal gardens with geometric layout can be seen at **Hampton Court**, Ham House and Pitmedden.

The most prevalent style is the famous English Landscape, promoted by Capability Brown and Humphry Repton – **Stourhead** and **Castle Howard**.

The art of **topiary** is practised at Levens Hall and Earlshall in Scotland. The vogue for follies, usually an artificial ruin at the end of a vista, produced **Studley Royal**, which achieves its climax with a view of the ruins of Fountains Abbey. Less contrived gardens incorporate natural features, such as **Glendurgan**, which occupies a deep coastal combe.

Gardens range from the most southerly, Tresco **Abbey Gardens** in the Scilly Isles, created and maintained since 1834 by successive generations of the same family, to the most northerly, **Inverewe** in Wester Ross, where, despite the northern latitude, the gardens are frost-free, owing to the warm North Atlantic Drift. Sissinghurst and Crathes Castle are examples of themed gardens, where the enclosures are distinguished by colour, season or plant species.

Kirkcudbright, Dumfries and Galloway

Vernacular Architecture

The idealised British dwelling may still be the thatched cottage by the village green, but this is increasingly at odds with modern Britain where city folks inhabit anonymous boxes with little or no sense of community.

From the end of the medieval period, relative peace meant that security was no longer paramount and the fortified castle gave way to the rural residence designed as a setting for artistic patronage, culture, the social round, field sports and farm management; each generation of the rich and powerful seeking to establish or consolidate its status by building or rebuilding in accord with architectural fashion.

It is, however, the everyday architecture of the British cottage, farmhouse and barn that expresses most strongly the individuality of particular places. The range of materials used is enormous. Every type of stone has been quarried and shaped, from the most intractable of Scottish and Cornish granites to the crumbling chalk of the south. Limestones are often exploited to wonderful effect, as in the **Cotswolds** or the **Yorkshire Wolds**. Where stone is lacking, timber is used as in the **cruck-built cottages** of Herefordshire and the elaborate half-timbered houses of much

of the Midlands, or as 'weather-boarding' cladding in the south-east. In the claylands, most villages once had their own brickfield, producing distinctive tiles as well as bricks, while reedbeds provided thatch for roofing.

Building forms vary too: from the solid **timber frame** of a Kentish Tudor house to the humble one-roomed dwelling of a crofter in northwest Scotland. Scotland is also notable as the home of Scottish-Baronial architecture, a form of Gothic-Revival, influenced by late-Medieval castles and tower houses.

Settlement patterns are also almost infinitely varied: a few cottages and farms may be loosely grouped to form a hamlet; elsewhere, true villages may predominate, street villages accompanying a road for part of its way, others clustering sociably around the green. Modern town planning is much less community based, with densely packed estates, many lacking in any social or shopping facilities. Instead these are found in out-of-town complexes.

VERNACULAR ARCHITECTURE

CRUCK COTTAGE, HEREFORDSHIRE
Late medieval

The simplest form of timber construction, using the two halves of a massive, curving branch or tree-trunk

HOUSE AT CULROSS, SCOTLAND 16C

Crow-stepped gable

Rubble walls covered in rough cast ("harling") and colour-washed

WEALDEN HOUSE, KENT c 1500

Upper floor jettied out

Hipped roof, originally thatched, now tiled

Close-studded vertical timbers

Smoke vent, later replaced by chimney stack

TIMBER-FRAMED HOUSE, Kent 17C

Timber frame clad in contrasting materials: upper floor with hung tiles, ground floor in weather-boarding

STONE COTTAGES, Gloucestershire

Built of oolithic limestone, possibly as a 14C monastic sheephouse and converted into cottages in 17C

Steep-pitched roof with graded stone slates

SEMI-DETACHED SUBURBAN HOUSES
Urban outskirts anywhere in Britain c 1930

Picturesque Arts and Crafts outline and detail. Contrasting treatment: pebble-dash on left, applied "half-timbering" on right

R. Corbel/MICHELIN

© Y. Duhamel / MICHELIN

Choir, Canterbury cathedral

Architectural Terms

I f you don't know your flying buttresses from your clerestory or your machicolations from your narthex, fear not – help is at hand...

Aisle – lateral divisions running parallel with the nave in medieval churches and other buildings.
Ambulatory – passage between the choir and apse of a church.
Apse – rounded or polygonal end of a church.
Arcade – a series of arches, resting on piers or columns
Architrave – the beam, or lowest portion of the entablature, extending from column to column. Also used as the moulded frame around the head and side of a window or door opening.
Baldachin – canopy supported by pillars set over an altar, throne or tomb
Baptistery – building, separate from the church, containing the font.
Barbican – outwork of a medieval castle, often with a tower, defending a gate or bridge.
Barrel vaulting – continuous arched vault of semicircular section.
Battlements – parapet of medieval fortifications, with a walkway for archers or crossbowmen.
Broach spire – octagonal spire rising from a square tower without parapets.
Buttress – vertical mass of masonry built against a wall, so strengthening it and resisting the outward pressure of a vaulted roof.
Capital – crowning feature of a column or pillar.
Chancel – part of the church set aside for clergy and choir, to the east of the nave.
Chantry chapel – endowed for religious services for the soul of the founder.
Chapter house – place of assembly for the governing body of a monastery or cathedral. In medieval England, often multi-sided, with vaulting supported on a central pillar.
Chevron – Norman decoration of zigzag mouldings used around windows and doorways.
Choir – western part of the chancel, used by the choir, immediately east of the screen separating nave and chancel.
Clerestory – upper storey of the nave of a church, generally pierced by a row of windows.
Corbel – stone bracket, often richly carved, projecting from a wall to support roof beams, the ribs of a vault, a statue or an oriel window.

Cornice – crowning projection, the upper part of the entablature in Classical architecture. Also used for the projecting decoration around the ceiling of a room.

Crossing – central area of a cruciform church, where the transepts cross the nave and choir. A tower is often set above this space.

Crypt – underground chamber beneath a church, used as place of burial or charnel-houses. They often also housed the bones or relics of a saint or martyr

Cupola – hemispherical roof.

Drum – vertical walling supporting a dome, sometimes with windows.

Embrasure – the space between two merlons, on a battlement, through which archers could fire, whil protected by the merlons.

Entablature – in Classical architecture, the entire portion above the columns, comprising architrave, frieze and cornice.

Fan vaulting – system of vaulting peculiar to English Perpendicular architecture, all ribs having the same curve, resembling the framework of a fan.

Finial – top or finishing portion of a pinnacle, gable, bench end or other feature.

Fluting – narrow concave channelling cut vertically on a shaft or column.

Flying buttress – external arch springing over the roof of an aisle and supporting the clerestory wall, counteracting the thrust of the nave vault.

Frieze – central division of the entablature – horizontal decorative design.

Gable – triangular end section of a wall of a building, enclosed by the line of the roof.

Hammerbeam roof – late Gothic form of roof construction with no tie-beam. Wooden arches rest on corbels and beams bracketed to the walls and eaves.

Harling – wall plastered with roughcast. Often painted or with colour incorporated.

Jamb – upright side of a window or door opening.

Keep – inner tower and strongest part of a medieval fortress.

Keystone – central, wedge-shaped stone which locks an arch together.

Lancet – Early English (13C) sharp-pointed arch.

Lantern – glazed construction, for ventilation and light, often surmounting a dome.

Lierne – short intermediate rib in Gothic vaulting.

Loggia – open-sided gallery or arcade.

Machicolation – in medieval military architecture, a row of openings below a projecting parapet through which missiles could be rained down on the enemy.

Misericord – tip-up seat in choir stalls, with a small projection on the underside, to support a person having to stand through a long service. Often fancifully and grotesquely carved.

Mullions – vertical ribs dividing a window into a number of lights.

Narthex – western portico at the entrance to early Christian churches.

Nave – central main body of a church, west of the choir, into which lay persons were admitted, chancel and choir being reserved for the priests.

Ogee – arch used in late Gothic period, combining convex and concave curve, ending in a point.

Oriel – window projecting from a wall on corbels.

Pediment – triangular termination above the entablature, in Classical architecture sometimes "broken" in Renaissance designs.

Pilaster – rectangular pillar, projecting from the wall.

Rose window – circular window with mullions converging like the spokes of a wheel.

Screen – partition, often richly carved, separating nave from choir and chancel.

Spandrel – triangular space between the curves of arches and the frame in which they are set.

Squinch – arch placed diagonally across the internal corner angles of a square tower, converting the square into an octagonal form.

Tierceron – secondary rib in Gothic vaulting.

Transept – arms of a cruciform church set at right angles to nave and choir.

Transom – horizontal cross-bar or division of a window.

Tympanum – space between the flat lintel and the arch of a doorway.

Undercroft – vaulted chamber partly or wholly below ground, in a medieval building.

Volute – spiral scroll used at the corners of Ionic, Corinthian and Composite capitals.

Sculpture

Despite having a glorious past, in statuary at least, sculpture has rarely occupied a place in the heart of the British public. Modern artists are trying to redress the issue with some startling new works.

Angel of the North *(1998) by*
Antony Gormley near Gateshead

© Marc Jackson/age Fotostock

The idea of erecting statues, in stone and bronze – introduced largely by the Romans – fell into disuse in Britain in the Dark Ages. Gradually, however, pagan influences and Celtic scroll-work were put to Christian service, in standing crosses and in church decoration. Massive carving in Norman churches gave way to glorious tracery, windows, ribs and vaults in Early English and Perpendicular churches and cathedrals, complemented by carved wooden misericords, bench ends, altar screens and font covers. Impressive statuary such as that on the west front of Wells Cathedral has survived Reformation and Puritan depredations, to give an idea of the skills of early craftsmen.

First Classical and then Baroque memorials began to grace both cathedrals and churches in the flowering of British sculpture which took place between 1720 and 1840. In the Victorian age in many towns and cities statues were erected to the memory of industrialists and benefactors, municipal worthies and military heroes. There are also some very fine sculpted memorials executed in commemoration of those who died in battle. In the 20C British sculpture has been enlivened by the sometimes controversial works of **Jacob Epstein** and also of **Henry** Moore, whose technique of "natural carving" allowed the grain and shape of the material to dictate the final form. **Barbara Hepworth**, who settled in St Ives in 1943, **Reg Butler** and **Kenneth Armitage** are among other famous modern sculptors.

Monumental sculptures by Jacob Epstein, Eric Gill, Frank Dobson, Henry Moore, Barbara Hepworth and Eduardo Paolozzi among others set the standard for public art in cities, by the sea and in the countryside. Spectacular modern schemes – Broadgate in London, Herne Bay Sculpture Park, Brighton seafront, sculpture at Goodwood near Chichester, Stour Valley Art Project, Yorkshire Sculpture Park, the Gateshead Riverside Sculpture Park, the Northern Arts Project, Glenrothes in Scotland – have inspired major artists to create large-scale outdoor sculptures and promote interest in art in a wider public.

The most popular sculptor of recent times has been **Antony Gormley** whose *Angel of the North (1998)* (♦*see p483*) has become a modern icon for the North East and follows his much admired *Another Place (1997)* in which 100 cast iron figures look out to sea on Crosby Beach, near Liverpool.

Into the 21C scene the trend is a break with the past as many artists (Damien Hirst, Anish Kapoor, Richard Deacon, Cornelia Parker, Tracey Emin, Alison Wilding, Stephen Hughes, Tony Cragg, Rachel Whiteread among others) invent new idioms, such as in Kapoor's twisted ArcelorMittal Orbit.

Painting

British art has thrown up many inspired and distinctive talents throughout the centuries: from Hogarth to Blake, Turner to Mackintosh, Spencer to Hockney, and latterly Bacon and Banksy.

EARLY ART

The Celtic peoples loved rhythm and curvilinear scroll patterns, which they used in jewellery and later in manuscripts. The Romans brought their wall paintings and mosaics and both later inspired the didactic medieval church murals, which are some of Britain's earliest paintings. Surviving painting from the Saxon and medieval periods consists largely of exquisite work on illuminated manuscripts, such as the **Lindisfarne Gospels** from Holy Island, though the drawings of **Matthew Paris** are notable departures from this stylised work. One of the earliest surviving English paintings is the **Wilton Diptych** (c.1400), now in the National Gallery.

16C–18C

British artists never enjoyed that scale of patronage given to European artists by absolute monarchs and the Papacy. Much early portraiture, other than the **Holbein** pictures of Henry VIII and his court, tend to be flat and stiff but the art of the miniature flourished at the court of Elizabeth, where **Nicholas Hilliard** and **Isaac Oliver** created their masterpieces, capturing both the likeness and something of the spirit of the sitters.

The Dutchman **Sir Anthony van Dyck**, knighted by Charles I, enjoyed his patronage and was the first to record the atmosphere of the Stuart Court, in full-size paintings, before the Civil War. Canaletto, a Venetian, enjoyed some aristocratic support in the 1740s, as did **Sir Peter Lely** and **Godfrey Kneller**, both of German origin, who worked in England for long enough to be considered founders of the English portrait painting school. **William Hogarth**, English born and bred, famous for his vivid commentaries on the life of his day, started the idea of public exhibitions of painting, leading ultimately to the founding in 1768 of the **Royal Academy**. **Sir Joshua Reynolds**, its first president, and his contemporary, **Thomas Gainsborough**, raised the status of English painting, especially portraiture, though it was still much influenced by Dutch and Italian example. **Richard Wilson**, a founder of the Royal Academy, was much inspired by the French masters, Claude and Poussin, and founded the English school of **landscape painting**, a fashion which developed in England and spread to include marine scenes as well as country houses and estates.

19C TRENDS

The visionary **William Blake** heralded the dawn of English Romanticism. Portraiture by **Sir Thomas Lawrence** and the works of **Sir Henry Raeburn** in Scotland added **Romanticism** to the traditions of Reynolds.

John Crome founded the Norwich School in 1803, a regional treatment of landscape painting which was uniquely English. It was continued after his death by **John Sell Cotman**. **John Constable** and **Joseph M W Turner** carried this tradition and its studies of the effects of ever-changing light into the 19C. From 1840 to 1850 **Dante Gabriel Rossetti's** group, the **Pre-Raphaelites** and **Sir Edward Burne-Jones**, made a short-lived return to primitive values and religious and moral subjects. Their designs inspired Art Nouveau, best expressed by the work of **William Morris** (◖*as seen in the Morris Room in London's V&A p176*) and particularly **Charles Rennie Mackintosh** whose work is still so prevalent and loved in his native city, Glasgow.

Scottish National Gallery, Edinburgh

© Hartmut Krinitz/hemis.fr

Alfred Sisley, born in Paris of English parents, was an Impressionist whose sense of colour and tone owed much to the founder of the movement, Claude Monet, with whom he painted *en plein air* in France. The **Camden Town Group**, around **Walter Sickert**, returned to the realism of the Post-Impressionists, whose work **Roger Fry** had exhibited in 1911 and the next 20 years saw many short-lived and loose "movements" such as the **Bloomsbury Group**. **Augustus John** was known for his fashionable portraits in an almost Impressionist style.

20–21C

Artists influenced by the horrors of what they had witnessed during the World Wars include **Paul Nash and Sir Stanley Spencer**. Nash's landscapes are infused with symbolism described the killing fields of the First World War. He was also a pioneer of modernism in Britain, promoting the European styles of abstraction and surrealism in the 1920s and 1930s. Although similarly traumatised by his experiences, **Spencer** took a gentler route, painting biblical scenes in familiar British settings, mostly in his home village of Cookham (*see p261*).

Graham Sutherland, a Second World War official artist, also specialised in religious themes. He is most famous for his huge tapestry of Christ in Coventry Cathedral (*see p383*). In the 1950s **Ben Nicholson** was the major abstract artist. The optimistic 1960s brought Pop Art: **Peter Blake**, **David Hockney**, **Bridget Riley** ("Op Art"), while the portraits and figures of **Francis Bacon** and **Lucian Freud** show a much darker outlook.

Contemporary artists who have won acclaim include Gilbert and George, Paula Rego, Beryl Cooke, Ken Currie, Adrian Wizniewski, Stephen Conroy, Peter Howson, Lisa Milroy, Richard Wentworth, Julian Opie and **Damien Hirst**. Hirst himself was partially responsible for founding The **Young British Artists** group (Angela Bulloch, Michael Landy, Gary Hume, etc.) in the late 1980s. Their work is still championed by the **Saatchi Gallery**, though many YBAs have now been assimilated into the mainstream. **Banksy**, the satirical street artist from Bristol, famous since the 1990s, continues to poke fun at the Establishment and remains in the headlines, reportedly selling original prints in New York Central Park in 2013 for just $60 each. Grayson Perry is an interesting 21C newcomer working in several media.

Music

B ritain has been world famous for its music ever since the 1960s, but its musical heritage goes back an awful lot further.

POLYPHONY TO COMPOSITION

As with painting and sculpture, early and medieval English music was largely inspired by religion. The **Chapel Royal** – an institution, not a building – has fostered English music since 1135. **Thomas Tallis** (c.1505–85), organist at Waltham abbey near London (until it was dissolved) and later at Queen Elizabeth's Chapel Royal, can be credited with beginning the particularly rich tradition of **church music** for which England is famous. He arranged the harmony for the plainsong responses of Merbecke's English church service (Festal Responses in four and five parts), which are still widely in use and also arranged a setting of the Canticles in Dorian Mode and composed numerous anthems, Latin mass settings, lamentations and motets, of which his most famous is the magnificent *Spem in Alium* for forty voices, and of course his equally famous Canon (c.1567). Together with **William Byrd** (1542/3–1623), himself a prolific composer of high-quality church music with whom Tallis was joint organist at the Chapel Royal, he was granted a monopoly on music printing in England (1575).

By the early 17C, **madrigals**, originally an Italian form, with amorous or satirical themes, were being produced in large numbers by English composers, such as Byrd and **John Dowland** (1562–1626), a talented lute player. Folk music dating back much further accompanied the country dance, which survives today as the **Morris Dance**. Composers such as **Byrd** and **Thomas Morley** (1557–1602), who wrote settings for several of Shakespeare's plays, spread music into the theatre. **John Bull** (1562–1628), a skilled performer and composer for the virginals, ranks for many as one of the founders of the English keyboard repertoire. He is also sometimes linked with the original tune for *God Save the Queen*. **Ben Jonson** (1573–1637) and **Henry Lawes** (1596–1662) among others were leading exponents of the **masque**, which became popular in the 17C, combining music, dance and pageantry.

Orlando Gibbons (1583–1625), organist of the Chapel Royal under James I and one of the finest keyboard players of his day, wrote quantities of superb church music, madrigals and music for viols and virginals. **Henry Purcell** (1659–95), considered the greatest British composer of his generation (and by some of all time), wrote much splendid church music, stage music (opera *Dido and Æneas*), music for State occasions and harpsichord and chamber music.

MUSIC APPLIED TO DRAMA

Chamber music (music not intended for church, theatre or public concert room) truly came into its own in the 18C, which also saw great strides taken in the development of English **opera** and the emergence of a new form, the **oratorio**, under the German-English composer **George Frideric Handel** (1685–1759), perhaps its greatest exponent. His vast output included more than 40 operas, 20 or so oratorios, cantatas, sacred music, and numerous orchestral, choral and instrumental works. In 1719–28 the **Royal Academy of Music** was founded as an operatic organisation linked with Handel. The following century (1822) it became an educational institution, later to be joined by the Royal College of Music (1883) and the Royal School of Church Music (1927).

POST ROMANTICISM AND THE MODERN AGE

The composer **Thomas Arne** (1710–78) set to music the words of James Thomson, *Rule Britannia*, in a masque for Alfred, Prince of Wales in 1740. The late-18C to early-19C was rather a fallow period for Britain in terms of musical composition, although the Romantic movement that swept through Europe made itself felt in other arts such as literature (Wordsworth, Coleridge, Scott), and Romantic song cycles were fashionable with the British public in the 19C.

The next British composer of note was **Sir Edward Elgar** (1857–1934), the first to win international acclaim in almost 200 years. His love of the English countryside (he lived not far from the Malvern Hills) shaped his music, which is infused with an Englishness that captures the spirit of a nation in its heyday as a world power. Works such as *The Enigma Variations* and *The Dream of Gerontius* placed him on the world stage, and his many orchestral works exhibit the composer's masterly orchestration (Symphonies in A flat and E flat, Cello Concerto). **Frederick Delius** (1862–1934), championed by the conductor Sir Thomas Beecham, composed orchestral variations, rhapsodies, concerti and a variety of other orchestral and choral works stamped with his very individual, chromatic approach to harmony. The compositions of **Ralph Vaughan Williams** (1872–1958) were influenced by his study of English folk songs and Tudor church music; throughout his life he took an active interest in popular movements in music. **Gustav Holst** (1874–1934), prevented from becoming a concert pianist by neuritis in his hand, studied music at the Royal College of Music under Sir Charles Villiers Stanford (1852–1924), an Irish composer of church music and choral works. Holst, an ardent socialist, influenced by his love of the works of Grieg and Wagner as well as a certain innate mysticism, produced his most famous work, the seven-movement orchestral suite *The Planets*, in 1914–16.

Sir William Walton (1902–83) rose to fame with his instrumental settings of poems by Edith Sitwell (*Façade*, 1923) and went on to compose symphonies, concerti, opera, the biblical cantata *Belshazzar's Feast* and film music (Laurence Olivier's *Henry V*, *Hamlet* and *Richard III*). **Sir Michael Tippett** (1905–98) won recognition with his oratorio *A Child of Our Time*, reflecting the unrest of the 1930s and 40s, and went on to produce a rich and varied output, including operas (*The Midsummer Marriage, King Priam*), symphonies and other orchestral works in which he exhibits formidable powers of imagination and invention, combining inspiration from earlier sources such as Purcell with his interest in popular modern music such as blues and jazz. **Sir Benjamin Britten** (1913–76) studied under **John Ireland** (1879–1962) at the Royal College of Music and after a couple of years in the USA returned to England where he produced mainly vocal or choral works (one exception being his *Variations and Fugue on a Theme of Purcell*, or *Young Person's Guide to the Orchestra*), notably the operas *Peter Grimes*, *Billy Budd* and *A Midsummer Night's Dream*, *A Ceremony of Carols* and the immensely moving *War Requiem*. **John Tavener** (b.1944), whose haunting *Song for Athene* ended the funeral service of Diana, Princess of Wales, at Westminster abbey in September 1997, draws the inspiration for his predominantly religious music from his Russian Orthodox faith.

Still popular since their inception by **Sir Henry Wood** (1869–1944) in 1895 are the **Promenade Concerts**, which are held at the Royal Albert Hall every summer (mid-July–mid-September). The chorus *Jerusalem* sung as an unofficial anthem at the end of each season of Promenade concerts is perhaps the best-known work of **Sir Hubert Parry** (1848–1918). Conductors and composers such as Sir Peter Maxwell Davies, Sir Neville Mariner, Sir John Eliot Gardner, Sir Colin Davis, Sir Simon Rattle, Christopher Hogwood and Andrew Davies ensure the continuation of healthy and creative British music.

Eisteddfods in Wales and Mods in Scotland carry on a tradition of the Celtic bards. Festivals, such as the **Three Choirs** at Hereford, Worcester and Gloucester cathedrals and – in completely different spheres – opera productions at **Glyndebourne** and the **English National Opera** contribute to the aim of maintaining public interest in live classical music. However, Glyndebourne remains the reserve of the rich, while opera is usually targeted at the wealthy middle and upper classes.

Coda

On a lighter note, the meeting in 1875 of **Sir William Gilbert** (1836–1911) and **Sir Arthur Sullivan** (1842–1900) produced an enduring and well-loved English musical tradition in the form of "Gilbert and Sullivan" operettas, staged by Richard D'Oyly Carte. **Musical comedy**, an English development of the European operetta, was born in the 1890s at the Gaiety Theatre in London, with shows like *The Gaiety Girl*.

Another typically British institution, the **music hall**, also became popular – variety entertainment with the audience being able to eat and drink while watching the performance. Two names, **Ivor Novello** (1893–1951) and **Sir Noël Coward** (1899–1973), will always be associated with British musical comedy between the world wars. The tradition of British musicals has since been continued most notably by **Sir Andrew Lloyd Webber** (b.1948).

POP AND ROCK

British pop music began in the 1950s with early pioneers being **Lonnie Donegan** with his skiffle sound and a very youthful **Cliff Richard** doing his best to emulate Elvis Presley. It was **The Beatles**, however, who did more than any band to bring the new genre of "popular music" to the fore. Their first chart hit was in 1962 and they broke up in 1970. During that short but explosive period of creativity, they spawned a whole "Liverpool Sound". Their influence, not only on British but also on world pop and rock music, is incalculable, and

reverberates around concert halls and in recording studios even today. **The Beatles**' most famous contemporaries are the equally iconic **Rolling Stones** (from London), still touring and recording today.

The 1960s closed to the sound of **Black Sabbath**, **Deep Purple** and **Led Zeppelin** – heavyweights, who were to rule the burgeoning rock music scene for much of the decade until the advent of punk rock in 1977, led most (in)famously by the **Sex Pistols**.

The 1980s saw the dance and club scene take off and the rise of Manchester bands such as **The Smiths**, **Stone Roses** and **Happy Mondays**. The decade is best remembered for its frothy pop and pop-soul sounds, however, typified by **Wham** (featuring George Michael), **Culture Club** (Boy George) and **Simply Red** (Mick Hucknall).

The 1990s was the era of Britpop, most famously **Blur** and **Oasis**; both quintessentially English bands drawing heavily on 1960s influences. It was also the decade of 'boybands' (**Take That**, **Westlife**, **Blue**) and 'girlbands' (**The Spice Girls**, **All Saints**), a vocals-only genre which continues to defy critical disdain and sells millions of albums well into the 21C. The first decade of the new Millennium was notable (many would say notably depressing) for television talent shows such as *Pop Idol*, which was replaced by *The X Factor* 'manufacturing' some of Britain's cheesiest pop stars, with occasional bright spots such as **Will Young** and **Leona Lewis**. Meanwhile, bands such as **Coldplay** and **Radiohead** maintained credible mainstream British rock.

Notable recent successes include: **Adele**, who in 2011 became the first artist to sell more than 3 million copies of an album in a year in the UK; **Mumford & Sons** whose unlikely style of "Nu Folk" has been as hugely popular in the US as in the UK; and the **Arctic Monkeys**, with their own brand of streetwise indie rock.

Literature

B ritish literature has a prominent place on the bookshelves of the world, from the plays of Shakespeare to the adventures of Harry Potter.

MIDDLE AGES

Geoffrey Chaucer (c.1340–1400), the first great English poet, was influential in the evolution of "standard" English from cruder medieval dialects. The language of the *Canterbury Tales* is consequently as recognisable to us today as are Chaucer's vividly etched characters. **William Langland** (c1330–1400) in the *Vision of Piers Plowman*, and **Sir Thomas Malory** (d. 471) in *Le Morte D'Arthur* also brought a new depth and expressiveness to literature.

THE ENGLISH RENAISSANCE AND THE ELIZABETHAN AGE

The sonnet was introduced and blank verse became the regular measure of English dramatic and epic poetry. The supreme achievement of this dynamic, expansive period was in the theatre. Ambitious dramatic forms developed by the fiery **Christopher Marlowe** (1564–94) were perfected by the genius of **William Shakespeare** (1564–1616), the greatest dramatist and poet of this or any age. His monumental 37 plays appealed to all classes. **Ben Jonson** (1572–1637) created the English comedy of humours.

17C

John Donne (1572–1631), courtier, soldier and latterly Dean of St Paul's, was the most important of the Metaphysical poets whose "witty conceits" were concerned with the interaction between soul and body, sensuality and spirit. **John Milton** (1608–74), after Shakespeare arguably England's greatest poet, was also a powerful pamphleteer for the Puritan cause. He overcame blindness and political disappointment to write his epic masterpiece *Paradise Lost*, concerning the Judeo-Christian story of the Fall of Man, in 1667.

Puritan control was responsible for closing the theatres for nearly 20 years until the Restoration of Charles II in 1660. Restoration drama primarily reflected the licentiousness of the Court by the use of broad satire, farce, wit and bawdy comedy.

In prose, the language of the Bible exerted a strong influence, most notably in the work of **John Bunyan** (1628–88), whose *Pilgrim's Progress* was more widely read than any book in English except the Bible itself. The diaries of **John Evelyn** (1620–1706) and **Samuel Pepys** (1633–1703) detailed the minutiae of everyday life at the time.

18C

The early development of the novel is probably best exemplified in the work of **Daniel Defoe** (1660–1731). While his *Journal of the Plague Year* is a lively but primarily factual piece of journalism, *Robinson Crusoe*, though it utilises similar reporting techniques, is entirely fiction. Defoe's style was imitated and developed by **Samuel Richardson** (1689–1761), **Henry Fielding** (1707–54) and **Laurence Sterne** (1713–68).

The rise of the novel, the newspaper) and the expansion of a newly literate middle class were part of the Age of Reason. **Alexander Pope** (1688–1744), the finest satirical poet of the time, was matched in both poetry and prose by **Jonathan Swift** (1667–1745), famous for the incisive political and social satire of *Gulliver's Travels*. The era was dominated, however, by the influence of **Samuel Johnson** (1709–84), the subject of Boswell's famous biography and author of the first *English Dictionary* in 1755.

19C

The French Revolution was a primary inspiration for the Romantic movement, which stressed intensity of emotion and freedom of expression. This rebellious spirit was epitomised in the life of **Lord Byron** (1788–1824) though perhaps a better representative of Romantic poetry is **William Wordsworth** (1770–1850), whose best poems reflect his belief that intense joy could arise from deep harmony with Nature. **Percy Bysshe Shelley** (1792–1822) wrote more directly of the power of joy as a reforming influence, while the intense, lyrical verse of **John Keats** (1795–1821) stressed the power of beauty. Though lyricism, nature and the exotic continued to attract Victorian poets such as **Robert Browning** (1812–89), faith in joy and the senses waned and the verse of **Alfred, Lord Tennyson** (1809–1902) is noble but sombre.

The novel, meanwhile, had continued to develop in range and appeal from the carefully structured domestic comedies of **Jane Austen** (1775–1817) to the more popular, if less deep, historical novels of her contemporary, **Sir Walter Scott** (1771–1832). Popular too were Scott's Victorian successors, **William Makepeace Thackeray** (1811–63), **Anthony Trollope** (1815–82) and, above all, **Charles Dickens** (1812–70), whose sentimental but funny and sometimes despairing vision of city life in the Industrial Revolution struck a sharp chord with the reading public. Mary Ann Evans (1819–80), under the pseudonym **George Eliot**, wrote realistic works about the problems of the provincial middle class. The **Brontë** sisters, **Charlotte** (1816–55) and **Emily** (1818–48), took inspiration from their upbringing on the wild moors of Yorkshire to write their respective masterpieces, *Jane Eyre* (1846) and *Wuthering Heights* (1847). Most important of the writers of the century is **Thomas Hardy** (1840–1928), whose novels express a passion for man's tragic involvement in Nature and estrangement from it.

Influenced by the new drama in Europe, **George Bernard Shaw** (1856–1950) brought a new purpose and seriousness to the English theatre which had, for nearly two centuries, failed to find a clear direction.

The witty comedies of **Oscar Wilde** (1854–1900) were less profound but equally well crafted. They reflected the aims of the Decadent movement, which stressed flagrantly amoral beauty – a direct reaction against Victorian moral earnestness.

20–21C

The early modern masters of the **novel** – **Henry James** (1843–1916), **Joseph Conrad** (1857–1924) and **E M Forster** (1879–1970) – were still working in a recognisably Victorian tradition. The Dubliner **James Joyce** (1882–1941) used the stream-of-consciousness technique in the highly experimental *Ulysses* (1922) and *Finnegans Wake* (1939). This insistent excavation of personal experience is also found in the very different novels of **Virginia Woolf** (1882–1941) and of **D H Lawrence** (1885–1930), who challenged the taboos of class and sex, particularly in his novel *Lady Chatterley's Lover*. Concurrent with the serious "literary" novel, there developed a growing market for lighter fiction – entertainments – to serve the needs of an increasingly literate public; from the adventure novels of **Robert Louis Stevenson** (1850–94) and the *Sherlock Holmes* stories of **Arthur Conan Doyle** (1859–1930) to the spy thrillers of John Le Carré and Len Deighton in our own time. **George Orwell**'s (1903–50) dark political novels *(Animal Farm, 1984)* condemned the evils of communism.

Throughout the century there have been a number of important and stylish writers – less iconoclastic than their more innovative peers – who have continued to work with more traditional subjects and themes. The novelists **Aldous Huxley** (1894–1963), **Evelyn Waugh** (1903–66), and **Graham Greene** (1904–91) achieved considerable critical as well as commercial success, while **Somerset Maugham** (1874–1965) and **J B Priestley** (1894–1984) triumphed equally as playwrights and novelists.

The novel has, in all its forms, become the dominant vehicle of literary expression in the modern age. Eminent contemporary writers include Anthony Powell *(A Dance to the Music of Time)*; Paul Scott ((1920–78) *The Raj Quartet* and *Staying On*); **Anthony Burgess** *(A Clockwork Orange* and *Earthly Powers)*, Lawrence Durrell *(Alexandria Quartet* (1957); William Golding, *Lord of the Flies* (1954) and *Rites of Passage* (1980), studies of human behaviour, Iris Murdoch ((1919–99) *Under the Net* and *The Sea, The Sea*, which deal with complex psychological issues), John Fowles' haunting stories *(The French Lieutenant's Woman* and *The Magus)*. Doris Lessing *(The Golden Notebook)*, Muriel Spark *(The Prime of Miss Jean Brodie)*, **Daphne du Maurier** *(Rebecca* and *Jamaica Inn)* and Olivia Manning *(The Balkan Trilogy)* are also distinguished authors.

Among the new generation of writers who have won acclaim are **Martin Amis** *(London Fields* and *The Information)*, Julian Barnes *(The History of the World In 10½ Chapters)*, J G Ballard *(The Empire of the Sun, Crash* and *Cocaine Nights)*, Angela Carter *(Wise Children* and *The Magic Toyshop)*, A S Byatt *(Possession)*, Anita Brookner *(Hotel du Lac)*, Beryl Bainbridge *(Every Man for Himself)*, Jeanette Winterson *(Oranges Are Not the Only Fruit)*, Graham Swift *(Last Orders)*, Pat Barker *(Regeneration Trilogy)*, Irvine Welsh *(Trainspotting)*.

The English-language tradition is also enriched by writers from the Commonwealth and other countries who bring different perceptions: V S Naipaul, Caryl Phillips from the Caribbean, Nadine Gordimer, André Brink, J M Coetzee, Ben Okri from Africa; Peter Carey, Thomas Keneally, J G Ballard from Australia, Keri Hume from New Zealand, **Salman Rushdie**, Vikram Seth, Arundhati Roy from the Indian subcontinent and Kazuo Ishiguro from Japan.

During the 1990s, **J K Rowling** almost single-handedly revived the children's adventure story (in the process becoming richer than the Queen and a dollar billionaire) and introduced a new generation of children to reading with her record-breaking *Harry Potter* series. In 2012 she broke the mould by writing *The Casual Vacancy*, a million-selling adult novel under the pen-name of Robert Galbraith, following this up in 2013 with *The Cuckoo's Calling*. She also writes crime fiction under the pseudonym Robert Galbraith.

The previous year's erotic romance, *Fifty Shades of Grey* by E L James surpassed *Harry Potter* as the fastest selling paperback of all time, with the trilogy going on to sell over 100 million copies worldwide.

POETRY

Comparatively speaking, this is much-less widely read than in previous times. The Romantic decadence of the early-20C was swept aside by the Modernist poets **Ezra Pound** (1885–1972) and T S Eliot (1888–1965), whose *The Waste Land* (1922) is a dense and highly literary meditation on the situation of modern man. Less dramatically modern but equally influential was the slightly earlier poetry of **Thomas Hardy** and **W B Yeats** (1865–1939). The poets of the First World War, particularly **Wilfred Owen** (1893–1918) and **Siegfried Sassoon** (1886–1967), voiced their horror of mass warfare. **W H Auden** (1907–73) led a prominent group of intellectual left-wing poets in the 1920s and the exuberant imagery and lyrical rhetoric of **Dylan Thomas** (1914–53) caught the public's imagination. Only **John Betjeman** (1906–84), has achieved comparable popularity in recent times. Philip Larkin (1922–91) was the leading figure of the Movement group; the tone and form of his poetry expressing melancholic sensibilities in reaction to the romantic excesses of the 1940s. Poet Laureate Ted Hughes (1930–98), known for his violent and symbolic nature poems, is one of the most influential contemporary poets alongside Tom Paulin, Andrew Motion, Roger McGough, Benjamin Zephaniah, Carol Ann Duffy, Wendy Cope and Helen Dunmore.

Books

I t would be impossible to recommend a comprehensive reading list for your trip. Instead we concentrate on some favourites from the last two decades, plus a few evergreens that capture the flavour and atmosphere of Britain past and present.

Reference/Biography

A Brief History of British Kings & Queens - Mike Ashley (2002). A useful and insightful biography of all the country's rulers.

Travel

Notes from a Small Island - Bill Bryson (1995: 2001). Wry account of Bryson's first trip to Britain and its many foibles, followed up in 2015 with *The Road to Little Dribbling*.

Fiction

Oliver Twist - Charles Dickens (1838). Dickens' most famous work is a strident social commentary on a grim and unforgiving London, albeit with a happy ending. Also see: *Great Expectations, David Copperfield, Our Mutual Friend*.

Tess of the D'Urbervilles - Thomas Hardy (1891). This tragedy of class consciousness and sexual double standards paints an indelible picture of England's fading rural West Country. see: *Far from the Madding Crowd*.

Brighton Rock - Graham Greene (1938). Violence and gang war are the themes of this murder thriller set in the 1930s in Brighton.

Rebecca - Daphne du Maurier (1938). A brooding dark romantic novel set on the Cornish coast. see: *Jamaica Inn (1936).*

Cider With Rosie - Laurie Lee (1959). A tale of childhood in rural Gloucerstershire after the First World War. The trilogy continues with *As I Walked Out One Midsummer Morning* (1969) and *A Moment of War* (1991).

The Prime of Miss Jean Brodie -Muriel Spark (1961). Education, pupil control, love and betrayal in 1930s Edinburgh.

Knots and Crosses - Ian Rankin (1987). The first of the 18 Inspector Rebus novels, mostly based in and around Edinburgh, by Britain's top-selling crime author.

The Buddha of Suburbia - Hanif Kureishi (1990). A darkly comic romp through the lives, hopes and fears of young Asians in the London of the 1980s.

Fever Pitch - Nick Hornby (1992). Hornby specialises in the modern British male, in this case, an autobiographical obsession with football and specifically Arsenal Football Club. see: *High Fidelity*.

England England - Julian Barnes (2000). A satire on the country's obsession with heritage featuring a "theme park England" on the Isle of Wight.

White Teeth - Zadie Smith (2000). Multiculturalism in modern North London with three families – white, Indian and mixed.

Atonement - Ian McEwan (2001). A tragic-romantic family saga spanning 1935 to the present day (*see opposite*).

Brick Lane - Monica Ali (2003) London's multi-cultural issues centring around the Bengali community in the East End.

Never Let Me Go - Kazuo Ishiguro (2005) This romantic tragic "quasi sci-fi" novel is set in a boarding school in a dystopian alterative 1990s England.

Wolf Hall and *Bring up the Bodies - Hilary Mantel* (2010 and 2012) describe life in Tudor England and the influence of Thomas Cromwell, in writing styles and on themes that are equally annoying and enjoyable. Both titles won the Man Booker Prize.

Films

B ritain has always been one of the great filmmaking nations, in quality if not quantity, and often turns the camera on its own characteristics and foibles. Here is a modern day selection.

Educating Rita (1983). The film focuses on a young woman who wants to better herself by studying literature.

Four Weddings and a Funeral (1994). A romantic comedy drama set in the 1990s following the lives and loves of a group of friends set around the title events.

Trainspotting (1996). The mean (non-tourist) streets of Edinburgh is the setting for this disturbing story about disaffected youths turning to heroin

The Full Monty (1997). Six unemployed steel workers from Sheffield form an unlikely male striptease act in this comedy drama set in the post-industrial North of England.

Billy Elliot (1999). An inspiring and sometimes gritty tale set in a northern England mining town during the Miners Strikes of 1984 where a young boy discovers his talent for ballet.

Bend it Like Beckham (2002). Heart-warming comedy-drama involving women's football and culture-clash in the Asian community in 1990s suburban London.

Calendar Girls (2003). Based on a true story, a group of mature Women's Institute ladies in North Yorkshire decide to raise funds for charity by posing nude for a calendar and in the process become internationally famous.

Pride and Prejudice (2005). Beautiful costume drama adaptation of the Jane Austen novel, set in an idyllic Georgian England.

The Queen (2006). Concerning the intriguing interaction between Queen Elizabeth II and Prime Minister Tony Blair following the death of Diana, Princess of Wales in 1997.

Atonement (2007). A 13-year-old irrevocably changes the course of several lives when she accuses her older sister's lover of a crime he did not commit in this haunting romantic drama. Beautifully shot, very atmospheric.

This Is England (2008). Racism, xenophobia and class warfare via the violent teen movements of the early-1980s. Not for the fainthearted.

An Education (2009). This tender coming-of-age story about a teenage girl evokes the spirit of 1960s London and the suburbs.

Sherlock Holmes (2009). Movies about London's most famous detective come and go, but this action-packed blockbuster starring Robert Downey Jnr and Jude Law puts all the right pieces into place. If you like this you'll also enjoy its sequel, *A Game of Shadows* (2011).

The King's Speech (2010). The unlikely true tale of the fascinating relationship between King George VI and his unorthodox speech therapist.

Woman in Black (2012). A long-running British stage horror yarn, given the classic Hammer Films treatment, starring Daniel Radcliffe.

Posh (2014). A fictionalised account of the infamous Bullingdon Club, a hedonistic exclusive Oxford undergraduate dining society formerly patronised by leading members of the current political elite, including the Prime Minister.

Kingsman (2015). A humourous and well-acted, slightly off-beat spy story based on the comic book *The Secret Service*. A sequel – *Kingsman: The Golden Circle* – was released in 2017.

Nature

The picture-postcard image of rural Britain is usually that of gently rolling hills where sheep graze, a wisp of smoke emerges from a distant cottage and where little has changed since the 1950s, or indeed the 1850s. This domesticated idyll still holds true in many places but also belies the great variety and drama of completely natural wild landscapes to be found elsewhere. Much of Snowdonia, the Brecon Beacons and Black Mountains, the less commercialised Lake District, the Peak District and the Scottish Highlands remain untamed, while the Cairngorms is still largely wilderness. There are lonely moors in north and south west England, and in Scotland small offshore islands are colonised by tens of thousands of gannet, puffin, guillemot, razorbill and cormorant, and patrolled by seals, dolphin, porpoise, sharks and whales. Indeed, Scotland's Northern Isles are closer in every sense to the Faroe Islands and Norway than to most of the British mainland.

» 'Green and Pleasant Land' p144

Wye Valley from Symonds Yat Rock, Herefordshire © Craig Joiner/age fotostock

'Green and Pleasant Land'

The exceptionally diverse geological foundation of Britain has given rise to landscapes of great variety, a natural heritage enhanced by a continuous human presence over several millennia which has shaped and reshaped the material to form the present uniquely rich pattern of fields and fells, woods and parks, villages and farmsteads. Celebrated in literature and art, this densely textured landscape, usually domesticated but with its wilder beauties too, has become a kind of national emblem, lived in lovingly and vigorously defended against change by its inhabitants.

LANDSCAPE

The country can be broadly divided into **Upland** and **Lowland** Britain. The former, generally of older, harder material, comprises much of the North and South West of England and virtually the whole of Wales and Scotland.

As well as rolling, open moorlands, where the eye ranges freely over vast expanses of coarse grass, bracken or heather, there are mountain chains, modest in elevation but exhibiting most of the features of much higher and more extensive systems, attracting serious climbers as well as walkers. To the south and east the gentler relief of Lowland Britain is mostly composed of less resistant material. Much is "scarp and vale" country where undulating chalk and limestone hills terminate in steep escarpments commanding grand panoramas over broad clay vales.

Most of the course of the Earth's history can be traced in these landscapes. From the unimaginably distant Pre Cambrian, more than 600 million years ago, came the Torridonian sandstone and Lewisian gneiss of northwest Scotland as well as the compact, isolated uplands of Charnwood Forest in Leicestershire and the Malvern Hills in Worcestershire. The violent volcanic activity of Ordovician times left the shales and slates of **Snowdonia** and the **Lake District**, which in 2017 became the UK's newest World Heritage Site. Extreme pressure from the southeast in the Caledonian mountain-building period produced the northeast/southwest "grain" of ridges and valleys so evident in much of Wales

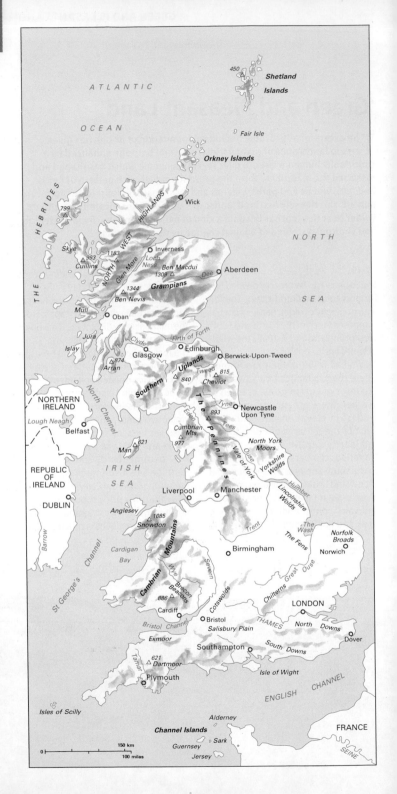

ATLANTIC

OCEAN

Shetland
Islands
450

Fair Isle

Orkney Islands

THE HEBRIDES

NORTH WEST HIGHLANDS

Wick

799

Skye

Inverness

993
Cuillins

1183

Glen More

Loch Ness

Ben Macdui

1309

Dee

Aberdeen

NORTH

SEA

1344

Ben Nevis

Grampians

Mull

Oban

Jura

Clyde

Firth of Forth

Islay

Glasgow

Edinburgh

Berwick-Upon-Tweed

Southern

Uplands

874

Arran

840

Tweed

Cheviot

815

NORTHERN
IRELAND

North Channel

Lough Neagh

Belfast

Man

621

REPUBLIC
OF
IRELAND

DUBLIN

Barrow

IRISH

SEA

Tyne

Newcastle
Upon Tyne

893

Cumbrian
Mts.

977

Eden

Tees

The Pennines

North York
Moors

Vale of York

Ouse

Yorkshire
Wolds

Liverpool

Manchester

Humber

Lincolnshire
Wolds

Anglesey

Snowdon

1085

Cambrian Mountains

Wye

Cardigan
Bay

St George's Channel

Trent

Severn

Birmingham

The Wash

The Fens

Norfolk
Broads

Norwich

Brecon
Beacons

886

Cardiff

Cotswolds

Chilterns

Great Ouse

LONDON

THAMES

North
Downs

Bristol Channel

Bristol

Salisbury Plain

Dover

Exmoor

Tamar

Southampton

South Downs

621

Dartmoor

Isle of Wight

ENGLISH CHANNEL

Plymouth

Isles of Scilly

Alderney

Channel Islands

Sark

Guernsey

Jersey

FRANCE

SEINE

0   150 km
    100 miles

and Scotland. Most of the abundant reserves of coal originated in the tropical vegetation of Carboniferous times. Except for the extreme south, the whole country was affected by the action of the often immensely thick ice sheets of the series of Ice Ages. The characteristically sculpted forms of the high mountains testify to the great power of the glaciers as they advanced and retreated, eroding and transporting vast quantities of material, much of which was spread over the lowlands by the mighty ancestors of today's rivers. As the last of the ice melted, the sea level rose, the land bridge joining Britain to the continent of Europe was flooded, and a truncated **Thames**, hitherto a tributary of the Rhine, acquired its own outlet to the sea.

DOMESTICATION

The taming and settling of the landscape can be traced back to the 5th millennium BCE when Neolithic farmers began to clear the wildwood, the dense forests that had spread northwards in the wake of the retreating ice. The imprint of each succeeding age may be traced, not only in the obvious features of prehistoric stone circles, burial mounds and hill-forts, the planned network of Roman roads or the countless medieval churches, but also in the everyday fabric of the working countryside, where a track may first have been trodden in the Bronze Age or a hedge planted by Saxon settlers.

The many-layered landscape is now characterised by **enclosure**, a web of fields bounded by hedges in the lowlands, by drystone walls in the uplands and by dykes in areas reclaimed from the sea. Small fields with irregular boundaries are likely to be ancient in origin; a regular chequerboard of hawthorn hedges is the result of agricultural "improvement" in the 18C and 19C.

In spite of conditions which are ideal for tree growth, only eight percent of the land surface is wooded. About half of this consists of recent coniferous plantations, mostly in the uplands. In many parts of the lowlands, the lack of great forests is compensated for by an abundance of small woods and by the countless individual trees growing in parks and gardens, and above all, in the hedgerows.

Standing out from this orderly pattern are the "commons", rough open tracts of grass and scrub. Once the villager's source of fodder, food and game, they now provide fresh air and exercise for both town and country people.

The country is well watered. The abundant rainfall, carried off the hills by a multitude of streams, feeds the rivers which, though of no great length, often end in splendid estuaries which bring salt water and the feel of the sea far inland.

The irregular outline of the country and the complex geology combine to form a long and varied coastline. Where the mountains meet the sea there is exceptionally fine coastal scenery, such as the spectacular chalk-white cliffs near Dover, symbol of English insularity. Many of the better stretches of sand and shingle have been appropriated by seaside resorts but there are some quieter beaches as well as remote marshlands and lonely sand dunes.

FAUNA

Britain's largest native mammal is the **red deer**. The stag, with full antlers, known in Scotland as the **Monarch of the Glen**, is a splendid sight. Roe, fallow and sika deer proliferate in some areas. The most unusual British bird is the **Puffin**, found just offshore of North Devon (Lundy), in Pembrokeshire, and in various locations in Scotland and its islands. Most impressive however is the sight of around 150 000 **gannet** at Bass Rock, North Berwick; or the great flocks in St Kilda in the Outer Hebrides, home to almost a million seabirds.

Many kinds of **whales** and **dolphins** are frequently seen off Scotland and the outer islands, plus in Pembrokeshire, Cornwall and Dorset. Seals are also common in Scotland, as well as at Cardigan Bay, Northeast England, Lincolnshire, and Blakeney Point, Norfolk.

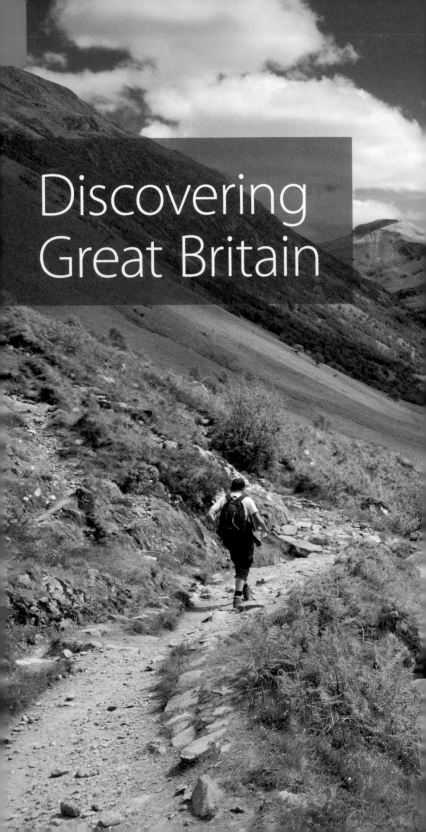

Discovering
Great Britain

Walking trail to Ben Nevis,
Glen Nevis, Highland
© Sébastien Wasek/Loop Images/Photononstop

London

Introduction

London is not only the commercial, political and artistic capital of the United Kingdom, but also one of the great financial centres and tourist destinations of the world. The only problem for the visitor is knowing how best to allocate time and which areas will suit his or her particular tastes: preparatory research will save time.

The main visitor centre is **Westminster**, incorporating the West End, famous for its royal palaces and Houses of Parliament, art galleries, theatres, shopping streets, nightlife and entertainment. West of here lie **Kensington** and **Knightsbridge** with three world-class museums, a royal palace and park, and Britain's most famous store, Harrods. On the western edges of London are two unmissable warm weather excursions: Kew Botanic Gardens and Hampton Court Palace.

To the east of Westminster lies **The City of London** ('The City' – with a capital C), famous for trade and commerce, but also home to the Tower of London, St Paul's Cathedral, a host of exquisite Wren-designed churches, as well as cosy traditional wine bars and pubs. Adjacent are the fascinating historic enclaves of **Southwark** and **Spitalfields**, haunts of Dickens, Jack the Ripper and the Young British Artists. The skyscrapers of London's

Highlights

1 Gaze dizzily down from **St Paul's** Whispering Gallery (p168)

2 Discover the 21C **Docklands** on the elevated DLR line (p163)

3 Take a blast on the river with a white-knuckle **RIB ride** (p163)

4 Come face to face with a dinosaur at the **Natural History Museum** (p175)

5 Feast your eyes and stomach at **Borough Market** (p190)

Docklands mark London's modern financial area, a fascinating contrast to neighbouring **Greenwich**, a favourite of Henry VIII, and an essential day out for anyone with an interest in maritime history.

Portobello Road Market, Notting Hill © Maremagnum/Photolibrary/Getty Images

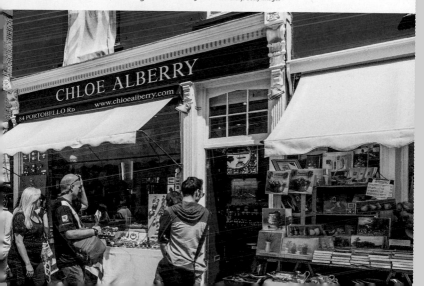

Grenadier Guards in front of Buckingham Palace

© Peter Phipp / World Pictures / Photoshot

A Bit of History

London goes back over 2000 years, and despite suffering from fires, bombing and the vagaries of contemporary town planning, there are still visible remains of every period of its long colourful past, from Londinium to the Swinging Sixties.

London first began to take shape under the Romans, who made it the hub of their road system. They enclosed it within walls and built the first London Bridge. Remains of the Roman walls, together with medieval additions, are still visible on the street called London Wall and near the Tower of London. It was Edward the Confessor (1042–66) who established the rival centre at Westminster, when he built a royal palace and founded an abbey, its minster in the west, as opposed to St Paul's Cathedral, its minster in the east.

In fact, London did not become the official capital of England until the mid-12C, taking over from Winchester. The City and its busy port gained considerable freedom and independence from the crown, which was often dependent on City merchants for raising money for military expeditions. The great houses of the nobility lined the Strand along the north bank of the Thames, while merchants built elegant mansions in the less crowded West End, or nearby villages like Islington, Holborn and Chelsea. Overcrowding was somewhat reduced by the ravages of the **Great Plague** (1665), in which 75 000 out of 460 000 people died, and of the **Great Fire** (1666), which

destroyed 80 percent of the buildings. Within six days of the end of the fire, Christopher Wren, then 33 years old, submitted a plan to rebuild the city with broad straight streets. It was rejected, though Wren was commissioned to build the new St Paul's Cathedral and the majority of the city's churches.

As the population continued to expand, poor-quality housing proliferated, accompanied by limited investment in sanitation. The appalling conditions of the 18C are strikingly illustrated in the work of **William Hogarth**.

Charles Dickens continued to document the poverty and dreadful living conditions well into the 19C. Eventually, in 1855, the government established the Metropolitan Board of Works, a central body with special responsibility for mains sewerage, and the tide of filth began to turn.

Destruction was to again play a role in the modernisation of the city when the piles of rubble left by German bombers during The Blitz of 1940–41 provided opportunities for modern and imaginative redevelopment such as the arts centres at the **South Bank** and the **Barbican**.

London Today

While London is loved the world over for its history, it is a city at the forefront of national change: in its fashions, its skyline, even its ethnicity. No matter how many times you visit you'll always see something new.

The City remains a financial powerhouse, thronged with pin-striped suits by day but deserted by night and on weekends. Its itinerant citizens almost all commute to the suburbs or much farther afield. The rest of London, and particularly the West End, is lively at all hours – by day with shoppers and office workers and by night with people going to the theatre, pubs, restaurants and nightclubs. London has grown organically over the centuries, absorbing other towns and villages as it sprawls ever outwards. Most Londoners live in the old belt of "villages" (such as Hampstead, Chiswick, Kensington or Chelsea), which have retained their own character.

The cosmopolitan atmosphere of London was greatly reinforced in the latter half of the 20C by easier foreign travel, higher standards of living, immigration from the former Empire and Britain's membership of the European Union, as reflected in the large number of foreign restaurants and food stores.

Modern multicultural London has many of its own traditions from Hindu Diwali to the **Notting Hill Carnival** *(last weekend of Aug)*, London's biggest festival and the second-largest street festival after Rio. Between one and two million visitors turn this area of London into a giant free party each year.

The 1980s and 1990s saw the large-scale regeneration of 8sq mi/21sq km of derelict warehouses and dock basins east of The City in the **Docklands**, which were converted into offices of epic proportions. Around the Docklands modern flats, low-rise housing and sports facilities have been laid out. More recently, the Swiss Re Building and London Bridge's Shard – the fourth tallest building in Europe – have joined the skyline.

- ▶ **Population:** 8 788 000.
- ⊘ **Michelin Map:**
  Michelin Atlas pp19–21
  or map 504 T 29.
- ⊛ **Don't Miss:** The London Eye; British Museum; National Gallery; Covent Garden; Westminster Abbey; St Paul's Cathedral; Natural History Museum; Science Museum; Tower of London; Kew Gardens; Hampton Court Palace; Greenwich (by river boat); London Zoo.

A massive building programme saw the creation of the **2012 Olympic Park**. The Olympic Park in the Lea valley, just east of the Docklands, was one of the largest construction and engineering projects in Europe. It features the Aquatics Centre, Hockey Stadium, Multi-sport arenas, 80 000-seat Olympic Stadium and Velopark, as well as the Olympic Village and Media Centre. Following the hugely successful games, the Park is now used regularly for events such as music concerts and festivals.

Traditional London

Tradition still plays a vital role in London life. The following are the most colourful and famous, but dozens more take place throughout the year.

The ceremonial **Changing of the Guard** at Buckingham Palace *(summer daily 11.30am, in summer; otherwise every other day)* and **Horse Guards** *(Mon–Sat 11am, Sun 10am)* is an evergreen favourite with British and oversees visitors and continues to draw the crowds. Get there early!

There is more pageantry and military precision when the Queen attends **Trooping the Colour** on Horse Guards Parade *(2nd or 3rd Sat in Jun)* and the **State Opening of Parliament** *(Nov)*.

In the **Lord Mayor's Show** *(2nd Sat in Nov)* the newly elected Lord Mayor of London proceeds through The City in the Golden State Coach before taking his oath at the Royal Courts of Justice in the Strand.

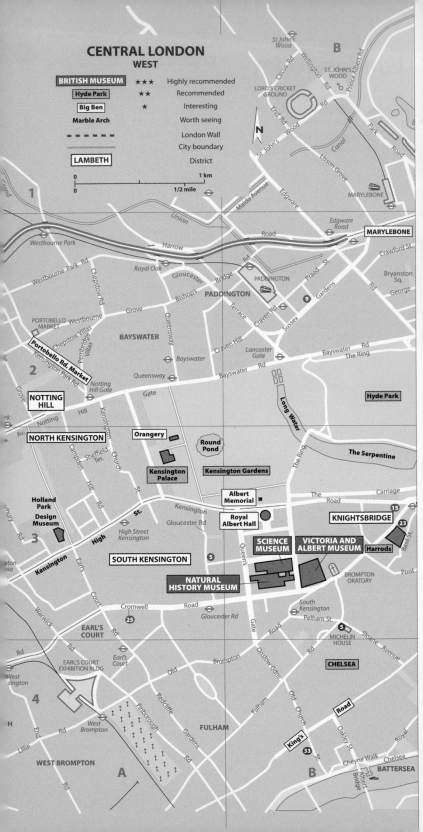

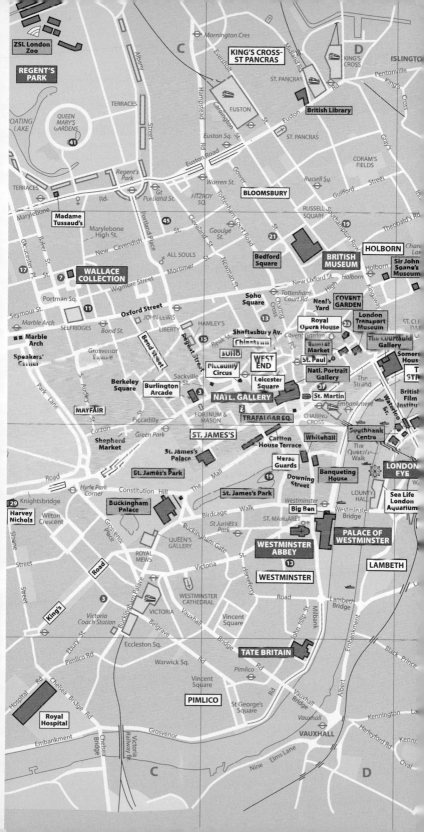

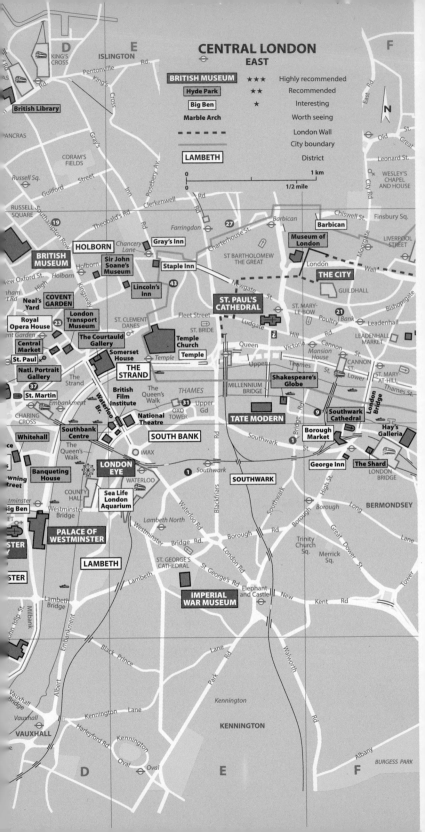

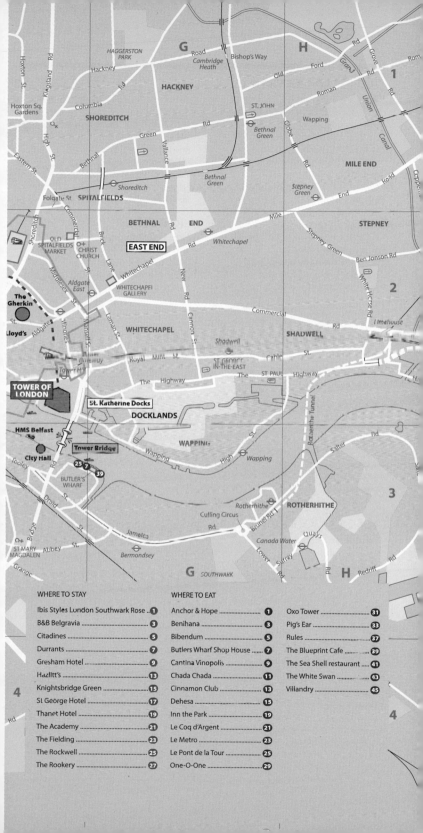

TOURIST INFORMATION

There are central tourist information offices open daily in the underground stations at Piccadilly Circus and Liverpool Street and in the mainline stations at Victoria, Euston and King's Cross St Pancras. There is a kiosk at Kingsway Holborn (Mon–Fri 9am–6pm). These are all walk-in only centres; for telephone enquiries call the London Information Line (0870 156 6366 (infoline); www.visitlondon.com). For what is happening specifically in The City, go to the City of London Information Centre (St Paul's Churchyard; www.cityoflondon.gov.uk). Out of the centre, there are offices at Twickenham (020 8891 1411; www.visitrichmond.co.uk), Greenwich (0870 608 2000; www.visitgreenwich.org.uk) and other London suburbs. For more information visit www.visitlondon.com.

PUBLIC TRANSPORT

London's **airports** are each connected to the city by public transport. Express trains to central London run from Gatwick, Heathrow, Stansted and Luton (the latter via a shuttle bus). London City Airport is the most central, but is business oriented, only servicing a limited number of European cities. The most enjoyable way of travelling to France or Belgium is by the **Eurostar** (www.eurostar.com) high-speed train from St Pancras via the Eurotunnel.

Transport for London (0343 222 1234; www.tfl.gov.uk) runs the tube (Underground), buses, Docklands Light Railway and Thames riverboats, while regional train companies service the majority of the suburbs. TfL's online **journey planner** is very useful.

Tickets are available by the journey, day, multiple days or longer. The **Visitor Oyster card** (http://visitorshop.tfl.gov.uk) is the cheapest and easiest way to travel, valid on all public transport (except taxis). This credit card-style ticket can be used repeatedly and loaded as you wish. They can be bought online or from any station. Simply top-up credit and the card automatically calculates the cheapest overall ticket for journeys made that day.

Trains run out of London from: Euston and King's Cross/St Pancras (northern destinations and Eurostar); Paddington and Marylebone (western destinations); Waterloo, Victoria and London Bridge (the south); and Liverpool Street and Fenchurch Street (the east).

Taxis are expensive. Always catch a licensed taxi cab (*see www.tfl.gov.uk for taxi fares*).

SIGHTSEEING

Most sightseeing and tourist activities are confined to Westminster, the West End and Kensington. Although the tube doesn't allow you to see the layout and character of London, it is the fastest way of getting around town. But, do try to avoid using the Underground in central London at rush hours; it's manic. If you are touring Westminster you are often better off walking, or using buses. Certain **bus routes**, such as the No. 11, give a fantastic tour of the city for little money. Remember, in Westminster buses may require you to buy a ticket before you board. Bus drivers only accept coins; use an Oyster card instead (*see above*).

Tours on **open-topped buses** start from Victoria, Green Park, Piccadilly, Coventry Street, Trafalgar Square, Haymarket, Lower Regent Street, Marble Arch, Baker Street, Tower Hill. Some tours are non-stop; some allow passengers to hop on or off and continue on a later bus. Pick up details of guided walking tours from information centres, or see press listings, particularly the excellent, free magazine *Time Out* (www.timeout.com/london).

Thames cruises depart from Westminster Pier, London Eye Tower Pier and Greenwich Pier. The major operator is City Crusises (www.citycruises.com). Public river transport (www.tfl.gov.uk) is expensive and offers limited options.

The **London Waterbus Company** operates a regular service along the Regent's Canal (020 7482 2550; www.londonwaterbus.com). Other operators are Jason's Trip (www.jasons.co.uk) and Jenny Wren (020 7485 4433; www.walkersquay.com). Probably the best walking tours are the Original London Walks (020 7624 3978; www.walks.com).

Westminster★★★

SIGHTS

Westminster Abbey★★★

⊖Westminster. Abbey: General opening times: year-round 9.30am–3.30pm, but see website for current details. £20 online, £22 at the abbey (incl. entry to all areas; cloister and garden free). Verger guided tours +£5. ⅙. **Cloister:** Open daily 9.30am–4.30pm. **Chapter House:** Open daily 10am–4.30pm. Closed 1 Jan, 24–26 Dec and except services. **College Garden:** Open Tue–Thu, 10am–4pm. ℘020 7222 5152. www.westminster-abbey.org.

The abbey, in which William the Conqueror was crowned as **William I** on Christmas Day 1066, and in which **Prince William** married **Kate Middleton** on 29 April 2011, was built by **Edward the Confessor** in the Norman style. It was only after the rebuilding by the Plantagenet Henry III in 1220 that it acquired its present Gothic appearance. Henry III began with the Lady Chapel, to provide a noble shrine for the Confessor, who had been canonised in 1163. Gradually the existing building was demolished as new replaced the old. When Henry VII constructed his **chapel** at the east end (1503–19) he produced the jewel of the age. The west towers by Wren and Nicholas Hawksmoor (1722–45) and repairs by George Gilbert Scott kept to the Gothic spirit. Inside, the vaulting is glorious, the carving on screens and arches delicate, often beautiful, sometimes humorous; the ancient tombs in **Henry VII's, St Edward's** and the ambulatory chapels are dignified. The transepts and aisles abound with sculpted monuments, particularly in the famous **Poets' Corner★** *(south transept)*, where there are monuments to many great poets though few are actually buried here; the tomb of Geoffrey Chaucer was the first in this corner, others interred here include Alfred Lord Tennyson and Robert Browning.

Westminster abbey

The **sanctuary** beyond the **choir** is where the **coronation ceremony** is performed. To the right hangs a 16C tapestry behind a large 15C altarpiece of rare beauty. Beyond is an ancient 13C sedilia painted with full-length royal figures (Henry III, Edward I).

The **Henry VII Chapel★★★** with its superb fan-vaulted roof is the most glorious of the abbey's many treasures. The banners of the Knights Grand Cross of the **Order of the Bath** hang still and brilliant above the stalls with inventive 16C–18C misericords. The **Chapel of Edward the Confessor★★** is rich in history, with the Confessor's shrine ringed with the tombs of five kings and three queens. In the centre against a carved stone **screen** (1441) stands the Coronation Chair, which until recently contained the Stone of Scone beneath the seat *(⅙see EDINBURGH and PERTH).* The **Chapter House★★** (1248–53) is an octagonal vaulted chamber (18m in diameter) with Purbeck marble columns. Its walls are partially decorated with medieval paintings.

Palace of Westminster (Houses of Parliament)★★★

⊖Westminster. Open by guided tour (75min) starting from the Victoria Tower. Sat throughout year; Mon–Fri Aug–Sept (summer recess). £25.50–£28. Book tickets online or call ✆020 7219 4114 (Mon–Sat 9am–5pm). Advance booking strongly advised.

When Parliament is in session the general public are allowed into the Visitors' Gallery free of charge to watch the proceedings in the House of Commons. If you do not have advance tickets, be prepared to queue for popular sessions such as Prime Minister's Question Time. www.parliament.uk/visiting.

The palace built by Edward the Confessor was enlarged and embellished by the medieval English kings, but most of the surviving buildings, by then occupied by Parliament, were destroyed in a disastrous fire in 1834. The oldest part is **Westminster Hall★★**, which William Rufus added to his father's palace between 1097 and 1099. This scene of royal banquets and jousts in the Middle Ages was altered and re-roofed by command of Richard II between 1394 and 1399. For this the upper parts were rebuilt and what is perhaps the finest timber roof of all time was built, a superb **hammerbeam★★★** designed by the king's master carpenter, Hugh Herland. After the 1834 fire, which, fortunately, did not damage Westminster Hall, **Charles Barry** and **Augustus Pugin** won a competition for a new design for the palace, which became known as the Houses of Parliament. Together they created a masterpiece of Victorian Gothic architecture. It was completed in 1860, with over 1 000 rooms, 100 staircases and 2mi/3km of corridors over 3ha.

The Clock Tower (96m), the most famous feature of this distinctive building, was completed by 1859. The name **Big Ben★** applied originally to the great bell, probably so-called after Sir Benjamin Hall, the Commissioner of Works and a man of considerable girth. The clock, which has an electrically wound mechanism, proved reliable for 117 years, until it succumbed to metal fatigue in 1976 when it required major repairs. Big Ben was first broadcast on New Year's Eve 1923 and its chimes are the most famous in the world.

The **House of Commons★**, rebuilt after being bombed in 1941, seats 437 of the 659 elected Members of Parliament; at the end of this simply decorated chamber is the canopied Speaker's Chair. Red stripes on both sides of the green carpet mark the limit to which a Member may advance to address the House – the distance between the stripes is reputedly that of two drawn swords.

The **House of Lords★★** is a masterpiece of design and workmanship. The throne and steps, beneath a Gothic canopy mounted on a wide screen, all in gold, occupies one end of the chamber. The ceiling is divided by ribs and gold patterning above the leather benches and the Woolsack, seat of the Lord Chancellor since the reign of Edward III, adopted as a symbol of the importance to England of the wool trade.

Whitehall★★

The wide street, which leads north from Parliament Square and Parliament Street, is lined by government offices. In the middle stands the Cenotaph, the austere war memorial designed by Sir Edwin Lutyens. On the left is **Downing Street** *(no public access)* where a relatively modest Georgian house (No. 10) has been the official residence of the prime minister since 1732. **Banqueting House★★** (⊖Westminster; open (functions permitting) year-round daily 10am–5pm; closed Good Fri, 1 Jan, 24–26 Dec, and bank holidays; £5.50; ⚹; ✆0844 482 7777; www.hrp.org.uk), the only part of the great Whitehall Palace to survive destruction by fire, was designed by Inigo Jones in 1619, but much altered in the early-19C. The hall is a double cube with a delicate balcony on gilded corbels; the ceiling is divided by richly decorated beams into compartments filled with magnificent

Woolsack, House of Lords

paintings (1634–35) by Rubens. It was on a platform erected in front of this building that Charles I was executed in January 1649.

Opposite stands **Horse Guards**★ famous for the presence of the **Household Cavalry sentries**. The ceremonial mounting of the **Queen's Life Guard**★★★ occurs daily at 11am (10am Sun) in summer on Horse Guards Parade. The dismount ceremony is daily at 4pm in the Front Yard of Horse Guards. The cavalry rides along The Mall between Horse Guards and their barracks in Hyde Park. Behind is the parade ground, where Trooping the Colour takes place in June.

St James's Park★★

St James's Park.

The oldest and most beautiful royal park in London dates from 1532 when Henry VIII had **St James's Palace**★★ built. The park was landscaped in the 19C by John Nash, who was also responsible for the majestic **Carlton House Terrace**★ in the northeast corner. From the bridge over the water there is a fine **view** of Whitehall and Buckingham Palace.

Buckingham Palace★★

St James's Park, Victoria. Open late Jul–Sept daily, 9.30am–7pm (6.30pm Sept; last entry 2h15 before closing). £23. Joint tickets: with garden highlights tour £32.50; with Royal Mews and Queen's Gallery £39.50. 020 776 7300. www.royalcollection.org.uk.

Buckingham House was built by the Duke of Buckingham in 1703 and purchased in 1762 by George III. Under George IV it was converted into a palace (1825–37) by John Nash and Edward Blore; the east front containing the famous balcony was added in 1847. The tour includes Throne Room, Drawing Rooms, Dining Room and the Picture Gallery, hung with royal portraits and old masters (*Charles I* Van Dyck; portraits by Rembrandt and Frans Hals; seascapes by Van de Velde; *A Lady at the Virginals*, Vermeer; pastoral and religious scenes by Rubens…) and furnished with many pieces collected by George IV. When the sovereign is in residence, the Royal Standard flies over the palace.

The **Changing of the Guard**★★ (for security reasons the schedules are not normally released until the month prior, and can change; check website for current details. www.changing-the-guard.com) takes place in the palace forecourt. Arrive early for a good view. The **Queen's Gallery**★★ (open daily Oct–mid-Jul 10am–5.30pm; mid-Jul–Sept 9.30am–5.30pm. £11; 020 7766 7300; www.royalcollection.org.uk) exhibits portraits, paintings, drawings and furniture in the priceless Royal Collection.

West End★★

Trafalgar Square★★

⊖Charing Cross.

Begun in 1829, the square was completed in the 1840s, when Charles Barry levelled it and built the north terrace for the National Gallery (☉see below). In 1842 **Nelson's Column** was erected; the monument is 56m tall, with the pedestal, fluted granite column, bronze capital and a 5.2m statue of the great admiral who lost his life in victory at the Battle of Trafalgar.

Note the equestrian statue (south) of **Charles I** cast by Le Sueur in 1633. A plaque in the road next to it marks the spot from where all road distances to/from London are measured. Ironically the square is now pedestrianised. Note the four plinths at each corner of the square. While three of these are occupied by conventional historical statues, the fourth plinth is now the location for specially commissioned artworks.

The church of **St Martin-in-the-Fields★** (Trafalgar Square; open daily, see website for times; &✗; ℘020 7766 1100; www.stmartin-in-the-fields.org) was built by James Gibbs in 1722–26, with a Corinthian portico and elegant spire. Today it is one of London's most active churches, staging free **lunchtime concerts** (Mon–Tue and Fri at 1pm; donation suggested); regular evening **classical concerts**; is home to a **Brass Rubbing Centre** (Mon–Wed 10am–6pm Thu–Sat 10am–7.45pm, Sun 11.30am–5pm; from £4.50) and the award-winning Café in the Crypt restaurant.

National Gallery★★★

⊖Leicester Square, Charing Cross. Trafalgar Square. Open year-round daily 10am–6pm (9pm Fri). Closed 1 Jan, 24–26 Dec. Charge for temporary exhibitions. &✗; ℘020 7747 2885. www.nationalgallery.org.uk.

This landmark building was completed in 1838, its pedimented portico of Corinthian columns forming a climax to Trafalgar Square. The sixth and latest extension to the original building is the Sainsbury Wing (1991) by Robert Venturi.

There are now more than 2 000 paintings in the collection; they represent the jewels in the public domain from early to High Renaissance Italian painting, early Netherlandish, German, Flemish, Dutch, French and Spanish pictures and masterpieces of the English 18C. The fuller representation of British art, particularly the more modern and 20C work of all schools is in Tate Britain.

The galleries are arranged chronologically starting with the period 1260–1510 in the **Sainsbury Wing**. Leonardo's fragile preparatory "cartoon" of Virgin and Child with St Anne and John the Baptist is spectacular while his Virgin of the Rocks is similarly enigmatic and engaging. Uccello exploits strong lines and colour in his epic Battle of San Romano. Haunting realism and solemn stillness are the keywords in the works of Van Eyck and Van der Weyden, particularly in the former's legendary Arnolfini Portrait. Botticelli is represented by Venus and Mars and Portrait of a Young Man while other Italian masters in this gallery are Raphael, Mantegna and Bellini, whose perfect use of oils is encapsulated in his Madonna and Child. Earlier German and Netherlandish work is also represented by Dürer, Cranach, Bosch and Memlinc. Paintings in the **West Wing** range from 1510 to 1600. The Ambassadors by Holbein is a wonderful large-scale historical portrait and its famous trompe l'œil skull is a great favourite with gallery visitors. Tintoretto, El Greco, Michelangelo and Veronese are also here.

In the North Wing are paintings by the French school, the Spanish school and from the Low Countries. Works by Claude and the great British landscape artist J M W Turner are shown together and should not be missed. Rembrandt and Rubens, Caravaggio, Velázquez and Van Dyck (his huge Equestrian Picture of Charles I is unmissable) also star here.

Paintings from 1700 to 1900 are exhibited in the **East Wing**. The British school is exemplified by classics such as The Haywain by Constable, The Fighting Temeraire and Rain, Steam and Speed by J M W Turner. There are works by Canaletto, Goya, Tiepolo and Delacroix but many visitor's favourites are the Impressionist collection starring Pissarro, Renoir, Monet, Manet, Degas and Cézanne. Van Gogh's *Chair* and *Sunflowers* (once the world's most expensive painting) stand out as crowd pleasers. Seurat's *Bathers at Asnière* is another favourite. Another distinctive and popular artist is Henri Rousseau, whose *Tiger in a Tropical Storm* is a classic.

National Portrait Gallery★★

⊖ Leicester Square, Charing Cross. St Martin's Lane. Open year-round daily 10am–6pm (9pm Thu–Fri). Closed 24–26 Dec. Charge for temporary exhibitions only. ♿✕ ✆020 7306 0055. www.npg.org.uk.

Here you will find portraits of almost every British person of significant public or historical interest from the Middle Ages to the present day, some painted, sculpted or photographed by the famous artists of the day. They range from the raffish picture of **William Shakespeare** (his only known contemporary portrait) to Sir Winston Churchill and Margaret Thatcher to modern icons such as Diana, Princess of Wales and David Beckham.

MAYFAIR★

The most luxurious district of London takes its name from a cattle and general fair held annually in May until it was closed in 1706 for unruly behaviour. It contains the most elegant hotels and most exclusive shops in all of London: **Burlington Arcade★** (1819), where the bow-fronted boutiques sell fashion, jewellery, leather goods; **Bond Street★** famous for art auctioneers and dealers (Sotheby's, Phillips, Agnew's, Colnaghi), jewellery (Asprey, Cartier) and fashion (Fenwick, Yves St Laurent); **Regent Street** well known for elegant stores (Austin Reed, Aquascutum, Burberry, Jaeger and **Liberty★★**); **Oxford Street** lined with the more popular department stores (John Lewis, Debenhams, D H Evans, Selfridges and Marks & Spencer). Less well known is **Shepherd Market**, a charming maze of lanes, alleyways and paved courts linked by archways

River Cruises

There's no better way to spend a sunny day in London than an excursion to **Greenwich★★★** by river cruiser from Westminster, Charing Cross or Tower Pier. For a more adrenaline fuelled ride, take a **RIB** (rigid inflatable boat; www.thamesrockets.com; www. thamesribexperience.com). On a cruise, make sure you pick one with a live (rather than a pre-recorded) commentary. You can return a different route, by the foot tunnel under the Thames to Island Gardens. There is a fine **view★★** of Greenwich Palace from Island Gardens on the north bank, which can be reached via the foot tunnel. From here return west on the **Docklands Light Railway** (DLR), enjoying the scenic ride on its elevated track (✆0343 222 1234; www.tfl.gov.uk).

with a village atmosphere. Victorian and Edwardian pubs and houses, antique shops and small inserted shop fronts which serve in summer as pavement cafes line its streets.

You will find it hard to hear a nightingale singing in **Berkeley Square** (laid out in 1737) these days, but it is still a very impressive plane-tree-lined ensemble – the trees are not much younger, many dating from the 1780s. Look for the late-18C houses on the west side with ironwork balconies, lamp holders at the steps and torch snuffers.

Piccadilly Circus★

This famous road junction (circus), once considered the hub of the British Empire, is still dominated by **Eros**, the Angel of Christian Charity, surmounting the fountain erected in memory of the philanthropist Lord Shaftesbury in 1892. It is famous for its garish neon advertising hoardings and as a meeting place. Appropriately, London's gaudiest attraction, a branch of **Ripley's Believe It or Not! London★** 👥👤 (⊖ Piccadilly Circus; open year-round daily

10am–midnight, last entry 10.30pm; £27.99, child £20.99 (save by booking in advance); ♿✖; ☎020 3238 0022; www. ripleyslondon.com) is located here and wows the crowds with its inimitable mixture of amazing facts and over 700 jaw-dropping artefacts.

Off the Circus, **Shaftesbury Avenue** is the heart of London "theatreland".

MARYLEBONE
Wallace Collection★★★

⊖Bond Street. Manchester Square. Open daily 10am–5pm. Closed 24–26 Dec. ♿✖ ☎020 7563 9500. www.wallacecollection.org.

This gathering of one of the world's finer collections of 18C French art was the life's work of the 4th Marquess of Hertford (1800–70). These sit along Italian masters, 17C Dutch painting, 18C French furniture (note the magnificent cabinets by A C Boulle), and Sèvres porcelain. Don't miss the formidable display of European weapons and arms, nor the **Great Gallery.** This is traditionally hung with the larger 17C pictures and Old Master paintings including works by Rubens, Murillo, Velázquez, Rembrandt, Van Dyck, Gainsborough and the most popular work in the museum, *The Laughing Cavalier* by Frans Hals.

👥 COVENT GARDEN★★

Covent Garden Piazza, the first London square, was designed by Inigo Jones in 1631. It was originally surrounded by colonnades, long demolished.

St Paul's church is an original survivor, its elegant portico dominating the west side of the square.

At the centre are the **Central Market Buildings★★**, designed in 1832 by Charles Fowler, to house the fruit and vegetable market, which moved out in 1974. The tiny shops and market stalls which now occupy it sell all kinds of goods, much of it aimed at visiting tourists (fashion, jewellery, crafts, etc.) and there are dozens of refreshment options.

One of the biggest draws is the high-quality (licensed) musicians and street artists who perform on the open cobblestones.

Covent Garden has long been synonymous with opera, and its **Royal Opera House★** has been magnificently refurbished. Its design incorporates the original framework of the old Floral Hall. Also recently revamped with great success, **London Transport Museum★★ 👥** (open daily 10am–6pm, Fri 11am–6pm; £17.50, child under-16 free; ♿✖; ☎020 7379 6344; www.ltmuseum.co.uk) tells the fascinating story of the capital's public transport history with a large collection of historic vehicles, interactive displays and archive materials that really bring its subject to life. It also has one of London's best museum shops.

It is well worth exploring the narrow side streets in and around Covent Garden, particularly **Neal's Yard** (off Shorts Gardens, a 2-min walk from Covent Garden Underground station) complete with period hoists, dovecotes, trees in tubs, geranium-filled window boxes and a whole raft of eco-friendly shopkeepers, vegetarian and wholefood restaurants and food outlets. It's a particularly attractive spot in summer.

The Courtauld Gallery★★

⊖Temple, Embankment. Somerset House, Strand. Open year-round daily 10am–6pm. Closed 25–26 Dec. £7 (but varies according to exhibitions). ♿✖ ☎020 7848 2526. www.courtauld.ac.uk.

The gallery is housed in one of central London's finest riverside buildings, **Somerset House**, designed by **Sir William Chambers** and built 1776–86. Samuel Courtauld's splendid private collection of **Impressionists** is the heart of the gallery, including famous canvases by Manet *(Bar at the Folies-Bergère)*, Degas, Bonnard, Gauguin (Tahitian scenes), Van Gogh *(Peach Trees in Blossom, Self-Portrait with Bandaged Ear)* Cézanne *(Lake at Annécy)* and Seurat. Other outstanding pieces include 30 oils by **Rubens** and six drawings by **Michelangelo** as well as works by Bruegel, Leonardo, Tiepolo, Dürer, Rembrandt, Bellini, Tintoretto and Kokoschka; paintings of the Italian Primitive school and of the Renaissance;

paintings by the **Bloomsbury Group**. In the summertime Somerset House stages open-air events; in winter it is home to a spectacular ice-rink.

SOHO★

This very cosmopolitan district (⊖Leicester Square, Piccadilly Circus), where immigrants once tended to congregate, is the home of the music and film trades, and night-life of every kind. Soho is particularly popular with the gay community.

In the latter decades of the 20C it became synonymous with sex clubs, prostitution and low-life. Today, although sex clubs and sex shops can still be found, the night scene is more reputable and much safer.

The area is also famous for its concentration of good places to eat and drink, with many top French, Italian, Greek and Chinese restaurants in particular, many of the last can be found in and around Gerrard Street, London's small **Chinatown★** district. This colourful area is marked by Oriental gates and other exotic street furniture, and abounds in eating places, supermarkets selling eastern foodstuffs and Oriental goods. At **Chinese New Year** this is the scene of one of London's most colourful street festivals.

Gerrard Street leads onto **Old Compton Street**, the spiritual heart of bohemian Soho, lined with pubs, wine merchants, pastry shops and Italian food stores. In summer grab a sandwich or snack and retreat to bucolic **Soho Square** (est. 1680), between Greek and Frith streets.

At **Leicester Square★** the bohemian character of Soho dissipates with the huge crowds that traverse this tree-shaded pedestrian precinct, made garish by the bright lights of many cinemas and tawdry cheap food outlets. In the run-up to the 2012 Olympics the square is being redeveloped, so you may notice lots of hoardings.

Theatre fans should note the **TKTS Leicester Square** building (formerly known as the Half-Price Ticket), where you can buy tickets for leading West End shows at a discount (⊚*see p191*).

HOLBORN★

The medieval manors at this former crossroads have been transformed into Lincoln's Inn and Gray's Inn, two of the four Inns of Court (⊚*see below*). The fields where beasts once grazed are less in extent but still open; on the north side stands the remarkable time capsule of **Sir John Soane's Museum★★** (⊖ Holborn; 13 Lincoln's Inn Fields; open Tue–Sat 10am–5pm; Candlelight tour 1st Tue of month 6–9pm; closed bank holidays; free entry; guided tours Tue, Thu–Sat at noon, and also 11am on Tue and Sat; £10, book online, limited to 8 places per tour; ℘020 7405 210/; www.soane.org). This remarkable little museum presents the highly individual collection of Classical sculpture, architectural fragments, drawings, prints and paintings, assembled by Soane, the architect, in his own house and left virtually untouched as stipulated in his will in 1833. The highlight is the **collection of pictures** mostly assembled on folding and sliding planes which make the most of the very limited available space. There are drawings by Piranesi, paintings by Canaletto, Reynolds and Turner and 12 of Hogarth's minutely observed paintings of London's unpleasant 18C underbelly including *The Election* and *The Rake's Progress*.

The area around High Holborn and Fleet Street has been the centre of legal London since the 14C, housing some of the world's oldest surviving legal training establishments: Lincoln's Inn, Gray's Inn, Inner Temple and Middle Temple, known collectively as the **Four Inns of Court**. Each inn (which meant lodgings in Old English) resembles a small university campus, comprising rooms for practising barristers, a dining hall, a library and a chapel. They are oases of calm, little known even to most Londoners. The grounds and some of the buildings are open to the public from Monday to Friday.

Lincoln's Inn★★ (⊖Holborn; Entrances on Chancery Lane, Carey Street and Serle Street; grounds: open year-round Mon–Fri

7am–7pm except bank holidays; Chapel open Mon–Fri (except bank holidays), 9am–5pm; ☏020 7405 1393; www.lincolnsinn.org.uk) is the grandest of the four Inns of Court, dating back to the late-15C. The Old Hall dates from 1490; the Old Buildings are Tudor, while the Chapel was rebuilt 1620–23.

The **Temple★** (⊖Temple; entrances on Fleet Street and Embankment; www.innertemple.org.uk), another remarkable ancient complex, comprises two of the four Inns of Court, **Inner Temple** and **Middle Temple**. The gabled, half-timbered three-storey Tudor **Inner Temple Gateway** leads off Fleet Street into the Temple, past 19C buildings and the houses *(right)* where Dr Johnson (of Dictionary fame) lived in the 1760s. It leads to **Temple Church** (usually open Mon–Fri 11am–1pm, 2–4pm see website for current details; £5. ☏020 7353 8559; www.templechurch.com) made famous by *The Da Vinci Code* movie. This was built in the 12C in the round style of the Church of the Holy Sepulchre in Jerusalem. On the stone floor lie 10 effigies of knights in armour dating from the 10C to the 13C. The highlight of Middle Temple is the magnificent **Middle Temple Hall** *(open Mon–Fri 9am–noon (functions permitting, call ahead)* ☏020 7427 4800; www.middletemple.org.uk). The Elizabethan Great Hall has ancient oak timbers, panelling and fine carving, heraldic glass, helmets and armour and a remarkable double hammerbeam construction roof (1574). The splendid dining table is reputedly made from the hatch of Sir Francis Drake's flagship *Golden Hinde*, and the suits of armour standing guard around the hall are of similar vintage.

On High Holborn, **Gray's Inn★** (⊖Holborn; gardens: open Mon–Fri, noon–2.30pm; squares: open Mon–Fri 9am–5pm; closed (all areas) bank holidays; ☏020 7458 7800; www.graysinn.org.uk) was founded in the 14C. Its buildings date from the 16C though many have had to be renewed since the war. On the opposite side of the road, a contempo-

rary survivor, from the late-16C, is the row of **half-timbered houses** (1586–96), forming the front of **Staple Inn★**, which was also once a legal training establishment, albeit never an Inn of Court.

Just around the corner is another remarkable little half-timbered house, known as the **Old Curiosity Shop** *(Portsmouth Street, SW corner of Lincoln's Inn Fields)* immortalised by Dickens in his eponymous novel (1841). It is a very rare example of an Elizabethan building (c.1567) to survive intact in London. It has had many recent guises and currently sells shoes (open Mon–Sat 10.30am–7pm; ☏020 7405 9891).

BLOOMSBURY★

This former residential area with its many squares is dominated by two learned institutions, the British Museum *(see below)* and the **University of London**. The development of Bloomsbury Square in 1661 brought a new concept in social planning; the 4th Earl of Southampton erected houses for the well-to-do around three sides of the square, a mansion for himself on the fourth, northern side and a network of service streets all around. A century later, in 1775, the elegant **Bedford Square★★** was developed. It is still complete, with its three-storey brick terrace houses with first-floor balconies. More squares, now partly incorporated into the university precinct, followed. The most famous residents were the 1920s **Bloomsbury Group** of writers, artists and philosophers, including Virginia Woolf, Vanessa Bell and Roger Fry.

British Museum★★★

⊖Russell Square. Great Russell Street. Open year-round daily 10am–5.30pm (8.30pm Fri). Closed 1 Jan, 24–26 Dec. Charge for temporary exhibitions only. Various guided tours (see website). ♿✗ ☏020 7323 8299. www.thebritishmuseum.ac.uk. Since the Millennium the British Museum has undergone the biggest revolution in its centuries-old existence. **The Great Court**, designed by Sir Norman Foster, is now the hub of the museum – its glass-and-steel roof spans the space to the Reading Room – and makes for a stunning entrance foyer.

It all began back in 1753 when Sir Hans Sloane's collection was bequeathed to the nation. This augmented the old Royal Library of 12 000 volumes assembled by monarchs since Tudor times. Acquisitions increased dramatically in the 19C and 20C with finds by archaeologists attached to the museum, bringing the museum its reputation as one of the greatest centres of world antiquities. Notable among the Egyptian antiquities are the **mummies**, and the **Rosetta Stone**, which provided a key for deciphering heiroglyphics. No less fascinating is **Ginger** (so-named after the colour of his hair), a 5 000-year-old corpse buried in hot sands c.3300 BCE and naturally preserved intact.

The collection of Western Asiatic antiquities is particularly wide-ranging, including the world-famous **Elgin Marbles** (*see below*). Look carefully at the exquisite Roman **Portland Vase** and you can see that it has been carefully pieced back together again after it was smashed it into 200 pieces in 1845. **Lindow Man** (1C), garrotted and preserved in a peat bog, is evidence of human sacrifice. Reminders of Roman Britain include the 4C silver set of tableware known as the **Mildenhall Treasure**, found in Suffolk, and considered to be the finest pieces of their kind anywhere in the Roman Empire. This was eclipsed in 1994 by the **Hoxne Hoard** – thousands of coins, jewellery and silver plate, also found in Suffolk. In the Medieval, Renaissance and Modern Collections is the **Sutton Hoo Ship Burial**, which shows the rich variety of artefacts retrieved from a royal tomb including fabulous gold jewellery, weapons and armour. Note too the beautifully carved mid-12C walrus ivory **Lewis Chessmen** found on the Isle of Lewis in the Outer Hebrides. The Western Asiatic section, covering Mesopotamia and Asia Minor, includes breathtaking **Assyrian sculptures** from the cities of Nimrud, Khorsabad and Nineveh. From ancient Iran the rich artistic tradition of the Persian Empire shines through in the **Luristan Bronzes** c.1200 BCE, and the fabulous **Oxus Treasure** (5C–4C BCE).

The circular, domed **Reading Room** (12m wide) dates from 1857, and was designed to ensure that the "poorest student" as well as men of letters should be able to have access to the library. It accommodates 400 readers and 25mi/40km of shelving (1 300 000 books). The restored blue-and-gold decoration of the dome re-creates the original setting, where Karl Marx, Lenin and George Bernard Shaw, among many others, have sat and studied.

British Library★★

Euston Square. 96 Euston Road. Galleries: Open Mon–Thu 9.30am–8pm, Fri 9.30am–6pm, Sat 9.30am–5pm), Sun and bank hols 11am–5pm. 0330 333 1144. www.bl.uk.

The British Library houses the world's second-largest collection of written works after the Library of Congress in the USA. Opened in 1997, the St Pancras building (there are other branches) is a monumental free-form, asymmetric structure of red brick, Welsh slate and metal and granite. The entrance piazza is dominated by a huge bronze statue of Newton by Sir Eduardo Paolozzi.

The library's most famous treasures, on display in the **Sir John Ritblat Gallery**, include a copy of **Magna Carta**, the **Lindisfarne Gospel**, **Codex Sinaiticus**, the Gutenberg Bible, the Diamond Sutra, Nelson's last letter, Shakespeare's signature and **First Folio** (1623), and Beatles' manuscripts. Advanced technology makes it possible to turn the pages of rare books (if only virtually) at the touch of a button. There are two other permanent galleries, devoted to philately and conservation, as well as temporary exhibitions.

REGENT'S PARK★★

This beautiful park (Regent's Park), bounded to the north by the Regent's Canal, surrounded by dazzling white Regency terraces and splendid villas, was laid out in the early-19C by John

Nash. Regent's Park is famous for its zoo, and is much loved for its rose garden and boating lake. Bordering it to the south is the busy Marylebone Road and Madame Tussaud's.

⚐⚐ ZSL London Zoo★★

⊖ Regent's Park, Camden Town. Outer Circle, Regent's Park. Open daily Apr–Aug 10am–6pm; Sept–late Oct 10am–5.30pm; late Oct–Mar 10am–4pm. Closed 25 Dec. Online tickets from £24.30, child (3–15) from £18; prices are higher at the gate. Book online for discount and to beat queues. ♿✕ ✆0844 225 1826. www.zsl.org/zsl-london-zoo.

The Zoological Society of London (ZSL) opened on a 2ha site in Regent's Park in 1828. Today it covers 14ha with around 8 000 animals from 900 species. The emphasis nowadays is placed on breeding endangered animals and on foreign conservation projects. Family favourites include the lions, tigers, rhinos, gorillas, monkeys, penguins and giraffes. Pick up a programme of activities and plan your visit around that.

Madame Tussaud's★

⊖ Baker Street. Open daily year-round 9.30am–5.30pm (9am–6pm weekends and school holidays). Closed 25 Dec. Online tickets from £29, child £24; prices are higher at the gate. Book Online to avoid queues and for discount). ♿ ✆0871 894 3000. www.madame-tussauds.com.

The oldest waxwork in this world-famous collection is of Louis XV's mistress, portrayed as Sleeping Beauty, made by Madame Tussaud herself. There are over 300 other famous likenesses, from the worlds of film (with a special Bollywood feature), sport, culture, British royalty, world leaders and murderers in the Chamber of Horrors (complete with live actors). A Spirit of London Ride and a Marvel Super Heroes 4D movie completes the visit.

City of London★★★

SIGHTS

St Paul's Cathedral★★★

⊖ St Paul's. Open Mon–Sat 8.30am–4.30pm. Galleries 9.30am–4.15pm (last entry). Sun open for worship only. £18 (£16 online). Guided tours at no extra cost. ♿✕ ✆020 7246 8357; 020 7246 8348 (recorded info). www.stpauls.co.uk.

The present cathedral, the fourth or fifth on a site dating back to 604, is the masterpiece of **Sir Christopher Wren** (1632–1723). After the Great Fire of 1666, Old St Paul's was a ruin. The foundation stone of the new cathedral was laid on 21 June 1675 and 33 years later Wren saw his son set the final stone in place – the topmost in the lantern. When Wren died 15 years later he was buried within the walls. Beneath the dome his own epitaph reads in Latin: "Reader, if you seek his monument, look around you."

Exterior – The most striking feature is the **dome**, even today a dominant feature of the City skyline. Unlike the dome of St Peter's, which influenced Wren, it is not a true hemisphere. The drum below it is in two tiers, the lower encircled by columns and crowned by a balustrade, the upper recessed behind the balustrade so as to afford a circular viewing gallery, the **Stone Gallery**. On top of the dome, the lantern features columns on all four sides and a small cupola serving as a plinth to the 2m-diameter golden ball.

The **west end**, approached by two wide flights of steps, is composed of a two-tier portico of columns below a decorated pediment surmounted by St Paul. On either side rise Wren's Baroque spires. A notable feature of the exterior is the profuse carving by **Grinling Gibbons** and others.

Interior – The impression is one of space, of almost luminescent stone and, in the distance, gold and mosaic.

St Paul's Cathedral

A 270-degree film exhibition, *Oculus; An Eye into St Paul's* traces both the cathedral's 1 400 year-history and its daily life. "Virtual access" films also cover the dome and galleries.

In the **nave** the entire space between two piers in the north aisle is occupied by the Wellington monument; in the south aisle hangs Holman Hunt's *The Light of the World*. From the **Whispering Gallery** in the dome *(259 steps)* there are impressive views of the concourse below, and close views of the interior of the dome, painted by Thornhill. A whisper spoken close to the wall can be clearly heard on the diametrically opposite side. The **views★★★** from the **Golden Gallery** at the top of the dome are even more dizzying than from the Stone Gallery *(543 steps)*. In the **choir** the dark oak stalls are the exquisite work of Grinling Gibbons. The iron railing, the gates to the choir aisles and the great gilded screens enclosing the sanctuary are the work of Jean Tijou. The graceful sculpture of the Virgin and Child in the north aisle is by Henry Moore (1984). In the south aisle is a rare pre-Fire relic, a scorch-marked statue of **John Donne**, the great poet and Dean of St Paul's 1621–31. The **Crypt** contains tombs of many illustrious individuals and memorials, too numerous to list.

Barbican★

⊖Barbican. The Barbican complex (built 1962–82) combines residential accommodation with a world-class arts centre (*www.barbican.org.uk*), a medieval church and the Museum of London.

Museum of London★★

⊖Barbican, Moorgate, London Wall. Open daily 10am–6pm. Closed 24–26 Dec. ⅙✖ ℘020 7001 9844. www.museumoflondon.org.uk.
The biggest city history museum in the world presents the story of London from prehistory to the present day, with exhibits as various as the sculptures from the Roman temple of Mithras, medieval pilgrim badges, the Cheapside Hoard of Jacobean jewellery, a diorama of the Great Fire, the doors from Newgate Gaol, 19C shops and interiors, the Lord Mayor's Coach, souvenirs of the women's suffrage movement… right through the swinging 60s and into 21C issues.

≗ Tower of London★★★

⊖Tower Hill. Open Mar–Oct Tue–Sat 9am–5.30pm, Sun–Mon 10am–5.30pm. Nov–Feb closes 4.30pm. Closed 1 Jan, 24–26 Dec. £24.80, child £11.50. Buy tickets online (at a discount), or ℘0844 482 7799 (booking line only: +£2 service charge) to reduce queuing time. Guided tour (1h) by Yeoman Warders, daily every 30min. Last tour: summer 3.30pm, winter 2.30pm. Free. ⅙✖ ℘0844 482 7777. www.hrp.org.uk.
In 1067, William I constructed a wooden fortress then replaced it with one in stone (c.1077–97) in order to deter Londoners from revolt; its river site also gave immediate sighting of any hostile

White Tower, Tower of London, the Shard in the background

© D. Brenes/age fotostock

force coming up the Thames. Norman, Plantagenet and Tudor successors recognised its value and extended it until it occupied 7ha.

From 1300 to 1810, the Tower housed the Royal Mint; because of its defences it became the Royal Jewel House and also served as a feared prison.

Monarchs have been associated with the Tower from William the Conqueror to Elizabeth I.

The **Jewel House** (🕘 *queues tend to be shorter early in the day*) displays the **Crown Jewels★★★** which date from the Restoration to the present day, almost all of the earlier regalia having been sold or melted down by Oliver Cromwell. The **Chapel of St Peter ad Vincula**, consecrated in the 12C, rebuilt in the 13C and 16C, is the burial place of several dukes and two of Henry VIII's queens, beheaded in the Tower.

Traitors' Gate was the main entrance to the Tower when the Thames was still London's principal thoroughfare; later, when the river served only for secret access, the entrance acquired its chilling name. The Bloody Tower gained its name in the 16C and was perhaps the place where the "Princes in the Tower" were murdered in 1483. Sir Walter Raleigh was imprisoned here 1603–1615.

The **White Tower★★★** keep is one of the earliest fortifications on such a scale in western Europe, begun by William I in 1078 and completed 20 years later by William Rufus. The 30m-high stone walls form an uneven quadrilateral, its corners marked by one circular and three square towers. The **Armour Collection**, one of the world's greatest, was started by Henry VIII and increased under Charles II. On the second floor, **St John's Chapel★★** remains much as it was when completed in 1080, a 17m-long stone chapel rising through two floors. An inner line of great round columns with simply carved capitals bears circular Norman arches and is echoed above in a second tier.

Beauchamp Tower★, built in the 13C, has served as a prison since the 14C. The walls of the main chamber are inscribed with prisoners' graffiti.

Tower Bridge★★

⊖Tower Hill, London Bridge. Riverboat to Tower Pier. Tower Bridge Road. Open daily, Apr–Sept 10am–5.30pm; Oct–Mar 9.30am–5pm. Closed 24–26 Dec. £9.80 (online discount available). ♿ ☏020 7403 3761. www.towerbridge.org.uk.

The familiar Gothic towers, high-level walkways and the original engine rooms form part of the tour which traces the design of the bridge by Sir John Wolfe-Barry and Horace Jones, its construction (1886–94) and explains the functioning of the hydraulic mechanism which, until 1976, raised the 1 100ton drawbridge-like bascules (now driven by electricity).

St Katharine Docks★

In 1828, **Thomas Telford** developed this series of basins and warehouses next to The City and they prospered for over a hundred years. After wartime bombing, however, the dock was abandoned until 1968, when moorings were organised for private yachts. Telford's main Italianate-style building was restored as **Ivory House** with apartments above a shopping arcade. Restaurants and bars now proliferate around the dock.

Southwark★

SIGHTS

In the 16C, the borough of Southwark was infamous for its brothels and theatres, on account of its location outside the jurisdiction of the City of London. Near the site of the original Globe Theatre, where Shakespeare's plays were performed, now stands the landmark **Shakespeare's Globe★★** which replicates the original 16C structure. The Elizabethan playhouse's stage thrusts into a large circular yard surrounded by three tiers of roofed seating in the round. **Stage productions★★** are held in this authentic outdoor setting each summer (*late Apr– early Oct*) and the site also has an excellent permanent **exhibition★** (◯Mansion House, London Bridge; 21 New Globe Walk; open daily 9am–5pm, tours every 30 minutes; closed 24–25 Dec; £16 ♿✗; ✆020 7902 1500; www.shakespearesglobe.com).

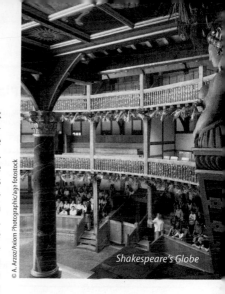

Shakespeare's Globe

The most spectacular local medieval building is the **George Inn★**, still a functioning pub, built round three sides of a courtyard, although only one of the galleried ranges has survived. Along the river old warehouses have been converted to new uses – **Hays Galleria** with its shops, pubs and modern sculpture, and the acclaimed **Design Museum** (◯High Street Kensington; 224–238 Kensington High Street; open year-round daily 10am–6pm; closed 25–26 Dec; £13; ♿✗; ✆020 7940 8790; www.designmuseum.org), are two examples. The latter illustrates the evolution of contemporary design via temporary exhibitions featuring the works of nationally and internationally renowned designers.

LONDON BRIDGE

With the relocation of long-time resident and teen-favourite, the London Dungeon to the South Bank (♺see p173), horror seekers will have to get their kicks at the **London Bridge Experience** (◯London Bridge. Tooley Street; open year-round Mon–Fri 10am–5pm, Sat–Sun 9.30am–6pm; closed 25 Dec; from £19.95 online, buy timed tickets in advance to make savings and to avoid waiting time; ♿✗; ✆020 7403 6333; www.thelondon bridgeexperience.com). This weaves ghostly happenings and special effects into the colourful history of London Bridge. It does have some historical interest and not a little humour, but also features a good dose of terror and *is unsuitable for young children.*

A five minute walk to the river from here is **HMS Belfast** (◯London Bridge; Morgan's Lane. Tooley Street; open daily 10am–6pm, £14.50, child 5–15 £7.25; closed 24–26 Dec; ✗; ✆020 7940 6300; http://hmsbelfast.iwm.org.uk). This great grey cruiser (built 1938), moored against the south bank of the Thames, saw service with the North Atlantic Convoys, and also on D-Day in 1944.

Just beyond is the landmark **City Hall** (◯London Bridge; The Queen's Walk open Mon–Thu 8.30am–6pm, Fri 8.30am–5.30pm; ✗; ✆020 7983 4000; www.london.gov.uk/city-hall). This striking rounded glass building by Foster + Partners is home to the Greater London Authority and the office of the Mayor of London. It's well worth a look inside for its architecture, views of the river, and its exhibitions.

Retrace your steps to follow the riverbank west and just on the other side of London Bridge is **Southwark Cathedral★★** (◯London Bridge; open year-round daily 8am–6pm (Sat–Sun and bank hols 8.30am–6pm); £4 contribution requested; ♿✗; ✆020 7367 6700; http://

Blue Plaques

All over the capital you will find blue plaques affixed to buildings where famous people have lived. In total there are over 900 in London including actors, authors, politicians, painters, scientists, sportsmen, campaigners and reformers – people from different countries, cultures and backgrounds have all been commemorated in this way. In order to be eligible for a plaque there are a number of criteria to be met: the person must have been dead for 20 years, or have passed the centenary of their birth, whichever is the earlier; be considered eminent by a majority of members of their own profession or calling; have made an important positive contribution to human welfare or happiness; be recognisable to the well-informed passer-by; deserve national recognition; have resided in a locality for a significant period, in time or importance, within their life and work. To illustrate their diversity, in Mayfair there is a plaque to George Frideric Handel at 25 Brook Street and next door at No. 23 a plaque to Jimi Hendrix.

cathedral.southwark.anglican.org). **The** cathedral began life in 1106 and its earliest work is the fragment of a Norman arch in the north wall. The massive piers supporting the central tower and the Early English **chancel** date from the 13C. The **altar screen** (1520) appears in sumptuous Gothic glory; it remained empty until 1905 when statues were carved to fill the niches. The nave was rebuilt in 1890–97 to harmonise with the chancel. Notable features are the **Harvard Chapel**, the 1616 **monument** to Alderman Humble and his wives, and the 12 **bosses** rescued from the 15C wooden roof which collapsed in 1830. The cathedral bounds **Borough Market★** (&see p190). This is not only London's oldest food market but also the country's most important retail market for fine foods and a great place to sit down and eat too.

Continuing west from here along the river, you come to the **Golden Hinde** (⊖London Bridge, Monument. St Mary Overie Dock; programmes and events are suspended; check the website for current details; ℘020 7403 0123; www. goldenhinde.com), a full-size seaworthy replica of the 16C ship in which Sir Francis Drake's circumnavigated the world. "Hands-on" learning with costumed interpreters is the order of the day.

SOUTHBANK AND LAMBETH

Head west along the river from London Bridge to the landmark **Tate Modern★★** (⊖Southwark, Blackfriars. Bankside; open year-round daily 10am–6pm (Fri–Sat 10pm); closed 24–26 Dec; charge only for temporary exhibitions; &🅿(disabled visitors only) ✕; ℘020 7887 8888; www.tate. org.uk). The former Bankside Power Station, with its single chimney (99m) and giant internal dimensions, makes a striking home for this major gallery, devoted to international 20C and 21C art. The wealth of the collection is largely due to the bequests of Sir Roland Penrose, one-time friend of Picasso and Ernst, and that of Edward James, a former patron to Dalí and Magritte. Gigantic sculptures by contemporary artists are set off by the vast spaces of the Turbine Hall (152m long and 35m high), where overhead cranes recall the building's working life. Themed displays mean that you can never quite be sure what will be here at any one time. World-class special exhibitions are regularly staged. Further west is the **Southbank Centre★★** (⊖Waterloo; www.southbankcentre. co.uk, www.nationaltheatre.org.uk, www. bfi.org.uk), the UK's most important arts and theatre complex. The Brutalist-style grey concrete buildings house: the **National Theatre**, which stages the finest theatre productions in the country outside London's West End; the **BFI (British Film Institute) Southbank**, formerly known as the National Film Theatre, which screens both classic and cult movies; the **Royal Festival Hall** specialises in orchestral concerts; the **Queen Elizabeth Hall** hosts chamber orchestras, quartets, choirs, dance performances and opera (and also contains the Purcell Room); the **Hayward Gallery** has a rotating exhibition of contemporary art. Bookshops, cafés, restaurants and live foyer events ensure that the South Bank is lively for much of the day as well as during evening performances. In the last couple of years this has also become a vibrant nightlife district on summer nights thanks to a variety of temporary entertainment venues, in particular the London Wonderground's cabaret, circus and slideshows.

Carrying on west along the river bank you will find the **London Eye★★** (⊖Westminster, Waterloo; South Bank; ticket office in County Hall; open daily year-round, 10am/11am–6pm/9.30pm; closed for annual maintenance second and third week Jan; due to its huge popularity, visitors should book a time slot in advance; a limited number of tickets are sold on-site every day; from £23.45(up to 15 percent discount online); ⅍✗; ✆0800 093 0123 (enquiries); 0871 781 3000 (bookings); www.londoneye.com). On the opposite side of the river to Parliament this giant observation wheel is a spectacular Millennium landmark on the Thames. Sightseers are accommodated in glass pods to enjoy unparalleled **views★★★** of London 135m high during their 30-minute ride.

Next to the Eye, inside County Hall are a number of visitor attractions. New to the location, though long established in the capital, is the infamous **London Dungeon★** (👤👤;⊖Westminster, Waterloo; open year-round daily; Mon–Fri 10am–5pm (11am Thu), Sat–Sun 10am–6pm; closed 25 Dec; from £21 online; buy timed tickets in advance to avoid waiting time; ⅍✗; ✆0871 423 2240; www.thedungeons.com/london). **Newly revamped**

and more terrifying than ever, this gruesome all-too-lifelike exhibition of death, disease, disaster and torture in past centuries features theme-park-style rides and is hugely popular with gore-loving teens.

The **Sea Life London Aquarium★** (👤👤; ⊖Westminster, Waterloo. County Hall; open year-round Mon–Fri 10am–6pm, Sat–Sun 9.30am–7pm; £20.40 (online saver price); ⅍✗; 0871 663 1678; www.visitsealife.com/london) is one of Europe's largest aquariums with sharks in spectacular large-scale tanks, piranhas at feeding time and stingrays in a touch-tank. There are also exhibits on local and British marine life.

The **London Film Museum, Covent Garden** (⊖Leicester Square, Charing Cross, Covent Garden; open year-round, Sun–Fri 10am–6pm, Sat 10am–7pm; £14.50, child (5–15) £9.50; ⅍; ✆020 7836 4913; www.londonfilmmuseum.com) concentrates mostly on British films, but also has enough of international interest for most regular cinema fans. On the other side of Westminster Bridge, is the **Imperial War Museum★★★**(⊖Lambeth North, Elephant and Castle; Lambeth Road; open year-round daily 10am–6pm; charge for temporary exhibitions; ⅍✗; ✆020 7416 5000; www.iwm.org.uk). One of the world's finest war museums, this sensitive and thought-provoking exhibition honours both civilians and those who have served during wartime.

A wide range of weapons and equipment is on display: armoured fighting vehicles, field guns and small arms, together with models, decorations, uniforms, posters and photographs, masses of archive material, including moving first-hand oral accounts of warfare, as well as a selection from the museum's outstanding collection based on the work of two generations of official war artists.

Inner Suburbs★★

CAMDEN

Set immediately north of Regent's Park, gritty **Camden** (⊖Camden Town) provides a stark contrast to grand Palladian villas. This is one of London's more bohemian areas and is famous for its **markets★★** (Camden Market, Camden Lock Market and Canal Market), which sell antiques, fashion and bric-a-brac, catering to a young and alternative lifestyle. The area also bustles by night with buzzing **live music** venues, down-to-earth pubs and cheap ethnic eats.

KNIGHTSBRIDGE

One of London's most exclusive suburbs, Knightsbridge (⊖Knightsbridge) is synonymous with **Harrods★★** (est 1849), the world's most famous department store, and its neighbour, **Harvey Nichols★**, where "ladies who lunch" come for the very best in fashion, beauty and home accessories. Both stores are renowned for their displays; "Harvey Nicks" for its window dressing and Harrods for its cornucopian turn-of-the-century **Food Halls**. By night, Harrods' terracotta façade, added in 1901, illuminated by around 11 000 lightbulbs, is a famous London sight.

KENSINGTON★★

Kensington is one of London's wealthiest suburbs and **Kensington High Street** (⊖) offers local as well as brand-name shops, with The **Design Museum**, (*see p171*) moving here in November 2015. Just off the High Street, **Holland Park** (⊖) is a pretty, bucolic retreat from the crowds. Immediately north is **Notting Hill** (⊖), famous for its **carnival** *(last weekend Aug)*, and weekly *(Sat)* **Portobello Road Market** (*see p190*). The antiques market here is claimed to be the world's largest and includes many shops, also open in the week. South Kensington is home to three world-famous national museums (*see below*).

Kensington Palace★★

⊖Queensway, High Street Kensington. Open daily 10am–6pm (Nov–Feb 4pm. Closed 24–26 Dec. £15.50 (online price). ᵹ ✆0844 482 7799. www.hrp.org.uk.

This early-17C Jacobean house has passed through three principal phases: under the House of Orange it was William III's private residence, with **Sir Christopher Wren** as principal architect; under the early Hanoverians it became a royal palace, with William Kent in charge of decorative schemes; since 1760 it has been a residence for members of the royal family, most famously the late **Diana, Princess of Wales**, and now the official London residence of William and Kate, Duke and Duchess of Cambridge, and their children, George and Charlotte. The **State Apartments** are approached by the Queen's Staircase, designed by Wren. The **Queen's Gallery** has carving by Grinling Gibbons and portraits by Kneller and Lely. The **Privy** and lofty **Presence Chamber**, **Cupola** and **Drawing Rooms**, added for George I in 1718–20, were decorated by William Kent during 1722–27, covering the walls and ceiling with *trompe l'œil* paintings. The palace has recently reopened after two years of major renovations, making for a much richer and less formal visit than in the past. The "Fashion Rules" collection of 12 000 items worn by royalty and courtiers from the 17C to the pres ent day, from George III and Queen Victoria, to the Queen, and Diana, Princess of Wales, is a long-established favourite. Brand new are the multi-media installations and live interactive theatre, examining the sometimes tragic lives of the palace's inhabitants, and this is certainly the first royal residence with talking cushions; take a seat and tune into court gossip from years gone by!

Kensington Gardens★★

⊖Queensway, High Street Kensington. At weekends these gardens are a favourite walk with Kensington locals, most famously nannies with their small charges. The **Round Pond** is the focal point for avenues radiating northeast,

east and southeast to the **Serpentine**, where rowing boats may be hired, and **Long Water**. The early-18C **Orangery★**, Hawksmoor's splendid Baroque centrepiece (1705), now houses a restaurant. Beyond the Flower Walk on the south side of the gardens stands the **Albert Memorial★** (1876), designed by George Gilbert Scott. Beneath a highly ornamented Gothic Revival spire surrounded by statues and a frieze of 169 named figures of poets, artists, architects and composer, sits a bronze statue (4.2m) of the Prince Consort who did so much to further the arts and learning, until his premature death in 1861. Opposite stands the **Royal Albert Hall★** (1867–71), a splendid venue for meetings, conferences and concerts, notably the eight-week summer season of **Promenade Concerts ("the Proms")**.

Hyde Park★★
⊖Marble Arch, High Street Kensington, Hyde Park Corner)

Adjoining Kensington Gardens to the east, Hyde Park is less formally laid out and very popular with office-workers and tourists alike, who come to enjoy the fresh air.

In the corner of the park nearest Oxford Street stands **Marble Arch**, the triumphal arch designed by John Nash in 1827 as a grand entrance to Buckingham Palace in commemoration of the battles of Trafalgar and Waterloo. Embarrassingly it was never used, as it was too narrow to accommodate the royal Gold Stage Coach, and eventually ended up here. Beside the arch is **Speakers' Corner**. In 1872, the government recognised the need for a place of public assembly and free discussion. Anyone can stand up and speak here, as they frequently do on a Sunday morning, as long as they observe certain rules including no blasphemy, nor must they incite a breach of the peace.

▲▲ Natural History Museum★★★
⊖South Kensington. Cromwell Road. Open year-round daily 10am–5.50pm. Closed 24–26 Dec. Charge for temporary

exhibitions. ♿✖ ℘020 7942 5000. www.nhm.ac.uk.

Alfred Waterhouse's vast palace, inspired by medieval Rhineland architecture, was opened in 1881 to house the British Museum's ever-growing natural history collection, which today illustrates all forms of life, from the smallest bacteria to the largest creatures. This is now one of the country's favourite family museums, superbly combining education and entertainment with spectacular exhibits such as the famous **blue whale** model and huge **dinosaur skeletons**. Dinosaurs and fossils are still most visitors' favourite area and the diplodocus skeleton in the foyer has become a museum icon.

Elsewhere you can learn about human biology, creepy crawlies, the origin of the species, take a behind-the-scenes tour, visit the Earth Galleries and get caught in a real earthquake simulation. The latest major development is the fascinating **Darwin Centre**, dedicated to evolution.

▲▲ Science Museum★★★
⊖South Kensington Exhibition Road. Open daily 10am–6pm (7pm during school holidays). Closed 24–26 Dec. Free except IMAX cinema, simulators and special exhibitions. ♿✖ ℘0870 870 4868. www.sciencemuseum.org.uk.

This world-beating factory-laboratory of Man's continuing invention extends over 3ha. Large-scale exhibits range from early beam engines to actual spacecraft, the first biplanes to jet aircraft, historic railway engines, road vehicles, and it is quite easy to spend a whole day here simply marvelling at the hardware without the need for any technical knowledge.

For more enquiring minds there are innumerable working models, handles to pull, buttons to push, huge floor areas devoted completely to **hands-on** experiments and cutting-edge technology. Children (and adults) also love the **IMAX** theatre with its 3-D films. Don't miss the **Wellcome Galleries** or the **History of Medicine**, on the upper floors.

Victoria and Albert Museum★★★

⊖South Kensington. Entrances in Cromwell Road and Exhibition Road. Open year-round daily 10am–5.45pm (Fri 10pm). Closed 24–26 Dec. Charge for some exhibitions. 🚻✕
℘020 7942 2000. www.vam.ac.uk.
This fabulously rich and varied collection was started, in part, with the purchase of contemporary works manufactured for the Great Exhibition of 1851. It includes the national collection of furniture, British sculpture, textiles, ceramics, silver and watercolours, as well as world-famous displays of fashionable dress, jewellery, Italian Renaissance sculpture, and art from India and the Far East.

Renaissance sculptures – The most highly prized work is Michelangelo's *Slave*, a wax model for a figure intended for the tomb of Pope Julius II.

Cast courts – Plaster casts made 1860–1880 for art students who could not go abroad to see the real thing, include Trajan's Column, *St George* (Donatello) and *Dying Slave* (Michelangelo).

Prints, drawings and paintings – The most valuable collection here is the **Raphael Cartoons**, seven huge tapestry patterns, commissioned in 1515 by Pope Leo X for the Sistine Chapel.

Furniture and woodwork – The collection ranges from the Middle Ages to the present day and encompasses just about every culture. **The Great Bed of Ware**, mentioned by Shakespeare, is the most remarkable piece of ancient British furniture. It is said to have once slept 52 people (26 butchers and their wives).

Textiles and dress – one of the world's most extensive collections of textiles.

Metalworks and jewellery – This is perhaps the most diverse and eclectic national collection, ranging from the 2C BCE to present times, and encompasses a very broad spectrum and some magnificent pieces.

The **Gilbert Collection** of gold, silver, micro-mosaics and gold boxes is a beautiful recent addition.

Eastern works of art – Some 60 000 artefacts from China, Korea and Japan.

CHELSEA★★

Riverside Chelsea (⊖Sloane Square, Pimlico) has always attracted artists, architects, writers and actors. Chelsea has long had a reputation for fashionable bohemian living, but it is currently better known as a well-heeled suburb. In 1955 the opening of Bazaar clothes boutique by Mary Quant led to a radical change in dress with the launch of the mini skirt. During the 1960s, the **King's Road★** became 'the navel of swinging London', then in 1971, Chelsea fashion was re-invigorated by Vivienne Westwood, who opened her clothes shop at 430 Kings Road. The road became the launching point for the Punk movement. Punk fashions are rarely seen here today, but you may spot a celebrity.

Royal Hospital★

Royal Hospital Road. Open: Museum Mon–Fri (except bank holidays) 10am–4pm. Grounds: open daily 10am (Sun 2pm)–dusk. ℘020 7881 5200. www.chelsea-pensioners.co.uk.
The Royal Hospital was founded by King Charles II in 1682 as a retreat for veterans of the regular army who had been retired from duty after 20 years' service, or had become unfit for duty as a result of wounds or disease. The **Chelsea Flower Show** is held here.

PIMLICO
Tate Britain★★★

⊖Pimlico, then 5min walk (signed). Millbank. Open year-round daily, 10am–6pm. Closed 24–26 Dec. Charge for temporary exhibitions only. 🚻✕
℘020 7887 8888. www.tate.org.uk.
In 1897, Henry Tate, sugar broker and British art collector, offered his collection to the nation and £80,000 for a building, if the government would provide a site. The museum is devoted exclusively to British art from 1500 to the present day. The **Clore Gallery Turner Collection** is a highlight and is one of the relatively few permanent exhibits.

Outer London★★

GREENWICH★★★
London's Maritime Centre

(⊖Cutty Sark DLR). The Tudors preferred Greenwich to their other royal residences, and Henry VIII, who was born here, built a vast palace with a royal armoury; he also founded naval dockyards at neighbouring Deptford and Woolwich. During the Commonwealth, however, the palace became derelict and only the Queen's House survived. William and Mary granted a charter for the foundation of a Royal Hospital for Seamen at Greenwich, with **Wren** as surveyor. In 1873 the buildings were transformed into the Royal Naval College, and eventually the Queen's House became part of the Maritime Museum. **Greenwich Park★** is the oldest enclosed royal domain, extending for 73ha, rising to a point 4/m above the river. It is a wonderful place for a picnic with **views★★** across to Docklands, west to St Paul's and beyond.

👥 National Maritime Museum★★★

Park Row, Greenwich. Open daily 10am–6pm. Royal Observatory Flamsteed House and Meridian Courtyard £9.50, child £5; Solar Storms Show and Sky Tonight live show £7.50, child £5.50 (book timed ticket in advance). Cutty Sark (see below). ♿✕ ☎020 8312 6608 (ticket office); ☎020 8312 6565 (recorded information). www.rmg.co.uk.

As part of its £20 million Millennium makeover, this museum of Britain's naval past – the largest maritime collection in the world with over two million objects – added an impressive single-span glazed roof, the largest in Europe, above its neo-Classical courtyard. The museum's centrepiece gallery is the Sammy Ofer wing, home to "Voyagers", telling the story of Britain and the sea, illustrating the contemporary significance of maritime histories.

The O2

Built to celebrate the Millennium and sited right on the Meridian Line, the Millennium Dome is the largest single-roofed structure in the world. Its external appearance is that of a huge (365m diameter) white marquee held up by twelve 95m-high towers. Its circumference exceeds 0.62mi/1km and the floor space is large enough to park 18 000 London buses. Now known as the O2, it stages major concerts and other events (*www.theo2.co.uk*). The O2 also has one of London's more unusual and thrilling experiences, climbing the iconic roof (while safely tethered) via a tensile fabric walkway suspended over 52m above ground.

For hands-on fun there's the Children's Gallery and Ship Simulator Interactive Galleries. Within the complex is the Queen's House★★. This elegant white Palladian villa was designed by Inigo Jones in 1615 as Britain's very first Classical mansion.

Royal Observatory★★

The Old Royal Observatory was built by Christopher Wren in 1675 "for finding out the longitude of places for perfect navigation and astronomy".
Inside Wren's brick **Flamsteed House** is the lofty Octagon Room, beautifully proportioned, equipped with what John Evelyn called "the choicest instrument". The **Meridian Building** was added in the mid-18C to house the growing **telescope collection★★**. Note Airey's Transit Circle, through which the meridian passes, and outside, in the Meridian Courtyard, a brass rail marking the meridian of 0°, which visitors enjoy standing astride (thus being in two meridians at once). Adjacent is the **Astronomy Centre** including three galleries and the state-of-the-art **Peter Harrison Planetarium**.

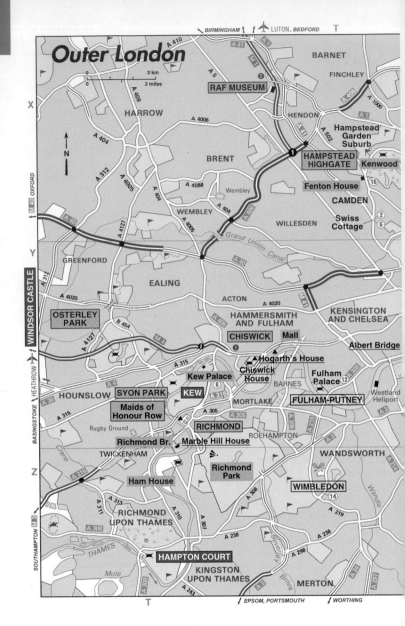

Outer London

BIRMINGHAM · LUTON, BEDFORD · T

A 410 · A 41 · M1

BARNET

FINCHLEY

A 5 · A 406 · A 1000

RAF MUSEUM

X

HARROW

A 4006

HENDON

Hampstead Garden Suburb

A 409

A 404

BRENT

HAMPSTEAD HIGHGATE

Kenwood

A 312

A 4005

A 404

A 4088

Wembley

A 502

Fenton House

CAMDEN

M10 OXFORD

A 40

A 4127

WEMBLEY

A 404

WILLESDEN

Swiss Cottage

Grand Union Canal

Y

GREENFORD

A 317

A 40

M11

EALING

A 4020

ACTON

A 4020

KENSINGTON AND CHELSEA

OSTERLEY PARK

B 454

A 4127

M4

HAMMERSMITH AND FULHAM

Mall

CHISWICK

Hogarth's House

Albert Bridge

WINDSOR CASTLE

HEATHROW / BASINGSTOKE

A 4

A 315

Chiswick House

Kew Palace

Fulham Palace

Westland Heliport

HOUNSLOW

SYON PARK

KEW

A 316

BARNES

MORTLAKE

FULHAM-PUTNEY

A 30

A 315

Maids of Honour Row

A 305

A 205

Rugby Ground

Crane

RICHMOND

ROEHAMPTON

WANDSWORTH

TWICKENHAM

Richmond Br.

Marble Hill House

A 3

Z

Ham House

Richmond Park

WIMBLEDON

Westland

A 313

A 310

A 308

Wandle

SOUTHAMPTON M3

A 311

RICHMOND UPON THAMES

A 307

A 219

A 308

THAMES

A 238

A 238

Beverley Brook

HAMPTON COURT

KINGSTON UPON THAMES

MERTON

Mole

A 243

A 3

T · EPSOM, PORTSMOUTH · WORTHING

3 km
2 miles

N

Cutty Sark★★

King William Walk. Open daily 10am–6pm. £13.50, child £7. &(limited number of spaces, call ahead) ✗. 📞020 8312 6608. www.rmg.co.uk/cutty-sark.

Most famous as a tea clipper, though carrying many other cargoes, Cutty Sark visited every major port in the world through the course of her working life (1869–1922) during which time she was the fastest ship of her type. She came to her present resting place in 1954, but was badly damaged by fire in 2007 and only reopened to the public in 2012. A spectacular new viewing arrangement however allows visitors to walk right beneath the keel.

Onboard you can learn all about the fascinating history of the ship and see the largest collection of ships' figureheads in the world.

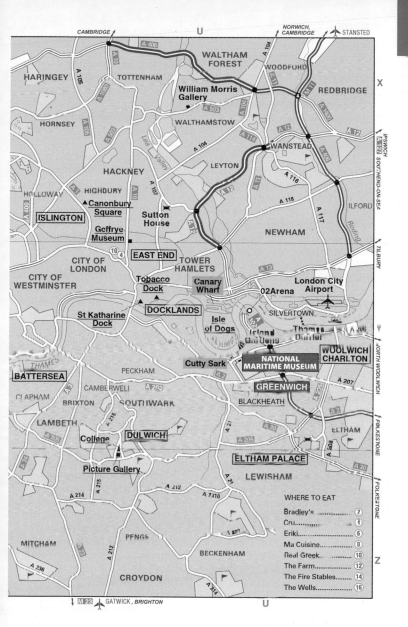

WALTHAM FOREST

WOODFORD

HARINGEY

TOTTENHAM

William Morris Gallery

WALTHAMSTOW

REDBRIDGE

HORNSEY

WANSTEAD

LEYTON

HACKNEY

HIGHBURY

Canonbury Square

ISLINGTON

Sutton House

Geffrye Museum

EAST END

CITY OF LONDON

CITY OF WESTMINSTER

Tobacco Dock

Canary Wharf

TOWER HAMLETS

NEWHAM

London City Airport

02Arena

SILVERTOWN

St Katharine Dock

DOCKLANDS

Isle of Dogs

Island Gardens

Thames Barrier

Cutty Sark

NATIONAL MARITIME MUSEUM

WOOLWICH CHARLTON

THAMES

PECKHAM

GREENWICH

BATTERSEA

CAMBERWELL

BLACKHEATH

CLAPHAM

BRIXTON

SOUTHWARK

LAMBETH

College

DULWICH

ELTHAM

Picture Gallery

ELTHAM PALACE

LEWISHAM

IPSWICH / SOUTHEND-ON-SEA

ILFORD

TILBURY

NORTH WOOLWICH

FOLKESTONE

FOLKESTONE

MITCHAM

PENGE

BECKENHAM

CROYDON

WHERE TO EAT	
Bradley's	②
Cru	①
Eriki	⑥
Ma Cuisine	⑧
Real Greek	⑩
The Farm	⑫
The Fire Stables	⑭
The Wells	⑯

Old Royal Naval College★★

Painted Hall and Chapel and Discover Greenwich Visitor Centre. Open daily, 10am–5pm. ℘020 8269 4799. www.ornc.org. After the demolition of the old Tudor Palace, Wren retained the King Charles Block to which he added three symmetrical blocks named after King William, Queen Mary and Queen Anne. For the Queen's House (℘see p177) he provided a river vista (46m) flanked by twin cupolas over the Chapel and the Painted Hall down to a new river embankment. The result is a Baroque masterpiece of English architecture set in landscaped grounds.

The **Painted Hall★** in the domed refectory is the work of **Sir James Thornhill**. The ceiling is covered by the **largest painting** (32m by 16m) in Great Britain, the *Triumph of Peace and Liberty*, by Sir James Thornhill.

WEST AND SOUTHWEST
Osterley Park★★

⊖ Osterley then 20min walk. Jersey Road, Isleworth. **House:** check website for opening hours. **Park:** open year-round daily 8am–7.30pm/dusk. £10.90 (during winter £8.80). **P** £7. ⚬✗ ✆020 8232 5050.
www.nationaltrust.org.uk/osterley-park.
Osterley is the place to see **Robert Adam** rich interior decoration at its most complete – room after room just as he designed them between 1761 and 1780, in every detail from ceilings and walls to the furniture. This magnificent neo-Classical house also has a land-scaped park and 18C gardens.

Royal Botanic Gardens, Kew★★★

Open daily from 10am, closes Mon–Thu 6.30pm, Fri–Sun and bank holidays 8.30pm. Closed at differing times throughout the year; check website for details. £15.50 (online price, includes Kew Palace). ⚬✗ ✆020 8332 5655. www.kew.org.
The **Royal Botanic Gardens**, the finest in the land, are a wonderful place to visit at any time of year. However, this 121ha garden is not just a pleasure garden but the offshoot of laboratories engaged in the identification and conservation of plants from every corner of the earth, for economic, medical and other purposes.
The gardens were begun in 1756 by **Sir William Chambers**. The same architect designed the **Orangery★**, the three small Classical temples and in 1761 the 50m-high 10-storey **Pagoda★**. As the gardens grew, more buildings were added, notably Decimus Burton's **Palm House★★** in 1848, which has recently been completely refurbished. In 1899 Burton completed the **Temperate House★**, which contains camellias, rain-forest and dragon trees. The **Princess of Wales Conservatory★**, a steel-and-glass diamond-shaped structure, boasts 10 different tropical habitats ranging from mangrove swamp to sand desert.

Kew Gardens' latest treat is the **Treetop Walkway**, which takes visitors 18m up in the air. Don't leave without seeing the beautiful and fascinating, oft-overlooked **Marianne North Gallery★**; a Victorian treasure house of botanic art, opened in 1882.
Also within the grounds, close to the river, stands **Kew Palace★★** (*open Apr–Sept 10.30am–5.30pm*) built for a London merchant in 1631. It was leased by George II for Queen Caroline in about 1730 and purchased by George III in 1781. The interior is that of a small late-18C country house.

🚻 Hampton Court Palace and Gardens★★★

East Molesey, Surrey. **Palace:** Open daily, 10am–6pm (4.30pm late-Oct–late-Mar). Closed 24–26 Dec. **Grounds:** Open daily 7am–dusk. £18.40, child £9.20 (online prices; gate prices are higher). **P** (charge). ⚬✗ ✆0844 482 7777 (information line). www.hrp.org.uk.
This magnificent Tudor palace was begun (1514–29) by **Cardinal Wolsey,** who rose to become one of the most powerful figures in the land under King Henry VIII. However, his great wealth and his failure to obtain papal approval for the king's divorce angered the king, and when Wolsey died in disgrace in 1530, Henry appropriated the palace. He then enlarged it, including the splendid Great Hall with its hammerbeam roof, and lavishly transformed the chapel. The Astronomical Clock (in Clock Court), made in 1540, was brought here from St James's Palace in the 19C.
In 1688 Wren rebuilt the east and south fronts, the **State Apartments** and the smaller royal apartments. These rooms were decorated with carvings by **Grinling Gibbons** and painted ceilings by **Verrio**. The apartments and rooms contain a superb collection of **paintings** and **furniture**, while the **kitchens** and the **King's Beer Cellars** and the **wine cellars** offer a glimpse of life in Tudor times, all enhanced by costumed actors who interact with visitors.

The **gardens**★★★ as seen today are the results of various schemes. The famous triangular **maze** was planted in 1690. In 1768 under George III, Lancelot Capability Brown planted the **Great Vine**★, now a plant of remarkable girth which produces an annual crop of around 500–600 bunches of grapes.

Syon Park★★

⊖Gunnersbury then bus 237 or 267. Brentford. **House:** open mid-Mar–Oct Wed–Thu, Sun and bank holidays 11am–5pm. **Gardens:** open daily 10.30am–5pm. £12.50; gardens and conservatory only £7.50. ♿🅿✗. ℘020 8560 0882. www.syonpark.co.uk.
The 1st Earl of Northumberland remodelled this ancient house in 1762, commissioning **Robert Adam**, who richly ornamented and furnished it. A number of notable Stuart portraits by Van Dyck, Lely and others further embellish the interior. **Lancelot Capability Brown** re-designed the gardens and extended them to the river; two of his mulberry trees still survive and a vast rose garden is in bloom from May to August. The **Great Conservatory**, a beautiful semi-circular building with a central cupola and end pavilions, dates from 1827.

Ham House★★

⊖Richmond then bus. Ham Street. **House:** Open early Mar–early Nov noon–4pm. **Garden:** Open mid-Feb–early Nov Sun–Thu 10am–5pm/dusk. Garden History tours daily; Kitchen Garden Tours Wed, 2pm. House and gardens £10.80. ♿🅿✗ ℘020 8940 1950. www.nationaltrust.org.uk/ham-house.
This is an exquisite three-storey 17C brick house. Much of the original furnishing has survived and is lavish even by the standards of the age. The house is rich in ornate plasterwork on the ceilings and splendid carved wood panelling on the walls. The Great Staircase of 1637, built of oak around a square well and gilded, has a beautiful balustrade of boldly carved trophies of arms.

Richmond★★

Set around possibly the most beautiful "urban village" green in England, Richmond grew to importance between the 12C and the 17C as a royal seat. Today private houses stand on the site of Henry VII's Royal Palace in which he died in 1509 (as did his granddaughter, Elizabeth I, in 1603). Among other fine Georgian houses in the "village" note the **Maids of Honour Row**★★ on the Green, built in 1724.

Climb **Richmond Hill**'s steep road, lined by 18C houses with balconied terraces, to enjoy the excellent views immortalised by artists such as Turner and Reynolds. At the top **Richmond Park**★★ is the largest of the Royal Parks and is known for its herds of red and fallow deer. From the top of Henry VIII's Mound, near Pembroke Lodge and the Richmond Gate, on a clear day the **panorama**★★★ extends from Windsor Castle to St Paul's cathedral in The City.

NORTH

Kenwood House★★ (The Iveagh Bequest)

⊖Archway or Golders Green, then 210 bus. Hampstead Lane. **House:** open daily 10am–5pm during summer, but check website for seasonally variable hours. Closed 1 Jan, 24–26 Dec. **Grounds:** Open daily 8am–dusk. ♿🅿✗ picnic area. ℘020 8348 1286. www.english-heritage.org.uk.
Set in leafy grounds beside Hampstead Heath, this is one of London's outstanding country houses, remodelled by Robert Adam 1764–79. It reopened in late 2013 following major conservation and enhancement works.

The richly decorated **library**★★ is one of Adam's great masterpieces. Kenwood also possesses superb paintings including a Rembrandt (Self Portrait in Old Age). Its lakeside summer concerts are a highlight of the northwest London social scene.

Windsor★★

Berkshire

Windsor is synonymous with its castle, but there is more to the town than just one building. Windsor Great Park stretches out for miles beyond the castle and is a perfect place for summer walks and picnics.

TOWN

The network of old **cobbled streets** bordered by High Street, Castle Hill, Church Lane, Church Street and Albans Street, contains a number of fine 16C–18C timber-framed houses with oversailing upper floors rising to pointed gables. The short High Street is distinguished by St John's parish **church**, rebuilt in 1822, and the **Guildhall**, begun by Sir Thomas Fitch c.1637 and completed by Sir Christopher Wren in 1690.

WINDSOR CASTLE★★★

Open daily 9.30am–5.30pm (9.45am–4.15pm Nov–Feb). St George's Chapel closed Sun. Changing of the Guard Apr–Jul Mon–Sat 11am, and on alternate days for rest of year (weather permitting). Closed 25–26 Dec and various days throughout year (see

▶ **Population:** 32 160.

◔ **Michelin Map:** Michelin Atlas p 20 or Map 504 S 29.

🛈 **Info:** The Old Booking Hall, Windsor Royal Shopping, Thames Street. ℘01753 743 900. www.windsor.gov.uk.

◗ **Location:** 23mi/37km due west of London. There are two stations, Windsor & Eton Riverside and Windsor & Eton Central, both centrally located, both with direct London services. The town comprises two main streets, **Thames Street** (by the castle) intersected by Peascod ("Pescot") Street, opposite the castle gate,

👪 **Kids:** Legoland.

website). £20.50 (£11.30 when the state apartments are closed). ♿ ℘020 7766 7304. www.royalresidences.com.

England's biggest castle is also the largest inhabited stronghold in the world and has been a favourite royal residence, frequently extended and rebuilt, since William the Conqueror first built a motte and bailey on the site c.1080.

A Bit of History

By 1110, the castle had become a royal lodge where Henry I held his first court. Henry II erected the first stone buildings between 1165 and 1179, constructing one range of royal apartments in the Upper Ward (to the east of the Round Tower) and one in the Lower Ward. Faced with rebellion by his sons he modernised the defences, rebuilding the earthen walls and wooden Round Tower in stone. Under Henry III (1216–72) this work was virtually completed. Edward III (1327–77) reconstructed the royal apartments for his newly founded Order of the Garter. Under Charles II the State Apartments were rebuilt in an ambitious renovation project which included the reconstruction of

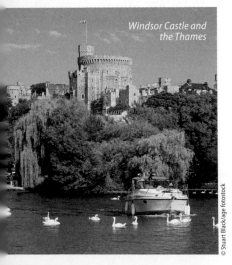

Windsor Castle and the Thames

© Stuart Black/age fotostock

St George's Hall and the King's Chapel, in which the architect Hugh May concentrated on fitting out the interior in a manner fit for a king, insulating the rooms with oak panelling festooned with Grinling Gibbons carvings. However, the principal changes were made in the early-19C when George IV commissioned Sir Jeffry Wyatville as his architect; he built the machicolated walls and several towers, raised the massive Round Tower, giving the castle its famous outline, and remodelled the State Apartments, adding the Waterloo Chamber. This section was badly damaged by fire in 1992. The principal change under Queen Victoria was the addition of a private chapel in memory of Prince Albert, who died here on 14 December 1861. Queen Mary, wife of George V, carried out careful restoration work on the castle at the turn of the 20C century, and it became the childhood home of HRH the Princesses Elizabeth and Margaret during the Second World War, since which it has remained the royal family's principal home. The Court is in official residence throughout April and for Ascot Week in June and the annual Garter Day ceremonies.

The impressive 65m-tall tall **Round Tower** stands on the site of William I's original fortress and houses the Royal Archives. In 2011 it was opened to the public for the first time for visitors to enjoy **views★★** of the castle the Great Park, the Thames Valley and the London skyline. Adjacent, the **North Terrace** (c.1570) affords **views★★** of Eton College and London.

Chapels
St George's Chapel★★★

This great Perpendicular chapel was begun by Edward IV to replace the chapel of Henry III to the east which Edward III had enlarged and dedicated to his **Most Noble Order of the Garter**. The slender clustered piers lead the eye to the crowning glory of the chapel, the **lierne vault**, rich with coloured bosses – completed in 1528. The blank panelling between the tall arcades and the clerestory windows is topped with

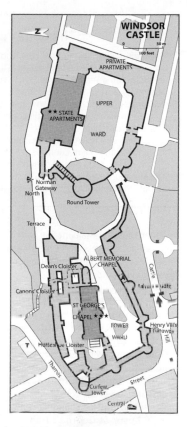

smiling angels. The aisles are notable for their **fan vaulting**. The impressive Perpendicular **west window** depicts 75 figures mainly in early 16C glass.

The ornate **stalls★★★**, abounding in misericords and other carvings, were built in 1478–85; the top tier, surmounted by a richly carved canopy, is for the Knights of the Garter. Edward III's **battle sword** (2m) is in the south chancel aisle. The glorious **east window** (9m high and 8.8m wide; 52 lights) commemorates Prince Albert (incidents from his life illustrated in the lower tier, below the Resurrection and the *Adoration of the Kings*).

Albert Memorial Chapel

The original chapel (1240) was given its magnificent Victorian embellishment by Sir George Gilbert Scott after the death of Albert and is a supreme example of the 19C revivalist age with

The Order of the Garter

The highest order of chivalry in the land is also the oldest to survive in the world. It was established by Edward III in 1348 when England was engaged in the Hundred Years War with France and may have been modelled on the legendary story of 5C King Arthur and his Knights of the Round Table. It was to reward men who had shown valour on the battlefield, and also to honour those who manifested the idealistic and romantic concept of Christian chivalry. Tradition relates how at a ball celebrating the conquest of Calais in 1347, the king retrieved a fallen garter and returned it to its rightful owner, the young and beautiful Joan of Kent, Countess of Salisbury, with the words, "Honi soit qui mal y pense" (Shame on him who thinks evil of it) – the emblem and motto of the Order. A more likely derivation is a strap or sword-belt from a suit of armour to denote the bond of loyalty and concord.

Venetian mosaics, inlaid marble panels and statuary. Prince Albert's tomb was later removed to Frogmore Mausoleum (♿see Box, Frogmore House).

State Apartments★★
Public Rooms
In the Waterloo Chamber hangs a series of portraits by Sir Thomas Lawrence, of the monarchs and leaders involved in Napoleon's final defeat. The Grand Reception Room features Gobelins tapestries and is decorated with gilt plasterwork, massive chandeliers and bronze busts. St George's Hall hall was built by Edward III for the Knights of the Garter and the Baroque chapel was built for Charles II. The 700 past Garter Knights' escutcheons are set in the panelling of the plaster ceiling. Note the award-winning octagonal Lantern Lobby, created after the fire in 1992.

The Queen's Rooms
The Queen's Guard Chamber leads into the panelled Queen's Presence Chamber which, with the adjoining Queen's Audience Chamber, is essentially unchanged since the time of Charles II. The Queen's Drawing Room contains some of the earliest plate glass in England. Eight Van Dyck portraits hang in the ballroom while Holbeins hang in the drawing room.

The King's Rooms
The King's Drawing Room contains paintings by Rubens and his followers

and Chinese porcelain. The King's Bed-chamber has a grandiose "polonaise" bed made for the visit by Emperor Napoleon III and his wife Eugénie in 1855. On the walls of the King's Dressing Room are a number of master-pieces★★ by Dürer, Memling, Clouet, Holbein, Rembrandt, Rubens and Van Dyck. The King's Dining Room retains much of the character it had under Charles II.

Queen Mary's Dolls' House
This fascinating miniature masterpiece, designed by Sir Edwin Lutyens, was presented to Queen Mary in 1924. Everything is exactly on a 1:12 scale – not only the furniture, but even the printed leather-bound books in the library, paintings and the cars in the garage.

WINDSOR PARK★
In the mid-18C George II charged his son, William Duke of Cumberland, with the task of organising the vast Windsor Forest, hunting ground of Saxon leaders and medieval knights. 1 942ha of overgrown woodland were cleared and streams were diverted to drain the marshes into newly dug ponds, which eventually flowed into the especially created 53ha of Virginia Water. George III continued this land reclamation work and established two farms.
The park is now divided into Home Park, which is private, and Great Park, most of which is public. A significant feature of the park is the Long Walk, a

3mi/5km avenue running south as far as the **Copper Horse**, an equestrian statue of George III. Under Charles II the avenue was planted with elm trees, in 1685, the year in which he died, but in 1945 the trees, which had fallen victim to Dutch Elm disease, had to be replaced by chestnuts and planes. Two former royal residences are tucked away in the park: Royal Lodge, used as a retreat by George IV and by the late Queen Elizabeth the Queen Mother, and Cumberland Lodge, where William Duke of Cumberland resided while redesigning the park. Smith's Lawn is an area reserved for polo matches, and beyond it stretch the beautiful **Valley Gardens**. The **Royal Mausoleum**, Frogmore Garden, in Home Park was begun in 1862, the year after Prince Albert's death, specifically so that Queen Victoria and Albert could be buried side by side. The rich interior reflects the Consort's passion for the Italian Renaissance. **Frogmore House** (1684) is furnished largely with possessions accumulated by Queen Mary.

Although it is no longer a royal residence, Frogmore House is still used by the Royal Family for entertaining (*see box above*).

ETON COLLEGE★★

10min on foot across Windsor Bridge.
⊶ Closed for building work until 2016, see website for details. ✆01753 671 177. www.etoncollege.com/PublicVisits.aspx.
The most prestigious of all British schools, Eton was founded in 1440 by Henry VI to give free education to 70 poor scholars and choristers.
Henry then founded King's College, Cambridge, so the boys could continue their education and it soon became fashionable for the nobility to send their sons to Eton.
The paved **School Yard**, centre of college life, is dominated by the 16C red-brick **Lupton's Tower** on the east side. To the north is **Lower School**, the 15C brick building originally constructed by Henry VI to house the Scholars. **Upper School** on the west side was built in the 17C to accommodate the increas-

Frogmore House

The last resting place of both Victoria and Albert is the Frogmore Mausoleum. It is attached to Frogmore House, set in a very peaceful area of Home Park (the private part of Windsor Park) and renowned for its beautiful landscaped garden and 18C lake. The house also contains works of art by Queen Victoria and her children (house only open to group tours for a few days each year, see www.royalresidences.com for details; ✆020 7766 7305; www.royalcollection.org.uk).

ing number of boys. In the centre of the yard stands a 1/19 bronze statue of the founder.
The **College Chapel★★**, built in 1449–82, is one of the best examples of Perpendicular architecture in England. The 15C **wall paintings★** are also the finest in the country. The modern stained glass (Evie Holme, John Piper), and the tapestry reredos and panelling by William Morris from designs by Burne-Jones are notable. The brick **Cloister Court** dates back to Henry VI's time. It contains the 15C College Hall where the "collegers" eat; in the undercroft is the **Museum of Eton Life**.

LEGOLAND WINDSOR★★

▶ 2mi/3km SW of Windsor on the B 3022. Bus from Windsor town centre, by both railway stations. Open daily from 9.30am/10am mid-Mar/Apr–late Oct; closing times and admission prices vary seasonally; day tickets from £30 (see website). ♿🅿✕ ✆0871 2222 001. www.legoland.co.uk.
Millions of Lego building blocks are used to impressive effect in this landscaped theme park.
Moving models and miniature European towns, 50+ theme park rides, attractions and live shows (geared for children up to the age of 12).

ADDRESSES

🏠 STAY

👁 **Top Tips** – Staying in London can be very expensive. Consider bed and breakfasts (B&Bs) instead: **London Bed and Breakfast Agency Ltd** (☎020 7586 2768 ; www.londonbb.com). Or check out no-frills budget chain hotels such as **Premier Inn** (www.premierinn.com) and **Travelodge** (www.travelodge.co.uk). Beware that breakfast is not included in the room rate for many London hotels. Always check in advance.

MARYLEBONE

🛏🍽🛎 **St George Hotel** – Plan C2. 49 Gloucester Place. ⊖ Marble Arch. ☎020 7486 8586. www.stgeorge-hotel.net. 16 rooms. This historic townhouse, a short walk from Oxford Street and Baker Street, offers very comfortable period bedrooms and a warm welcome .

🛏🍽🛎🛎 **Durrants** – Plan C2. 26–32 George Street. ⊖Bond Street. ☎020 7935 8131. www.durrantshotel.co.uk. 92 rooms. A London institution since 1790, Durrants guarantees a very British take on old-fashioned charm. Very pricey, so look for special offers.

COVENT GARDEN

🛏🍽🛎 **The Fielding** – Plan D2. 4 Broad Court, Bow Street. ⊖ Covent Garden. ☎020 7836 8305. www.thefieldinghotel. co.uk. Perhaps the main attraction of this comfortable (air-conditioned) period house is its location at the heart of Covent Garden, and free access to the area's premier spa complex.

SOHO

🛏🍽🛎🛎 **Hazlitt's** – Plan D2. 6 Frith Street . ⊖ Tottenham Court Road. ☎020 7434 1771. www.hazlitts.co.uk. 22 rooms. This small hotel at the heart of Soho is a Georgian-cum-Victorian gem full of character and luxurious antique fittings.

BLOOMSBURY

🍽🛎 **Thanet Hotel** – Plan D2. 8 Bedford Place. ⊖Russell Square. ☎020 7636 2869. www.thanethotel.co.uk. 16 rooms. Situated on a quiet Georgian terrace, near the British Museum, this simple cheerful good-value hotel is run by a friendly husband-and-wife team.

🛏🍽🛎🛎 **The Academy** – Plan D2. - 21 Gower Street. ⊖ Goodge Street. ☎020 7631 4115. www.theacademyhotel.co.uk. 49 rooms. Five Georgian townhouses make up this elegant luxurious four-star boutique hotel with private garden.

THE CITY

🛏🍽🛎🛎 **The Rookery** – Plan E2 - 12 Peter's Lane. Cowcross Street. ⊖Barbican. ☎020 7336 0931. www. rookeryhotel.com. 32 rooms/suites. A sister hotel to Hazlitts (🕯 **see above**) with the same mix of bohemian luxury and charm, located in trendy Clerkenwell.

SOUTHWARK

🛏🍽🛎🛎 **Ibis Styles London Southwark Rose** – Plan E3 – 43–47 Southwark Bridge Road. ⊖London Bridge. ☎(020) 7015 1480. www.ibis.com. 114 rooms. Impressive stylish modern minimalist hotel, near the Globe and Tate Modern. Prices inc Breakfast.

KNIGHTSBRIDGE

🛏🍽🛎🛎 **Knightsbridge Green** – Plan B3. 159 Knightsbridge. ⊖Knightsbridge. ☎020 7589 6700. http://159knightsbridge.com. 30 rooms. Luxury hotel, located in the heart of Knightsbridge, with light spacious, contemporary rooms.

SOUTH KENSINGTON

🛏🍽🛎🛎 **Citadines** – Plan A3. 35a Gloucester Road. ⊖ Gloucester Road. ☎0800 376 3898. www.citadines.com. 92 apartments. Beautifully furnished, comprehensively equipped studios and apartments.

HYDE PARK

🛏🍽🛎 **Gresham Hotel** – Plan B2. 116 Sussex Gardens. ⊖Paddington. ☎020 8166 0990. http://londongresham hotel.com. 57 rooms Location (close to the major museums) and value are the selling points for this simple but comfortable central London hotel.

CHELSEA

🛏🍽🛎 **The Rockwell** – Plan A3. 181–183 Cromwell Road. ⊖ Earl's Court. ☎020 7244 2000. www.therockwell.com. 40 rooms. Elegant contemporary and traditional English style mix at this Kensington hotel with a large south-facing landscaped garden. Garden rooms available.

BELGRAVIA

🍴🛏️ **B&B Belgravia** – Plan C3.
64–66 Ebury Street. 🔄 Victoria. 📞020
7259 8570. www.bb-belgravia.com.
17 rooms. Stylish up-to-the-minute
boutique accommodation in a historic
Georgian townhouse. Full English
organic breakfasts. No lifts.

🍴 EAT

😊 **Top Tips** – London's cosmopolitan
character is typified by its huge range
of places to eat and its global range of
cuisines. For lunch, you'll have no trouble
finding something decent to eat on the
run; high-quality sandwiches, bagels,
soups, noodles… whatever you fancy!

WESTMINSTER

🍴🛏️ **Cinnamon Club** – Plan D3.
The Old Westminster Library, Great Smith
Street. 🔄St James's Park. 📞020 7222 2555.
www.cinnamonclub.com. Closed Sun and
hols. This stylish upmarket Anglo-Indian
restaurant is set in the atmospheric
surrounds of Old Westminster Library

🍴🛏️ **Inn the Park** – Plan D3. St James's
Park. 🔄St James's Park 📞020 7451 9999.
Set in the middle of St James's Park,
Oliver Peyton's eco-friendly restaurant
enjoys a terrific terrace. The British
menu uses many small suppliers,
cooking is straightforward and
wholesome.

MAYFAIR

🍴 **Chada Chada** – Plan C2. 16-17 Picton
Place. 🔄 Bond Street. 📞020 7622 2209.
www.chadathai.com. Closed Sun and hols.
One of the best budget Thai restaurants
in town, this elegant little place serves
traditional favourites, alongside original
recipes.

PICCADILLY

🍴🛏️ **Benihana** – Plan C2.
37 Sackville Street. 🔄 Piccadilly Circus.
📞020 7494 2525. www.benihana.co.uk.
The Japanese food is good here but
the "show cooking", with ingredients
flamboyantly prepared and served in
front of diners on a hibachi hot plate, is
what most customers come for.

COVENT GARDEN

🍴🛏️ **Rules** – Plan D2 - 35 Maiden
Lane - 🔄Charing Cross/Covent Garden.
📞020 7836 5314. www.rules.co.uk.

London's oldest restaurant (est. 1798)
specialises in atmosphere and hearty
traditional British cooking.

SOHO

🍴🛏️ **Dehesa** – Plan C2. 25 Ganton
Street, 🔄 Oxford Circus. 📞020 7494 4170.
www.saltyardgroup.co.uk/dehesa. Closed
Sun evening. This calm charcuterie and
tapas bar takes inspiration from Spain
and Italy, and boasts an impressive
wine list.

TEMPLE

🍴🛏️ **The White Swan** – Plan E2. 108
Fetter Lane. 🔄 Temple. 📞020 7242 9696.
www.thewhiteswanlondon.com. Closed
weekends. Just off Fleet Street this
new gastropub serves traditional and
modern English dishes, in a very smart
dining room above the pub.

REGENT'S PARK

🍴 **The Sea Shell** – Plan C1. 49-51 Lisson
Grove. 🔄 Marylebone. 📞020 7224 9000.
www.seashellrestaurant.co.uk. Closed Sun.
One of London's best fish and chip
places with a smart traditional black-
and-white dining room to save your
fingers getting messy. Ideal after a day
at Regent's Park/London Zoo.

🍴🛏️ **Villandry** – Plan C2.
170 Great Portland Street. 🔄Regent's Park.
📞020 7631 3131 www.villandry.com.
Closed Sun evening. This all-day French
restaurant, café, foodshop, bakery and
bar (all under one roof) is as good for a
quick takeaway as it is for a full-blown
elegant classic French dinner.

CITY

🍴🛏️ **Le Coq d'Argent** – Plan F2.
1 Poultry. 🔄Bank. 📞020 7395 5000.
www.coqdargent.co.uk. Closed Sat lunch,
Sun evening and hols. At the heart of
The City, this vast sixth-floor restaurant
features one of the most remarkable
roof gardens in London with a
wonderful view from its terrace. Classic
French menu with contemporary
flavours.

TOWER BRIDGE

🍴🛏️ **The Blueprint Cafe** – Plan G3. 28
Shad Thames. 🔄Tower Bridge. 📞020 7378
7031. www.blueprintcafe.co.uk. Closed Sun
evening. This long-standing restaurant
enjoys a classy location among the
converted warehouses of Butler's Wharf.

Superb riverside views complement excellent Modern British cuisine.

🍽️ **Le Pont de la Tour** – Plan F3 - 36D Shad Thames, Butlers Wharf. ⊖ Tower Bridge. 📞020 7403 8403. www.lepontdelatour.co.uk. This elegant establishment, serving fine French cuisine, is a favourite for business and pleasure with a riverside terrace and perfect views of Tower Bridge. Try its Bar & Grill (🍽️) for a less formal meal.

🍽️ **Butlers Wharf Chop House** – Plan F3 36e Shad Thames. ⊖Tower Bridge. 📞020 7403 3403. www.chophouse-restaurant.co.uk. Classic down-to-earth British food, such as chops and steaks and a famous steak and kidney pudding are the signature dishes at this wood-panelled restaurant by the Thames which evokes the style of a boating or cricket pavilion. Great views of Tower Bridge from its terrace.

SOUTHWARK

🍽️ **Anchor & Hope** – Plan E3. 36 The Cut. ⊖ Southwark. 📞020 7928 9898. www.anchorandhopepub.co.uk. Mon lunch and Sun. One of London's best gastropubs, serving its own original unfussy take on Modern and traditional British cuisine. No bookings taken, so arrive early.

🍽️ **Cantina Vinopolis** – Plan F2. 1 Bank End. ⊖ Southwark. 📞020 7940 8333. There's a wide choice of menus in this "shrine to wine" (part of visitor attraction, Vinopolis), tucked away under massive Victorian arches beside the Thames in handsome brick-vaulted dining rooms.

SOUTH BANK

🍽️ **Oxo Tower** – Plan E2. Oxo Tower Wharf, 8th floor. Barge House Street. ⊖ Southwark. 📞020 7803 3888. www.harveynichols.com/restaurants. Magnificent views of the capital across the Thames are complemented. by fine pan-Asian and Modern British cuisine. On the same level, the **Oxo Tower Brasserie** is cheaper but with equally fine views and excellent cooking.

KNIGHTSBRIDGE

🍽️ **The Knightsbridge Metro** – Plan B3. 28 Basil Street - ⊖Knightsbridge. 📞020 7589 6286. www.thelevinhotel.co.uk. Near Harrods, this modern bistro breaks no new ground with its menu but is ideal for a shoppers' lunch or afternoon tea.

CHELSEA

🍽️ **Pig's Ear** – Plan B4. 35 Old.Church Street. ⊖ Sloane Square. 📞020 7352 2908. www.thepigsear.info. Tucked away between the King's Road and the Thames, this smart gastropub offers British/French brasserie food, in the bar or in its two formal dining rooms.

🍽️ **Bibendum** – Plan B3. Michelin House, 81 Fulham Road. ⊖ South Kensington. 📞020 7581 5817. www.bibendum.co.uk. Housed in London's finest Art Nouveau building and celebrating Michelin's famous "Mr Bibendum", this 20-year-old establishment serves consistently excellent classic French food with a strong British influence. Also in the building is the Oyster Bar, Crustacea Stall and a cafe.

🍽️ **One-O-One** – Plan C3. William Street. ⊖ Knightsbridge. 📞020 7290 7101. www.oneoonerestaurant.com. One of the country's top seafood dining rooms, located at The Park Tower Knightsbrisge hotel. Only sustainable and farmed produce are used.

PUBS

Pubs usually open Mon–Sat 11am-11pm, Sun noon–10.30pm.

Anglesea Arms – Plan B4. 15 Selwood Terrace. ⊖ South Kensington. 📞020 7373 7960. www.angleseaarms.com. Set in a peaceful residential district, this is the ideal spot for a relaxing drink after a walk, particularly on the pretty outdoor terrace. The pub is also known for its excellent Modern British food, which can also be served on the terrace (🍽️–🍽️).

Dickens Inn – Plan G2. St Katharine Dock. ⊖ Tower Hill. 📞020 7488 2208. www.dickensinn.co.uk. Although it may look older, this rambling Dickens-themed pub, looking onto St Katherine Docks, only opened in 1976. Its restaurant is famous for its huge "Beast" pizzas serving five people at a time; its generous servings of pasta are also recommended.

George Inn – Plan F3. 77 Borough High Street. ⊖ London Bridge. ℘020 7407 2056. www.nationaltrust.org.uk/george-inn. London's last galleried inn, dating from the 17C, is such a treasure that the National Trust now cares for it, though it still functions as it has since Shakespeare's time. The Bard may well have performed in the original George Inn (which burned down in 1676) and Dickens mentions the present inn in *Little Dorrit*.

The Bunch of Grapes – Plan B3. 207 Brompton Road. ⊖ Knightsbridge. ℘020 7589 4944. www.bunchofgrapes-knightsbridge.co.uk. Just a few yards from Harrods, this classic Victorian pub is perfect for a relaxing drink after shopping. Note the remarkable carved wooden bunch of grapes bar partition.

The Nag's Head – Plan C3. 53 Kinnerton Street. ⊖ Knightsbridge. ℘020 7235 1135. Stepping into "the Nag's" is rather like walking into an old movie, with its small cosy rooms full of bric-a-brac from yesteryear. Mobile phones are banned!

Ye Grapes – Plan C3. 16 Shepherd Market. ⊖ Green Park, Hyde Park Corner. ℘020 7493 4216. This charming late-19C pub is tucked away in an alleyway in village-like Shepherd Market. Upstairs is a restaurant serving British and Thai food.

CAFÉS

Café in the Crypt – Plan D2. ⊖ Trafalgar Square. ⊖ Leicester Square, Charing Cross. ℘020 7766 1158. www.stmartin-in-the-fields.org. Located in the crypt of St Martin-in-the-Fields church, this self-service cafe serves good value snacks and light meals. Live jazz each Wed (tickets required after 6.30pm).

Fortnum and Mason's – Plan C2. 181 Piccadilly. ⊖ Piccadilly Circus. ℘020 7734 8040. www.fortnumandmason.co.uk. Founded in 1707, London's world-famous grocery shop boasts several restaurants. The most popular are the affordable **Fountain**, and the more expensive and chic **The Diamond Jubilee Tea Salon**, both of which feature a pianist. Afternoon tea can be taken in both).

Garden Café – Plan C1. Queen Mary's Gardens, Inner Circle. ⊖ Regent's Park, Baker Street. ℘020 7034 0722. www.companyofcooks.com. Open 9am–8pm; winter 9am–6pm. Simple but stylish café in elegant Regent's Park, serving high-quality teas, coffees, lunch and evening meals in summer.

Harrods – Plan B3. 87–135 Brompton Road. ⊖ Knightsbridge. www.harrods.com. Open Mon–Sat 10am–9pm, Sun 11.30am –6pm. The most famous shop in town includes some 30 restaurants and cafés: from sushi and seafood in their fabulous **Food Hall**, self-service to traditional afternoon tea in **The Tea Room** or on **Harrods Terrace**.

Harvey Nichols – Fifth Floor Café – Plan C3. 109–125 Knightsbridge. ⊖ Knightsbridge. ℘020 7823 1839. www.harveynichols.com. Knightsbridge shopping regulars appreciate this bright, light spacious café-bar, complete with open-plan-style kitchen and roof terrace. There's also a very chic restaurant and a champagne bar on the same floor.

SHOPPING

Window shopping is all part of the fun in London, particularly in stores like Harvey Nichols, Harrods and Selfridges which are renowned for their displays. For many people however the famous end of year sales (late Dec to mid-Jan) are worth the trip alone.

☺ **Top Tip**– **Museum shops** are a great source of inspiration when it comes to unusual gifts and souvenirs; try the British Museum, the Science Museum, the Natural History Museum, London Transport Museum…

SHOPPING AREAS

Around **Covent Garden** (www.covent gardenlife.com; www.coventgarden londonuk.com) you'll find all kinds of shops selling unusual gifts, fashion and perfumes. Don't miss **Penhaligon's**, at No. 41 Wellington Street). In The Market **Peter Rabbit and Friends** (No. 42) delights little ones.

In **St James's**, Jermyn Street is the place for classic gentlemen's fashion. Cheese lovers should follow their noses to no. 93, the home of **Paxton & Whitfield** for their wonderful Stiltons, Cheddars and many more cheeses from Britain (and beyond).

In **Mayfair**, Burlington Arcade and Old Bond Street specialise in many of the world's most exclusive fashion brands. Sloane Street in **Knightsbridge** is also synonymous with expensive designer shopping. Sloane Street joins Sloane Square at **Chelsea**, famous for the King's Road and its many one-off fashion shops. In The **City**, the old Royal Exchange building is home to several upmarket shops.

MARKETS

Portobello Road – Plan A2. Portobello Road. ⊖ Notting Hill Gate. www.portobelloroad.co.uk. On Saturdays the world's largest antique market is held; the rest of the week, antique shops, galleries, and all kinds of specialists and dealers in collectibles flourish here.

Borough Market – Plan F3. Stoney Street, Borough High Street. ⊖ London Bridge. Open Wed–Thu 10am–5pm, Fri 10am–6pm, Sat 8am–5pm; partially open Mon–Tue 10am–5pm. ✆020 7407 1002; www.boroughmarket.org.uk. London's oldest and finest food market delights both foodies (including some of the capital's top restaurateurs) and passing tourists. At some stalls you can sit down to eat, and there are established bona-fide cafés and restaerants here too.

BOOKS AND READING

Waterstone's Booksellers – Plan D2. 203–206 Piccadilly. ⊖ Piccadilly Circus. ✆0843 290 8549. www.waterstones.com. Occupying six floors of a lovely 70-year-old building, Waterstone's is the biggest bookshop in Europe. This is also the place to come for a comprehensive selection of foreign newspapers and magazines.

HOME FURNISHING

The Conran Shop Chelsea, Michelin House – Plan B3 – 81 Fulham Road. ⊖South Kensington. ✆0844 848 4000. www.conranshop.co.uk. Housed in the former UK headquarters of Michelin, and still boasting its famous stained-glass Bibendum windows, style-guru

Terence Conran presents the very best in contemporary home fashion, for both Londoners and visitors.

TEA

Twinings & Co – Plan E2. 216 Strand. ⊖ Temple. ✆020 7353 3511. www.twinings.co.uk. Closed Sun. Established in 1717, this is the oldest tea shop in the world, and sells hundreds of varieties of tea in all flavours and packages. There is a small museum at the back of the shop.

TOYS AND GAMES

Hamley's – Plan C2. 188–196 Regent Street. ⊖ Oxford Circus. ✆0871 704 1977. www.hamleys.co.uk. The world's most famous toyshop is six levels of heaven for children, though beware, it can be unbearably crowded and stressful for parents, particularly at peak periods.

ENTERTAINMENT

The capital's most famous theatres, cinemas and concert halls tend to congregate around Leicester Square, Piccadilly (particularly Shaftesbury Avenue) and Covent Garden. Some of London's most famous **West End musicals** have been running for over 20 years.

Even if you don't really understand all the language it's well worth attending a **Shakespeare play** at the beautifully rebuilt Globe Theatre, just to experience what it may have been like in those days (*see p171*). London also has great **concert halls** and it's always worth noting what's on at the Barbican, the Royal Albert Hall and the Southbank Centre (Royal Festival Hall, Hayward Gallery, Queen Elizabeth Hall, Purcell Room).

The best listings and reviews of all shows and events in town are in *Time Out* magazine every Tuesday (www.timeout.com/london), and *The London Evening Standard* (www.standard.co.uk), published daily. Both are free; pick up Time Out at tube stations, and selected retailers, museums, cafes and galleries, the Evening Standard is given away at mainline and tube stations.

TICKETS

The simplest way of buying tickets for any show is at the box office. Alternatively you can telephone or buy online, though there is a surcharge (of up to 10 percent).

Ticketmaster – ℘0333 321 9999 (0044 161 425 7563 from abroad); www.ticketmaster.co.uk.

TKTS Leicester Square – Plan D2. Leicester Square. ⊖ Leicester Square. open Mon–Sat 9am–7pm for matinée and evening shows, Sun 11am–4.30pm. www.tkts.co.uk. Formerly known as the Half-Price Ticket Booth, and (still) operated by the Society of London Theatres (SOLT), this kiosk offers the best seats in London's theatres at **half the normal price**, plus a "booking fee" per ticket. They are only valid for that day and are first come first served. You can pay by cash or credit card (surcharge for the latter); tickets are non-returnable and are limited to four per person.

Beware of half-price tickets imitators also located in Leicester Square. You can also book tickets for the theatre, and for many other events, through the official channels, online at www.visitlondon.com.

EVENTS

For more details on any of the events below visit www.visitlondon.com.

New Year's Day Parade (1 Jan) More than 10 000 performers in fancy dress parade through central London. http://lnydp.com.

Chinese New Year (late Jan–mid Feb) The largest Chinese New Year celebrations outside Asia take place in London's Chinatown. www.chinatownlondon.org.

Head of the River Race (Mar) Some 400, 8-man crews from around the globe take to the Thames in one of the capital's longest-running sporting traditions. www.horr.co.uk.

The Boat Race (Apr) The crews of Oxford University and Cambridge University compete, from Putney to Mortlake, in one of the world's oldest sporting events. www.theboatrace.org.

Chinese New Year, Chinatown
© C. Ochterbeck/MICHELIN

Chelsea Flower Show (May) The world's greatest flower show in the grounds of the Royal Hospital, Chelsea. ℘020 3176 5800. www.rhs.org.uk.

Trooping the Colour (2nd/3rd Sat Jun) Pomp and pageantry at the Queen's official birthday parade on Horse Guards Parade. www.householddivision.org.uk/trooping-the-colour.

Wimbledon (last wk Jun– 1st wk Jul) The world's finest Lawn Tennis Championships. www.wimbledon.com.

The BBC Proms (mid-Jul–1st wk Sept) The Royal Albert Hall is the venue for a world-beating series of classical concerts. www.bbc.co.uk/proms.

Notting Hill Carnival (last weekend Aug) Europe's largest carnival celebrations is a blaze of colour and music. www.thelondonnottinghillcarnival.com.

The Lord Mayor's Show (Nov) Over 6 000 colourful participants show off London's history and cultural diversity. www.lordmayorsshow.org.

Christmas Lights (Dec) Illuminations and dressed shop windows on Regent Street (www.regentstreetonline.com) and Oxford Street (www.oxfordstreet.co.uk); and an enormous Christmas tree in Trafalgar Square.

Surrey, Kent and Sussex

Introduction

The three counties south of London have been influenced not only by the proximity of the capital, but also by that of the continent. Many of the wealthy inhabitants of the county towns will have commuted at one time or another to London – indeed Brighton is still known as 'London-by-the-Sea' – while the remnants of, and deterrents to, foreign invaders can be seen in the Roman villas, medieval castles, famous battlefields, and historic naval dockyards. Christianity also established an early stronghold here, as witnessed by the great cathedrals at Canterbury and Chichester.

Surrey

The capital's southwest commuter belt, Surrey has the busiest road network outside London. Despite this, however, it is also England's most wooded county with many wealthy havens. Surrey's county town of Guildford has no major attractions, but is a pleasant base for exploring the region's houses and gardens, and maybe even theme parks.

Kent

Famous for the iconic White Cliffs of Dover, Kent faces France across the Channel. Formerly the cradle of British sea power, since Victorian times places such as Chatham and Rochester have become more famous for their connections with Charles Dickens. The county is known as 'the Garden of England' for its abundance of orchards and hop gardens, so it is no surprise that it boasts many fine gardens. Elsewhere are some of England's best-preserved and most beautiful castles, while Tunbridge Wells is a delightful spa town at the northern edge of the High Weald.

Highlights

1 Explore **Leeds Castle**, the most romantic in England (p197)
2 Make your own pilgrimage to **Canterbury cathedral** (p199)
3 Stroll in the footsteps of smugglers in sleepy **Rye** (p205)
4 Marvel at the Oriental Gothic **Brighton Pavilion** (p208)
5 Travel back to Tudor and Jacobean times at **Knole** (p213)

Sussex

Breezy, bohemian Brighton is the undisputed main centre of England's south coast, with its attractions, dining and nightlife. Beyond, the glorious South Downs and coastline of Eastbourne make Brighton a touring base too. West Sussex boasts Chichester cathedral and its water meadows, while Rye is the jewel of East Sussex.

Cloister, Canterbury cathedral © Jon Arnold/hemis.fr

North Downs★

The North Downs are a ridge of chalk hills that start in Farnham in Surrey, and run all the way to the White Cliffs of Dover in Kent.

GUILDFORD★

31mi/50km southwest of London

🛈 155 High Street. ✆01483 444333/4.
www.guildford.co.uk

Guildford's prosperity can be traced back to the 18C, when it was crowded with coaching inns, and travellers breaking their journey between Portsmouth and London. Today, it is an archetypal wealthy middle-class southern town, complete with university.

The elegant cobbled High Street descends towards the River Wey, with the green slopes of the Mount beyond. The High Street is dominated by the **Guildhall** (open May–Jul and Sept 11am–5pm, Aug Mon–Sat 10am–5pm; ✆01483 444 751; www.guildford.gov.uk/guildhall) with its ornate projecting clock. Nearby, the **Guildford House Gallery** (155 High Street; open Mon–Sat 10am–4.45pm, Sun May–Sept only 11am–4pm; ✕) is an elegant late-17C town house displaying changing exhibitions. Opposite the landmark **Angel Hotel**, is the fine vaulted-stone **Undercroft** built by a 13C wool merchant beneath a shop. It may be visited on the free **guided city tour**, which includes the Tudor-style **Abbot's Hospital**, founded by Arch-

bishop Abbot in 1619, and still in use as a home for the elderly. A five-minute walk from here, on Warren Road, is **The Spike**, built in 1906. This housed the forgotten classes of Edwardian England – the poor, the infirm, the ill and destitute. (Open Tue and Sat 10am–4pm, call in advance to book; £6 (child 5–16, £5); ✆01483 598 420; http://www.heritage.charlotteville.co.uk).

Guildford Castle

Grounds: Open daily dawn–dusk. Keep: Open Mar and Oct Sat–Sun 11am–4pm (daily during half-term); Apr–Sept daily 10am–5pm. £3.20. ✆01483 444 751. www.guildford.gov.uk/castle.

A 12C sandstone keep is virtually all that remains of the castle built by William the Conqueror shortly after the Battle of Hastings in 1066. Inside the grounds is Jeanne Argent's 1990 sculpture *Alice through the Looking Glass* commemorating Lewis Carroll, a frequent visitor to Guildford who rented a nearby house for his sisters. He died while visiting them and is buried in the Mount Cemetery.

WISLEY GARDEN★

6mi/10km NE of Guildford on the A3. Open Mon–Fri 10am–6pm, Sat–Sun and bank holidays 9am–6pm. Closed 25 Dec. £14. ♿🅿✕ ✆01483 224234. www.rhs.org.uk/gardens/wisley.

The flagship gardens of the Royal Horticultural Society are worth a visit in all seasons. Founded in 1903 and

---

🛈 **Michelin Map:** Michelin Atlas p 19 or Map 504 S 30.

🛈 **Info:** There is no one tourist information point for the North Downs, but all of the major towns have tourist offices.

▶ **Location:** The North Downs stretch from Farnham in Surrey to the White Cliffs of Dover in Kent..

👥 **Kids:** Thorpe Park; Chessington.

Surrey Theme Parks

Close to Guildford lie two of the UK's leading theme parks:

👥 **Thorpe Park** (✆0871 663 1673; www.thorpepark.com) and 👥 **Chessington World of Adventures** (✆0871 663 4477. www.chessington.com). Thorpe Park is better for older children, while Chessington focuses on younger children. Arrive early. Book online for big discounts.

boasting many fine trees, there is a great range of different sorts of gardens, including a pinetum, an alpine house, a rock garden, and state-of-the-art new Glasshouse.

BOX HILL★

5mi/24km E of Guildford via the A 246, 1mi/1.6km N of Dorking via the A 24.
This glorious countryside of rolling woodland and chalk downland has been a famous beauty spot for over a century and is now in the care of the National Trust. They have installed an information centre including a Discovery Zone, and the popular Box Tree café (open daily Apr–late Oct 9am–5pm, rest of year 10am–4pm, other areas from 11am; closed 25 Dec; ⬤🅿(charge); ☎01306 885 502; www. nationaltrust.org.uk/box hill). If you're feeling energetic, they also hire mountain bikes.

DORKING

12mi/19 km E of Guildford on A 25.
www.visitdorking.com.
The main interest in this well-to-do market town is **West Street**, with its fine old houses, many antique shops and the **Dorking Museum and Heritage Centre** (Open Thu–Sat 10am–4pm; £2, www.dorkingmuseum.org.uk).
The area around Dorking is Surrey's finest countryside, most notably **Leith Hill**, 5mi/8km south (open year-round dawn to dusk; closed 25–30 Dec, 1–3 Jan; 🅿✗; ☎01306 712 711; www.nationaltrust.org.uk/leith-hill). It is crowned by a fortified folly tower that peaks at 314m above sea level, making it the highest point in southeast England. You can climb its spiral staircase to enjoy panoramic views. Nearby, recently opened to the public is **Leith Hill Place** (open late-Jul–early Nov Fri–Sun 11am–5pm; £3; 🅿(charge) ☎01306 711 685; www.nationaltrust.org/leith-hill-place), once home to the Wedgwood family and composer Ralph Vaughan Williams, and visited by Charles Darwin.

FARNHAM

10.6mi/17km W of Guildford via the A 31.
www.farnham.gov.uk.
This attractive prosperous little market town by the River Wey centres on West Street/The Borough and Castle Hill. The latter is a beautiful wide street crowned by **Farnham Castle**. For 800 years, the Bishops of Winchester used the castle as a home and administrative centre (open Mon–Fri 9am–5pm, Sat–Sun and bank holidays 10am–4pm; ☎01252 721 194; www.english-heritage.org.uk).

POLESDEN LACEY★

5mi/8km NW of Dorking, 2mi/3km S of Great Bookham off the A 246.
House and gardens: Open Mar–Oct daily 11am–5pm. Guided tours only 11am–12.30pm, then free flow. £13.60;. ⬤🅿(£3). ✗. ☎01372 458 048. www. nationaltrust.org.uk/polesden-lacey.
This Edwardian country estate once entertained the highest people in the land and is set out to re-create its halcyon days. The house is notable for its interiors and collections, with lovely gardens offering superb views across the rolling Surrey Hills.

HATCHLANDS PARK

East Clandon. 5mi/8km E of Guildford ,via the A 246. Open Apr–Oct 2–5pm. £10. ⬤🅿✗ ☎01483 222 482. www. nationaltrust.org.uk/hatchlands-park.
Hatchlands Park was built in the 1750s and today is a family home, containing a fine collection of paintings and Europe's largest collection of keyboard instruments, associated with J C Bach, Chopin and Elgar.

CLANDON PARK★

West Clandon. 3mi/5km E of Guildford via the A 3/A 247. Open Wed–Sun 10am–5pm. £5. 🅿(250m from entrance, www.nationaltrust.org.uk/clandon-park.
Built c.1730, until a major fire in April 2015, Clandon Park was one of the country's most complete Palladian mansions. Although a fire devastated Clandon in 2015, the National Trust is currently rebuilding it and providing public access to many areas.

North Kent Coast★

Although this is one of England's least fashionable coastal stretches, the many Dickensian connections, magnificent Leeds Castle and the attractions of the Thanet Resorts (including the new Turner Contemporary gallery) make North Kent well worth a visit.

🗎 **Info:** Droit House, Stone Pier, Margate. ℰ01843 577 577. www.visitthanet.co.uk.

🚾 **Michelin Map:** Map 504 V 29.

🅯 **Don't Miss:** World Naval Base, Leeds Castle; Turner Gallery.

👪 **Kids:** World Naval Base, Dickens World.

ROCHESTER★

35mi/53km E of London.

🗎 95 High Street. ℰ01634 338 141. www.visitmedway.org. The train station is on the High Street with a frequent London service.

The Romans built Durobrivae to dominate the point where Watling Street crossed the River Medway. A 12C Norman castle now stands tall, while the walled town is cut in two by 'the silent High Street, full of gables with old beams and timbers' (Charles Dickens). In fact Rochester and the Medway area are the scene of a number of Dickens' novels, notably *Pickwick Papers* and *Great Expectations*.

The River Medway cuts Rochester in two. In the centre of town, on the south side of the river near the High Street bridge is the **castle★** (open daily Apr–Sept 10am–6pm, Oct–Mar 10am–4pm; closed 1 Jan, 24–26 Dec; £6.40; ℰ01634 335 882; www.english-heritage.org.uk), whose early **curtain walls** were built by Gundulf, Bishop of Rochester and

architect of Rochester Cathedral and the Tower of London. The present massive **keep** was built in 1127; its ruins are an outstanding example of Norman military architecture.

Close by, the **cathedral★** (open Mon–Fri 7.30am–6pm, Sat 7.30am–5pm), Sun 7.30am–5pm; guided tours Mon–Fri 10am–3.30pm, Sat 10am–2pm, Sun 12.30–2.30pm; ♿✕; ℰ01634 843 366; www.rochestercathedral.org) is where Bishop Gundulf (1024–1108) held England's second episcopal see, from 1077. The cathedral was extended at least twice and is mostly 12C and 13C. Of particular interest is the Norman west front, and its centrepiece, the exuberantly sculptured **west doorway** (1160). Beyond the six Norman **nave bays** the cathedral is essentially Early English. The painting on the choir wall is the *Wheel of Fortune* and dates from the 13C. Back on the High Street, the **Guildhall Museum** (open Tue–Sun 10am–5pm; closed Christmas; ♿; ℰ01634 8332 900; www.medway.gov.uk) is housed in

---

The Roman Conquest

The Medway area is rich in prehistoric and Roman sites. During Emperor Claudius' invasion of Britain, Roman legions landed near Richborough in Kent and moved westwards. An unhewn stone (5m high), erected near a ford on the Medway at Snodland, south of Rochester, in 1998, is a belated memorial to a decisive Roman victory in year 43 over the army of the Celtic king Cunobelinus – Shakespeare's Cymbeline. This event sealed the fate of Britain coming under the Roman Empire. The battle probably took place near a fordable point on the Medway – near Snodland, according to modern historians.

handsome Rochester Guildhall, built in 1687. Its star attraction is an actual-size section of a piece of an infamous Medway hulk (Victorian prison ship, made famous by Dickens) sitting alongside displays on more genteel 19C local life.

CHATHAM
👤👤 World Naval Base★★

2mi/3km NE of Rochester. Open mid-Feb–Nov daily 10am–4pm (Apr–Oct 10am–6pm); £24, child £14 (online booking discounts). ♿🅿✕.
℘01634 823 800.
www.thedockyard.co.uk.
Established in the reign of Henry VIII, this cradle of British sea power built nearly 500 ships, including *HMS Victory*, before the Royal Navy finally left in 1984. The large complex (32ha) of historic maritime buildings and docks now reinterprets the life of the dockyard through exhibits and demonstrations, from the **Victorian Ropery**, the award-winning **Hearts of Oak** (construction of large wooden ships), the **RNLI Historic Lifeboat Collection** and **3 Slip**. The last refers to the immense covered slipway built in 1838, then Europe's largest wide-span timber structure.

LEEDS CASTLE★★★

7mi/11km E of Maidstone, M20 (J8). Open daily Apr–Sept 10.30am–5.30pm; (Oct–Mar 4pm); Grounds open from 10am. Closed 25 Dec. £24.90. ♿🅿✕
℘01622 765 400.
www.leeds-castle.com.
Originally Norman, built on two islands in a lake, Leeds Castle was described by Lord Conway as '...the loveliest castle in the world', and is certainly one of the most picturesque in Britain. A romantic stone **bridge** links the keep, which rises sheer from the lake, with the turreted and battlemented main building. The interior is graced by splendid **works of art** (14C–19C): statues, carvings and tapestries. The glorious **park** and **gardens** include an aviary, grotto and maze.

WHITSTABLE

7mi/11km N of Canterbury via A290. Famed for its oysters and wide choice of fish and seafood eating places, this pleasant little fishing town makes for an ideal stroll along the pebbly seashore after a day in Canterbury.

THANET RESORTS★
Broadstairs

21mi/34km E of Canterbury via A 256.
The quietest and prettiest of the Thanet resorts, Broadstairs is also closely associated with Dickens, who made his holiday home here during his most prolific writing years, calling it 'Our English Watering Place'. It is now home to the **Dickens House Museum** (open daily Easter–mid-Jun and mid-Sept–Oct 1–4.30pm, mid-Jun–mid-Sept 10am–1.30pm, Nov–Sat–Sun only 1–4.30pm; ℘01843 861 232, or 01843 863 453 when museum closed; www.thanet.gov.uk).
In 2011, the sleepy seaside town of **Margate** (3.6mi/5.8km northwest) became host to the state-of-the-art **Turner Contemporary** Gallery (open Aug daily 10am–6pm, rest of year Tue–Sun 10am–6pm; no charge; ℘01843 233 000; ♿🅿✕, www.turnercontemporary.org), dedicated to Britain's greatest landscape artist, J M W Turner, who was a regular visitor to Margate. The gallery is the largest art space in the Southeast, outside London, and in its first two years received 1 million visitors.

Ramsgate

2.5mi/4km south of Broadstairs.
℘01843 598 750.
www.ramsgatetown.org.
The largest of the Thanet resorts, Ramsgate owes much of its character to its Georgian **Royal Harbour** – now a marina – and to its popularity as a Victorian bathing resort, which has left a rich legacy of Victorian architecture. The town's principal industries are tourism and fishing, and there is a thriving marina with more than 800 moorings. Undoubtedly, Ransgate's main attraction is its coastline, and the Main Sands, a Blue Flag beach.

Canterbury★★★

The ecclesiastical capital of England, rich in medieval atmosphere, is dominated by its renowned cathedral. The city lies on Watling Street, the great Roman thoroughfare linking London with the port of Dover. It is the terminus of the **Pilgrims' Way**, a trackway of prehistoric origin used by many of the worshippers at the shrine of St Thomas à Becket, England's renowned martyr.

A BIT OF HISTORY

Early settlement – Canterbury's recorded history begins with Emperor Claudius' invasion in year 43 and the foundation of the walled town of Durovernum. After the Roman withdrawal early in the 5C, the city was settled by Jutish invaders and renamed *Cantwarabyrig*, or 'Stronghold of the Men of Kent'.

A Christian see – In 597, **St Augustine** arrived in Kent to convert the pagan population to Christianity. The city became the centre of the English Church and Augustine was consecrated as first archbishop.

In 1170, a later archbishop, **Becket**, was assassinated in the cathedral by four of Henry II's knights who, legend has it, had resonded all too literally to their ruler's question 'Who will rid me of this meddlesome priest' (although the exact words have been lost to history). Becket was canonised two years later and his shrine immediately attracted pilgrims, many of whose stories are recounted in **Chaucer's** *Canterbury Tales*. The cathedral's monastery was the largest in the country and by the 13C Grey Friars and Black Friars were established here as well. This thriving monastic life came to an end with the Dissolution of the Monasteries; the cathedral's treasures were appropriated by Henry VIII, and the saint's shrine destroyed.

A prosperous city – The post-Reformation saw the arrival of French Huguenot refugees at the invitation of Elizabeth I.

▶ **Population:** 157 600

🕭 **Michelin Map:** Michelin Atlas p 13 or Map 504 X 30.

🚻 **Info:** The Beaney, 18 High Street, ℘01227 862 162, www.canterbury.co.uk. The town has two train stations. Canterbury East, just outside the old walls, receives trains from London Victoria and Dover; Canterbury West is five minutes' walking time from the western section of wall, with services from London Charing Cross and Waterloo (East). Fastest train time from London: St Pancras to Canterbury West, 55 min to 1hr 10min. The bus station is on St George's Lane inside the walls.

◖ **Location:** 56mi/90km east of London.

◔ **Don't Miss:** Canterbury's stunning cathedral and the Black Prince's tomb.

🕓 **Timing:** At least a day.

🐾 **Walking Tours:** Depart from the Buttermarket, Apr–Sept 11am & 2pm, Oct–Mar 11am, £7.50, ℘01227 459 779, www.canterburyguidedtours.com.

These skilled craftsmen contributed to Canterbury's prosperity and in spite of the depredations of the Puritans in the Civil War, the city continued to flourish. Greater damage was suffered in bombing raids of 1942, when part of the historic centre was reduced to rubble, though the cathedral remained undamaged.

Today, Canterbury is the thriving centre of eastern Kent and the seat of a modern university. The city exerts nearly as strong a pull on the modern tourist as in medieval times and remains a religious centre. The See of Canterbury remains the focal point of the worldwide Anglican Communion.

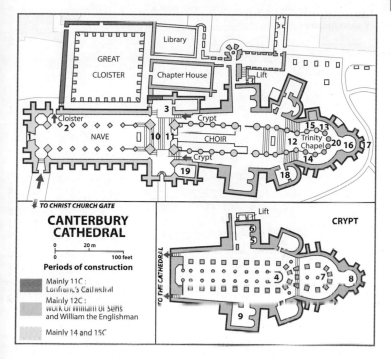

CANTERBURY CATHEDRAL

Periods of construction

Mainly 11C: Lanfranc's Cathedral

Mainly 12C: work of William of Sens and William the Englishman

Mainly 14 and 15C

CANTERBURY CATHEDRAL★★★

Open (services permitting) Mon–Sat summer 9am–5.30pm; winter 9am–5pm. Crypt opens 10am–5/5.30pm; Sun year-round 12.30–2.30pm (including the Crypt). £12.50. & ℘01227 762 862. www.canterbury-cathedral.org.

The original cathedral built by St Augustine was destroyed in 1067 and replaced by the first Norman archbishop, **Lanfranc**. Archbishop **Anselm** replaced his predecessor's choir with an ambitious structure. It too was gutted by fire in 1174, four years after Becket's murder, though the crypt and nave were spared. As the cathedral had become the most important centre of pilgrimage in northern Europe, the opportunity was seized to rebuild in a manner worthy of the martyr, in an early Gothic style which was to be of great subsequent influence in the development of English architecture. The work was started by the French architect **William of Sens**, completed by "William the Englishman". The nave and clois-

ters were rebuilt in Perpendicular style in the 14C; the transepts and towers, including **Bell Harry Tower**, crowning the entire building, were completed in the 15C. The north-west tower was demolished in 1832 and replaced by a copy of the southwest tower.

Along with St Augustine's Abbey and St Martin's church, Canterbury cathedral is listed as a World Heritage Site.

Christ Church Gate★ (D), built in the early-16C and decorated with coats of arms, is the main entrance to the cathedral. **Mercery Lane★**, a bustling street which has kept its medieval charm, offers an impressive view of Christ Church Gate and the western towers.

Interior

Enter through the SW porch.

In the **nave** built (1392–1404) by Henry Yevele, the slender columns soar majestically to the lofty vault and aisles. The great west window (1) contains 12C glass (note Adam delving). Near the north door stands a 17C Classical marble **font** (2) depicting the Four Evangelists and the Twelve Apostles. In the north

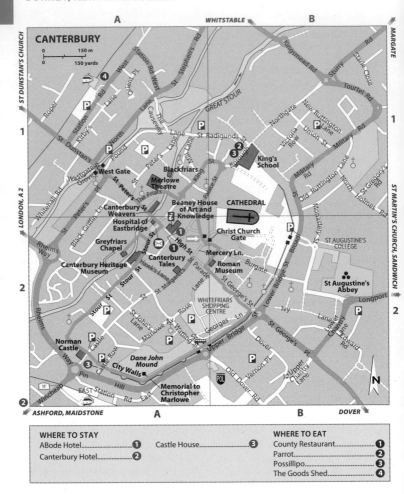

WHERE TO STAY

ABode Hotel	**1**
Canterbury Hotel	**2**
Castle House	**3**

WHERE TO EAT

County Restaurant	**1**
Parrot	**2**
Possillipo	**3**
The Goods Shed	**4**

transept the 'Altar of the Sword's Point' and a modern cruciform sculpture commemorate the **site of Becket's martyrdom** (3). Steps lead down to the 12C vaulted **crypt**. The delicate screens of the **Chapel of Our Lady Undercroft** (4) and the capitals are masterpieces of Romanesque carving. The transept houses the altars of St Nicholas (5) and St Mary Magdalene (6). In the eastern extension (post-1174) with its massive columns and pointed vaults is the site (7) where the body of St Thomas Becket was entombed until 1220. Beyond is the Jesus Chapel (8). The south transept was the Black Prince's Chantry (9), subsequently the Huguenots' Church; it is still used for services in French today.

Leave the crypt on the south side to return to the upper level.

Turn right into the crossing to admire the lace-like **fan vaulting underneath the Bell Harry Tower** (10); the bosses are decorated with coats of arms of those responsible for building the tower. Pass through the iron gates into the choir which contains a mid-15C **screen** (11) with figures of six kings, the High Altar and the 13C marble **St Augustine's Chair** (12) traditionally used for the enthronement of the Archbishop, Primate of All England.

From either of the choir aisles the long vistas back to the nave reveal the evolution of Gothic style over three centuries.

The wonderful medieval **stained-glass** windows include one depicting the Miracles (13) wrought by St Thomas in the Trinity Chapel. His shrine, placed here in 1220, has long gone, though the fine Roman mosaic pavement in front of it remains. Among the remarkable tombs is that of the **Black Prince** (14) (d.1376); above hang replicas of his helm, crest, shield, gauntlets and sword; the fragile originals are displayed nearby. Opposite is the alabaster **tomb of Henry IV** (15) (d.1413) and Queen Joan of Navarre. In the **Corona** (16), a circular chapel said to have housed the top of St Thomas' skull, there is an early-13C **Redemption window** (17) behind the altar.

The **Chapel of St Anselm** (18) – *(SW corner of Trinity Chapel)* is mostly Norman and contains a rare 12C wall painting (high up in the apse). Off the south transept *(main exit)* is the **Chapel of St Michael** (19) with Renaissance and Baroque memorials.

Exterior

The great cathedral with its soaring buttresses, pinnacles and towers above which Bell Harry rises to a height of almost 76m, is an impressive sight. The elaborate vaulting of the galleried **Great Cloister** (rebuilt c.1400) is ornamented with grotesque faces, religious symbols and scenes of everyday life.

Off the east walk is the **Chapter House** with its intricately ribbed oak roof and Perpendicular windows with glass depicting characters in the cathedral's history. On the eastern side of the cathedral precincts is the **King's School★**(B), an ancient foundation remodelled by Henry VIII in 1541. It occupies buildings of the former cathedral monastery grouped in the main around Green Court.

The immense length of the cathedral is best appreciated from this point. Note the splendid **Norman staircase** (12C).

🐾 CITY CENTRE WALK

Start your walk at Christ Church Gate and follow Burgate to the **Canterbury Roman Museum** (Butchery Lane; open Mon–Sat 10am–5pm; closed 1 Jan, Good Fri, 25–26 Dec; £8; &; ℘01227 785 575; www.canterbury-museums.co.uk).

Deep below current street level, part of Canterbury's excavated Roman levels have been transformed into this modern museum, which uses contemporary techniques to bring the Roman city of Durovernum Cantiacorum to life. Authentic reconstructions include a Roman marketplace with stalls and a house with kitchen.

Follow St George's Street to get to the **city walls**. If you leave the old walled city (and our marked tour) to the east on Church Street, you come to **St Augustine's Abbey★★** (open daily Apr–Sept 10am–6pm, Oct 10am–5pm, Nov–Mar Sat–Sun 10am–4pm; closed 1 Jan, 24–26 Dec; £6.20; &; ℘01227 767 345; www.english-heritage.org.uk), founded in 597 by St Augustine. Extensive ruins remain of the great Norman abbey church, such as the early-14C Great Gateway. There are also vestiges of Saxon burial places and of the church of St Pancras (7C); the walls are built of Roman brick. A museum interprets the site.

Continue on Longport to North Holmes Road and take a left for **St Martin's church★** (open Tue, Thu–Fri 11am–3pm, Sat 11am–4pm, Sun 9.45–10.23am; &; ℘01227 768 072; www.martinpaul.org) on St Martin's Hill, the oldest functioning church in England. When St Augustine arrived from Rome in 597 to convert the English, he set up his mission here. It has Roman brickwork in its walls and a Perpendicular tower. Inside there is a Norman font, a Norman *piscina* and a Leper Window.

Returning to the tour marked on the map, walk along the top of the well-preserved medieval **city walls**, stoutly built on Roman foundations. Follow them south and you will come to the **Dane John Mound**, which overlooks a charming park and a **memorial** to Christopher Marlowe, born in Canterbury. At the end of this stretch of the wall you will find the 11C **Norman castle** built of flint with bands of stone, of which only the keep remains.

Head north from here along Stour Street and you will come to the **Canterbury**

Heritage Museum★ 👥 (open days vary 11am–5pm, check website for details; closed 1 Jan, Good Fri, 25–26 Dec; £8, child free (up to 2 per adult); ☏01227 475 202; www.canterbury-museums.co.uk). This modern museum is housed in the Poor Priests' Hospital, founded in the 13C as an almshouse. It presents the history of Canterbury from prehistoric to modern times including lively interactive displays. Oliver Postgate and Peter Firmin created their much-loved children's programmes just outside Canterbury and here you can see the 'real' Bagpuss, original Clangers, Ivor the Engine and Noggin the Nog drawings. Rupert Bear, who was also created by a local lady, is also featured.

On leaving the museum, continue to No.6 Stour Street and take the little alley to your left, then cross the bridge for **Greyfriar's chapel and garden** (*for opening times, see Eastbridge Hospital, below*). This was the first English Franciscan friary, built in 1267. The undercroft was originally a pilgrims' dormitory. Upstairs are the refectory and the chapel. The chapel has a fine timber roof. **Greyfriar's House** is the only building now remaining of the first English Franciscan friary, built in 1267 in the lifetime of St Francis of Assisi, 43 years after the first friars settled in Canterbury. An exhibition explores the history of this important settlement.

Return to Stour Street, then take Hawks Lane and St Margaret Street to reach **The Canterbury Tales** 👥 (open Apr–Aug daily 10am–5pm, Sept–Oct daily 10am–4pm, Nov–Mar Wed–Sun 10am–4pm; closed 1 Jan, 25–26 Dec; £9.95, child £7.95; ♿; ☏01227 454 888; www.canterburytales.org.uk). The converted interior of St Margaret's Church is the setting for this entertaining multimedia attraction, which popularises and brings to life the vivid 14C characters created by Chaucer as they make their pilgrimage from London to Canterbury. Continue up St Margaret Street and turn left on the High Street to see **The Beaney House of Art & Knowledge★** (open Tue–Sat 9am–5pm, Sun noon–5pm; ♿✗; ☏01227 862 162, canterburymuse-

ums.co.uk/beaney), which takes its name from Dr James George Beaney, who died in 1891 and left money in his will to the city of Canterbury. It is worth the visit to see the interiors alone, but before entering, step back to admire its magnificent ornate beamed **facade★**, which dates from 1897, but looks much older. 'The Beaney' is now home to eclectic collections of local art, Dutch stained glass, Egyptology, Ancient Greek Art, a Cabinet of Curiosities, ethnography, natural history, weapons, and more, all of which feature pieces of national importance and are superbly displayed in modern award-winning fashion. The Beaney also houses the tourist information office and Canterbury Library.

Further up the High Street and across the road is the **Hospital of St Thomas the Martyr, Eastbridge** (open Nov–Feb Mon–Sat 11am–4pm; Mar–Oct Mon–Sat 10.30am–5pm; chapel open Easter Mon–Sept Mon–Sat 2–4pm; gardens open Easter Mon–Sept Mon–Sat 10.30am–4pm; ☏01227 471 688; www.eastbridgehospital.org.uk). Founded in 1180, the hospital served as lodgings (in those days hospital meant a place of hospitality) for poor pilgrims to the shrine of St Thomas. After the Dissolution in the 16C, the hospital was re-founded as a boys' school and then as an almshouse, a role it still fulfils today. The building presents a black flint exterior. The 14C door leads into a vaulted hall (11C).

Cross the bridge; on your right you will find the **Canterbury Weavers**. This group of picturesque Tudor houses (by tradition, c.1500) overlooking the River Stour takes its name from the refugee Huguenot weavers who settled in the area. Note the replica of the medieval **ducking stool** that was once located here and which was used to 'test' whether or not a woman was a witch. **Canterbury Historic River Tours** (tours run every 15–20 mins, daily Mar–Oct 10am–5pm; £10.50; ☏07790 534 744; www.canterburyrivertours.co.uk) operate from here. Continue up St Peter's Street to the **Westgate Towers★** (St Peter's Street; ☏01227 378 100). This city landmark is the last of the gatehouses that once formed part of the city walls. From 1830 it served as a gaol and the present museum is devoted to this period. From the battlements there are fine **views** of the city and cathedral.

Continue up St Dunstan's Street (leaving our marked tour) and turn left on London Road to see **St Dunstan's church** (open services only Tue and Sun; ☎01227 472 557). The church was founded in the late-1C and used by Henry II in 1174 when he changed into penitential garments for his involvement in the murder of St Thomas Becket. The head of Sir Thomas More is thought to be buried in the Roper family vault. Return back down St Peter's Street; up St Peter's Lane is **Blackfriars Monastery**. All that remains of this 13C Dominican friary are the Great Hall and the Refectory. Back on St Peter's Street, continue towards the West Gate and turn left on The Friars to see the splendid **Marlowe Theatre**. Cross the Stour and turn left on King Street; turn right on Palace Street and continue on Sun Street. The walk takes

in beautiful medieval buildings, including **Conquest House** and **Tudor House**.

EXCURSION
♣♣ Howletts Wild Animal Park
❯ Bekesbourne Road, Bekesbourne. 3mi/5km S off the A 2. Open year-round daily. Late Mar–late Oct 9.30am–6pm, winter 9.30am–5pm. Closed 25 Dec. £18.95, child £15.95 (discount online). ♿🅿✕ ☎01227 721 286. www.aspinallfoundation.org/howletts.

Set in 36ha of ancient parkland, Howletts is famous as the home of the world's largest family group of gorillas in captivity and the UK's largest group of African elephants. Among the 90 or so other rare and endangered species from around the world are tigers and clouded leopards, black rhinos, tapirs and giant anteaters.

The **Treetop Challenge** (additional charge) ropes, nets and zip-wires course gives adventurous visitors a monkey's-eye view of the park.

Cinque Ports★

Traditionally pronounced 'sink', even though it refers to the French for five, the Cinque Ports was a maritime league of Kent and Sussex towns established in the 11C by Edward the Confessor to supply ships and men for the defence of the realm. The five were Dover, Hastings, Hythe, New Romney and Sandwich, with Rye and Winchelsea later added, with the title of 'ancient towns'. This defence, and sometime offence, was against the French, who at the nearest point – from Dover to Cap Gris Nez – are just 21mi/34km distant. The towns today have very different functions and characteristics and modern Dover's remit is mostly to welcome, not repel, foreign visitors. Ironically, Hasting's most famous moment was in 1066 when William of Normandy won the final major battle in the conquest of England.

- ⓖ **Michelin Map:** 504
- ⓝ **Don't Miss:** Dover Castle, Bodiam Castle, Rye;
- ♣♣ **Kids:** Dover Castle Secret Wartime Tunnels.

DOVER★
84mi/134km southeast of London. Dover Priory train station (Approach Road) has a frequent service and shuttle buses to the docks. Fastest train time to London, St Pancras via Ashford Intl. 1h20. Bus station: Pencester Road. Both are a 5min walk from the centre.
🄸 Dover Museum, Market Square. ☎01304 201 066. www.whitecliffscountry.org.uk.

Flanked by the iconic white cliffs, Dover has been the southeast gateway to England since Roman times, receiving sailing ships, steamships and hovercraft. Despite the opening of the Channel Tunnel, the port's cross-Channel ferry traffic remains intense. Dover was badly damaged during the Second World War, but retains many historic properties giving the town islands of elegance rarely seen in a working port. German bombs and shells from batteries on the French coast devastated Dover but, with postwar redevelopment, helped reveal the archaeology of this ancient port.

Head east from Dover Priory train station and you come to York Street, then New Street, home to the **Roman Painted House** (open 10am–5pm: 1st 2 wks Apr Tue–Sun; last week Apr–end May Tue and Sat; Jun–Sept Tue–Sat; £3; ✆01304 203 279; www.theromanpaintedhouse.co.uk), which has the finest Roman wall-decorations to be seen in situ north of the Alps. Just around the corner is the **Dover Museum** (Market Square; open year-round Mon–Sat 9.30am–5pm (also Apr–Sept Sun 10am–3pm); closed 1 Jan, 25–26 Dec; £4.20; ♿; ✆01304 201 066; www.dovermuseum.co.uk), whose artefacts include a 15m section of the world's oldest known seagoing boat, the 3 000-year-old **Dover Bronze Age boat**.

Just outside the centre, at Langdon Cliffs, Upper Road is **The White Cliffs of Dover**, with dramatic clifftop countryside and a Visitor Centre managed by the National Trust (visitor centre open daily Mar–Oct 10am–5pm (5.30pm mid-Jul–early Sept), Nov–Feb 11am–4pm; closed 24–26 Dec; ♿; 🅿 (£3.50); ✗; ✆01304 207 326; www.nationaltrust.org.uk/white-cliffs-dover). This excellent modern facility offers spectacular views of the chalk cliffs and views across the world's busiest shipping lanes to France. You can also begin clifftop walks from here.

👥 Dover Castle★★

Open daily year-round from 10am. Late Mar–Sept (Aug 9.30am) closes 6pm; Oct closes 5pm; Nov–late Mar Sat–Sun 10am–4pm. Closed 1 Jan, 24–26 Dec. £19.40, child (5–15) £11.60. 🅿✗ ✆01304 211 067. www.english-heritage.org.uk.

The high land to the east, commanding town and port, has been fortified since the Iron Age. The Romans built a lighthouse (Pharos) which still stands within the castle walls, and the Saxons a church (St-Mary-in-Castro). The defences were strengthened by William the Conqueror, then by Henry II, who in the 1180s added the splendid **keep**. The spectacular **Constable's Tower** dates from the early-13C. The warren of tunnels and secret chambers beneath the castle dates from early times but was greatly added to in the Napoleonic period and during the Second World War. Operation Dynamo, the evacuation from Dunkirk in 1940, was planned and directed from here.

A guided tour (timed ticket system) of the **Secret Wartime Tunnels★ 👥** takes visitors through the dimly lit chambers and passageways of the underground hospital and communications centre for the Combined Headquarters. A dramatic exhibition vividly re-creates the Dunkirk evacuation, complete with dramatic projections of swooping Spitfires and real film footage.

SANDWICH★

3mi/21km E via the A 257. 🚹 Guildhall, Cattle Market. ✆01304 613565.

The road from Canterbury runs through the pretty village of **Wingham**. The fascinating medieval borough of Sandwich was one of the original Cinque Ports, is still largely contained within its earthen ramparts and seems to have changed little since the River Stour began to silt up in the 15C. Its pretty houses of all periods cluster around its three **churches**: St Clement's with a sturdy, arcaded Norman tower; St Peter's with a cupola reflecting Flemish influence; and St Mary's, much reduced by the collapse of its tower in 1668.

DEAL

8mi/13km N via A258.

🚹 Town Hall, High St. ✆01304 369 576.

Once one of the busiest ports in England, now a quiet resort, this is one of the most attractive seaside towns in Kent.

Deal Castle (&; open daily year-round from 10am; late Mar–Sept closes 6pm; Oct closes 5pm; Nov–late Mar closes 4pm; closed 1 Jan, 24–26 Dec; £6.60; P &01304 372 762; www.english-heritage. org.uk) marks the site where Julius Caesar is alleged to have first landed in Britain in 55 BCE. It is one of the finest Tudor artillery castles in England, and among the most elaborate of a chain of coastal forts that included Walmer Castle.

WALMER CASTLE

1mi/1.6km S of Deal. &Open daily year-round from 10am. Late Mar–Sept closes 6pm; Oct–late Mar closes 4pm. Closed 1 Jan, 5–7 Jul, 24–26 Dec. £10.70. P X &01304 364 288. www.english-heritage.org.uk.

Built by order of Henry VIII, this fine Tudor rose-shaped castle evolved into the official residence of the Lord Warden of the Cinque Ports (€ see Rye, below). The most notable incumbents were the Duke of Wellington – the armchair in which he died and an original pair of 'Wellington boots', worn at Waterloo, are on display – and the late Queen Elizabeth, the Queen Mother, who made regular visits to the castle. Beautiful gardens adjoin the house with fine coastal views.

ROMNEY AND DENGE MARSHES

31mi/50km southwest via the coast road. This area of reclaimed marshland and mile after mile of shingle is a marked contrast to the rest of Kent's green pasturelands. Locally, it is best known for Dungeness power station.

Close by, near Lydd, is the **RSPB Dungeness** bird reserve (open daily 9am–9pm, or dusk if earlier, visitor centre open Mar–Oct 10am–5pm, Nov–Feb 10am–4pm; closed 25–26 Dec; &01797 320 588; www.rspb.org.uk).

The most interesting way to arrive here is aboard the 'world's smallest public railway'. The **Romney, Hythe and Dymchurch Railway** (operates year-round, see website for schedule and fares; &01797 362 353; www.rhdr.org.uk) is a 15-in gauge line, built in 1927 and operating steam and diesel trains between Hythe and Dungeness via Dymchurch, St Mary's Bay, Romney Warren, New Romney and Romney Sands stations (journey time around 65 minutes).

RYE★★

36mi/58km SW of Dover.
🛈 The Old Sail Loft , Strand Quay, Rye. &01797 226 696. www.ryeheritage. co.uk, or www.visitrye.co.uk.

This exquisite little hill town standing at the confluence of three rivers is visible far across the vast expanse of eastward-stretching levels – a multitude of red-roofed houses building up to a massive squat-towered church. Tranquil centuries of decline and its former remoteness have preserved Rye's charming townscape, though much of its medieval fabric wears a Georgian exterior. Many artists and writers, among them Henry James, have lived here.

Rye's early history was one of struggle both on and with the sea. It lies just 40mi/64km northwest of Boulogne and was added to the Cinque Ports; despite this it suffered repeated sackings by the French. It was also battered by storms that changed the course of the River Rother in the 13C and later destroyed many of its buildings. The town is still a minor port, though the sea's retreat has left it 2mi/3km inland.

Old Town★★

With its steep narrow streets, a wealth of different building materials and sudden glimpses of the countryside, Rye is ideal for exploring on foot.

Cobbled **Mermaid Street★** rises sharply. Its varied buildings include the 15C **Mermaid Inn**, once the haunt of ruthless smuggler gangs. Looking towards Church Square is the handsome Georgian façade of **Lamb House** (open mid-Mar/Apr–late Oct Tue and Sat 2–6pm; £6; &01580 762 334), home of Henry James from 1897 and later of the satirical novelist E F Benson.

South of Cinque Ports Street is **St Mary's church** (open daily, except during services, 9.15am–5.30pm/winter 4.30pm; &; &01797 224 935, www.ryeparish

church.org.uk), a large impressive building, begun in the 12C. Note the 16C clock, its pendulum (5m) swinging inside, its elaborate face on the outside of the north transept, flanked by jolly painted quarter boys who strike the quarters (but not the hours). From the tower (donation requested) there is an incomparable **view★** of Rye's rooftops and its countryside.

BODIAM CASTLE★

13mi/21km NW on the A 268. After 11mi/18km turn left at Sandhurst and follow minor roads. Open mid-Feb–Dec daily 10.30am–5pm; 1st week Jan–mid-Feb Sat–Sun 10.30am–4pm. Closed 24–25 Dec. £9.30. ♿🅿 (charge). ✗ ✆01580 830 196. www.nationaltrust. org.uk/bodiam-castle.

In a pretty landscaped setting among low hills, overlooking the levels of the River Rother, this perfect example of a late medieval castle sits four-square within its protecting moat. It was built in 1385–88 to block movement inland by marauding Frenchmen up the (then navigable) river, and it retains its great gatehouse, curtain walls and drum towers (18m high) at each corner.

HASTINGS
Jerwood Gallery★

Rock-a-Nore Road. Open Tue–Sun (and Bank Holiday Mons) 11am–5pm. £9, 1st Tue month free 4–8pm. ♿✗ ✆01424 728377. www.jerwoodgallery.org.

Overlooking the historic fishing beach in Hastings' picturesque Old Town, the RIBA-award winning Jerwood Gallery opened in 2012. It is home to the Jerwood Collection of 20–21C art and hosts changing contemporary exhibitions. The collection includes works by well-known artists including Sir Stanley Spencer, L S Lowry, Walter Sickert and Augustus John.

Note from the gallery windows the unique local fisherman's black two-storey beach huts, called '**net shops**', used for equipment storage. Set among these huts, in a mid-19C church, is the **Hastings Fishermen's Museum** (Rock-a-Nore Road; open daily, except during services, Apr –Oct 10am–5pm, Nov–Mar 11am–4pm; ✆01424 461 446. www.ohps. org.uk).

Hastings Castle and The 1066 Story

Castle Hill Road. 12mi/19km SW on the A 259. Open Apr–Oct daily 10am–5pm; winter daily 11am–4pm. £4.75 (cash only). ✆01424 781 776. www. discoverhastings.co.uk.

The ruins of William the Conqueror's first English castle stand high above the old town and seaside resort below. The history of the castle and the famous battle of 1066 are told in an entertaining audio-visual presentation.

BATTLE★

18mi/29km southwest on the A 259, B 2093 and A 2100.

The momentous victory, on 14 October 1066, of the Normans over King Harold's English army is marked by the remains of the great commemorative **Battle Abbey★** (open Apr–Sept daily 10am–6pm, Oct daily 10am–5pm, Nov–Mar Sat–Sun 10am–4pm; closed 1 Jan, 24–26 Dec; £11.20; ♿🖨🅿(charge); ✗ ✆01424 775 705. www.english-heritage. org.uk), built on its hilltop site by William the Conqueror. The **1066 Battle of Hastings** exhibition features CGI film and interactive displays to tell the story of the great battle and paints a picture of England at the time of the Conquest. There is also an audio tour of the battlefield.

Over the humble buildings of the town's marketplace rises the imposing 14C **gatehouse**, battlemented and richly decorated. Most of the great Benedictine abbey beyond was dismantled at the Dissolution. The church altar, erected at William's command, is above the spot where Harold fell.

A **museum** in the gatehouse presents the history of the abbey.

Battlefield★

From the **terrace walk** there is a view of the tranquil scene over which the battles was fought. The day-long battle was fierce and bloody; a pathway with topographical models at intervals follows its course along the fateful slopes.

WINCHELSEA

40mi/65km SW of Dover.

Winchelsea was founded by Edward I to take the place of an older town of the same name, which had been lost to the sea in a series of great storms and now lies beneath the waters of Rye Bay. It rose to become one of the major ports of the region and was added to the Cinque Ports. Like Rye it was pillaged by the French; the ruined St Thomas church is a reminder of this period as are its three medieval gates. Unlike Rye, however, the town today is quiet and not on the tourist trail.

BATEMAN'S

Bateman's Lane. 0.5mi/0.8km S of Burwash. 58mi/93km W of Dover via the A 20 and A 259. Open Apr–Oct daily 11am–5pm; 1st 3 wks Dec daily 11am–3pm. £10.40. ♿🅿️✖️ ✆01435 882 302. www.nationaltrust.org.uk. Surrounded by the wooded landscape of the Sussex Weald, this handsome sturdy 17C house, with its mullioned windows and oak beams, was the home of Rudyard Kipling from 1902 until he died here in 1936. When Kipling moved in it had no bathroom, no running water upstairs and no electricity but he still loved it. Today the rooms, described by Kipling as 'untouched and unfaked', remain much as he left them, with Oriental rugs and artefacts reflecting his strong association with the East, as immortalised in his poetry such as 'Mandalay' and 'Gunga Din' and, of course, in his classic stories *The Jungle Book*.

Brighton to Eastbourne★★

If Brighton is the trendy young star of the south coast, Eastbourne is the reliable old timer, now with a fashionable important gallery of its own, and some stunning coastline. Lewes is a charming inland detour.

BRIGHTON★★

55mi/88km due S of London.
🚩 Royal Pavilion Shop, Royal Pavilion. ✆01273 290 337. www.visitbrighton.com. Trains and buses run here frequently from London (London Bridge or Victoria, around 1h) ; the train station (Queen's Road) is a 5–10-min walk from the centre, while the bus station (Old Steine) is centrally located just back from the seafront. The town is compact and easily explored on foot. To get an overview, jump aboard the **City Sightseeing** open-top bus (✆01273 886 200;

- ⛪ **Michelin Map:** Map 504.
- 👁 **Don't Miss:** In Brighton: The Royal Pavilion; The Lanes and the North Laine. The Bluebell Railway, running on the East/West Sussex border.
- 🕐 **Timing:** In summer you'll want to spend at least one night in Brighton to catch some of its famous evening nightlife. The Brighton Festival runs for three weeks every May, and is the biggest mixed arts festival in England. www.brightonfestival.org.
- 👥 **Kids:** Pier; Sea Life Centre.

www.city-sightseeing.com), or take the Volks Railway for a 1.2mi/2km ride along the beachfront (www.volkselectric railway.co.uk).

Brighton is where the English seaside tradition was born and brought to a pitch of perfection. Within easy reach of the capital, the town has long been a weekend retreat for Londoners. Its south-facing beach is punctuated by piers and backed by a wide promenade and elegant Georgian, Regency and Victorian architecture. The labyrinthine lanes of the old fishing town, with their jewellers and trendy shops, contrast with lavishly planted open spaces and parkways.

Modern Brighton began in the mid-18C with the promotion by Dr Richard Russell of the healthy effect of drinking and bathing in seawater.

The town received a royal seal of approval from the Prince of Wales, following his first visit in 1783. From the 1840s the London, Brighton and South Coast Railway brought ever-increasing numbers of holidaymakers of all social classes to what had truly become 'London-by-the-Sea'. Today's mature town has remained young, stage-managing its raffish appeal to attract successive generations of visitors, while acquiring all the ingredients of a miniature metropolis: specialist shops, trendy restaurants, entertainments of all kinds, including a year-round calendar bursting with festivals, and on its outskirts, the modern University of Sussex.

Royal Pavilion★★★

Open daily Apr–Sept 9.30am–5.45pm (last tickets 5pm); Oct–Mar 10am –5.15pm. Closed from 2.30pm on 24 Dec and all day 25–26 Dec. £11.70 (10% online discount, bought at least 1 day in advance). & (ground floor only). ✕ ℰ0300 0290 900. http://brighton museums.org.uk/royalpavilion.

This fantastic Oriental confection in stucco and stone reflects the brilliant personality of George Augustus Frederick, Prince of Wales 1762–1811, Regent 1811–20, finally **King George IV**.

Its exotic gateways and extraordinary silhouette, all bulbous domes, pinnacles, turrets and spikes pricking the skyline, are a free interpretation of 'Hindoo' architecture. Within, throughout

a series of gorgeously furnished and decorated interiors, Chinoiserie prevails, taken to astonishing lengths in the **Music Room**, lit by lotus-shaped gaseliers, where painted serpents and dragons writhe beneath the gilded scales of a great dome. Equally sumptuous is the great **Banqueting Room**; from its dome (14m high) hangs a one-ton crystal lighting device, at its apex a huge winged dragon in silver outlined against enormous *trompe l'œil* plantain leaves. The refurbished **royal apartments** on the first floor are reached by a staircase whose cast-iron bannister is cunningly disguised as bamboo.

All this exuberance is set in restored **gardens**, remodelled and planted as near as possible to its Regency state.

Also in the gardens, the Pavilion's former stables are home to the splendid **Brighton Museum and Art Gallery★** (open Tue–Sun and Bank Holiday Mons 10am–5pm; closed 1 Jan, from 2.30pm on 24 Dec and all day 25–26 Dec; £5.20; & ✕; ℰ0300 0 290 900; http://brightonmuseums.org.uk/brighton). In addition to its local history collection, Dutch and English paintings, porcelain and pottery, and its fashion and ethnographical gallery, the intimate interior also houses a well-presented display of 20C decorative arts.

Seafront★★

The meeting of Victorian Brighton and the sea is marked by a broad **promenade**, carried on massive brick vaults and with generous ramps and stairs leading to a roadway at beach level. A wealth of light-hearted detail, from splendid decorative ironwork to jaunty little kiosks and shelters, sets the holiday mood, and is extended into the sea on the **West Pier** of 1866 and Palace Pier, now **Brighton Pier** 👥 (open daily from 10am, 9am school summer holidays, closed 25 Dec; &; ℰ01273 609 361; www.brightonpier.co.uk), a lively place of fun-fair-style rides and amusements – from traditional to the 21C thrill variety – and refreshments. Close by is the **Sea Life Centre** (👥 Marine Parade open from 10am daily, except 25 Dec; tickets from

£10.50; &; ℘0871 423 2110; www.vis-itsealife.com) offering a variety of ways to view marine life at close quarters in the original Victorian vaulted aquarium – the largest in the world when it opened in 1872. The pioneering electric **Volks Railway** of 1883 runs eastwards along the foot of the cliff to the **Marina** (☝see above).

Within the continuous wall of seafront building is a succession of architectural set-pieces: the most distinguished is **Brunswick Square** (1825–27), with stucco, bow windows, Classical details and elegant ironwork; the earliest is **Royal Crescent** (1798–1807), in black mathematical tiles; the grandest, to the east, is the Victorian panache and elegance of **Lewes Crescent/Sussex Square**, (1823 onwards), exemplified in the many-storeyed and richly decorated Grand and Metropole hotels.

Town Centre

The Lanes★, a maze of animated old town alleyways, lined with countless boutiques and antique shops, focuses on **Brighton Square**.

To the east lie the quirky, bohemian boutique, music, clothes and alternative lifestyle shops, not to mention a huge range of places to eat and drink, of the **North Laine**. Tucked away behind the train station to the northeast, **St Bartholomew's★** (Ann Street; open Mon–Sat 10am–1pm, 2–4.30pm; ℘01273 620 491; www.stbartholomewsbrighton.org.uk) is the most outstanding of Brighton's many Victorian churches. The sublime simplicity of patterned brick walls carrying the nave to the awesome height of 41m contrasts with rich **furnishings** (Lady Altar, main altarpiece, giant candlesticks), masterworks of the Arts and Crafts Movement.

EASTBOURNE

22mi/35km E of Brighton.
🛈 Cornfield Road. ℘01323 415 415. www.visiteastbourne.com.
This attractive but rather staid resort, where Charles Dickens and Lewis Carroll once holidayed, is these days known mostly for being a retirement town. Its handsome Victorian seafront, Grand Parade, features most of the usual favourite British seaside icons including a very fine traditional pier.

A couple of blocks inland is the town's main cultural attraction, the ultra-modern **Towner Art Gallery** (open year-round Tue–Sun and Bank Holiday Mons 10am–5pm, &✕; ℘01323 434 670; www.townereastbourne.org.uk). It hosts major exhibitions of contemporary and historic visual art, alongside changing displays from the Towner Collection. From the windows of the Towner café you can see the **South Downs**, Britain's newest national park. Spend a day walking or cycling through this beautiful landscape, perhaps along the coast to the famous lighthouse at **Beachy Head★** or a little further to the spectacular **Seven Sisters★** chalk cliffs.

LEWES★

9mi/14km NE of Brighton.
🛈 187 High Street, ℘01273 483 448. www.staylewes.org.
Perched on a hilltop, Lewes was originally a strategic Saxon stronghold on account of its commanding coastal views. The value of the site was also appreciated by William de Warenne, who built his castle here soon after the Conquest. In 1264 Simon de Montfort's rebellion against Henry III led to the defeat of the royal forces at the **Battle of Lewes**, fought on nearby Mount Harry. The religious conflicts of the 16C were marked by the burning at the stake of 17 Protestant martyrs, commemorated (along with Guy Fawkes and the Gunpowder Plot) on 5 November with torchlit processions, tar-barrel rolling, fireworks and giant bonfires. Today Lewes is one of the few places in Britain where the rolling of burning tar barrels on Bonfire Night still happens and the spectacle draws huge crowds.

For the other 364 days of the year it reverts to being a charming, characterful little county town with a fine architectural heritage.

Town and Castle

The well-preserved **High Street★**, with its independent shops, features a delightful variety of traditional building materials: flint, stone, brick, timber, stucco, hung tiles, and the local speciality, 'mathematical tiles', which in the 18C were used on older timber buildings to simulate a fashionable brick façade. Cobbled **Keere Street★** is very pretty, dropping steeply downhill to a fragment of the old town walls and to **Southover Grange**, built of stone taken from the priory.

In Southover High Street is the beautiful Tudor timber-framed **Anne of Cleves' House**, now a local history museum (open Mar–Oct Tue–Sat 10am–5pm, Son–Mon and bank holidays 11am–4pm; Feb and Nov Tue–Sat 10am–4pm: 11am on Sun, Mon and Bank Holidays; ℘01273 474 610; £5.90; www.sussexpast.co.uk).

Entry to **Lewes Castle** is via **Barbican House**, a fine 16C timber-framed building with a late Georgian façade. It too is now home to a local museum (open Nov–Feb Tue–Sat 10am–3.45pm, 11am on Sun–Mon and bank holidays; Mar–Oct 10am–5.30pm: 11am on Sun, Mon and Bank Holidays; closed 1 Jan; £7.70; ℘01273 486 290; www.sussexpast.co.uk). A perfect flint-built 14C **barbican** also guards the castle precinct. From one of its towers there are fine **views★** of the town and the gracefully sculpted outlines of the chalk hills all around.

SHEFFIELD PARK AND GARDEN★

9.5mi/15km N via the A 275. Open daily: Jan–Feb and mid-Nov–Dec 10am–4pm; Mar–mid-Nov 10am–5pm. £11.20. &🅿✕ ℘01825 790 231. www.nationaltrust.org.uk.

This magnificent informal landscape garden was laid out in the 18C by 'Capability' Brown with four **lakes** linked by cascades. It was enriched early this century with thousands of trees and shrubs from around the world.

BLUEBELL RAILWAY

Operates year-round, visit website or call for schedule and fares. &🅿✕ ℘01825 720 800 (general enquiries). www.bluebell-railway.com.

Nostalgically preserved **steam trains** of Britain's first preserved standard gauge passenger railway run along 11mi/17.6km of the old London Brighton and South Coast Railway company track. This is one of the best known steam railway lines in the country and at peak holiday times is very busy.

GLYNDEBOURNE

3mi/5km E of Lewes.

A picnic on the lawn at the **Glyndebourne Festival** (http://glyndebourne.com) is, for some people, as indispensable a part of the English summer as strawberries and cream at Wimbledon. Glyndebourne is the only unsubsidised opera house in the country and during the festival presents six productions each year, from mid/late May to August, in a 1 200-seat opera house. Prices and quality are high.

CHARLESTON

7mi/11km E of Lewes, between Firle and Selmeston. Open Mar–Oct Wed–Sun and bank holiday Mon 11.30am–5.30pm. £12.50. 🅿✕ ℘01323 811 626; www.charleston.org.uk.

In 1916, this handsome former farmhouse became the country home and meeting place for the writers, painters and intellectuals known as the **Bloomsbury Group**, the most famous of these being Virginia Woolf. The interior was painted by the artists Duncan Grant and Vanessa Bell (Virginia Woolf's lover and sister respectively), and there is a changing programme of exhibitions in the gallery, including works by Renoir, Picasso, Derain, Sickert and Delacroix. There is also a charming walled garden created by Bell and Grant to designs by Roger Fry.

Chichester★★

and around

On the flatlands between the South Downs and the sea, Chichester and its picturebook cathedral spire present a quintessential English scene.

CHICHESTER★★

Many English towns grew up around their cathedral, but Chichester was already a thousand years old before the cathedral was considered. The main arteries of North, South, East and West Streets, which run off the ornamental **Market Cross** (1501), still conform to their original Roman plan. Chichester enjoyed a golden age in the 18C and the harmonious Georgian townscape is best seen in **The Pallants**. In the heart of Chichester, close to the Market Cross (the centrepoint of the city's main pedestrianised shopping streets), is the **cathedral★★** (West Street; open Mon–Sat 7.15am–6.30pm, Sun 7.15am–5pm; guided tour (45min) Mon–Sat 11.15am and 2.30pm; ＆.✕. ℘01243 782 595; www.chichestercathedral.org.uk).

The cathedral took almost 100 years to build, from 1091 to 1184. The interior is Romanesque in style and spirit and its austere nave is Norman, though every architectural movement of the Middle Ages has left its mark. The nave is best viewed looking west, when it appears small, almost intimate. Its splendid screen is Perpendicular Gothic. The Lady Chapel ceiling paintings are notable but the cathedral's greatest treasures are the 12C **stone panels★★** in the south choir aisle; they depict scenes from the Raising of Lazarus and are among the finest examples of Norman sculpture in England. In the south transept, lit by a Decorated window, are early-16C paintings of the cathedral. In the north transept is the grave of the composer Gustav Holst (1874–1934); east of this is a stained-glass window by Marc Chagall (1887–1985).

One block due east from the cathedral is North Pallant Street, home to the

---

👤 **Michelin Map:** 503.

ℹ **Info:** The Novium, Tower Street, ℘01243 775 888. www.visitchichester.org.

▷ **Location:** 81mi/130km SW of London on the River Lavant, very close to the south coast. Trains and buses run regularly from London (Victoria 1h30). The train station is on Stockbridge Road, the bus station close by at South Street; both are a 10min walk from the centre.

🅿 **Parking:** Park by the river for the classic view.

🕓 **Timing:** Allow half a day for Chichester and a few more for the area.

👀 **Don't Miss:** Chichester Cathedral's Norman stone panels; Arundel castle, the home of the Duke of Norfolk.

Pallant House Gallery★ (9 North Pallant; open Tue–Wed, Fri–Sat 10am–5pm, Thu 10am–8pm, Sun and Bank Holidays 11am–5pm; £11, Tue and Thu £5.50 ＆; ℘01243 774 557; www.pallant.org.uk). Built in 1712. This Queen Anne town house is now home to one of the best collections of 20C British art. Chichester's latest visitor attraction is **The Novium** (Tower Street; open Apr–Oct Mon–Sat 10am–5pm, Sun 4pm; Nov–Mar Mon–Sat 10am–5pm; ＆; ℘01243 775 888, www.thenovium.org), the town's principal history museum, now on a new site in a new building, above Chichester's Roman bath house remains, which are open to the public for the first time.

PETWORTH HOUSE★★

14mi/23km NE on the A 27 and A 285. **House**: open mid-Mar–early Nov daily 11am–5pm. **Grounds**: Open mid-Jan–Dec. £13.50 (park and grounds only, free). ＆🅿(£4) ✕ ℘01798 342 207. www.nationaltrust.org.uk.

This grand 17C mansion (1688) contains the National Trust's finest collection of art. The **grounds★★**, by Lancelot 'Capability' Brown, enjoy fine views of the South Downs.

Interior – The rooms contain exquisite carvings, antique statuary and a superb collection of paintings. The most spectacular feature is the **Grand Staircase** with its painted walls and ceiling by Laguerre. The **Turner Room** contains the largest collection of his works outside the Tate Gallery. Other famous artists represented are Reynolds, Van Dyck and Kneller. Lely's *Children of Charles I* hangs in the Oak Hall, Bosch's *Adoration of the Magi* in the Dining Room. **Grinling Gibbons'** carvings adorn the **Carved Room**.

WEALD & DOWNLAND OPEN AIR MUSEUM★★

6mi/10km N on the A 286. Open Mar–23 Dec daily 10.30am–5.30pm (winter 4pm). £13.50. ♿🅿✕ ✆01243 811 363. www.wealddown.co.uk.

Fifty historic buildings have been re-erected on the beautiful Downland slopes. They include a cottage, shop, farmhouse, Tudor market hall, working watermill, toll cottage and school. Many of the interiors have also been re-created and there are daily demonstrations of typical bygone rural activities.

FISHBOURNE ROMAN PALACE★★

1.5mi/2.4km W on the A 259. Open Feb and Nov–mid-Dec daily 10am–4pm; Mar–Oct daily 10am–5pm. £9.20. ♿🅿✕ ✆01243 785 859. www.sussexpast.co.uk.

This splendid palace, built c.75, was probably the home of Cogidubnus, an ally of Imperial Rome. The lavish complex, the largest Roman home in Britain, included guest lodgings and grand colonnades, burned down in the 3C.

The rich **mosaics★** and the tableaux tracing the history of the palace are highlights.

BIGNOR ROMAN VILLA

Pulborough. 13mi/21km NE on the A 27 and A 29. Open daily Mar–Oct 10am–5pm. £6. ♿🅿✕ ✆01798 869 259. www.bignorromanvilla.co.uk.

Some of the finest Roman **mosaics★** in England are preserved here at this Roman farm uncovered in 1811 by a farmer's plough.

Also of interest are the Georgian covering buildings that have protected the site so well for nearly 200 years and a modern traditional farm, set in beautiful South Downs countryside.

ARUNDEL

11mi/18km E on the A 27.
✆01903 885866. www.arundel.org.uk.

This prosperous hilltop town, picturesquely situated beside the quiet River Arun, is the most attractive small town in West Sussex. Its old characterful streets manage to retain a local feel even though they are also dotted with contemporary art galleries, antique and chichi shops, aimed at London day-trippers, and are a delight to wander, particularly during the August Festival. The town is dominated by **Arundel Castle★★** (open Apr–Oct Tue–Sun and Aug Mons 10am–5pm; £13–£20; ♿🅿✕; ✆01903 882 173; www.arundelcastle.org). This spectacular fortress is the home of the Duke of Norfolk, the premier duke of England. The original Norman **gatehouse and keep** (1138) survive after 750 years of assaults and sieges. Climb up its 131 steps to enjoy panoramic views. In the castle's Victorian rooms are the **Chapel** and **Barons' Hall** (paintings by Mytens, Kneller, Van Loo and Van Dyck); in the **Drawing Room** hang portraits by Van Dyck, Gainsborough and Reynolds. The Gothic Revival-style **Library** (37m long) dates from c.1800. On the boundary of the castle grounds stands the Decorated private **Fitzalan Chapel**, crowded with tombs and monuments to the Norfolk dynasty.

The great French Gothic-style hulk of **Arundel cathedral** (open year-round daily 9am–6pm; ✆01903 882 297. www.arundelcathedral.org), is metaphorically and, at certain times of the day, literally overshadowed by the castle above. Built in 1870, its exterior is arguably more impressive than its interior.

Kent Weald★

Weald derives from the German Wald (meaning woods) and although the forest has mostly long gone, the bucolic nature of Kent's rolling hills remains. In harmony with the landscape are some of England's finest gardens, country houses and pretty villages, while the regional centre, Tunbridge Wells is the very epitome of a genteel southern English town.

Don't Miss: Knole, Ightam Mote.
Kids: Hever Castle.

ROYAL TUNBRIDGE WELLS

42mi/68km SE of London. Train station south end of High Street: London service – London Bridge Station 48 min. The Corn Exchange, The Pantiles. 01892 515 675. www.visittunbridgewells.com.

A graceful combination of Georgiana and Victoriana, amid parks, vistas and a vast semi-wild common, Tunbridge Wells owes its good fortune to the accidental discovery of its mineral springs in 1606 by Lord North. As a result it soon became a draw for the fashionable, most famously, Queen Henrietta Maria, who spent six weeks here, in a tent, after the birth of her son, Charles II. Queen Anne provided the tiled paving after which The Pantiles are named and Queen Victoria, who spent holidays here, commented "Dear Tunbridge Wells, I am so fond of it."

The Pantiles★

This perfect pedestrian precinct is on two levels, with an Upper Walk and a Lower Walk. The **Bath House** (1804) still shows off its spring; the **Corn Exchange** (1802), once a theatre, displays Doric columns and Ceres, Goddess of the Harvest, on the roof; and the **Music Gallery** remains a reminder of the town's past elegance. **Union House** (1969, by Michael Levell) at one end of The Pantiles is an object lesson on how old and new can stand together in dignity. The 17C **Church of King Charles the Martyr** at the other end is also worth a visit. **Calverley Park★** – Not so much a park as a Neoclassical new town by Decimus Burton. Inspired by Bath, it is best seen around Calverley Park Crescent.

KNOLE★★

Sevenoaks. 15mi/24km north on the A 26, A 21 and A 225. **House**: limited opening due to conservation work Tue–Sun noon–4pm. £3.15. ♿; P (£4); ✕. 01732 462 100. www.nationaltrust.org.uk.

This great late medieval, Tudor and Jacobean mansion – the childhood home of **Vita Sackville-West**, English poet, novelist and gardener (1892–1962) – is one of the finest buildings of its kind in England. The present building and its collection reflects the efforts of the Earls of Dorset in the 17C–18C. The **Great Hall** with its exquisite Jacobean screen is impressive. The elaborate grisaille décor of the **Great Staircase** sets off a life-size nude of the beauty Gianetta Baccelli in the lobby; the second-oldest harpsichord case made in England in 1622 is displayed in the **Spangle Dressing Room**. The rooms are ornamented with splendid friezes, ceilings, panelling and chimney-pieces, in particular the **Ballroom**, **Crimson Drawing Room** and **Cartoon Gallery**, where are displayed ornate furnishings and fine paintings (17C–18C family portraits, works by Lely, Reynolds and copies of Raphael's Cartoons).

Pick of the Weald

Surrounding Tunbridge Wells are some of southern England's loveliest villages: Beneden, Brenchley and Goudhurst in particular, and the market town of Cranbrook with its picturesque working windmill, are all well worth the detour.

Ightham Mote

© Y. Duhamel/MICHELIN

The highlight of Knole is the **King's Room**, with its gaudy grisailles, ostrich feathers, expensive embroidery and silver ornamentation.

IGHTHAM MOTE★★

Ivy Hatch. 10mi/16km N on the A 26 and A 227. House open Mar–Oct Wed–Mon 11am–5pm; Nov–Dec daily 11am–3pm. £11.50, Oct–Dec Sat–Sun £5.40. ♿🅿✕ ✆01732 810 378. www.nationaltrust. org.uk /ightham-mote.

Ightham (pronounced 'item'), built of stone and timber in 1340, is the best-preserved moated manor house in England; its survival is probably largely due to its secluded site. The crenellated gatehouse leads into the courtyard, where the atmosphere is one of calm and privacy. Opposite is the **Great Hall**, built in the 1340s. The carved **frieze** above the fireplace and the **panelling** were designed by Norman Shaw in the 1870s. In the stairwell beyond, the **Jacobean staircase** has a Saracen's head, the Selby family crest, carved on the newel post.

The **New Chapel** has a unique **barrel-vaulted roof**, dating from 1470–80 and with early-16C painted panels.

SISSINGHURST CASTLE GARDEN★

Near Cranbrook. 13mi/21km E via the A 264, A 21 and A 262. Open year-round. Mar–Oct daily 11am–5.30pm; for other dates see website. £12.50, reduced charges during winter. ♿🅿(£2); ✕ ✆01580 710 701. www.nationaltrust.org.uk.

In 1930 **Vita Sackville-West** (👁see p213) and her husband Harold Nicolson took over the Sissinghurst estate. At its heart was (and still is) a garden in the ruin of an Elizabethan house, set in the middle of its own woods, streams and farmland, and with views on all sides across the fields and meadows of the Kentish landscape. "*I fell in love… I saw what could be made of it… a castle running away into sordidness and squalor, a garden crying out for rescue.*" The beautiful Elizabethan **tower** of the house became her study and the **garden** their monument.

PENSHURST PLACE★

8mi/13km W via the A 26 and B 2176. House and Toy Museum: Open Apr–Oct daily noon–4pm. Grounds: Open daily Apr–Oct 10.30am–6pm/dusk). £11, garden only, £9. ♿🅿✕ ✆01892 870 307. www.penshurstplace.com.

This splendid mansion, the home of the Elizabethan poet **Sir Philip Sidney** (1554–86), is set in a pretty Tudor Revival village, clustering around the 13C church of St John the Baptist, with its Sidney Chapel.

The original Great Hall (1346), built of coarse sandstone, has been added to with early Tudor, Jacobean and Gothic Revival wings. Inside the hall, the chestnut **timber roof** is held up by unusual life-size carvings of humble peasants. The open hearth is a rare feature and the screens are decorated with tracery. The elegant **furnishings** of the formal rooms include rare furniture, tapestries and portraits.

The great terrace is the focus of the formal **gardens** with their clipped hedges. There is a traditional adventure playground, a nature trail, a farm museum and an enchanting **Toy Museum** with puppets, rocking horses and 19C dolls.

CHIDDINGSTONE

16mi/26km NW on the A 26, B 2176, B 2027 and local roads.

The delightful 16C–17C dwellings, timber framed, tile hung, pargeted and gabled, clustered around St Mary's church, present a rare combination of 14C Gothic and Jacobean styles. The village is owned by the National Trust. To the west, near Edenbridge, stands **Chiddingstone castle** (open Apr–Oct, Sun–Wed and bank holidays 11am–5pm; £9.50; ᴗ🅿(charge); ✖; 𝒫01892 870 347; www.chiddingstonecastle.org.uk), a 19C setting for Buddhist, Egyptian, Japanese and English Stuart period works of art amassed by the colourful Denys Eyre Bower, an antiquarian with a remarkable eye and great enthusiasm.

ᴗ HEVER CASTLE★

13mi/21km W on the A 264 and B 2026. House: Open Apr–Oct daily noon–6pm; Nov Wed–Sun 3–4.30pm. Gardens: Open daily 10.30am, close as house. £16.90; Gardens only, £14.20 (discount for online booking). ᴗ🅿✖ 𝒫01732 865 224. www.hevercastle.co.uk.

This fortified manor house, protected by a moat, and the drawbridge and portcullis of its massive gatehouse stand in idyllic countryside. Formerly the childhood home of **Anne Boleyn**, the neglected castle was bought in 1903 by William Waldorf Astor, who lavishly restored both castle and grounds.

Much of the **woodwork** is a re-creation of the finest Renaissance craftsmanship. There are portraits of Anne, and one, by Holbein, of Henry; in her little room is the Book of Hours the young queen took to her execution in 1536. A costumed figure exhibition and tableaux represent the life and times of Anne Boleyn.

Gardens★

The lake (15ha) is approached via an elaborate loggia and an **Italian garden** with **antique statuary** and **sculpture**. It has recently won a 'most romantic garden in the South East' award. However, two mazes, an adventure playground and a lively summer-long programme of activities, including jousting, make this a very good place for children too.

CHARTWELL

Mappleton Road. 15mi/24km NW via the A 264 and B 206. **House**: open Mar–Oct daily 11.30am–5pm. Studio open year-round daily but times vary. **Garden and exhibition**: open daily Mar–Oct 10am–5pm (11am–4pm Nov–Feb, weather permitting). Entry to house by timed ticket; buy immediately on entry as they run out fast £13.50, garden and studio only, £7.50 ᴗ🅿(£3), ✖ 𝒫01732 868 381. www.nationaltrust.org.uk.

This restored Tudor house was the home of **Sir Winston Churchill** (1874–1965). It is packed with Churchilliana, including many of his paintings, and reflects comfortable domestic life.

The **walls** of the fine gardens were partly built by Churchill himself, who loved the splendid prospect over rolling Weald of Kent countryside and was a principal reason why he bought the estate.

ADDRESSES

⌂ STAY

CANTERBURY

⊜⊜⊜ **Castle House** – 28 Castle Street. 𝒫01227 761 897. www.castlehousehotel.co.uk. 🅿. 7 rooms. The main part of this house was built in the 1730s, incorporating part of the Norman city walls, though the interior lacks historical character. Rooms are spacious and some have a view of the cathedral.

⊜⊜⊜⊜ **Canterbury Hotel** – 140 Wincheap. 𝒫01227 453 227. www.thecanterburyhotel.co.uk. 🅿. 15 rooms. Just outside the city wall, this charming small hotel was originally an 18C farmhouse. On sunny days you can enjoy breakfast in the walled garden and at any time you can use the indoor pool. A spa was added in 2013.

⊝⊜⊜⊜ **ABode Hotel** – High Street. ☏01227 766 266. www.abodecanterbury. co.uk. **P**. 72 rooms. Canterbury's best hotel is set in the very heart of town. ABode has maintained the old wooden beams and traditional fabric of an ancient and historic building, while adding contemporary design features and every modern comfort, with understated British style. Superb eating and drinking (*see opposite*).

DOVER

⊝⊜ **Castle Guest House** – 10 Castle Hill Road. ☏01304 201 656. www.castle-guesthouse.co.uk. This attractive Grade-II-listed building guesthouse is close to the town centre, port and castle. Rooms are light and mostly spacious and there is a very warm welcome. Good value.

RYE

⊝⊜ **The Rise** – 82 Udimore Road. ☏01797 222 285. **P**. 3 rooms. This five-star luxury 1920s-built B&B, a 10-minute walk from town, offers large elegant rooms, pleasant gardens and south-facing terraces with superb countryside views.

Mermaid Inn, Rye

© Clive Sawyer/Travel Pictures

⊝⊜⊜ **Windmill Guest-House** – Mill Lane, off Ferry Road. ☏01797 224 027. www.ryewindmill.co.uk. **P**. 10 rooms. Near the town centre, this unusual B&B has bags of character, with two rooms (a suite and four-poster room ⊝⊜⊜– ⊝⊜⊜⊜) actually in the windmill itself; the others are in the mill building. All are beautifully decorated.

⊝⊜⊜⊜ **Mermaid Inn** – Mermaid Street. ☏01797 223 065. www.mermaid inn.com. **P**. 31 rooms This famous ancient smugglers' haunt has retained some of its 15C atmosphere with exposed beams and period furnishings. Several rooms have four-poster beds. Modern British cuisine (⊝⊜).

BRIGHTON

⊕ **Top Tip** – Most B&Bs tend to be on the streets running off Marine Parade.

⊝⊜ **Amblecliffe Hotel** – 35 Upper Rock Gardens. ☏01273 681 161. 13 rooms. Just a few minutes' walk from the centre of town, four-poster beds and a warm welcome are the main attractions of this Victorian boutique hotel.

⊝⊜⊜ **Paskins** – 18–19 Charlotte Street. ☏01273 601 203. www.paskins.co.uk. **P** 19 rooms. Each bedroom is decorated individually in this pleasantly quirky very eco-friendly Victorian B&B with Art Nouveau and Art Deco flourishes. Home-made organic breakfasts and vegan-friendly options.

⊝⊜–⊝⊜⊜ **Nineteen** – 19 Broad Street. ☏01273 675 529. www.hotel nineteen.co.uk. 7 rooms. This luxury B&B is in a tastefully converted Victorian townhouse in the Kemp Town area, just a pebble's throw from the beach. Bright airy contemporary bedrooms.

⊝⊜⊜⊜ **Hotel du Vin** – Ship Street. ☏01273 855 221. www.hotelduvin.com. 49 rooms. Situated in The Lanes, this flamboyant Gothic Revival/mock Tudor building was erected by a wine merchant on the site of an old inn; the original double-height hall now houses a wine bar. The luxurious rooms feature contemporary/traditional styling. Classic French bistro (⊝⊜–⊝⊜⊜).

EASTBOURNE

⊖⊖ Sea Beach House Hotel – 39–40 Marine Parade. www.seabeach house.com. ☎01323 410 458. 10 rooms. Sea Beach House is the only Grade II-listed seafront accommodation in Eastbourne. The owners are a mine of local information.

⊖⊖ Albert & Victoria Guest House – 19 St Aubyns Road. ☎01323 730 948. www.albertandvictoria.com. 4 rooms. Elegant Victorian house, 40m from Eastbourne beach with period-style canopied beds.

CHICHESTER

⊖⊖ Cherry End – City centre. ☎01243) 779 495. www.chichesterbed andbreakfast.net. 2 rooms. This Victorian house is a five-minute stroll from the town centre and offers two pretty blue-and-white rooms.

ℱ/EAT

CANTERBURY

Ⓖ Try north-east of the town centre (Peter Street, The Borough, Palace Street) and also on Dunstan Street.

⊖⊖ Parrot – 1–9 Church Lane. ☎01227 454 170. www.theparrotonline.com. One of Canterbury's oldest pubs, tastefully and traditionally renovated, with a lovely courtyard, serving an eclectic mix of fajitas, gourmet burgers and locally sourced pub meal favourites.

⊖⊖ Posillipo – 15–17 The Borough. ☎01227 761 471. www.posillipo.co.uk. This acclaimed Italian restaurant serves gourmet pizzas and rustic pasta dishes but is renowned for its fish.

⊖⊖ The Goods Shed – Station Road West. ☎01227 459 153. http://thegoodsshed.co.uk/restaurant. Closed Sun dinner and Mon. This smart rustic restaurant is part of the daily farmers' market and serves only seasonal locally sourced top-quality food.

⊖⊖⊖ County Restaurant – Abode Hotel, High Street. ☎01227 766 266 www.abodecanterbury.co.uk. Highly accomplished, contemporary cooking, stylishly presented, with classic combinations of ingredients. Excellent value for food of this quality and bargain prix-fixe menus.

BRIGHTON

Ⓖ North Laine and The Lanes include most of the best restaurants and pubs.

⊖⊖ Bill's – 100 North Road. ☎01273 692 894. http://bills-website.co.uk. Arranged in the style of a farmers' market/deli/trendy rustic bar, this informal and locally famous buzzing café-restaurant and shop serves only the best and freshest produce with its mouthwatering all-day dishes made up in the open kitchen.

⊖⊖ The Chilli Pickle – 17 Jubilee St. ☎01273 900 383. www.thechillipickle.com. Relaxed colourful trendy modern restaurant with passionate chef, buzzy vibe and friendly, welcoming service. Changing menu of tasty, thoughtfully prepared, authentic Indian dishes.

⊖⊖ Terre à Terre – 71 East Street. ☎01273 729 051. www.terreaterre.co.uk. Closed Mon and bank holidays. This is one of the most acclaimed and most inventive vegetarian restaurants in the country.

⊖⊖–⊖⊖⊖ The Gingerman – 21a Norfolk Square. ☎01273 326 688. www.gingermanrestaurants.com. Closed Mon. This small intimate stylish modern venue serves excellent Mediterranean cuisine. Bargain prix-fixe lunches.

EASTBOURNE

⊖⊖ Belgian Cafe – Burlington Hotel. 11–23 Grand Parade. ☎01323 729 967. www.thebelgiancafe.co.uk. Come here for mussels and chips and a Belgian beer to wash it down; there are over 50 kinds of beer to choose from.

CHICHESTER

⊖⊖ Trents Wine Bar – 50 South Street. ☎01243 773 714. www.trents-chichester.co.uk. This modern restaurant-bar offers a Mediterranean/British menu featuring the usual favourite grills and salads.

Hampshire, Dorset, Wiltshire, Channel Islands

Stourhead © Robert Harding/age fotostock

Introduction

These three counties of southern England were once the heartland of the kingdom of Wessex, ruled, most famously, by King Alfred. During the 10C Wessex unified much of England and was the last English kingdom before it was subdued by the Danes in the 11C. Its romantic appeal was revived during the 19C. Much older historic relics can be found in Wiltshire (Stonehenge and Avebury) and Dorset (the Cerne Abbas Giant, Maiden Castle and prehistoric fossils at Lyme Regis). Hampshire, meanwhile, is home to ancient forest land and England's naval heritage. It all makes for a rich mix where the ancient past is never far away.

Hampshire

England's second most wooded county (after Surrey) is a region of both rolling countryside and a coastline with a long naval history. Its best-loved landscape is the New Forest, new in name and national park status only. Ironically, precious little forest remains, but its atmosphere, traditions and village settlements still go back many centuries.

The county town, Winchester, retains echoes of King Arthur's rule, when it was capital of all England, and its magnificent cathedral and atmospheric college go back to medieval times. It is also a modern lively regional hub, however, and makes a good base. On the coast, Portsmouth is home to the Royal Navy past and present, from HMS *Victory* to nuclear submarines; it's Historic Dockyard is a sepia-tinted look at how Britannia once ruled the waves, as well as modern naval cutting-edge technology. Neighbouring Southampton has a proud commercial shipping history; every great British ocean liner has sailed from here, including Titanic. A short ferry ride away is the Isle of Wight, a favourite resort where Queen Victoria built a magnificent holiday home.

Dorset

For many English visitors, Dorset is the transition between the London-influenced southeast and the provincial West Country. It is also the heart of the ancient kingdom of Wessex, which comes most readily to life, particularly around Dorchester, through the late-19C works of its most famous literary figure, Thomas Hardy. The Dorset coastline is hugely popular, from the typical seaside charm of resorts like Bournemouth,

Highlights

1 Clamber aboard historic ships at **Portsmouth** (p220)

2 Pack a picnic and join the scenery at **Stourhead** (p239)

3 Go on safari at **Longleat** (p240)

4 Get a spiritual high on the Tower Tour at **Salisbury cathedral** (p241)

5 Try to solve the puzzle of over five millennia at enigmatic **Stonehenge** (p243)

Swanage, Weymouth and Lyme Regis, to uncommercialised natural beauty spots like Durdle Door and Lulworth Cove.

Wiltshire

Landlocked Wiltshire's most famous attraction is Stonehenge. In fact the county is rich in prehistoric remains and the savvy visitor may even prefer visiting Avebury to its world-famous neighbour. The main town is Salisbury, quintessentially English with its cathedral – arguably England's finest – rising above the water meadows, in a scene unchanged over centuries.

In Stourhead and Longleat, Wiltshire possesses two of Britain's finest outdoor attractions, at opposite ends of the cultural spectrum. The former is the apogee of English landscape gardening; the latter is the zenith of how to turn your estate into a commercially successful venture, which in this case has meant transforming swathes of Wiltshire into the plains of Africa, complete with native animals!

Portsmouth★

Britain's premier naval base is set between two almost landlocked harbours. In the early 15C the naval base developed and in 1495 the first dry dock in the world was built. By the end of the 17C Portsmouth had become the principal naval base in the country. In the 18C when France was Britain's major enemy, fortifications were strengthened. After heavy bombing in the Second World War, the city was rebuilt and expanded onto the mainland.

PORTSMOUTH HISTORIC DOCKYARD★★

Victory Gate, Queen Street and The Hard. Open daily Apr–Oct 10am–5.30pm; Nov–Mar 10am–5pm. Closed 24–26 Dec. All attractions ticket: £28 (child £12). Individual attraction prices also available (👜plus discount for booking online. 👤🅿️ (£4 per day) ✗ 🖋023 9283 9766. www.historicdockyard.co.uk.

HMS Warrior 1860★★ – Once the pride of Queen Victoria's Navy, Britain's first iron-clad battleship was commissioned in the 1860s. After 100 years of service as the largest and most powerful ship of its day, she has been restored and now displays an exhibition of life in the Victorian Navy.

Action Stations 👥 – This exciting hands-on centre is all about today's Royal Navy with high-tech exhibits and simulators which let you take charge of a helicopter, fire ship's guns, control the bridge of a warship, climb the rigging and much more.

National Museum of the Royal Navy★★ (www.nmrn.org.uk) – These fascinating galleries, currently being updated and refurbished, are full of mementoes and stories of those who have served their country at sea through 1000 years of peace and war.

HMS Victory★★ (www.hms-victory.com) – On 21 October 1805 Admiral Horatio Nelson's splendid three-masted flagship (built Chatham 1759) led the victorious attack on a combined French

▶ **Population:** 205 400.
👥 **Michelin Map:** Michelin Atlas p 10 or Map 504 Q 31.
🅸 **Info:** The Hard, Portsmouth – outside Historic Dockyard. 🖋023 9282 6722. www.visitportsmouth.co.uk. Harbour Station, on The Hard (includes the bus station), is adjacent to the main sights. Portsmouth Station is a 10–15 minute walk from the centre. Fastest train to London: Waterloo to Portsmouth Harbour 1hr 39mins. The Southsea Land Train is a useful way of getting around.
▶ **Location:** 81mi/130km south of London.
👁 **Don't Miss:** The Historic Dockyard; the view from the Spinnaker Tower.
🕐 **Timing:** At least 2 days minimum.
👥 **Kids:** Historic Dockyard (*HMS Victory* and Action Stations); Blue Reef Aquarium, Southsea; Explosion Museum of Naval Fire Power.

and Spanish fleet off Cape Trafalgar in Spain – at the cost of her admiral's life. In the 1920s the *Victory* was brought into dry dock after 150 years at sea. Today she continues to serve as the flagship of the Commander in Chief Naval Home Command, still manned by serving Royal Naval and Royal Marines personnel.

Mary Rose Museum★★ (www.mary-rose.org) – On 19 July 1545, the four-masted *Mary Rose* (built 1509), vice-flagship of Henry VIII's English fleet, keeled over and sank while preparing to meet a French attack. In the 1960s, the wreck was found, preserved in the Solent silt; in 1982 the hull was raised and it is now a unique Tudor time-capsule preserved after 437 years on the seabed. A stunning new £35 million gallery opened in 2013 to house the remains of the vessel.

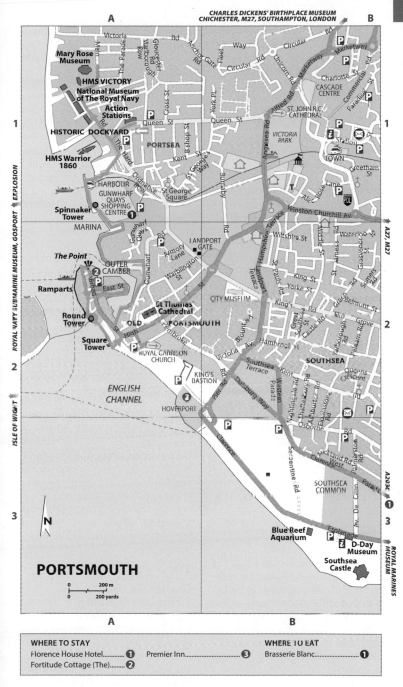

CHARLES DICKENS' BIRTHPLACE MUSEUM
CHICHESTER, M27, SOUTHAMPTON, LONDON

PORTSMOUTH

WHERE TO STAY
Florence House Hotel............ ❶   Premier Inn.................................. ❸
Fortitude Cottage (The)........... ❷

WHERE TO EAT
Brasserie Blanc............................. ❶

Here, you can peer through windows to see the impressive ship's carcass for the first time with its preserving sprays switched off, as up to 100 tons of water is removed from the timbers. Artefacts displayed in superb mirror-image context galleries running the length of the ship give a sense of what the decks would have looked like moments before Mary Rose sank. Themed galleries tell the personal stories and working lives of the crew on board, together with many of the 19 000 artefacts that were raised with her from the seabed in 1982.

OLD PORTSMOUTH★
Harbour ramparts

The original town which grew up around the **Camber** south of the dockyard was once entirely enclosed by ramparts; today only those on the harbour side are complete, forming a pleasant promenade with **views** of Gosport and Spithead. At the end of Broad Street, The **Point** affords fine **views**★★ of ships entering and leaving the port. The **Round Tower**, built on the orders of Henry V, was modified in Henry VIII's reign and again in the 19C. The **Square Tower** was built in 1494.

Portsmouth (St Thomas') cathedral★ was built c.1180 as a chapel to honour **Thomas Becket**, martyred in 1170. Only the Early English **choir** and **transepts** survived the Civil War; in around 1690 the nave and tower were rebuilt and the attractive octagonal wooden **cupola** was added in 1703. The church became a cathedral in 1927.

▲▲ Spinnaker Tower★
Gunwharf Quays. Open daily 10am–6pm (Aug 9.30am–7pm (6pm Fri, Sat). Closed 25 Dec. £9.50, child £7.50 (online discount). ♿(visitors with mobility impairments must call in advance); ✗ ✆023 9285 7520.
www.spinnakertower.co.uk.
Soaring 170m into the sky above the historic harbour, the Spinnaker is the tallest public viewing tower in the UK, with wonderful panoramic views that stretch across the Isle of Wight. It has three viewing decks complete with interactive multi-touch screens and a glass floor walk for those undaunted by heights!

SOUTHSEA
The strip of land at the south of Portsea Island was rough marshland until the 19C when a coastal resort began to grow and the Common became a pleasure area. At the southernmost tip of the island stands **Southsea Castle** (Clarence Esplanade; open Apr–Oct Tue–Sun and bank holiday Mons 10am–5pm; closed 24–26 Dec; ♿✗; ✆023 9284 1625; www.southseacastle.co.uk), **built by Henry VIII in 1544 as part of the chain of forts protecting the ports along the south and east coast. The central keep, surrounded by a dry moat, is still mainly Tudor; inside are displays of the growth of Portsmouth's fortifications.**

The **D-Day Museum and Overlord Embroidery** (Clarence Esplanade; currently closed for refurbishment, re-opening in 2018; call or check website for details; ✆023 9282 7261; www.portsmouthmuseums.co.uk) **illustrates major events of the Second World War. The centrepiece is the Overlord Embroidery with 34 panels telling the story of D-Day.**

Blue Reef Aquarium ▲▲ (Clarence Esplanade; open daily 10am–5pm/6pm during school holidays; closed 25 Dec; £10.70, child £8.25 (discount for online booking); ♿ ✗; ✆023 9287 5222; www.bluereefaquarium.co.uk), **is one of the country's new-wave aquaria with large high-visibility tanks and special viewing features.**

The former **Royal Marines Museum**★ (closed until 2020 pending move to Historic Dockyard; check website for latest information; ✆023 9281 9385; www.royalmarinesmuseum.co.uk), **set in the original 19C officers' mess, described the past and present of the Royal Marine Corps.**

ADDITIONAL SIGHTS
Charles Dickens' Birthplace Museum
393 Old Commercial Road.
Open Apr–Sept Fri–Sun 10am–5.30pm. £4.20. ♿ ✆023 9282 1879.
www.charlesdickensbirthplace.co.uk.
The small, neat city-centre terrace house where Dickens was born in 1812, and spent the first four months of his life, has been restored and furnished in the style of the period.

Royal Navy Submarine Museum

Gosport: cross harbour by shuttle ferry; Waterbus Service links with Gunwharf Quays and Historic Dockyard. Haslar Jetty Road. Open Apr–Oct daily 10am–5.30pm; Nov–Mar Wed–Sun 10am–4.30pm). Closed 24–27 and 31 Dec, 1–3 Jan. £13.50 (child 5–15, £9) – online discounts. ⊓✕ ✆023 9251 0354. www.submarine-museum.co.uk.

Tour an actual submarine, see torpedoes and a Polaris missile and get hands-on with periscopes and diving equipment; all tell the story of submariners and their role in peace and war.

⚨ Explosion Museum of Naval Fire Power

Gosport: cross harbour by shuttle ferry alternatively, a Waterbus Service links with Gunwharf Quays and Historic Dockyard. Priddy's Hard. Open Apr–Oct daily 10am–5pm; Nov–Mar Sat–Sun only, 10am–4pm. Closed 1 Jan, 25–26 Dec. £10 (child 5–15, £6) – online discounts. ⬥⊓✕ ✆012 9250 5600. www.explosion.org.uk.

Southampton

and around

This important south coast port, naturally favoured with a double tide, began as a Roman coastal garrison, Clausentum, on the east bank of the Itchen. By the 8C it had become the Saxon port of **Hamwic**, serving the royal city of Winchester and it has continued to grow until the present day, becoming one of Britain's major container ports. After severe bombing in the Second World War, the town began a successful recovery in the 1950s and, alongside medieval remains, a modern city has grown up, with a lively university and renewed industry.

The story of naval firepower is traced through audio-visual presentations, workers' testimonies and exhibits on mines, torpedoes, missiles and more.

EXCURSION
ROYAL ARMOURIES FORT NELSON

⊳ Fort Nelson, Portsdown Hill Road, Fareham. 9mi/14km NW on the M 27. Open daily Apr–Oct 10am–5pm; Nov–Mar 10.30am–4pm. Closed 24–26 Dec. ⬥⊓✕ ✆01329 233 734. www.armouries.org.uk.

This superbly restored Victorian fort is one of a chain built high across Portsdown Hill to defend Portsmouth from French invasion. There are sweeping **views** from the fort walls.

Alongside re-created barracks, the collection of artillery includes ornate medieval bronze cannons from India, China and Turkey, anti-aircraft guns and three sections of the immense 'Supergun' impounded in 1990, en route for Iraq in the guise of petrochemical piping.

▸ **Population:** 253 651.
⚇ **Michelin Map:** Michelin Atlas p 9 or Map 504 P 31.
▯ **Info:** (online only) www. discoversouthampton.co.uk. Southampton Central train station has a regular direct London service (Waterloo, fastest train 1h15). The bus station is on the other side of the Civic Centre. Blue Funnel Cruises (✆02380 223 278; www.bluefunnel. co.uk) offer several day trip options on the water.
⊳ **Location:** South coast, 78mi/125km SW of London;
⚨ **Kids:** Birds at the Hawk Conservancy Trust.

OLD TOWN WALK

A good deal of the medieval defences and town buildings can still be seen today.

The impressive northern gate to the town, the **Bargate★**, built c.1180, was given its large towers c.1285 and its forbidding north face in the 15C. The **west wall** of the early defences rises spectacularly above the **Western Esplanade**, where Southampton Bay once lapped the shore. Note the 15C **Catchcold Tower** and The **Arcade** running from the site of **Biddlesgate** to the **Blue Anchor Postern**. At the top of Blue Anchor Lane the large late-15C **Tudor House and Garden★** (open Mon–Thu 10am–3pm, Sat–Sun and bank holidays 10am–5pm; closed 24 Dec–1 Jan; £5; ✗; ℘023 8083 4242; www.tudorhouseandgarden.com) is the city's most important historic building, encompassing over 800 years of history on one site, and incorporating an earlier banqueting hall. It now houses a museum which tells the story of the house and the people who lived and worked there; outside, a lovely 16C **garden** of flowers and herbs and a formal knot garden have been re-created. At the far end steps lead down to the shell of the **Norman House**, a fine example of a 12C merchant's house, which was incorporated into the town wall defences in the 14C. **St Michael's Church** is the oldest building in the medieval town, built soon after the Norman Conquest and enlarged throughout the Middle Ages and in the 19C.

Back on the Western Esplanade is the old Wool House, a fine red 14C stone warehouse. Close by, **God's House** was founded c.1185 as an almshouse and hostel for travellers. To its east stand the early-14C **God's House Gate**, and the early-15C **God's House Tower**.

East of the rail station on Commercial Road within the Civic Centre is the **Southampton City Art Gallery★** (open Mon–Fri 10am–3pm, Sat 10am–5pm; ⚭ ℙ (charge); ℘023 8083 3007; www.southampton.gov.uk), which has an excellent collection of modern art including works by Spencer, Sutherland and Lowry. Beside the Civic Hall the Grade-II-listed Old Magistrates' Court building has been transformed into the **Sea City Museum** (Havelock Road; open daily 10am–5pm; ⚭; £8.50; ✗; ℘023 8083 4356, www.seacitymuseum.co.uk), opened in 2012 as Southampton's major new museum and gallery. its permanent exhibitions are The Titanic Story (including a 1:25 scale, interactive model of the ship) and Gateway to the World, telling the stories of people who have departed from or arrived in the port of Southampton.

🚗 DRIVING TOUR

TEST VALLEY

Circular tour approx 75mi/20km.

▷ Leave Southampton heading NW on the A 3057.

The River Test runs swiftly through a fertile valley of often-flooded meadows, passing small market towns and pretty villages with thatched cottages, most notably the Tytherleys, Broughton, the Wallops, the Clatfords, Wherwell and Chilbolton.

Broadlands★

8mi/13km NW on the A 3057, or 1mi/2km short of Romsey. Guided tours only Mon–Fri 1pm. £10. ⚭ ℘01794 505080. www.broadlandsestates.co.uk. In 1736 the first Viscount Palmerston bought a small Tudor manor near Romsey and set about transforming its grounds. His son commissioned **Lancelot 'Capability' Brown** to continue this work and rebuilt the house in the Palladian style. **Henry Holland** created the east entrance front and the elegant dining room – the setting for three splendid **Van Dyck** paintings. The house is notable for the **Wedgwood Room** with its friezes and mouldings, a fine collection of 18C Wedgwood pieces

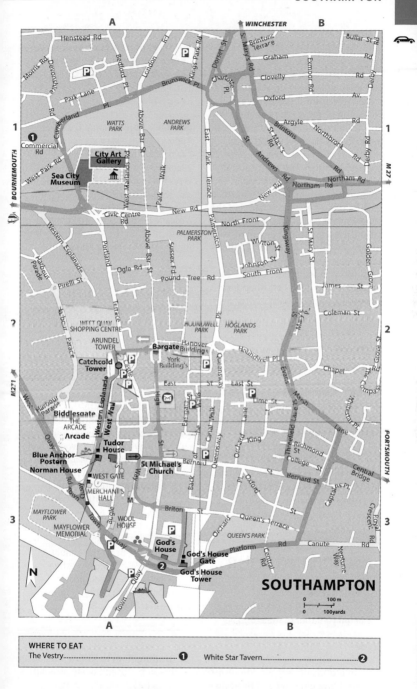

SOUTHAMPTON

and four portraits by Sir Peter Lely. The white-and-gold plasterwork of the **saloon** and the medallions in the drawing room ceiling are exquisite. In the 20C the house was Lord Mountbatten of Burma's (1900–79) residence.

Romsey abbey★

9mi/15km NW on the A 3057. Open daily 7.30am (11am Sun)–6pm. ✆01794 513 125. www.romseyabbey.org.uk.

The town of Romsey grew up around a nunnery founded by Edward the Elder, son of Alfred the Great, in 907 and rebuilt c.1120–1230. At the Dissolution the buildings were destroyed but the abbey church survived to serve as the parish church. The purity and simplicity of the **interior★★** make this an excellent example of late Norman architecture. In the east chapel of the south choir aisle is a **Saxon crucifix** of c.1100, depicting Christ crucified, with two angels, the Virgin and St John. A second Saxon sculpture, the 11C **rood**, is outside on the south side. Opposite the abbey on Church Street, **King John's House** is a 13C merchant's house with original roof timbers. It now serves as the **King John's House and Heritage Centre** incorporating Tudor and Victorian museum sections (open Mon–Sat 10am–4pm; ✖; ✆01794 512 200; www. kingjohnshouse.org.uk).

▲▲ Hawk Conservancy Trust

Andover. Open daily early Feb–Oct 10am–5.30pm; Nov–early Jan 10am–4.30pm. Closed early Jan–first week Feb. Adult £14.65, child (4–15) £10.30. ♿🅿✖; ✆01264 773 850. www.hawk-conservancy.org.

Majestic birds of prey are kept in large enclosures on the wooded grounds, with free-flying demonstrations.

Isle of Wight★

The Isle of Wight has been a holiday destination ever since Queen Victoria chose Osborne House for her country retreat. Visitors are attracted mainly by the quiet pace of life, the sandy beaches and the yachting. It is also increasingly popular for its music festivals.

🚗 DRIVING TOUR

ISLAND TOUR

◐ Begin your tour of the island here.

Ryde

This is the island's main ferry terminal and an old-fashioned seaside resort. The attractive old village of **Brading★** lies 4mi/6.5km south.

St Mary's church★, built c.1200, boasts impressive 17C family tombs while southwest is the remains of the

▶ **Population:** 140 500.
◔ **Michelin Map:** Michelin Atlas p 9 or Map 504 P, Q 31 and 32.
🖹 **Info:** www.visitisleofwight.co.uk. Many towns and villages have tourist information points.
◑ **Location:** English Channel, SW of Portsmouth, between 2mi/3km and 5mi/8km from the mainland.
◉ **Beware:** The island is packed out for the annual Isle of Wight Music Festival (second weekend June).
◉ **Don't Miss:** Osborne House.
▲▲ **Kids:** Dinosaur Isle.

3C **Brading Roman Villa★** (open daily 10am–5pm; closed Christmas holidays; £9.50; ♿🅿✖; ✆01983 406 223; www. bradingromanvilla.org.uk), with some fine 4C **mosaics** and a display of artefacts in the exhibition centre. Close by, **Nunwell House and Gardens★** (Coach

GETTING AROUND

Three operators service the island. The fastest route takes about 15 minutes, the slowest 40 minutes. **Red Funnel** runs a vehicle ferry and a high-speed passenger-only ferry, both between Southampton and Cowes (☎0844 844 99 88; www.redfunnel.co.uk). **Hover-travel** operates a hovercraft service (passenger only) between Southsea and Ryde (☎08434 87 88 87; www. hovertravel.co.uk). **Wight Link** operates vehicle ferries between Portsmouth and Fishbourne, and Lymington and Yarmouth, and a passenger-only catamaran between Portsmouth and Ryde (☎0871 376 1000; www.wightlink.co.uk).

Lane; 1mi/1.6km W; open early May–mid-Jul and 10 days in Sept Mon–Wed 1–4.30pm, Sun garden only; guided tour only of house 1.30pm and 3pm; £7, garden only, £4; 🅿✗; ☎01983 407 240; www.nunwellhouse.co.uk) has been a family home since 1522.

🚹🚺 Dinosaur Isle

6mi/10km S of Ryde. Culver Parade, Sandown Bay. Open daily Apr–Aug 10am–6pm; Sept–Oct 10am–5pm; Nov–Mar 10am–4pm. £5 (child 3–15, £4). &🅿✗; ☎01983 404 344. www.dinosaurisle.com.

Housed in a striking modern building in the shape of a giant pterodactyl, moving models and intelligent interpretations bring to life prehistoric times when dinosaurs ruled the Isle of Wight.

Shanklin

3mi/5km S of Sandown.

With its clifftop setting, beach, and pretty Old Village, Shanklin is a favourite stop on the island. A short walk from the Old Village, **Shanklin Chine** (Chine Hollow or Everton Road; open daily early Apr–Sept 10am–5pm/10pm late May–Sept when illuminated; £4.50; ✗; ☎01983 866 432; www.shanklinchine.co.uk) is a lovely leafy gorge that charmed the poet John Keats, who lived nearby. It includes rare plants, a delightful waterfall and a heritage centre.

Ventnor

3.5mi/5.6km S of Shanklin.

Another of the island's low-key seaside resorts, Ventnor is known for its tranquil 9ha subtropical **Ventnor Botanic Garden** (Undercliff Drive; open daily 10am–4pm; £9; &🅿✗; ☎01983 855 397; www.botanic.co.uk). East of the centre, secluded **Bonchurch beach** is where Charles Dickens once stayed. A detour north (3.5mi/5.6km on the B 3327) will take you to **Appuldurcombe House**, an 18C country estate, now also home to an Owl and Falconry Centre (flying times Apr–Sept Sun–Fri 11.30am and 2pm; house open Apr–Sept Sun–Fri 10am–4pm; &🅿✗; ☎01983 852 484; www.appuldurcombe.co.uk).

St Catherine's Point

5mi/8km W of Ventnor.

The island's southernmost point is marked by **St Catherine's Oratory**, (www.english-heritage.org.uk) nicknamed the 'Pepper Pot' for its shape. This medieval octagonal tower, allegedly once a lighthouse, dates from 1328.

Alum Bay

6.5mi/26km W of St Catherine's.

The westernmost bay of the island, where alum was once mined, is a remarkable geological phenomenon, its sandstone cliffs richly coloured with more than 20 mineral hues. In the afternoon sun, a boat trip to the **Needles**, sea stacks 30m offshore, gives fine views of the colourful slopes and chalk cliffs.

The Needles Park (open daily 10am–4pm with later openings in summer months; chairlift return £6, but check out the Supersaver ticket prices which give up to 25% saving; &🅿(£4); ✗(summer only); ☎01983 752 401; www.theneedles.co.uk)

227

Alum Bay with the Needles

© Alexey_Fedoren/iStockphoto.com

offers a chairlift giving fine views of the rock pinnacles, plus a 4D cinema, and various funfair-style family attractions.

Carisbrooke Castle★★

12mi/9km due E of Alum Bay (1.2mi/2km S of Newport). Open daily Apr–Sept 10am–6pm (Oct 5pm). Nov–Mar Sat–Sun only 10am–4pm. Feb half-term hol daily 10am–4pm. Closed 1–2 Jan, 24–26 Dec. £9.40. ♿🅿 ✕(summer only). ✆01983 522 107. www.english-heritage.org.uk.

In 1100, Richard de Redvers built the keep and curtain walls on the site of a Roman stronghold. The castle was further fortified against the Spanish in the late-16C. During the imprisonment of King Charles I in 1647–48, prior to his trial in London, the **bowling green** was created for his entertainment. He is said to have walked daily around the **battlements**, perhaps planning his escape (he made two attempts). The last resident governor, Queen Victoria's daughter, Princess Beatrice, died at Carisbrooke in 1944.

The Norman curtain wall encloses the high motte and 12C **keep** (with **views★** for miles around).

The late-12C **Great Hall** houses a museum of island history. An interactive exhibit in the Old Coach House explores life in the castle and the donkey centre houses the famous Carisbrooke donkeys, who give regular demonstrations in the **well-house** of the unique 1587 treadmill used to draw water from the 49m-deep well.

Cowes

6mi/10km N of Carisbrooke.

Cowes is the premier yachting centre in Britain, with nautical events throughout the summer, culminating in the world-famous **Cowes Week** regattas in August. Across the River Medina (1mi/1.6km) is East Cowes and Osborne House.

Osborne House★★

1mi/1.6km SE of East Cowes. Open Apr–Sept 10am–6pm (Oct 5pm); rest of year, days and times vary; check website for details. Closed 1–2 Jan, 24–26 Dec.. £16.20. ♿🅿✕ ✆01983 200 022. www.english-heritage.org.uk.

In a delightful position with views of the sea which reminded him of Naples, Prince Albert worked with Thomas Cubitt to create this enormous Italianate villa with terraced gardens, completed in 1851. For Queen Victoria, Osborne was a favourite home for family holidays with three generations of children.

After Albert's death in 1861 she spent much of her widowhood at Osborne, dying there in 1901. Her insistence that everything should be kept exactly as it had been during Albert's life gives a remarkable picture of royal family life, from richly furnished state rooms to the intimacy of the **Queen's Sitting Room**, where she worked beside her husband at twin desks. The only major addition to the house after Albert's death was the **Durbar Wing★★** built in 1890; its amazing principal room celebrating Victoria's role as Empress of India.

A carriage ride through the **grounds** takes visitors to the **Swiss Cottage**, imported from Switzerland and erected in 1853, where the royal children learned to cook on small ranges and entertained their parents. Their natural history collections are displayed in a smaller chalet **museum**, near their miniature **fort** with cannon, the queen's bathing hut and a collection of tiny wheelbarrows, each bearing the initials of its royal owner.

Winchester★★

and around

This ancient cathedral city was the capital of King Alfred's **Wessex** and then of England, from the early-9C to about 100 years after the Norman Conquest. Today it is a lively regional shopping, historical and cultural centre.

A BIT OF HISTORY

It was only after the Roman invasion of year 43 that the city known as **Venta Bulgarum** was founded. After the Romans withdrew, the city declined until the Saxons rebuilt a church and created a bishopric in 662.

After 878, **Alfred the Great** consolidated his defence of Wessex against Danish attacks by setting up a series of fortified **burghs**, of which Winchester was the largest.

At the time of the Norman Conquest the city was already of such importance that **William I** was crowned here as well as in London. He built a castle in the southwest angle of the city walls and established a new cathedral in 1070. After the 12C Winchester yielded to London as the preferred royal residence. During the Civil War the Norman castle was largely destroyed, the cathedral damaged and the city looted by Parliamentary troops. After the Restoration the city recovered.

CATHEDRAL★★★

Cathedral, Crypt and Treasury open Mon–Sat 9.30am–5pm, Sun 12.30–3pm. Tower (213 steps) check website for times, £6. No children under 12 on tower tour. ⚒✕ ✆01962 857 200. www.winchester-cathedral.org.uk. The cathedral stands surrounded by lawns on the same site as the 7C Saxon minster, the foundations of which were located in the 1960s. An early bishop of Winchester, **St Swithin**, was buried outside the west end of the minster in 862. There was torrential rain on the day in 1093 when his grave was transferred inside the new church, though he had

▶ **Population:** 116 600.
◔ **Michelin Map:** Michelin Atlas p 9 or Map 504 P, Q 30.
🛈 **Info:** Guildhall, High Street. ✆01962 840 500. www.visitwinchester.co.uk. The train station, with direct London service (Waterloo 53 mins), is 1mi/1.6km from the centre, on Stockbridge Road. The bus station is right in the centre, on Broadway. Winchester is a small city and can easily be covered on foot.
◑ **Location:** Winchester is 66mi/106km southwest of London.
☺ **Don't Miss:** The cathedral; St Cross Hospital; Winchester College.
◔ **Timing:** Allow a full day in Winchester.
🛉🛉 **Kids:** Mid-Hants Watercress Line specials; Marwell Zoo.

expressly asked to be buried in the open air; this gave rise to the legend that if it rains on St Swithin's Day (15 July) it will rain for 40 days.

William Walkelyn, appointed bishop by William I, began building the new cathedral in 1079. In 1202 the east end was reconstructed and in the early-14C the Norman choir was rebuilt in the Perpendicular style and the nave and west front were rebuilt between 1346 and 1404. After further remodellings of the nave, Lady Chapel and chancel in 1486–1528, the longest Gothic church in Europe (169m) was complete.

When, in 1652, Parliament ordered the cathedral (ransacked in the Civil War) to be destroyed, it was saved only by a petition of the citizens. Early in the 20C the east end, built on marshland and supported on a 13C beech tree raft, began to sink, causing the walls to crack and the roof to fall; the cathedral was saved by a diver, William Walker, who worked alone from 1906 to 1912 replacing the rotting rafts with cement.

Exterior

Built largely of stone from the Isle of Wight, the cathedral's exterior, with its squat Norman **tower**, is impressive, though less exciting than the interior.

Interior

Bishop William of Wykeham (1324–1404) rebuilt the Norman pillars in the lofty 12-bay nave, with its bosses and **stone lierne vault**, to support the graceful Perpendicular arches surmounted by balconies with clerestory windows. Of special note are the **west window**, the ornate William of Wykeham's chantry, Jane Austen's tomb, window and brass, the 12C black Tournai marble **font** and the Jacobean pulpit. The **Holy Sepulchre Chapel** has exquisite 13C wall paintings. In the chancel the **choir stalls** (1308) are ornamented with remarkable **misericords**; the marble tomb of the "ungodly" King William Rufus (d.1100) stands under the tower. The **stone reredos** with statues above the altar is early-16C; the early Tudor **vault** has outstanding **bosses**.

In the Early English retro-choir (13C) the chapels and chantries are dedicated to 15C–16C bishops. The early-13C Lady Chapel lit by seven-light windows is adorned with fine Tudor woodwork and **wall paintings**.

The 12C **Winchester Bible** is the jewel of the rich collection of manuscripts and books in the 12C Library (access from south transept).

In the north aisle of the nave is the grave of the great author **Jane Austen** (1775–1817), who moved to Winchester for treatment in her last illness.

The **Crypt** (open by guided tour only) houses the beautiful and critically acclaimed *Sound II* sculpture by Antony Gormley, creator of *Angel of the North* (⌖*see NEWCASTLE-UPON-TYNE, p481*).

Cathedral Close

The few remaining monastic buildings south of the cathedral include the **Deanery**, formerly the Prior's Lodging, with a three-arched porch and a 15C hall. The 14C **Pilgrims' Hall** (3 The Close; call for opening times; ☎01962 854 189),

part of the The Pilgrims' School, the choir school of Winchester Cathedral, has possibly the oldest **hammerbeam roof** in the UK. Beside the sturdy **St Swithin's Gate** stands the 15C timber-framed **Cheyney Court** and early-16C stables, also timber framed and now part of the Pilgrims' School.

CITY

Winchester College★

Guided tours: Apr–Aug Mon, Wed, Fri–Sat 10.15am, 11.30am, 2.15pm, 3.30pm, Tue and Thu 10.15am, 11.30am (Jul–Aug also 2.15pm, 3.30pm), Sun 2.15pm and 3.30pm; Sept–Mar Mon, Wed, Fri–Sat 10.15am, 11.30am, 2.15pm, Tue and Thu 10.15am, 11.30am, Sun 2.15pm, 3.30pm (no 3.30pm tour during Dec–Jan). Closed Christmas, New Year, and for college events throughout the year. £6. ☎01962 621 209. www.winchestercollege.org.

The college was founded in 1382 by **Bishop William of Wykeham** (pronounced 'wick-um'), to provide an education for poor scholars, as well as 'commoners' from wealthy families, to be continued at New College, Oxford, which Wykeham had already founded in 1379. Pupils are still known as 'Wykehamists' and Winchester has the longest history of any school in the country. The school is entered by the 14C **Outer Gate** in College Street. Through the Middle Gate is **Chamber Court**, the centre of college life, surrounded by Wykeham's original late-14C buildings. The **hall** on its south side *(1st floor)* has fine 16C wooden panelling on which hang portraits of former pupils and a 16C portrait of the founder. The **chapel**, with its prominent 15C pinnacled tower, was heavily restored in the 19C, but retains its medieval **wooden vault**, one of the first attempts at fan vaulting in England, and the original 14C **choir stalls** with fine misericords. In the centre of Wykeham's 14C cloister stands the early-15C **Fromond's Chantry**, the only example in England of a chapel so placed. The red-brick and stone **school** *(west of cloister)*, was built in 1683–87 for the increasing number of commoners. Sir Herbert Baker's simple peaceful **War**

Cloister, built in 1924, commemorates Wykehamists who fell in world wars.

Castle Great Hall★

Normally open daily 10am–4.30pm, but check website for variations. Closed 25–26 Dec. £3. ☏01962 846 476. www3.hants.gov.uk/greathall.

The Great Hall is the only surviving part of Winchester Castle, built in Norman times. It was slighted by order of Parliament in the Civil War but the hall (34m x 17m x 17m), dating from 1222–36, survived and is a splendid example of a medieval hall, with its timber roof supported on columns of Purbeck marble. On the west wall hangs a famous oak **Round Table** (5m diameter) which dates from the 14C; it is decorated with paintings of the Tudor rose in its centre, King Arthur and a list of his knights around the edge.

High Street

At the east end (The Broadway) stands a statue to Alfred the Great, erected in 1901. Among the buildings in the pedestrian street are the former **Guildhall** (now a bank), built in 1713, opposite the timber-framed **God Begot House★** dating from 1558 (now a restaurant). Note also the 15C stone-carved **Butter Cross**, where markets were held.

St Cross Hospital★★

1mi/1.6km S. Open Apr–Oct Mon–Sat 9.30am–5pm, Sun 1–5pm; Nov–Mar Mon–Sat 10.30am–3.30pm. Closed Good Fri, 25 Dec. £4.50. ♿🅿✕(Apr–Oct Mon–Sat, 10.30am–12.30pm, 2.30–4.30pm). ☏01962 851 375. http://hospitalofstcross.co.uk.

A lovely walk from the city centre across the water meadows leads to the oldest charitable institution in England. Founded by Bishop Henry de Blois in 1136, its almshouses are still in use today. The **chapel** (late-12C–late-13C) is a fine example of Norman architecture, rich in zigzag stone carving on the arches and chancel vaulting. In the **Lady Chapel** is a **Flemish triptych** of c.1530. The **Brethren's Hall** has a min-

strels' gallery and an impressive late-15C timbered roof.

EXCURSIONS

🧑‍🦽👤 Mid-Hants Railway Watercress Line

▶ Alresford. 8mi/13km NE on the A 31 and B 3046. Station and rolling stock open daily. For train times see website; standard fare £16 (child 2–16, £8). ♿🅿 (charge) ✕ ☏01962 733 810. www.watercressline.co.uk.

Named for the watercress beds which can still be seen in and around the handsome small Georgian town of Alresford (pronounced 'Arlsford'), the Watercress Line carries old-fashioned steam engines for 10mi/16km over the hills to the market town of Alton, with special themed services, for both adults and children, throughout the year.

Jane Austen's House

▶ Chawton. 18mi/29km NE via the A 31 and B 3006. Open Mar–May and Sept–Dec 10.30am–4.30pm; Jun–Aug 10am–5pm. Closed 25–26 Dec. £8. ♿ ☏01420 83262. www.jane-austens-house-museum.org.uk.

The eight years Jane spent sharing this peaceful red-brick house with her mother, and sister, Cassandra, were some of her happiest and most productive. The tiny table at which she wrote and revised her novels stands in the dining parlour. Early editions are displayed alongside letters, family portraits and pieces of needlework.

🧑‍🦽👤 Marwell Zoo

▶ Colden Common. 6mi/10km SE on the B 2177. Open daily 10am–4pm/5pm/6pm, see website for details. Closed 25–26 Dec. £17.26 (child 3–16, £13.62) – reduced prices Nov–Mar. ♿🅿✕ ☏01962 777 407. www.marwell.org.uk.

The grounds of 16C Marwell Hall are home to over 200 species of animals and birds, including large cats, primates, giraffes and rhinos, with the emphasis on education and conservation.

New Forest★★

This ancient landscape near the coast has remained more or less unchanged since William the Conqueror named the area his 'new hunting forest' in 1079. The ancient system to protect and manage the woodlands and wilderness heaths is still in place and today, a National Park since 2005, where New Forest ponies, donkeys, deer and cattle roam in England's largest remaining tract of unenclosed pasture.

- ⚜ **Michelin Map:** Michelin Atlas p 9 or Map 503 O, P 31
- ℹ **Info:** Main Car Park Lyndhurst. ℘023 8028 2269. www.thenewforest.co.uk.
- ▶ **Location:** Hampshire.
- 👀 **Don't Miss:** Beaulieu National Motor Museum; Buckler's Hard.

BEAULIEU★★

This pretty village (pronounced '*bew-ley*') at the head of the Beaulieu river is famous for the National Motor Museum, one of the world's most comprehensive collections of motor vehicles, set in the grounds of a Cistercian monastery founded in 1204 by King John. After the Dissolution of the Monasteries, the **abbey** fell into ruin, its stone being in demand for Henry VIII's coastal forts; only the footings remain. The cloister has partly survived, notably the lay brothers' quarters, now housing the **Monastic Life Exhibition** and the 13C refectory, converted into the parish church. **Palace House**, the home of the first Lord Montagu, is a strange mixture of medieval monastic architecture and Victorian comforts.

The **National Motor Museum★★** 👫 (open daily late Sept–late May 10am–5pm; late May–late Sept 10am–6pm; closed 25 Dec; £24.75, child 5–17, £12.50 – discounts for advance purchase online; ♿🅿✖; ℘01590 612 345; www.beaulieu.co.uk) has a collection of over 250 vehicles and celebrates the story of motoring from 1895 to the present day. The Hall of Fame presents the great motoring pioneers and veteran and vintage cars while racing and record-breaking heroes are also commemorated. You can take a ride through 100 years of motoring with 'Wheels' and browse a re-created 1930's country garage before coming bang up to date with a *Top Gear* exhibition and – from the movies, Harry

Potter's 'Flying' Ford Anglia, and the world's largest official collection of original James Bond vehicles. Hands-on stations encourage children to explore how vehicles work.

BUCKLER'S HARD★

2mi/3km SE of Beaulieu. Open daily 10am–4.30pm (Easter–Sept 10am–5pm). £6.90, includes museum. 🅿✖ ℘01590 616 203. www.bucklershard.co.uk.

This charming hamlet comprises one very wide street lined with 18C cottages running down to the Beaulieu river. In the 1740s, the village became a shipbuilding centre for the Navy. The **Maritime Museum and Buckler's Hard Story★** illustrates many aspects of life and work in the 18C with the reconstructed interiors of two cottages and the New Inn, furnished in the style of the 1790s. Boat trips run from the wharf.

LYNDHURST

Capital of the New Forest, this attractive town was where the forest rulers held court in the 17C **Queen's House**. The **New Forest Museum**, housed in the visitor centre (High Street; open daily Jul–mid-Sept 9am–5pm; mid-Sept–Oct 10am–5pm; rest of year 10am–4pm; closed 25–26 Dec; ♿; ℘023 8028 3444; www.newforest museum.org.uk), gives an excellent introduction to the area.

MINSTEAD

This attractive unspoiled village just north of Lyndhurst is home to the 13C **All Saints church**. North of the church is **Furzey Gardens** (Garden: open daily

10am–sunset; Gallery and tea rooms: open 10am–5pm, Mar–Oct daily, Nov–mid-Dec Fri–Sun; garden £8, gallery free; &✗; ☎023 8081 2464; www.furzey-gardens.org), with a 16C thatched cottage showing how New Forest workers lived over 400 years ago.

BROCKENHURST

This may well be your arrival point in the New Forest as it is the main bus and train interchange. The village itself is peaceful with a pretty green often full of grazing ponies and cattle. You can **hire cycles** from **Cyclexperience Ltd**. (open daily 9am–5.30pm; ☎01590 624 808; www.newforestcyclehire.co.uk).

LYMINGTON★

Lymington is the liveliest town in the New Forest, full of good shops and places to eat and drink. The High Street leads down to the picturesque small bustling **quayside** and marina

area, lined with pretty period cottages, where fishing boats and yachtsmen mingle, fresh fish is sold and people come to enjoy the seaside holiday atmosphere.

FOREST DRIVES

Bolderwood Ornamental Drive★ – 2mi/3km from Lyndhurst on the A 35 towards Christchurch, take a right turn for this lovely drive through enclosures created in the 19C with many fine, mature trees. **Walks** enable visitors to see forest deer up close from observation platforms. At the end of the drive is the venerable Knightwood Oak, said to be over 375 years old.
Rhinefield Ornamental Drive★ 2mi/3km from Lyndhurst on the A 35 towards Christchurch, take a left turn for this magnificent drive along an avenue of trees planted in 1859. Today they are Britain's finest collection of mature conifers. Some stand 46m high.

Bournemouth Coast★

The seaside resort of Bournemouth is surrounded by attractive towns like Poole and Christchurch, home to one of the area's best beaches.

BOURNEMOUTH

The Grand Old Lady of England's south central coast, Bournemouth has been a popular summer and winter resort since the late-19C. It is famous for its two piers and the ever-colourful public gardens. A lively student population ensures a good number of busy pubs and nightclubs.

Russell-Cotes Art Gallery and Museum★★

East Cliff, Russell-Cotes Road. Open Tue–Sun and bank holiday Mons 10am–5pm. Closed Good Fri, 25–26 Dec. £6. &✗ ☎01202 451 858. http://russellcotes.com.

▶ **Population:** 183,491
◔ **Michelin Map:** Michelin Atlas p 9 or Map 503 O 31.
🖪 **Info:** Tourist Information Centre, Pier Approach. ☎01202 451 734. www.bournemouth.co.uk. The bus station and train station (Waterloo 1h45) are together, 1mi/1.6km east of the centre. To navigate the seafront jump aboard the cliff lifts and land-train, which runs for 6mi/10km along the promenade.
◐ **Location:** 105mi/169km southwest of London.
◉ **Don't Miss:** Russell-Cotes Art Gallery and Museum; Compton Acres; the view of Old Harry Rocks from the Southwest Coast Path.
◔ **Timing:** In summer allow at least 2 days.
👥 **Kids:** The beaches.

Housed in **East Cliff Hall**, decorated in archetypal ornate High Victorian taste, with inlaid furniture, painted ceilings, decorative windows and coloured wallpaper, the collections include numerous paintings (William Frith, Landseer, Leighton, Rossetti, Alma-Tadema…), fine English china, gold and silver plate, and souvenirs from abroad (the Orient, Germany, Egypt).

EXCURSIONS
Compton Acres★★
◗ 164 Canford Cliffs Road. 2mi/3km W by the A 338. Open daily Easter–Oct 10am–6pm; Nov–Easter 10am–4pm. Closed 1 Jan and 25–26 Dec. £8.45. &🅿✕ ℘01202 700 778. www.comptonacres.co.uk.
This series of nine distinct **gardens** (Italian, rock, water and Japanese) spreads over 6ha in a rift in the sandstone cliffs; it is famous for having flowers in bloom throughout the year. The **English Garden** lies open to sunsets and a westerly **view★★★** of Poole Harbour, Brownsea Island and the Purbeck Hills.

Poole★
◗ 4mi/6km W on the the A 338. 🄱 ℘01202 262600. www.pooletourism.com.
With its fine sandy beach at Sandbanks and its situation on one of the largest harbours in the world, Poole is a holiday resort, yachting haven and a major roll-on, roll-off port. By the quay is **Poole Museum** (4 High Street; open Apr–Oct daily 10am–5pm; Nov–Mar Mon–Sat 10am–4pm, Sun noon–4pm; &; ℘01202 262 600; www.poolemuseum.co.uk) telling the history of the port and town. Adjacent is **Scaplen's Court** (open Aug only, contact details as Poole Museum), a domestic building from the late medieval period. Note the attractive 18C **old town** and Guildhall.

Brownsea Island★
◗ Access by boat from Poole Quay and Sandbanks. Open daily from mid-Mar 10am–5pm. Entry to island £6.75; ferry with Brownsea Island Ferries (℘01929

462 383. www.brownseaislandferries. com), from Poole Quay, £10.75, from Sandbanks £6.50. &✕ ℘01202 707 744. www.nationaltrust.org.uk.
This 200ha island, covered in heath and woodland and fringed by inviting beaches along its south shore, consists of two nature reserves, either side of **Middle Street** along the central spine of the island.
The north reserve is a sanctuary for waterfowl and other birds, and the south reserve, where visitors can wander at will, is likewise home to numerous birds, including peacocks.
There is an excellent **view★★** across Poole Bay to the Purbeck Hills from **Baden-Powell Stone**, which commemorates the first Boy Scout camp held here in 1907.

Christchurch★
◗ 6mi/10km E on the A 35.
At the heart of this pretty and prosperous little coastal town is the Norman **Christchurch Priory★** (open Mon–Sat 9.30am–5.30pm, Sun 2.15–5.30pm; £3 suggested donation; tower tours £3; museum 50p; priory tours £10, see website for dates, prior booking essential; ℘01202 485804, www.christchurchpriory.org) and Norman castle, grouped around a harbour filled with fishing and pleasure craft.

The Blue Pool★
◗ 17mi/27km SW (on the Isle of Purbeck). Furzebrook Road. Open Mar–Nov daily 9.30am–5pm, later in summer. £7. &🅿✕ ℘01202 551 408. www.bluepooltearooms.co.uk.
This beautiful blue-green (1.2ha) lake (no bathing) is fringed by silver birch and pine woods, gorse and heather, through which sandy paths meander, giving views of the Purbeck Hills. There is a small museum of local clay mining and tea rooms plus the Wareham Bear collection of over 200 miniature dressed bears.

Wimborne Minster★

⏵ 10mi/16km NW.
Open Mar–Oct 10am–5pm; Nov–Feb
10am–4pm. ♿ ✆01202 884 753.
www.wimborneminster.org.uk.

This huge church dominates the small town of Wimborne. The present structure is mainly Norman (1120–80) with 15C additions. It has a wealth of detail to enjoy; note the 'Quarter Jack' grenadier figure on the west tower striking the time, the astronomical clock, and the splendid stained-glass windows. Ascend the 600-year-old spiral staircase to the old Treasury, and the second-largest chained library in the country with manuscripts on lambskin, dating back to 1343.

Kingston Lacy★

⏵ 12mi/19.3km NW. **House:** open Mar early Nov Wed–Sun and Bank Holiday Mons 11am–4pm/5pm. **Gardens:** open daily year-round 10am–dusk. £12.70 (timed tickets). ♿🅿✕ ✆01202 883 402. www.nationaltrust.org.uk.

This striking 17C house with lavish interiors has an outstanding art collection including paintings by Rubens, Van Dyck, Titian and more… plus the largest private collection of Egyptian artefacts in the UK. Outside are beautiful lawns and a restored Japanese tea garden.

🚗DRIVING TOUR

ISLE OF PURBECK

30mi/48km. Allow a full day not including visiting time.

The Isle of Purbeck is in fact a 60sq mi/155sq km peninsula of mostly unspoiled villages, seaside and castles.

⏵ Begin by crossing the water from Poole, on the Sandbanks Ferry.

Studland

3mi/5km S of the ferry via A 351.
This National Trust-owned beach is one of the finest in the West Country and is famous for its (signposted) nudist area.

Swanage★

3mi/5km S of Studland via B 3351.
🛈 The White House, Shore Road.
✆01929 422885.

A scenic stretch of road leads to this quarry town and harbour, from which stone and marble were shipped to build Westminster Abbey and the cathedrals of Exeter, Lincoln and Salisbury. Swanage also boasts a good beach and a range of seaside leisure facilities. Take the Southwest Coast Path east of Swanage to discover **Old Harry Rocks★★**, two stacks of gleaming chalk once part of an unbroken shoreline from The Needles, but now separated from the mainland and each other (Old Harry is the larger stack, his 'wife' is the slimmer!) Just over 1mi/1.6km south of Swanage, the road ends at **Durlstone Head** and its Country Park. In the park is **Durlstone Castle**, built 1889, as a Victorian folly, complete with its 40-ton, 3m diameter 'Great Globe' of the world in its grounds (www.durlston.co.uk).

⏵ Return to Swanage, then head west on the A 351 5mi/8km.

Corfe Castle★

Open daily Jan–Mar and Nov–Dec 10am–4pm; Apr–Sept 10am–6pm; Oct 10am–5pm. Closed 25–26 Dec. £9.54 (peak)/£9 (off-peak). ♿🅿 (charge); ✕ ✆01929 481 294.
www.nationaltrust.org.uk.

Corfe Castle has dominated the landscape since the 11C, first as a towering stronghold and since 1646 as a dramatic ruin. The **views★★** are spectacular from the high mound on which it stands.
In 987 the 17-year-old King Edward, son of Edgar, visiting his half-brother at the castle, was murdered by his stepmother, Queen Aethelfrith; in 1001 he was canonised as **St Edward, King and Martyr**. It became home to Sir John Bankes, Chief Justice to King Charles I. His wife resolutely defended it in the Civil War, but when it fell, owing to the treachery of one of the garrison, it was looted and blown up by the Parliamentarians. Below the ruins is a picture-postcard

village★ of low stone houses and several inns, many dating from the 16C and 17C. Visit the quaint model village (www.corfecastlemodelvillage.co.uk).

▶ Head north briefly on the A 351, then turn left to join the B 3070 to East Lulworth.

Lulworth Castle

Open Easter–Dec Sun–Fri 10.30am–5pm. Closed Jan–Easter. £5. ♿ 🅿 (£3) ✗ ✆01929 400 352. www.lulworth.com. This was built in the early 17C as a hunting lodge and in 1929 was gutted by fire. Restoration was completed in 1998.

▶ Continue on the same road for 2.5mi/4km; look for the brown signs to Lulworth Cove car park.

Lulworth Cove and Durdle Door★

The circular sweep of Lulworth Cove is almost enclosed by the downland cliffs. From here, the Dorset Coast Path leads to the striking cliff archway of **Durdle Door** to the west, a dramatic climax.

▶ Head back to East Lulworth and follow the B30370 north, then turn right onto the A352.

Wareham

The centrepiece of this quiet town in summer is its picturesque flower-filled **quay** on the languorous River Frome, plied by colourful pleasure craft. An old granary house (now a restaurant) and the Anglo-Saxon Lady St Mary's church and priory complete an idyllic composition.

Dorchester★

and the Jurassic Coast

The Romans built the southwest settlement of Durnovaria in the 1C on the London–Exeter highway, but Dorchester today is famous for being 'Hardy Country', home to the great British novelist, Thomas Hardy and the setting for many of his 19C tales.

VISIT
DORSET COUNTY MUSEUM★

High West Street. Open Apr–Oct Mon–Sat 10am–5pm; Nov–Mar 10am–4pm. £6.35. ♿ ✆01305 262 735. www.dorsetcountymuseum.org.
A splendid **Victorian gallery**, with painted cast-iron columns and arches supporting a glass roof, houses **Thomas Hardy** memorabilia: furniture and paintings and papers from **Max Gate**, the house Hardy built for himself in 1885, as well as a reconstruction of his study.

▶ **Population:** 19 060.
◉ **Michelin Map:** Michelin Atlas p 8 or Map 503 M 31.
▮ **Info: Dorchester Library and Learning Centre, Charles Street**. ✆01305 267 992. www.visit-dorset.com. London trains (Waterloo 2h30) arrive at Dorchester South, Bath (1h50) and Bristol (2h18) trains at Dorchester West.
▶ **Location:** 126mi/203km southwest of London.
◉ **Don't Miss:** Abbotsbury Village and Swannery.
🧒 **Kids:** Abbotsbury Children's Farm and Swannery.

EXCURSIONS
Bere Regis church★

▶ 11mi/18km E on the A 35.
The fine Perpendicular church of **St John the Baptist** is the only building in the village to have survived the last of a series of fires in 1788. Its **roof★★** is a particular joy.

Maiden Castle★

◐ 2mi/3km SW on the A 354.
Open daily dawn-dusk.
Britain's finest **earthwork ramparts** were begun c.350 BCE on the site of a Neolithic settlement. There were four main building phases before this massive 19ha complex was fully equipped with defences c.60 BCE.

Chesil Beach/Abbotsbury★★

◐ 10mi/16km SW via Martinstown and Portesham.
Chesil Beach is a remarkable 8mi/13km shingle bank which forms a lagoon; at one end is the charming thatched golden ironstone village of **Abbotsbury** with its three very popular visitor attractions ('Passport' Ticket: adult £14.40, child £12, family £36) – the Swannery, the Children's Farm and the Sub-tropical Gardens (www.abbotsbury-tourism.co.uk).
The **Abbotsbury Swannery★** ☒☒ (New Barn Road; open late Mar–Oct daily 10am–5pm; £12.50, child (5–15) £9.50 ♿🅿✗; ☎01305 871 858) was founded by monks c.1390 and now accommodates more than 400 mute swans. You can walk right through the middle of the beautifully located nesting grounds and observe the birds at close quarters. The highlight is the mass feeding of up to 600 swans at noon and 4pm daily.
A short walk away, the **Children's Farm** ☒☒ (Church Street; open as Swannery, Sept–Oct Sat–Sun only; £11 (child 5–15) £9.50; ♿✗ ☎01305 871 817) is housed in and around a splendid **Tithe Barn** built in the 1390s. The lush acclaimed neighbouring **Subtropical Gardens★** (Bullers Way; open daily 10am–4pm/5pm; £12.50; (child 5–15) £9.50; ♿🅿✗; ☎01305 871 387; www.abbotsbury-tourism.co.uk) contrast with the rugged setting of the wind-blown **St Catherine's chapel★** on its 76m crest.

🚗DRIVING TOUR

JURASSIC COAST★★

Stretching from Purbeck in the east to Exmouth in the west, this coastline

Jurassic Coast viewed from St Aldhelm's Head

© Robert Harding/hemis.fr

takes its name from the large number of Jurassic-age fossils that have been found in its cliffs. This short route (46mi/74km) along the coast covers the westernmost stretch *(distances are from Abbotsbury)*.
Begin at **Abbotsbury★★** (*◐see above*). Follow the coast road west to **Lyme Regis★** (18.5/30km). This small genteel resort is famous for its Cobb (breakwater) and palaeontology heritage – as explained in the **Lyme Regis Museum** (www.lymeregismuseum.co.uk).
Beer (28mi/45km) is a classic small Devon fishing village with a broad shingle beach where boats rest overnight. **Sidmouth** (34mi/55km) is another genteel resort, framed between high red cliffs, with its Regency vintage lovingly preserved. The road diverts inland (signposted) to **Bicton Park Botanical Gardens** (40mi/64km; www.bictongardens.co.uk). On the broad sandy Exe estuary, **Exmouth** *(46mi/74km)* is a mix of dignified Georgian houses and 'smugglers' alleys'. Don't miss **A La Ronde★** (www.nationaltrust.org.uk), a unique 16-sided, 18C house with an extraordinary interior decor of shells and feathers.

Dorset and Wiltshire Border★★

The rolling countryside of the Wiltshire/Dorset borders boasts two picture-postcard small historic towns, England's finest landscaped gardens, Britain's most exotic (and child-friendly) aristocratic estate, and its rudest chalk figure.

🅸 **Info:** www.visitwiltshire.co.uk; www.visit-dorset.com.

🅐 **Don't Miss:** Stourhead; Longleat; Wilton House.

🅺 **Kids:** Longleat Safari Park.

SHERBORNE★

With its imposing abbey church, public school and fine warm **Ham Hill stone** buildings, Sherborne has the charm of a miniature cathedral city.

Sherborne Abbey★★

Open daily 8am–6pm (winter 4pm). Guided tours Apr–Sept Tue 10.30am, Fri 2.30pm (call to confirm). ♿ ☎01935 812 452. www.sherborneabbey.com.

The abbey church, rebuilt during the 15C, contains elements which date back to Saxon times when Sherborne was made the See of the Bishop of Wessex, **St Aldhelm**, in 705. The Norman church extended as far west as the Saxon church, as the late Norman **south porch** proves. The 15C **crossing tower** on massive Saxon-Norman piers and walls has paired bell openings and 12 pinnacles. Inside, the **chancel** shafts rise directly from the floor up to the earliest large-scale **fan vault** in the country, and the effect is breathtaking. Even more impressive is the late-15C **nave vault**. A splendid, unadorned Norman **tower arch** divides the nave from the chancel. An original **Saxon doorway** can be seen at the end of the north aisle.

Sherborne Castle★

Open Apr–Oct Tue–Thu, Sat–Sun and bank holidays 10am–5pm (castle 11am). £12, grounds only, £6.50. ✕ ☎01935 812 072. www.sherbornecastle.com.

The original **Old Castle**, now a ruin, was built in 1107–35. In 1592 it was acquired by **Sir Walter Raleigh**, who decided to build a new Sherborne Castle on the far bank of the River Yeo.

Raleigh created a four-storey house beneath a Dutch gable and balustrade, built of Ham Hill stone. Sir John Digby, who acquired the property following Raleigh's imprisonment, enlarged the castle in 1620–30, keeping to Raleigh's style. The house, set in parkland modelled by Lancelot 'Capability' Brown in 1776–79, contains fine collections of paintings, furniture and porcelain. Note the painting (1600) of Queen Elizabeth I, and the 17C plaster ceiling in the Red Drawing Room.

CERNE ABBAS★

11mi/18km S of Sherborne.

The **village★** is notable for the beautiful range of timber-fronted 16C houses in Abbey Street, and for **St Mary's Church**, a mix of Early English and Perpendicular, with a spectacular **tower**.

However, it is the spectacular 55m-long chalk outline of the naked **Cerne Abbas Giant**, one of the largest hillfigures in Britain, that attracts most visitors. 'He' has been connected, for obvious reasons, with local fertility rituals, although his origin and date remain unclear.

SHAFTESBURY

16.5mi/26km E of Sherborne.

This little town is perched on the crest of a 213m spur, an excellent **vantage point★**, used by King Alfred as a strongpoint in his wars against the Danes. And even today Shaftesbury's joy is the steep cobbled picture-book **Gold Hill★**, lined on one side with small 16C–18C houses and on the other by a massive buttressed 13C ochre-coloured wall. It is famous in Britain as the scene of the sepia-tinted nostalgia-laden Hovis bread TV adverts. At the top is the small **Gold Hill Museum** (open Apr–Oct Thu–Tue 10.30am–4.30pm; ☏01747 852 157; http://goldhillmuseum.org.uk) covering local history.

Shaftesbury **Abbey** (museum and garden open Apr–Oct, daily 10am–5pm; £3; ☏01747 852 910; www.shaftesburyabbey.org.uk), founded in 888 by King Alfred, became the wealthiest nunnery in England. In the 15C–16C the saying went that if the Abbess of Shaston (Shaftesbury) were to marry the Abbot of Glaston (Glastonbury) their heirs would own more land than the king. In 1539, Henry VIII dissolved both abbeys and now only the ground plan of Shaston remains visible.

WILTON HOUSE★★
3mi/5km W of Salisbury.

House: open Easter weekend, May–Aug Sun–Thu and bank holiday Sats 11.30am–5pm. **Grounds**: open 1 wk before and after Easter; May–mid Sept daily 11am–5.30pm Sun–Thu and bank holiday Sats. £15, grounds only, £6.25. ☏01722 746 714. www.wiltonhouse.com.

In 1544 the first Earl of Pembroke was given the land of the dissolved Benedictine convent at Wilton by Henry VIII and built a house here. The 4th Earl commissioned Inigo Jones to design the house anew in 1630 and the 11th Earl called in James Wyatt in 1801, who greatly altered the house.

The suite of State Apartments by Inigo Jones has a wealth of Classical detail. The furniture includes pieces by William Kent and the younger Chippendale.

The ceiling of the Colonnade Room boasts fantastical 17C monkey motifs. In the Great Ante Room are portraits by Rembrandt, Van Dyck and Clouet.

The white-and-gold Double Cube Room, measuring 18m x 9m x 9m, was specially designed by Inigo Jones to house the 4th Earl's unique collection of splendid Van Dyck portraits. It was here that strategic plans were laid by Eisenhower and Churchill (a frequent visitor) during the Second World War, when Wilton House was the Southern

Command headquarters. The house sits square on a flat lawn which stretches south to the river, marked by the much-photographed **Palladian bridge** (1737). The grounds also include an excellent adventure playground.

STOURHEAD★★★
Stourton. Nr Warminster, 18.5mi/30km S of Bath. ♿. **Garden**: open daily 9am–5pm (Apr–Sept 6pm). **House**: open mid-Mar–Oct and late Nov–late Dec daily 11am–4.30pm (late Nov–late Dec daily 11am–3.30pm). **Tower**: open Mar–late Oct Sat–Sun noon–4pm.
Garden and house £16, tower £4.20. 🅿(£4). ✗ ☏01747 841 152. www.nationaltrust.org.uk.

One of the most celebrated gardens in the country, Stourhead is a supreme example of English landscape style including a Palladian mansion, delightful garden architecture and rare planting around a tranquil lake.

Garden
This idyllic scenery was created by the banker Henry Hoare II (1705–85), influenced by the landscapes he saw on his travels. Perhaps an even greater influence were the paintings of Claude Lorrain and Nicolas Poussin, in which nature is presented in luminous shades and focal points are provided by statuary or Classical buildings. He first had the great triangular lake formed, then began the planting of trees, 'ranged in large masses as the shades in a painting'. In collaboration with his architect, Henry Flitcroft, he began to build his garden architecture: the Temple of Flora, the Grotto, the Gothic Cottage, the Pantheon, the Temple of Apollo, and **Palladian bridge**. He also created a quintessential English vista of lake, Turf Bridge, Cross, and, in the background, Stourton church and village. His planting, now wonderfully mature, has been added to by his successors to give a wealth of exotic specimens and of ever-changing seasonal effects. At the far end of the 'outer circuit' stands **Alfred's Tower**, a triangular brick folly built on the spot where Alfred

Longleat Safari Park

© C. Ochterbeck/MICHELIN

allegedly raised his standard resisting the Danes; it also commemorates the succession of George III and peace with France (1762). At the top of the narrow tower is a viewing balcony (205 steps).

House

The original house of 1721 was built for the father of Henry Hoare II. In 1902 a fire destroyed the early-18C interiors, although the contents of the ground floor state rooms were largely saved. The **hall**, a perfect 9m cube, is hung with family portraits. The long barrel-vaulted **library**, a particularly fine Regency interior, contains some splendid pieces of **Chippendale** furniture and **Canaletto** drawings of Venice. Further treasures are to be found in the South Wing (furniture) and **Picture Gallery**: landscapes by **Claude** and **Poussin**.

LONGLEAT★★★

Warminster. 19mi/31km S of Bath and well signed from the main roads.
Open: see website for dates and times.
£28.85, child (3–15) £21.62 (online prices). Closed 25 Dec. ☏01985 845 420.
♿🅿✕ ☏01985 844 400.
www.longleat.co.uk.

Set in 360ha of Capability Brown-landscaped parkland, the house is one of the best examples of High Elizabethan architecture in Britain. It caused great controversy in 1949, when it became the first stately home to open to the public on a commercial basis, and an even bigger furore in 1966 when it opened the first safari park outside Africa.

House

On the ground floor, the late-16C Great Hall with its fine hammerbeam roof contains a splendid pillared fireplace. The Ante-Library is graced by Italian furniture. The Red Library boasts *trompe l'œil* ceiling panels, while the gilded coffered ceiling of the Lower Dining Room is modelled on one in the Doge's Palace. In the Breakfast Room family portraits look down on Chippendale-style chairs and japanned gaming tables, while the walls are hung with modern art.

Upstairs, highlights include the State Dining Room with its Cordoba leather walls and a Meissen table centrepiece (c.1760); the 27m 17C Long Gallery with a massive marble fireplace copied from one in the Doge's Palace; the State Drawing Room paintings and various pieces of 18C French furniture; the Apartments, dress collection and cabinets of porcelain. The Royal Bedrooms comprise an elegant dressing room hung with hand-painted Chinese wallpaper. The outbuildings comprise a butchery and stable block (containing the eclectic 'Lord Bath's Bygones'). **Lord Bath's Murals** is a collection famous for its Kama Sutra-type murals.

🏃🏃 Safari Park and Other Attractions

The 'drive-in zoo' is famous for its lions and monkeys, the latter being notorious for clambering onto cars. There are also enclosures for wallabies, giraffes, zebras, llamas, dromedaries, camels, white rhinos, fallow deer, wolves, tigers, and elephants. Popular features include: **hand-feeding giraffes** at the Watering Hole in the East Africa Reserve; **Jungle Kingdom;** feeding lorikeets; walking through the meerkat enclosure, and so on… Once out of your car a **safari boat** takes you on a lake among seals and hippos. There's also a batcave, birds of prey and animals with ranger shows, Pets Corner, a steam railway, motion simulators and various other family activities. Another Longleat claim to fame is its **hedge maze**, made up of more than 16 000 English yews (20–90 mins to complete).

Salisbury★★

Salisbury (pronounced "sauls-bur-ee") is the archetypal English cathedral town. The view, as you approach it, is much as John Constable painted it more than two centuries ago, unencumbered by high-rise modernity or sprawling suburbs. The spire, the tallest in England, is the city's focal point.

▸ **Population:** 45 000.

◔ **Michelin Map:** Michelin Atlas p 9 or Map 503 O 30.

▯ **Info:** Fish Row. ℘01722 342 860. www.visitwiltshire.co.uk. Salisbury is a transport hub with frequent services (London Waterloo 1h30, Bath 56 min). The station is on South Western Road 0.5mi/0.8km from the centre. The bus station is central, on Endless Street.

◖ **Location:** Near Southampton and just north of the New Forest.

A BIT OF HISTORY

The earlier city of **Old Sarum★** (2mi/3km N), originally an Iron Age hilltop fort (11ha), had been modified by the Romans and Saxons and became a Norman stronghold where two successive cathedrals were built. By the beginning of the 13C the citizens and clergy of Old Sarum began to build their third cathedral on the banks of the River Avon. The hilltop buildings fell into ruin and New Sarum, or Salisbury, was born.

MEDIEVAL STREETS

Between the cathedral and the 19C **Market Square** extend medieval streets, lined by gabled half-timbered houses dating from the 14C–17C. At the centre in a small square stands the 15C hexagonal **Poultry Cross**.

At the northeast end of the high street is **Sarum St Thomas church★**, a Perpendicular church dating from 1220 with a low square tower of 1390. It features a **doom painting** (c.1475), with Christ in Majesty and the New Jerusalem.

CATHEDRAL★★★

Open Mon–Sat 9am–5pm, Sun noon–4pm. £7.50, voluntary contribution requested. Tower Tour (105min) run once daily (see website for details); £12.50, advance booking recommended. ㅤ℘01722 555 120. www.salisburycathedral.org.uk.

For many people, Salisbury cathedral epitomises the Early English style at its best; Medieval Gothic in its purest, most ascetic form. It is unique among England's older cathedrals, having been built in a single style, in just 38 years, with the tallest spire in England (123m). Outside, the ornate **west screen** extends from the gabled portals up through lines of statue-filled niches, lancet windows and arcading to the pointed gable and corner towers with their miniature angel pinnacles and ribbed spires. The most spectacular feature of the cathedral, the **spire** over the heightened tower, was added almost a century later but harmonises perfectly. Inside, the **nave** (70m) extends over half the length of the whole building (137m), its vault towering to a height of 26m. Note on the south side the tomb chests of **Bishops Roger** (d.1139) and **Joscelin** (d.1184), the shrine of **St Osmund** (d.1099) and the chain-mailed **William Longespée** (d.1226), half-brother of King John. Giant piers of clustered black marble columns mark the **crossing**, intended to support the original tower, but since the 14C required to bear the additional 6 500 tons of the heightened tower and spire. The piers have in fact buckled a noticeable 9cm, despite reinforcing.

A brass plate in the crossing marks the spot where a plumb-line let down from the spire point by Sir Christopher Wren in 1668 reached the floor; 75cm off-centre to the southwest. In the north aisle is the oldest working clock in England (c.1386).

A **Tower Tour** climbs 332 steps in easy stages by narrow winding spiral staircases to reach the foot of the spire 69m) above ground level. From here you can see up into the spire through the medieval scaffold, and from the outside you can look over the city and surrounding countryside.

Construction of the Decorated Gothic–style **chapter house** and **cloisters** was begun c.1263, making the latter the earliest in any English cathedral; they are also the longest (55m). The vault of the octagonal chapter house (18m across) is supported on a central column, surrounded by eight ringed Purbeck marble shafts which rise from their foliated capitals as ribs to ceiling bosses, before dropping to clusters of slim columns framing the windows. An Old Testament frieze (restored 19C) fills the niches on either side of the canons' seats. The main floor display is dedicated to one of four original copies of the **Magna Carta**.

Cathedral Close★

The Close is spacious and mellow with its 16–18C houses composed of ancient stone and terra-cotta bricks. The Close walls are of stone from the abandoned cathedral and castle of Old Sarum.

The medieval flint-and-brick house **Salisbury & South Wiltshire Museum★** (open Mon–Sat and bank holidays 10am–5pm, Sun noon–5pm; Closed 24–25 Dec; £7.50; &✕; ℘01722 332 151; www.salisburymuseum.org.uk) contains nationally important archaeological displays including **Stonehenge galleries**, Roman and medieval Salisbury, and relics from Old Sarum. Other areas include the Pitt-Rivers collections of ethnography and antiquities; art; glass, porcelain and pottery.

The Museum of the Infantry Regiments of Berkshire and Wiltshire is housed in **The Wardrobe★** (open Feb–Nov Mon–Sat 10am–5pm; £5; &✕; ℘01722 419 419; www.thewardrobe.org.uk), one of the first houses to be built in the Close (1254) as the bishop's document storehouse and wardrobe.

In Chorister's Close, **Mompesson House★** (open Apr–early Nov 11am–5pm; £6.50; &✕; ℘01722 335 659; www.nationaltrust.org.uk) was built in 1701 by Charles Mompesson. It is notable for its ornate Baroque plasterwork and Turnbull Collection of some 370 types of English drinking glasses dating from 1700.

EXCURSION
OLD SARUM★

◗ 3.5 mi north of Salisbury.
Open daily Apr–Sept 10am–6pm; Oct 10am–5pm; rest of year 10am–4pm. Closed 1 Jan, 24–26 Dec. £4.80. ℗
℘01722 335 398.
www.english-heritage.org.uk.

The mighty ramparts of this great earthwork were raised c.500 BCE by Iron Age peoples, then occupied by the Romans, the Saxons and, eventually, the Normans. Here, William the Conqueror paid off his troops in 1070, and in 1086 summoned the great landowners of England to swear an oath of loyalty.

A castle was built, then a royal palace. By the mid-12C a town had arisen complete with a new Norman cathedral, but the lack of water on the scorched hilltop made life almost unbearable.

The answer was a move downhill to the burgeoning New Sarum (Salisbury), where a new cathedral was founded in 1220. Old Sarum went into rapid decline. Its cathedral was demolished and used for building materials and its castle was abandoned.

Today, Old Sarum remains an atmospheric place, the remains of its fortress palace, castle and cathedral still clear, and well interpreted in-situ.

© gravision/iStockphoto.com

Stonehenge

Salisbury Plain★★★

and North Wiltshire

This area is dominated by the enigmatic presence of Stonehenge, though this is but one of many important prehistoric sites on and around the 300sq-mile (780sq-km) Salisbury Plain, much of which is occupied by the Army and is out of bounds. Well-preserved traces of the less distant past are in evidence at Malmesbury, Devizes and Lacock.

👪 STONEHENGE★★★

Just N of Salisbury, 84mi/135km SW of London. Open (timed tickets in operation; advance booking essential) daily Jun–Aug daily 9am–8pm; Sept–mid-Oct 9.30am–7pm; mid-Oct–May 9.30am–5pm. In poor weather, access may be restricted and visitors may not be able to use the walkway around the stone circle. Closed 24–25 Dec. £16.50. ♿🅿✕ ☎0370 333 1181. www.english-heritage.org.uk.

Britain's most celebrated prehistoric monument is between 4 000 and 5 000 years old; radiocarbon dating indicates that its construction was begun in c.2950 BCE and completed in three phases by c.1550 BCE. For centuries man has speculated upon its purpose but it remains an enigma. Although many of the stones have fallen or disappeared it

- 👣 **Michelin Map:** Michelin Atlas p 9 or Map 503 O 30.
- 🔋 **Info:** www.visitwiltshire.co.uk.
- 👁 **Don't Miss:** Stonehenge; Avebury; Lacock; Grand Avenue, Savernake forest; Corsham Court.
- 👪 **Kids:** Stonehenge.

is still possible, from the centre of the circle, to see the sun rise over the Heel Stone (at the entrance) on midsummer's day; there are suggestions that it was constructed as an astronomical observatory or a sanctuary for a sun-worshipping cult, or even a combination of the two. The main axis has always been aligned with the midsummer sunrise, so Stonehenge must have been linked to the seasons.

A Bit of History

The period – When work began the area was inhabited by nomadic hunters and early farming settlers who had crossed the Channel and North Sea in skin boats. By 2000 BCE the Beaker Folk spread into Wessex along the chalk upland tracks, growing into a community of 12–15 000, ruled by the cattle-barons of Salisbury Plain, who also controlled the metal industry. There was a growing priesthood who, at peak periods in the construction of Stonehenge, could call on the population to provide the 600 men needed to haul a sarsen stone up the Vale of Pewsey, or 200 to erect it on-site.

The building design – Like many a medieval cathedral, Stonehenge was much remodelled after its foundation. In the **first phase**, 2950 BCE–2900 BCE, a ditch with an inner bank of chalk rubble (nearly 2m high) was dug. This, with a ring of 56 holes, known as the Aubrey Holes, after the 17C pioneer of field archaeology John Aubrey (1626–97), encloses an area 91m in diameter. To the northeast the bank and ditch were cut to make an entrance marked inside by two upright stones and outside by the **Heel Stone** (near the road). Inside the enclosure four **Station Sarsens** were set up at the cardinal points of the compass.

In the **second phase**, c.2100 BCE, a double ring of undressed **bluestones** was set up towards the centre; these stones, weighing up to 4 tons each, were transported 240mi/386km from the Presely Hills in southwest Wales, mainly by water, and finally along the wide **Avenue**, which was built from the River Avon to the entrance of the henge. In the **third phase**, c.2000 BCE, the structure was transformed. The bluestone rings were replaced by a circle of tall trilithons. These standing stones were tapered at one end and tenoned at the top to secure the curving mortised lintels, which were linked to each other by tongues and grooves, having been levered gradually into position. Inside the circle five separate giant trilithons rose in a horseshoe, opening towards the Heel Stone. The entrance was marked by new uprights, one of which, the Slaughter Stone, now fallen, remains.

By the end of this **final phase**, c.1550 BCE, the dressed bluestones were reintroduced in their present horseshoe formation, within the sarsen horseshoe.

DEVIZES

24mi/39km E of Bath and 90mi/145km W of London.
🅱 ☎01380 800 400.
www.devizes.org.uk.

Devizes flourished as a cloth market from medieval times to the 19C; from the 17C it profited from tobacco, which was then grown widely in the area and it is now probably best known for its local brewery, Wadworths, whose shire horses make daily deliveries in town. All this accounts for the number of handsome 18C town houses, pubs and not one but two town halls.

St John's church★★

39 Long Street. Open daily during daylight hours. ☎01380 723 705.
This important Norman parish church has a mighty oblong **crossing tower** with, on the inside, round arches towards the nave and chancel and an early example of pointed arches towards the transepts. Inside, the vaulted east end is typically Norman, decorated with interlaced arches articulated with chevron and zigzag mouldings. The side chapels (1483) are separated from the chancel and sanctuary by decorative stone screens and have fine lacunar roofs resting on carved corbels.

Wiltshire Heritage Museum★

41 Long Street. Open Mon–Sat 10am–5pm, Sun noon–4pm. £6. ♿
☎01380 727 369.
www.wiltshiremuseum.org.uk.
In addition to geology and natural history collections and an art gallery, the museum has a renowned archaeological department. Models of nearby Stonehenge and Avebury are displayed among a collection of local finds including those from Bush Barrow, described as "the Crown Jewels of the King of Stonehenge"

AVEBURY★★

7mi/11km NE of Devizes on the A 361.
Stones: Open any reasonable time during daylight hours.
Museum: open daily Apr–Oct 10am–6pm; Nov–Mar 10am–4pm; closed 24–26 Dec, 1 Jan; £4.40.
Manor house and Garden: open Thu–Tue mid-Feb–Mar and Nov–Dec 11am–4pm, Apr–Nov 11am–5pm (by timed ticket); £7.20.

White Horses

Within a 30mi/50km radius of Marlborough are no fewer than seven white horse figures carved into the chalky landscape. The oldest, largest and most famous is the **Uffington White Horse**, 20mi/32km northeast of Marlborough on White Horse Hill, Berkshire Downs. It is visible from the A 420 or B 4508 or B 4507 east of Swindon. This is one of England's oldest chalk hill figures.

It is 111m long, though it can only be seen fully from the air, so leading to the theory that perhaps it was a sign to ancient gods. It was once thought that it might be from the Iron Age, as its shape is similar to those found on coins from the period; or perhaps Anglo-Saxon, constructed to celebrate King Alfred's victories over the Danes in AD 871. However, new testing methods on soil samples have revealed that the horse is in fact about 3,000 years old (late Bronze Age). But who carved it and why remains a mystery.

♿⛶ (£7, or £4 after 3pm) ✕ ✆01672 539 250. www.nationaltrust.org.uk; www.english-heritage.org.uk
Though less famous than Stonehenge, for many visitors Avebury is more rewarding. The surrounding district is extremely rich in prehistoric monuments and earthworks, the earliest dating from c 3700 BCE–3500 BCE. The site is all the more fascinating as the village lies inside the circle of 30-ton–40-ton sarsen stones within the earth ramparts.

The Stones★

It is difficult to make out the plan of the stones, since the only vantage points are on the earth banks, reinforced by an inner ditch, around the 28 acre/11ha site. These are broken at the cardinal points of the compass to allow access to the centre (now used by modern roads) and enclose a circle of 100 sarsens from the Marlborough Downs and two inner rings. From the south exit, an avenue of about 100 pairs of stones (only some of which can still be seen) once led to the burial site known as the Sanctuary on Overton Hill (excavated in 1930).

The **Alexander Keiller Museum** and its **Barn Gallery** give a valuable insight into this and neighbouring sites. The early 16C manor house, **Avebury Manor,** reopened in 2012 following a major transformation that was followed by a BBC TV series (*The Manor Reborn*).

SILBURY HILL★

2mi/3km S of Avebury.
A 40m high man-made chalk mound, one of the largest of its kind in Europe. The reasons for its construction remain a mystery.

The **West Kennet Long Barrow★** (3mi/5km S) is England's finest burial barrow (104m x 23m), dating from 3500–3000 BCE. The entrance at the east end is flanked by giant sarsens, and the passage, lateral vaults and chamber at the far end are roofed with massive capstones supported on upright sarsens and drystone walling. Some 50 skeletons from the early Neolithic period were discovered in these atmospheric internal burial chambers, which may be explored.

THE RIDGEWAY PATH★★

Overton Hill is around 1mi/1.6km S of Avebury. www.nationaltrail.co.uk.
This ancient trade route was already in use by the nomadic peoples of the Palaeolithic and Mesolithic ages, who followed the line of the chalk ridge, as it was easier going than the lower slopes covered in forest or scrub. The modern path, opened in 1973, runs from Overton Hill, via the Uffington White Horse, to the Ivinghoe Beacon near Tring in Hertfordshire (85mi/137km).

Kennet and Avon Canal

In 1794, a scheme to build a canal between navigable sections of the River Avon and River Kennet, thereby linking Bristol and Bath with Newbury and Reading, began. In 1810, it was completed with its most spectacular section being the flight of locks up Caen Hill. However, just three decades later the advent of the Great Western Railway meant canal traffic had declined to the point where the waterway was abandoned.

Following restoration, southern England's most picturesque canal is once more open to navigation, threading its way through the Avon valley, the Vale of Pewsey and on into Berkshire. To see how the canal was built and for details of **boat trips** (Apr–Oct Wed, Sat–Sun and bank holidays 2pm), **visit the Kennet and Avon Canal Trust Museum** (Canal Centre, Couch Lane, Devizes; &01380 721 279; www.katrust.org).

MARLBOROUGH★

6mi/10km E of Avebury.

This former market town, strategically placed on the London–Bath road (A 4), has been home to the famous exclusive public school of **Marlborough College** since the 19C.

To the north of the town stretch the **Marlborough Downs**, crossed by the Ridgeway Path and home to flocks of sheep (every town in Wiltshire was originally a wool town). The attractive **High Street** leads from The Green to Marlborough College. **St Mary's church**, also at the east end, was rebuilt after a fire during the Commonwealth, hence its Puritan austerity. The High Street boasts a couple of interesting 17C **coaching inns** (Castle and Ball, Sun Inn). At the west end, the **Church of St Peter and St Paul** (now an arts and crafts centre) is Norman in origin, but was rebuilt in the 15C and extensively restored in the mid-19C.

A couple of miles southeast of Marlborough lies **Savernake Forest★★**, a privately owned but publicly accessible forest. Its 1 619ha is a wonderful place to explore on foot or by bicycle. Cutting through the forest northwest to southeast is the **Grand Avenue★★★**, lined with superb beeches laid out by Lancelot "Capability" Brown.

LACOCK★★

5.5mi/25km W of Avebury.
www.nationaltrust.org.uk.

This peaceful picturesque stone-and-brick village is owned by the National Trust. It comprises little more than four streets laid out in a square but has provided the film set for numerous period TV dramas and movies, including appearances in two *Harry Potter* films, *Cranford* and *Pride and Prejudice*.

The wide **High Street★** leading to the abbey is lined with cottage-shops and houses of various heights, sizes and designs, some of which date from as long ago as the 14C and 16C. **West Street** and **East Street** are enclosed by interesting old houses and inns (the **George Inn** is the oldest inn in the village, built 1361). **Church Street** (note the 14C Cruck House and 15C Sign of the Angel Inn) runs parallel to the High Street, leading into the village's original Market Place on the right.

The church of **St Cyriac★** (open year-round daily 10am–5pm; &01249 730 272) is a superb example of a Perpendicular "wool church" reflecting the village's prosperity from the 14C to the 17C.

Lacock Abbey and Fox Talbot Museum of Photography★

Museum, cloisters and grounds: open daily mid-Feb–Oct 10.30am–5.30pm; Nov–mid-Feb 11am–4pm.

Abbey: open 2nd wk Feb–Oct Wed–Mon 11am–5pm; Nov–Dec Sat–Sun noon–4pm.

Closed 1 Jan, 25–26 Dec. ♿ ✆01249 730 459. www.nationaltrust.org.uk.

To the east of the village lies Lacock abbey, founded in the 13C and converted into a stately home following the Dissolution (the cloisters, sacristy and chapter house survive). Successive generations of the **Talbot family** added decorative features following the tastes of their day. The pioneer photographer, **William Henry Fox Talbot** (1800–77), added three oriels to the south front in 1827–30, the central one of which was the subject of his historic first successful photograph in 1835. The **Fox Talbot Museum**, housed in a 16C barn at the abbey gate, is devoted to Talbot and his contemporary photographers.

CORSHAM COURT★★

5mi/8km N of Lacock. Open Apr–Sept Tue–Thu, Sat–Sun and bank holidays 2–5.30pm; Oct–Mar Sat–Sun 2–4.30pm £10; gardens only, £5. ♿⌨ ✆01249 712 214. www.corsham-court.co.uk.

This Elizabethan mansion built in 1582 was bought by Paul Methuen in the mid-18C. Corsham was altered and enlarged on several occasions, by architects such as Lancelot 'Capability' Brown in the 1760s, John Nash in 1800 and Thomas Bellamy in 1845–49, to house the extensive Methuen Collection of Master **paintings** (16C and 17C Italian and 17C Flemish), **statuary**, **bronzes** and **furniture**. It includes works by Caravaggio, Tintoretto, Veronese, Rubens and Van Dyck, as well as pieces by the Adam brothers and Chippendale. The **Cabinet Room** contains Fra Filippo Lippi's Annunciation (1463), while the highlight of the **Octagon Room**, designed by Nash, is Michelangelo's *Sleeping Cupid*.

MALMESBURY★

12.5mi/20km N of Lacock. 🛈 ✆01666 823 748. www.malmesbury.gov.uk.

The centre of this small south Cotswold market town is graced by a **market cross★★**, one of England's finest, built of local stone in 1490, when the town was known for its tanning, wool weaving and other textile industries. Malm-esbury is a hilltop town shaped by the course of two rivers, the Bristol and Tetbury Avons.

Malmesbury Abbey★

Open daily 9am–5pm (winter 4pm). £5–£10 donation requested. ♿✗ ✆01666 826 666. www.malmesburyabbey.com.

The present church was begun in the 12C and by the 14C extended 98m from east to west. However, a storm in the late-15C and the collapse of its tower (with subsequent damage) a century later means that the existing structure is about one-third the size of the building at its largest. The ruins are a dramatic backdrop to the present church. The masterpiece of the abbey is the **south porch**, an outstanding example of Norman sculpture and decoration featuring geometrical patterning and magnificent carved figures in a style reminiscent of that found in the churches of southwest France. The massive Norman pillars inside have scalloped capitals. On the south side is the **watching loft** from where the abbot could follow the service beyond the chancel screen.

Abbey House Gardens★★

Open Apr–Oct 11am–5.30pm. £7.50. ♿✗ ✆01666 822 212. www.abbeyhousegardens.co.uk.

Planted on neglected land in 1994, these gardens, adjacent to the abbey, have become one of the best loved in the south of England. A large part of their appeal is their location, adjacent to and in sympathy with the beautiful 16C abbey house and abbey ruins. Keeping the historical link are ancient stones from the abbey complex, a herb garden, arcading (reminiscent of cloisters), statues of monks and a monk's stone coffin. The formal part of the gardens are divided into a series of delightful rooms and lawns with knot gardens. Tens of thousands of bulbs are planted each year to create a real splash of colour including the county's largest private collection of roses. The wilder part of the gardens tumble down to the river and monastic fish ponds.

Channel Islands★★

Blessed by better weather than mainland Britain and unspoiled rural countryside, the Channel Islands have developed tourist facilities to attract sailors, surfers and swimmers, birdwatchers, walkers and cyclists. Life in general is lived in the slow lane and a characteristic feature is fresh, home-grown produce along the road with adjacent 'honesty box'.

A BIT OF HISTORY

The islands are rich in prehistoric tombs and monuments indicating human habitation in 7500 BCE–2500 BCE. They were annexed by the Normans in 933 and later attached to the English Crown by William the Conqueror. Some customs and traditions and the Norman–French dialect heard on these islands, which have only been universally English-speaking since the early 20C, date back to this period. In 1204 King John was forced to cede Normandy to the French, but the Channel Islanders chose to remain loyal to the English Crown in return for certain privileges, one of which was an independent parliament.

Despite this, the French tried repeatedly to capture the islands. Threats of invasion by Napoleon account for the many Martello defence towers built along the coasts. The islands were occupied by the Germans from 1940 to 1945, the only British territory to fall to the enemy during the Second World War.

The Channel Islands are divided into the **Bailiwick of Jersey** and the **Bailiwick of Guernsey**. The original Norman laws and systems have been renewed and modified by subsequent monarchs, though in matters of defence and international relations the islands are subject to decisions made by the Home Office in London. The Channel Islanders benefit from a **VAT-exempt** economy and lower rates of income tax. Coins,

▶ **Population:** 163 857.

⌖ **Michelin Map:** Michelin Atlas p 5 or Map 503 P, Q 33.

🅱 **Info:** Jersey: The Weighbridge, St Helier. ☎01534 859 000. www.jersey.com. Guernsey: North Esplanade, St Peter Port. ☎01481 723 552. www.visitguernsey.com.

⊗ Stay on either Jersey or Guernsey and use it as a base from which to visit the other main island and the smaller islands.

◖ **Location:** The Channel Islands lie west of the Cherbourg peninsula, off the Normandy coast.

☺ **Don't Miss:** Durrell Wildlife Park; Jersey War Tunnels; St Peter Port, Guernsey; if you seek peace and quiet, Sark and Herm.

◕ **Timing:** Allow a few days to relax here.

👪 **Kids:** Durrell Wildlife Park.

bank notes, and postage stamps are issued locally and are not legal tender elsewhere. The islands have therefore become a tax haven for wealthy British citizens and have developed a buoyant industry in **financial services**. **Farming** still plays an important part in the local economy and maintains a supply to mainland Britain of early vegetables (potatoes, tomatoes, grapes), cut flowers and rich Channel Island milk, produced by the famously pretty local cattle.

JERSEY★★

The Jersey Heritage Pass gives unlimited access to 4 sites for the price of 3 and passes are valid for 7 days. £32.85. www.jerseyheritage.org/heritage-pass. The largest and southernmost of the group, only 12mi/19km from the coast of France, Jersey possesses a charming combination of English and Norman–French traditions and local features echo both Normandy and Cornwall. Being so close to the Gulf Stream, it is thick with flowers in spring and summer. The sandy bays which characterise the coastline occur even among the steep pink granite cliffs of the sparsely populated north.

St Helier

The capital is named after the 6C hermit saint who brought Christianity to the island. On an islet (access on foot via causeway at low tide, at other times DUKW vehicle) stands **Elizabeth Castle** (open Apr–Oct daily 10am–5.30pm; £11.25 (including ferry £13.95); ✆01534 723 971; www.jerseyheritage.org), begun in the mid-16C. In the Civil War it was adapted to resist attacks by the Parliamentarians and during the Second World War the occupying German forces made their own additions. Past the **Militia Museum** (mementoes of the Royal Jersey Regiment) the Upper Ward encloses the Mount (keep) affording **views★** across St Aubin's Bay. Today a breakwater leads south to the 12C hermitage chapel on the rock on which St Helier lived (procession on or about 16 Jul, St Helier's Day). The centre of the town is marked by the charming **Royal Square** with a statue of George II dressed as a Roman emperor. St Helier's two main collections are both near the harbour. The **Jersey Museum and Art Gallery★** (The Weighbridge; open Apr–Oct Mon–Sat 8.30am–5pm, Sun 10am–5pm; Nov–Dec Mon–Sat 9am–4pm, Sun 10am–4pm; £9.95; ♿; ✆01534 633 300; www.jerseyheritage.org) contains award-winning displays of maritime exhibits and the story of Jersey. The **Maritime Museum** (New North Quay; open Oct–mid-Dec Sun 10am–4pm; Apr–Oct daily 10am–5pm; £9.80; ♿; ✆01534 811 043; www.jerseyheritage.org), installed in converted 19C warehouses, celebrates the importance to Jersey of the sea and displays a 12-panel tapestry (2m x 1m) illustrating the Occupation of Jersey during the Second World War, based on an archive photos.

GETTING THERE
By Air
There are flights to Jersey, Guernsey and Alderney:

Jersey, Guernsey and **Alderney airports** are served by British Airways (www.britishairways.com), Flybe (www.flybe.com), Air Southwest (www.bravofly.com), Jet2 (www.jet2.com), Blue Islands (www.blueislands.com) as well as Swiss (www.swiss.com) from Zurich.

Aurigny Air Services offers flights between Guernsey, Jersey and Alderney and several British airports as well as Dinard in France. www.aurigny.com.

By Sea
Fast catamaran ferries run to the Channel Islands from England (Poole, Weymouth and Portsmouth) and France (Granville, Diélette, Carteret, St-Malo).
Contact www.condorferries.co.uk; www.manche-iles.com.
Scheduled ferries run among the islands.
Note that, for all ferry services, where they land and at what time depends on tides.

♿♿ Durrell Wildlife Park★★
Trinity. 4mi/6km N of St Helier.
Open daily 9.30am–5pm/6pm. Closed 25 Dec. £16, child £11.50. ♿🅿✕
✆01534 860 000. www.durrell.org.
The remit of this famous wildlife park – the word zoo is never used – named after its founder, the naturalist **Gerald Durrell**, is to preserve and breed rare and endangered species that live in an environment as similar as possible to their natural habitat. Its success has led to exchanges with other leading UK wildlife parks and zoos and the re-introduction of a number of threatened species to the wild.

Eric Young Orchid Foundation★

Victoria Village, Trinity. Open early Feb–mid Dec Wed–Sat 10am–4pm. £5. ♿ ✆01534 861 963. www.ericyoungorchidfoundation.co.uk.
A fabulous show of prize plants appealing to amateurs and professionals.

La Hougue Bie★

Grouville. 2.5mi/4km NE of St Helier. Open Apr–Oct daily 10am–5pm. £8.95. ♿ P ✆01534 853 823. www.jerseyheritage.org.
La Hougue Bie is a cruciform **Neolithic tomb★** dating from 3000 BCE, a 10m passage grave, roofed with granite slabs leading to a 3m x 9m funeral chamber and three side chambers.

Hamptonne Country Life Museum★

La Rue de la Patente, St Lawrence. 3mi/5km from St Helier. Open daily late May–mid-Sept 10am–5pm; £8.70. ♿ ✆01534 863 955. www.jerseyheritagetrust.org.
Thatched and with bags of atmosphere, Hamptonne House is thought to have been completed in 1637. It provides an insight into family lifestyle during the 17C and early-18C.

Jersey War Tunnels★

Meadowbank, Les Charrieres Malorey. Open Mar–Oct daily 10am–6pm; Nov daily 10am–2.30pm. £12. ♿ P ✕ ✆01534 860 808. www.jerseywartunnels.com.
This large complex of tunnels is kept as a memorial to the forced labourers who worked on its construction for three and a half years under the harshest conditions. Wartime films, archive photographs, newspaper cuttings, letters and memorabilia document the personal suffering and trauma of those caught up in the events.

Mont Orgueil Castle★

The charming old port of **Gorey** is dominated by Mont Orgueil Castle (open mid-Mar–Oct daily 10am–6pm; Nov–21 Dec Fri–Mon 10am–4pm; 22–23 and 27–30

Mont Orgueil Castle

© Jon Arnold/hemis.fr

Dec 10am–4pm. Closed 1 Jan, 24–26 and 31 Dec. £12.20, children 6–16, £7.40. ✆01534 853 292; www.jerseyheritage.org), which dates to the 13C. Set on a rocky promontory, its position and defensive strength account for the name (Mount Pride). A spiral network of steps and passages between separate defence systems leads up to excellent **views★★** at the top.
Also in Gorey is the 15m **Faldouet Dolmen** passage grave, dating from 2500 BCE, with a 6m-wide funeral chamber.

St Matthew's church

Millbrook. ✆01534 720 934. www.glasschurch.org.
The 'Glass Church', built in 1840, is remarkable for **René Lalique**'s rich **glasswork★** interior, executed in 1934.

GUERNSEY★

The second principal Channel Island, Guernsey features wild, dramatic **southern cliffs**, while the sandy beaches and rocky promontories of the west and north coasts are excellent for bathing, surfing and rock-pool exploring.

St Peter Port★★

The island capital, attractively situated on a hillside on the east coast, overlooks a sheltered harbour. A late-18C building boom produced a delightful

Regency town built in local granite. **Castle Cornet★** (open–Oct 10am–5pm; Jul–Aug 9.30am–5pm. £10.50. **P ✗**; ☎01481 721 657; www.museums.gov.gg), dating back to c.1206 and reinforced under Elizabeth I, remained loyal to the king in the Civil War, being the last of the royal strongholds to surrender, after eight years of siege.

In 1672 an explosion destroyed much of the structure and the castle was subsequently rebuilt. Today it also includes five small museums; The Story of Castle Cornet, the Maritime Museum and collections dedicated to the Royal Guernsey Militia, Royal Guernsey Light Infantry and 201 Squadron RAF respectively. The Ceremony of the **Noonday Gun** is performed daily.

St Peter Port **Town Church★** dates back as far as 1048, when it also served as a fort, and was completed around 1475. It now contains several memorials to famous Guernseymen. **Victor Hugo** lived on Guernsey in political exile at **Hauteville House★** (open Apr–Sept Mon–Sat (except Wed) 10am–4pm; £8; ☎01481 721 911; www.victorhugo.gg), which he decorated in a highly individual way.

Set in **Candie Gardens**, with its statue and historic greenhouses, the **Guernsey Museum and Art Gallery** (open daily late Jan–Dec 10am–4pm; £6.50; �& ✗; ☎01481 726 518; www.museums.gov.gg) contains art and archaeological collections.

Around the Island

At **St Martin** is the elegant Queen Anne period **Sausmarez Manor** (Sausmarez Road; visit house by guided tour only, Apr–Oct; see website for details; Subtropical Gardens and Art Park open year-round daily 10am–5pm; �& P ✗; ☎01481 235 571; www.sausmarez-manor.co.uk, www.artparks.co.uk), also home to a subtropical garden and an art park with over 100 pieces of sculpture. Other attractions are coppersmiths at work, golf and train rides. Not to be confused with the manor, **Saumarez Park★**, at Castel, is home to The **Guernsey Folk & Costume**

Museum★ (open mid-Mar–Oct daily 10am–5pm; £5; **P**; ☎01481 255 384; www.nationaltrust.gg) set within a cluster of meticulously renovated traditional buildings. The park is also the venue for the annual **Battle of Flowers**, a famous parade held on the fourth Thursday in August, originally started in 1902 for the coronation of Edward VII. Afterwards the floats are broken up and the crowd pelt each other with flowers. Between St Peter Port and Guernsey Airport is the La Valette **Military Underground Museum★** (La Valette; open Mar–mid-Nov daily 10am–5pm; £6; ☎01481 722 300, http://lavalette.tk). The largest construction in the Channel Islands, yet almost invisible from the surface, this tunnel complex covers 0.7ha. It was hewn out of solid rock by slave workers of many nationalities. The island's most notable **prehistoric remains** are the burial chambers **Déhus Dolmen** (N), **le Trépied Dolmen** (W) and **La Gran'mère du Chimquièra**, a Stone Age figure at the gate to St Martin's churchyard.

Guernsey's satellite islands, **Alderney**, **Herm** and **Sark★★** are well worth a visit. Sark has stayed remarkably remote from modern society, and is totally free of cars.

Sons and Daughters

The most famous name connected with Jersey is **Lillie Langtry** (1853–1929), the 'Jersey Lily' who became an actress and captivated British high society with her beauty and who was also a close friend of Edward VII – she is buried in St Saviour's churchyard.

The fashionable 19C painter **Sir John Everett Millais** (1829–96) grew up in Jersey and belonged to an old island family. The well-known French firm which makes Martell brandy was founded by **Jean Martell** from St Brelade.

ADDRESSES

🏠 STAY

PORTSMOUTH/SOUTHSEA

⊜⊜ **Fortitude Cottage** –
51 Broad Street. ✆02392 823 748.
www.fortitudecottage.co.uk. 6 rooms. This
charming guesthouse with up-to-the-
minute decor is right in the heart of Old
Portsmouth, with a great view of the
fishing boats and ferries. Spectacular
penthouse bedroom (⊜⊜⊜⊜).

⊜⊜ **Premier Inn** – Long Curtain
Road, Southsea. ✆0871 527 9014. www.
premierinn.com. This modern budget
hotel by the sea is a 1-minute walk from
Clarence Pier and less than a mile from
the Spinnaker Tower. What you see
is what you get with this Premier Inn.
Great value.

⊜⊜⊜ **Florence House Hotel** –
2 Malvern Road, Southsea. ✆023 9200
9111. www.florencehousehotel.co.uk.
7 rooms. Set just off the seafront, this
small Edwardian boutique hotel is a
lively combination of contemporary and
period styles. Attentive owners.

ISLE OF WIGHT

⊜⊜⊜ **The Royal Hotel** – Belgrave Road,
Ventnor, Isle of Wight, PO38 1JJ. ✆01983
852186. http://royalhoteliow.co.uk. One of
the oldest hotels on the island, and still
one of the best. Restaurant ⊜⊜⊜.

WINCHESTER

⊜⊜⊜ **No. 5 Bridge Street** – 5 Bridge
Street. ✆01962 863 838. www.no5bridge
street.co.uk. 6 rooms. Set in an artfully
modernised old property a 2-min walk
from the centre of town, this lively
restaurant bar offers stylish boutique
rooms with a whole array of amenities,
including DVD players and oversized
showers.

⊜⊜⊜⊜ **Hotel du Vin** – 14 Southgate
Street. ✆01962 896 329. www.hoteldu
vin.com. 24 rooms. This handsome early-
18C red brick house is located in a quiet
part of the city centre and its elegant
decor reflects the wine theme with
very stylish contemporary/traditional
bedrooms. Acclaimed restaurant
(⊜⊜⊜⊜) has a champagne bar.

NEW FOREST

⊜⊜⊜⊜ **The Montagu Arms Hotel** –
Beaulieu. ✆01590 612 324. www.montagu
armshotel.co.uk. 23 rooms. This luxury 17C
country house hotel, complete with
its Monty's Inn restaurant and free spa
membership, is an oasis of calm.

BOURNEMOUTH

🏠 For affordable lodgings try the
streets running off the seafront and on
Tregonwell Road (in the Westcliff area).
There are plenty of guesthouses and
B&Bs on the Isle of Purbeck.

⊜⊜ **Mount Stuart** – 31 Tregonwell Road.
✆08450 554 639. www.mountstuarthotel.
co.uk. 18 rooms. This large Victorian villa
a short walk from town has been run
by the same family for over 20 years.
Rooms are small but pleasant.

⊜⊜⊜⊜ **Highcliff Marriott** –
St Michael's Road, West Cliff. ✆01202
557 702. www.bournemouthhighcliff
marriott.co.uk. 157 rooms. Perched on the
clifftop with a pool and magnificent
views, this is one of the town's top
hotels with contemporary design rooms
and every comfort. Last-minute deals.

DORCHESTER

⊜⊜ **Westwood House** – 29 High Street
West. ✆01305 28 018. www.westwood
house.co.uk. 7 rooms. Georgian
townhouse (1815) in the centre of
town, run by resident owners.

SALISBURY

⊜⊜⊜⊜ **Milford Hall** –
106 Castle Street. ✆01722 417 411. www.
milfordhallhotel.com. 45 rooms. This
beautiful 19C building is a five-minute
walk from the centre of town. Both
modern and more formal Georgian-
style interior and rooms.

JERSEY

⊜⊜ **Au Caprice** – Route de la Haule,
St Brelade. ✆01534 722 083. www.
aucapricejersey.com. Next to a large
sandy beach this guesthouse offers
pretty, comfy rooms; the small seaview
surcharge is very good value.

GUERNSEY

⊜⊜⊜ **La Michele** – Les Hubits,
St Martin. ✆01481 238 065. www.
lamichelehotel.com. This 16-room hotel
enjoys a quiet country location, a
short walk from picturesque Fermain

Bay. Conservatory lounge, beautiful secluded garden and small pool. No children under-16.

℉ EAT

PORTSMOUTH

🅖 Gunwharf Quays and Port Solent are bursting with cafés and restaurants.

⊜🅑 **Brasserie Blanc** – 1 Gunwharf Quays. ☎02392 891 320. www. brasserieblanc.com.Part of the empire of masterchef Raymond Blanc, this lively place serves classic brasserie dishes; large outdoor terrace. Excellent value prix-fixe menus.

SOUTHAMPTON

🅖The town boasts a good choice of independent restaurants.

⊜🅑 **White Star Tavern** – Town Quay. ☎02380 337 232. www.platformtavern.com. Award-winning bar and restaurant in a tastefully modernised Victorian building serving tapas-style small plates or modern British classics and locally sourced meat and fish dishes.

⊜🅑 **The Vestry** – 61 Commercial Road. ☎02380 231 101. www.thevestryrestaurant andbar.co.uk. This is an atmospheric conversion of a church to an all day restaurant and bar, serving up an interesting Modern British dinner menu and various live entertainments.

ISLE OF WIGHT

⊜🅑 **Pond Café** – Bonchurch. ☎01983 855 666. www.thehambrough.com/the-pond-cafe. Intimate neighbourhood eatery with an attractive terrace overlooking the duck pond. Bistro-style interior with tablecloths and candles in the evenings; Mediterranean-inspired dishes.

WINCHESTER

⊜🅑🅑 **Wykeham Arms** – 75 Kingsgate Street. ☎01962 853 834. www.wykeham armswinchester.co.uk. This famous 18C inn, tucked away on a cobbled street, is packed with Winchester College memorabilia. Dishes range from simple soups and pies to full traditional roasts and continental cuisine. Bar meals are best for value and atmosphere.

⊜🅑 **No. 5 Bridge Street** – 5 Bridge Street. ☎01962 863 838. www.no5bridgestreet. co.uk. 6 rms. Stylish bar and restaurant with glass doors that lead onto a patio seating area. The menu is a heady mix of British/Mediterranean influences, with a selection of tapas-style market plates charcuterie, and interesting locally sourced modern meat and fish dishes

BOURNEMOUTH

⊜🅑 **Beau Monde** – Exeter Park Road. ☎01202 311 181. Tables in the restaurant overlook Bournemouth's beautiful Lower Gardens, while the bistro opens onto the terrace allowing seasonal al fresco dining. Both traditional English and contemporary European dishes feature.

DORCHESTER

⊜🅑🅑 **Sienna** – 36 High West Street. ☎01305 250 022. www.siennadorchester. co.uk. Lunch Wed–Sat, dinner Tue–Sat. Reservations required. Chef Marcus Wilcox is a 'Masterchef' semi-finalist, and offers modern British food with a twist.

SHAFTESBURY

⊜🅑 **The Mitre Inn** – 22 High Street. ☎01747 853 002. www.themitredorset. co.uk. Tasty home-cooked traditional pub food in a nicely old-fashioned inn with great views over the Dorset countryside from the outside terrace.

SALISBURY

⊜🅑 **The Victoria & Albert Inn** – Netherhampton, via A 36 to Warminster or a 40-min walk from town. ☎01722 743 174. The village pub: a warm welcome, log fires in winter and a good variety of local dishes. Excellent choice of drinks.

JERSEY

⊜🅑🅑 **Old Court House Inn** – St Aubin's Harbour. ☎01534 746 433. www.oldcourthousejersey.com. This atmospheric, rustic (in parts) 15C inn, right on the picturesque harbourfront, offers a choice of bars, bistro and formal 'white-linen dining'. Their cosmopolitan menus have a seafood emphasis.

GUERNSEY

⊜🅑 **Fleur du Jardin** – Kings Mills, Castel. ☎01481 257 996. www.fleurdujardin.com. Set in the heart of the island, the beamed pub-like restaurant of this smart 15C hotel offers fresh, seasonal, locally sourced gastro-pub food cooked simply. Outdoor dining in the summer.

Chilterns,
Oxfordshire,
Cotswolds

Choir vault, Tewkesbury Abbey © Eurasia Press/Photononstop

Introduction

Within easy day-tripping distance of the capital, the Cotswolds are a prime draw for visitors who have only a short time to experience idyllic English villages and rural scenery. They are a 'must-see', but at peak times can be unbearably busy. Oxford justifies its reputation as one of Britain's top attractions and although better equipped to handle the crowds, is still much more comfortable out of season. The Chiltern Hills, like the Cotswolds, are designated an Area of Outstanding Natural Beauty: situated close to London, they have less appeal in terms of 'quaintness'; but, for walkers and seekers of solitude, they are a better bet.

Chiltern Hills

Providing a breath of fresh air, pastoral scenery and good walking territory within easy commuting distance of London, the Chilterns are a very desirable part of south-east England. There are few set-piece visitor attractions or even obvious places to stay for more than a night or two so you'll probably want to keep moving between their small towns and villages.

Oxford

The glittering spires of Oxford are deservedly world famous. Easily covered on foot, the town is, as you would expect from an internationally renowned University, young, lively and cosmopolitan. However the university is also the oldest in Britain and imparts a very British sense of history and tradition, matched elsewhere in the UK only by Cambridge. The peaceful tiny college 'quads' (quadrangles/squares) and cloisters have a real sense of history and old-world atmosphere, but a walk around the old alleyways of the city centre, particularly by night, admiring the city's stunning architecture at almost every turn, is to take a step back several centuries in time. Just outside Oxford, Blenheim Palace is one of England's greatest treasures.

Cotswolds

If you want to find the England you've seen on old-fashioned jigsaws, chocolate boxes and picture calendars, then you won't be disappointed by the Cotswolds. Wool brought it untold riches in medieval times, as celebrated by the number of 'wool churches' erected in gratitude by wealthy merchants, but the Industrial Revolution simply passed it by. This meant that the

Highlights

1 Stroll among some of Europe's finest landscaping at **Stowe Landscape Gardens** (p257)
2 Be awestruck at **Christ Church College, Oxford** (p266)
3 See where Churchill lived at **Blenheim Palace** (p267)
4 Find the medieval Cotswolds at **Chipping Campden** (p274)
5 Feel like Alice in Wonderland at **Hidcote Garden** (p274)

glorious golden-stone Cotswold villages were preserved until they were popularised for the birth of modern tourism in the 1920s and 30s. Some places may have sold their souls to tourism and wealthy out-of-towners, but it's done in the best possible rural taste with cream teas on manicured lawns beside thatched cottages in summer, and roaring log fires and foaming pints of real ale in winter. Fast-food chains and shopping malls are still a century away. There are some very atmospheric period houses (Chastleton and Snowshill Manor) and wonderful gardens here too, notably the Alice-in-Wonderland-like Hidcote.

Gloucester

The glory of Gloucester is undoubtedly its cathedral. Its docks make an interesting diversion while in autumn, Westonbirt Arboretum is a splash of New England colour in the heart of old England. Spend the night out of town, at posh Regency neighbour, Cheltenham.

Chiltern Hills★

The chalk downs known as the Chiltern Hills run some 60mi/97km on a southwest to northeast axis bordered by the River Thames and Luton respectively. They rise gently to their highest point at Coombe Hill (260m), topped by a gibbet. Two of Britain's ancient roads, the **Icknield Way** and the **Ridgeway**, follow the line of the hills.

WALK

The gentle rolling Chilterns are ideal for walkers. The **Ridgeway National Trail** was one of Iron Age Britain's main highways; today it is a waymarked long-distance footpath.

Another easy route is the Thames Path, which follows the river and crosses the Ridgeway. Tourist offices will be able to provide detailed walking maps, and www.chilternsaonb.org is also useful.

AYLESBURY AREA

Aylesbury, Buckinghamshire's county town, was a major market town in Anglo-Saxon times and played a large part in the English Civil War.

The **Buckinghamshire County Museum** on Church Street (open Apr–Oct Tue–Sat 10am–5pm, plus extra days during school holidays; museum free; ♣♣ Dahl Gallery £7.70, child 4–17, £5.50; entry by timed ticket; visits last an hour and

---

Roald Dahl

Roald Dahl lived and wrote for 36 years in Great Missenden village; it is now home to the award-winning **Roald Dahl Museum and Story Centre** (♣♣ open year-round Tue–Fri 10am–5pm, Sat–Sun and bank hol/half-term Mons 11am–5pm; £6, child £4; ♣✗; ✆01494 892 192; www.roalddahlmuseum.org; book ahead if possible).

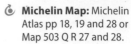

♣	**Michelin Map:** Michelin Atlas pp 18, 19 and 28 or Map 503 Q R 27 and 28.
▯	**Info:** The Old Gaol, Market Hill, Buckingham. ✆01280 823 020. www.visitsoutheastengland.com.
▶	**Location:** Main tourist centres are Buckingham, Aylesbury, Marlow and Henley-on-Thames.
♨	**Don't Miss:** Waddesdon Manor; Stowe Gardens.
◔	**Timing:** At least two days.
♣♣	**Kids:** Roald Dahl Gallery; Roald Dahl Museum.

---

entry is on the hour, booking is advised, additional £1 fee; ✗; ✆01296 331 441; www.buckscountymuseum.org) traces local history but many visitors head straight for the **Roald Dahl Children's Gallery** – a delight for fans of the great author.

South of Aylesbury in the village of Hartwell is **Hartwell House**, now a luxury-hotel, first mentioned in the Domesday Book, once the home of an illegitimate son of William the Conqueror.

Five mi/8km northwest of Aylesbury via the A 41 is **Waddesdon Manor★★** (open late Mar–Oct Wed–Fri, noon–4pm, Sat–Sun 11am–4pm; £20; gardens only, £10; National Trust members, free; entry by timed tickets; ♣▣✗; ✆01296 820 414; www.waddesdon.org.uk), built in 1874–89 in French Renaissance style, for Baron Ferdinand de Rothschild, set in 61ha of landscaped grounds. It contains the acclaimed **Rothschild collection** of Dutch, French and English paintings, French furniture, porcelain, carpets and many other works of art. Twenty rooms are furnished with French 18C royal furniture, Sèvres porcelain and Savonnerie carpets. Works by Gainsborough, Reynolds and Romney, plus pictures by Rubens, Cuyp, Van der Heyden and Dutch masters grace the walls.

Some 10mi/16km northwest of Aylesbury, off the A 41 to Waddesdon, is **Claydon House**★ (Middle Claydon; open mid-Mar–Oct Sat–Wed 11am–5pm; £7.50; garden £6; ♿🅿✕; ✆01296 730 349 infoline, 01296 730 349; www.nationaltrust.org.uk), famous for its extravagant Rococo work, the parquetry staircase and the 'Gothic Chinoiserie' woodwork of the Chinese Room. There are mementoes of Florence Nightingale, who was a frequent visitor.

BUCKINGHAM AREA

Buckingham was Buckinghamshire's county town until Aylesbury took over in the 16C. Today it is best used as a base for walks in the surrounding area and for visiting **Stowe Landscape Gardens**★★★ (3mi/5km NW, off the A 422; gardens open daily: Jan–Feb and Nov–Dec 10am–4pm; Mar–Oct 10am–5pm; Stowe House (not National Trust) times vary, visit www.stowe.co.uk/house for information, Guided walks Mon–Fri 1pm, closed 25 Dec, last Sat May; gardens £11.20; house £6.50 (not National Trust); 🅿✕; ✆01280 817 156, www.nationaltrust.org.uk). These magnificent landscaped gardens were created over a period of 200 years starting in 1700.
In 1733, **William Kent** began work and in 1741 **Lancelot 'Capability' Brown** was appointed head gardener. The long, straight approach up the **Grand Avenue** (1.5mi/2.5km) gives glimpses through the trees of the temples, columns and arches and also a full view of the north front of **Stowe House**, part of the exclusive Stowe School. A full tour of the gardens would take a couple of hours but a shorter walk close to the house provides a visit or a view of the major features, which include over 40 temples, follies and monuments. Nearby, the **parish church** is the sole survivor of the medieval village of Stowe.

VALE OF WHITE HORSE

This shallow valley lying between the Ridgeway and the River Thames, and bounded by Wantage and Farringdon, stretches from the edge of Oxford to the threshold of the Cotswolds. Its name comes from the oldest chalk figure in Britain dating back to around 1000 BCE.

Wantage

In the centre of this small market town stands a statue of its most famous son, King Alfred the Great. You can learn more about him and the region in the **Vale and Downland Museum** (Church Street open Mon–Sat except bank holidays, 9.30am–4pm; ♿✕; ✆01235 771 447; wantage-museum.com).
One of the most rewarding short stretches of the famous **Ridgeway** footpath is 2mi/1.2km south of here.

White Horse Hill

This stylised, almost modern-art figure of a 114m-long horse (or perhaps a dragon) has perplexed scholars for centuries. It was carved out of the chalk hillside some 3 000 years ago but by whom, and for why, remains a mystery. One school of thought says that the figure represents a horse goddess connected with the local Belgae tribe.

Woolstone and Uffington

Just below the White Horse, **Woolstone** is possibly the prettiest of the region's many attractive villages. It has a beautiful 12C church and a pretty thatched pub – The White Horse Inn (naturally...). Neighbouring **Uffington** also has a fine church, known locally as 'The Cathedral of the Vale'. Thomas Hughes (1822–96), author of *Tom Brown's School Days*, was born here. Hughes' books are based on local people and places; and the 17C schoolhouse featured in his most famous work is now **Tom Brown's School Museum** (open Easter–Oct Sat–Sun and bank holiday Mons 2–5pm; www.museum.uffington.net). It includes mementoes of the late poet laureate Sir John Betjeman (1906–84), who also lived for many years in Uffington.

St Albans★

and around

The Romans built the first real settlement here on the south bank of the River Ver and named it Verulamium. Around the year 250, so the legend goes, Alban, a pagan living in the town, was converted to Christianity when he sheltered a Christian priest. Facing imminent discovery, Alban switched cloaks with the priest, was arrested in his place by Roman soldiers and executed, thus becoming England's first Christian martyr. Following the Romans' departure the town's building blocks were transferred to the other bank of the river to build an abbey, beside which the town of St Alban's developed.

▶ **Population:** 144 800.
⏁ **Michelin Map:** Michelin Atlas p 19 or Map 504 T 28.
ℹ **Info:** Alban Arena, Civic Centre. ✆01727 864 511. www.enjoystalbans.com. Train station (London St Pancras 20 mins) is a 10-min walk from the centre. Most buses stop at the central clock tower.
▷ **Location:** 27mi/43km northwest of London.
⌾ **Don't Miss:** Verulamium Museum; cathedral; Woburn abbey; Hatfield House.
⏱ **Timing:** Allow half a day.
🧑‍🧒 **Kids:** Woburn Safari Park; Whipsnade Wild Animal Park; Hatfield Park Farm.

CATHEDRAL★

Open daily 8.30am–5.45pm. £3 contribution requested. Guided tours Mon–Sat 11.30am plus Sat 2pm, Sun–Fri 2.30pm; Highlights tour, daily 1.05pm; Tower tours (193 steps) £9; check website for times. ♿✗ ✆01727 890 210. www.stalbanscathedral.org.uk.

The original abbey was a Saxon shrine to St Alban. The present building, dominated by its Norman tower, began in 1077. The impressive Norman nave was lengthened in the Early English style; the Victorian west front dates from 1879, the chapter house from 1982. The beauty of the interior lies in the furnishings – the exquisite medieval wall paintings and ceiling panels, the nave screen (1350), the reredos (1484), the Lady Chapel (1320) and the **shrine**.

VERULAMIUM★

Western outskirts of St Albans just off the A 4147/Bluehouse Hill.

Verulamium, the third-largest city in Roman Britain, was established in AD 49 on Watling Street and rebuilt at least twice – once after being sacked by Boadicea in AD 61 then again c.155 after a major fire. When the Romans withdrew, Verulamium fell into ruins, was lost and not uncovered until the 20C. **Verulamium Park**, beside the river, includes town wall remains, the hypocaust of a large villa in situ (open during museum opening hours, see below, free entry). and the remains of the **Roman Theatre of Verulamium** (open daily: Mar–Oct 10am–5pm; Nov–Feb 10am–4pm; £2.50; ✆01727 835 035; www.romantheatre.co.uk). Also in the park, the **Verulamium Museum★** (St Michael's Street; open daily 10am (2pm Sun)–5.30pm. £5. ♿🅿(Charge). ✆01727 751 810. www.stalbansmuseums.org.uk) displays some of the most impressive Roman works to be unearthed in Britain – ironwork, jewellery, coins, glass, pottery and **exceptional mosaics**. The museum is 'invaded' every second weekend in the month by Roman soldiers who demonstrate the tactics and equipment of the Roman Imperial Army.

EXCURSIONS
Hatfield House★★

▷ 6mi/10km E of St Albans on the A 414. **House:** open late Mar–Sept Wed–Sun and bank holidays. House

Hatfield House

11am–5pm. **Park and West Garden**: open Tue–Sun and bank holidays 10am–5.30pm. **East Garden**: open Wed only 11am–5pm. House, park and West Garden £19; East Garden +£4; Park and West garden only, £11. **Park farm** (inc Play Area): open Tue–Sun and bank holidays 10am–5.30pm or dusk. £5, child £2.50. &P✕ ℘01707 287 010. www.hatfield-house.co.uk.

This is one of the finest and largest Jacobean houses in England, the home of the Cecil family since the time of Henry VIII. The **interior** is notable for its hall, staircase and long gallery. In the **Marble Hall** the magnificently carved screen, minstrels' gallery and panels are Jacobean;, the gigantic 17C allegorical tapestry is from Brussels. The **Ermine Portrait** of Elizabeth I is attributed to Nicholas Hilliard while the one of her cousin Mary Queen of Scots is said to be by Rowland Lockey. The **grand oak staircase** is Jacobean carving at its best.

Note the relief of John Tradescant, gardener to Charles I, who was employed at Hatfield, and the *Rainbow Portrait* of Elizabeth I. In the library is the execution warrant for Mary Queen of Scots. The extensive **gardens** include a scented garden and fountains, and a spectacular knot garden. The **West Garden** includes a scented garden and herb garden. The **East Garden**, best viewed from the first floor of the House, has elegant parterres, topiary, rare plants and a maze. The estate also includes the 12C **St Etheldreda's church** and the **Hatfield Real Tennis Court**. For children there's the **Bloody Hollow Play Area** ▲⚊ and **Hatfield Park Farm**, featuring traditional breeds.

Knebworth House★

◐ 5mi/8km N by the A 1 junction 7. Open Easter Sat–last weekend Sept noon–5pm. See website for exact dates. House noon–5pm, gardens 11am–5pm.

Elizabeth I at Hatfield

It was at Hatfield under an oak tree in what is now **Hatfield Park** that Elizabeth I heard of her succession – "It is the Lord's doing and it is marvellous in our eyes". All that remains of her childhood home, a palace built by Cardinal Morton, is the old Tudor Palace **Hall** – '…one of the foremost monuments to medieval brickwork in the country' according to the acclaimed architectural historian, Pevsner. The adjacent **knot garden** is said to be where Elizabeth I spent much of her childhood and in November 1558, she held her first Council of State here. Sadly, it is only open today as a venue for social and corporate functions. The **long gallery** holds the queen's silk stockings, hat and gloves.

Entry by guided tours only, except on busy weekends. £13. ♿ 🅿 ✕ ☎01438 812 661. www.knebworthhouse.com.

The great hall with its richly carved screen and minstrels' gallery has hardly changed since the house was built in the 15C. The Gothic style was introduced by **Edward Bulwer-Lytton**, Victorian novelist, playwright and politician; it is best seen in the **State Drawing Room** with its turreted fireplace, painted panels and stained-glass windows, often used as a film set in Hollywood movies. Knebworth is famous for its rock concerts.

▲▲ Whipsnade Wild Animal Park★

▶ Dunstable. 13mi/21km NW via the A 5183. Open daily from 10am, with seasonal closing times. Closed 25 Dec. ♿ 🅿(£4) ✕. £22.90, child £16.60; small reduction winter ☎01582 872171. www.zsl.org.

The biggest zoo in the country, Whipsnade (part of London Zoo), plays a major role in animal conservation and welfare. Star attractions are elephants, sea lions, bears, lions, tigers, zebras, rhinos, penguins, chimpanzees and a walk-through lemur area.

Woburn Abbey★★

▶ 22mi/35km N via the M 10, then M 1 to junction 12 and minor road W.
Abbey, **Deer park, gardens and grounds**: open mid-Apr–Oct 11am–5pm. £17. 🅿✕ ☎01525 290 333. www.woburnabbey.co.uk.

Woburn was a Cistercian abbey for 400 years before becoming a private mansion. The north range was refurbished in 1630 but the more significant changes date from the 18C. The **interior** contains sumptuously furnished apartments including the **Mortlake Tapestries**, based on Raphael's *Acts of the Apostles*.

The **State Rooms** include **Queen Victoria's Bedroom** with etchings by Victoria and Albert; **Queen Victoria's Dressing Room** with walls adorned by superb 17C Dutch and Flemish paintings including works by Aelbert Cuyp, and Van Dyck; the **Blue Drawing Room** with its ceiling (1756) and its fireplace by Duval and Rysbrack; the **State Saloon** with its ornamental ceiling and Rysbrack chimneypiece; the **State Dining Room** graced by a Meissen dinner service and a portrait by Van Dyck; the **Reynolds Room** displaying 10 of his portraits; and the **Canaletto Room** hung with 21 Venetian views.

The **Library**, the finest room in the Holland range, is divided into three parts by Corinthian columns; on the walls hang *Self-Portrait* and *Old Rabbi* by **Rembrandt**. The **Long Gallery**, also divided by columns, by Flitcroft, is hung with 16C paintings including the *Armada Portrait* of Elizabeth I.

The **Deer Park** (1 200ha) was landscaped by Humphry Repton and is home to some one thousand deer from nine different species.

▲▲ Woburn Safari Park★

▶ Entrance 1mi/1km from Woburn Abbey. Open mid-Feb–early Nov daily 10am–5pm (last entry). Closed 23–26 Dec. £22.99, child £15.99 (online discounts). ♿🅿✕ ☎01525 290 407. www.woburnsafari.co.uk.

This is the country's largest drive-through safari park, with white rhino, elephant, tiger, lion, giraffe, bear, wolves, monkeys, eland, oryx, gemsbok, zebra, camel, bison and many more. You can **drive your own vehicle** through the reserves as often as you wish before parking in the Wild World Leisure Area. From here you can make another trip on the off-road **Safari Lorry**, hop aboard a small **safari train,** take a foot safari, attend feedings and talks, or let the kids blow off steam in the play areas. The park is also home to the **Go Ape** high-wire forest adventure course (additional charge).

Upper Thames Valley★★

The Thames gently winds between Kew and its source in the Cotswolds, offering many varied pleasures as it passes through an often idyllic English countryside of low hills, woods, meadows, country houses, pretty villages and small towns.

- **Michelin Map:** Michelin Atlas p 18 or Map 504 Q, R 28 and 29.
- **Info:** Town Hall, Henley-on-Thames. ℘0149 578 034. www.southernoxfordshire.com.
- **Location:** The London service, from Paddington to Henley takes 1h direct, or 37mins via Twyford.

SIGHTS

Cookham

This pretty village has been immortalised by the artist **Sir Stanley Spencer** (1891–1959). The chapel which Spencer attended as a boy is now the **Stanley Spencer Gallery★** (open Apr–Oct Tue–Sun 10.30am–5.30pm; Nov–Mar Thu–Sun 11am–4.30pm; £6, &; ℘01628 471 885; http://stanleyspencer.org.uk). Cookham features in many of his paintings.

Henley-on-Thames

In the first week of July some of the world's best oarsmen visit this charming town for the **Henley Royal Regatta**, England's premier rowing event.
The **River and Rowing Museum** ♣♣ (Mill Meadows; open daily 10am–5pm, May–Aug 5.30pm; Closed 1 Jan, 24–25 and 31 Dec; £12.50, child £9.95; &PX; ℘01491 415 600; www.rrm.co.uk) illustrates the evolution of rowing; the River Thames as a habitat for wildlife, a means of trade and source of pleasure; and the history of Henley-on-Thames. Its **Wind in the Willows** gallery celebrates the famous story set on the Thames, by Kenneth Grahame, who lived in nearby **Pangbourne** (1922–32).

Mapledurham★

Open Apr–Oct Sun and bank holidays except Aug 2–5.30pm. £9.50. &PX ℘0118 972 3350. www.mapledurham.co.uk.
An Elizabethan **manor house** beside a 14C church and a fully operational **watermill** dating back to the 15C, form an idyllic riverside picture.

Basildon Park★

House open daily: noon–3pm. £12.70. &PX ℘01491 672382. www.nationaltrust.org.uk.
The splendid Palladian villa overlooking a lush part of the Thames Valley was built by John Carr in 1776. It is rich in exquisite **plasterwork** and boasts a fine collection of 18C paintings.

Goring and Streatley

These two villages, with the weir and Goring Lock, are set in one of the most beautiful parts of the Thames, offering enjoyable riverside walks.

Cliveden★★

House: Apr–Oct Thu and Sun 3–5.30pm. £13.70. **Garden and woodlands**: open all year 10am–5.30pm (4pm Jan–mid-Feb and Oct–Dec). £11.70. X ℘01628 605 069. www.nationaltrust.org.uk.
Set high above one of the most glorious stretches of the Thames, Cliveden has entertained every monarch from George I onwards. From 1893 to 1966 it was the home of America's richest family, the Astors; in 1963 John Profumo first met Christine Keeler here to begin their scandalous affair.
The house is now a luxury hotel and its magnificent gardens and majestic woodlands – formal Parterre, secluded glades, tree-lined avenues and riverside woodland walks – capture the grandeur of a bygone age.

Oxford★★★

Blenheim Palace and around

The city of Oxford is famous as the home of England's oldest university. Its romantic townscape of 'dreaming spires', as Matthew Arnold described it, mellow golden stone walls and students in black gowns on bicycles has been the setting for any number of works of fiction, from *Harry Potter* to *Inspector Morse* and *Jude the Obscure*.

A BIT OF HISTORY

Oxford developed in Saxon times around the 8C nunnery of St Frideswide, now Christ Church, and still maintains its original street plan and parts of its city walls. Religious foundations sprang up and in about 1200 the university emerged as a federation of monastic halls; it is still a federation of autonomous colleges today. Oxford was the headquarters of the Royalists during the Civil War (Charles I staying at Christ Church and Henrietta Maria at Merton College). Reform came in the 19C, with the Anglo-Catholic Oxford Movement – which revived the Catholic tradition within the Anglican Church – and the growth of scientific research. In the 20C women were admitted and most of the colleges are now co-educational. However, the essence of Oxford remains unchanged.

The bicycle shop opened in Longwall Street by **William Morris** in 1902, where he began to make motorcycles, has since developed into a vast motor manufacturing enterprise in the suburb of Cowley, where BMW now produces Minis.

MUSEUMS AND TRINITY COLLEGE

Oxford's finest collections can be found in the **Ashmolean Museum★★** (Beaumont Street; open Tue–Sun and bank holiday Mons 10am–5pm; ♿;✖; ☎01865 278 000; www.ashmolean.org). Built in 1845, this museum houses

▶ **Population:** 161 300.
♿ **Michelin Map:** Michelin Atlas p 18 or Map 504 Q 28.
🚩 **Info:** 15–16 Broad Street. ☎01865 686 430. www.experienceoxfordshire. org. The train station (55 mins to London Paddington) is a 10-minute walk from the centre. The bus station is in the centre at Gloucester Green. Oxford is compact and can be covered on foot, or from an open-top bus (☎01865 790 522; www. citysightseeingoxford.com).
▶ **Location:** 58mi/93km northwest of London.
☺ **Don't Miss:** Punting on the river; Christ Church; Bodleian Library; Ashmolean Museum; University Museum of Natural History/ Pitt Rivers Museum.
🕐 **Timing:** At least 3 days. Many of the colleges are open only in the afternoon; visiting times are usually displayed at the porter's lodge. Opening times at www.ox.ac.uk.
👪 **Kids:** Oxford Castle Unlocked.
🚶 **Walking Tours:** Contact the tourist office. The **tour** marked on the map (*p264*) explores the city's highlights.

the university's archaeology and art collections. Greek and Roman sculptures, Egyptian antiquities, and the decorative and fine arts of China, Japan, Tibet, India and Persia are well represented. The outstanding object here is the exquisite late-9C Alfred Jewel, probably made for Alfred the Great. The principal art collections are: Italian paintings, with masterpieces by Uccello and Piero di Cosimo; Renaissance works by Bellini, Veronese, Tintoretto and Giorgione; outstanding Pre-Raphaelite paintings including works by Hunt and Charles Collins; a good selection of

French Impressionists; and 20C British works from the Camden Town school. From the Ashmolean, head east on Beaumont Street, past the **Martyr's Memorial** and enter **Balliol College** (note the scorch marks on the inner and outer quad doors from the 16C burning of two Protestant bishops in Broad Street) to access **Trinity College** (Broad Street; call to check opening hours and access to the College. ℘01865 279 900; www.trinity.ox.ac.uk), founded 1555. Standing well back from Broad Street, behind gardens in the Front Quad, is the **chapel★**, with Grinling Gibbons' exquisite carvings. Note in the Durham Quad the 17C Library and in the Garden Quad, facing **Trinity Gardens★**, the north range by Sir Christopher Wren.

Head north from Trinity, up Parks Road to visit the **University Museum of Natural History★** (Parks Road, off Broad Street; open 10am–5pm; closed over Christmas; ℘01865 272 950; www.oum.ox.ac.uk). Founded in 1860, the museum's natural history contents (including the famous Oxford Dodo) arguably tell us more about the Victorians than the natural world, though both sink into insignificance beside the extraordinary building: a cast-iron neo-Gothic Revival cathedral designed like a railway station, with 19C decorated stone carvings of animals and plants by the Irish sculptor-mason family, the O'Sheas. A doorway at the end leads to the **Pitt Rivers Museum★** (open Tue–Sun and bank holiday Mons 10am–4.30pm; other Mons noon–4.30pm; closed over Christmas; ℘01865 270 927; www.prm.ox.ac.uk), Oxford's splendidly eclectic and highly colourful anthropological collection of masks, musical instruments, jewellery, skulls, totem poles, armour, and more…

CITY CENTRE

The route marked on the map (☞see p264) offers a tour of all of the colleges, but you may prefer simply to wander and admire the architecture.

Oxford's heart is Radcliffe Square and the landmark Baroque **Radcliffe Camera★**, which contains two reading rooms, mainly used by undergraduates (open only on the Bodleian Library Extended Tour). This rotunda, designed by James Gibbs, is a useful reference point when exploring the many colleges that branch off it.

North of the Quadrangle

On the north side of the quadrangle you will find one of the world's great libraries, the **Bodleian Library★★** (Broad Street; see website for varying times and charges; ℘01865 277 162; www.bodleian.ox.ac.uk/bodley), which contains a copy of every book printed in Britain. Established in the 14C and rebuilt in the 17C, the Bodleian contains more than 6 million books, manuscripts and maps. The main entrance leads to th Old Schools Quadrangle, built in 1439 in the Jacobean Gothic style. On the right is the Tower of the Five Orders, richly decorated with the five classical orders of architecture. Opposite is the 15C Divinity School – Harry Potter fans may recognise it from the first two films – famous for the bosses and pendants of its **lierne vaulting★**. Above is Duke Humphrey's Library (1610–12), with its decorated **ceiling★★**.

Just north of the Bodleian you will find the **Clarendon Building** and, next door, the **Sheldonian Theatre★** (Broad Street, open Feb–Nov (university functions permitting) Mon–Sat 10am–4.30pm (May–Sept also Sun 10am–4.30pm); Nov–Jan Mon–Sat 10am–3pm; £3.50; ℘01865 277 299; www.sheldon.ox.ac.uk). Built 1664–69, Oxford's first Classical building and Sir Christoper Wren's first work of architecture was designed to accommodate formal university ceremonies, a function it fulfils today, alongside its role as a recital room for small music concerts. Next door is Hawksmoor's 1713 Palladian **Clarendon Building,** now part of the Bodleian Library.

East of the Quadrangle

On the east side of the quadrangle you first come to **All Souls College** (High Street; College Front and Great Quadrangles and Chapel open daily when col-

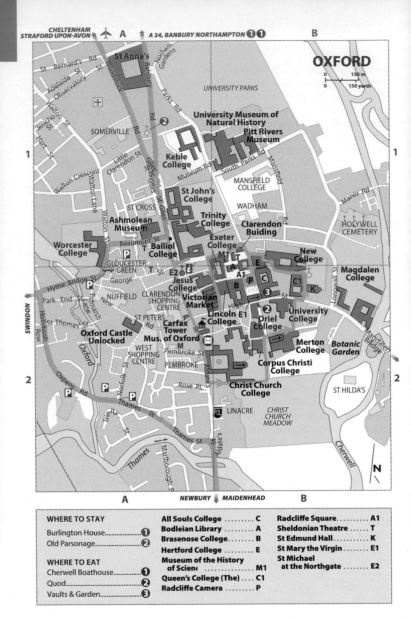

lege is open 2–4pm; ☏01865 279 379; www.asc.ox.ac.uk). **Founded in 1438 as a memorial to those killed in the Hundred Years War, the Front Quadrangle is mid-15C and the larger North Quad, by Nicholas Hawksmoor, is 18C. Between them is the 1442 Perpendicular chapel★, with 15C glass in the antechapel, and a magnificent medieval reredos.**

Further east are **Hertford College** and **New College** (New College Lane gate

summer, Holywell Street gate winter; open daily Easter–early Oct 11am–5pm; early Oct–Easter 2–4pm; £4 (winter free); ☏01865 279 555; www.new.ox.ac.uk). **Founded by William of Wykeham in 1379, New College still maintains some of its original buildings. The Great Quad is quintessential English Perpendicular; the hall is the oldest in Oxford. The 15C chapel★ is vast, complete with 14C glass. The cloister is a place of calm, offering a view of the 1400 Bell Tower.**

Bridge of Sighs, Hertford College, New College Lane

In the gardens is Oxford's finest section of city walls, including five bastions. Across Longwall Street from New College is **Magdalen College**★★ (open Oct–late Jun 1pm–dusk or 6pm; late Jun–Sept noon–7pm; £6; ✗; ℘01865 276 000; www.magd.ox.ac.uk). Founded in 1458 Magdalen (pronounced 'mordlin') was originally the Hospital of St John the Baptist; the wall running along the High Street is even earlier, dating from the 13C. The chapel, bell tower and cloisters are sumptuous late Perpendicular. The chapel is adorned with gargoyles and pinnacled buttresses.

The 46m bell tower is still '...the most absolute building in Oxford' (James I). The gargoyles on the cloister buttresses are a familiar feature of the Great Quadrangle.

Beside Magdalen Bridge is a boat house and punting station (you will also find these at Folly Bridge and Bardwell Road). A relaxing trip on a flat-bottomed **punt** along the Cherwell or the Thames is almost de rigueur for many visitors, and self-hire and chauffered punts are available by the hour (£22 per hour; for more details visit *www.oxfordpunting.co.uk*).

West of the Quadrangle

Just west of the quadrangle is **Brase-nose College** (Radcliffe Square; open Mon–Fri 10–11.30am, 2–4.30pm (5pm in summer), Sat–Sun 9.30–10.30am (10am–11.30am non-term time) 2–4.30pm; closed Christmas; £2; ℘01865 277 030, www.bnc.ox.ac.uk). Founded 1509, the Gatehouse, Front Quad and Hall are early-16C, the Library and Chapel mid-17C and the old kitchen a 14C relic of Brasenose Hall (the name refers to a doorknocker from the hall). Adjacent to Brasenose is **Lincoln College**★ (Turl Street; open year-round Mon–Fri 2–5pm, Sat–Sun 11am–5pm; closed 1 Jan, 25–26 Dec; ℘01865 279 800; www.linc.ox.ac.uk). Founded 1427, the Front Quad and Hall were built in 1436 and provide a rare glimpse of medieval Oxford. The 1610–31 chapel in the Back Quad contains original 17C Flemish stained glass. Between the two quads are the rooms of **John Wesley**.

Christ Church and South

The **Botanic Gardens** (Rose Lane; open Mar–Apr and Sept–Oct Tue–Sun 9am–5pm, Mon noon–5pm; May–Aug 9am–6pm (Mon May only noon–6pm); Nov–Feb Tue–Sun 9am–4pm, Mon noon–4pm; closed Good Fri, 25 Dec; £5; ♿; ℘01865 286 690; www.botanic-garden.ox.ac.uk) to the southeast were established in 1621; these are the oldest botanic gardens in England. They provide a view of both the college towers and spires and the River Cherwell.

Christ Church

West of here is **Merton College★★** (Merton Street; open Mon–Fri 2–5pm/dusk, Sat–Sun 10am–5pm/dusk; £3; ☏01865 276 310; www.merton.ox.ac.uk). Founded in 1264, Merton has the oldest and most picturesque college buildings in Oxford. The oldest square is **Mob Quad**, a complete 14C quadrangle with the **Library** (1371–78) – the first medieval library to put books on shelves – on two sides. Adjacent is the **Decorated Chapel** (1294–97) with 14C transepts, and stained glass.

Leaving the chapel you immediately see **Corpus Christi College** (open daily 1.30–4.30pm; closed Easter and Christmas; ☏01865 276 700; www.ccc.ox.ac.uk). Founded in 1517, the gateway and Front Quad are early Tudor. The Pelican Sundial in the centre of the quad was designed in 1581, the 16C Hall has a splendid hammerbeam roof and the 16C chapel contains an altarpiece attributed to the studio of Rubens.

Just beyond Corpus Christi is **Christ Church★★** (college, cathedral and hall: open Mon–Sat 10am–5pm, Sun 2–5pm; closed 25 Dec; college, cathedral, hall £7–£9; ☏01865 276 492; www.chch.ox.ac.uk). Founded in 1525 by Cardinal Wolsey, 'The House' is Oxford's biggest and grandest Renaissance college. Oxford's largest quadrangle is **Tom Quad★**. Above the gatehouse is Wren's synthesis of Baroque and Gothic, **Tom Tower★**, a fine domed gateway. The **Tudor Hall★★**, by James Wyatt, boasts a magnificent fan-vaulted entrance stairway, hammerbeam roof and portraits by Kneller, Romney, Gainsborough, Lawrence and Millais. The **Picture Gallery** at Christ Church holds one of the most important private collections of Old Master drawings in the country and includes work by Leonardo, Michelangelo, Dürer, Raphael and Rubens. Picturesque Christ Church Meadow stretches from St Aldate's to the River Thames. **Christ Church Cathedral★**, originally the church of St Frideswide's Priory, is late Norman with a 16C roof. Its glory is its 15C stellar vaulted **choir roof★**.

Nearby, just off Cornmarket Street, in the Town Hall on St Aldates, is the **Museum of Oxford** (open Mon–Sat 10am–5pm; ☏01865 252 334; www.museumofoxford.org.uk). Here you will discover the story of the city including its earliest residents' medieval crafts, Civil War Oxford, famous literary connections and the growth of the modern city.

A little further up Cornmarket Street is **Carfax Tower** (open daily Apr–Sept 10am–5pm, rest of year 10am–4pm; ☏01865 792 653; £3.50; ☺No children under five admitted), **the centre of the**

Saxon and medieval city. This 14C tower is all that remains of St Martin's Church. There are good views of the High Street from the top of the tower (99 steps).

There are four entrances from the High Street to the delightful **Victorian Covered Market★**, which dates back to 1774.

West of Carfax, along Queen Street and Castle Street is **Oxford Castle Unlocked★ ♟♟** (open daily 10am–5.30pm (last tour 4.20pm); closed 25 Dec; £10.95, child £7.75; discount online; ♿✕; ✆01865 260 666; www.oxford-castleunlocked.co.uk). The city's most recent visitor attraction, this is a brilliant restoration of the former castle/prison complex, including a hotel and restaurants, and is worth a visit if only to see the exterior. George's Tower is a striking survival from Oxford Castle, built 1071. Since then the site has been used as a place of incarceration until its closure in 1996. The more colourful events – violence, executions, escapes, betrayal, romance – which shaped its grim history are explored with relish by the castel guides.

WOODSTOCK

8hmi/13km N of Oxford.

Effectively the lobby to Blenheim Palace, the elegant little mellow Cotswold-stone town of **Woodstock** is well worth a visit in its own right. Old coaching inns and antique shops cluster round the Classical town hall.

Across the street, the **Oxfordshire Museum** (open Tue–Sat 10am–5pm, Sun 2–5pm (closes 4.30pm Tue–Fri Nov–Feb); ♿✕; ✆01993 814 106; www.oxfordshire. gov.uk) tells the story of both town and county. Kids enjoy its Dinosaur Gallery.

BLENHEIM PALACE★★★

Woodstock. **Park**: open daily (except 25 Dec) 9am–6.30pm/dusk; closed 25 Dec. **House**: open daily 10.30am–5.30pm. **Gardens**: open 10am–6pm on dates when house open: Park open year-round daily 9am–6pm. Palace and park £24.90, park & gardens £15.30. ♿🅿✕ ✆01993 810530. www.blenheimpalace.com.

The greatest building of the English Baroque, residence of the Dukes of Marlborough, is matched in splendour by the sublime landscaping of its vast park.

A Bit of History

The Royal Manor of Woodstock once the hunting ground of Saxon kings, was the birthplace of Edward the Black Prince (b.1330). In the 18C the royal manor was given to **John Churchill, Duke of Marlborough** (1650–1722), to mark his victory in 1704 over the armies of Louis XIV at Blenheim in Bavaria. Seemingly limitless funds from the national purse were made available for a *'Royall and National Monument'* to be erected in celebration of this decisive check to France's pan-European ambitions. Leading architects and craftsmen were employed, foremost among them **Sir John Vanbrugh**, one of England's most original architects, whose inventiveness and sense of drama found full expression here. The grandiose project, a monument rather than a home, was completed in 1722. A century and a half later, on 30 November 1874, his direct descendant, **Winston Churchill**, grandson of the 7th Duke, was born here. This most illus-

Water Terraces, Blenheim Palace

trious of Englishmen is buried in the churchyard at Bladon (3mi/5km south). On the first floor 'Blenheim Palace: The Untold Story' is a good introduction to the estate's 300-year history.

Palace★★★

The palace's huge scale and fortress-like character are relieved by almost theatrical composition and exuberant detail. Its silhouette has a romantic, even medieval air, with an array of turrets, pinnacles and disguised chimney-pots, and the Great Court (137m long) is like a stage set, a succession of colonnades, towers and arcades leading the eye inexorably to the main façade with its imposing portico. Symbols of military prowess and patriotism abound; over the courtyard gateway the cockerel of France is mauled by the English lion.

Interior

A series of splendidly decorated rooms continues the monumental theme. In the **Great Hall** (20m high) the ceiling is painted with an allegory of Marlborough's victory. Sir Winston Churchill's life is celebrated in a suite of rooms, including the one in which he was born. State apartments are furnished with original pieces. There are portraits by Reynolds, Romney, Van Dyck and one, by Sargent, of the 9th Duke with his family and American-born wife Consuelo. The vast **Saloon** has a great painted colonnade, apparently open to the sky. The **Long Library**, with a magnificent stucco ceiling, runs the entire length (55m) of the west front. In the chapel is the bombastic **tomb** of the 1st Duke.

Grounds★★★

The ancient hunting park, with its venerable trees and deer-proof wall, was worked upon in the early-18C by the royal gardeners. The **Italian Garden** to the east of the palace and the spectacular **Water Garden** to the west are modern, as is the symbolic maze of trophies, cannon and trumpets in the walled garden, but they capture something of the spirit of the formal avenues

and geometrical parterres which were mostly swept away by **Lancelot 'Capability' Brown**, the greatest of English landscape architects. The redesigned park is his masterpiece, offering, from the Woodstock Gate, what has been described as '...the finest view in England'. Sweeping grassy slopes, noble groves of trees and the curving outline of the great lake, crossed by Vanbrugh's **Grand Bridge**, provide a more than worthy setting for the palace.

The huge **Doric column** (41m high) is topped by a statue of the 1st Duke with Victory in his grasp. Downstream, Brown's water engineering terminates in his **Grand Cascade**, over which the little River Glyme foams to rejoin its former bed.

In the **Pleasure Grounds** ♟♟ (the area nearest the house) are various attractions including Blenheim Bygones, a lavender garden, a maze, a butterfly house (closed winter) and an adventure play area. A land train (free) saves weary feet. You are also free to wander the 850ha of beautiful parkland.

DORCHESTER★

10mi/16km S of Oxford.

This historic village dates back to the Bronze Age and boasts a fine Norman **abbey church** (open daily 8am–6pm/ dusk, abbey museum open early Apr–Sept daily 2–5pm; 🅿 ✕(seasonal); ✆01865 340 007; www.dorchester-abbey.org.uk).

ABINGDON ON THAMES★

11mi/17km S of Oxford.

🅱 Old Abbey House. ✆01235 522711. www.southernoxfordshire.com.

The town grew up around an abbey founded in the 7C, though the only remaining abbey buildings are the 13C **Chequer** with its tall chimney, the c.1500 **Long Gallery** with an oak-beamed roof and the 15C **gateway** beside the medieval church of St Nicholas. Abingdon's skyline is characterised by the 15C spire of the wide five-aisled **St Helen's Church**. Delightful 15C **almshouses★** border the churchyard.

© nadger/iStockphoto.com

Market Hall, Chipping Campden

Cotswolds★★★

Cirencester to
Chipping Campden

Rising gently from the Upper
Thames Valley in the southeast to
a dramatic escarpment overlooking the Severn Vale in the west, the
Cotswolds cover around
770sq mi/2 000sq km), encapsulat-
ing rural England in concentrated
form. Airy open uplands, sheltered
in places by stately belts of beech
trees, alternate with deep valleys enfolding venerable golden
limestone villages and small
county towns.

A BIT OF HISTORY

The region has long been favoured for
settlement. The commanding heights in
the west are crowned more often than
not by the hill forts of prehistoric man,
whose burial places also abound, from
the chambered tombs of the Neolithic
to the round barrows of the Bronze Age.
Great estates were farmed from the
Roman villas lying just off Ermin Street
and the Fosse Way. In the Middle Ages
it was the wool from countless sheep
grazing on the fine pasture of the wolds
which gave rise to a trade of European
importance and to a class of prosperous
merchants, whose monuments are the
great "wool" churches which they built
from the underlying oolitic limestone.
Ranging in colour from silver or cream

Michelin Map: Michelin
Atlas pp 17 and 27 or
Map 503 O 27 and 28.

Info: Stow on the
Wold: St Edward's Hall.
℘01451 870 998.
Chipping Campden: The
Old Police Station, High
Street. ℘01386 841 206.
Cirencester: Corinium
Museum, Park Street.
℘01285 654 180.
Bourton-on-the-Water:
Victoria Street.
℘01451 820 211.
www.cotswolds.com.

Location: Most of the central
villages make a good base.
Alternatively, stay in Oxford,
Stratford, Cheltenham or
Bath. Regular Cotswolds
bus tours depart from all
of these in summer.

Don't Miss: The villages
of Bibury and Chipping
Campden; Chastleton House;
Snowshill Manor; Hidcote
Manor Garden; the view
from Broadway Tower.

Beware: Busy roads and
crowds during school
summer holidays.

Timing: At least 3 days.

Kids: Cotswold Wildlife
Park and Bourton-on-
the-Water's many child-
friendly attractions.

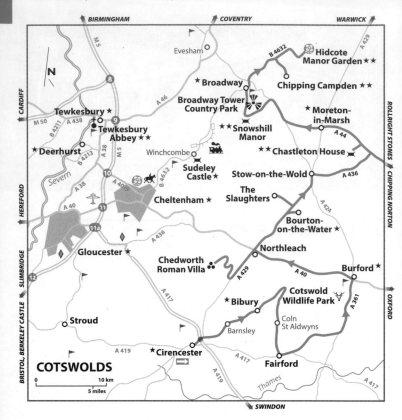

to deepest gold, this loveliest of building stone is synonymous with 'Cotswold character'. Yielding the sophisticated masonry of manor houses, the tiles of cottage roofs, rough-dressed walls of barns and even the drystone boundaries of fields, it creates a rare harmony of building and landscape. Far removed from coalfields and big cities, the area escaped the effects of industrialisation; its rural pattern is intact, an idyllic setting for quiet exploration of the past.

🚗 DRIVING TOUR

CIRENCESTER TO CHIPPING CAMPDEN

▶ 40mi/64km; Allow a day.

This tour runs north through some of the region's most delightful small towns and villages towards the escarpment

above Broadway with its spectacular views.

Cirencester★

The 'Capital of the Cotswolds' is still the market town for a prosperous rural region. It was founded as a Roman fort, Corinium, established early in the Roman occupation at the junction of three major roads – Ermin Street, Akeman Street and the Fosse Way. By the 2C, it had become a walled city, second only to London in size, the centre of a flourishing countryside of villa estates. The old town is compact and has kept a traditional townscape, little marred by incongruous intrusions. It is hemmed in by the green spaces of two ancient estates: the gardens of the abbey sloping down to the pretty River Churn (the abbey buildings were demolished at the Dissolution) and the grandiose formal landscape of **Cirencester Park**, which contains the magnificent **Broad**

Avenue (5mi/8km) and the great house, concealed from the town by a high wall and an even higher yew hedge.

On Coxwell Street, the **Church of St John the Baptist★** (open daily 9.30am–5pm, except during services; closed 25–Dec except for services; ℘01285 659 317; www.cirenparish.co.uk) is one of the largest parish churches in the country, and an important example of a Cotswold 'wool church'. The lofty tower of 1400–20, supported by powerful spur buttresses, rises grandly above the town. The unusual three-storey porch opening into the marketplace once served as the town hall. The nave is exceptionally high and spacious; its immensely tall piers carry angels bearing the coats of arms of those pious townsfolk responsible for the ambitious rebuilding of 1516–30. Throughout the interior there is a wealth of detail: an unusual pre-Reformation pulpit; the **Boleyn Cup**, a gilt cup made for Anne Boleyn; memorial brasses grouped in the Chapel of the Holy Trinity; and, in the Lady Chapel, the charming effigies of Humfry Bridges (d.1598), his wife and their numerous children.

On Park Street, the **Corinium Museum★** (open daily Mon–Sat 10am–5pm, Sun 2–5pm; closes 4pm daily Nov–Mar; closed 1 Jan; 23–26 Dec; £5.40; ⅊✕☞ ℘01285 655 611; http://coriniummuseum.org) is a modern well-arranged museum explaining Cotswold history from geological to recent times. It holds one of the finest and most extensive Roman collections in the country, including a series of superb **mosaic pavements★**. The building also houses the local tourist information office.

▷ From Cirencester drive east on the A 429 and the B 4425.

Bibury★

William Morris' epithet of '...the most beautiful village in England' is justified by the combined prospect of the River Coln, stone bridges, Arlington Row weavers' cottages and the gables of Bibury Court against a wooded background.

▷ From Bibury return SW by the B 4425; at the crossroads turn left; in Poulton turn left on to the A 417.

Fairford

This old coaching village is famous for the **Church of St Mary★** (open daily 10am–5pm/3.30pm in winter; ℘01285 712 611; www.stmaryschurchfairford.org.uk), harmoniously re-built in the late-15C. Sculptures, some humorously grotesque, enrich the exterior. Inside, the screens, stalls and misericords of the choir are of exceptional quality. But the church's glory is its wonderful set of **stained-glass windows★★** (c.1500), tracing in colour the Bible's story from Adam and Eve to the Last Judgement.

▷ From Fairford take the A 417 E and the A 361 N.

▲▲ Cotswold Wildlife Park★

Open Apr–Oct daily 10am–6pm (Nov–Mar 5pm/dusk). £15, child 5–16, £10 (discount for e-tickets). ⅊⅊✕ ℘01993 823 006. www.cotswoldwildlifepark.co.uk.

The peaceful natural habitat of the park and gardens (65ha), set around a listed Victorian manor house, is home to a wide variety of wildlife. Come eye to eye with giraffes on a high-level walkway; see rhinos, zebras, lions, leopards and ostriches behind unobtrusive moats; spot monkeys and otters; walk through the aviary in the old walled garden, or through the tropical house. Other attractions include an adventure playground, brass rubbing centre, children's farmyard and narrow-gauge railway.

▷ Continue north on the A 361.

Burford★

One of the focal points of the wool trade, later an important coaching town, Burford's growth stopped when the turnpike road (A 40) bypassed it in 1812. With its wealth of beautifully preserved buildings, nearly all of Cotswold limestone, it is one of the region's 'show' villages. The single main street descends to cross the pretty River Windrush. About half-way down, the black-

and-white timber-fronted building on stone pillars is the 16C **Tolsey**, once the courthouse, and toll collecting point, now the local museum (open Apr–Oct Tue–Sun 2–5pm; ✆01993 823 196, www.tolseymuseumburford.org).

Slightly apart from the town is the large **Church of St John the Baptist★**, its tall spire rising gracefully above the water-meadows. Norman in origin, the church exhibits a rich variety of work from many periods; the pinnacled three-storey 15C porch is outstanding. Note the exuberant monument to Edward Harman (d.1569), decorated with American Indians, and rows of kneeling children.

▷ Take the A 40 west to Northleach.

Northleach

This small market town is graced with many fine historic buildings but its 'wool church' takes pride of place. It boasts Britain's finest collection of memorial brasses, dedicated (unsurprisingly) to the merchants whose money built the church. Note the huge brass dedicated to John Fortey (d.1458), over 1.5m long, beneath the North Arcade. On the High Street is **Keith Harding's World of Mechanical Music Museum**, (open daily 10am–5pm; closed 25–26 Dec; £8; &; ✆01451 860 181, www.mechanicalmusic.co.uk), a showcase of ingenious self-playing musical instruments and automata, introduced and played by expert guides.

▷ Take the A 429 south and turn right to Chedworth.

Chedworth Roman Villa

Yanworth, nr Cheltenham. Open mid-Feb–Nov daily 10am–4pm (late Mar–late Oct 5pm). £9.50. 🅿 ✕ ✆01242 890 256. www.nationaltrust.org.uk.

This large wealthy villa stood at the head of a small valley beside its own spring. It was undoubtedly one of the grandest buildings of the Roman Cotswolds. The remains, including good mosaic floors, have been carefully excavated and are well presented. The museum displays items found on the site.

▷ Return to Northleach and continue N on the A 429.

Bourton-on-the-Water★

The village owes its special charm to the clear waters of the Windrush, which run between well-tended grass banks beside the main street and under elegant small stone bridges. It is the most commercialised of the Cotswolds villages, due in no small part to three very popular family attractions: The **Model Village** (Rissington Road, behind Old New Inn; open daily 10am–6pm/winter 4pm; £3.60, child £2.80; &; ✆01451 820 467; www.theoldnewinn.co.uk; the excellent **Cotswold Motoring Museum & Toy Collection** (The Old Mill; open daily 10am–6pm mid-Feb–mid-Dec; £5.75, child £4.10; &; ✆01451 821 255; www.cotswoldmotoringmuseum.co.uk), home to the popular children's TV character Brum; and **Birdland Park and Gardens** (Rissington Road; open daily 10am–6pm/Nov–Mar 4pm; £9.95, child 3–15, £6.95; &✕; ✆01451 820 480; www.birdland.co.uk), complete with penguins.

▷ Make a detour west of the A 429 by a minor road to the Slaughters.

The Slaughters

Frequently cited as two of the prettiest villages in the Cotswolds, both **Lower** and **Upper Slaughter** are picturesquely sited by the River Eye. The word 'Slaughter' is in fact derived from the Old English word 'Slohtre' meaning muddy place.

The **Old Mill** (open daily, Mar–Oct 10am–6pm, Nov–Feb 10am–dusk; ✕; £2.50; ✆01451 820 052, www.oldmilllowerslaughter.com) at Lower Slaughter is worth a stop, not just for its local history museum but also for its riverside tearooms and handmade organic ice cream parlour.

▷ Take the minor road north east into Stow-on-the-Wold.

Stow-on-the-Wold

This is the highest settlement in Gloucestershire and probably originated as a Roman lookout post on the Fosse Way. It is a regular stop for visitors on the traditional Cotswold circuit, to browse in the antique shops, admire the 14C cross in the marketplace or the Crucifixion by Caspar de Crayer (1610) in the church.

▶ Take the A 436 north east; at the crossroads turn right onto the A 44.

Chipping Norton

This is one of the Cotswold's liveliest towns with a good number of pubs, restaurants and shops and an acclaimed theatre. It has a fine wool church and a modest local museum.

Take a detour 2.6mi/4.2km north via the B 4026 to Little Rollright, where you will see signs to the **Rollright Stones**, (open daily sunrise–sunset; £1 honesty box; www.rollrightstones.co.uk). Set in a field is an ancient small stone circle – 70 stones, 31m in diameter – which according to the local legend represents a future king of England and his knights, turned to stone by a witch. The circle, some 4 000–4 500 years old, is known as The Kings Men. There is the (separate) King Stone, and the remains of a 5 000-year-old megalithic tomb, known as The Whispering Knights.

▶ Return along the A 44.

Chastleton House★★

Chastleton, nr Moreton-in-Marsh. Open early Mar–early Nov Wed–Sun 1–5pm; 1st 2 wks Dec Sat–Sun only 11am–3pm. Entry by timed ticket, issued at reception on first-come, first-served basis (limited numbers available) from 12.30pm. £10.50. **P**✗ (in church); ℘01608 674 981. www.nationaltrust.org.uk.

This rare gem of a Jacobean country house was built in the early-17C by a wool merchant and is a near-perfect time capsule. The absence of shop, tearoom and other modern accretions adds to the atmosphere.

The **Great Hall**, one of the last of its kind to be built, the richly decorated **Great Chamber** and the tunnel-vaulted Long Gallery, running the whole length

of the top floor, evoke the atmosphere of domestic life in the 17C.

On the forecourt are the 17C stables and the little **Church of St Mary**. To the east of the house is a great rarity, a small formal **garden** surviving from about 1700.

▶ Continue west on the A 44.

The route passes through **Moreton-in-Marsh★**, an attractive little market town, on the Fosse Way and dating from the 13C. Most properties on the wide main street, however, are 18C, and feature elegant inns and houses, including the Redesdale Market Hall. The oldest building is probably the 16C curfew tower, its bell being rung nightly until 1860, and more than once has guided travellers in poor visibility to safety.

▶ After 6mi/10km turn left onto the B 4081.

Snowshill Manor and Garden★★

Snowshill, nr Broadway. House: Open Jul–Aug Wed–Mon noon–5pm; Apr–Jun and Sept–Oct Wed–Sun and bank holidays noon–5pm. House and garden £10.80, garden only £6.10; Entry to house by timed ticket only, issued at reception on first-come, first served basis. &**P**✗ ℘01386 852 410. www.nationaltrust.org.uk.

This typical Cotswold manor house (c. 1500) is snugly sited below the rim of the escarpment. The low-lit house is very atmospheric and crammed with a fascinating jackdaw's nest of objects, acquired by the eccentric owner Charles Wade (1883–1956), the most striking of which is the **Samurai armour** collection displayed to its full menacing effect on brooding warrior mannequins in the gloom of the Green Room. Stepping out into the light, Wade also laid out the enchanting **terraced garden★**.

▶ Return northeast on the B 4081; turn left onto a minor road.

Broadway Tower

Open daily 10am–5pm (may vary in poor weather). £5. &🄿 ✕ ℘01386 852 390. www.broadwaytower.co.uk.

Broadway Tower, a battlemented folly (1800), marks one of the highest points (312m) in the Cotswolds. It houses exhibitions on three floors about the history of its occupants. On a clear day the **panorama★★★** extends to the Welsh borders. The surrounding country park includes a red deer enclosure and beautiful nature walks.

▷ Continue on the minor road; turn left into the A 44, down a long hill.

Broadway★

This handsome village, more formal than its neighbours, is famous for its variety of genteel upmarket antique and craft shops, cafés and restaurants, hotels and guesthouses.

The long, partly tree-lined 'broadway' rises gently from the village green at the western end to the foot of the escarpment, flanked by mellow stone buildings, from picturesque thatched cottages to the stately Lygon Arms hotel.

▷ Take the B 4632 and B 4035 north then east to Chipping Campden.

Chipping Campden★★

The long curving High Street, lined with buildings of all periods in the mellowest of limestone, makes Chipping Campden the embodiment of the Cotswold townscape. The town has been quietly prosperous since the great days of the medieval wool trade and something of its present state of preservation is due to the care and skill of the artists and craftspeople who were attracted to Chipping Campden in the early-20C. Many of the houses in the **High Street** are substantial but, more than individual distinction, it is the overall harmony of the street scene which impresses. The centre of the town is marked by the arched and gabled **Market Hall** of 1627. Further north, distinguished by its two-storeyed bay window, is the **house of William Grevel**, "the flower of the wool merchants of all England", who died in 1401 and is commemorated by a fine brass in the splendid **St James's Church** (open daily; donation requested; ℘01386 841 927; www.stjameschurch-campden.co.uk). In Church Street stand the almshouses built in 1617 by Sir Baptist Hicks. His own mansion *(opposite)* was destroyed but two pavilions survive, together with pepperpot lodges and the gateway, near the entrance to the church.

▷ Take the B 4081 north (signed).

Hidcote★★

Hidcote Bartrim. Open May–Sept daily 10am–6pm; Oct daily 10am–5pm; mid-Mar–Apr Sat–Wed 10am–6pm; Nov–mid-Mar, except Jan and Christmas period Sat–Sun 11am–4pm. £11.80 (Feb, Nov–Dec £7.25). &🄿✕ ℘01386 438 333. www.nationaltrust.org.uk/hidcote.

The horticulturalist Lawrence Johnstone has managed an enchanting variety of effects in such a small space (4ha) and created one of the greatest English gardens of the 20C, an Arts and Crafts masterpiece. Calm expanses of lawns (one of which is open for croquet), vistas down avenues or into the countryside contrast with luxuriant but carefully controlled wildness. A labyrinth of "garden rooms" encloses an arrangement of herbs, plants entirely in white, and a mysterious pool.

CHELTENHAM★

55mi/88km N of Bath and 96mi/155km W of London.

🄱 ℘01242 237 431. www.visitcheltenham.com.

The benefits of the waters of this elegant English spa town were discovered early in the 18C, but it was at its most fashionable in the Regency period, when it developed the Classical architecture, squares, terraces and crescents, all in a delightful setting of trees and gardens, which are still its pride today. Despite its older residents and retirement-home status, it has an animated cultural life, with internationally important musical and literary festivals.

Town Centre★

Of pre-spa Cheltenham there remains little except the secluded Church of St Mary and the line of the much rebuilt High Street. At right angles is the **Promenade**; its spacious lower part is lined on one side by the **Municipal Offices**, an imposing terrace of 1823; its upper part, twice as broad, rises gently to the stately stuccoed façade of the **Queen's Hotel** of 1838. To the east are the **Imperial Gardens**, a floral cocktail in summer; to the west, behind an avenue of trees, are some of the refined **Regency houses** with classical details and exquisite balcony ironwork which characterise the town. Farther south is **Montpellier Walk**, whose mid-19C shopfronts are divided up by Grecian caryatids; it terminates in the colonnade and dome of the old **Montpellier Spa** (now a bank).

Cheltenham Art Gallery and Museum

Open Mon–Sat 9.30am–5.15pm, Sun 11am–4pm. Closed 25–26 Dec and Easter Sun. www.cheltenhammuseum.org.uk
The highlight of the town gallery is its **collection of applied art** illustrating the importance of the Cotswolds in the Arts and Crafts movement. The redeveloped stylish new building (opened in 2013) houses galleries dedicated to local heroes, including the great Edward Wilson (one of Scott's key men on his 1912 expedition to Antarctica), and temporary exhibition galleries.

Pittville

This distinguished district of Classical terraces and villas *(1mi/1.6km N of the High Street)* was laid out in the early-19C by Joseph Pitt. In romantic Pittville Park great trees and sweeping lawns surround a picturesque lake.

Pittville Pump Room★

Open year-round (events permitting) Wed–Mon 10am–4pm. Closed bank holiday Mons, 25–26 Dec. ▣ ℘0844 576 2210. www.pittvillepumproom.org.uk. During the Regency this was the most magnificent of several buildings where the spa waters were taken. This outstanding Grecian building (1825–30), with its Ionic colonnade and domed interior, was designed by Joseph Pitt. You may enter, as long as there is not a function on, and sample a glass of water.

Holst Birthplace Museum

4 Clarence Road, Pittville. Open Tue–Sat 10am–5pm, Sun 1.30–5pm. £5. ℘01242 524 846. www.holstmuseum.org.uk.
Near the park entrance is the Regency house where Gustav Host, composer of *The Planets*, was born in 1874.

DEERHURST★

7mi/11km N of Cheltenham via the A 4019, A 38 and a minor road W.
This tiny village possesses two important Anglo-Saxon buildings. Once part of a flourishing monastery, vestiges of **St Mary's church★** (open daily 8.30am–dusk; &; ℘01684 292 562) date from the 8C, and it is typically Saxon.
Odda's Chapel (open daily Apr–Oct 10am–6pm; Nov–Mar 4pm; closed 1 Jan, 25–26 Dec; ▣; www.english-heritage.org.uk) was dedicated by Earl Odda in 1056 and consists of a nave and chancel, both of touching simplicity. It was rediscovered in the 19C, having served as the kitchen of the adjoining farmhouse.

TEWKESBURY★

8mi/13km N of Cheltenham on the A 4019 and A 38.
This little Saxon town is dominated by the great Norman abbey.
Tewkesbury grew little in the 19C and has conserved its historic character almost intact.

Tewkesbury Abbey★★

Church Street. Open Mon–Sat 8.30am (Sun, Wed, Fri 7.30am)–5.30pm/6pm Sun. Guided tours £5, Apr–Oct Mon–Fri. &✗ ℘01684 850 959. www.tewkesburyabbey.org.uk.
Once part of a wealthy and important Benedictine abbey, the church combines a noble simplicity of structure with great richness of detail, and many of the abbey's important benefactors are buried here.

There are two survivals from monastic days – the **Abbey House** and the **Gatehouse**, just outside the precinct. At the Dissolution it was saved from demolition by the townsfolk. The most impressive elements are the huge 12C **tower** and the grandeur of the **west front**, with its recessed arch (20m high).

The Norman **nave**★★ is covered by a beautiful 14C vault which replaced an earlier timber roof. The church's many monuments are grouped around the choir. Bishop Wakeman is grotesquely commemorated by the *memento mori*, of a decomposing cadaver crawling with vermin. The 14C **stained-glass windows** of the choir depict local notables. The choir **vault**★ is a glorious web of ribs and bosses.

SUDELEY CASTLE★

Castle Street, Winchcombe. 7mi/ 11km NE of Cheltenham via the B 4632. Castle Street, Winchcombe. Open daily mid-Mar–Oct 10am–5pm. £14.95. &🅿✕ ☎01242 604 308. www.sudeleycastle.co.uk.

The house is surrounded by the dramatic scenery of the Cotswold escarpment. Once a medieval stronghold, it became the home of **Katherine Parr**, widow of Henry VIII. During the Civil War it was besieged and largely destroyed. In the 19C the house was restored, although some parts were left ruined. The collection includes Turner, Van Dyck and Rubens. The **gardens** are glorious, with the centrepiece Queens' Garden billowing with hundreds of varieties of old-fashioned roses. The grounds also include St Mary's Church, a rare breeds Pheasantry and adventure playground.

STROUD

The most westerly and least typical of the major Cotswold settlements, Stroud is the only one to have been affected significantly by the Industrial Revolution. Its interesting history can be traced in the **Museum in the Park** (Stratford Park; open Jan–Nov Tue–Fri, 10am–5pm, Sat–Sun and bank holidays 11am–4pm;

Oct–Mar Tue–Fri 10am–4pm, Sat–Sun 11am–4pm; &🅿✕; ☎01453 763 394, www.museuminthepark.org.uk) housed in a 17C wool merchant's mansion.

The Wildfowl and Wetlands Trust, Slimbridge★

15mi/24km SW of Gloucester. Open daily 9.30am–5.30pm (5pm Nov–Mar). £12.72. &🅿✕ ☎01453 891 900. www.wwt.org.uk.

Bordering the extensive wetlands of the tidal Severn, this pioneering waterbird sanctuary, created by the late Sir Peter Scott, has acquired an international reputation for research and conservation and as a place where a great variety of native and exotic wildfowl can be observed from hides, observatories and a canoe safari at close quarters. Visitors can also enjoy the spectacular winter arrival of thousands of wild ducks, geese and swans.

Berkeley Castle★★

20mi/32km SW of Gloucester. Open Apr–Oct Sun–Wed, 11am–5pm. Butterfly House open May–Sept. £11 🅿✕ ☎01453 810 303. www.berkeley-castle.com.

This archetypal medieval stronghold commanded the narrow strip of lowland between the Cotswolds and the Severn; its defences could be strengthened by flooding the surrounding water meadows. The inner courtyard is dominated by the great drum of the **keep** of 1153. The **interior** is a confusion of twisting passages and stairways, vaulted cellars, ancient kitchens and deep dungeons. In the King's Gallery can be seen the chamber where the deposed **Edward II** was kept prisoner and then horribly murdered, possibly by agents of his former queen. Other rooms are richly furnished with reminders of the castle's continuous occupation since the 12C. In the **Butterfly House** are hundreds of exotic and rare free-flying species.

Gloucester★

Gloucester (pronounced 'Gloster') is a busy centre of administration, manufacturing and commerce, dominated by its glorious cathedral.

CITY

City Centre

The point where the Roman streets intersect is marked by **St Michael's Tower**. The late-medieval timber **Bishop Hooper's Lodging★** in Westgate Street houses **Gloucester Life Museum** (open generally Tue–Sat 10am–5pm but check website for additional opening hours; £5; ✕; ☏01452 396 868; www.gloucester.gov.uk), where the lively exhibits include fishing on the Severn, toys, games and agricultural bygones. Nearby, just off Eastgate Street, is the recently renovated **Gloucester City Museum and Art Gallery** (Brunswick Road; open Tue–Sat 10am–3pm (Apr–Sept 10am–4pm); ✕; ☏01452 396 868), where highlights include an Interactive Roman Kitchen exhibition, a toys and games gallery, and a garden gallery.

Gloucester Docks★

The fine 19C inland port and ware houses have been conserved. The **Gloucester Waterways Museum** (Llanthony Warehouse; open daily mid-Mar–mid-Nov 10am–5pm; closed 1 Jan, 25–26 Dec; ♿ 🅿(charge) ✕; ☏01452 318 200; www.canalrivertrust.org.uk) explores the long history of river and canal navigation in Britain through models, displays, text panels, video simulations and a variety of historic vessels moored by the quay. Take a 45-minute boat trip on either the River Severn, or the Gloucester and Sharpness Canal, complete with commentary by the captain.

▲▲ Beatrix Potter Museum

9 College Court,. Open daily 10am–4.30pm (winter 4pm). ☏01452 422 856. www.tailor-of-gloucester.org.uk. *The Tailor of Gloucester*, published 1903, was Beatrix Potter's personal favourite among her Peter Rabbit Books. In 1897, when on holiday here, she became fascinated by a local folk tale about John Pritchard, a tailor who had been commissioned to make a fine suit of clothes for the Mayor of Gloucester, and so the story was born. The shop, set in a lovely little alley, still exists today, selling a full range of Beatrix Potter merchandise alongside a small museum.

CATHEDRAL★★

Open year-round daily 7.30am–6pm in term time (closed term time Mon–Fri 8.45–9.15am for school assembly). £5 minimum contribution requested. ♿✕ ☏01452 508 210. www.gloucestercathedral.org.uk. The present structure is essentially the creation of the Norman Benedictine abbot, Serlo, and of his 14C successors, who pioneered the Perpendicular style and adorned the transepts and choir

▶ **Population:** 125 600.
🚗 **Michelin Map:** Michelin Atlas p 17 or Map 503 N 28.
ℹ **Info:** 28 Southgate Street. ☏01452 396 572. www.thecityofgloucester.co.uk. The train (London Paddington 1h53, Bath 1h20) and bus stations face each other, just off Bruton Way, a five-minute walk from the compact city centre. The docks are a short walk further on.
▶ **Location:** 104mi/167km west of London and 47mi/76km north of Bath.
👁 **Don't Miss:** Gloucester Cathedral; excursions to Berkeley Castle, Painswick and Wildfowl and Wetlands Trust, Slimbridge (◉ *see opposite*).
🕐 **Timing:** Allow 3–4 hours.
▲▲ **Kids:** The House of the Tailor of Gloucester.

Village of Painswick

using funds provided by royal patronage, or by pilgrims visiting the tomb of Edward II, who was murdered in 1327 at nearby Berkeley castle (&see Cotswolds, p276). The building was extended in the 15C by the addition of the Lady Chapel. Massive Norman columns, reddened at the base by a fire in 1122, give an impression of enormous strength, while Perpendicular elegance prevails in the exquisite tracery of the high **vault** (28m), the **east window** – the largest of its kind in medieval glass, commemorating the Battle of Crécy – and in the wonderfully light **Lady Chapel** c.1500.

Severn Bore

The village of Minsterworth (4mi/ 6.5km W of Gloucester by the the A 40 and A 48) is a good place from which to observe the phenomenon known as the Severn Bore, a roaring wall of water (up to 2m high) advancing up the Severn estuary, which occurs most vigorously at the time of the equinoxes.

Edward's effigy, north of the choir, is protected by a 14C stonework canopy of rare delicacy. The **Cloisters** (which have featured in three *Harry Potter* films) contain the **lavatorium** where the monks washed their hands at the entrance to the refectory; the 14C fan vaulting, the earliest of its kind, is exceptionally rich. The mid-15C **tower** (69m), with its unmistakable crown of parapet and pinnacles, rises gracefully above **College Green**, a pleasant combination of mainly 18C houses, replacements of earlier monastic buildings. **St Mary's Gate** is an impressive medieval survival.

EXCURSIONS
Tetbury/Westonbirt (The National Arboretum)★
❍ Tetbury. 22mi/35km S of Gloucester via the A 38 and A 4135.

The road passes through **Tetbury**, an elegant Cotswold town, built of silver-grey stone round a quaint Market House (1655) and **St Mary's church**, a refined 18C interpretation of medieval motifs. Take the A 433 3mi/5km southwest to reach the **Westonbirt (The National Arboretum)**, first planted in 1829 (open daily except 25 Dec 9am–5pm; £7–£10. ♿ ✕; ☎0300 067 4890). This important plant collection has grown steadily over the last 180 years to comprise some 14 000 trees and shrubs from all over the world. There are many miles of signed walks and an attractive visitor centre. Some trees here are the largest of their kind in Britain.

Painswick★
The streets of this beautiful little hilltop village contain many old buildings of golden Cotswold stone. The elaborate Baroque tombstones in the parish churchyard are accompanied by 99 clipped yew trees.
On the outskirts of the village (take the B 4073) is the **Painswick Rococo Garden** (open mid-Jan–Oct daily 10.30am–5pm; £7.20; Ⓟ; ☎01452 813 204, www.rococogarden.org.uk). Originally laid out in the early-18C, and set in a hidden valley, it boasts magnificent views of the surrounding countryside.

ADDRESSES

🏨 STAY

CHILTERN HILLS

🍴🍴 **The Nag's Head** – London Road, Great Missenden. ☎01494 862 200. www.nagsheadbucks.com. 7 rooms. This delightful characterful award-winning 15C contemporary-styled pub serves excellent Anglo-French food (🍴🍴–🍴🍴🍴).

OXFORD

🛏 A large number of B&Bs can be found on Banbury Road, Iffley Road and Abingdon Road.

🍴🍴 **Burlington House** – 374 Banbury Road. ☎01865 513 513. www.burlington-hotel-oxford.co.uk. 12 rooms. This Victorian merchant's house, dating from 1889, a 10-minute ride from town, has been beautifully renovated into a luxurious boutique-style B&B.

🍴🍴🍴 **Old Parsonage** – 1 Banbury Road. ☎01865 310 210. www.oldparsonage-hotel.co.uk. 35 rooms. This small luxurious 17C boutique hotel is just a five-minute walk from town. The atmosphere is calm, almost rural, but also chic and clubby. Live jazz and summer barbecues in the beautiful garden.

COTSWOLDS

🍴🍴 **Old Manse Hotel** – Victoria Street, Bourton-on-the-Water. ☎01451 820082. www.oldenglishinns.co.uk. 15 rooms. Dating from 1748, the Old Manse encompasses traditional Cotswold charm and has a lovely riverside location.

🍴🍴 **Noel Arms Hotel** – Lower High Street, The Square, Chipping Campden. ☎01386 840 317. www.noelarmshotel.com. 28 rooms. One of the oldest Cotswolds inns, reputably visited by Charles II during the English Civil War. Integral restaurant (🍴🍴🍴), bar and coffee shop.

🍴🍴🍴 **Lamb Inn** – Sheep Street, Burford. ☎01993 823 155. www.cotswold-inns-hotels.co.uk. 15 rooms. This charming 14C Cotswold inn with antique furnished bedrooms, gourmet restaurant (🍴🍴🍴🍴) and pub bar and log fires.

CHELTENHAM

🍴🍴 **Mercure Queen's Hotel** – The Promenade. ☎01242 514 754. www.mercure.com. 79 rooms. Set behind large white neo-Classical colonnades, this beautiful Regency hotel overlooks the Imperial Gardens and Promenade. Contemporary British cuisine and grills in the hotel's Napier restaurant (🍴🍴).

🍴 EAT

OXFORD

🍴 **Vaults & Garden** – Radcliff Square. ☎01865 279 112. www.vaultsandgarden.com. Open 8am–6pm. On Radcliffe Square, dine in either in the vaults of the university's Old Congregation House, or alfresco surrounded by architectural treasures, flowers and aromatic herbs.

🍴 **Old Quod** – Old Bank Hotel, 91–94 High Street. ☎01865 799 599. www.oldbank-hotel.co.uk. 42 rooms. Set in the boutique-style Old Bank Hotel (🍴🍴🍴) – this Modern British/European bistro is one of the trendiest places in Oxford.

🍴 **Cherwell Boathouse** – Bardwell Road. ☎01865 552 746. www.cherwellboathouse.co.uk. Dine on simple Modern English dishes at this charming riverside restaurant while watching the punts go by. Lovely summer terrace.

COTSWOLDS

🍴🍴 **The Porch House** – Digbeth Street, Park Street, Stow-on-the-Wold. ☎01451 870 048. www.porch-house.co.uk. Thought to be the oldest inn in England this newly refurbished historic pub serves top quality locally sourced Modern British food. (12 rooms. 🍴🍴).

🍴 **Rose Tree** – Riverside, Bourton-on-the-Water. ☎01451 820 635. Classic British dishes and simple continental favourites, all cooked well, have made this a favourite with visitors.

🍴🍴 **Eight Bells Inn** – Church Street, Chipping Campden. ☎01386 840 371. www.eightbellsinn.co.uk. This 14C inn features exposed beams, log fires, secret passages, a summer terrace and Modern British cuisine. (7 rooms. 🍴🍴).

Bristol, Bath and Somerset

Introduction

Gateway to the West Country, this region includes two of Britain's finest cities. Cultured Bath, with its eponymous Roman springs and glorious architecture, is probably the finest 18C city in the world, and is the only World Heritage city in the UK. By contrast, neighbouring Bristol has a raw energy, built upon maritime and engineering trade. However, while it exploits this rich heritage with many superb waterside attractions, and a Georgian appeal of its own, Bristol also has a vibrant contemporary scene. Rural Somerset is famous for its cider apples, the UK's most popular caves, mythical Glastonbury, and Wells – a gem of a cathedral city that is too often overlooked.

The revitalised dockside and magnificent churches of **Bristol** are the main attractions in the city centre, while the beautiful suburb of Clifton and its breathtaking bridge sit amid bucolic splendour. **Bath** is admired as much for its natural springs as is architecture. Just outside town the American Museum and Bradford-on-Avon are well worth a visit. In **Somerset**, Cheddar Caves and Wookey draw underground explorers, while Glastonbury is the focus of both Christian and Arthurian legends, and a New Age shrine. Wells, England's smallest city, is almost a time capsule.

Highlights

1 Board Brunel's *SS Great Britain* in **Bristol Docks** (p283)

2 Going back in time with the ingenious Romans in **Bath** (p288)

3 Bathing al fresco with a view over **Bath**'s cathedral (p289)

4 The magnificent 13C front of the cathedral in **Wells** (p293)

5 Go underground in the caves of **Cheddar Gorge** (p294)

Cheddar Gorge, North Somerset © Craig Joiner / age fotostock

Bristol★★

and around

In the 10C, Bristol was a settlement at the western limit of Saxon influence, trading with Ireland. Its port, on the site of today's Harbourside, flourished, and during the Middle Ages Bristol was England's second city. By the 17C trade had expanded to the Canaries, the Americas, Africa and the West Indies. In the 18C–19C, new industries developed: iron, brass, copper, porcelain, glass, chocolate and tobacco. To overcome the problems caused in the port by the exceptionally high tidal range (the second highest in the world), an elaborate system of locks was constructed in 1804–09 to maintain a constant water level along the city's quaysides, thus creating the **Floating Harbour★★★**. When the Industrial Revolution drew interests north however, the city declined, and today's modern docks on the estuary of the Severn enable commercial shipping to avoid the difficult Avon Gorge passage.

▶ **Population:** 428 100.

🖦 **Michelin Map:** Michelin Atlas p17 or Map 503 M 29.

🛈 **Info:** E Shed, 1 Canons Road, Harbourside. ℰ0906 711 2191 (50p/min plus network charges). www.visitbristol.co.uk. Bristol has two mainline stations, Parkway (out of town) and Temple Meads, a 20-minute walk from the centre. Fast train services: London Paddington 1h20, Bath 15mins (both to/from Temple Meads). The bus station is in Marlborough Street, a 10-minute walk from the centre.

◖ **Location:** 118mi/190km west of London and 13mi/21km northwest of Bath.

☺ **Don't Miss:** *SS Great Britain*; Clifton.

🕐 **Timing:** At least 2 days.

👪 **Kids:** Zoo; At-Bristol; *SS GB*.

🚢 **Boat Trips:** The Bristol Packet Ltd city docks tour and river trips.

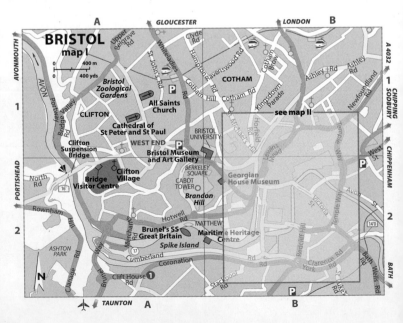

Floating Harbour

© Olaf Protze/age fotostock

MODERN BRISTOL

Bristol is strongly linked with the visionary engineer **Isambard Kingdom Brunel** (1806–59), designer of the Clifton Suspension Bridge, the *SS Great Britain* and architect of the Great Western Railway, which reached its terminus here, at the Station Building, in 1841. In 1940–42 the city was heavily bombed and much of today's centre is the result of post-war rebuilding. Bristol's present affluence and regeneration is underpinned by the electronic age: high-technology research and assembly continues to maintain Bristol's strong engineering tradition. The quaysides have become thriving leisure and recreation areas and are the setting for several arts centres including the **Arnolfini** (*see below*) and the **Watershed Media Centre**, which specialises in films.

HARBOURSIDE WALK
Route marked on Map II.

Harbourside is Bristol's fastest-growing and most exciting area, where bold modern designer buildings such as **Canons House** (Arup for Lloyd's Bank) rub shoulders with warehouse conversions such as **Bordeaux Quay**, the **Old Leadwork** and **M Shed** (*see p284*). A host of small **ferries** criss-cross the water and are an excellent way to explore the Floating Harbour.

Millennium Square features sculptures of famous locals, fountains and lights, and lots of places to eat and drink.

At-Bristol★

Harbourside. Open Mon–Fri 10am–5pm; Sat–Sun and school holidays 10am–6pm. Closed 24–25 Dec. £15.30, child £9.90. &☐✕ ☎0845 345 1235. www.at-bristol.org.uk.
This 21C science centre combines hands on activities with the very latest multimedia techniques. Science is brought alive through stunning visuals and over 170 interactive experiences. There is also a planetarium (additional £3).

Bristol Aquarium

Open except 25 Dec 10am–6pm. £14.75, child 3–12, £9.75 (online discounts). &☐✕ ☎0117 929 8929. www.bristolaquarium.co.uk.
The city's aquarium, opened in 2011, includes over 40 naturally themed habitats from the British coast to tropical seas. An underwater tunnel brings you within inches of reef sharks and rays.

Pero's Bridge

The distinctive feature of this pedestrian bascule bridge is its pair of horn-shaped sculptures which act as counterweights for the lifting section. Pero was the slave of wealthy merchant John Pinney (*see p286*).

Arnolfini

Galleries open Tue–Sun 11am–6pm, Wed 11am–8pm. Closed Mon. ♿✕ ☎0117 917 2300. www.arnolfini.org.uk.
Established in 1961, this is the oldest and most acclaimed arts centre in Bristol, staging live music, films, contemporary live art, performance and dance.

M Shed

Princes Wharf, Wapping Road. Open Tue–Sun 10am–5pm. ♿✕
☎0117 352 6600.
www.bristolmuseums.org.uk/m-shed.
Bristol's latest museum is a busy modern interactive place where visitors explore over 2 000 years of city history. Topics include Bristol's inglorious role in the transatlantic slave trade, the city's war-time experiences, industrial and engineering history and its present-day successes in technology, music and art.

👥 SS GREAT BRITAIN★★★

Map I. Open Apr–Oct 10am–5.30pm; Nov–Mar 10am–4.30pm. Closed 24–25 Dec, 2nd Mon Jan. £14, child 5–17, £8. ♿🅿✕ ☎0117 926 0680.
www.ssgreatbritain.org.
Launched in 1843, Brunel's revolutionary steamship *SS Great Britain* was the very first iron-built, propeller-driven Atlantic liner. She sailed until 1886, travelling 32 times around the world covering nearly one million miles. She was finally abandoned and scuttled in the Falkland Islands, in 1937, after more than 40 years' use as a floating warehouse. In 1970 the most ambitious salvage project ever attempted finally brought her home to Bristol, where she is now conserved.
Sitting in her original dry dock, above the waterline the ship has been meticulously restored to her halcyon days, when she transported both freight and passengers around the world. Below the waterline, glass plates, covered in a thin layer of water, form a sealed space, which is dehumidified to inhibit the rusting process of the ship's fragile hull. The ingenious facilities allow visitors to walk around the bottom of this leviathan (98m long and 16m across) viewing the giant propeller and anchor, with water high above. Back on the dockside is a superb **museum** that tells the fascinating story of the ship, the many colourful characters who sailed in her, the epic salvage operation and the emotional homecoming to Bristol. The ship itself has been meticulously restored, right down to the dirty plates and the ship's cat chasing rats in the galley. Audio guides relate the story of what it was like to travel both steerage (3rd class) and Upper Saloon (1st class) in colourful detail.

OLD TOWN WALK

Map II.
Occupying a peninsula formed by St Augustine's Reach and the port of Bristol, the old town area is set around Queen Square, a large grassy area with a few early-18C houses and an impressive equestrian statue of King William III.

King Street

This historic cobbled street contains 18C and 19C warehouses, 17C almshouses and pubs, notably the **Llandoger Trow**, and the 18C **Theatre Royal★★**. The latter opened in 1766 and is the oldest playhouse in the country still in use. The **Merchant Venturer's Almshouses★** was built in 1544 and enlarged in 1696.

St Stephen's church★

www.saint-stephens.com.
The 15C tower of the city parish church rises 40m to a distinctive crown. The interior houses memorials to local merchants, 17C wrought-iron gates and a medieval eagle lectern.

Corn Street

The imposing **Exchange** was built in 1741–43 by John Wood the Elder. Its original function was a corn and general trade exchange, recalled by the four bronze-topped pedestals dating from the 16C and 17C, where deals were concluded; these were known as 'nails', hence the expression to pay on the nail, meaning immediate payment.

The Exchange and its precincts is now home to the home to the largest collection of independent retailers in Bristol, the lively **St Nicholas Market**. To the left of the 19C Council Hall is the exuberant façade of Lloyd's Bank (1854–1858). At No. 56, Café Revival is the latest incarnation of the coffee shop, built in the 18C, where Georgian merchants once met to trade.

Church of St John the Baptist★

This 14C church with its battlemented tower and spire stands over one of the six medieval gateways in the city walls. It contains a vaulted crypt and some interesting 17C woodwork (lectern, communion table, hour-glass).

Lord Mayor's Chapel▲

St Mark's Chapel was once part of a medieval hospital. The impressive Perpendicular chapel beside the narrow nave contains 15–17C **tombs**. Note the 16C continental **glass**, the mayors' hatchments, the gilded sword rest (1702) and the fine wrought iron gates.

Bristol cathedral★

College Green. Open Mon–Fri 8am–5pm, Sat–Sun 8am–3.15pm. Guided tours most Sats 11.30am and 1.30pm. £5 donation suggested. ✕ ℰ0117 926 4879. www.bristol-cathedral.co.uk.
A church has stood here for over a thousand years. The cathedral is a 14C–15C Perpendicular Gothic church; the nave and twin west towers are 19C. Note the screen, the choir stalls (lively **15C misericords**), the 19C reredos and, over the nave, the early-14C vault, unique in English cathedrals. The **East Lady Chapel** (added 1298–1330) has a riot of medieval colour highlighting the elaborately carved stone. The **Harrowing of Hell**, a remarkable 1 000-year-old Saxon carved stone coffin-lid, stands in the south transept. Note too the late Norman rib-vaulted **chapter house** and columned vestibule.

REDCLIFFE

Map II. Separated from the old town by an arm of the port, Redcliffe can be reached by Bristol Bridge, via Baldwin Street or by Redcliffe Way, off Queen Square.

St Mary Redcliffe★★

Redcliffe Hill. Open Mon–Fri 8.30am–5pm, Sun 8am–8pm (except during services). ℰ0117 231 0060. www.stmaryredcliffe.co.uk.
'The fairest, goodliest, and most famous parish church in England', according to Queen Elizabeth I, St Mary represents the perfect expression of the Gothic style, and has stood for over 800 years. The **spire** (1872) rises 89m above the city. The Decorated hexagonal **north porch** (1290) is the antechamber to the shrine of Our Lady, in an inner, more modest Early English porch (1185). The church contains a number of interesting furnishings, most notably the late-16C wooden statue of Queen Elizabeth I, and armour of Admiral Sir William Penn, in the **American chapel**.

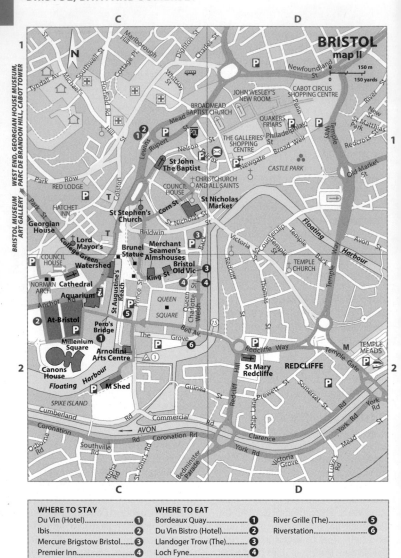

WHERE TO STAY		WHERE TO EAT			
Du Vin (Hotel)	❶	Bordeaux Quay	❶	River Grille (The)	❺
Ibis	❷	Du Vin Bistro (Hotel)	❷	Riverstation	❻
Mercure Brigstow Bristol	❸	Llandoger Trow (The)	❸		
Premier Inn	❹	Loch Fyne	❹		

BRANDON HILL
Georgian House★★

Map I. Open Apr–Dec Sat–Tue 11am–4pm, except 25–26 Dec. ℰ0117 921 1362. www.bristolmuseums.org.uk. This handsome, typical Bath stone house was built c.1790 for the merchant and sugar planter **John Pinney**. Among the fine furniture note the mid-18C **bureau-bookcase**, the **desk** and the **long-case clock** (c.1740) in the hall; the elaborate gilded **girandoles** in the first-floor drawing room; the **double secretaire bookcase** (c.1800) and his collector's cabinet. Note the **cold-water plunge bath** which Pinney used daily.

Bristol Museum and Art Gallery★

Map I. Queen's Road. Open Tue–Sun 10am–5pm (Mon bank and school holidays. Closed 25–26 Dec. �&✕ ℰ0117 922 3571. www.bristolmuseums.org.uk.

Housed in an Edwardian Baroque building this substantial collection of artefacts includes antique, Oriental and locally produced glassware, pottery, porcelain and silverware, local archaeology and geology, fine art (works from the Italian, 19C French and 19C–20C British schools), important costume jewellery, Assyrian and Egyptian antiquities, scale models of locomotives, and maritime history.

CLIFTON★★

Map I. The elegant suburb of Clifton took shape on the heights above the Avon Gorge in the early-1790s; distinguished crescents, squares and terraces are generously interspersed with greenery. Streets such as The Mall, Caledonia Place, Princess Victoria Street and Royal York Crescent make up the delightful **Clifton Village★** with terraced houses, small shops and G E Street's 1868 **All Saints Church (A1)** (*see map p282*).

Clifton Suspension Bridge★★

Visitor Centre open daily 10am–5pm. Guided tours (free) Sat–Sun and bank holidays Easter–Oct 3pm from the Clifton toll booth. ℘0117 974 4664. www.cliftonbridge.org.uk.

Designed by Brunel in 1829, this is arguably the most beautiful of early English suspension bridges. Unfortunately funds ran out and Brunel never saw his 214m-long bridge completed; he died five years earlier, in 1859.

A **Visitor Centre** at the Leigh Woods end relates the history of its construction. On the opposite side of the bridge, the **Clifton Observatory, Camera Obscura and Cave** (Litfield Place; open daily 10am–4pm/5pm; Camera Obscura £2.50, child £1.50; Giant's Cave £2.50, child £1.50; joint ticket £4, child £2.50; ℘0117 974 1242; https://cliftonobservatory.com), stands on a cliff. At the top is an 18C **camera obscura** while below, at the cave mouth, visitors can enjoy a spectacular view of the Bridge and Avon Gorge below.

Cathedral of St Peter and St Paul★

This Roman Catholic cathedral is an impressive hexagonal edifice in white concrete, pink granite, black fibreglass, lead and glass; it was consecrated in 1973. Note the windows and the stations of the cross carved in stone.

♟♟ Bristol Zoo Gardens★★

Open daily 9am–5.30pm. Closed 25 Dec. £22.00, child 2–14, £15 (online discounts). ♿✖ ℘0117 428 5300. www.bristolzoo.org.uk.

This venerable institution opened in 1836, making it the fifth oldest zoo in the world. Today it features over 400 species of animals – from gorillas in their landscaped compound to Bug World – accommodated in various architect-designed houses; see the Reptile and Ape Houses in particular. A popular recently added attraction is **Explorers' Creek** including a wet play area, a tropical bird house and a walkthrough parrot-feeding area.

EXCURSION

Clevedon Court★

⊙ 11mi/18km W on the A 370, the B 3128 and the B 3130. Open Apr–Sept, Wed–Thu, Sun and bank holiday Mons 2–5pm. £8.35, garden only £4.35. ✖ 📇 ℘01275 872 257. www.nationaltrust.org.uk.

William Makepeace Thackery often stayed at Clevedon, sketching and writing. This well-preserved early-14C house features a 12C tower and 13C Great Hall. The exterior dates to 1570, but inside you will find evidence of earlier centuries. The **Great Hall** has Tudor windows and fireplaces; the remarkable Hanging Chapel, with its unusual reticulated window tracery, contains 17C prayer desks and 15C and 16C biblical carvings. The contents of the 14C State Bedroom reflect 10 generations of family taste, while the Justice Room displays local Nailsea glass made between 1788 and 1873. In fine weather, enjoy the Georgian terraced gardens.

Bath★★★

and around

Set in rolling Somerset countryside, Bath's hot springs, Roman Baths, splendid abbey and Georgian stone crescents have attracted visitors for centuries. The city combines the grace and elegance of the 18C with a long and varied past.

A BIT OF HISTORY

In 500 BCE, according to legend, **Prince Bladud** (the father of King Lear) was cured of his leprosy by wallowing in the mud here. The **Romans**, in the 1C, made Bath England's first spa resort with baths and a temple. In the 11C the Bishop of Wells bought Bath for £500. He began a vast Benedictine cathedral priory, and built a palace, new baths and a school. Bath became a prosperous wool town, but at the Dissolution the monks were forced to sell off parts of the abbey. In 1574, Queen Elizabeth I set up a fund to restore the abbey and enhance the town.

In the following centuries **Ralph Allen** (1694–1764) and John Wood (1700–54) transformed its architecture and urban plan. Inspired by Bath's Roman past they built in the Palladian style with the local honey-coloured stone, now known as **Bath-stone**. But it was in the early 18C that Bath saw its golden age. In 1704 **Beau Nash** (1673–1762) came to Bath, opened the first Pump Room for taking the waters and organised concerts, balls and gambling. Bath prospered – as did Nash – and, for a while at least, became England's most fashionable city.

CITY WALK
Roman Baths★★

Pump Room, Stall Street.
Open Jan–Feb and Nov–Dec 9.30am–6pm; Mar–Jun and Sept–Oct 9am–6pm; Jul–Aug 9am–10pm; last entry 1h before closing. Closed 25–26 Dec. £15, Jul–Aug £17 (combined ticket with Fashion Museum and Art Gallery

▶ **Population:** 100 231.
Ò **Michelin Map:** Michelin Atlas p17 or Map 503 M 29.
▤ **Info:** Abbey Churchyard. ℘0844 847 5256; www.visitbath.co.uk. Bath Spa train station (London Paddington 1h24) and Bath bus station are on Manvers Street in the centre. The city centre is compact and most major sights are within walking distance. Bath Bus Company operate a hop-on hop-off bus tour (℘01225 444 102; www. bathbuscompany.com).
◖ **Location:** 107mi/172km southwest of London.
◉ **Don't Miss:** The Baths; Royal Crescent; American Museum.
◔ **Timing:** Allow at least 2 full days.
◕◕ **Walking Tours:** The Mayor's Honorary Guides free walking tours depart from outside the Pump Room daily Sun–Fri 10.30am, 2pm, Sat 10.30am; May–Sept also Tue and Thu 7pm. There are many other different themed walking tours; for details visit www.visitbath.co.uk.
▣ **Parking:** A park and ride system is in operation (follow the signs).

£21.50). ♿✗ ℘01225 477 785. www.romanbaths.co.uk.

One of the best-preserved Roman spas in the world, the baths are fed by a spring which pours out 1 136 000 litres of water per day at a temperature of 46°C. The Roman complex consisted of the Great Bath, a large warm swimming pool, now open to the sky (sadly, bathing is not allowed), and two baths of decreasing heat; later a *frigidarium* was built on the west side with openings at the north, overlooking the sacred spring, and two more heated

© Onfokus/iStockphoto.com

Roman Baths, Bath Abbey in the background

chambers (*tepidarium* and *caldarium*). The east end was enlarged, the baths were elaborated and the *frigidarium* transformed into a cold-plunge circular bath.

After the Romans had left, the drains soon clogged through lack of attention and mud covered the site. In the early Middle Ages the Normans constructed the King's Bath around the tank which the Romans had lined with Mendip lead. Modern excavations have revealed the temple and baths complex and a wide variety of artefacts.

Pump Room★

Open daily for morning coffee, lunch and afternoon tea. Closed 25–26 Dec. & 01225 444 477 (table reservations). www.romanbaths.co.uk.

The present Pump Room was built in 1789–99. The interiors are elegantly furnished with ornamental pilasters, gilded capitals, a coffered ceiling, antiques and a glass chandelier. The bay overlooking the King's Bath contains the drinking fountain, from which visitors can still taste the water, complete with its 43 minerals.

Thermae Bath Spa★★

The Hetling Pump Room, Hot Bath Street. Open daily – New Royal Bath: 9am–9.30pm; last entry 7pm. Cross Bath: 10am–8pm; last entry 6pm. Visitor centre: Open Apr–Sept Mon–Sat 10am–5pm, Sun 11am–4pm. Closed 25–26, 31 Dec. New Royal Bath 2h session Mon–Fri £35, Sat–Sun £38 (additional hour £10). Cross Bath 1½h session Mon–Fri £18, Sat–Sun £20. 01225 33 1234. www.thermaebathspa.com.

Opened in 2006, Britain's original and only natural thermal spa is a combination of the best of the original Georgian spa, housed partly in an 18C building and partly in a glass-sided ultra-modern building, offering 21C comforts and facilities, including four thermal baths and the latest therapies. The flagship **New Royal Bath** gives access to the open-air rooftop pool, which looks directly onto the abbey, particularly romantic at twilight.

Bath Abbey★

13 Kingston Buildings. & 01225 422 462. www.bathabbey.org.
Abbey: Open Mon 9.30am–5.30pm, Tue–Fri 9am–5.30pm, Sat 9am–6pm, Sun 1–2.30pm and 4.30–5.30pm. £4 contribution suggested.
Tower Tours (on the hour): Jan–Mar and Nov–Dec 11am–4pm; Apr–Aug 10am–5pm; Sept–Oct 10am–4pm. £6.

The present sanctuary, on the site of an abbey founded early in the reign of King Offa (757–96), was begun in 1499 by Bishop Oliver King. From the pillars of the Norman church arose the pure late Perpendicular abbey. At the Disso-

Royal Crescent

© George Clerk/iStockphoto.com

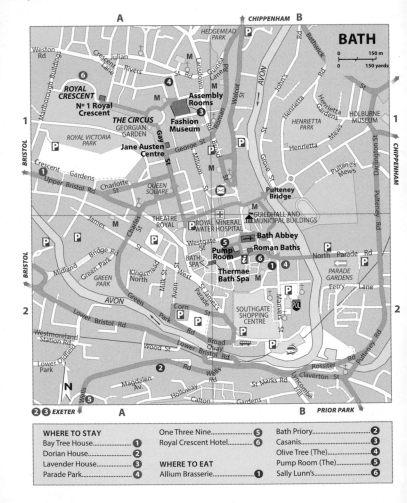

WHERE TO STAY	One Three Nine.......................⑤	Bath Priory....................................❷
Bay Tree House..........................❶	Royal Crescent Hotel..............⑥	Casanis...❸
Dorian House.............................❷		Olive Tree (The).......................❹
Lavender House.........................❸	WHERE TO EAT	Pump Room (The).....................⑤
Parade Park................................❹	Allium Brasserie.......................❶	Sally Lunn's.................................⑥

lution, the incomplete building fell into disrepair, but restoration was begun in the late-16C. Inside, the nave, chancel and narrow transepts soar to **fan vaulting** by Robert and William Vertue (of Westminster Abbey fame).

Pulteney Bridge★

This magnificent bridge, built in 1769–74 to Robert Adam's design, has small shops on both sides, domed end pavilions and a central Venetian window. It is best viewed from Parade Gardens by the crescent weir.

Jane Austen Centre

40 Gay Street, Queen Square. ℘01225 443 000. www.janeausten.co.uk. Open: Apr–Oct daily 9.45am–5.30pm; Nov–Mar Sun–Fri 10am–4pm, Sat 9.45am–5.30pm. Closed 1 Jan 24–26 Dec. £11

Jane Austen knew Bath as a visitor and a resident, and this exhibition is devoted to every place in Bath associated with Jane or her novels.

The Circus★★★

The King's Circus is a tight circle of identical houses, pierced by three equidistant access roads. Although one of John Wood the Elder's earliest concepts, it was not built until the year of his death, 1754. The houses of pale Bath stone, decorated with coupled columns, rise three floors to a frieze and acorn-topped balustrade.

Royal Crescent★★★

The great arc of 30 terrace houses, in which the horizontal lines are counterbalanced by 114 giant Ionic columns rising from the first floor to the pierced parapet, was the great achievement of John Wood II, built 1767–74.

No. 1 Royal Crescent★★ (open Feb–mid-Dec Tue–Sun 10.30am–5.30pm, Mon noon–5.30pm. £10; ℘01225 428 126; http://no1royalcrescent.org.uk) has been authentically restored, providing a perfect setting for Chippendale, Sheraton and Hepplewhite furniture and for porcelain and 18C glassware.

Jane Austen (1775–1817)

Jane visited Bath when staying with her aunt and uncle, the Leigh Perrots, at No. 1 The Paragon, and it was in Bath that she set much of *Northanger Abbey*. In May 1799, the Austen family took lodgings at 13 Queen Square; later, they resided at 4 Sydney Place; it was during their time at 27 Green Park Buildings that Jane's father died in January 1805; on two further occasions, the remaining ladies of the family lived both at 25 Gay Street and in Trim Street.

Bath Assembly Rooms/Fashion Museum★

Bennett Street. Assembly Rooms open daily 10.30am–6pm (Nov–Feb 5pm) if not in use for functions (check ahead). Closed 25–26 Dec. &; ℘01225 477173. www.nationaltrust.org.uk.

These elegant rooms were built in 1769–71 for the evening assemblies at which high society met to dance, play cards, drink tea and to gossip. The **Octagon** was intended as a small card room. The **Tea Room** has a rich interior with a splendid two-tiered screen of columns at its west end.

Within the Assembly Rooms, the fascinating **Fashion Museum** (open Mar–Oct 10.30am–5pm, Nov–Feb 10.30am–4pm £9; &; ℘01225 477 173; www.fashionmuseum.co.uk) presents a colourful and elegant display of every sort of garment from the Stuart period to Lady Gaga. Note the museum's oldest complete attire, the **Silver Tissue Dress** (1660s), and its selection of superb gloves.

EXCURSIONS
The American Museum in Britain★★

◖ Claverton. 3mi/5km E on the A 36. Open mid-Mar–Oct Tue–Sun noon–5pm (Closed Mondays, except during August and on bank holidays); Late Nov–mid-Dec Tue–Sun noon–4.30pm. £12.

Bradford–on–Avon

© Y. Duhamel/MICHELIN

♿🅿✕ ☎01225 460 503.
www.americanmuseum.org.
Housed in historic Claverton Manor, located in an area of outstanding natural beauty, with spectacular views over the valley of the River Avon, this is the only museum of Americana outside the United States. Its remarkable collection of folk arts and decorative arts shows the diverse and complex nature of American culture over 200 years. The collection is shown off to great effect in a series of furnished rooms dating from the late-17C to the middle of the 19C. A major annual exhibition on a popular US theme is also staged (for example, Marilyn Monroe, or the Wild West).

Bradford-on-Avon★★

⊙ 8mi/13km via the A 4 and A 363.
🅱 ☎01225 865797.
www.bradfordonavon.co.uk.
The old houses picturesquely rising up the hillside from the River Avon give Bradford-on-Avon its charm and character. The nine-arched **bridge★**, built in 1610 with a small square, domed chapel topped by a weathervane, is the best starting point for the walk to the top of this attractive town. It's thought that the Saxon **Church of St Laurence★** (open daily 10am–6pm/4pm Oct–Mar; ♿; ☎01225 865 797) may date from the 7C–8C when St Aldhelm built a church here. Having served as a school, cottage and charnel house, the church was rediscovered in 1856.
A short walk along the River Avon lies a vast early-14C stone **tithe barn★** (open daily 10.30am–4pm; ♿🅿(charge); www.english-heritage.org.uk) with gabled doorways and a superb wooden cruck roof.

The American Museum in Britain

© Y. Duhamel / MICHELIN

Mendips and Quantocks★★

This quiet rural part of North Somerset features England's smallest cathedral city in Wells and its two most visited show caves, Wookey Hole and Cheddar Gorge. Meanwhile, Glastonbury continues its centuries-old tradition as a place of pilgrimage, these days for music festival lovers and New Agers.

- **Michelin Map:** Michelin Atlas p16 or Map 503 M 30.
- **Don't Miss:** Wells cathedral; Cheddar Gorge; the view from Glastonbury Tor.
- **Kids:** Wookey Hole; Cheddar Gorge and Caves.

WELLS

23mi/37km SW of Bath.
☎ ✆01749 671 770.
www.wellssomerset.com.
The calm of the cathedral within its precinct contrasts with the bustle of the Market Square. In the Middle Ages Wells prospered as a wool centre.

Wells Cathedral★★★

Open daily 7am–7pm (Oct–Mar 6pm).
Guided tours (free) Mon–Sat hourly. &✖
✆01749 674 483.
www.wellscathedral.org.uk.
Wells was the first cathedral church in the Early English style; it took more than three centuries to plan and build, from c.1175 to 1508.
Despite weathering and much destruction by the Puritans, the **west front** is one of England's richest displays of 13C sculpture – with its figures coloured and gilded, it would have once resembled an illuminated manuscript or sumptuous tapestry. Although now monochrome, it is tinted at sunset and gilded by floodlights at night. The screen front is nearly 46m across, twice as wide as it is tall, with some 300 statues rising to a climax in the centre gable.

Inside the cathedral, set into the west wall of the north transept is a **quarterjack** – 15C knights who strike the bells with their pikes at the quarters. The most striking feature of the **nave** is the **scissor arch**, constructed in 1338–48, when the west piers of the crossing tower began to subside.

The nave was completed in 1239. There are interesting carvings in the **south transept**: men's heads, animal masks and everyday scenes such as a man with toothache and two men caught

Wells cathedral
© Corrado Piccoli/Sime/Photononarstop

in the act of stealing apples from an orchard. The medieval **misericords** show a man killing a wyvern and Alexander the Great being lifted to heaven by two griffins. In the north transept is an **astronomical clock** of 1390, with the sun and a star revolving round the 24-hour dial and, above, a **knights' tournament** in which one knight is struck down each quarter-hour.

A wide curving flight of steps, laid c.1290, leads to the splendid octagonal **chapter house**, completed 1306.

Cathedral Precinct

Three 15C **gates** lead from the city streets to the calm of the Green and the spectacular view of the cathedral exterior. The **Chain Gate** gives access to **Vicars' Close**, a street of identical cottages built c.1348.

On the south side of the cathedral stands the 800-year-old **Bishop's Palace★** (open Apr–Oct 10am–6pm; Nov–Mar 10am–4pm; occasional closure for private functions, see website; £7.25; ᵟ✗; ℘01749 988 111; https://bishopspalace.org.uk), stoutly walled and encircled by a moat. Inside are walled gardens and the well springs from which the city gets its name – belching out over 15 million litres a day, or 180 litres a second.

There are also the ruins of the old banqueting hall, the present palace and an excellent **view★★** of the cathedral.

THE MENDIP HILLS

Immediately north of Wells and some 8mi/13km south of Bristol, the Mendip Hills is a triangular-shaped Area of Outstanding Natural Beauty, reaching a modest height of 325m. It is composed of porous limestone and is most famous for its outstanding caves at Wookey Hole and Cheddar Gorge.

ᵃᵗ Wookey Hole★

2mi/3km NW. Open Apr–Oct daily 10am–5pm, Nov–Mar 10am–4pm (Dec–Jan Sat–Sun and school holidays only). Closed 25–26 Dec. £19, child £15 (onnline discount). ▣ ✗ ℘01749 672 243. www.wookey.co.uk.

Spectacular **caves** have been formed by the River Axe, which gushes in a torrent through a hole in a 61m-high cliff-side, then descends into a series of six chambers. The river is always present, in echoing cascades and deep blue-green pools. The tour leads through some 320m of extravagantly lit caverns featuring **stalactites**, **stalagmites**, petrified waterfalls and translucent pools. These were inhabited by Iron Age man in 300 BCE and later by Romano-British and Celtic peoples.

However, the caves mix history and legends fairly liberally, and are now a mini-theme park, with the 'mistress of ceremonies' being the Witch of Wookey. Family attractions in the caves and its gardens include the Circus Show, a Fairy Garden, life-size dinosaur replicas, a mirror maze, a Victorian games arcade, adventure golf, and much more. The most interesting "add-on" is the **handmade papermill★**– paper was first made at Wookey Hole c.1600.

ᵃᵗ Cheddar Gorge and Caves★★

9mi/14km NW. Open daily 10am–5pm. Closed 24–25 Dec. £19.95, child 5–15, £16.95 (online discounts). ▣✗ ℘01934 742 343. www.cheddargorge.co.uk.

Evidence of human settlement at Cheddar Gorge dates back to the Upper Late Palaeolithic era. The gorge is 2mi/3km long with a one in six gradient, twisting and turning in its descent from the Mendips, and the cliffs rise vertically 107m–122m.

The caves are near the gorge bottom on the south side (left, going down). **Cox's Cave** was discovered in 1837 and **Gough's Cave** in 1890. The series of chambers follows the course of underground streams through the porous limestone, past stalagmites, stalactites and petrified falls.

As with neighbouring Wookey Hole, the caves have become heavily commercialised. Also included in the ticket price is the **Cheddar Man Museum of Prehistory**; the **Crystal Quest** (a dark-walk fantasy adventure); **The Lookout Tower**, a staircase of 274 steps which

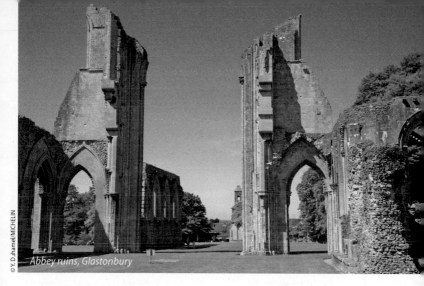

Abbey ruins, Glastonbury

leads up to a panoramic **view★**; a 3mi/5km **clifftop gorge walk**, offering more stunning views, and an **open-top bus tour** (Mar–Oct only). Also on offer are rock climbing, abseiling and caving all suitable for beginners (see website for details).

This is, of course, also the home of the famous **cheese** (⌖*see above*), on sale in the shop, and in **Cheddar** village, which lies at the foot of the gorge.

GLASTONBURY★★

29mi/47km SW of Bath. 🚍 ℘01458 447 384. www.glastonburytic.co.uk.
Glastonbury Abbey, a ruin since it was dissolved in 1539, was once one of the richest abbeys in the land and renowned as a centre of learning. The town, which grew up around the abbey, has become an important centre of spiritualism and is now synonymous with an alternative lifestyle. Its most public face however is the hugely successful annual open-air Glastonbury music festival (www.glaston buryfestivals.co.uk), attended by over 130 000 people.

A Bit of History

According to the Holy Grail legends, an abbey was founded by Joseph of Arimathea, who donated his own prepared tomb for the burial of Jesus and caught the blood of the crucified Christ in the cup of the Last Supper. When he planted his staff in the ground here, it sprouted and became the famous **Glas-**

West Country Cheese

According to one fanciful legend, the history of West Country cheese began when monks on a pilgrimage to Glastonbury took shelter from a terrible storm in the Cheddar caves and found that the milk they were carrying in leather pouches had turned into a delicious cheese: Cheddar has since become synonymous with English cheese, notably abroad. In fact the Cheddar caves were inaccessible to all but climbers until the 19C. The truth is that itinerant holy men, especially early Celtic monks from Ireland, developed the art of cheese-making not only as a means of saving what otherwise might be wasted milk, but also for eating on days of fasting when meat was forbidden.

tonbury Thorn, a tree whose descendant still flowers here at Christmas and in May. The dual flowering was once considered miraculous.

Another legend links **King Arthur** with Glastonbury: mortally wounded by his stepson Mordred, Arthur sailed to the Isle of Avalon, held to be near Glastonbury. He and Guinevere were

Glastonbury Tor

supposedly buried in Glastonbury, and in 1191 their bodies were 'discovered' in the abbey cemetery (a plaque marks the spot).

Abbey ruins★★

Open daily from 9am, closes: Jun–Aug 8pm, Nov–Feb 4pm, rest of year 6pm. ⚐ ✗ (May–Sept). Guided tours by costumed guides Mar–Oct. Closed 25 Dec. £7.50 (online discounts). ✆01458 832 267. www.glastonburyabbey.com.

The ruins extend far across the lawns, standing tall amid majestic trees. The Lady Chapel in Doulting stone has a corner turret, decorated walls, and rounded doorways, the one to the north enriched by carved figures. On the impressive Gothic transept piers remain the chancel walls and beyond them the site of the Edgar Chapel, a mausoleum for the Saxon kings.

The 14C **Abbot's Kitchen★**, the sole building to survive intact, features an eight-sided roof with lanterns, which served to draw the smoke from the corner fires in the kitchen up the flues in the roof. North of the abbey stands the **Glastonbury Thorn Tree** (⚐see above).

Town

Glastonbury's two main streets are Magdalene Street, lined with attractive little 17C–19C houses, and High Street, overlooked by the 15C George and Pilgrims Hotel and the 14C Tribunal. The latter houses the tourist information centre and Lake Village Museum (open Mon–Sat 10am–4pm, closed 23 Dec–1 Jan; £3.50; ✆01458 832 954; www. english-heritage.org.uk), featuring excavated artefacts from an **Iron Age Lake Village** near the town.

Looming above the High Street is the 41m tower of the 15C **church of St John the Baptist★★** (open Mon–Sat 10.30am–12.30pm/summer also 2–4pm; ✗; ✆01458 830 060; www.stjohns-glastonbury.org. uk), one of the finest churches in Somerset. Inside, its St Katherine's Chapel survives from the 12C building.

A ten-minute walk away, the **Somerset Rural Life Museum★** (Chilkwell Street; open Tue–Sat and bank holiday Mons 10am–5pm; closed Good Fri; ⚐ P ✗ (summer only); ✆01458 831 197; www.somerset.gov.uk/museums), illustrates daily life on a Somerset farm in the 19C. The outstanding exhibit is the splendid 14C **barn** of Glastonbury Abbey.

Glastonbury Tor★

The tor (meaning hill, or rocky peak), is 159m high and a landmark visible for miles around. The tower at its summit is the last remnant of a Church to St Michael, built in the 14C. On a fine day, the **view★★★** embraces the Quantocks, Bristol Channel and the Mendips.

BRIDGWATER

41mi/66km SW of Bath.

Bridgwater's place in history was secured in 1685 at the **Battle of Sedgemoor** (3mi/5km outside town), when the Duke of Monmouth, an illegitimate son of Charles II, proclaimed himself king and fought the superior forces of James II. Monmouth was routed, and the bloody reprisals that followed (see below) left a historic stain on the area.

The **Blake Museum** (Blake Street; open Tue–Sat 10am–4pm; 01278 456 127; www.bridgwatermuseum.org.uk) relates the story of the battle and stages other exhibitions of local history. Today Bridgwater is famous for its November **Carnival**, Europe's largest illuminated procession.

TAUNTON★

53mi/85km SW of Bath.

01823 336 344.

The county town of Taunton, gateway to the West Country, is an agricultural and commercial centre at the heart of the fertile Vale of Taunton (Taunton Deane), famous for its cider apples.

Taunton Castle

The castle, dating from the 11C–12C, has been owned by successive Bishops of Winchester. The Civil War put Taunton, and the castle in particular, under siege three times. In 1685 the **Duke of Monmouth** and many of his followers were tried in the castle's Great Hall; 508 of them were condemned to death in what came to be known as the notorious **Bloody Assizes** and another thousand or so were transported to the West Indies. Monmouth was executed on Tower Hill a month later. Part of the castle houses the **Museum of Somerset★** (open Tue–Sat and bank holiday Mons 10am–5pm; 01823 255 088, www.somerset.gov.uk/museums).

Also on display is the **Frome Hoard**, the largest collection of Roman coins discovered in Britain in a single container.

St Mary Magdalene church★

01823 272 441.

www.stmarymagdalenetaunton.org.uk.

In the Somerset tradition, this splendid medieval church culminates in a soaring tower (1488–1514) built of lovely red and tawny-gold Ham Hill stone. Inside, the roof carvings are also typical of Somerset craftsmanship.

St James's church★

Call for opening times, 01823 272 931.

www.stjamestaunton.co.uk.

St James's dates mostly from the 14C–15C and features a 37m tower of Quantock red sandstone with Ham Hill stone decoration.

ILMINSTER★

45mi/72km SW of Bath.

This Ham stone market town, which flourished from the wool trade in the 15C–16C, was listed as having a **minster★★** in the Domesday Book. The most impressive feature is its 27m crossing tower, modelled on that of Wells cathedral. The 15C Perpendicular building with nave, transepts, chancel and tower was extended with aisles in the 16C. Note the fan vaults inserted at the crossing and **Wadham Chapel**, built in 1452 to house the tomb chest of Sir William Wadham, founder of Wadham College, Oxford.

QUANTOCK HILLS

Rising to a peak of 384m and extending for around 12mi/19km, the Quantock Hills are a peaceful Area of Outstanding Natural Beauty where pretty villages, such as Combe Florey and Crowcombe, nestle in wooded valleys known as combes. The hills start just west of Bridgwater and run northwest to the Bristol Channel. A good way to see the landscape is to either drive along the A358 or hop aboard one of the historic **West Somerset Railway** (see website for timetable and fares; www.west-somerset-railway.co.uk) steam locomotives. The line runs for around 20mi/32km) between the pleasant village of **Bishops Lydeard** and the commercialised seaside resort of Minehead.

South Somerset★

Midway between the Somerset and Dorset coastlines, this quiet region of traditional towns and villages contains two top attractions.

YEOVIL

Yeovil was an important leather and glove centre from the 14C onwards, and was later known for its flax.

The opening of the railway link with Taunton in 1853 broadened the town's horizons. The population increased and the buildings we now see are mainly 19C–20C, albeit with a few scattered 18C–19C Georgian houses and older inns on the likes of Princess Street, High Street and Silver Street.

👥 FLEET AIR ARM MUSEUM★★

RNAS Yeovilton, Ilchester. 6mi/10km N. Open Apr–Nov daily 10am–5.30pm; Dec–Mar Wed–Sun (daily during school holidays) 10am–4.30pm. Closed 24–26 Dec. £11.20, child £8.40. ♿🅿✖ ℘01935 840 565. www.fleetairarm.com.

Europe's largest naval aviation collection is set within aircraft hangars next to the Royal Naval Air Station, where helicopters are put through their paces daily. The display includes over 90 aircraft including the second prototype of **Concorde**, the famous Anglo-French jet airliner. A highlight is the **Aircraft Carrier Experience**, where visitors feel the noise and rush of jets around them.

MONTACUTE HOUSE★★

Montacute. 5m/8km W.
House: open mid-Mar–Oct daily 11am–4.30pm, Nov–mid-Mar Wed–Sun noon–3pm. £11.40, winter £8.20 (house and garden).
Garden: open Jan–mid-Mar and Nov–Dec Wed–Sun 11am–4pm; mid-Mar–Oct daily 10am–5pm. £5.60.
♿🅿✖ ℘01935 823 289.
www.nationaltrust.org.uk.

ⓘ Michelin Map: Michelin Atlas p8 or Map 503 M 31.
ℹ Info: Petters Way. ℘01935 462 781. www.visitsomerset.co.uk. Yeovil has two stations, Yeovil Junction and Yeovil Pen Mill. Bath to Yeovil Pen Mill 1h11.
▶ Location: Yeovil lies 41mi/66km south of Bristol.

This handsome Elizabethan three-storey mansion was built 1597–1601 for Sir Edward Phelips, a successful lawyer, Speaker of the House of Commons (1604) and Master of the Rolls (1611). Entrance to the house is through the original east doorway into the screens passage. At the far end of the **Great Hall**, the charming **Skimmington Frieze** is a 17C plaster relief depicting the ordeals of a hen-pecked husband. The **Parlour**, with its original Ham Hill stone fireplace, Elizabethan panelling and frieze of nursery animals contains some fine 18C furniture (beautiful centre table by Thomas Chippendale the Younger), as does the **Drawing Room**. **Lord Curzon's Room** *(first floor)* contains his lordship's bath stowed in a 'Jacobean' cupboard, a 17C overmantel of King David at Prayer, an 18C bed, a Dutch oak drop-leaf table and an 18C japanned skeleton mirror. The **Crimson Room**, so-called since the 19C when red flock wallpaper replaced the tapestries below the plaster frieze, contains a sumptuous oak four-poster bed carved with the arms of James I. The **Library**, once the formal dining room, features some remarkable heraldic glass. Other interesting features in this former state room are the stone mantelpiece, plaster frieze, Jacobean inner porch, 19C moulded plaster ceiling and bookcases. **The Long Gallery** (52m), lit with oriels at either end, is the longest in existence and provides the perfect setting for a Tudor and Jacobean portraits.

ADDRESSES

🛏 STAY

BRISTOL

Ibis – Explore Lane, Harbourside. ✆0117 319 9000. www. ibis.com. 182 rooms. Modern comfortable rooms with clean lines are on offer at this low-price chain hotel just off Millennium Square.

Premier Inn – King Street. ✆0871 527 8158. www.premierinn.com. 60 rooms. This budget chain hotel enjoys a great dockside location in one of Bristol's oldest streets. Next door is the hotel's 'dining room', the famous Llandoger Trow pub.

Mercure Brigstow Bristol – 5–7 Welsh Back. ✆0117 929 1030. www. mercure.com. 116 rooms. This four-star contemporary boutique hotel is in the heart of old Bristol on the water's edge.

Hotel du Vin – The Sugar House, Narrow Lewins Mead. ✆0117 403 2979. www.hotelduvin.com. 40 rooms. Bristol's finest hotel is a five-minute walk from the waterfront. It occupies a magnificently restored 18C sugar refinery and warehouse complex, with wine-themed, post-industrial chic loft-style rooms (including stunning double-height suites) with every comfort, including walk-in showers and large freestanding baths. The atmospheric public areas include a beautiful bar with courtyard and a superb bistro (🍴 *see below*). Staff are exemplary.

BATH

Bay Tree House – 12 Crescent Gardens. ✆01225 483 699. www.baytree housebath.co.uk. 5 rooms. A perfect location 5 mins walk from the centre (but with free parking), bedrooms in this highly acclaimed Bathstone house B&B are stylish, modern, light and airy, with iPod docking stations, DVDs, etc. Very friendly and thoughtful owners.

Parade Park – 8–10 North Parade. ✆01225 463 384. www.nilvihotelsgroup. com. 35 rooms. Good-value, few-frills accommodation with crisp white linen, in a Georgian townhouse built by John Wood in the 1740s. Four-posters available. A few steps to the Roman Baths and bus and railway stations.

Lavender House – 17 Bloomfield Park. ✆01225 314 500. 5 rooms. This elegant spacious Edwardian house just outside the town centre has delightful gardens and a family atmosphere.

One Three Nine – 139 Wells Road. ✆01225 314 769. www.139bath. co.uk. 10 rooms. Detached Victorian house within walking distance of the city centre. Stylish, sizeable bedrooms, some with four-poster beds and spa baths.

Dorian House – 1 Upper Oldfield Park. ✆01225 426 336. www. dorianhouse.co.uk. 11 rooms. This beautifully-furnished 1880 Bath stone house offers Victorian-meets-contemporary styled rooms with bags of period charm. Marble bathrooms and high-pressure showers, a breakfast orangery and lovely garden. Off-street parking available.

Royal Crescent Hotel – 16 Royal Crescent. ✆01225 823 333. www.royalcrescent.co.uk. 35 rooms. The top address in Bath, this 18C townhouse is an exclusive de-luxe hotel with one of the UK's most renowned hotel spas, and a gourmet restaurant overlooking leafy secluded gardens.

WELLS

The Crown – Market Place. ✆01749 673 457. www.crownatwells.co.uk. 15 rooms. This 15C coaching inn in the centre of town (once visited by William Penn) provides a mix of contemporary and traditional styles. Four-posters available. Anton's Bistrot (🍴) is recommended (🍴 *see below*).

The Ancient Gate House Hotel – Sadler Street. ✆01749 672 029. www. ancientgatehouse.co.uk. 9 rooms. This family-run hotel and restaurant has a wonderful aspect facing the famous west front of Wells cathedral and its green. Four-posters available. Rugantino restaurant (🍴) offers al fresco dining.

The Swan Hotel – Sadler Street. ✆01749 836 300. www. swanhotelwells.co.uk. 50 rooms. The bedrooms at this former coaching inn feature period antique furniture and some boast original four-poster beds.

Several have views of the cathedral. Restaurant (🍽🍽🍽🍽).

GLASTONBURY

🏠 There are few hotels in town but plenty of B&Bs, several run by vegetarians, with meat-free breakfasts.

🍽 EAT

BRISTOL

🍽🍽 **The Llandoger Trow** – King Street. ☎0870 990 6424. www.brewersfayre.co.uk. Bristol's most famous historic inn, now with wine bar and restaurant, serving standard pub food.

🍽🍽🍽 **Bordeaux Quay** – First Floor, V Shed, Canons Way. ☎0117 943 1200. www.bordeaux-quay.co.uk. This large multi-award-winning complex of restaurant (closed Mon), brasserie, bar, deli, bakery and cookery school ticks all the boxes, serving acclaimed organic European-style dishes by the waterside.

🍽🍽🍽 **Loch Fyne** – King Street. ☎0117 930 7160. www.lochfyneseafoodandgrill.co.uk. Situated in the Old Granary – a beautiful listed building on the waterfront – this branch of a nationwide chain specialises in fish and seafood.

🍽🍽🍽 **Riverstation** – The Grove. ☎0117 914 4434. www.riverstation.co.uk. Closed Sun dinner. This stylish modern restaurant and bar on the harbourside has al fresco terraces overlooking the water. Excellent Modern European cuisine using fresh, local carefully sourced ingredients.

🍽🍽🍽 **Hotel du Vin Bistro** – The Sugar House, Narrow Lewins Mead. ☎0117 925 5577. www.hotelduvin.com. This beautifully decorated though unfussy incarnation of a fin-de-siècle French bistro shimmers romantically at night as candlelight reflects off its myriad wine glasses, bottles and gleaming wooden surfaces. Excellent cooking, faultless friendly informal service.

🍽🍽🍽 **The River Grille** – Bristol Hotel, Prince Street. ☎0117 923 0333. This light, airy, quayside restaurant uses fresh local food in its Modern British dishes.

BATH

🍽🍽 **The Pump Room** – ☎01225 444 477. www.romanbaths.co.uk. Take coffee, lunch or afternoon tea where Bath's

Georgian High Society met, in the place where the original spa waters bubbled up.

🍽🍽 **Sally Lunn's** – 4 North Parade Passage. ☎01225 461 634. www.sallylunns.co.uk. Bath's oldest and most famous eating house dates from 1482. In cosy small rooms try the signature Bath Bun, or a traditional Trencher Bread meal.

🍽🍽 **Casanis** – 4 Savile Row. ☎01225 780 055. www.casanis.co.uk. Gallic bistro tucked away near the Assembly Rooms, run by a French chef and his wife. Authentic cooking with a focus on local produce.

🍽🍽🍽🍽 **Bath Priory** – Weston Road, 1.2mi/2km west on A 4. ☎01225 448 267. www.thebathpriory.co.uk. Set in a beautiful Georgian country house and under the direction of Michelin-starred chef Sam Moody, this has probably the finest food in the area.

🍽🍽🍽🍽 **Allium Brasserie** – Abbey Hotel, 1 North Parade. ☎01225 809 965. www.abbeyhotelbath.co.uk. A modern hotel restaurant close to the river in the city centre. Cooking is skilfull and ambitious, influenced by Britain, Asia and the Mediterranean.

🍽🍽🍽🍽 **The Olive Tree** – Queensberry Hotel, Russell Street. ☎01225 447 928. www.thequeensberry.co.uk. Stylish contemporary dining room serving expertly produced Modern European cuisine. Good-value prix-fixe lunch menu and an acclaimed wine list.

WELLS

🍽🍽🍽 **Anton's Bistrot** – The Crown, Market Place. ☎01749 673 457. www.crownatwells.co.uk. Satirical cartoons decorate the walls. Good-value prix-fixe lunches. Modern British dishes at dinner.

CHEDDAR

🏠 There are several restaurants between the village and the gorge.

TAUNTON

🍽🍽 **Brazz** – Castle Row. ☎01823 252 000. www.brazz.co.uk. Lively modern all-day brasserie-style restaurant-bar, housed within a luxury hotel that is part of Taunton Castle. Good cheese selection.

St Nicholas Market, Bristol
© csfotoimages/iStockphoto.com

Devon and Cornwall

St Michael's Mount   © David Noble/Travel Pictures

Introduction

With two very distinct coastlines, several historic towns and cities, a host of picture-postcard villages and fishing harbours, unspoilt moors and national parks, stately homes and even statelier gardens, plus a fascinating and unexpected industrial heritage, Devon and Cornwall pack a lot of interest into a small geographical area. This is England's main holiday playground and, whatever the weather, it is not simply a cliché to say that there is always plenty to see and do. The north coast is generally rugged and windblown (Newquay is a world-class surfing centre), while the south is characterised by sheltered coves and creeks reaching far inland, though both coasts have sheltered resorts boasting beautiful golden beaches. While the coast is commercialised in parts and farming is still strong inland, much of the region and many of its inhabitants, both locals and newcomers, have a bohemian and arty character; from the hippy culture of Totnes to the modern art of St Ives. It is 284mi/454km from London to Penzance and this relative remoteness leads some locals to think of it an independent state. If you have more time, you can leave the English mainland altogether, and explore the quiet unspoilt Scilly Isles.

Coast and Country

Devon's county town, **Exeter** is a thriving university city with a famous cathedral, old quarter, and historic quayside. Due south, the '**English Riviera**' comprises Torquay, Paignton and Brixham. This is archetypal British seaside holiday territory; from donkey rides at Paignton to bracing clifftop walks at Berry Head; a working fishing fleet at Brixham to Torquay marina's glamorous powerboats; from sunbathing on golden sands to exploring caves on rainy days.

A short distance from the glitziest part of the English Riviera, **Dartmoor** is the largest remaining wilderness in southern England. It has two distinct faces: crowded cream-tea show villages, and paths less trodden, leading to prehistoric remains and mighty tors (rock outcrops). Devon's southernmost tip is the **South Hams**. For many visitors this quiet understated area is the most beautiful and charming part of the whole West Country. You can explore the River Dart and Kingsbridge estuary by rail, road or boat. Totnes and Dartmouth are two of southern England's most attractive small towns. **Plymouth** is Devon's second city, the place from which Drake famously sailed to repel the Armada. It still has a salty maritime air, particularly around the cobbled Barbican from where the Pilgrim Fathers set sail. West of Plymouth begins the **south Cornish coast**. Some of England's loveliest seaside villages and scenery can be found along this heavily indented coast-line, where magnificent gardens frequently tumble down to picture-postcard bays. The meandering seashore continues west via the beautiful creeks and inlets around Falmouth, the dramatic rocky Lizard peninsula, via Penzance, to spectacular Land's End. The **north Cornish coast** is blessed with some of Britain's finest beaches. St Ives is for families and art lovers, the crashing surf at Newquay is for surfers and party people, and in between there's something for most tastes. Dramatic rocky shores characterise the **North Devon coast** with low-key resorts and pleasant market towns inland. East of Ilfracombe lies **Exmoor** National Park, comprising sparse uplands, rolling verdant pastures, and streams and ravines meeting in dramatic beauty spots.

Highlights

1 Sail along the glorious River Dart at **Dartmouth** (p308)

2 Pretend you're in a Mediterranean village at **Clovelly** (p320)

3 Leave the 21C behind by sailing to **Lundy Island** (p320)

4 Go green in gardener's heaven at the **Eden Project** (p324)

5 The giant 'sandcastle' that is **St Michael's Mount** (p331)

Exeter★★

Devon

A visit to Exeter, the regional centre of this part of the Southwest, is rewarding for the charm of its crescents and terraces and in particular for its cathedral, standing out in elephant grey against the red sandstone of the city churches and city wall, and red brick Georgian houses.

A BIT OF HISTORY

The Saxon town that succeeded the ancient Roman stronghold was devastated by the Danes in the 9C and 10C, but was rebuilt for the bishop's see to be transferred from Crediton to Exeter in 1050. Medieval trade prospered thanks to the city's position at the head of the navigable waters of the River Exe and it became one of the chief markets of country woollens. With steam power and machinery, however, Exeter's woollen trade declined and the city settled down to the calm life of a county town. Heavy bombing in 1942 destroyed much of the city's medieval fabric.

CATHEDRAL★★

Open year-round Mon–Sat 9am–5pm, Sun 11.30am–5pm. £7.50. Guided tours several times during the day. Tower and Roof tours: call for details. &✗ ✆01392 285 983. www.exeter-cathedral.org.uk.

The cathedral is set in its **Close**, an island of calm amid the city's traffic and surrounded by buildings from many periods. The west front rises through tier upon tier of carved angels, bishops and monarchs, through decorated tracery to castellated parapets. The **Norman transept towers** are the earliest part of the cathedral, since the majority of the building was remodelled and improved in the 13C. Inside the cathedral, the most striking feature is the **nave vaulting**, extending 91m from west to east. Also impressive are the 14C **corbels** between

▶ **Population:** 129 800.
⏾ **Michelin Map:** Michelin Atlas p 4 or Map 503 J 31.
▯ **Info:** Dix's Field. ✆01392 665 700. Custom House, Exeter Quay. ✆01392 271 611. www.exeter.gov.uk. There are two train stations; Central, in the heart of town, and St David's (Bath Spa 1h20, London Paddington 2h12), around 0.5mi/0.8km northwest of the centre. The bus station is on Paris Street in the centre. The city can be covered on foot.
◗ **Location:** 84mi/135km SW of Bath and 171mi/275km SW of London.
😊 **Don't Miss:** The cathedral; the Devon Gallery and ethnography collection in the Royal Albert Memorial Museum.
🕐 **Timing:** Allow a day.
🧑‍🧒 **Kids:** Have fun at the play areas at Bicton Gardens.
🌿 **Walking Tours:** The route marked on the map offers a pleasant stroll. Free Red Coat Guided Tours (90min) operate daily. ✆01392 265 203. www.exeter.gov.uk.

the pointed arches of the arcade. Note the 14C **minstrels' gallery** (north side) with 14 angels playing instruments and the west rose window with reticulated tracery (20C glass).

Behind the high altar stands the **Exeter Pillar**, the prototype of all the others in the cathedral. Sir Gilbert Scott's canopied choir stalls (1870–77) incorporate the oldest complete set of **misericords** in the country, carved in 1260–80. The exquisite bishop's throne was carved in 1312. Above the high altar the late-14C east window contains original glass.

Cathedral Close

© George-Standen/iStockphoto.com

TOWN
Royal Albert Memorial Museum & Art Gallery★

Queen Street. Open Tue –Sun
10am–5pm, 🚻 ✕ ☏ 01392 665 858.
www.rammuseum.org.uk

This dynamic museum is housed in what has been called, '...an exquisite jewel box of a (Victorian) building', which re-opened in 2011 following the biggest refurbishment in its 150-year history. The **natural history** collection is one of the most comprehensive outside London of animal, vegetable and mineral specimens, from all five continents; the **Birds of a Feather** display is particularly dazzling. The **World Cultures** galleries reflect the number of Exeter families with far-flung trade contacts; specimens of tribal art include artefacts collected by Captain Cook. The art gallery features a rolling programme of fine art and also holds local artists' exhibitions.

Quayside

Access via the Butts Ferry or the Cricklepit Footbridge.
Quay House Visitor Centre, 46 The Quay.
Open Apr–Oct daily 10am–5pm.
Nov–Mar weekends 11am–4pm.
☏ 01392 271 611. www.exeter.gov.uk.
The quay, a 10-minute walk from the city centre, dates from the days when Exeter was a tidal river port, during a period of prosperity which was brought to an

abrupt end in the 13C, when Isabella, Countess of Devon, built a weir across the river and successfully diverted all trade from Exeter to Topsham.

The visitor centre presents models, paintings and artefacts and an audio-visual history of Exeter. There is a regular programme of music and events throughout the summer months including spectacular dragonboat racing and other regattas. Free Redcoat boat tours and (conventional paid-for)river cruises (11.30am–5pm; £3.50; ☏ 07984 368 442; www.exetercruises. com) operate in summer from the quayside.

EXCURSIONS
👥 Bicton Park Botanical Gardens★

🕐 8mi/13km SE on the B 3182 and B 3179, then a minor road. Open daily 10am–5pm/4.30pm in winter. Closed 25–26 Dec. £10.95, child (2–16) £8.95.
🚻✕ ☏ 01395 568 465.
www.bictongardens.co.uk.
The grounds of Bicton House have been designed in formal Italian style and planted with specimen trees over the last 200 years. There are four glasshouses, the most notable being the beautiful **Palm House**, built in the 1820s to a daring curvilinear design, using 18 000 small glass panes in thin iron glazing bars. Among other features are an **American Garden** (started in the

305

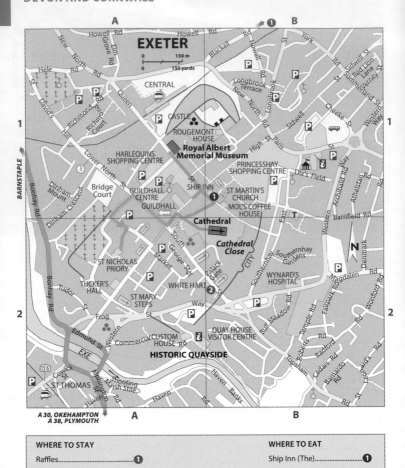

EXETER

WHERE TO STAY		WHERE TO EAT	
Raffles	❶	Ship Inn (The)	❶
White Hart (The)	❷		

1830s), a secluded **Hermitage Garden**, a **Countryside Museum**, a collection of motorcycles and cars, a woodland railway, an adventure playground, an indoor play area and mini golf.

Queen Victoria, George VI and the late Queen Mother are among the monarchs who have worshipped at **St Mary's Church**, which adjoins the gardens.

Ottery St Mary★

🡲 12mi/19km E. 🯅 ☎01404 813 838. www.otterystmarytourism.co.uk.

This attractive little town of winding streets and small squares with 17C and Georgian houses is attractively situated on the River Otter, surrounded by green hills. Its jewel is the twin-towered parish church of **St Mary's★**, consecrated in 1260 and converted into a collegiate foundation in 1336: the chancel, nave, aisle and Lady Chapel were remodelled in the Decorated style and many of the furnishings belong to this period, including **Grandisson's clock** in the south transept and the gilded wooden **eagle lectern**, one of the oldest and grandest in England. A special feature of the church is its varied **vaulting**, superb coloured **bosses** and **corbels**.

Ottery St Mary is famous for its flaming **Tar Barrels** and Tar Barrel rolling on 5 November, and its **carnival**, held on the Saturday before.

English Riviera★★

The English Riviera is a marketing term coined in the 1980s to evoke images of sophisticated French coastlines, and encompasses the resorts of Torquay, Paignton and Brixham, also known collectively as Torbay. Originally fishing villages, the three towns have capitalised on natural advantages, which include a mild climate, exotic palm-tree vegetation, sea views and wide sandy beaches by adding hotels, promenades, piers, pavilions and public gardens to become fully fledged holiday resorts.

- **Michelin Map:** Michelin Atlas p 4 or Map 503 J 32.
- **Info:** 5 Vaughan Parade Torquay. ℘01803 659 790 . www.englishriviera.co.uk. 36mins by train from Exeter St David's, over 3h by train from Paddington.
- **Location:** 23mi/37km south of Exeter, 194mi/310km southwest of London.
- **Don't Miss:** Dartmouth Steam Railway & River Boat.
- **Kids:** Paignton Zoo; Kents Cavern; Plymouth Aquarium; Dockyards.
- **Sailing:** The English Riviera and South Hams offer some of the UK's best sailing waters.

TORQUAY

This is the most popular resort in Devon and of the three Torbay towns, the one that most lives up to its glamorous 'English Riviera' billing.

Most activity takes place around the bustling harbour/marina and beaches.

Living Coasts★

Beacon Quay, Torquay Harbourside. Open daily from 10am–4pm/5pm/6pm, closing times vary seasonally. Closed 25 Dec. £13, child (3–15) £9.80; &⊡✕ www.livingcoasts.org.uk.

A sister attraction to Paignton Zoo (&see p308) this first-class attraction features marine creatures, both local and exotic. Feeding time with the penguins, otters and octopus and seals are particularly popular.

Kents Cavern★

(Wellswood, Ilsham Road. Entry by guided tour only, daily from 9.30am; tour times 10.30am–4pm (10.15am–4.30pm in Jul–Aug). Closed 25 Dec. £10, child (3–15) £9. ⊡£2. ✕ ℘01803 215 136. www.kents-cavern.co.uk.

Excavations have shown that this group of limestone caves were inhabited by prehistoric animals and by men for long periods from the Paleolithic era, 100 000 years ago, until Roman times.

The tour (0.5mi/0.8km) leads through contrasting chambers with petrified 'waterfalls' beautiful white, red-brown and green crystals and many **stalactites** and **stalagmites** all beautifully lit. There are lots of activities for children in and around the caves.

Torre Abbey

Torbay Road. Open daily 10am–5pm. £8. &✕ ℘01803 293 593. www.torre-abbey.org.uk.

Set in luxuriant gardens, Torre abbey consists of an 18C house, the so-called Spanish Barn, and the ruins of the medieval abbey. The house is home to Torbay's art collection, including about 600 oils and watercolours from the 18C to the mid-20C. They include Pre-Raphaelite works, with paintings by artists such as Holman Hunt and Burne-Jones. There is a lively programme of contemporary arts events.

PAIGNTON

2.5mi/4km S of Torquay.
℘0844 474 2233.
www.theenglishriviera.co.uk.

Despite the Riviera tag, Paignton remains the poor relation to upwardly

Dame Agatha Christie (1890–1976)

Agatha Christie was born and brought up in Torquay. At the outbreak of the First World War she worked in the town hall while it doubled as a Red Cross Hospital. This inspired her to create Hercule Poirot, distilled from the many Belgian refugees stranded in Torquay at that time. After nursing she trained in a pharmacy – perfect inside information on the poisons that feature in her novels. In 1938, she bought **Greenway House** on the River Dart as a holiday home and lived here until 1959. Today, it belongs to the National Trust and, in 2009, the beautiful 12ha gardens and house were opened to the public (open Mar–Oct Wed–Sun 10.30am–5pm; Nov–Dec Sat–Sun 11am–4pm; house visit by timed ticket only, on busy days there may be a wait; £11; ☐(£3) ✕; ✆01803 842 382; www.nationaltrust.org.uk).

mobile Torquay. It has a good beach and one of England's best zoos.

♚♙ Paignton Zoo★★

Totnes Road, 1mi/1.6km from town centre. Open daily from 10am, closing times vary seasonally, see website. Closed 25 Dec. £16.50, child (3–15) £12.35. ♿☐✕ ✆01803 697 500. www.paigntonzoo.org.uk.
This is one of Britain's largest zoos, home to over 3 000 animals, set in 32ha of luxuriant botanical gardens. The animals are kept as part of a far-reaching conservation programme.

BRIXHAM

8 mi /13km S of Torquay.
🛈 ✆0844 474 2233.
www.englishriviera.co.uk.
Unlike its sister resorts, Brixham has a life aside from tourism, as a major fishing port which lands among the highest-value catch in England. It has

no major visitor attractions as such; most people are happy to look around its compact picturesque harbour, perhaps board the replica **Golden Hind** ♚♙ (open daily normally from 10am–4pm, but closing times vary seasonally, see website; £7, child £5; ✆01803 856 223, www.goldenhind.co.uk), take a boat trip around the bay and, of course, enjoy a fish supper. The short excursion, 2mi/3km)west, to the unspoiled clifftop nature reserve of **Berry Head**, for its **sea views** is very worthwhile.

SOUTH HAMS★★

A different world to the English Riviera, the South Hams, lying immediately to the south and west, is agricultural, studded with small villages. The countryside is beautiful, particularly around the River Dart and Kingsbridge estuary.

Dartmouth★★

10mi/16km S of Torquay.
🛈 ✆01803 834 224.
www.discoverdartmouth.com.
Dartmouth enjoys one of the most beautiful and unspoilt settings in southwest England, occupying a deepwater haven in a tidal inlet encircled by verdant hills. It grew wealthy on maritime trade and the quay was constructed in 1548, when it served as the centre of the town's activities. In appearance little has changed since, still lined with elegant merchants' houses, built in the early–mid-17C. In the late-17C, trade moved to Bristol and London, and Dartmouth became purely a naval port.

Rail and River

The **Dartmouth Steam Railway & River Boat Company** synchronises river and rail trips between Lower Street Dartmouth (river) and Queen's Park Station, Paignton (rail) (Apr–Oct and Christmas; see website for timetable and prices). They also run stand-alone river boat trips and coastal cruises daily in summer (✆01803 555 872; www.dartmouthrailriver.co.uk).

Dartmouth Harbour, Britannia Royal Naval College in the background

The Town

The **Butterwalk**★ *(Duke Street)* is a terrace of four shops with oversailing upper floors supported on 11 granite pillars (built 1635–40). Just off here is St Saviour's Church *(Anzac Street)*. The tall square pinnacled tower has been a landmark for those sailing upriver since it was constructed in 1372. Note especially the south door with its two ironwork lions and rooted Tree of Life, and the medieval altar with legs carved like ships' figureheads. Farther along Duke Street is the old cobbled market square and building (1829), at its liveliest on a Friday when the pannier market takes place.

The Shambles, the main street of the medieval town, is still lined with houses of that period – the early-17C four-storey **Tudor House** and the **Carved Angel**, a late-14C half-timbered merchant's house, now an inn.

Britannia Royal Naval College

Public tours Jul–Nov (£13) start in Dartmouth, then to the college by coach for 2¼h walking tour. Places can be reserved online www.britanniaassociation.org.uk/tours or by contacting the Britannia Association Office (01803 677565). ✆01803 832 141. www.royalnavy.mod.uk.

On the hill above town, this huge, majestic building (1905) is a naval school where many members of the Royal Family received their training, most recently Prince William and Prince Andrew.

Dartmouth Castle

1mi/1.6km SE by Newcomen Road, South Town and Castle Road. Open daily Apr–Sept 10am–6pm; Oct 10am–5pm; Nov–Mar Sat–Sun only 10am–4pm. Closed 1 Jan, 24–26 Dec. £0.60. (charge). ✆01803 833 588, www.english-heritage.org.uk.

The fort was begun in 1481 by the merchants of Dartmouth to protect their homes and deepwater anchorage, and modified in the 16C and 18C. It commands excellent **views**★★★ out to sea and across and up the estuary.

Salcombe★

20mi/32km SW of Dartmouth.
🛈 ✆01548 843 927.
www.salcombeinformation.co.uk.

Brilliant blue Salcombe Bay, aflutter with white triangular sails, fringed by golden pocket-handkerchief-sized beaches and perfectly framed by rolling green hills, is one of the finest sights in Devon. Salcombe is one of the largest yachting centres in England and several old wharf houses are workshops for boat makers and marine engineers. Other old properties have been converted to fashionable places to eat and drink.

Totnes★

13 mi /21km NW of Dartmouth.
🛈 ✆01803 863 168. www.visittotnes.co.uk.

Ancient Totnes is one of the most rewarding small towns in England, standing at the highest navigable and lowest bridging point on the River Dart

View over Totnes town

© Ann Taylor-Hughes / iStockphoto.com

on the south Devon coast. The narrow main street runs steeply between 16C–17C wealthy merchants' houses built of brick and stone or colour-washed. Totnes is unusual for a town of its size, eschewing chain stores, devoted almost entirely to small individual shops and cafés, many catering for the bohemian-chic lifestyle for which the town is famous.

Fore Street

The half-timbered **Elizabethan House and Museum★** (70 Fore Street; open Apr–Sept Tue–Fri 10am–4pm; Aug also Sat 10am–2pm; ✆01803 863 821; www. totnesmuseum.org), a dark red-brick **mansion** (now a community education centre), a late-18C Gothic house (in Bank Lane), and other attractive buildings (Nos. 48 and 52) testify to Totnes' former prosperity.

High Street

Interesting features include the mid-16C **Guildhall** (open Apr–Oct, Mon–Fri, except Bank Holidays,11am–3pm; ✆01803 862 147), which occupies the site of an earlier Benedictine priory; the house at No. 16, now a bank built in 1585 by a local pilchard merchant; and the granite pillared **Butterwalk★**, which has protected shoppers from the rain since the 17C.

St Mary's★

The 15C parish and priory church with its red sandstone tower adorned with gruesome gargoyles contains a beautiful late-15C rood screen.

Castle

Open daily Apr–Sept 10am–6pm; Oct 10am–5pm; Nov–Mar Sat–Sun 10am–4pm. £4.30. 🅿 ✆01803 864 406. www.english-heritage.org.uk/totnes. High on a mound sits the castle, encircled by 14C ramparts built to strengthen the late-11C motte and bailey earthworks. The castle walls command excellent **views★★★** of the Dart River valley.

PLYMOUTH★★

Plymouth is on the border between Devon and Cornwall, delineated by the River Tamar.
🛈 ✆01752 306 330.
www.visitplymouth.co.uk.
Plymouth is the principal town of the southwest with nearly 260 000 inhabitants. It is arranged in three distinct areas: the Hoe and its environs, adorned with the splendour of Victorian and Edwardian buildings; the older, bustling Barbican district by the harbour with its narrow streets; the commercial post-war centre, with wide shop-lined avenues.

A Bit of History

The Plantagenet period brought trade with France, and by the Elizabethan period trade had spread worldwide, so that for a time Plymouth was the fourth-largest town in England after London, Bristol and York. In the Second World War the city suffered terrible bomb damage. From the 13C Plymouth also played a prime role as a naval and military port, from which warriors and

explorers such as Drake, Raleigh, Hawkins and Grenville (all Devonians), Cook and the Pilgrim Fathers set sail.
The Royal Naval Dockyard was founded by William III in 1691 at Devonport and today employs some 4 800 workers.

WALKING TOUR

National Marine Aquarium★

Rope Walk, Coxside. Open daily 9.30am–6pm. Closed 25-26 Dec. £15.95, child 3-15, £11.95 (online booking discount). & P(charge).
✗ ℘0844 893 7938 (info line). www.national-aquarium.co.uk.
Opened in 2001, this was the first aquarium in the UK to be set up solely for the purpose of education, conservation and research, and remains Britain's largest aquarium. The tanks represent different environments, such as a fresh stream, shallow sea and coral reef; with an array of fish, from delicate sea horses to mighty sharks.

Barbican

Old Plymouth survives in the Barbican, an area extending a quarter of a mile inland from Sutton Harbour, combining modern amenities with medieval houses, Jacobean doorways and cobbled alleys. The **Mayflower Stone** on the pier commemorates the voyage of the **Pilgrim Fathers**, who set sail in 1620 in their 27m ship, the *Mayflower*. Many other famous voyages are commemorated in the numerous stones and plaques on the pier.

Mayflower Museum

3–5 The Barbican. Open Apr–Oct Mon–Sat 9.30am–5pm, Sun 10.30am–4pm; Nov–Mar Mon–Fri 9.30am–5pm, Sat 10.30am–4pm. £3. ℘01752 306 330. www.visitplymouth.co.uk.
In the same building as the tourist office, this traces the voyage of the *Mayflower* (&see above) and contemporary events.

Elizabethan House

Currently losed for conservation work; check website for information. ℘01752 304 774. www.plymouth.gov.uk.
This house and its neighbour were built in the late-16C as part of a development for wealthy merchants and sea-captains.

Plymouth Gin Distillery

60 South Side Street. Visit by guided tour only (40min) Mon–Sat 10.30am–5pm, Sun 11.30am–5pm. &✗ £7. ℘01752 665 292. www.plymouthdistillery.com.
The distillery is housed in what was once a Dominican Friary founded in 1425. You can take a guided tour to see how gin is made, then enjoy a drink and bite to eat in the 500-year old surroundings of the Refectory Cocktail Lounge and Barbican Kitchen (&sec p337).

Merchant's House

Currently closed to conservation work; check website for details. ℘01752 304 774. https://plymhearts.org/merchants-house.
This mid-16C timbered house, its upper floors supported on stone corbels, houses the **Museum of Old Plymouth** including a reconstruction of an old city **Edwardian pharmacy★**.

St Andrew's church

www.standrewschurch.org.uk.
Founded in 1050 and rebuilt in the 15C, the church was firebombed in 1941, leaving only the walls, granite piers, chancel arches and the 41m tower standing. The rebuilt church features six vividly coloured **windows** by John Piper (1904–92). On a window ledge is the so-called **Drake crest scratching** showing the *Golden Hinde*. It is thought to have been carved by a mason working in the church at the time of Drake's return from circumnavigating the world (3 November 1580). Among the **memorials** are tablets to Frobisher and Drake. Just south of the church stands the **Prysten House** (Finewell Street; enquire while you're at St Andrew's, or ℘01752 661 414), dating from 1490 and thought

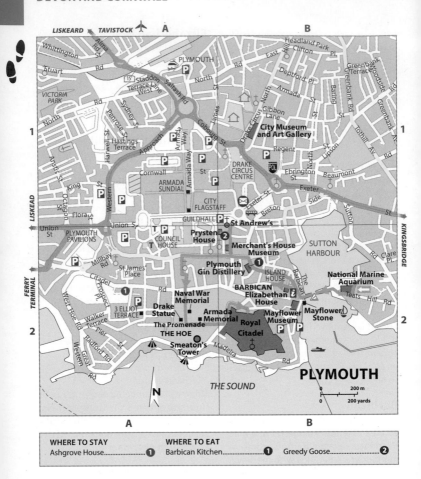

WHERE TO STAY
Ashgrove House........................①

WHERE TO EAT
Barbican Kitchen........................①   Greedy Goose........................②

to be the oldest house in Plymouth. It is a fine three-storeyed building around an inner courtyard with open timber galleries.

City Museum and Art Gallery★

Closed until 2020 for redevelopment work; check website for updates. ☎01752 304 774. https://plymhearts.org/thebox. The spacious Victorian building housed splendid collections relating to the city's **maritime history**.

Plymouth was also the home of **William Cookworthy**, discoverer of the Cornish kaolin which made the production of **hard paste porcelain** a reality in this country from 1768.

Plymouth Hoe

On '...that loftie place at Plimmouth call'd the Hoe', **Sir Francis Drake** (1540–96) is said to have seen the 'invincible' Spanish Armada arriving one day in 1588 and decided to finish his game of bowls (perhaps waiting for the tide to turn) before going to battle. It remains an ideal point to **view** maritime traffic on the Sound, the natural harbour at the mouth of the Tamar and Plym rivers. **Smeaton's Tower** (open daily 10am–5pm; £4; ☎01752 304 774; https://plymhearts.org/smeatons-tower), a red-and-white-painted lighthouse, was erected on the Hoe in 1884 after 123 storm-battered years on Eddystone Rocks, some 14mi/23km southwest of Plymouth.

The present **Eddystone Lighthouse**, built in 1878–82, can be seen from the Hoe and even better from the top of Smeaton's Tower, from where there is a splendid **view★★**. Other monuments testifying to Plymouth's role in history include Boehm's 1884 **Drake Statue**, the **Armada Memorial** and the **Naval War Memorial**. Also on the Hoe is **Tinside Lido** (open Jun–early Sept; www.visitplymouth.co.uk), a restored 1935 Art Deco outdoor pool.

Royal Citadel

Visit by guided tour only mid-Apr–Sept Mon-Tue, Thu and Sun 2.30pm. £6. ℘01752 306 330. www.english-heritage.org.uk.

In 1590–91 Drake began a fort intended to protect the Sound against marauding Spaniards and it was here that Charles II had the present castle built in 1666–71. The **ramparts** command **views★★** of the Sound, the Barbican and the Tamar.

EXCURSIONS

Buckland Abbey★★

◗9mi/14km N of Plymouth.
Open mid-Feb–early Mar and Dec 11am–4pm; early Mar–Oct 11am–5pm; Nov tours at 11.30am and 4pm. Gardens open daily (Nov Fri–Sun only) 10.30am–5.30pm. £11. ♿🅿✕ ℘01822 853 607. www.nationaltrust.org.uk/buckland.

Buckland was founded in 1278. At the Dissolution of the Monasteries, the property was sold to the Grenvilles and converted into an Elizabethan mansion before their famous cousin, **Sir Francis Drake**, purchased the estate in 1581. The property has since been transformed from Tudor mansion to Georgian family home. The garden is largely 20C with the striking exception of the 14C **Great Barn**, buttressed and gabled, built to store the abbey's tithes and dues. A new addition is the **Cider House Garden**, including a walled kitchen garden and wild garden.

The house accommodates elements of the original church in its domestic context in a fascinating way, outlined in the **Four Lives Gallery**. The **Drake Gallery**, which dominates the first floor, was added in the 1570s and houses an exhibition on the great seaman explorer. The panelled **Drake Chamber** is hung with a series of 16C–17C portraits and contains English and continental furniture of the same period. The **Great Hall**, at the heart of the old abbey, is paved in pink-and-white tiles, lined with oak panelling, and features striking original plasterwork. The furniture is predominantly 16C–17C. The kitchen, with French-style brick charcoal ovens and a range of old-fashioned kitchen utensils, was added in the 17C.

Saltram★★

◗3.5mi/5.5km E on the A 374 then S on the A 38 to Plympton.
House: open Mar–Oct Sat–Thu 11am–3.30pm/4.30pm. £11. **Garden**: daily 10am–4pm (5pm Mar–Oct); **Park**: open year-round daily dawn–dusk. ♿🅿 (£3) ✕ ℘01752 333 503. www.nationaltrust.org.uk/saltram.

This is a magnificent Georgian house with some of the finest 18C rooms in the country, with opulent Robert Adam interiors, gardens, follies and landscaped parkland. To complete Adams' interior design, Chippendale contributed furniture, Reynolds portraits and Angelica Kauffmann paintings.

Mount Edgcumbe

◗Mount Edgcumbe Country Park, Cremyll. 25mi/40km by road.
Park: open year round daily 8am–dusk. **House**: open Apr–Sept Sun–Thu and bank holiday Mons 11am–4.30pm. £7.20. ♿🅿✕ ℘01752 822 236. www.mountedgcumbe.gov.uk.

Built in the 1500s, and now restored to its 18C appearance, the house include paintings by Sir Joshua Reynolds and William van de Velde, Irish Bronze Age horns, 16C tapestries and 18C Chinese and Plymouth porcelain.

However, for many people, the best reason to visit is its large **country park**, looking out to sea. This includes the National Camellia Collection, the majority of the formal gardens and the Orangery Restaurant.

Haytor Rocks, Dartmoor

© Black Beck Photographic/iStockphoto.com

Dartmoor★★

Devon

The largest of the five granite masses that form the core of Southwest England, Dartmoor National Park welcomes 8 million visitors each year. Many are curious holidaymakers taking a day out from the coastal Torbay resorts visiting the pretty villages on the edges of the moor. Others are serious walkers, delving deep into the heart of the park and into the bleak unpopulated western areas.

THE MOOR

Dartmoor offers two contrasting faces. The centre is open moorland, often bleak and windswept rising 300m high, while the **tors** (rocky outcrops), mainly to the north and west, are as much as 600m. To the east and southeast, however, are **wooded valleys**, cascading streams and small villages. Ponies, sheep and cattle graze freely on the moor, while a myriad of birds flock above. The whole area is a walker's paradise with hundreds of routes and trails mapped out to accommodate every level of walker. You can join one of the many Dartmoor National Park Authority walks led by a guide with a wealth of local knowledge or simply blaze your own trail.

Michelin Map: Michelin Atlas p 4 or Map 503 H, I 32.

Info: Ashburton: Town Hall, North Street. ℘01364 653 426. Okehampton: 3 West Street. ℘01837 52295. www.dartmoor.co.uk.

National Park Info: Dartmoor National Park Authority, Bovey Tracey, Newton Abbot, Devon TQ13 9JQ. ℘*01626 832093 (general enquiries).* www.dartmoor.gov.uk. There are **visitor centres** at Haytor (℘*01364 661520),* Princetown (℘*01822 890414) and Postbridge* (℘*01822 880272).*

Location: 365sq mi/ 945sq km of moorland in the centre of Devon.

Don't Miss: South Devon Railway; Castle Drogo; Lydford; view from Brent Tor.

Kids: Miniature Pony Centre (Moretonhampstead); the adventure centres at Becky Falls and River Dart Country Park.

Warning: On enclosed land, access is by public footpaths and bridleways only and it is an offence to drive or park more than 15m from a road.

⌂ DRIVING TOUR

▷ Leave Plymouth E on the A 398.

Buckfastleigh
This small market town is the terminus of the steam-driven **South Devon Railway** (operates Apr–late Oct daily, rest of year see website; Buckfastleigh–Totnes £15 return fare; ♿ P ✕; ℘01364 644 370; www.southdevonrailway.co.uk), one of the most picturesque railway lines in England.

Buckfast Abbey
Abbey and grounds: Open Mon–Sat 9am–6pm. Sun noon–6pm. ♿ P ✕ ℘01364 645 506.
www.buckfast.org.uk.
The present abbey church was consecrated in 1932, some 900 years after the original foundation under King Canute. Norman in style, it follows the plan of the Cistercian house dissolved by Henry VIII. The interior of white Bath stone rises to a plainly vaulted roof, 15m above the nave floor. Note the ornate **high altar** and the modern **Blessed Sacrament Chapel** (1966) with walls of stained glass. An exhibition in the **crypt** traces the abbey history.

▷ Return to the A 38.

Ashburton
This former stannary (coinage) town stands on a tributary of the River Dart at the beginning of the old road (B 3357) across the moor to Tavistock. The church was built in the 15C when the town was a significant wool centre. Slate-hung houses indicate its importance as a slate mining centre from the 16C to the 18C. Signposted from town is the **River Dart Country Park** 👪 (open: Apr–Sept daily 10am–dusk; Oct–Mar daily 10am–4pm; £9.80, 3–4 year-olds £5.50; P £4–£7; ℘01364 652 511; www.riverdart.co.uk), a popular country park with a range of outdoor facilities and family amusements.

▷ Take the road to Buckland.

Buckland in the Moor
Thatched stone cottages set in a wooded dell and the medieval moorstone church form this characteristic Devon village.

▷ Go back to the B 3357; turn right.

At **Dartmeet** the West and East Dart rivers converge from the uplands to flow through a gorge-like valley lively with bird- and animal-life.

▷ Turn right on the B 3387.

Widecombe-in-the-Moor
A cluster of white-walled thatched cottages, grouped around the church, stands in the shallow valley (wide combe) surrounded by granite ridges which rise to 460m. The vast Perpendicular **Church of St Pancras**, with its imposing pinnacled 41m-tall tower, is known as the Cathedral of the Moor. The church house dates back to 1537, when it was an alehouse.
The road to Bovey Tracey runs close by **Haytor Rocks** (454m), from where there is a fine **view★**

Bovey Tracey
This small town is a gateway to Dartmoor. Many of its cottages are built of moor granite, mellowed by thatch. The 15C **Church of St Peter, St Paul and St Thomas of Canterbury★** was founded in 1170 by Sir William de Tracey, possibly in atonement for his part in St Thomas Becket's murder. The church contains interesting Jacobean tombs, a 15C-lectern, carved pulpit, and rood screen.
The **Riverside Mill** is home to the **Devon Guild of Craftsmen** (open daily 10am–5.30pm; ♿ P ✕; ℘01626 832 223; www.crafts.org.uk), founded in 1954. This is the largest contemporary crafts centre in Southwest England, and exhibits a variety of top-quality local work.

▷ Retrace your steps and turn right towards Manaton.

The Becka Brook tumbles some 20m from the moor into the beautiful wooded glade occupied by **Becky Falls Woodland Park** ♣♣ (open mid-Feb–Oct daily 10am–5pm/dusk; £8.25, child £7.25; 🅿✕; 𝒫01647 221 259, www.beckyfalls-dartmoor.com). Children's activities include animal shows and feeding. The estate is criss-crossed by nature trails.

Moretonhampstead

The old market town of 'Moreton' was a coaching stage on the Exeter–Bodmin road. The 14C–15C granite **church** has a commanding west tower; note the unusual row of thatched, colonnaded granite **almshouses**, dating from 1637. About 2mi/3km west, in 20 acres/8ha of beautiful parkland, the **Miniature Pony Centre** ♣♣ (open daily Easter–Oct 10.30am–4.30pm/5pm in Jul–Aug; £8.50, child 3–16, £7.50; ♿🅿✕; 𝒫01647 432 400; www.miniatureponycentre.com) is a great favourite with young children.

◗ B 3212 towards Exeter, turn off for Dunsford and continue, passing the triple-arched 16C Fingle Bridge, to Drewsteignton.

Castle Drogo★

Open Mar–Oct daily 11am–5pm; but currently undergoing restoration. £11. Garden: open daily 10am–5.30pm, then 11am–4pm from Nov. ♿🅿✕ 𝒫01647 433 306. www.nationaltrust.org.uk/castle-drogo.

On discovering his descent from the 12C Norman nobleman Dru/Drogo, the grocery magnate, Julius Drewe, commissioned **Edwin Lutyens** (1869–1944) to create an extravagant castle to the glory of his name. The castle was built in 1911–30 of granite partly from Drewe's own quarry; the exterior shows Norman and Tudor influences while the interior is very much Lutyens at his best, including superb oak fittings.

Sticklepath

This attractive rural village is home to the **Finch Foundry** (open mid-Mar–Oct/Nov daily 11am–5pm; £6.70;

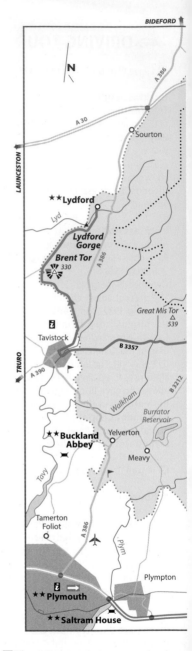

🅿✕ 𝒫01837 840 046; www.national-trust.org.uk/finch-foundry), a restored 19C edge-tool factory and water-powered forge, offering demonstrations of tools and waterwheels.

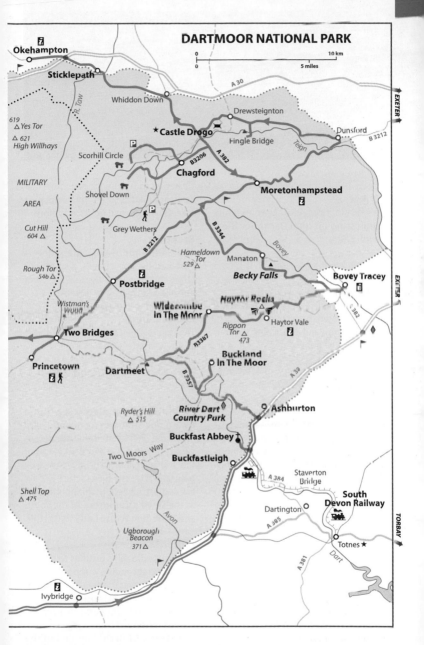

DARTMOOR NATIONAL PARK

0 _____ 10 km
0 _____ 5 miles

EXETER

Okehampton

Sticklepath

Whiddon Down

A 30

Drewsteignton

Dunsford

B 3212

★ Castle Drogo

Fingle Bridge

Teign

619 △ Yes Tor

△ 621
High Willhays

Scorhill Circle

B3206

Chagford

A 382

Moretonhampstead

MILITARY

AREA

Shovel Down

Cut Hill
604 △

Grey Wethers

B 3212

Hameldown
Tor
529 △

Manaton

Bovey

Becky Falls

Bovey Tracey

Rough Tor
546 △

Postbridge

Wistman's
Wood

Widecombe
in The Moor

Haytor Rocks

Rippon
Tor △
473

Haytor Vale

EXETER

A 382

Two Bridges

B3367

Princetown

Dartmeet

B 3357

Buckland
In The Moor

A 38

Ryder's Hill
△ 515

River Dart
Country Park

Ashburton

Buckfast Abbey

Two Moors Way

Buckfastleigh

Staverton
Bridge

A 384

South
Devon Railway

Shell Top
△ 475

Dartington

A 385

TORBAY

Avon

Ugborough
Beacon
371△

Totnes ★

A 381

Dart

Ivybridge

Okehampton

This market town was a Norman strongpoint and prospered during the great wool period. The ruins of **Okehampton Castle** (&. open Apr–Oct 10am–5pm (6pm Jul–Aug); £4.80; P; ✆ 01837 52844; www.english-heritage.org.uk), enjoy a picturesque setting. Initially a Norman motte and bailey, rebuilt in the 13C, it includes the gatehouses, barbican, outer and inner baileys, keep and stair turret. In town, an 18C mill is home to the **Museum of Dartmoor Life** (3 West Street; open

317

View from Brent Tor

Apr–Oct Mon–Fri 10am–3pm/1pm Sat; £3; &X; ✆01837 52295; www.museumofdartmoorlife.org.uk), with exhibits reminiscing on rural Dartmoor life a century ago.

▶ Return to the A382; left on B 3206.

Chagford

This thriving village, formerly a stannary (coinage) town, boasts several shops, cafés, old pubs and a charming covered market ('The Pepperpot').

▶ Return to Moretonhampstead and turn right (SW) on the B3212.

Postbridge

Clapper bridges – simple ancient structures of large flat granite slabs – are a feature of the moor. The famous Postbridge example has three openings spanned by slabs weighing up to 8 tons, each about 5m long, and is believed to date from the 13C, when tin-mining and farming were being developed.

Two Bridges

The Two Bridges, one a medieval clapper bridge, cross the West Dart at the junction of two ancient tracks.

Princetown

The town is dominated by a famous prison. Built 1806–08 to hold Napoleonic prisoners of war, it became one of the most feared prisons in the country. It is still in use, and the adjacent **Dartmoor Prison Museum** (open Mon–Thu and Sat 9.30am–4.30pm; Fri and Sun 9.30am–4pm; £3.50; www.dartmoor-prison.co.uk) relates its often grim history.

▶ Return to Two Bridges and take the Tavistock road (B 3357). In Tavistock, take the minor road right for Lydford.

Brent Tor

The 344m-hill of volcanic stone is crowned by St Michael's, a small 13C stone church with a low stalwart tower affording far-reaching **views★★**.

Lydford Gorge

The Stables. Open daily early-Mar–Sept 10am–5pm; Oct 10am–4pm; Nov–Christmas 11am–3.30pm. £8.90 (reduced rate in winter). &P X ✆01822 820 320. www.nationaltrust.org.uk/lydford-gorge.

This lush oak-wooded steep-sided river gorge stretches for 1.5mi/2.5km and is the deepest in the southwest. A variety of walks give excellent **views** of the river and glimpses of Dartmoor. One path leads via Pixie Glen to the Bell Cavern via the thundering whirlpool known as the **Devil's Cauldron**. At the south end is the 30m **White Lady Waterfall**.

Lydford★★

Lydford Castle ruins testifies to the village's ancient military importance as a Saxon outpost; the two-storey **keep** dates from 1195. Alongside is the 16C oak-timbered Tudor **Castle Inn**, which at one time served as the rector's house. **St Petroc's Church**, founded in the 6C, was rebuilt and enlarged on Norman foundations in the 13C, the south aisle and tower in the 15C, and further changes were made in the 19C.

North Devon★★

North Devon changes in character from east to west. The long sandy beaches of traditional resorts such as Ilfracombe end at Westward Ho!, with dramatic rocky foreshores at Clovelly and Hartland Point. Inland are relaxed market towns, such as Barnstaple and Bideford.

ILFRACOMBE★

The most popular resort on the North Devon coast, pretty coves and cliff scenery are set against a backdrop of attractive wooded hills and valleys.

The hills around the town provide good vantage points for surveying the area: **Capstone Hill** (47m) offers a good **view★** of the town, the harbour mouth, the rock-enclosed bays and beaches; **Hillsborough** at the centre of the pleasure ground, rises to 136m and affords an extensive coastal **view★★**.

A 20m high bronze-clad sculpture, *Verity*, created by Damien Hirst, was unveiled in 2012 beside the harbour on Ilfracombe's pier.

The **Holy Trinity** parish church is Norman (enlarged 14C) and has an ancient, elaborately carved **wagon roof★★**.

In the early 14C the beacon set as a marker on Lantern Hill was replaced by a **mariners' chapel** (St Nicholas' Chapel; Lantern Hill, open Easter–Oct daily 10am–4pm (May–Sept 6pm); www.visitilfracombe.co.uk), which still shines a red light to guide shipping. From the rock platform on which the chapel stands there is a good **view★** over the almost land-locked harbour and out to sea.

In the 19C the hill between the road and the sea was tunnelled and the rock cove, on the far side, made accessible. The cove was then equipped with a sea wall to prevent the tide running out and so provide all-day **bathing beaches** 👪 (Granville Road; open subject to tide: Apr and Oct 10am–5pm; May–Jun and Sept 10am–6pm; Jul–Aug 10am–7pm; £2.50, child £1.95; ♿✗; www.tunnelsbeaches.co.uk).

👁 **Michelin Map:** Michelin Atlas p 6 or Map 503 H 30.

ℹ **Info: Ilfracombe:** Landmark Theatre, The Seafront. ☎01271 863 001; www.visitilfracombe.co.uk; **Barnstaple:** The Square, . ☎01271 346 747. www.staynorthdevon.co.uk.

◐ **Location:** Ilfracombe lies on the coast, just west of Exmoor National Park.

◉ **Don't Miss:** Arlington Court; Clovelly; Lundy Island.

👪 **Kids:** Tunnels Beaches; Watermouth Castle.

👪 Watermouth Castle

1ml/1.6km SE on the A 399. Open: check website for variable opening hours. £14, child under 92cm, free. 🅿 ✗ ☎01271 867 474. www.watermouthcastle.com. Overlooking picturesque Watermouth Cove, this Victorian folly castle is a handsome sight. Its landscaped gardens and buildings host a lively theme park for young children.

BARNSTAPLE★

13mi/21km S of Ilfracombe.
ℹ Museum of Barnstaple and North Devon, The Square. ☎01271 375 000.
Barnstaple is the regional centre and its 19C cast iron-and-glass **Pannier Market** (open Mon–Sat 9am–4pm; ☎01271 379084; www.barnstaple.co.uk/pannier-market), is always busy selling local produce (Tue, Fri and Sat) arts and crafts (Mon and Thu) and antiques and collectables (Wed). For the best in fresh meat, visit adjoining **Butchers' Row**.
Long Bridge★ (158m) was first built c.1273; three of its 16 stone arches were replaced c.1539.
The 13C **parish church** is notable for its memorial monuments and its 17C lead-covered spire. The 17C **Horwood Almshouses** and **Alice Horwood School** (*Church Lane*) have attractive wooden mullioned windows. The 19C **Guildhall** (*High Street*; open Apr–Oct

319

Sat 10am–2pm; to visit at other times call ℘01237 373 003) contains the Dodde-ridge Parlour, panelled in 17C oak, in which the town's collection of corpora-tion plate is displayed.

The **Museum of North Devon** (The Square; Mon–Sat 10am–4pm/5pm; ♿✕; ℘01271 346 747; www.barnstapl-emuseum.org.uk) traces regional history. Downriver from the bridge is the colon-naded **Queen Anne's Walk** (1609), built as a merchants' exchange and crowned by a statue of Queen Anne. Amid the colonnades in a former 19C bathhouse is a local heritage centre.

On the road between **Clovelly** and Barnstaple lie two of Devon's best and most popular children's attractions, the **Milky Way** (www.themilkyway.co.uk) and **The Big Sheep** (www.thebigsheep. co.uk). Both are farm-themed but with lots of rides, shows and activities.

ARLINGTON COURT★★

8mi/13km NE of Barnstaple on the A 39. Open Feb half-term week and mid-Mar–Oct daily 11am–5pm (Feb 4pm). Nov–21 Dec Sat–Sun only, 11am–4pm. £11. ℘01271 850 296. www.nationaltrust. org.uk/arlington-court.

This Classically styled house (1820–23) contains the varied collections of *objets d'art* accumulated by its former owner, Miss Rosalie Chichester (1865–1949), the most remarkable of which is her collection of **model ships**, including 36 made by Napoleonic prisoners of war. The house is also home to the National Trust **Carriage Museum**.

CLOVELLY★★

30mi/48km SW of Ilfracombe. Entry via visitor centre: summer 9am–6pm; rest of year call for details. £7.25, child 7–16, £4.40. 🅿✕ ℘01237 431 781. www.clovelly.co.uk.

This appealing and attractive village, mentioned in the Domesday Book, is now privately owned. The **visitor centre** outlines its history as a fisher-men's community and its preservation. The steep, stepped and cobbled **High Street**, known as **Down-a-long** or **Up-a-long** (depending on the direc-tion being faced), is lined with small, whitewashed 18C and 19C houses decked with bright flowers. Donkeys and mules are still the only form of transport up and down the High Street. En route are two small museums (one devoted to **Charles Kingsley** who lived in the village as a child) and, just before the Visitor Centre, **Clovelly Court Gar-dens**. At the bottom of the High Street lies **Quay Pool**, the small, restored 14C harbour protected from the open sea by a curving breakwater which offers a **view** extending from Lundy to Baggy Point. The pebble beach is backed by stone-built cottages and balconied houses, the old harbour lime-kiln, the inn and the lifeboat store.

Just west (4.5mi/7km) is the village of Hartland, the gateway to **Hartland Point** (3mi/5km north), the spectacular rocky apex of North Devon, comparable to Land's End for its drama and a ship-ping graveyard over the centuries.

LUNDY ISLAND★★

2h by MS *Oldenburg* from Bideford Quay all year, also from Ilfracombe Pier (summer only). £65 day return, child £33. ℘01271 863 636.
www.lundyisland.co.uk.

Lying 12mi/19km north west of Clo-velly, Lundy derives its name from the Icelandic word for puffin, *Lunde*. The attraction is its fascinating bird- and marine-life, in a peaceful setting free of many of the trappings of modern life including cars.

Despite the name, however, there are reportedly only 30 breeding pairs of puffins here (May–Jul). Lundy has been designated a **Marine Nature Reserve** since 1986, with grey seals, basking sharks and porpoises. Clear waters and several wrecks mean excellent diving. A complete circuit of the island is 11mi/18km (4h on foot), with a pub and various points of historical inter-est en route.

TORRIDGE ESTUARY

The principal settlement along the Torridge is the small market town of **Bideford (**10mi/16km W of

Barnstaple); its 17C quay is from where fishing boats and the Lundy ferry sail. Don't miss the views from the new bridge over the River Torridge, which take in its 24-arch 16C stone bridge. Bideford hosts a lively pannier market (Tue and Sat).

Appledore (3mi/5km north) is a charming old-fashioned fishing village with narrow cobbled streets, pastel-washed cottages and the small **North Devon Maritime Museum** (open Apr–Oct 10.30am–5pm; £3; ☎01237 422 064; www.northdevonmaritimemuseum. co.uk), which offers and insight into the shipbuilding and seafaring history of the region.

Exmoor★★

This great southwest moor (267sq mi/692sq km) on the boundary between North Devon and Somerset is one of Britain's national parks. Red deer, wild Exmoor ponies, sheep and cattle still roam the moor, which is vividly described in R D Blackmore's classic novel *Lorna Doone* (1869). Exmoor's coastline is in places rugged and wild but also home to popular seaside resorts, such as Minehead.

Michelin Map:
Michelin Atlas pp 6, 7 or Map 503 8 I, J 30.

Info: www.visit-exmoor. co.uk, www.visitsomerset. co.uk, www.exmoor-nationalpark.gov.uk. Visitor centres give information on paths, cycle routes, bridleways, guided walks and nature trails.

Location: On the Bristol Channel coast of Southwest England.

Don't Miss: The views from Dunkery Beacon; Dunster Castle; Watersmeet; Tarr Steps.

DULVERTON★

Southern Exmoor off A 396.
National Park Centre, 7–9 Fore Street. ☎01643 323 841.
www.exmoor-nationalpark.gov.uk.
The southern gateway to Exmoor National Park, Dulverton sits amid beautiful scenery and boasts a solid church (rebuilt in the 19C) with a 13C west tower and pretty cottages.
Set in a National Nature Reserve, **Tarr Steps★★**, the finest **clapper bridge** (see Dartmoor) in the country, dating back to the Middle Ages or earlier, crosses the River Barle near Liscombe, 6mi/10km north of Dulverton,.

DUNSTER★★

16mi north of Duverton, near the coast.
National Park Centre, Dunster Steep. ☎01643 821 835.
The beautiful old town of Dunster, right on the northeast edge of Exmoor, enjoyed a flourishing coastal and continental trade until the sea retreated in the 15C–16C, whereupon it became a wool market and weaving centre. It is now a popular tourist destination in season. The red sandstone **castle★★** (castle open early Mar–Oct daily 10am–5pm; £11; P(£3); ☎01643 821 314, www. nationaltrust.org.uk), dominates the town from the tor on which a fortification has stood since Saxon times. The castle was begun by the Norman baron William de Mohun and in 1867 transformed to its present fortified Jacobean mansion.
Dunster Working Watermill★ (Mill Lane; open daily 10am–5pm/dusk; £7 inc NT members; ☎; ☎01643 821 759; www. nationaltrust.org.uk) on the River Avill, rebuilt and improved since Domesday,

Literary Associations

The 14C thatched pub, the **Rising Sun Inn** Lynmouth, is said to have sheltered **R D Blackmore** while he wrote *Lorna Doone*. In 1797 the poets **Wordsworth** and **Coleridge** arrived here, having walked 30mi/48km from Nether Stowey. While staying at Culbone nearby (now called Ash Farm), Coleridge began his poem *Kubla Khan*. In 1812, the disowned young poet **Shelley** came to Lynmouth with his 16-year-old 'bride' Harriet Westbrook and attendants. During his stay, Shelley distributed his revolutionary pamphlet, the *Declaration of Rights*: some he sealed inside bottles wrapped in oiled cloth and packed into crates fitted with a sail before being launched from the beach; others he despatched in balloons.

ground corn until the late-19C, came back into use during the Second World War and was rebuilt and restored to working order in 1979–80.

The long, wide **High Street** lined by 17C–19C houses is graced by the unique 17C octagonal, dormered **Yarn Market**. Many of the buildings along **Church Street** are related to the priory founded in 1090, including the 14C nunnery and Priest's House (restored 19C) and 6m-high early medieval **dovecote★** (beyond the gate in the end wall of the Priory Garden). **St George's Church★** was originally built by the Normans in the 12C then rebuilt by the monks in the 14C. Its 34m **tower**, dating from 1443, houses a carillon. Inside are **wagon roofs**, a splendid 16m carved **screen**, a 16C Perpendicular **font** and the **Luttrell tombs**.

WINSFORD★

8mi/13km N of Dulverton.

Tucked away in a valley Winsford is often cited as Exmoor's most attractive village and is notable for its series of eight bridges crossing its many small streams in quick succession, the oldest being the **packhorse bridge**, possibly from the 17C.

EXFORD

Central Exmoor, 10mi northwest of Dulverton.

On the River Exe, at the very heart of Exmoor National Park, lies Exford with its attractive village green surrounded by shops, restaurants and hotels. It is a busy walking, fishing and equestrian centre. Some 6mi/10km north east is **Dunkery Beacon**, at 520m, the highest point on the moor, visible for miles around, with commanding **view★★★**.

MINEHEAD

19mi north of Dulverton, on the coast.
🛈 ☎01643 702 624.
www.mineheadtowncouncil.co.uk.
Minehead is the region's only real 'bucket-and-spade' resort, boasting a large sandy beach. It is dominated by Butlins holiday camp, the largest in the UK. It has a good beach and is the northern terminus of the **West Somerset Railway** (☞*see Mendips and Quantocks*).

LYNTON AND LYNMOUTH★

🛈 Town Hall, Lee Road, Lynton. ☎0845 458 3775. www.lynton-lynmouth-tourism.co.uk.
🛈 National Park Centre, The Esplanade, Lynmouth. 01598 752 509.
www.exmoor-nationalpark.gov.uk
These complementary towns sit in a hollow at the top, and at the foot of 152m North Devon cliffs, and enjoy glorious **views★** across the Bristol Channel to the distant Welsh coast.

Lynmouth, at the foot of the cliffs, remains a traditional fishing village with small stone cottages and houses. Directly above, Lynton is predominantly Victorian–Edwardian in character.

Linking the two is the small funicular **Cliff Railway** (open mid-Feb–mid-Nov, daily, 10am–dusk; ☎01549 753 486; ♿; www.cliffrailwaylynton.co.uk), which operates at a gradient of 1:1.75 ascending approx 152m. There are two cars, each of which has a huge water tank which is filled at the top and emptied at the bottom, thus causing the lower car to be pulled up to Lynton, while the heavier car from the top descends to Lynmouth. The railway was officially opened in 1890 and offers spectacular **views**.

Most visitors make the ascent to visit the **Valley of the Rocks★** (1mi/1.6km W of the railway), great jagged formations spectacularly carved by the wind rising from a wide grass-covered valley. Housed in Lynton's oldest surviving domestic dwelling, the **Lyn & Exmoor Museum** (open Easter–Oct Tue Thu and Sat; £2, ✆ 01392 265967; www. devonmuseums.net) includes the story of the tragic Lynmouth flood of 1952 that killed 34 people.

OARE

6mi/10km E of Lynmouth.

This tiny village owes its fame entirely to **Lorna Doone**. The Doone family is said to have lived here and it was in the restored 14C 15C church that Lorna was married to John Ridd. A path leads to **Doone valley★** (6mi/10km), made famous by Blackmore's novel, based on tales of a group of outlaws and cutthroats in the 1620s.

PORLOCK★

11.5mi/18.5km E of Lynmouth.
🚹 ✆01643 863 150.
www.porlock.co.uk/visitors.

This is an attractive much-visited village with old thatched cottages and a good selection of shops, cafés, restaurants and places to stay. It was made famous by 'the man from Porlock', who interrupted Coleridge as he was writing *Kubla Khan* (☾ *see Box opposite*).

The 13C **St Dubricius church★** with its truncated shingle-covered spire is dedicated to a legendary figure who lived until he was 120 and is said to have been a friend of King Arthur. Inside is a remarkable canopied tomb with alabaster effigies. Motorists should beware

that **Porlock Hill**, part of the A39, is one of the UK's steepest roads, with a gradient that reaches 1-in-4 (25 percent). It can be by-passed by a toll road.

WATERSMEET★

1.5mi/2.4km E of Lynmouth. Open: site freely accessible dawn–dusk. www.nationaltrust.org.uk/watersmeet.

This very popular beauty spot is where the rivers East Lyn and Hoaroak meet in a deep wooded valley, the riverbed picturesquely strewn with boulders around which the water swirls endlessly. It is worth a visit alone for its charming **Edwardian tearoom and gardens**.

COMBE MARTIN★

12.8mi west of Lynmouth.
🚹 ✆01271 889 031.
www.visitcombemartin.com.

This sprawling village is situated in a beautiful fertile valley and its two headlands – Great Hangman and Little Hangman – funnel visitors into the village, then down to the pretty, sheltered harbour and beach.

Just outside the village (1mi/1.6km south), set in over 12ha of spectacular gardens, is **The Wildlife and Dinosaur Adventure Park** 👥 (open mid-Feb–early Nov daily 10am–5pm; £14.50, child £12.50 – online booking discounts; ✕; ✆01271 882 486; www.devontheme-park.co.uk). This features lions, sea lions, meerkats, lemurs, birds of prey shows, a tropical house, Earthquake Canyon, Tomb of the Phaoraohs, and animatronic dinosaurs.

On the same road, heading further south (7.5mi/12km south of Combe Martin), **Exmoor Zoo** 👥 (open daily mid-Feb–May and mid-Sept–Oct 10am–5pm/dusk; mid-May–mid-Sept 10am–6pm; Nov–mid-Feb 10am–4pm/dusk; closed 24–26 Dec; £12.95, child £9.50, ♿✕; ✆01598 763 352; www.exmoorzoo. co.uk) features mostly smaller animals among its 175 species though the star attractions are its two black leopards.

South Cornwall Coast★

Immediately west of bustling historic Plymouth (⊙see p310) the picture-postcard villages and beaches of holidaymakers' Cornwall begin. The relatively sheltered conditions make this a yachtsman's paradise. Inland, the climate is benevolent, encouraging some of England's finest gardens.

⊷DRIVING TOUR

1 PLYMOUTH – MORWENSTOW

◐ Leave Plymouth on A 38. After Landrake, take the left to St Germans. ⊙Map pp326–327.

St Germans

In the centre of this delightful old village are a group of Tudor **almshouses** (1583) and a beautiful **church★** with a carved-stone **Norman arch** at the west front and a **window** by Burne-Jones and William Morris.

◐ Take the A387 towards Looe.
At Polperro you must park at the entrance to the village and take the horse-drawn cart or electric bus to the centre.

Polperro★

The closely packed cottages and winding alleys of this attractive old fishing village lie at the bottom of the steep road which follows the stream down to the double harbour in the creek.
A converted pilchard factory on the waterfront houses the small **Heritage Museum** (open Mar–Oct daily 10.30am–5.30pm; £1.60; ✆01503 272 423; www.polperro.org/museum.html), devoted to fishing and smuggling.

◐ Follow the coast road to Polruan, where a ferry crosses the Fowey estuary.

- **Michelin Map:** Michelin Atlas pp 2, 3 or Map 503 D to H 32, 33.
- **Info:** Boscawen Street, Truro. ✆01872 261 735. www.visitcornwall.com.
- **Don't Miss:** The Eden Project; Trewithen Garden; Fowey.
- **Kids:** National Seal Sanctuary; Kynance Cove; Mullion Cove.
- **Parking:** Park on the edge of towns and villages as the streets can be narrow.

Fowey★★

✆01726 833 616.
www.fowey.co.uk.
This small town (pronounced 'foy'), dates from the 11C, and was once one of England's busiest ports. It is set on the hillside above a superb natural harbour at the mouth of the River Fowey.
In town, **Fore Street** is lined with picturesque old houses. The 14C–15C **church of St Nicholas** (on the site of a Norman church dedicated to St Fimbarrus) boasts a tall, pinnacled tower, a two-storey porch in Decorated style, a fine wagon roof and a Norman font. Walk out to **Gribbin Head**, from where there are **views★★** for miles around, and take a **boat trip** round the harbour and coast, where the cliffs rise dark and sheer from the water, or up river between wooded hillsides.

◐ Take the road towards St Austell and at the town entrance go right at the roundabout on the A391, then follow the signs to the Eden Project.

Eden Project★

Open daily 10am/10.30am–4pm/6pm; see website for seasonal opening details. Closed 25 Dec. £27.50; advance online booking discount, and reduced rates Mon–Thu from Aug onwards after 3.30pm. ⅏🅿✕ ✆01726 811 972. www.edenproject.com.

As one of the Landmark Millennium Projects in the UK, an abandoned china-clay pit (60m deep) was converted into an extraordinary gigantic botanical 'green theme park' project. It has been both critically acclaimed and a huge commercial success. Here the plant world, the conservation of natural habitats and indigenous species and man's dependence on plants for food and medicine can be studied by visitors in the context of global biodiversity.

The star features are the **Rainforest Biome**, and **The Mediterranean Biome,** vast multi-faceted glasshouses, the larger of the two measuring 60m high with a 100m span. The highlight, quite literally, is the Rainforest Aerial Walkway, where you can take a spectacular walk among the treetops.The most recent addition to this stunning architectural ensemble is **The Core**, which takes its inspiration from the tree, incorporating a central trunk and canopy roof that shades the ground and harvests the sun. This is devoted mostly to educational aspects and art exhibitions. All sorts of events and tours are staged throughout the year, the dining facilities are first class and the latest attraction is **SkyWire** (£18), the UK fastest and longest zipwire with speeds of up to 60mph over its course.

▷ Return to St Austell, take the A 390, then almost immediately turn left onto the B 3273.

Mevagissey★
This picturesque old fishing village, with its old quayside boathouses and sail lofts, maze of twisting backstreets and nets of all shapes and colours drying on walls, attracts crowds of visitors all summer. It boasts an unusual double harbour with a 1770s pier.

▷ Follow the St Ewe road for 1mi/1.6km.

Lost Gardens of Heligan★
Pentewan. Open daily (except 24–25 Dec) 10am–6pm (5pm Oct–Mar). £14.50.
&🅿✕ ☎01726 845 100.
www.heligan.com.

Coastal Paths

Remoteness and wildness are the charms of the Cornwall peninsula with its long rugged coastline. The Cornwall Coast Path – part of the larger Southwest Coast Path – winds a sinuous course (268mi/431km) above the sheer cliffs and indented coves and is the ideal way to discover the scenic splendours of the peninsula. The footpath is clearly waymarked and there is a wide choice of inland paths.

These 23ha gardens, originally laid out in the 18C by Thomas Gray but left to grow wild by the 20C, have been painstakingly recovered from dereliction since 1991. They include Flora's Garden (rhododendrons), a walled vegetable garden, fruit orchards, 'The Jungle' (exotic trees planted in the 19C) and 'The Lost Valley' (indigenous species and a water-meadow).

Roseland peninsula
Veryan★ – This village's unique charm comes from four curious little white-walled **round houses** with Gothic windows and conical thatched roofs, surmounted by a cross.

St Just-in-Roseland★★ – The **church** here, built on a 6C Celtic site in the 13C and restored in the 19C, has a remarkable setting in an enchanting churchyard garden, close to the creek and little harbour.

St Mawes Castle★ – In 1539–43 Henry VIII constructed this cloverleaf-shaped **castle★** (open Apr–Sept daily 10am–6pm; Oct 10am–5pm; rest of year times vary, check website for details; £5.40; ☎01326 270 526; www.english-heritage.org.uk), with motte and bailey, as a pair with Pendennis Castle (on the opposite bank of the River Fal) to safeguard the 1mi/1.6km entrance to the estuary. Situated in lovely gardens, it affords excellent **views★** right out to Manacle Point (10mi/16km).

◐ Take the B 289 towards Truro and the ferry across the waterway of the Carrick Roads.

Trelissick Garden★★

House: Open mid-Feb–Oct daily 11am–5.30pm; check website for rest of year times. £10.90. ♿🅿(£4). ✗ ✆01872 862 090. www.nationaltrust.org.uk/trelissick.

From the gardens beyond the Classical, porticoed house (built 1750, remodelled 1825), there are superb **views★★** over the park, Falmouth and out to sea. The woodland dropping down to the river has a variety of trees, shrubs, exotics and perennials. Spacious areas of lawn feature hydrangeas (over 130 varieties), azaleas and rhododendrons.

◐ Turn right onto the A 390.

Truro

🚉 ✆01872 274 555. www.visittruro.org.uk.

Once a river port and mining centre, Truro is the finest Georgian town west of Bath, with a host of 18C houses.

Just south of St Clement Street is **Truro cathedral** (open Mon–Sat 7.30am–5pm, Sun noon–4pm. Bank Holidays 9.30am–6pm; £5 suggested donation; Guided tours Apr–Oct Mon–Thu 11am; ♿✗; ✆01872 276 782, www.truro cathedral.org.uk). Completed 1910, this Gothic Revival building features upswept vaulting, vistas through tall arcades and, outside, three steeple towers which give the building its characteristic outline.

A short walk west, via Boscawen Street, is the **Royal Cornwall Museum★** (River Street; open Tue–Sat 10am–4.45pm, Sun 10am–4pm: £5.50; ♿✗; ✆01872 272 205, www.royalcornwallmuseum.org.uk). Cornwall's oldest and most prestigious museum is home to a variety of artefacts relating to the geology, archaeol-

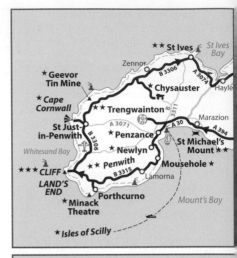

ogy and social history of Cornwall, a section on World Cultures, and a collection of significant works by nationally and internationally important artists from all over the world.

◐ Rejoin the A 390; E for 6mi/10km.

Trewithen★

Grampground Road. **Garden**: open Mar–Jun daily 10am–4.30pm. **House**: Visit only by

CORNISH COAST

guided tour Mar–Jun Mon and Tue only
2–4pm (booking advisable).
£8.50 house or gardens, £15 combined
tariff. ♿🅿✕ ☎01726 883 647.
www.trewithengardens.co.uk.
Trewithen estate is famous for its 11ha
of beautiful landscape and woodland
gardens which include, in season,
magnificent banks of rhododendrons,
camellias and magnolias.
The gardens provide an elegant setting for a fine Georgian **country house**
(1715–55) containing period furniture,
paintings and porcelain.

▶ Turn left onto the A 39.

Falmouth★

Once the busiest provincial port in
England, Falmouth is now one of Cornwall's principal holiday resorts, though
it has retained much of its unspoiled
marine atmosphere. Standing guard
seaward, **Pendennis castle★** (open

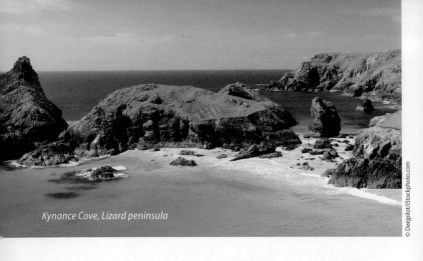

Kynance Cove, Lizard peninsula

© Deejpilot/iStockphoto.com

Apr–Sept daily 10am–6pm; Oct 5pm; Nov–Christmas and Jan–mid-Feb Sat–Sun 10am–4pm; Feb holidays daily 10am–4pm; closed 1 Jan, 24–26 Dec; £8.40; &P✕; ℘01326 316 594; www.english-heritage.org.uk), is the sister to **St Mawes** (℘*see above)* across the Fal, on the point.

In the centre of town, Falmouth **Art Gallery** (open Mon–Sat 10am–5pm; closed 25 Dec–1 Jan; &; ℘01326 313 863; www.falmouthartgallery.com), contains a good selection of maritime, Victorian and early-20C paintings.

Housed in a new waterfront building, with spectacular views, the recently refurbished **National Maritime Museum Cornwall★** (open daily 10am–5pm; closed 25–26 Dec; £12.95; &P✕; ℘01326 313 388; www.nmmc.co.uk), is one of the region's finest collections, with many historic small boats plus superb displays on smuggling, local shipbuilding and much more.

Dancing Furries

On 8 May (or the previous Saturday if this falls on a Sunday or Monday), Helston town is closed to traffic for the famous **Flora Day Furry Dance★★**. Five processional dances are performed along a 1.8–2.4mi/3–4km route (beginning and ending at the Guildhall), including the children's procession at 10am and the Invitation Dance for couples at noon.

Glendurgan Garden★★

Mawnan Smith. 4mi/6km) south of Falmouth on a minor road. Open spring and summer Tue–Sun and bank holiday Mons (Aug Mon–Sat) 10.30am–5.30pm. £9; P (£2) &✕ ℘01326 252 020. www.nationaltrust.org.uk/glendurgan. This beautiful garden, richly planted with subtropical trees and shrubs, drops down to Durgan hamlet on the Helford River. It is home to an interesting laurel maze and a maypole.

Lizard peninsula★

This southernmost part of England is famous for its rocky coves and its glossy green-and-black serpentine stone. **The Cornish Seal Sanctuary★** (▲▲; Gweek; open daily from 10am, call for closing times; closed 25 Dec; from £10.46, online discounts; &P✕; ℘01326 221 361, www.sealsanctuary.co.uk), set on the picturesque **Helford estuary**, has been rescuing seals for 50 years and always has a number of residents.

On the south side of the estuary is the **Manacles** (an underwater reef responsible for many a shipwreck); the famous old fishing and smuggling village of **Coverack★**; **Landewednack★** with its thatched roofs and **church★** decorated with serpentine stone; the Lizard and its 1751 lighthouse (altered in 1903) on the southernmost tip of England; and the popular picture-postcard **beaches** of **Kynance Cove★★** ▲▲ and **Mullion Cove★★** ▲▲. **Helston** is the peninsula's market town.

North Cornwall Coast★

This is probably the most dramatic stretch of the Cornish peninsula, in places harsh and forbidding, formerly feared by mariners for its wrecking potential. Yet it is also home to beautiful golden sand beaches, the most popular of which are at Newquay, Britain's premier surf resort.

🚗 **DRIVING TOUR**

② MORWENSTOW TO ST AGNES BEACON

◖ North–south on the A 39 and coastal B roads. *Map pp326–327*

Morwenstow

Cornwall's northernmost parish boasts a fine **church★** with a Norman door and spectacular **cliffs★★** (137m high) reaching out to offshore rocks.

Bude

This cliffside harbour town is a popular resort with golden sandy beaches and breakers ideal for surfing. The **breakwater★★** has a good sea view.

Poundstock★

The 13C–15C **church★**, with its square unbuttressed tower and square 14C font, the lychgate and the unique, sturdily built 14C **guildhouse★** form a secluded group in a wooded dell.

Boscastle★

🛈 ℘01840 250 010.
www.visitboscastleandtintagel.com.
The pretty village straggles downhill to a picturesque natural harbour inlet between 91m headlands.

Tintagel

17mi/27km SW of Bude. 🛈 ℘01840 779 084. www.visitboscastleandtintagel.com.
Tintagel in particular and the West Country in general are associated

◖ **Michelin Map:** Michelin Atlas pp 2, 3 or Map 503 D to H 32, 33.
🛈 www.visitcornwall.com.
◎ **Don't Miss:** Tate St Ives; Land's End cliff scenery; Minack Open-Air Theatre; St Michael's Mount.
👫 **Kids:** Newquay Zoo; the Southwest's sand beaches, Land's End; Geevor Tin Mine.
🅿 **Parking:** Park on the edge of towns and villages as the streets can be narrow.

with the elusive legend of **Arthur**, '… the once and future king'. According to the 12C romantic novelist Geoffery of Monmouth, Arthur was fathered at **Tintagel castle★** (open daily Apr–Sept 10am–6pm, Oct 10am–5pm, Nov–Mar daily half-term hols, otherwise Sat–Sun only 10am–4pm; closed 1 Jan, 24–26 Dec; £8.40; ✗; ℘01840 770 328; www.english-heritage.org.uk), which occupies a dramatic **site★★★** overlooking the sea from precipitous rocks. The site is more impressive than the fragmentary castle ruin, which includes walls from the 1145 chapel and great hall, built on the site of a 6C Celtic monastery, and other walls dating from the 13C – all centuries after Arthur's time.

On Fore Street is the **Old Post Office★** (open daily: Feb half-term week, then Mar–Oct 11am–4pm/Apr–Sept 10.30am–5.30pm; £4; ℘01840 770 024; www.nationaltrust.org.uk) a small atmospheric, compact manor house with thick walls and undulating slate roofs dating from the 14C. The house has simple country furniture and a delightful cottage garden.

Padstow★

The harbour is enclosed by quays lined with attractive old houses. Behind the quay a network of narrow streets ends at **St Petroc's Church** and **Prideaux Place★** (open Easter Sun–early Oct, Sun–Thu 1.30–4pm; grounds open Sun–

Coast viewed from Tintagel Castle

Thu 12.30–5pm; ✆01841 532 411; www.prideauxplace.co.uk), an Elizabethan house, set in gardens and landscaped parkland.

In recent years Padstow has become a shrine to **seafood**, thanks to chef, restaurateur and TV presenter **Rick Stein**. He first opened a seafood restaurant here in 1974 and now operates four restaurants, four shops and a cookery school.

Trevone

The **Cornwall Coast Path**★★ (5mi/8km on foot) is a spectacular way of reaching Trevone from Padstow, circling the 74m Stepper Point and passing the natural rock arches of Porthmissen Bridge. The village and chapel (with a slate spire) stand in a small, sandy cove guarded by fierce offshore rocks. A large blowhole leading directly down to the sea can be found in one of the cliffs.

Trevose Head★

6mi/10km W on the B 3276 and by-roads; last 0.5mi/0.8km on foot.
From the lighthouse on the 74m head, it is possible to see that of Hartland Point, 40mi/64km northeast, and that of Pendeen on West Penwith. The **views**★★ take in bay after sandy cove after rocky island.

Bedruthan Steps★

Cliff staircase open Mar–Oct. ✗.
A much-photographed long arc of sand (1mi/1.5km), spectacularly scattered with giant rocks worn to the same angle by waves and wind, is visible over the cliff edge. Legend has it that the rocks were the stepping stones of the giant Bedruthan.

Newquay

This popular, sometimes rowdy resort, with its sandy beaches, lies at the foot of cliffs in a sheltered, north-facing bay. By the 18C Newquay was a pilchard port, exporting salted fish to Italy and Spain. The **Huar's House** on the headland, from which the *huar* summoned the fishermen when he saw shoals of fish enter the bay, dates from this period. Newquay has recently enjoyed a surfing-led revival and hosts world-class competitions.

In Trenance Gardens in the centre of town, is **Newquay Zoo**★ (👥👤; open daily from 10am–4.30pm/5pm; closed 25 Dec; £13.20, child 3–15, £9.90; ♿️🅿️ (charge); ✗; ✆01637 873 342; www.newquay-zoo.co.uk). This is Cornwall's biggest zoo, with over 130 species and is at the forefront of conservation, education and innovative enclosure design. Set in beautiful gardens, it specialises in breeding many endangered smaller species.

Trerice★

Kestle Mill. **House and garden:** Open mid-Feb–Oct daily 11am–5pm. **Great Hall and garden: early** Nov–21 Dec Sat–Sun 11am–3.30pm; £9.45. ⚡🅿✕ 🕿 01637 875 404. www.nationaltrust. org.uk/trerice.

This small, silver-grey stone Elizabethan **manor house** was rebuilt 1572–73. The east front has a highly ornate exterior and interior notable for the quality of its 16C **plasterwork** and fine furniture.

St Agnes Beacon★

The beacon, at 191m, affords a **panorama★★** from Trevose Head to St Michael's Mount, with the typical north Cornish landscape, windswept and punctuated by old mine stacks.

Penwith★★

Cornwall

Penwith is the most westerly headland in England, famous for **Land's End** with its spectacular cliffs and coastal scenery staring out to America. Much of the area is a semi-bare plateau standing around 130m above sea level. This sparsely populated region has its own bleak beauty deriving from its granite foundation, the wind, the blue of the ocean and its small granite churches and Celtic wayside crosses. The principal settlements of this largely rural district are Penzance and Newlyn, both continuing the age-old Cornish fishing tradition, and St Ives, one of the West Country's favourite resorts. **Leave the coast road for clifftop views and to enjoy Penwith's many beautiful golden sandy beaches.**

🚗DRIVING TOUR

Penwith Coast (🕑map pp326–327)

St Michael's Mount★★

Causeway from Marazion. Access at high tide by ferry; at low water on foot across the sands and causeway. **Castle:** open Apr–Oct Sun–Fri 10.30am–5pm (Jul and Aug 5.30pm). **Garden:** open mid-Apr–Jun Mon–Fri 10.30am–5pm. Jul–Sept

😊 **Don't Miss:** Land's End and St Michael's Mount views.

open Thu–Fri only. £9.50 castle; £14 inc garden. ⚡🕿 🕿 01736 710 265. www.stmichaelsmount.co.uk.

According to Cornish legend, in the year 495, fishermen saw the archangel Michael on the granite rock rising out of the sea. The island became a place of pilgrimage and a Celtic monastery is said to have stood on the rock from the 8C to the 11C. In c.1150 Abbot Bernard of Mont St-Michel, off the coast of Normandy, built a Benedictine monastery here. It was appropriated by the crown in 1425 and dissolved in 1539. The rock frequently served as a strongpoint from the Middle Ages to 1647, when its last military commander, Colonel John St Aubyn, bought the **castle** as a family residence. It is now a hybrid of 14C–19C styles, with a Tudor doorway bearing the St Aubyn arms, a 14C entrance hall, a restored 14C church with 15C windows, and an 18C Rococo-Gothic drawing room.

Trengwainton Garden★★

Open mid-Feb–Oct Sun–Thu and Good Fri, 10.30am–5pm. Early to mid-Dec Fri and Sun 10.30am–4pm. £8.10. ⚡🅿✕ 🕿 01736 363 148. www.nationaltrust.org.uk.

The garden's splendid rhododendron and azalea collection stems from the late-1920s when specimens were brought back from Burma, Assam and China. From here is a **view★★** of Mount's Bay. A series of walled gardens contains magnolias and other flowering trees.

Penzance★

🚉 Station Approach. ℘01736 335530.
This busy market town, built largely post-1800, has been a popular holiday resort for over 150 years (since the arrival of the Great Western Railway). The 0.5mi-/0.8km-long **Western Promenade** reflects 19C Penzance's importance as a resort. The harbour area has a wonderful **outlook★★★** over Mount's Bay and St Michael's Mount. It is from here that the *Scillonian III* sails to the **Isles of Scilly**.

The town centre, particularly **Market Jew Street** and **Chapel Street★**, boasts some attractive 17C, 18C and 19C buildings including the grand Classical Market House, the exotic Egyptian House (1835) with its extraordinary facade, Abbey House, and The Admiral Benbow pub. Close by, the **Penlee House Gallery and Museum★** (Morrab Road; open Apr–Oct Mon–Sat 10am–5pm, Nov–Mar 10am–4.30pm; £5; ♿🅿✕; ℘01736 363 625; www.penleehouse.org.uk) is a centre of art and heritage for West Cornwall including a fine collection of art from 1750 to the present with works by the Newlyn school. Modern and contemporary works of art can be found in the suitably contemporary styled **Exchange Gallery** (Princes Street; details as Newlyn Art Gallery, ♿*see below*).

Newlyn★

Newlyn is the major fishing village in the South West with a large fleet that brings in mackerel, whitefish, lobster, crab and – its signature fish – pilchards (large sardines), now also called Cornish sardines. The beautiful light and the charm of the cottages clustered round the harbour and on the hillside attracted a group of painters who founded the famous **Newlyn school** in the 1880s. Their works are on display in the **Newlyn Art Gallery** (open Mar–Oct Mon–Sat 10am–5pm; winter Tue–Sat 10am–

5pm; closed 1 Jan, 25–26 Dec; £2.20; ♿✕; ℘01736 363 715; www.newlyn artgallery.co.uk).

Mousehole★

Mousehole ('Mowzel') is an attractive little village. Its **harbour** is protected by a quay of Lamorna granite and a **breakwater** dating from 1393. Set back from the low granite fishermen's cottages at the water's edge is the half-timbered **Keigwin Arms** (once an inn, now a private dwelling), the only house left standing after a Spanish raid in 1595.

Porthcurno★

This idyllic sheltered cove is famous for the **Minack Theatre★**, founded in 1929 with its stunning ocean backdrop and views over Lamorna. The theatre's fascinating history is recounted in the **visitor centre** (open Mar–Oct daily from 9.30am; Nov–Mar daily from 10am–4pm; £5; 🅿✕; ℘01736 810 181; www.minack.com) which gives access to the theatre.

Land's End★

The attraction of Land's End is less its physical beauty (and much less its visitor attractions) than its position at the western most point of England, overlooking **cliff scenery★★★** perpetually assailed by the surging swell of the Atlantic. For a peaceful view, come early and walk along the coastal path, or come at sunset and wait for the beams from the lighthouses to add a magical touch. Ramblers and walkers can approach along the Cornwall Coastal Path.

The tip of Land's End is occupied by a mini theme park, also known as **Land's End** ♟♟ (visitor centre: Mon–Sun 10am–4pm; all attractions daily 10am–4pm; ♿🅿 (£5) ✕; ℘01736 871 844; www.landsend-landmark.co.uk). This comprises Arthur's Quest (an interactive walk-through attraction), the 'Lost World' (a **4D film**), the **Air Sea Rescue** motion-theatre experience, the **End to End Story exhibition**, devoted to the select band who have completed the length of Britain from Land's End

Cliffs of Land's End

to John o' Groats, and the child-friendly **Greeb Farm** collection of small animals.

St Just-in-Penwith

The prosperity enjoyed by this 19C mining town is reflected in the substantial buildings lining the triangular square, the fine terraces of cottages and the large Methodist chapel. The **church★** features a 15C pinnacled tower, dressed granite walls, an elaborate 16C porch, wall paintings and a 5C tomb in the north aisle.

About 1mi/1.6km west, the hillock of **Cape Cornwall★** rises 70m, giving **views★★** of Brisons Rocks, Land's End and the Longships Lighthouse. Just before reaching Land's End, the road passes through the little village of Sennen, home to the most westerly church in England (walk down to **Sennen Cove★**, 20 minute there and back, for a good **view★** of Whitesand Bay, Brisons Rocks and Cape Cornwall).

🅰🏃 Geevor Tin Mine★

Near Pendeen lighthouse. Pendeen. Open Apr–Oct Sun–Fri 9am–5pm. Nov–Mar 10am–4pm. Closed 1 Jan, Christmas week. £13.95, child £8. 🅿 ✗ ✆01736 788 662. www.geevor.com.

Until its closure in 1990 Geevor was a working tin mine, with almost 300 years of history. The miners searched for tin not only deep underground but also in shafts which went far below the sea.

Today it is the largest preserved mining site in the UK with many surface buildings open to the public and a guided underground tour through 10C and 19C workings, often with former employees who worked the mine. It also features a museum, which explains how tin was extracted and processed, as well as a mineral gallery.

Chysauster Ancient Village★

Open Apr–Oct daily 10am–5pm (6pm Jul–Aug, 4pm Oct). £4.60. 🅿 ✆07831 757 934. www.english-heritage.org.uk.

This well-preserved prehistoric Cornish village was inhabited c.100 BCE–250 CE. It consists of at least eight circular stone houses, which would originally have been roofed with turf or thatch, in two lines of four just below the crest of the hill.

ST IVES★★

17mi/27km NE of Land's End.
🅸 The Guildhall, Street-an-Pol, ✆01736 796 297. www.stives-cornwall.co.uk.

This picturesque fishing harbour on the North Cornish coast is a much-visited summer resort and has been a favourite with artists since the 1880s when Whistler and Sickert followed Turner.

Today its network of stepped winding alleys and hillside terraces, lined by shoulder-to-shoulder colour-washed fishermen's houses, is still home to a thriving artists' community.

Tate St Ives★★
Porthmeor Beach.
Open daily 10am–5.20pm. Galleries
closed during exhibition re-hanging.
Closed 24–26 Dec. £7.50, joint entry
to Barbara Hepworth Museum £10.
℘01736 796 226.
www.tate.org.uk/stives.
This splendid building (1993) enjoys
a view over the sands of Porthmeor
Beach. The asymmetrical gallery
consists of swirling forms spiralling
upwards while inside, stairways clim
through airy space for access to the
changing exhibitions of historic and
contemporary displays that embrace
the best of international modern and
contemporary art.

Barbara Hepworth Museum★★
Barnoon Hill. Entry details as Tate
St Ives (☙see above). Entry at peak times
may be restricted.
Barbara Hepworth (1903–75) came
to St Ives with Ben Nicholson in 1943,
decided to settle, and stayed here until
her death. The house she lived in, filled
with sleek, polished wood and stone
abstract sculptures spanning a life's
work, and workshops with unfinished
blocks of stone, left pretty much as they
were at the artist's death, contrast with

the small garden, which provides a
serene setting for some twenty abstract
compositions in bronze and stone.

Parish Church★
The church dates mostly from the 15C
and is dedicated to the fishermen-
Apostles St Peter and St Andrew, and
St Ia, the early missionary who arrived
in the area from across the sea on a leaf
and after whom the town is named. It
stands by the harbour, distinguished
by its pinnacled 26m tower of Zennor
granite. Note the **wagon roof**, carved
bench ends and stone **font**. The **Lady
Chapel** contains the tender *Mother and
Child* (1953) by Barbara Hepworth.

Smeaton Pier
The pier and its octagonal domed lookout were constructed 1767–70 by the
builder of the third Eddystone lighthouse, John Smeaton. At its shore end
is the small St Leonard's sailors' chapel.

St Nicholas Chapel
This small ancient chapel, surrounded
on three sides by the sea, is also a traditional seamen's chapel, built as a
beacon. It commands a wide **view★★**
across the bay.

Plaster workshop, Barbara Hepworth Museum

© Tate

Old Town beach, St Mary's

Isles of Scilly★

Cornwall

This wind battered archipelago off England's southwesterly tip is designated an Area of Outstanding Natural Beauty, a Heritage Coast, and its waters have been granted Marine Park status. The approach by sea or air gives a partial view★★★ of the 5 inhabited islands, 40 uninhabited islands, and 150 or so named rocks in a close group in the clear blue-green ocean.

VISIT
St Mary's
3mi/5km across at its widest, with a coastline of 9mi/15km, St Mary's is the largest and principal island on which all but a few hundred Scillonians live. The main settlement is **Hugh Town**, formerly home to the **Garrison**. The mid-18C **Guard Gate** gives access to **Star Castle★** *(now a hotel, freely accessible to the public)* built in 1594 at the time of Elizabeth I's feud with Spain. From the rampart walls are excellent **views★★**.

Tresco★
On being appointed Lord Proprietor in 1834, Augustus Smith built a Victorian medieval castle mansion near the ruins of a priory. Around these ruins he created the subtropical **Abbey Gardens★★** (open daily 10am–4pm; ♿️🅿️✕; ℘01720

- **Population:** 2 203 (2011).
- **Michelin Map:** Michelin Atlas p 2 or Map 503 A, B
- **Location:** 34 – 28mi/45km southwest of Land's End
- **Info:** Porthcressa Bank, St Mary's. ℘01720 424 031. www.visitislesofscilly.com.

GETTING THERE
The *Scillonian III* operates a summer boat service from Penzance to St Mary's. Fixed-wing aircraft services operate from Exeter, Newquay and Land's End.
Skybus is the fastest way to Scilly (℘01736 334 220, www.Islesofscilly-travel.co.uk).

424 108; www.tresco.co.uk), from seeds and plants brought back by Scillonian sailors and plant collectors. The garden is home to species from 80 countries, ranging from Brazil to New Zealand and Burma to South Africa, and due to the micro-climate, even at the winter equinox more than 300 plants will be in flower. From the terraces, there are fine **views★★** over the gardens.
On the edge of the gardens is **Valhalla**, an extraordinary collection of figure-heads.

335

ADDRESSES

🛏 STAY

DEVON

Exeter

🛏🍽 **Raffles** – 1 Blackall Road. ☎01392 270 200. www.raffles-exeter.com. 7 rooms. This sympathetically restored Victorian townhouse is furnished with antiques.

🛏🍽 **The White Hart** – 66 South Street. ☎01392 279 897. www.whitehartpub exeter.co.uk. 55 rooms. Historic pub between the town centre and Quayside, with refurbished rooms, including four-posters.

Torquay

😊 Guesthouses and hotels can be found on King's Drive. Book well ahead for anywhere on the English Riviera in summer.

Dartmouth

🛏🍽🍽🍽 **The Royal Castle** – The Quay. ☎01803 833 033. www.royalcastle.co.uk. 24 rooms. Superb location with many of its traditionally furnished bedrooms enjoying river views. Four-poster beds and spa baths available.

North Devon

😊 **Ilfracombe** is well stocked with B&Bs. The Landmark Trust (www.landmarktrust. co.uk) offer several unusual historic properties on **Lundy Island**.

Plymouth

😊 There are a series of small Victorian hotels and B&Bs behind the Hoe on Citadel Road. **Dartmoor National Park** has a wide selection of both hotels and campsite. You can even camp 'wild' on the moor as long as you observe certain park regulations (www.dartmoor-npa.gov.uk).

🛏 **Ashgrove House** – 218 Citadel Road. ☎01752 664 046. www.ashgrove-house.com. 9 rooms. Simple well-kept traditionally furnished grade-II listed Victorian town house with a warm welcome and a good location.

CORNWALL

😊 For high-quality B&Bs, and self-catering farm and cottage holidays try www.cornishfarmholidays.co.uk.

Polperro

🛏 **Claremont** – The Coombes. ☎01503 272 241. www.theclaremonthotel.co.uk.

12 rooms. Set on the main street going down to the port, but free of passing traffic noise, this large fisherman's cottage, parts of which date from the 17C, is ideally placed to enjoy Polperro. No breakfast, just 'bed on a budget'.

Fowey

🛏🍽🍽🍽 **Fowey Hall** – Hanson Drive. ☎01726 833 866. www.foweyhallhotel. co.uk. 23 rooms. This beautiful historic luxury landmark property occupies a spectacular location overlooking Fowey and the bay. It boasts a splendid spa and gourmet restaurant yet still manages to be very family-friendly.

Truro

🛏🍽🍽 **Mannings** – Lemon Street. ☎01872 270 345. www.manningshotels. co.uk. 26 rooms. In 1876 Prince Albert stayed here, though not in the well-equipped, stylish, bright airy contemporary rooms we see today. Smart fashionable bar and restaurant.

Falmouth

🛏🍽🍽🍽 **Greenbank** – Harbourside. ☎01326 312 440. www.greenbank-hotel. co.uk. 57 rooms. The restaurant 🛏🍽🍽 and many of the contemporary-styled bedrooms here enjoy a magnificent view (small supplement) over the River Fal.

Padstow

🛏🍽🍽 **Cross House** – Church Street. ☎01841 532 391. 11 rooms. This charming Georgian house right in the centre of Padstow has a lovely front garden where afternoon teas are served. Traditional Victorian furnishings.

Penzance

🛏🍽🍽 **Chy-An-Mor** – 15 Regent Terrace. ☎01736 363 441. www.chyanmor.co.uk. Closed Dec–Jan. 10 rooms. This elegant Regency house sits in an elevated position on Penzance's finest street and some of its prettily decorated rooms have sea views.

St Ives

🛏🍽🍽🍽 **The Garrack** – Burtwallan Lane. ☎01736 796 199. www.garrack.com. 18 rooms. Just five minutes from the centre, overlooking the main beach, but in an elevated country setting with lawns and an indoor pool, this is the perfect St Ives location. Rooms are very stylish and the award-winning restaurant serves Modern British cuisine.

St Mary's (Scilly Isles)

⊜⊜ **Evergreen Cottage Guest House** – The Parade, Hugh Town. ☏01720 422 711. www.evergreencottageguesthouse. co.uk. 5 rooms. This pretty 300-year-old cottage offers simple rooms, just a few steps away from the port.

⟨ EAT

DEVON

Exeter

⊛ On **Quayside**, good places for a snack or lunch include The Riverside Café, in the Antiques Centre and The Prospect Inn, in the **city centre**; try Tea on the Green, beside Cathedral Green.

⊜⊜ **The Ship Inn** – 6 Martin's Lane. ☏01392 272 040. Historic pub with a restaurant on the first floor.

Dartmouth

⊜⊜⊜⊜ **Seahorse** – 5 South Embankment. ☏01803 835 147. www. seahorserestaurant.co.uk. Picturesque location overlooking the estuary and harbour, with some alfresco tables. Mediterranean influenced dishes with a strong seafood slant, much of which is cooked over an open charcoal fire. Good value early-bird menu Wed–Fri before 7pm.

Plymouth

⊜⊜⊜ **Barbican Kitchen** – Plymouth Gin Distillery, 60 Southside Street. ☏01752 604 448. www.barbicankitchen.com. Top-quality wine bar/brasserie food in the atmospheric award-winning setting of a 16C distillery.

⊜⊜⊜ **Greedy Goose** – Prysten House, Finewell Street. ☏01752 252 001. www. thegreedygoose.co.uk. Closed Sun–Mon. The oldest house in town is now home to innovative contemporary cooking.

CORNWALL

Polperro

⊜⊜ **Nelsons** – The Saxon Bridge. ☏01503 272 366. www.polperro.co.uk. Closed Mon. This long-established village centre restaurant has the feel of a nautical-themed Victorian pub and serves a wide range of classic local

dishes, both in its upstairs restaurant, and as bar meals.

Padstow

⊜⊜⊜⊜ **The Seafood Restaurant** – Riverside. ☏01841 532 700. www.rickstein. com. A celebrated seafood restaurant, thanks to its celebrity chef owner (Rick Stein), and undoubtedly also one of its best.

⊜⊜⊜⊜ **Paul Ainsworth at No. 6** – 4 New Street, Padstow. ☏01841 532 093. www.number6inpadstow.co.uk. It may be No. 6 by name, but you soon realise that this Michelin-starred eatery is really No. 1 in Padstow.

Port Isaac

⊜⊜⊜⊜ **Restaurant Nathan Outlaw** – 6 New Road, Port Isaac. ☏01208 880 896. www.nathan-outlaw.com. With two Michelin stars, this is arguably the finest seafood fine-dining restaurant in the country; a celebration of ultra-fresh fish and shellfish landed at the harbour.

Penzance

⊜⊜⊜ **Harris's** – 46 New Street. ☏01736 364 408. www.harrissrestaurant. co.uk. Closed Sun–Mon. This small, elegant, long-established town centre restaurant serves classic traditional local dishes using the finest and freshest ingredients.

St Ives

⊜⊜⊜ **Alba** – Old Lifeboat House, The Wharf. ☏01736 797 222. www.alba-stives.co.uk. Housed in the old lifeboat house on the harbourfront, this smart seafood restaurant is renowned for its contemporary menu produced from local produce. Daily lunch specials.

Port Isaac

© fisfra/iStockphoto.com

East Anglia

Introduction

In popular imagination, East Anglia is a flatland, devoid of interest, fringed by a handful of old-fashioned seaside resorts, and chilled even in summer by the winds from Europe. Its climate and soils mean that much of its gently undulating farmland is in arable cultivation supplying much of England's food crop, and as a result fields are large from which trees and hedges removed. However, this aside, England's largest area of low relief is also a region of surprising individuality. Densely populated and wealthy in medieval times, it boasts a valuable legacy of ancient villages and small towns. In the early-19C, Constable painted it as a rural idyll and pockets of such countryside still remain.

Many visitors make their only regional stop in **Cambridge,** and while this is an undoubted highlight, a tour of the **Stour valley** and an excursion to **Bury St Edmunds** are also rewarding.

The **Suffolk Coast** has an unspoilt beauty while only geographical isolation prevents the regional capital, **Norwich**, from being more widely renowned.

West of here, great cathedrals arise from **Ely** and **Peterborough** to cast their gaze over the marshy Fenlands, the watery playground of the **Norfolk Broads**, and the **North Norfolk** coast, which includes **King's Lynn** and many fine historic houses.

Highlights

1. Attending Evensong, **King's College, Cambridge** (p340)
2. Put yourself in the picture in **Constable Country** (p343)
3. Go boating on the **Norfolk Broads** (p352)
4. The **Holkham** estate with its palatial Palladian **Hall** and beautiful **beach** (p353)
5. The magnificent medieval cathedral at **Ely** (p356)

Ely cathedral © Rod Edwards / Loop Images / Photononstop

Cambridge★★★

and around

England's second-oldest university city (after Oxford), Cambridge established its academic reputation in the early-13C (c.1209), attracting groups of scholars from Oxford and Paris interested in studying theology, church and civil law, and logic. The oldest Cambridge college, Peterhouse, was founded in 1284 and by 1352 seven more colleges had been built, all with their characteristic four-sided enclosed monastic courtyard.

CITY AND COLLEGES WALK

Today, the 31 colleges are self-governing bodies while the university undertakes all public teaching and confers the degrees. Each college is an independent institution, with its own property and income.

Cambridge is a showpiece for new architecture, some controversial, both on college sites and on the west side of the city. Some colleges charge for entry from March to September; most are closed during the examination period May–June.

Kettle's Yard★

Castle Street. Closed for redevelopment; check website for current status.
℘01223 352 124.
www.kettlesyard.co.uk.
In complete contrast to the academic atmosphere of the Fitzwilliam is Kettle's Yard, which, according to its creator Jim Ede, is '...a living place where works of art can be enjoyed inherent in the domestic setting'.
This collection of 20C art includes works by Ben Nicholson, Henry Moore, Barbara Hepworth, Eric Gill, Henri Gaudier-Brzeska and Miró, most of whom were friends of Ede; the pieces are customarily set about the house among the furniture so that visitors may sit to admire the exhibits or read the books.

▶ **Population:** 123 900.

◌ **Michelin Map:** Michelin Atlas p29 or Map 504 U 27.

Info: The Guildhall, Peas Hill. ℘01223 791 500. www.visitcambridge.org. The train station (London King's Cross 45 mins) is 1mi/1.6km southeast of the centre, off Hills Road. The bus station is on Drummer Street, in town. The main colleges and the Fitzwilliam Museum are tightly clustered in the centre.

◖ **Location:** 58mi/93km north of London on the western edge of the East Anglian fenlands situated on the River Cam.

◉ **Don't Miss:** St John's College; King's College Chapel, particularly listening to the choir; punting on the River Cam.

◷ **Timing:** At least 2 days.

▲▲ **Kids:** Imperial War Museum.

🐾 **Walking Tours:** Contact the Visitor Information Centre for daily guided walking tours, including King's College Chapel, and Cambridge ghost tour.

🅿 **Parking:** Parking in the city centre is expensive. 'Park and Ride' service in operation. Use the 'Just Park' app or website (www.justpark. com). City centre closed to motor vehicles during the week 10am–4pm.

St John's College★

Visitors must enter via the Great Gate, St John's Street. Open daily Mar–Oct 10am–5pm; Nov–Feb 3.30pm. Closed 25 Dec–3 Jan. ⴠ ℘01223 338 606. www.joh.cam.ac.uk.
St John's (founded 1511) is the second-largest college in Cambridge; its turreted gatehouse is impressive.

First, Second and Third Courts are predominantly Tudor; Ruskin called the Second the most perfect in Cambridge. Behind Third Court is the 18C Kitchen Bridge, with its view of Hutchinson's exquisite **Bridge of Sighs**. The 13C **School of Pythagoras** is the oldest medieval stone house in Cambridge.

Trinity College★★

Visitors must enter via the Great Gate. Open most days 10am–5pm, but call ahead for details, or ask the tourist porter at the Great Gate. £3.
Wren Library: open Mon–Fri noon–2pm, also Sat in Full Term time 10.30am–12.30pm. ✆01223 338 400. www.trin.cam.ac.uk.
The largest Cambridge college, Trinity, was founded in 1546 by Henry VIII; its oldest buildings surround the **Great Court** – the 1432 **King Edward's Tower** (clock tower) and the **Great Gate**, completed in 1535.
In cloistered **Nevile's Court** (1612) stands the **Wren Library**, completed in 1695 and named after its designer. The bookcases are decorated with limewood carvings by Grinling Gibbons. Among the manuscripts are the 8C Epistles of St Paul, Shakespeare's First Folio and illuminated 15C French Books of Hours.

Trinity Hall

Down Senate House Passage. Open Tue and Thu 10am–noon, 2–5pm, Sun 9am noon. College may be closed without prior notice. ✆01223 332 531. www.trinhall.cam.ac.uk.
Trinity Hall College was founded by Bishop Bateman of Norwich in 1350. Behind the 18C ashlar of **Principal Court** are three ranges (best viewed from North Court) which date from 1350. Beyond the delightful Elizabethan Library is the garden Henry James called '...the prettiest corner of the world'.

Clare College★

Old Court, Hall, chapel and gardens. Open Easter–start of term time (around first week Oct) 10.30am–5pm. £5. ✆01223 333 200. www.clare.cam.ac.uk.

Bridge of Sighs, St John's College
© oversnap/iStockphoto.com

The college was founded in 1326. The 17C ranges are the work of father and son **Thomas** and **Robert Grumbold** and are among the most serene in Cambridge.
Clare Bridge was built by Thomas Grumbold, before the 17C ranges. Note the missing segment of one of the stone balls on the bridge's parapet. He had vowed never to complete the bridge unless he was paid. He never was.

King's College★

Tickets: The Visitor Centre on King's Parade. **Entrance**: North Gate of the Chapel. **College**: open (functions permitting) Term-time Mon–Fri 9.30am–3.30pm, Sat 9.30am–3.15pm, Sun 1.15–2.30pm; Out of Term Mon–Sun 9.30am–4.30pm. £9. Guided tours (45min) Aug Mon–Fri 11am and noon, Sept Sat only 11am, noon. +£6. ✆01223 331 212. www.kings.cam.ac.uk.
Founded in 1441 and set back behind **William Wilkins'** Gothic Revival **screen** and **gatehouse**, King's is dominated by **Gibb's Building** in the Classical style and the soaring late Perpendicular buttresses of King's College Chapel.

King's College Chapel★★★

Built between 1446 and 1515 mainly by three kings (Henry VI, Henry VII and Henry VIII), King's College Chapel is the

King's College Chapel

© Adrian Zenz/Dreamstime.com

final and most glorious flowering of Perpendicular. Turner painted its exterior, Wordsworth wrote three sonnets about it, and Wren, marvelling at the largest single-span vaulted roof in existence, offered to make one himself, if only someone would tell him where to lay the first stone.

The dimensions (88m long, 29m high, 12m wide) suggest a cathedral choir rather than a college chapel; the 18 side chapels and door emphasise the height of the 22 buttresses which take the weight of the roof. The 12-bay nave rises upwards on stonework so slender that it forms a mere frame to the 25 stained-glass windows (16C) illustrating episodes from the Old Testament (above) and from the New Testament (below). The vaulting (nearly 2 000 tons) appears weightless. The architect was **John Wastell**.

Note the splendid early Renaissance **screen** and **stalls** by foreign craftsmen and **Rubens'** *Adoration of the Magi*. Above the screen is the organ in its 17C case used for services broadcast live on Christmas Eve across the world featuring the famous King's College Choir. You don't have to wait for Christmas however as you can attend Evensong (free of charge) daily, particularly atmospheric in the winter months, by candlelight.

Queens' College★

Visitors' Gate, Queens' Lane. Open most days 10am–4.30pm or 2–4pm. Closed 3rd week May–3rd week Jun (exams). ℘01223 335 511. www.quns.cam.ac.uk.

Named after the patronage bestowed by two successive queens, Margaret of Anjou, wife of Henry VI, and Elizabeth Woodville, wife of Edward IV, the college was granted its first charter in 1446. **Old Court**, completed in 1449, shows late medieval brickwork; in charming **Cloister Court** the half-timbered building is the **President's Lodge**.

The Dutch philosopher **Desiderius Erasmus** taught Greek at Queens' but his rooms (Erasmus' Tower) cannot be definitely identified; his name, however, lives on in the brick Erasmus Building (1960) by Basil Spence. Another recent addition is the glass, and, concrete Cripps' Court (1981) by Powell, Moya and Partners. The famous wooden **Mathematical Bridge** over the river is a 20C copy (1904), the second, of the original one (1749) designed by James Essex.

The Backs★★

The 'Backs' (of the colleges) along the River Cam are as fine as the fronts; they form a wonderful combination of buildings and lawns in a riverside setting and are best viewed from a punt (on hire at Silver Street Bridge).

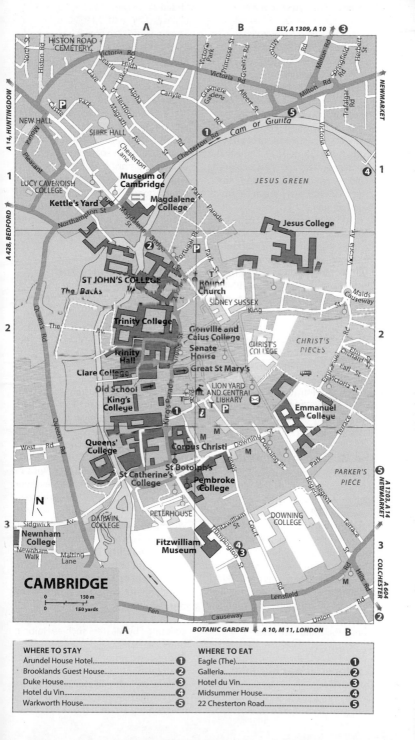

CAMBRIDGE

0 — 150 m
0 — 150 yards

WHERE TO STAY		WHERE TO EAT	
Arundel House Hotel	❶	Eagle (The)	❶
Brooklands Guest House	❷	Galleria	❷
Duke House	❸	Hotel du Vin	❸
Hotel du Vin	❹	Midsummer House	❹
Warkworth House	❺	22 Chesterton Road	❺

Fitzwilliam Museum★★

Trumpington Street. Open Tue–Sat 10am–5pm, Sun and bank holidays noon–5pm. ♿✖ ☎01223 332 900. Guided tours available, call ☎01223 791 501. www.fitzmuseum.cam.ac.uk.

Founded in 1816, the Fitzwilliam Museum houses world-class collections of art and antiquities from Egypt, Sudan, the Ancient Near East, Greece, Rome (look for the marble **Pashley sarcophagus**, dating from 130–150 CE), English and European pottery and glass, sculpture, furniture, armour, illuminated manuscripts, Oriental art, Korean ceramics, coins and medals.

The art collection includes 25 watercolours by J M W Turner (donated by John Ruskin) and a selection of some of William Blake's best works in addition to works by Gainsborough, Reynolds, Stubbs and Constable and an outstanding collection of prints by Rembrandt. The paintings include **Old Masters** of exceptional quality with works by Domenico Veneziano, Leonardo da Vinci, Titian, Rubens and Van Dyck. The collection of French Impressionists includes landscapes by Monet, Seurat and Cézanne as well as studies by Renoir and Degas. Representing the 20C are pieces by Picasso, Nicholson and Sutherland.

The Museum of Cambridge

Castle Street. Open Tue–Sat 10.30am –5pm, Sun and bank holidays noon– 4pm. £4. ♿ ✖ (Sat). ☎01223 355 159. www.folkmuseum.org.uk.

This charming friendly small museum is set in a higgledy-piggledy 17C building which served as the White Horse Inn for 300 years. It now features nine themed rooms (kitchen, bar, Fens and folklore, childhood…), which explore the lives of ordinary Cambridgeshire people as far back as the 1660s, using original memorabilia and exhibits.

EXCURSIONS

♟ Imperial War Museum, Duxford★

❯9mi/14km S on the M 11.
Open daily 10am–4pm.

Closed 24–26 Dec. £16.35, child 5–15, £8.15. ♿🅿✖ ☎01223 835 000. http://duxford.iwm.org.uk.

Duxford is Europe's premier aviation museum as well as having one of the finest collections of tanks, military vehicles and naval exhibits in the country. It began as an airfield in the First World War and also played a vital role in the Second World War. Today its vast hangars, and notably **AirSpace**, its stunning main exhibition space, house dozens of civil and fighter aircraft, several of which, including Concorde, you can climb aboard. To celebrate the Second World War associations of this former Battle of Britain base with the USAAF it is also home to the **American Air Museum in Britain**.

Audley End House and Gardens★★

❯13mi/21km S. House: open Apr–Oct daily noon–6pm (5pm Sept); Oct–Mar Sat–Sun only noon–4pm. The gardens are often open when the house is closed; check website for details. £17.50. ♿🅿✖ ☎01799 522 842; www.english-heritage.org.uk.

When this estate came into the possession of Thomas Howard, Earl of Suffolk and Lord High Treasurer in the early-17C, it was one of the greatest Jacobean houses in England. 'Too large for a king, but might do for a Lord Treasurer' said James I, who unintentionally helped to finance it at a cost of £200 000, and later imprisoned the earl for embezzlement. It was partially demolished in 1721 when the interior was redesigned by **Robert Adam** and the grounds by **Lancelot 'Capability' Brown**.

The present house, vast enough, is but a shadow of its former self. The interior is laden with the possessions of the 3rd Baron Braybrooke, who inherited Audley End in 1825, filling it with paintings by Masters such as Holbein and Canaletto.

The restored historic **stables**, complete with resident horses and a Victorian groom, includes an exhibition where you can find out about the workers who lived on the estate in the 1880s.

Stour Valley ★

and Ipswich

The valley of the River Stour is the southernmost part of East Anglia, where Essex, on the fringe of London, meets rural Suffolk. It is best known for its association with John Constable (1776–1837), whose landscapes of this area are among the most popular and valuable in British art. However, while the Lower Stour is **Constable Country**, the Upper Stour is **Gainsborough Country**, named after another great 18C English painter, Thomas Gainsborough (1727–88).

IPSWICH

🆔 ℰ01473 258 070.
www.allaboutipswich.com.

This bustling county town is mostly Victorian and modern in character. All that remains of the distant past is its Anglo-Saxon street layout and about a dozen medieval churches, some just towers, built when the town was a rich port and trading centre. The area once covered by the **Victorian Wet Dock**, once the largest in the world, is now known as the Waterfront, with its recently converted warehouses, merchants' houses and maltings, and makes for an interesting walk.

In the centre of town, within Christchurch Park is **Christchurch Mansion** (open Mar–Oct Tue–Sat 10am–5pm, Sun 11am–5pm; Nov–Feb Tue–Sat 10am–4pm, Sun 11am–4pm; closed 1 Jan, 24–27 Dec; 🅿✕; ℰ01473 433 554; www.cimuseums.org.uk), a much-restored Tudor manor house, set in pleasant parkland and full of treasures from Ipswich and the surrounding countryside. It holds a good collection of paintings by Suffolk-born artists, including works by Thomas Gainsborough and the largest collection of art by John Constable outside London.

Head due south on Northgate Street and take a right onto Buttermarket to see the **Ancient House** (open Mon–Sat

- **Michelin Map:** Michelin Atlas p23 or Map 504 X 27.
- **Location:** Ipswich is at the head of the Orwell estuary on the southeast Anglian coast

9am–5.30pm). The exterior of this 15C house abounds in Restoration plasterwork, pargeting (ornamental plastering) and stucco reliefs of nymphs, pelicans and the four (then-known) continents. The coat of arms is that of Charles II who visited the building in 1668. Now a shop, visitors can view several panelled rooms (c.1603) with wall pargeting – a form of exterior decorative stucco work which is a speciality of Suffolk – ornamental ceilings and 18C ceramic tilework.

🚗 DRIVING TOUR

STOUR VALLEY ★

This tour is quite literally a drive through England's artistic heritage.

▶ Take the A 12 south for 8mi/13km, go left on the B 1070 and follow signs.

Flatford Mill ★

The mill (1773) at East Bergholt was the home of Constable (his father was the miller) and inspired some of his best-loved landscapes – *The Haywain*, *Boatbuilding* and *Flatford Mill*. It is now home to a field studies centre and there is no entry for individuals although group tours may be arranged (ℰ01206 297 110).

Adjacent is the picturesque thatched **Bridge Cottage**, formerly known as Willy Lott's Cottage (open Apr–Sept daily 10am–5pm; Oct 10am–4.30pm; Nov–mid-Dec Wed–Sun 10.30am–3.30pm; Jan–Feb Sat–Sun 10.30am–3.30pm; closed 1 Jan, 25 Dec; 🅿(£3.50) ✕; ℰ01206 298 260; www.nationaltrust.org.uk), which has a free-admission exhibition on Constable and the valley, plus a lovely riverside tearoom.

> Take the A 12 south (3.7mi/6km) or walk along the riverbank path.

Dedham

This lovely English village, its main street lined with timber-framed houses, was often painted by Constable and is still recognisable from his works.

> Return to the A 12 and head south.

Colchester

Once the capital of England, Colchester is well worth a visit for its castle and collection of Roman antiquities. Built with 4m-thick walls on the vaults of the Roman Temple of Claudius, **Colchester Castle**★ (Castle Park; open Mon–Sat 10am–5pm, Sun 11am–5pm; £7.75; ⅍✕; ✆01206 282 939; www.cimuseums.org. uk) is the largest keep ever built by the Normans (46m by 34m), half as big again as the White Tower at the Tower of London. It houses one of the largest collections in Britain of **Roman antiquities** gathered from one site.

> Take the A 134 north and turn right on the B 1087 to Nayland, where the 15C church contains *The Last Supper* by Constable. Continue on the B 1087.

Stoke by Nayland

With its many traditional cottages and timber-framed houses this picturesque village is often cited as the prettiest in the region. The Church of St Mary was a favourite painting subject of Constable.

> Return to the A 134, head north.

Sudbury

The regional centre of the upper Stour valley, Sudbury is best known as the birthplace of Thomas Gainsborough, the leading English portrait painter of the 18C. His birthplace, **Gainsborough's House**★ (46 Gainsborough Street; open Mon–Sat 10am–5pm; Sun 11am–5pm; closed Good Fri, 24 Dec–2 Jan; £7; ✆01787 372 958; www.gainsborough. org) is a medieval building set behind an elegant 18C façade. It houses a large collection of Gainsborough's paintings, drawings and prints. There is also a walled garden with a 400-year-old mulberry tree and used for exhibitions of sculpture during the summer months.

> Take the A 134 north for 3mi/5km.

Long Melford

The long main street (2mi/3km) is lined with 16C, 17C and 18C timbered and pink-plastered houses. It terminates in a spacious triangular **green**, overlooked by **Trinity Hospital** (1573), **Holy Trinity Church** (late-15C) – one of the great 'wool churches' of East Anglia – and Melford Hall★ (open Apr–Oct Wed–Sun and bank holiday Mons noon–5pm; £7.80; ⅍🅿✕ ✆01787 376 395. www.nationaltrust.org.uk/melford-hall).

The house is early Elizabethan, built around three sides of a courtyard, but only the **Main Hall** has preserved its Elizabethan features. The Drawing Room is splendidly Rococo. The West Bedroom contains the original Jemima Puddle-Duck watercolours by **Beatrix Potter**, who was a frequent visitor.

Lavenham★

Now a picture-postcard backwater, Lavenham was once one of the wealthiest places in Tudor England. Bypassed, in all senses, by modern developments, it is a superbly preserved medieval wool town, crowded with timber-framed houses. These are zealously preserved and the town is also renowned for its pargeting (*see above, Ipswich*).

The late-15C **Church of St Peter and St Paul**★ (open 8.30am–5.30pm/3.30pm; ⅍), is one of the great 'wool' churches with a noble tower and porch and enchanting misericords.

The impressive timber-framed **Guildhall of Corpus Christi** facing the Market Place dates from c.1520. It stages exhibitions and houses a **museum** (open Apr–Oct daily 11am–5pm, Mar Wed–Sun 11am–4pm, Nov–Dec Thu–Sun 11am–4pm; £6.50; ⅍🅿✕; ✆01787 247 646; www.nationaltrust.org.uk/lavenham) on the East Anglian wool trade and local history.

Bury St Edmunds★

The historic market town of Bury St Edmunds boasts the ruins of what was once one of the richest abbeys in Christendom, as well as a perfect late Perpendicular cathedral and a wide range of English architectural styles, from secular medieval (**The Guidhall**) to Georgian (**Athenaeum**), and Regency (**Theatre Royal**) to grand Victorian.

TOWN

On Angel Hill in the eastern part of town is the parish church, **St Edmundsbury cathedral**★(open daily 8.30am–6pm; suggested donation £3 per adult; guided tours May–Sept Mon–Sat 11am; &; ℘01284 748 720; www.stedscathedral.co.uk), which dates from 1530 and was originally dedicated to St Denys. It changed its name when it was granted cathedral status in 1914. A composition of nine bays leads the eye to the chancel and transepts (1960) by Stephen Dykes Bower. Note the Flemish stained-glass Susanna window (c.1480) and hammer-beam roof (19C) with angels. It was not until 2005 however that the cathedral was finally completed by the addition of the Millennium Tower, a 46m Gothic **lantern tower**. This and other recent works – the North Transept, the Chapel of the Transfiguration, a crypt and East Cloisters – were all added employing traditional materials and methods. The Chapel of the Transfiguration was consecrated by the Archbishop of Canterbury in 2009, and in 2010 a colourful painted and gilded vault was unveiled under the tower. Another popular recent addition is the **Edmund Gallery** exhibition space.

In the grounds behind the cathedral lie the **Abbey ruins**★(open dawn–dusk). Founded in 633 and later renamed in honour of the Saxon king and martyr Edmund (d.870), it was rebuilt by Benedictine monks in the 11C. Today only two of its monumental crossing towers still stand upright. Remnants of nave, chancel and transepts, together

▶ **Population:** 40 664.
& **Michelin Map:** Michelin Atlas p22 or Map 504 W 27.
🛈 **Info:** The Apex, Charter Square. ℘01284 764 667. www.visit-bury stedmunds.co.uk. The train station (40 mins from Cambridge) is a 10-minute walk north of the centre; the bus station is central, on St Andrew Street North. Bury's medieval grid layout makes orientation easy. Guided tours from the tourist office.
◗ **Location.** 28mi/45km east of Cambridge.
🕐 **Timing:** Market days are Wednesday and Saturday.

with the **Abbey Gate**, give some idea of its vastness (154m long). The **Norman Tower**'s richly decorated gateway frames a bronze of St Edmund by Elisabeth Frink and the cathedral precinct houses, built into the abbey's west end. Today it is surrounded by beautiful gardens.

Moyse's Hall Museum

Cornhill. Open Mon–Sat 10am–5pm, Sun noon–4pm. Closed 24 Dec–2 Jan. £4. & ℘01284 706 183. www.moyseshall.org.

A rare and important example of Norman domestic architecture, Moyse's Hall dates from the second half of the 12C. It comprises a medieval gallery, exhibitions on social history, a regimental gallery and museum, and a permanent exhibition that showcases the museum's very fine horological collection.

Under ornate plasterwork ceilings the collection concentrates on clocks but also includes costumes, textiles, portraits and local *objets d'art*.

Suffolk Coast★

North of Ipswich is a delightful stretch of unspoiled coastline now known as the Suffolk Heritage Coast. It includes Aldeburgh, home of a famous classical music and arts festival, and fashionable Southwold, a fine, unspoiled genteel resort.

ORFORD & ORFORD NESS

One of the prettiest villages on the Suffolk Heritage Coast, in the Middle Ages Orford was a thriving seaport from where Eleanor of Aquitaine set off to ransom her son King Richard I (the Lionheart). The gradual silting up of the river has left it a quiet village of brick and timber houses. **Orford Castle** (open Apr–Oct 10am–5pm, Nov–26 Dec and Jan–Mar Sat–Sun 10am–4pm; 27–31 Dec daily 10am–4pm; £7.50; ℘01394 450 472; www.english-heritage.org.uk/orford), built by Henry II in the 12C, and the fine medieval church dominate the skyline. The unique polygonal castle tower keep looks across the water to the largest shingle spit in Europe (some 10mi/16km long), home to **Orford Ness National Nature Reserve** (access by NT ferry only 10am–2pm, every 20 mins: mid-Apr–late Jun and mid-late Oct Sat only; Jul–Sept Tue–Sat; site £10 plus ferry charge; ℘01728 648 024; www.nationaltrust.org. uk/orford-ness). This mysterious place, closed to the public for many decades, was formerly administered by the Ministry of Defence, which until 1971 conducted secret military tests here during both world wars and the Cold War. You can access some of these dramatic, once potentially deadly, buildings (albeit now empty shells).

ALDEBURGH

In the 16C Aldeburgh was a thriving port and shipbuilding area. By Victorian times it had become a seaside resort. Notable town landmarks include the **Moot Hall**, the meeting place of the Town Council for the last 400 years, and the **Church of St Peter and St Paul**, its memorial window designed by

🛈 **Info**: www.visit-suffolkcoast. co.uk; www.visitsuffolk.com.

John Piper, dedicated to the memory of Benjamin Britten (1913–76). Britten, acclaimed as one of England's finest ever composers, co-founded the Aldeburgh Festival in 1948 (*www.aldeburgh. co.uk*) for which the village is famous.

DUNWICH

The 'Lost City' of Dunwich sparks the imagination of most visitors. It may have possessed as many as 18 churches at the height of its fortune when it was the main port of East Anglia during the 12C and 13C. However, it was swept away in a great storm in 1286 and today continues to be eroded by the sea at the rate of around a metre each year. Nowadays it's a tiny village with a few fishing boats, a 17C pub, a beach café and Dunwich Museum (open Mar Sat–Sun 2–4.30pm, Apr–Oct 11.30am–4.30pm; ℘01728 648 796; www.dunwich-museum.org.uk).

SOUTHWOLD★

Favoured by well-heeled weekenders, Southwold is one of England's most attractive little seaside resorts, retaining vestiges of its maritime history, but embracing none of the crassness of modern-day resorts. It is much loved for its pastel-hued beach huts, its greens, an award-winning pier, a 30m-tall lighthouse and its seaside walks. On the attractive, mainly Georgian, High Street, the **Sailors Reading Room** (open 9am–dusk; www.southwoldsailorsreadingroom.co.uk) contains pictures, ship models and other items of seafaring interest. For more local history visit **Southwold Museum** (Victoria Street; open Apr–Oct 2–4pm; ℘01502 726097; www.southwoldmuseum.org). The **Church of St Edmund, King and Martyr** has an imposing flint tower. Note the screens, the 15C pulpit, the vast font cover and the choir stalls.

Norwich★★

and around

In 1066, Norwich was the fourth most populous city in England, and later grew rich as the centre of the East Anglian wool trade. Today, it is one of the country's best-preserved medieval cities and the surviving towers and spires of over 30 flint churches, many now redundant, etch the skyline. The city is dominated by the hill-top castle; below is the centre of old Norwich, where cobbled streets, lined with half-timbered houses, lead through stone gateways to the cathedral. Its star attractions are its Norman cathedral, castle, and the Sainsbury Centre for Visual Arts (part of the University of East Anglia).

▶ **Population:** 132 512.
Michelin Map: Michelin Atlas p31 or Map 504 Y 26.
Info: The Forum, Millennium Plain. ℘01603 213 999. www.visitnorwich.co.uk. Train station 10 minutes from centre (London Liverpool Street 1h50, Cambridge 1h15). Buses – Surrey Street Station (10 minutes from centre), or Castle Meadow (central). Tourist buses (www.city-sightseeing.com).
▶ **Location:** 62mi/100km northeast of Cambridge.
Don't Miss: Cathedral; Blickling Hall.
Walking Tour: Marked on the map.

NORWICH CATHEDRAL ★★

Palace Street. Open daily 7.30am–6pm, Hostry Visitor Centre open Mon–Sat 9.30am–4.30, Sun 10am–3pm. Contribution requested. &✕ ℘01603 218 300. www.cathedral.org.uk.

The Norman cathedral was begun in 1096 and consecrated in 1278. Its choir clerestory was rebuilt in Early English style in the 14C and Perpendicular vaults added in the 15C and early-16C. The 15C **spire** (96m) is the second-tallest in England after Salisbury.

Inside, above the steadfast Norman nave and transepts the 400 carved and painted bosses on the vaults portray '...a strip cartoon of the whole story of God's involvement with man from creation to last judgement'. Note the **misericords** of the choir stalls, the ambulatory, St Luke's Chapel (displaying the famous 14C five-panelled Despenser Reredos) and Jesus Chapel (displaying Martin Schwarz's *Adoration of the Magi* (1480). The **Prior's Door**, leading from the nave to the cloisters, with its sculptured figures of Christ flanked by two angels, two bishops and two monks, is one of the most beautiful doors of the early Decorated style. The unusual two-sto-reyed cloisters, the largest in England, were rebuilt (c.1297–1430).

CITY CENTRE

▲▲ Norwich Castle Museum and Art Gallery★

Castle Meadow. Open Mon–Sat 10am–4.30pm, Sun 1–4.30pm (late Jun–late Sept daily until 5pm). £9.15. Twilight ticket £2, one hour before closing. Closed 1 Jan, 24–26 Dec. &✕ ℘01603 493 625. www.museums.norfolk.gov.uk.

The castle was begun in 1160, built on a commanding hilltop. The high-walled stone **keep** has retained many of its original features – Norman arches, windows, chapel niche and the well (34m deep) and makes for an atmospheric display. The art gallery *(ground floor)* displays an outstanding collection of works by the **Norwich school** of painters, greatly influenced by Dutch landscape artists. Also on display are works by 20C **East Anglian** artists – Alfred Munnings, Edward Seago – as well as Victorian and Dutch works.

History galleries are devoted to **Queen Bouadicea; Anglo-Saxon and Viking**

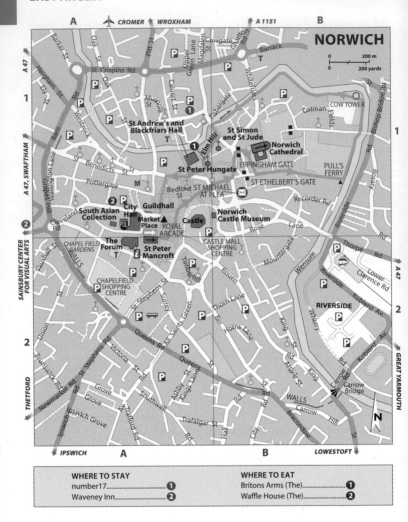

WHERE TO STAY		WHERE TO EAT	
number17	❶	Britons Arms (The)	❶
Waveney Inn	❷	Waffle House (The)	❷

life in East Anglia, including a remarkable reconstruction of a grave site, and an Egyptian tomb with mummies. The **decorative arts** galleries trace 600 years of style and design in 'The Arts of Living', while 'Trade and the Exotic' exhibits objects brought back from the east.

Market Place★

The square, which is 900 years old and the largest in East Anglia, is occupied six days a week by market stalls mostly selling local produce. To the north is the chequered flint **Guildhall**, begun in 1407. To the west is the modern **City Hall**, considered by Pevsner to be '...

probably the foremost English public building of between the wars'.

The Forum

2 Millennium Plain, Bethel Street. Open daily 7am–midnight. ♿🅿✕ ℘01603 727 950. www.theforumnorwich.co.uk. This spectacular glass building – the landmark Millennium project for the East of England – houses an eclectic mix of free exhibitions, stages events, activities, catering, shopping and learning opportunities (including the most popular public library in the UK), and also the tourist office.

© Linda Steward/iStockphoto.com

Blickling Hall

The huge glass atrium windows face south to Norwich's grandest parish church, **St Peter Mancroft**, an exemplar of the Perpendicular style, with a fine hammerbeam roof, a great east window with medieval glass, and a 15C font. Another colourful museum, the **South Asian Decorative Arts and Crafts Collection** (open Mon–Sat 9.30am–5pm; closed bank holidays and Sun; &; ℘01603 663 890, www.southasiandecorativearts andcrafts.co.uk) lies on adjacent Bethel Street in an intriguing restored building which was originally a Victorian skating rink, then a vaudeville theatre. It exhibits pictures and prints, architectural items, vernacular furniture and objects which illustrate the everyday arts and crafts of the region.

Elm Hill

This quaint cobbled street, formerly the centre of the weaving industry, is lined with medieval brick and timber houses. At the Tombland end stands the church of **St Simon and St Jude**, now put to commercial use. Farther along sits the thatched 15C **Britons Arms Coffee House & Restaurant**, and **Hungate Medieval Art** (open Mar–Nov Sat, 10am–4pm, Sun 2–4pm; & ℘01603 623254, www.hungate.org.uk), an interpretation centre occupying the church of St Peter Hungate, re-built 1460.

Across the street can be seen the east window of **Blackfriars Hall**, which together with **St Andrew's Hall** once formed the choir and nave of the Convent Church of the Blackfriars.

Both halls, with fine hammerbeam roofs, are now used for public, private and civic functions.

Sainsbury Centre for Visual Arts

University of East Anglia. 3mi/5km W of the city centre. Open Tue–Fri 10am–6pm, Sat–Sun 10am–5pm. &✕ ℘01603 593 199. www.scva.org.uk. This important gallery is housed in one of the most acclaimed buildings of the 1970s, designed by Norman Foster. Works by Degas, Seurat, Picasso, Epstein, Bacon, Modigliani, Moore and Giacometti, plus African, Pacific, Oriental and Native American art.

EXCURSION
Blickling Estate★★

▶ 15mi/24km N on the A 140. House: open mid-Mar–Oct Wed–Mon noon–5pm; mid–end Feb daily 11am–3.30pm; rest of year from 11am with varying closing times; check website for details. £13.55 (winter £9.50); garden only summer £8.10, winter £5.70. & ▣ (£5). ✕ ℘01263 738 030. www.nationaltrust.org.uk/blickling. The splendid turreted and gabled brick-built Blickling Hall was built 1619–25 by Robert Lyminge, the architect of Hatfield House, and is one of the most intact of great Jacobean houses, famed for its long gallery, fine tapestries, paintings and the National Trust's most important collection of books. A plastered ceiling (36m) portrays the *Five Senses* and *Learning* in the Long Gallery.

River Ant near How Hill

© Laurence Gough/Fotolia.com

Norfolk Broads★

One of Britain's premier wildlife habitats, the Broads – 14 large lakes formed from medieval peat diggings – are the home of Chinese water deer, kingfisher, bittern, heron and great crested grebe. Peaceful waterways wind their way through misty fens, cutting between lush woods and open marshes beneath a seemingly endless sky. Over 125mi/200km of these are navigable by boat. The Broads' villages are famous for their churches, some of which have hammerbeam and thatched roofs.

WROXHAM

The 'capital of the Broads', on the River Bure, is usually the first port of call for the widest choice of boat hire.

HOW HILL

6mi/10km east of Wroxham.
Toad Hole Cottage (open Jun–Sept daily 9.30am–5pm; Apr–May and Oct Mon–Fri 10.30am–1pm, 1.30–5pm, Sat–Sun 10.30am–5pm; ℘01692 678 763, http://howhilltrust.org.uk), **built 1780–1820**, was once home to Broads 'marshmen'. Now a museum, it tells their story of landscape management.

🛈 **Info: Norwich:** 7 Oaktree Business Park, Basey Road, Rackheath. ℘01603 735573. www.norfolkbroads.com.
Broads Authority: Yare House, 62-64 Thorpe Road, Norwich. ℘01603 610734; www.visitthebroads.co.uk; www.broads-authority. gov.uk.
🐾 **Don't Miss:** Boating on the Broads in summer.

POTTER HEIGHAM

9mi/14km east of Wroxham.
This is a popular boating centre on the River Thurne. **St Nicholas' church** has a Norman tower and a hammerbeam and thatched roof.

RANWORTH

6mi/10km southeast of Wroxham.
The Perpendicular tower and Decorated south porch of **St Helen's church** give no hint of the splendour inside '...the cathedral of the Broads'. It is home to the finest rood screen (15C) in East Anglia, a brightly painted array of saints, apostles and martyrs. For a wonderful panorama, climb the winding stone staircase to the top of the tower.

North Norfolk Coast ★

Away from bustling Norwich and the busy boating centres of the Broads, Norfolk is a land of peace and quiet and big, empty skies; excellent for nature-watching.

Info: Louden Road, Cromer.
📞0871 200 3071.
www.visitnorthnorfolk.com.

Don't Miss: A visit to Holkham Hall, or a taste of Cromer crab.

Kids: Go seal spotting at Blakeney.

CROMER

24mi/39km north of Norwich.

Cromer reached its height as a fashionable resort with the coming of the railway in the 1880s. Despite, or perhaps because of, failing to keep up with the times, it still has a loyal following, thanks largely to its fine beach, exhilarating clifftop walks, its charming pier, unspoiled by seaside amusements, and the local delicacy of **Cromer Crab**. Don't miss the **view** from the tower (172 steps) of the medieval **Church of St Peter and St Paul**.

CLEY NEXT THE SEA AND BLAKENEY POINT

Cley is 12mi/19km west of Cromer.

Cley (pronounced 'cly') is renowned for its birdwatching, with a recently opened **Norfolk Wildlife Trust** visitor centre (open daily 10am–5pm; 4pm Nov–Feb; ♿✕; 📞01263 740 008, www.norfolkwildlifetrust.org.uk) offering superb views across Cley Marshes.

Some 4mi/6.5km west Blakeney Point is one of the best places in Britain to see **seals**. The 500-strong colony is made up of common and grey seals. The common seals pup between June and August. Local ferry operators (📞01263 740505; www.beansboattrips.co.uk) run seal watching trips from Moston Quay.

WELLS-NEXT-THE-SEA

9mi/14km) west of Cromer.

Despite the name you'll find this attractive little town a mile inland from the sea. Largely unaffected by 20C commercialisation, it retains many of its fine Georgian houses and is also the area's only working port. In summer a narrow-gauge railway runs out to the beach.

HOLKHAM ★★

11mi/18km west of Cromer.

The seat of the Earls of Leicester and of Coke of Norfolk (1754–1842) – the inventor of modern agriculture – the Holkham (pronounced 'holkum') Estate is the grandest in the region, and still a family home.

Holkham Hall★★ (open Apr–Oct Sun Mon and Thu noon–4pm; £15; private guided tours £21 per person; ♿; 🅿£2.50; ✕; 📞01328 710 227. www.holkham.co.uk) was designed in the palatial Palladian style by **William Kent**. Most monumental of the interiors is the Marble Hall. The Grand Drawing Room has works by Claude and Poussin and the Saloon boasts Rubens and Van Dyck. In the South Sitting Room hang works by Titian, Guido Reni, Gainsborough and Battoni; the Landscape Room is devoted to Poussin and Claude.

The sweeping **park** that surrounds the hall is home to fallow deer and a small herd of red deer.

The estate is also blessed with **Holkham Beach**★, voted the best beach in Britain in a survey of UK travel journalists, and winner of best beach category in The Kennel Club's Be Dog Friendly Awards. With 4mi/6.4km of golden sand and pine woods to explore, it has changed little in centuries and was famously used for the final scene in the movie *Shakespeare in Love*, when actress Gwyneth Paltrow waled across the sands at low tide.

King's Lynn★

North Norfolk Coast

Set amid the marshes, in what is known locally as the Fenlands, King's Lynn dates from the Norman Conquest (1066). In the Middle Ages it was a bustling port and member of the Hanseatic League, exporting cloth and wool. Today's fine townscape is especially rich in medieval merchants' houses; many with their own well-constructed warehouses line the River Ouse. Within a short distance are some outstanding country houses, including a royals' retreat, and some superb churches.

- ▶ **Population:** 42 800.
- **Michelin Map:** Michelin Atlas p30 or Map 504 V 25.
- **Info:** The Custom House, Purfleet Quay. ☎01553 763 044. www.visitwestnorfolk.com. The train station is a five-minute walk east.
- ▶ **Location:** On the River Ouse 44mi/71km north of Cambridge.
- **Don't Miss:** At least one of the area's stately homes.
- **Timing:** Allow 4–6 hours; more for excursions.
- **Walking Tours:** May–Oct Tue, Fri and Sat 2pm. Jun and Jul also 7pm. £5. ☎01553 763 044. www.visitwest norfolk.com.

TOWN CENTRE WALK

Begin at **Tuesday Market Place**, a large open space at the top of King Street, surrounded by well-preserved Georgian and Victorian buildings. **King Street** presents a delightful succession of houses of varied dates and materials including **St George's Guildhall**, the largest surviving medieval guildhall in England, where Shakespeare is supposed to have acted. On the right is the Dutch-inspired **Custom House** (17C), on the corner of Purfleet Quay, leading to the River Ouse, part home to the tourist information centre and part home to a **maritime exhibition** (open daily Mon–Sat 10am/10.30am–3.30pm/4.30pm, Sun noon–3.30pm/4.30pm; ☎01553 763 044; www.visitwestnorfolk.com) housing displays on the merchants, customsmen and smugglers of Lynn.

King's Staithe Lane, which is the next lane south, contains 16C and 17C warehouses; in cobbled King's Staithe Square stands a grand double-fronted red brick house, with a statue of King Charles I. In **Queen Street**, which is mainly Georgian in character, stands **Thorseby College**, founded in 1502 for training priests but later converted into a merchant's house with a 17C courtyard. This leads to Saturday Market Place and **Tales of the Old Gaol House**

(open daily 10am–4.30pm; £3.95; ☎01553 774 297; www.kingslynntownhall.com). Occupying the chequered flint **Guildhall** (1421), visitors pass through the old police station with its tiny cells and bleak history. The **Regalia Room** features civic silver and the **King John Cup** (1340).Turn right onto Church Street to see **St Margaret's church** (open daily; ☎01553 767 090; www.stmargarets kingslynn.org.uk), a twin-towered church originally built in the 13C. Surviving glories include 14C screens, a Georgian pulpit and a 17C moon clock.

Walk back towards Saturday Market Place and turn right onto St James Street, then left onto Tower Street, left into Blackfriar's Street, fork right onto Paradise Parade, which will lead you to Market Street and the **Lynn Museum** (open Tue-Sat 10am–5pm, also Sun noon–4pm Apr–Sept; £4.35, free Oct–Mar; ☎01553 775 001; www.museums. norfolk.gov.uk). This is the town's main collection and pride of place goes to **Seahenge**, a remarkable meticulously crafted c.4 000-year-old timber circle found on the beach.

Return to Paradise Parade, turn right onto New Conduit Street, then walk straight ahead via Broad Street, Chapel Street and St Anne's Street. Turn right onto North Street, home to **True's Yard** (open Tue–Sat 10am–4pm; closed 25 Dec–3 Jan; £3; ℘01553 770 479; www.truesyard.co.uk) where two cottages house a small museum illustrating the social history and hardships of the town's former fishing community.

EXCURSIONS
Houghton Hall★★
◗ 13mi/21km east via the A 148. Open mid-May–Sept, Wed–Sun and Bank Holidays 11am–5pm. £18. ♿🅿✕ ℘01485 528 569. www.houghtonhall.com.
Houghton Hall, which is transitional between Baroque and Palladian, was built (1722–35) for Sir Robert Walpole, Britain's first prime minister. Its main rooms by William Kent are dedicated to '...taste, expense, state and parade'. Its joys are its ceilings and Kent furniture, Sèvres porcelain, thrones by Pugin and 17C Mortlake tapestries.

Oxburgh Hall★★
◗ 18mi/29km SE. House: Open 11am–5pm (4pm in Oct), Sat–Wed, plus Thu–Fri in Apr, late May and Aug. £10.40. ♿🅿✕ ℘01366 328 528. www.nationaltrust.org.uk/oxburgh-hall.
This romantic moated manor house was built as a status symbol in 1482. Its **gatehouse** and flanking ranges are 15C; the hall range is 19C. The interior presents elaborate **embroideries** depicting mammals; letters from Henry VIII, Queen Mary and Queen Elizabeth I; woodcarvings by Grinling Gibbons and a secret priest's hole.

Sandringham★
◗ 8mi/13km NE. Open mid-Apr–Oct, see website for details. £14 (gardens, and museum only, £9). ♿🅿✕ ℘01485 545 408. www.sandringhamestate.co.uk.
'Dear old Sandringham, the place I love better than anywhere else in the world', wrote George V of the Royal Family's country home, a Revival Jaco-

© Cyril Privezentzev/Dreamstime.com
Oxburgh Hall

bean house acquired in 1862. The large Saloon is hung with family portraits and 17C tapestries. The corridor is adorned with intricately wrought Oriental arms and armour. In the main Drawing Room is Russian silver and Chinese jade.

FENLAND CHURCHES★
The glories of the Fens are its sunsets and churches, admirably complemented by the flat and featureless landscape.
St Clement's church (Terrington St Clement; ℘01553 828 430; www.tsc-church.org.uk) boasts a splendid west window and northwest tower. The interior has exquisite Georgian panelling.
St Peter's church (Walpole St Peter; ℘01945 781 228, www.walpolestpeter-church.org) Huge plain-glass windows illuminate the magnificent interior of the 14C 'Cathedral of the Fens'.
St Mary's church (West Walton, ℘01945 583667; www.ely.anglican.org/parishes/westwalton) is mid-13C Early English at its most profuse and extravagant.
All Saints' church (Walsoken; ℘01945 583 740; www.allsaintswalsoken.co.uk). Dating from 1146, "the grandest Norman parish church in Norfolk" presents a hammerbeam tie-beam roof, an eight-sided **font** portraying the Seven Sacraments and Crucifixion, and a 16C wall painting, the *Judgement of Solomon*.

Ely★

Once called Elig or Eel Island because of the abundance of eels, Ely lies on the River Ouse. It has been a place of worship since St Ætheldreda, a Saxon queen, founded a religious community and built an abbey here in the 7C. The small town is still dominated by the cathedral and monastic buildings and retains many medieval houses. In 1066, the legendary rebel, Hereward the Wake, made his last stand against the Normans in Ely. Oliver Cromwell lived here in the mid-17C.

▶ **Population:** 20 256.

♿ **Michelin Map:** Michelin Atlas p29 or Map 504 U 26.

🛈 **Info:** Oliver Cromwell's House, 29 St Mary's Street. ℘01353 662 062. www.visitely.org.uk.

▶ **Location:** 16mi/26km north of Cambridge. Ely station (Cambridge 15 mins) is a minute's walk from the centre. Regional buses stop by the cathedral.

CATHEDRAL★★

Open: daily 7am–6.30pm. (5.30pm Sun in winter). Stained Glass Museum closed 25–26 Dec, Good Fri.
Admission: £8 including guided tour; £15 cathedral and West Tower; the total experience £18. Guided tours (free) daily, except Good Fri. ♿✗ ℘01353 667 735. www.elycathedral.org.

The superb Norman nave and transepts contrast with the surprises beyond: the wonderful Decorated east end and Lady Chapel, and that 14C masterpiece, the Octagon. The present church was begun in 1083; in 1250 the east end of the original Norman building was reconstructed. In 1321 work started on the Lady Chapel. The following year the great Norman crossing tower fell down. The solution, cutting off the four Norman corners of the crossing and building an octagonal space on the eight points, was a triumph of engineering. The cathedral is best viewed from the northwest to appreciate its length, castellated west tower, Early English Galilee Porch, the Decorated Octagon and the wooden lantern above it.

The richness of the colours emanating from ceilings, stained-glass windows and stone pillars is awe-inspiring. The **southwest transept** (c.1200) is an outstanding example of the Romanesque period. Above all else, the eye is led to the **Octagon**. Its eight pillars support 200 tons of glass, lead and timber; below its high windows are panels decorated with angels. The Octagon is separated by a 19C **screen** (by George Gilbert Scott) from the beautifully vaulted Early English choir, with its splendid 14C **choir stalls**. In front of the High Altar lies the shrine of St Etheldreda. The light and spacious **Lady Chapel** was the largest single span of vaulting in its time; most of its treasures were lost during the Dissolution.

The **Stained Glass Museum** (www.stainedglassmuseum.com) in the triforium shows stained-glass and lead-cutting processes.

The group of medieval domestic buildings, together with the ruined cloisters, is the largest of its kind in England; some form part of the King's School.

CROMWELL'S HOUSE★

29 St Mary's Street. Open daily: Apr–Oct 10am–5pm; Nov–Mar 11am–4pm. £4.90. ♿ ℘01353 662 062. www.olivercromwellshouse.co.uk.
Born and bred in East Anglia, for 10 years Oliver Cromwell, Lord Protector of England, lived in this 13C house in Ely. The furnished rooms are few – kitchen, bedroom, study – but the flavour of the age is very well evoked.

Peterborough★

and around

Peterborough began life as a village around a monastery. It became a town around a cathedral and then a city dominated by brickworks. It is now a high-tech centre for financial institutions but ancient survivals include the cathedral, the 17C arcaded guildhall, the church of St John the Baptist in Cowgate and some Georgian houses in Priestgate.

CATHEDRAL★★

Open Mon–Sat 9am–5pm, Sun noon–3pm. Closed 26 Dec. Donation invited. ♿ P (wheelchair users only). ✕. Guided tours Mon–Sat 11.30am and 2pm; Tower tours Apr–early Nov, most Sats and Weds at 1.30pm (£10), booking recommended. ℘01733 355 315. www.peterborough-cathedral.org.uk.
Alongside Ely (♦see opposite), Peterborough was one of the two great monasteries of the Fens. The present building was started in 1118 and consecrated in 1238. In 1643 Cromwell's men destroyed the stained glass, the high altar, the cloisters and statues.
The Early English **west front** is fascinating with its three giant arches and its rich early Perpendicular (14C) porch. The interior is a superb example of Norman architecture. The nave has an uninterrupted vista towards the altar. The transepts and choir with their **Norman elevations** are a robust expression of faith. The 13C **nave ceiling** is a wonderful example of medieval art with figures of bishops, saints and mythical beasts. The 15C wooden ceiling in the sanctuary is decorated with bosses and the superb **fan vaulting** at the east end (in the New or Eastern Building) is late-15C Perpendicular. In the north choir aisle Catherine of Aragon is buried and in the south choir aisle Mary Queen of Scots was temporarily laid to rest (1587–1612).

▶ **Population:** 81 779.
♿ **Michelin Map:** Michelin Atlas p29 or Map 504 T 26.
▯ **Info:** 41 Bridge Street. ℘01733 452 336. www.visitpeterborough.com. The train station (London Kings Cross, 45 mins) is a short walk from the centre. Queensgate Bus Station is close by.
◐ **Location:** 25mi/40km north of Cambridge.
◉ **Don't Miss:** The cathedral's west front, 13C nave ceiling and fan vaulting.
◷ **Timing:** Allow half a day in Peterborough.
👥 **Kids:** One of the Specials Days at Nene Valley Railway.

EXCURSIONS

Flag Fen Archaeology Park★★

◑ The Droveway, Northey Road. 3mi/5km east via the A 47 and A 1130 (signposted) Open Apr–Sept daily 10am–5pm. ♿ P ✕. ℘01733 864 468. www.fensmuseums.org.uk.
Described as the finest Bronze Age archaeological site in Northern Europe, Flag Fen is one of the most important prehistoric sites in Britain; home to the country's oldest wheel and a 0.6mi/1km-long wooden causeway and platform that's been perfectly preserved in the wetland for 3 300 years.

👥 Nene Valley Railway★

◑ Wansford Station, Old Great North Road, Stibbington. 8mi/13km west on the A 47 and south on the A 1. Mar–Oct plus specials; visit website for times and dates. From £16, child £8. ♿ P ✕ ℘01780 784 444; www.nvr.org.uk.
Steam locomotives with shiny wooden fascias puff between Wansford and Peterborough (15mi/24km – 90min return) in a scene from yesteryear. At Wansford are displays of railway memorabilia and old rolling stock, some from abroad, and some from the movies.

ADDRESSES

🏨 STAY

CAMBRIDGE

⊜⊜ **Duke House** – 1 Victoria Street. 📞01223 314 773. www.dukehouse cambridge.co.uk. 5 rooms. Close to the main colleges, in a smartly refurbished Victorian house; breakfast can be taken in small courtyard on warm days.

⊜⊜ **Brooklands Guest House** – 95 Cherry Hinton Road. 📞01223 242 035. www.brooklandsguesthouse.co.uk. 🅿 7 rooms. One mile from the city centre, and five minutes from the train station, this simple guesthouse has lovely boutique-style bedrooms (one of which has a jacuzzi and four-poster bed).

⊜⊜ **Warkworth House** – Warkworth Terrace. 📞01223 363 682. www.warkworth house.com. 3 rooms. In the city centre, this small Victorian B&B offers a handsome spacious double room, and simple family and single rooms.

⊜⊜⊜⊜ **Arundel House Hotel** – 53 Chesterton Road. 📞01223 367 701. www.arundelhousehotels.co.uk. 🅿 103 rooms. Arundel House occupies one of the finest hotel sites in town, a few minutes' walk from the centre, overlooking the River Cam and open parkland. It has a beautiful garden and conservatory. Chintzy bedrooms.

⊜⊜⊜⊜ **Hotel du Vin** – 15–19 Trumpington Road. 📞01223 928 991. www.hotelduvin.com. 41 rooms. Opposite the Fitzwilliam Museum, set in an historic ex-University terrace, the luxurious ultra-stylish bedrooms and traditional Oxbridge lounge/library ooze atmosphere and class. Cosy cellar bar, exemplary staff, excellent dining.

IPSWICH

⊜⊜⊜⊜ **Salthouse Harbour Hotel** – Neptune Quay. 📞01473 226 789. www. salthouseharbour.co.uk. 🅿 30 rooms. On the marina, this rejuvenated warehouse has been converted into a striking contemporary space containing an eclectic blend of urban and country, vintage chic and cutting-edge design.

COLCHESTER

⊜⊜⊜ **The Red Lion** – High Street. 📞01206 577 986. www.red-lion-hotel. co.uk. 🅿 24 rooms. This 15C inn has been furnished and decorated sympathetically in period style with modern touches. Four-posters available.

BURY ST EDMUNDS

⊜⊜⊜⊜ **The Angel Hotel** – 3 Angel Hill. 📞01284 714 000. www.theangel. co.uk. 🅿 70 rooms. Opposite the abbey gardens, this fashionable hotel, behind a classic Georgian façade, offers contemporary-traditional styling, some rooms with shabby chic. The restaurant serves fine Modern British cuisine (⊜⊜⊜).

NORWICH

⊜⊜ **number17** – 17 Colegate. 📞01603 764 486. www.number17norwich.co.uk. 8 rooms. Family-run boutique-style B&B in the heart of the old city with bright cheery bedrooms and a small courtyard. Family suites also available.

⊜⊜⊜ **Waveney Inn** – Waveney River Centre, Burgh St Peter. 📞01502 677 599. www.waveneyinn.co.uk. 7 rooms. Part of the larger Waveney River Centre complex (www.waveneyrivercentre. co.uk), featuring luxury B&B rooms, lodges, cottage and penthouses, located right on the edge of the Norfolk/Suffolk marshes. Great restaurant, too.

WELLS-NEXT-THE-SEA

⊜⊜⊜⊜ **The Victoria Inn** – Holkham. 📞01328 711 008. www.holkham.co.uk/ victoria. 10 rooms. This beautiful 'Modern Colonial' themed hotel, formerly a pub, lies on the glorious Holkham Estate a few minutes' walk from Holkham Beach. The restaurant (⊜⊜⊜) serves excellent local dishes.

ELY

⊜⊜ **Cathedral House** – 17 Mary's Street. 📞01353 662 124. www.cathedralhouse. co.uk. 🖂 🅿. 3 rooms. Set almost in the shadow of the cathedral this lovely cosy quiet Georgian house offers simple pleasant white bedrooms. Minimum two-night stay at weekends.

⑪ EAT

CAMBRIDGE

Ⓐ Look on Regent Street, Bridge Street and along Quayside. There are over 100 pubs and bars throughout the town, the most famous being **The Eagle**, on Benet Street, off King's Parade.

Galleria – 3 Bridge Street. ✆01223 362 054. www.galleriacambridge.co.uk. This light airy brasserie serves excellent Modern European dishes (and snacks at lunchtime) on a pretty riverside terrace.

Hotel du Vin – 15-19 Trumpington Road. ✆0844/3 64253. Top quality candlelit French bistro-style dining in an atmospheric old ex-University building. Superb choice of wines expertly matched to uncomplicated dishes. Excellent service.

Midsummer House – Midsummer Common. ✆01223 369 299, www.midsummerhouse.co.uk. Michelin two-star establishment in East Anglia, Cambridge's finest enjoys an idyllic location beside the Cam, with conservatory dining. The French Mediterranean cuisine offers inventive detailed cooking.

22 Chesterton Road – 22 Chesterton Road. ✆01223 351 880. www.restaurant22.co.uk. Closed Sun–Mon. Critically acclaimed high-quality dining from a prix fixe dinner menu (hefty supplements on certain dishes).

NEAR CAMBRIDGE

The Three Horseshoes – High Street, Madingley, 5mi/8km west Cambridge. ✆01954 210 221. www.threehorseshoesmadingley.co.uk. A picture-perfect thatched pub, with an airy stylish interior and Modern British menu of bright, fresh, seasonal dishes.

IPSWICH

Mariners – Neptune Quay. ✆01473 289 748. www.marinersipswich.co.uk. High-quality French Brasserie cuisine is served from prix-fixe menus aboard a much-travelled late-19C wooden sailing ship, with polished beams and gleaming brass.

COLCHESTER

Victus Bistros – 48 St Johns Street. ✆01206 767 337. The exposed brickwork in this atmospheric restaurant is the town's historic city wall, though everything else is very contemporary, including the popular British and European dishes.

NORWICH

Ⓐ Look on St Giles Street, Upper St Giles Street, Elm Hill and St George Street.

The Britons Arms Coffe Housse and Restaurant – 9 Elm Hill. ✆01603 623 367. www.britonsarms.co.uk. Open Mon–Sat 9.30am–5pm. This long-established cosy place serves quiches, salads, cakes and more with a delightfully secluded terraced garden.

The Waffle House – 39 St Giles Street. ✆01603 612 790. www.wafflehouse norwich.co.uk. This buzzing café bar specialises in sweet and savoury Belgian waffles individually cooked to order using organic and free range ingredients.

KING'S LYNN

Bankhouse – King's Staithe Square. ✆01553 660 492. www.thebankhouse.co.uk. The restaurant of this beautiful Georgian hotel serves modern brasserie food, from burgers, steaks, pastas and salads, to the more exotic, and may be enjoyed in any of three dining areas, or in the summer on a riverside terrace.

ENTERTAINMENT

The Cambridge Folk Festival (late Jul/early Aug), is Britain's best music festival of its kind (✆01223 357 851; www.cambridgefolkfestival.co.uk).

SHOPPING

Cambridge is excellent for individual shops; try **Rose Crescent, Trinity Street, Bridge Street, Magdalene Street, St John's Street, Green Street. General Market in the Square** (Mon–Sat).

East Midlands

Burghley House, Stamford © Olaf Protze / age fotostock

Introduction

Comprising Nottinghamshire, Leicestershire, Northamptonshire and Lincolnshire, the East Midlands has never been a region that has figured highly on the itineraries of most visitors, foreign or domestic. Nottingham's Robin Hood is the star name – though there is little tangible evidence of the outlaw – and Lincoln's cathedral is the star attraction, but how many can even place Lincoln on a map?! The latter is certainly worth the detour, and Nottingham has more than just a legend to sustain visitor interest. Cosmopolitan Leicester, and its shire, is a pleasant surprise package, while Stamford is the hidden gem of this underrated region. Between the 9C and 10C the East (and North) Midlands was controlled by Danish conquerors, whose kingdom was known as the Five Boroughs of the Danelaw. Its five principal towns are still the region's centres: Nottingham, Leicester, Lincoln, Stamford and Derby.

Nottingham

The town and shire is best known for its connections with Robin Hood and Sherwood Forest. This 12C gentleman robber poached from the lands of the hated Sheriff of Nottingham, installed to enforce the law by the equally unpopular Prince John, who was the de facto ruler while King Richard (the Lionheart) was fighting the Crusades. Robin Hood, or Robyn Hode, therefore became the symbol of English resistance to Norman rule and it is unlikely that a single character like him ever existed at all. More likely 'he' was an amalgam of different people around this period. Robin would recognise nothing of modern Nottingham. Even D H Lawrence, the region's early-20C literary giant, would struggle, though the Lacemarket and castle would at least be familiar to him.

Highlights

1 Explore **Nottingham castle** and its caves (p362)

2 Beam yourself up to the National Space Centre, **Leicester** (p364)

3 Marvel at **Lincoln cathedral** both within and without (p367)

4 Be taken in by the Gothic fantasy of **Belvoir castle** (p371)

5 Wander around the 600 listed buildings of **Stamford** town centre (p373)

Leicestershire

Pronounced 'lester-sher', this was once the seat of the 8C East Mercian bishops and the capital of King Lear's kingdom. In recent times, Leicester was a centre for the hosiery trade, and this was a major factor in attracting Asian emigrants. Today, over a third of its population is Asian. Despite this accommodating nature, the city is a relative newcomer to welcoming tourists. The National Space Centre put Leicester on the day-visitor map and its new Curve Theatre has added to its cultural appeal.

Northamptonshire

Northants (as it is often abbreviated) is a pleasant county with ancient stone villages and some fine country houses. If you like shoes, you'll love the city museum.

Lincolnshire

A county of old-fashioned seaside resorts and industrial fishing ports on the windy east coast, Lincolnshire is never to going to attract much passing trade from visitors. The town of Lincoln, however, is well worth the dedicated journey. With a wonderful natural location, its magnificent cathedral is one of the finest in England, with the old town spreading around its feet is a delight. To the south of Lincoln are some fine country houses and Belvoir castle, while in the far southwest of the county Stamford has more in character with Northants or Leicestershire than Lincolnshire, and is probably the finest '...town built all of stone' in England. To the east of Lincoln is the haunting waterlogged landscape of the Fens.

Nottinghamshire★

This county is the home of Sherwood Forest, where Robin Hood and his band of medieval merry men famously robbed the rich and gave to the poor. Later, literary giants such as D H Lawrence would paint a much grittier local picture, while Lord Byron also has local associations.

⚐ **Michelin Map:** Michelin Atlas p36 or Map 504 Q 25.

🖥 **Info:** 1–4 Smithy Row, Nottingham. ℘08444 775 678. www.experience nottinghamshire.com.

NOTTINGHAM

Although this is the city that has adopted Robin Hood as its own, it is the outlaw's arch enemy, and chief villain, the Sheriff of Nottingham, who lures our hero into town from the safety of the forest. On safer historical ground, Nottingham made its early name from lace.

Nottingham castle★

Castle Road. Open daily: mid-Feb–Oct 10am–5pm; Nov–mid-Feb 10am–4pm. £8. ♿✕ ℘0115 876 1400. www.nottinghamcastle.org.uk.
Of the original Norman castle, only the subterranean passage, **Mortimer's Hole** (leading from the castle to the **Brewhouse Yard**, and now part of the Nottingham Castle Caves tour), and the 12C **Ye Olde Trip to Jerusalem** survive. The latter is probably the oldest inn in England, built into the foot of the castle walls, and accessed separately. The 'new' castle, a 17C ducal mansion, is home to a lively museum and art gallery, housing a large collection of silver, glass, decorative items, visual arts and paintings. Don't miss the fine examples of medieval Nottingham **alabasters★**. Beneath lie **Nottingham Castle Caves** (℘0115 876 1400; +£5), a labyrinth dating from medieval times, with over 300 steep and strenuous steps, alleviated by colourful tales.

If you want to get into the **Robin Hood** spirit of things, take a tour of the **city centre** (℘0844 477 5678, www.ezekial-bone.com, £12) with the man himself (or at least a lookalike!).

Just outside the gatehouse, next to Ye Olde Trip to Jerusalem pub, is the **Museum of Nottingham Life at Brewhouse Yard** (℘0115 876 1400; www.nottinghamcastle.org.uk) housed within five charming red-brick 17C cottages. Once a thriving small community of 20 houses, the surviving buildings contain a mixture of reconstructed room and shop settings depicting social history.

♟♙ National Justice Museum

Lave Market. Open: Mon–Fri 9am–5.30pm, Sat–Sun 10am–5.30pm. £10.95, child £7.95. Closed 24–26 Dec, 1 Jan. ℘0115 952 0555; www.galleriesofjustice.org.uk.
Behind the elegant 18C façade the turnkey takes visitors on a gruesomely entertaining actors-led 'performance' tour of caves, dungeons and prison cells featuring highwaymen (and women), convict ships, Great Train Robbers, Robin Hood (inevitably) and executions that took place just outside the cramped and squalid prison on this site that dates back to the 15C.
It is worth wandering around the narrow streets of the surrounding **Lace Market** area, particularly Stoney Street, to soak up its Victorian atmosphere. By night this is one of the city's buzzing hubs (though best avoided around pub closing time). Off Stoney Street, High Pavement leads into Weekday Cross and the modern **Nottingham Contemporary** (open Tue–Sat 10am–6pm, Sun 11am–5pm, bank holidays 10am–5pm; ✕℘0115 948 9750; www.nottingham contemporary.org), one of the UK's largest contemporary art centres.

EXCURSIONS

D H Lawrence Birthplace Museum

◉8a Victoria Street, Eastwood. 10mi/
16km NW on the A 610. Open for guided
tours only: Tue–Sun 10am–4pm. Timed
admission only, so booking ahead is
advisable for all tours (see website for
details). £6.90. ℘0115 917 3824.
www.dhlawrenceheritage.org.

This tiny terraced cottage, where Lawrence was born in 1885, was the first
of four Lawrence family homes in Eastwood. The tour gives an insight into the
writer's early life and influences in this
small mining town.

The **D H Lawrence Heritage Centre**
(closed in 2016, but the service has been
transferred to the Birthplace Museum),
housed exhibitions and artefacts about
the writer's life

Newstead Abbey★

◉12mi/19km N of Nottingham off the
A 60. **House:** open Sat–Sun and bank
holiday Mons noon–4pm. £8; **Grounds
and gardens:** daily 10am–5pm (4pm
mid-Oct–mid-Feb); £6 per vehicle.
🅿✕ ℘01623 455 900.
www.newsteadabbey.org.uk.

The medieval priory of the abbey was
converted in the 16C into a house that
became the ancestral seat of Lord
Byron. The 19C rooms include the apartments of Byron and a selection of his
manuscripts and memorabilia.

Sherwood Forest

◉21mi/34km N of Nottingham.

Once one of 65 'Royal' Forests that
covered much of England, Sherwood
was protected from agriculture and
development by royal hunting laws. In
this perfect environment for poaching,
outlaw bands became legends, and by
the 15C **Robyn Hode** had become a
charismatic folk-tale character embracing all their exploits.

The **Sherwood Forest Country Park**
Visitor Centre (1mi/1.6km N of Edwin-
stowe; open daily 10am–5pm; closed
25 Dec; ♿🅿 (£3; £5 during Robin Hood
Festival in late Jul–early Aug) ✕; ℘01623

823 202; www.nottinghamshire.gov.uk)
marks the area that was the legendary
haunt of Robin Hood. From the visitor
centre paths lead to the **Major Oak**,
beneath which the outlaw is supposed
to have sheltered. The tree is between
800 and 1 000 years old, and around
10m in diameter.

Southwell Minster★★

◉14mi/23km NE.

Open daily: Mar–Oct 8am–7pm/6.30 or
dusk in winter. £2. Guided and tower
tours £3–£5, see website for details.
♿🅿✕ ℘01636 812 649.
www.southwellminster.org.uk.

Southwell – pronounced 'su'thel' – is
dominated by the Norman Minster, well
known for the foliage carving of its late-
13C master masons. It is the only cathedral in England to boast a complete set
of three Norman towers and dates from
c.1108. Smooth lawns and well-spaced
graves frame the **west front**, pierced
by a Perpendicular seven-light window. The intimate **interior** combines
Norman severity with the glory of the
mid-14C **screen**, depicting 286 Images
of men, gods and devils, and the even
more glorious Early English **choir** and
chapter house (1288). The latter is the
first single-span stone-vaulted chapter
house in Christendom, decorated with
some of the finest medieval naturalism
(late-13C) carved in stone.

Rufford Abbey Country Park

◉Ollerton. 18mi/29km N. Open
daily summer 10am–5pm; winter
10.30am–4.30pm. Closed 25 Dec.
♿🅿 (£3). ✕ ℘01623 821 338.
www.nottinghamshire.gov.uk/ruffordcp.

The present-day park once formed part
of a 12C Cistercian abbey estate. Today's
abbey is a mixture of Cistercian remains
and one wing of a country house from
the early-1600s. The Stable Block, which
houses the Craft Centre, dates from the
1660s with Victorian renovations. The
grounds of the Abbey retain some fascinating features, such as its Ice Houses.

Leicestershire★

Once the capital of King Lear's kingdom, and the seat of the 8C East Mercian bishops, the wealth of Leicester was based on the manufacture of hosiery (legwear), and to a lesser degree, coal mining, from the medieval period until the mid-20C. Today, it is a cosmopolitan and increasingly fashionable town with the new £60 million Curve Theatre at the heart of its cultural regeneration. In 2012, archaeologists excavated the lost medieval Grey Friars church and within the ruins, found the grave and bones of King Richard III, who was later ceremoniously buried in Leicester cathedral.

- **Michelin Map:** Michelin Atlas p28 or Map 504 Q 26.
- **Info:** 51 Gallowtree Gate, Leicester. ✆0116 299 4444. www.goleicestershire.com.
- **Kids:** Space Centre; Snibston.
- **Tours:** Follow the route on the map.

LEICESTER★

In the city centre, between the River Soar and St Martin's Square, is the **Guildhall★** (Guildhall Lane; Open daily 11am–4.30pm; ✆0116 253 2569; www.leicestermuseums.ac.uk), one of the best-preserved timber-framed halls in the country, dating back six hundred years. Note the robust timber roof and uprights in the Hall, the early-16C glass in the mayor's parlour, and one of the earliest public libraries in England. It is now mainly a performance venue, but also holds a small museum, including Victorian cells with a couple of 'inmates' that amuse children.

Head southwest from the Guildhall to St Nicholas Circle, then turn down Castle Street for **St Mary de Castro church★** (✆01572 820 181; www.stmarydecastro.co.uk). The shadowy attractive interior goes back to 1107.

Southeast of the Guildhall, along Gallowtree Gate and Granby Street on New Walk (see Map I) at No. 53 is the town's major collection, the **New Walk Museum and Art Gallery★** (open Mon–Sat 10am–5pm, Sun 11am–5pm; ♿✕; ✆0116 225 4900; www.leicestermuseums.ac.uk). The art galleries showcase changing displays of Modern and Old Masters including works by Hogarth and Francis Bacon and a permanent display of Picasso ceramics. There are also galleries on biodiversity, World Arts, and popular dinosaur and Ancient Egypt sections.

Cathedral

Leicester's cathedral was built on the site of a Roman temple, and was dedicated to St Martin of Tours. Between the 13C and 15C it was the 'civic' church, with strong links both with merchants and the nearby Guildhall.

The cathedral saw its first bishop in the year 680, but within 200 years the attentions of the Vikings caused the then bishop to flee. For over 1 000 years, until as recently as 1927, the city had no bishop, when what was the Church of St Martin became Leicester cathedral.

More recently, the cathedral's fame has revolved around the discovery in a nearby council car park of the confirmed remains of Richard III, king of England from 1483 until 1485. In that year, Richard III was killed at the Battle of Bosworth Field (see below), and his body returned to Leicester in ignominy. Although the remains of the king were buried in the choir of Greyfriars Priory in August 1485, his precise last resting place was unknown for centuries until its discovery in 2012. In March 2015, the king was reinterred in the cathedral.

EXCURSIONS

National Space Centre★

2mi/3km N, just off the A6.

Open daily 10am–5pm. £14, child (5–16) £11. P (£3). ✕ ✆0116 261 0261, infoline ✆0116 261 0261; www.spacecentre.co.uk.

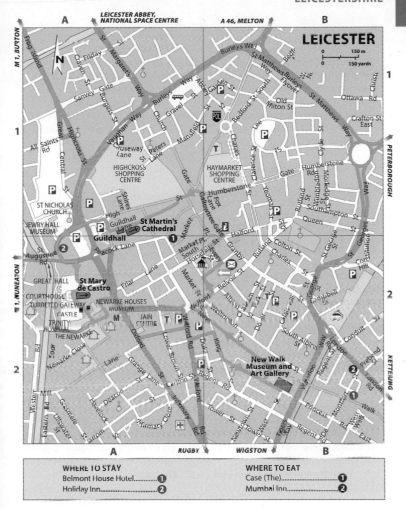

LEICESTER

WHERE TO STAY		WHERE TO EAT	
Belmont House Hotel	❶	Case (The)	❶
Holiday Inn	❷	Mumbai Inn	❷

Themed galleries include actual space hardware (a Russian Soyuz capsule, the British Blue Streak rocket…), hundreds of interactive hands-on activities and an exploration of the universe through the latest in audio-visual technology. The 42m-high landmark **Rocket Tower** includes the only lunar lander simulator outside of America. Another highlight for many visitors is a show, with laser and animation techniques, inside the UK's largest planetarium.

Bosworth Battlefield

❍ Sutton Cheney, Market Bosworth. 14mi/23km W. Heritage centre open daily: Apr–Oct 10am–5pm; Nov– and Mar 10am–4pm. £8.95, child (3–15) £5.75. 🅿 (charge). ✖ ✆01455 290 429. www.bosworthbattlefield.org.uk.

In 1485, Richard III was killed at the Battle of Bosworth and the first Tudor monarch, Henry VII, took the throne, ending years of dynastic war.

An excellent state-of-the-art visitor centre, on the edge of the rolling fields where the battle took place, interprets the event and a re-enactment takes place on the weekend closest to 22nd August. Regular guided walks and birds-of-prey demonstrations (additional charges) also take place during the summer.

Oakham

▶ 20mi/32km E of Leicester.
This traditional Georgian-period market town is at its best around the Market Place *(market days are Wed and Sat)* with its stocks and waterpump beneath its hexagonal medieval Buttercross. A few yards away stands **Oakham Castle** (open Mon, Wed–Sat 10am–4pm, Sun noon–4pm; ℘01572 757 578; www. oakhamcastle.org). In appearance little more than a large church, this is the Great Hall of long-gone Oakham Castle, one of the finest examples of late-12C domestic architecture in England.
Rutland Water Nature Reserve, less than 2mi/3km east of Oakham (www. rutlandwater.org.uk), is excellent for bird-watching (the closest visitor centre is at Egleton), or just a leisurely stroll in lovely natural surroundings.

Northamptonshire

Something of a forgotten corner, the area's main claim to fame is its shoemaking heritage. In Victorian times there were over 1 800 cobblers in town and Northampton supplied most of the boots to the British armed forces in the two world wars.

🄸 **Info:** County Hall, George Row, Northampton. ℘01604 367 997. www.visit northamptonshire.co.uk

NORTHAMPTON

The centre of town is marked by two handsome squares, Market Square and St Giles Square, the latter home to the impressive **Guildhall**, a flamboyant Victorian Gothic Revival design.
Close by **Northampton Museum and Art Gallery** (currently closed for expansion; check website for details; ℘01604 837 397, www.northampton.gov.uk/museums) boasts the world's largest collection of footwear from all over the world.

ALTHORP

Open daily May–Sept noon–5pm, also during Althorp Literary Festival in October. £18.50. ℘01604 770 107. www.spencerofalthorp.com.
Althorp has been the seat of the Spencer family for over 500 years. It is best known as the final resting place of **Diana, Princess of Wales,** but visitors should note that her grave is inaccessible (on an island in a lake) and there are no memorials or exhibitions to her at Althorp. The house holds one of Europe's finest private collections of furniture, ceramics, and paintings and photographs.

BOUGHTON HOUSE★★

Open for guided tours only: Aug daily 1–4pm. £10. ✗ ℘01536 515 731. www.boughtonhouse.org.uk.
Originally a monastic house owned by the Abbey of Edmundsbury, it was bought by Edward Montagu in 1528 and extended. More were made by the first Duke of Montagu, ambassador to Louis XIV, who built the north front and embellished the interior turning it into "the English Versailles". Among its paintings are masterpieces by El Greco, Murillo, Gainsborough, Van Dyck, Lely and Kneller.

Lincolnshire★★

The city of Lincoln and its cathedral rises physically and metaphorically above the wolds, marshes and north East Anglian seaside resorts like a beacon. Only Stamford is comparable in terms of metropolitan interest though there are many fine country houses to visit here in England's second largest county.

LINCOLN★★

Set high on a limestone plateau beside the River Witham and dominated by the triple towers of the cathedral, Lincoln is visible for miles around the eastern English countryside. Much of the lower part of the town is a pedestrianised shopping area dotted with the occasional medieval church; steep narrow streets lead to the upper town with its imposing cathedral, castle and Roman remains.

A Bit of History

Lindum Colonia, a settlement established since the Bronze Age and occupied by the Ninth Legion around the year 60, was turned into a *colonia* (colonial settlement) in about 96 CE, and confined to the plateau top (42 acres/17ha) surrounded by a wooden palisade. In the 3C, Lincoln, now one of the four provincial capitals of Roman Britain, doubled in size. The city spread down the southern slopes to the river and was encased in a gated stone wall (1.5m thick) – offering a good view from the Bishop's Old Palace. The surviving **Newport Arch**, the only Roman arch in England through which traffic still passes, was the city's north gate.

Lincoln survived the Roman decline, emerging as the capital of the Anglo-Saxon kingdom of Lindsey, and converted to Christianity in c.630. After the Conquest, it gained in importance, with the building of the castle and cathedral, and became one of the most prosperous cities in medieval England, shipping its wool direct to Flanders. Many half-timbered buildings survive from this time

Michelin Map: Michelin Atlas p36 or Map 502 S 24.

Info: 3-5 St Swithin's Square. ℘01522 545 458. www.visitlincoln.com. The train station and bus station are almost opposite each other in the lower part of the city centre. It's easy to cover the centre on foot, albeit a steep walk from 'downhill' to 'uphill'.

Location: Northeast Midlands, 88mi/142km from Birmingham and 39mi/63km from Nottingham.

Don't Miss: The cathedral, especially the roof tour (Saturday only) on a clear day, the High Bridge; Belvoir Castle

Timing: Allow a full day to see the cathedral and town.

Walking Tours: Lincoln Guild of Guides operates city centre tours on a daily basis. Ask at the tourist office.

CITY WALK
Cathedral★★★

Open: Jul–Aug Mon–Fri 7.15am–8pm, Sat–Sun 7.15am–6pm; Sept–Jun Mon–Sat. 7.15am–6pm, Sun 7.15–5pm. £8 (joint ticket with castle £16).
Libraries: Apr–Jun and Sept–Oct Mon–Fri 1–3pm, Sat 11am–3pm; Jul–Aug Mon–Sat 11am–3pm.
Tours: Cathedral floor: Mar–Oct Mon–Sat 11am, 1pm, 3pm; Nov–Feb 11am, 2pm; **Roof tours:** Mar–Oct Mon–Sat 11am, 2pm; Nov–Feb Mon–Fri 1.30pm, Sat 11am, 1.30pm; **Tower tours:** Mar–Nov Sat only 11.30am, 1pm, 2.30pm.
&X ℘01522 561 600.
www.lincolncathedral.com.

The first cathedral, built by Remigius, was early Norman, the result of a short and decisive programme between 1072 and 1092. Alexander, Lincoln's third bishop, builder of Newark castle,

Lincoln cathedral

© Jason Friend/age fotostock

re-roofed the cathedral following a fire in 1141. Hugh of Avalon, a French monk, built the present Early English cathedral following the earthquake of 1185, which virtually destroyed the original Norman building. Few cathedrals have achieved such even proportions: the chancel is as long as the nave, the west towers almost as high as the crossing tower. The **west front**, the most famous view, consists of early Norman central sections, surrounded by a cliff-face of Early English blind arcading.

The south side is graced by the intricate carving inside the **Galilee Porch** and **Judgement Porch** and the north side provides a splendid and varied view of the buttressed Decorated **east end**, the north transept and the flying-buttressed chapter house.

Interior – Lincoln limestone and Purbeck marble shafts combine to create piers of contrasted texture which support the triforium, clerestory and vaults, showing Early English architecture at its best. The **nave** is composed of seven bays; an exceptional font of Tournai marble stands in the second south bay; the windows are filled with Victorian stained glass. The crossing is flooded with light from the windows of the **Dean's Eye** (13C glass) in the north transept and the **Bishop's Eye** (14C leaf-patterned tracery, filled with fragments of medieval stained glass) in the south.

East of the magnificent 14C stone screen is **St Hugh's Choir**, furnished with 14C oak **misericords** and covered with the so-called 'crazy vault of Lincoln', the first rib-vault of purely decorative intentions in Europe, curiously asymmetrical yet '...easier to criticise than improve' (Pevsner). The **Angel Choir** is geometrical (late Early English), rich, light and spacious, so called after the 28 carved stone angels in the spandrels beneath the upper windows.

The soaring **East Window** of Victorian glass depicts biblical scenes in the earliest Gothic eight-light window (1275). High on the first pier from the east end on the north side, the **Lincoln Imp**, the grotesque little character that has become the city's emblem, looks down on the shrine of St Hugh.

The 13C **cloister** is vaulted in wood (note the bosses: a man pulling a face, a man sticking out his tongue). Forming the north range is Christopher Wren's **Library**, above a Classical loggia. East of the cloister is the **Chapter House** (early-13C) – the vaulting springing from a central shaft and externally supported by flying buttresses – where Edward I and II held some of the early English parliaments.

Precincts – Amid the mostly Georgian and Victorian houses the **Vicar's Court** dates from 1300–1400; the four ranges and mid-15C barn behind are a rare survival and among the prettiest examples of their kind in England.

Lincoln Medieval **Bishop's Palace** (currently closed for conservation work; check website for details; ☎01522 527 468; www.english-heritage.org.uk) is ruined

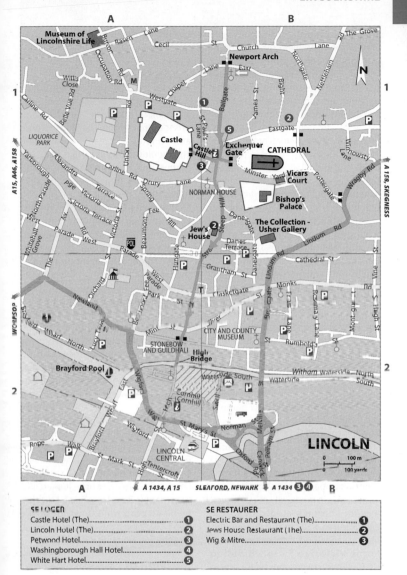

but redolent of its former grandeur and gives an idea of the richness of the city's medieval prelates. According to a description before its destruction in the Civil War, '…the great hall is very fair, lightsome and strong…one large middle alley and two out alleys on either side with eight grey marble pillars bearing up the arches and free-stone windows very full of stories in painting glass of the Kings of this land'.

Castle Hill

This street, which is lined by houses dating from the 16C to the 19C, links the 14C **Exchequer Gate** and the East Gate leading to the castle.

Castle★

Open daily Apr–Sept 10am–5pm; Oct–Mar 10am–4pm. Closed 1 Jan and 24-26 and 31 Dec. £13.50. ✕ ℘01522 554 559. www.lincolncastle.com.

The construction of the Norman castle was begun by William the Conqueror in 1068, though nothing remains of the original. The keep's mound is now crowned by the late-12C **Lucy Tower**, once surrounded by a ditch (6m deep) and a drawbridge. At the top is a circular Victorian burial ground for prisoners, marked by rows of small gravestones. The **East Gate** was added in the 12C, **Cobb Hall** in the 13C. This was a defensive tower and in the 19C the roof was the scene of public hangings. Iron rings, still fixed to the walls, were used to attach prisoners' chains.

A Norman tower was enlarged in the 14C and added to in the 19C when it became known as the Observatory Tower, from which there is a splendid **view** of the cathedral and the surrounding countryside. It is possible to walk round the walls along the east, north and west sides (not recommended for vertigo sufferers). Although besieged in the wars of 1135–54 and 1216–17, the castle gradually lost its military significance but became a centre for the administration of justice which continues to this day; it is still home to the Crown Court.

The Georgian **Prison Building**, constructed between 1787 and 1791, is used to display one of the four surviving copies of **Magna Carta** (1215) in a darkened room accompanied by a voice intoning its contents in medieval Latin. The vellum document is preceded by a small exhibition explaining the document's history and importance to democracy. In the **Victorian Prison Building** (1845/46), where prisoners were kept in solitary confinement, is a tableau showing oakum picking and the tiered **Prison Chapel** where a preacher addressed prisoners in their separate pews.

Jew's House★

Steep Hill.

The house, now home to a restaurant, features beautiful Norman windows and doorway, and original chimney buttresses dating from c.1170; the adjoining **Jew's Court** was once used as a synagogue.

Usher Gallery★

Danes Terrace. Open daily 10am–4pm. Closed 1 Jan, 24–26, 31 Dec. &✕ ✆01522 782 040. www.thecollectionmuseum.com.

This new space is devoted to art and archaeology in Lincoln. The latter comprises artefacts from the Stone, Bronze and Iron Ages, Roman, Saxon, Viking and medieval eras as well as fine, decorative and contemporary visual arts. Usher Gallery treasures are 16C–19C **miniatures**, 17C and 18C French and English clocks, Chinese, Sèvres, Meissen and English **porcelain** and English and continental glass. A room is devoted to the watercolours of **Peter de Wint** (1784–1849), who painted views of the Lincolnshire countryside and the Cathedral.

In the **Tennyson** room are many of the poet's personal items including hats, pens, the warrant appointing him Poet Laureate, and photos of his funeral. Other treasures include paintings by Turner, Stubbs and Lowry, and clocks with wooden movements by Robert Sutton.

High Bridge★★

Medieval, with the River Witham flowing through its Norman vaults (the Glory Hole), its timber-framed houses are a unique reminder of what Old London Bridge must have looked like. Upstream is **Brayford Pool**, Lincoln's medieval port, while downstream are two historic inns, the 14C Green Dragon and the 15C Witch and Wardrobe.

Museum of Lincolnshire Life

Open: **Museum:** daily 10am–4.30pm. Closed 1 Jan, 24–26, 31 Dec. ✕ ✆01522 782 040. www.lincoln.gov.uk.

This is the largest and most diverse community museum in Lincolnshire, with a rich and varied social history collection from 1750 to the present day. Exhibits illustrate commercial, domestic, agricultural, industrial and community life, and includes the interactive galleries of the Royal Lincolnshire Regiment. The authentic World War One tank, 'Flirt', is a favourite object. Behind the museum,

Belvoir castle

Ellis Mill (closed for conservation work) is a picturesque restored late-18C working windmill.

EXCURSIONS

Belvoir Castle★★

35ml/56km SW on the A 607 via Grantham, in Denton turn right (signs). Open Apr–Oct 11am–5.30pm. Guided tour, most days at 11.30am, 1.30pm, 3pm. £20; garden only £11.50.
  ♿ 🅿(£2) ✗ ℰ01476 871 001
www.belvoircastle.com.

Built by John Webb, a pupil of Inigo Jones, in 1654–68, Belvoir (pronounced 'beaver') was romanticised by James Wyatt into an early-19C 'castle on a hill'. The interior is part Gothic fantasy, part Baroque fantasy; the Ballroom contains Thomas Becket's illuminated breviary. The ceiling of the Elizabeth Saloon depicts Jupiter, Juno, Mercury and Venus. In the picture gallery are miniatures (Hilliard and Oliver) and paintings by Jan Steen, Cornelius Janssen, David Teniers II, Poussin and Gainsborough. The Regent's Gallery (40m long) is hung with vast Gobelins tapestries.

Belton House★

26mi/42km S on the A 607.
Open early Mar–early Nov Wed–Sun 12.30–5pm; park and gardens open all year, check website for details. £15, grounds only £11.50 (£8 early Nov–Dec).
♿🅿✗ ℰ01476 566 116.
www.nationaltrust.org.uk/belton-house.
Belton is the fulfilment of the golden age of English domestic architecture

from Wren to Adam. The Classical simplicity of the Marble Hall provides the setting for paintings by Reynolds, Hoppner and Romney; the woodcarvings in the Salon are possibly by Grinling Gibbons; and in the Red Drawing Room is Fra Bartolomeo's *Madonna and Child*.

Doddington Hall★

5ml/8km SW.
Open: **Hall and Gardens:** £10.50:
Easter–Sept Wed, Sun and bank holiday Mons noon–4.30pm; **Gardens only:** £7:
Aug Sun–Fri 11am–4.30pm; mid-Feb Easter and Oct Sun only 11am–4.30pm.
♿🅿✗ ℰ01522 694 308.
www.doddingtonhall.com.

Doddington Hall is late Elizabethan and outward-looking, abandoning the traditional internal courtyard. With the exception of the parlour, all the interior was refurbished in 1764 by Thomas Lumby, a local builder. The **parlour** itself is in Queen Anne style, its walls graced with paintings, including works by Sir Thomas Lawrence, Sir Peter Lely and Ghaerardt. The stairs are a masterpiece. The superb **Long Gallery** has displays of paintings and porcelain. The **West Garden** is a riot of colour from April through to September, with luxuriant, wide borders.

Gainsborough Old Hall★

18mi/29km W on the A 57 (Z) and N on the A 156. Open: Mar–Oct daily 10am–5pm; Nov–Feb Mon–Fri 10am–4pm, Sat 11am–4pm. £8.50.
♿🅿✗ ℰ01522 782 040.

www.gainsboroughdhall.co.uk;
www.english-heritage.org.uk.
One of the best-preserved late-medieval manor houses in England, this striking timber-framed hall was built between 1460 and 1480. Richard III visited it in 1483. It was originally all timber framed, except for the brick kitchen, brick tower and stone bay window, but Elizabethan features were added to the two ranges. The Hall itself has a sturdy single-arched braced roof; the **kitchen** gives an excellent impression of medieval life in the servants' quarters. The east wing contains great chambers, while the west wing is a unique example of 15C lodgings. The tower is furnished as a late-15C bedchamber. There is a permanent exhibition about the Old Hall and the Mayflower Pilgrims.

WOLDS AND COAST

⚹ www.visittheseaside.com.
Unless you have children in tow or you are a fan of the old-fashioned English seaside resort, you'll probably want to give a wide berth to Skegness/Ingoldmells, Mablethorpe and Cleethorpes. However, the rest of Lincolnshire's 50mi/80km of coastline is a wild and unspoiled haven for nature with a rich variety of reserves, sanctuaries and long sandy beaches to enjoy. The Wolds, low rolling hills and valleys are at their most attractive around Louth.

Louth

27mi/43km NE of Lincoln.
⚹ Town Hall, Cannon Street. ☏01507 601 111. www.explorelincolnshire.co.uk.
The 'historic capital of the Wolds', Louth is its most attractive town. Dating mostly from the 17C and 18C its skyline is dominated by the Church of St James, with a 90m-tall spire. It gained historical fame as the centre for an uprising against the religious reforms of Henry VIII, for which its vicar paid the ultimate price. The town champions independent shops and local produce, best seen on market days (Wed, Fri, Sat).

Skegness

43mi/69km east of Lincoln.
⚹ Embassy Theatre. ☏01507 613 100. www.visitskegness.co.uk.
With its broad golden sands, seaside pier, souvenir shops, amusement arcades/parks, caravan sites and boarding houses, Skegness is the quintessential English seaside resort of yesteryear. It reached its peak in the 1960s and in essence hasn't changed much since then. Its most worthwhile visitor attraction is the **Natureland Seal Sanctuary** (North Parade; open daily 10am–5.30pm; £9, child (3–15) £6.50; ☏01754 764 345; www.skegness natureland.co.uk), looking after abandoned baby seals since 1965.
If you prefer nature in the raw, head south to **Gibralter Point National Nature Reserve** (open all year; ♿**P**(£1–£3); ✗; ☏01754 898 057 ; www.lincstrust. org.uk/reserves/gib), home to a great variety of birdlife including wildfowl, waders and gulls.

LINCOLNSHIRE FENS

⚹ www.visitlincolnshire.com.
By turns, fascinating and monotonous, this pancake-flat, almost treeless territory, criss-crossed by narrow waterways, has been reclaimed from the sea to provide some of England's finest arable land.

Boston

32mi/51km SE of Lincoln.
This old market town is dominated by the bulk of the 14C **St Botolph's church** (open Mon–Sat 8.30am–4pm, Sun 7.30am–4pm; ☏01205 354 670; www.parish-of-boston.org.uk), whose 83m 16C-tower ('the Boston Stump') is a landmark for miles around.
The **Guildhall** (South Street; open Wed–Sat 10.30am–3.30pm; ☏01205 365 954; www.bostonguildhall.co.uk) is the best place to learn how the town developed from its Hanseatic League port and wool-trading origins, how Boston, Massachusetts was named after Boston Lincolnshire, and more.
A 10-minute walk (1mi/1.6km) from the High Street, is the spectacular **Maud**

Foster Windmill (open Wed and Sat 10am–5pm; £4;  01205 352 188; www.maudfoster.co.uk), one of the tallest windmills in the country. Climb its seven floors to see flour being made.

Stamford★★

45mi/72km S of Lincoln.

🛈 Arts Centre, 27 St Mary's Street. 𝄞01780 755 611. www.southwestlincs.com.

Stamford has a long history, being one of the five Danelaw towns. Sir Walter Scott called it '...the finest stone town in England', and it has maintained its elegance. In 1967 it was the first town in England to be designated a Conservation Area, boasting over **600 listed buildings** of mellow limestone in the town centre alone, and including five medieval churches.

St Martin's Church★

High Street St Martin's. Open daily 10am–4pm. Contribution requested.

The church was rebuilt c.1480 in the Perpendicular style. The north chapel is dominated by the alabaster monument to **William Cecil, Lord Burghley** (1520–98).

Lord Burghley's Hospital★

Station Road and High Street St Martin's.

These charming late Elizabethan almshouses were built on the site of the medieval hospital of St John the Baptist and St Thomas the Martyr in 1597.

Browne's Hospital★

Broad Street. 𝄞01780 763 153. www.stamfordcivicsociety.org.uk.

One of the best-preserved medieval hospitals in England, Browne's was built c.1475, with cubicles for 'ten poor men'. The chapel and the audit room are lit by late-15C stained glass.

Discover Stamford

Stamford Library, High Street. Open Mon–Wed and Fri 9am–5pm, Thu 9am–6pm, Sat 9am–4pm. Closed 1 Jan, 24–26 and 31 Dec. ♿ 𝄞01522 782 040. www.lincolnshire.gov.uk.

Old riverside building, Stamford

The centrepiece of this heritage display is the 6m long Stamford Tapestry, completed in the year 2000, depicting the history of the town in wool.

Burghley★★

2mi/3km E of Stamford. Open late-Mar Oct Sat–Thu 11am–5pm. House and gardens: £18, child (3–15) £9, Gardens only: £12, child £8 (all tickets are cheaper if bought in advance. ♿ 𝄞01780 752 451. www.burghley.co.uk.

This is one of the country's finest Elizabethan mansions, built by **William Cecil, Lord Burghley**. The extensive late-17C redecorations include Baroque ceilings painted by **Laguerre** and **Verrio**, at their most exuberant in the **Heaven and Hell Rooms**. The distinguished collection of **paintings** includes works by Veronese, Bassano, Gainsborough, Kneller and Lawrence and Brueghel the Younger. Capability Brown (by Nathaniel Dance) looks out over the grounds he created.

A fascinating recent addition to the grounds is **The Historical Garden of Surprises**, including a moss house, swivelling Caesar busts, jets of water, a mirrored maze and more. There is also a contemporary **Sculpture Garden**.

ADDRESSES

🛏 STAY

NOTTINGHAM

🍴🍴 **Best Western Westminster Hotel** – 312 Mansfield Road. 𝄞0115 955 5000. www.bw-westminsterhotel nottingham.co.uk. 🅿. 73 rooms. Adjoining

Victorian houses converted to a hotel, the Westminster is a family-friendly place 1mi/1.6km from the city centre.

◗◙ **Park Hotel** – 5–7 Waverley Street. ✆0115 978 6299. **P**. 27 rooms. This premium budget hotel combines original turn-of-the-20th-century features with a modern design and soft tones. A short walk from town, with a view of the arboretum, it enjoys both a quiet and a central location.

◗◙◙ **Nottingham Belfry Hotel** – Mellers Way, Off Woodhouse Way. ✆0115 973 9393. www.qhotels.co.uk. **P**. 120 rooms. Some 3mi/5km out of town, this luxury business-oriented hotel, in contemporary steel-and-glass boxy style, is superbly equipped including a top-class spa and indoor pool.

LEICESTER

⊛ The city centre has plenty of hotels but B&Bs are mostly on the outskirts.

◗◙◙ **Belmont House Hotel** – De Montfort Street. ✆0116 254 4773. www.belmonthotel.co.uk. **P**. 77 rooms. Ideally situated in a pleasant part of the town centre, this handsome family-owned and family-run characterful Victorian terrace hotel features recently refurbished sumptuous décor alongside contemporary furniture.

◗◙◙ **Holiday Inn** – 129 St Nicholas Circle. ✆0871 942 9048 . www.holidayinn. com. **P**. 188 rooms. Modern city-centre high-rise chain hotel with pool, sauna and jacuzzi.

LINCOLN

◗◙◙ **The Castle Hotel** – Westgate. ✆01522 538 801. www.castlehotel.net. **P** 20 rooms. The bedrooms at this luxury modern city-centre hotel feature timeless, classic styling, and most have excellent views of the castle walls or the cathedral.

◗◙◙ **Washingborough Hall Hotel** – Church Hill, Washingborough. ✆01522 790 340. www.washingboroughhall.com. **P** 20 rooms. This welcoming and comfortable country house hotel is just a short drive from Lincoln city centre. Remarkable history, and perfect for a quiet break. Restaurant ◗◙.

◗◙◙ **The Lincoln Hotel** – Eastgate. ✆01522 520 348. www.thelincolnhotel.com. **P**. 72 rooms. This light airy very modern

hotel features rooms stepping out to a garden or balcony with cathedral views. There are also fabulous views from the restaurant, lounge and terrace lawn bar.

◗◙◙ **White Hart Hotel** – Bailgate. ✆01522 526 222. www.whitehart-lincoln. co.uk. 59 rooms. Elegant very British luxury hotel with traditional furnishings, antiques and modern comforts. Many of the rooms have views of the cathedral or castle. Good grill restaurant (◗◙◙).

◗◙◙ **Petwood Hotel** – Stixwould Road, Woodhall Spa. ✆01526 352411. www. petwood.co.uk. This remarkable building was the intended home of Baroness Grace van Eckhardstein, but it was also the home of the legendary RAF 617 'Dambusters' Squadron in World War Two. Restaurant ◗◙.

STAMFORD

◗◙◙ **Garden House** – 42 High Street, St Martin's. ✆01780 430 310. http://garden housestamford.co.uk. **P**. 20 rooms. Near Burghley Park, a few minutes' stroll from the centre of town, and dating in part from the late-17C, the Garden House has retained much of its original charm to provide a haven of calm. It features one acre (0.4ha) of walled gardens, and a charming conservatory restaurant serving classic bistro dishes. The rooms are elegant and superior rooms include four-posters..

◗◙◙◙ **The George of Stamford** – 71 St Martin's. ✆01780 750 750. www. georgehotelofstamford.com. 47 rooms. The town's premier address, this 900-year-old inn, once used by the Knights Crusaders, then as a coaching inn (its current incarnation), has a walled garden and courtyard, oak-panelled dining rooms and exudes old-fashioned English luxury.

⏍ EAT

NOTTINGHAM

⊛ Nottingham is famous for the number of bars and pubs in the city centre. Two of its best known stand at the foot of the castle: **Ye Olde Trip to Jerusalem**, reputedly the oldest inn in England (Brewhouse Yard; www. triptojerusalem.com); **The Salutation Inn** (73–75 Maid Marian Way). Both have cellars that you can explore.

Intriguingly **The Bell Inn** (18 Angel Row, ℘0115 947 5241) claims to be the oldest pub in Nottingham, and is also worth a look in.

The **Cock & Hoop** (25 High Pavement) in the heart of the buzzing Lace Market, is a traditional Victorian alehouse has been tastefully restored with cosy corners, comfy armchairs, antiques and modern art.

LEICESTER

🦴 Leicester has a large Asian population and many excellent authentic Indian restaurants – try Belgrave Road/Melton Road ('Little India').

⊖⊖ **Mumbai Inn** – 1 De Montfort Street. ℘0116 247 0420. www.mumbaiinn.co.uk. A popular place serving Indian and Nepalese cuisine.

⊖⊖⊖ **The Case** 4 6 Hotel Street. ℘0116 251 7077. www.thecase.co.uk. Closed Sun and bank holidays. This stylish bustling modern restaurant is set on four floors of a light airy Victorian ex-luggage factory with lots of gleaming wood. Robust Modern British cooking (comfort food favourites also always on the menu) served in a lively atmosphere.

LINCOLN

⊖⊖ **Wig & Mitre** – 30-32 Steep Hill ℘01522 535 190. www.wigandmitre.com. Attractive old pub, tastefully renovated with a cosy bar, period dining rooms and an airy beamed restaurant. Menus offer interesting mostly British dishes with a Modern British/Mediterranean slant.

⊖⊖⊖ **The Jews House Restaurant** – 30 Steep Hill. ℘01522 524 851. www.jews houserestaurant.co.uk. Set in a beautiful 12C stone house (one of the oldest in all England) in the city centre, the Jew's House serves Modern European cuisine.

⊖⊖⊖ **The Electric Bar and Restaurant** – Brayford Wharf North. ℘01522 565 182. www.electricbarand restaurant.co.uk. Rising above a marina, and located on the 5th floor (accessed by a panoramic glass lift) this stylish restaurant offers contemporary British cuisine and a fine view of the cathedral.

STAMFORD

⊖⊖ **The Tobie Norris** – 12 St Paul's Street. ℘01780 753 800. www.kneadpubs. co.uk. Not only the best pub in town (arguably), but one of the finest of its kind in the country. Set in a very rustic 13C building, on three floors each of its seven spacious atmospheric rooms are decorated with country-style antiques, large wooden settles and comfy settees; outside is a large enclosed patio. It serves a wide range of real ales, and robust Modern British food in the evenings.

CALENDAR OF EVENTS

NOTTINGHAM

Goose Fair – One of Europe's largest fairs, held in early October.

Robin Hood Festival – www. nottinghamshire.gov.uk/robinhoodfestival. Aug. A week of light-hearted medieval-themed celebrations in Sherwood Forest.

LEICESTER

Indian festivals: Navaratri (Oct), music and dance; **Diwali** (http://visitleicester info), this festival of light (Nov) is one of the biggest outside India, with up to 35 000 people attending.

Leicester Caribbean Carnival – ℘0116 273 6649. Aug. The Afro-Caribbean community celebrates its culture with colourful floats and vibrant music in the second-largest carnival in Britain.

TOURS

NOTTINGHAM

Take a Nottingham City Walk, a Ghost Walk or explore the many caves (www. experiencenottinghamshire.com).

LINCOLN

By boat – On the River Witham departing from Brayford Pool:
Lincoln Boat Trips – ℘01522 881 200. www.lincolnboattrips.co.uk. Daily 11am, 12.15pm, 1.30pm, 2.45pm, 3.45pm.
Walking tours – ℘01522 874 056. Wed–Sat 7pm, depart from the tourist office, booking not required. Medieval and Ghost Walks.

BOSTON

By boat – Sailings from The Sluice Bridge, Witham Bank East, with the Boston Belle. ℘01205 460159. www.bostonbelle.co.uk. Lunch cruises also available.

West Midlands and the Peak

Chatsworth House   © Bill Allsopp/age fotostock

Introduction

The Industrial Revolution began in the Midlands, its raw material hammered out in the forges of Ironbridge and refined in the world's first industrialised conurbation. The region is still a major industrial centre, though increasingly tourism and retail are coming to the fore. Its industrial heritage is second to none, while unspoilt shires and countryside, magnificent country houses and some of England's best walking trails are only ever a short distance away. Shakespeare's Stratford-on-Avon is a world famous cultural pilgrimage.

Stratford-on-Avon may be inextricably linked with The Bard, but you don't have to be a fan of his works to appreciate its many beautiful timber-framed buildings or the picture-perfect thatch of Anne Hathaway's Cottage. There are more medieval properties to enjoy in neighbouring **Warwick**, which is even more compact than Stratford. Warwick castle however is the big attraction, famous nationwide as England's finest castle. By contrast, the city of **Coventry**, relentlessly bombed during World War II is a late-20C creation, renowned for its striking 1960s cathedral. Its recovery was based on being Britain's Detroit and it has a superb car museum to prove it.

At the very centre of England, **Birmingham** was formerly "the city of 1001 trades" and is often described as England's "second city" (in size/importance after London). Recently this former powerhouse of the Industrial Revolution has made huge strides from manufacturing centre to cultural hub.

To the south west, **Worcestershire** is the birthplace of a spicy sauce, the home of Royal Worcester Porcelain, and the site of the final battle of the English Civil War; but walkers know the county for the beautiful rolling landscapes of the delectable Malvern Hills. Adjacent, **Herefordshire** and the **Wye valley** butt up to the 'Marches', or borderlands, of Wales. This is also perfect walking territory, with romantic ruined abbeys and castles recalling the area's rich history. Now returned to its beautiful natural state, you would never guess that Shropshire, to the north, was the birthplace of the Industrial Revolution. Evoking the days of dark satanic mills, the living history museums of Ironbridge comprise the finest industrial heritage complex in the world.

Elsewhere, **Shropshire** is quiet and little explored, with the exception of the charming and historic Ludlow, now Eng-

Highlights

1   A midsummer's night at the theatre in **Stratford-on-Avon** (p378)

2   Storm the castle during summer festivities at **Warwick** (p382)

3   Explore Britain's industrial heritage at Ironbridge Gorge (p390)

4   A summer's day out in the glorious gardens and house at **Chatsworth** (p400)

5   Hold on for dear life at **Alton Towers** theme park (p405)

land's most important provincial food-lovers' town.

The **Peak District National Park** is another walking centre, where, along with the moors of Lancashire, freedom to roam was pioneered. Below rambling feet are a network of caves rejoicing in names such as the Devil's Arse, typical of the straight-talking character of northern folk. By contrast, magnificent halls and country houses also abound; Haddon Hall and Hardwick Hall are perfect showcases for the lives of 16C and 17C country nobility, but finest of all is Chatsworth, probably the finest country estate in Britain.

Outside the Park lie **Derby** and **Stoke**. The latter's famous Potteries date from the 14C, although it was Josiah Wedgwood who really put Stoke on the map in the 18C. Today's visitors are more likely to be in search of thrills at Alton Towers, Britain's top theme park. Derby's porcelain also gained fame in the 18C, and many splendid country houses are a short drive away.

Stratford-upon-Avon★★

and around

Stratford is not only Shakespeare country but Forest of Arden country, too. Its timber frames were hewn from the surrounding woods and its favourite son's mother was called Mary Arden. William Shakespeare (1564–1616) forsook his home town and his wife, Anne Hathaway, for London, where success came to him as a jobbing playwright, who was able to distil sex and violence, farce and philosophy into the most potent lines in the English language. He returned to Stratford in 1611, rich and famous enough to acquire a coat of arms, and lived at New Place until his death. Today, Stratford is one of England's most popular tourist destinations.

🐾 TOWN WALK

Shakespeare's Birthplace★

Open daily Apr–Oct 9am–5pm; Nov–Mar 10am–4pm.

Town, Cottage and Farm Pass £26.25 (*Shakespeare's Birthplace, Shakespeare's New Place, Hall's Croft, Anne Hathaway's Cottage and Mary Arden's Farm*).

Town Houses Pass £18.50 (*Shakespeare's Birthplace, Shakespeare's New Place and Hall's Croft*); 🕭 Save 10% by booking online. 📞01789 207 137. www.shakespeare.org.uk.

The half-timbered house where the dramatist was born is part museum and part shrine, visited by Dickens, Keats, Scott and Hardy. The Bard's plays are brought to life by the house's own troupe of professional actors, with live performances every day; you can even join in with the actors and request an excerpt from your favourite play!

Harvard House

This ornately carved half-timbered house bears the date 1596, when it was home to Katharine Rogers, the mother

▶ **Population:** 27 445.
🕭 **Michelin Map:** Michelin Atlas p27 or Map 503 P 27.
🛈 **Info:** Bridgefoot. 📞01789 264 293. www.visitstratford uponavon.co.uk.
The train station is a 10-min walk from the centre (London Marylebone 1h57; Birmingham Snow Hill 55mins). The regional Riverside bus station is a 5-min walk from the centre. Most attractions in Stratford can be comfortably covered on foot. A hop-on, hop-off City Sightseeing Bus visits the rest (📞01789 412 680; www.city-sightseeing.com).
▶ **Location:** 24mi/39km S of Birmingham.
🕭 **Don't Miss:** As many Shakespeare houses as you can fit in; a night at the theatre; Mary Arden's Farm.
👤👤 **Kids:** Tudor World, Ragley Hall Park and Gardens.
🕐 **Timing:** Allow two days; more for excursions. The town can be very congested during the summer months.

of **John Harvard** (b.1607), founder of Harvard University, which owns the building today.

👤👤 Tudor World

Sheep Street. Open daily 10.30am– 5.30pm. £6, child (6–15) £3. Closed 25 Dec. 📞01789 298 070. www.tudorworld.com.

Two huge oak gates open onto the oldest remaining cobblestones in Stratford, where you will find the cavernous 16C Shrieve's House Barn, formerly the site of The Three Tunn's Tavern, run by William Rogers, the model for Shakespeare's Falstaff. The barn holds exhibits relating to crime and punishment, the plague,

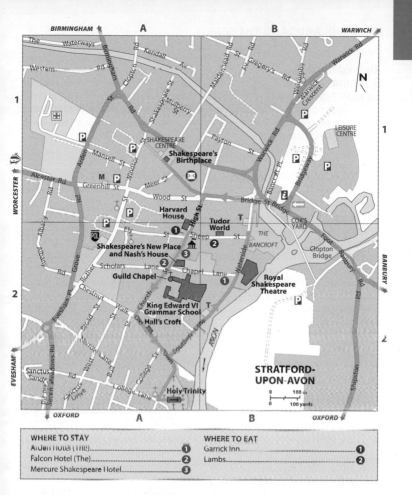

STRATFORD-
UPON-AVON

| 0 | 100 m |
| 0 | 100 yards |

medicine, alchemy, school (and more) and re-creates part of a Tudor Street. Actors add a touch of drama to the proceedings and a theatre has recently ben added where Shakespeare's plays are performed.The property is famous in paranormal circles – said to be one of the most haunted in the world – and **ghost tours** (£7.50; not suitable for children, 6pm each evening, Sat 6pm, 7pm, 8pm, 9pm) **depart nightly.**

Shakespeare Walking Tours of Straford take place at 2pm every Sat (£5, child 6–15, £3) **from Tudor World in** sheep Street.

Shakespeare's New Place and Nash's House★

Open daily Apr–Oct 10am–5pm; Nov–Mar 11am–4pm. ✗. All other details as Shakespeare's Birthplace.

New Place, Shakespeare's retirement home, was built in 1483, but today only the foundations remain, marked by a picturesque traditional knot garden. However, next door, **Nash's House**, home of Shakespeare's granddaughter, has been beautifully restored and houses exhibitions.

Guild Chapel

Open daily 10am–4.30pm. ✆01789 204 671. www.stratfordguildchapel-friends.org.uk.

Overlooking the site of New Place, the Chapel of the Guild of the Holy Cross (founded 1269) – the ruling body of Stratford before the Reformation – is predominantly Perpendicular, with wall-paintings of Christ, Mary, St John, St Peter and the Last Judgement.

King Edward VI Grammar School

Built c.1417 as the Holy Cross Hall and turned into a school after the Reformation, it lists among its former pupils a certain William Shakespeare.

Hall's Croft★

Open daily Apr–Oct 10am–5pm; Nov–Mar 11am–4pm. ✕. All other details as Shakespeare's Birthplace.

Shakespeare's eldest daughter, Susanna, married physician John Hall and the couple lived here until some time after 1616. The restored house, part 16C, part 17C, contains furniture and paintings from Hall's time, notes about his patients and a small exhibition on medicine in his day. There is also a lovely garden to visit.

Holy Trinity church

Open: Church free, but donation of £3 requested to view Shakespeare's grave (free with the various Shakespeare passes (⚲see above). ℘01789 266 316. www.stratford-upon-avon.org.

With an Early English tower and transepts and early Perpendicular nave and aisle, Holy Trinity would be notable even without **Shakespeare's grave** on the north side of the chancel. 'Blessed be the man who spares these stones, and cursed be he that moves my bones.'

Royal Shakespeare Company★

Royal Shakespeare Theatre (RST) and Swan Theatre open daily from 10am. Guided tours, see website. Closed 24–25 Dec. Tours from £8.50, tower £2.50; timed tickets for tours and the tower are available online, advance booking is recommended. ⚙✕ ℘01789 403 493 (box office). www.rsc.org.uk.

The new **Royal Shakespeare Theatre** (RST) reopened for business in 2010 after a three-year transformation and is open to visitors throughout the day with a variety of tours, free exhibitions and galleries, talks, children's activities and eating and drinking places enjoying wonderful riverside views. A highlight in every sense is ascending the theatre **tower**, which rises 36m above the River Avon, providing fantastic views. Sharing front of house space with the Royal Shakespeare Theatre is the **Swan Theatre**, built in 1986 with a Jacobean-style apron stage and galleried seating, within the shell of an earlier theatre.

EXCURSIONS

Mary Arden's Farm★

◗3mi/5km N, off the A 3400 in Wilmcote. Open daily mid-Mar–Oct 10am–5pm. £13.25 (free with Town, Cottage and Farm Pass, ⚲see Shakespeare's Birthplace, p378). ℘01789 293 455. www.shakespeare.org.uk.

The home of Shakespeare's mother, Mary Arden, is picture-perfect, featuring herring-bone timber framing and, mercifully, is unrestored. This was and still is a working farm where costumed characters re-enact the daily grind of Elizabethan times in the 16C farmhouse kitchen, preparing and cooking food using traditional methods. Visitors can even help if they wish, skep-making (bee hives with straw), basket-weaving, threshing, bread-making, gardening or animal-tending. Or you can try your arm at archery (school and bank holidays) visit the rare breed animals and watch the daily falconry displays.

Anne Hathaway's Cottage★

◗1mi/1.6km W via Shottery Road signed. Open daily Apr–Oct 9am–5pm; Nov–Mar 10am–4pm. £9.90 (free with Town, Cottage and Farm Pass, ⚲see Shakespeare's Birthplace, p378). ℘01789 295 517. www.shakespeare.org.uk.

This much-loved romantic picture-postcard building, where young William wooed his beloved Anne, is more a farmhouse than a cottage, and the rear was rebuilt after a fire in 1969. Upstairs are some dramatic tie-beams and the Hathaway bed. The award-winning **grounds** are equally picturesque, featuring a herb-scented garden, singing tree, giant willow sculptures, heart-shaped lavender maze, and Shakespeare Arboretum and Sculpture trail. During July, the annual **Sweet Pea Festival** provides a wonderful display of colour and scent.

© Jon Arnold Images/hemis.fr

Anne Hathaway's cottage

♟ Ragley Hall Park and Gardens★

◆Nr Alcester, 10mi/16km west, off the A 46. **House, Park and Gardens**: visit by guided tour only, Apr–Oct Wed–Sun and bank holiday Mon 10am–5pm (**State Room Tours** Sat–Sun only 10.30am and 11.30am). £10.50, child (5–16) £6.50. ♿🄿✗ ☎01789 762 090. www.ragleyhall.com.

This noble hall was designed and built by Robert Hooke in Palladian style, 1679–83. James Gibbs added some of the most perfect plasterwork ceilings he ever conceived around 1750, and 30 years later Wyatt built the gigantic portico. The walls are hung with paintings by Wootton, Van Loo, Reynolds, Hoppner, Lely and Cornelius Schut. The surprise is the **South Staircase Hall** decorated by Graham Rust between 1969 and 1983, with its ceiling of *The Temptation* and murals portraying Classical gods, monkeys, birds and contemporary members of the Seymour family.

The grounds include an adventure playground, a maze, boating, pony rides, woodland walks and an attractive lakeside picnic area.

Upton House★

◆Nr Banbury. 14mi/23km SE on the A 422. Open Jul–Aug daily 11am–5pm (House 1–5pm); check website for rest of year, when times vary. £10.90. ♿🄿✗ ☎01295 670 266. www.nationaltrust.org.uk/upton-house.

This late-17C house was bought by Viscount Bearsted, son of the founder of the Shell company, and exhibits his spectacular collection of porcelain and paintings in the setting of a 1930s millionaire's mansion. In the **Hall** is a view of Venice by Canaletto and a landscape by Wootton. In the **Long Gallery** are Dutch paintings – note Jan Steen's *Four Senses* as well as the Chelsea and Bow porcelain. The **Boudoir** is reserved exclusively for French 18C and 19C works, including Boucher's *Venus and Vulcan*.

The **Porcelain Lobby** is packed with Sèvres, Chinese, Chelsea and Derby china and porcelain. In the Games Room are Hogarth's *Morning* and *Night*. The pride of the collection is in the **Picture Gallery**, where among works by Holbein, Hogarth, Guardi, Tintoretto, Bruegel the Elder and Bosch hangs El Greco's *Christ Taken in Captivity*. By complete contrast is Lady Bearsted's gaudy red-and-silver Art Deco bathroom.

British Motor Museum

◆Gaydon: 13mi/21km W. Open daily 10am–5pm. Closed 24 Dec–1 Jan. Guided tours 11.15am, 2.15pm, included in admission charge. £14 (£17 on 5 special events days). ♿🄿✗ ☎01926 641 188. www.britishmotormuseum.co.uk.

In the 1960s the West Midlands was the centre of the thriving UK car industry and, fittingly, this motor museum is the repository for the world's largest collection of historic British cars.

The centre traces the story of the British motor industry with entertaining and educational interactive exhibitions and events. Optional extras include the hair-raising **Land Rover Experience**.

Warwick Castle and the River Avon

©Martin Lovatt/iStockphoto.com

Warwick★

and around

Much loved by visitors and locals alike – Pevsner called it '...this perfect county town' – Warwick is mostly built in the Queen Anne style. This both contrasts and complements its dominant 14C castle – '...the most perfect piece of castellated antiquity in the kingdom'.

TOWN

▲▲ Warwick Castle★★★

Open daily 10am–4pm/5pm/6pm. Closed 25 Dec. The **Castle Ticket** gives you access to the Castle, the grounds, attractions and shows: £29, child £26; **Castle and Dungeon tickets**: £34, child £31. Prices vary depending on time of year, and how far in advance you book. Get the cheapest prices by booking online, and at least 5 days in advance..

&♿🅿✗ ☎0871 265 2000 (information). www.warwick-castle.co.uk.

Britain's finest medieval castle occupies a picturesque location beside the River Avon. The curtain walls and gatehouse are 14C; the Bear Tower and Clarence Tower date from the 15C. The castle was begun by Thomas de Beauchamp, 11th Earl of Warwick (1329–69). Paintings and furniture are displayed in the 17C and 18C **State Rooms** including works by Lely, Van Dyck and Boulle furniture. Now part of the Tussauds Group, the

> **Population:** 31 345.
>
> **Michelin Map:** Michelin Atlas p27 or Map 503.
>
> **Info:** Jury Street. ☎01926 492 212. http://visitwarwick.co.uk. The train station is a 10-minute walk from town; the bus station is in the centre on Market Street.
>
> **Location:** 22mi/35km southeast of Birmingham.
>
> **Kids:** Warwick castle.

castle is brought dramatically to life by both historically accurate and fantasy characters. The former includes the **Royal Weekend Party** depicting a high society weekend in 1898. The latest addition is **Warwick Castle Unlocked**, four rooms rarely visited in recent history and opened for the very first time to visitors in 2013. One of these, perhaps inevitably, is haunted.

Merlin: The Dragon Tower, is an adventure experience based on the hit BBC TV series. Ascend the tower to meet 'The Great Dragon'. Braver souls meanwhile can descend to the gory **Castle Dungeons** horror house.

The magnificent riverside **grounds** host events year-round, but the highlight is the summer season when they come alive with **jousting knights**, **medieval** character actors of every persuasion, a spectacular **siege machine** that fires twice daily, **falconry** and lots more. Almost forgotten amid the razzmatazz is the Mill and Engine House, the Conservatory and Peacock Gardens and the Victorian Rose Gardens

Lord Leycester Hospital★

High Street. Open Tue–Sun and bank holiday Mons Apr–Sept 10am–5pm; Oct–Mar 10am–4pm. Closed Good Fri, 25 Dec. £8.50. ✆01926 491 422. www.lordleycester.com.

This picturesque black-and-white timber-framed ensemble was founded in 1571 by Queen Elizabeth's favourite, Lord Leicester. The oldest parts of the building, which surrounds a charming partly cloistered courtyard, are the chapel (1383) and the guildhall (1450).

Collegiate Church of St Mary★

Church Street. Open daily Apr–Sept 10am–6pm, Sun 12.30–4.30pm; Oct–Mar 10am–4.30pm, Sun 12.30–4.30pm. £2 suggested donation. & ✆01926 403 940. www.stmaryswarwick.org.uk.

Rebuilt after a fire in 1694, though it originally dates from 1123. Its glory is the 15C Beauchamp (pronounced 'bee-chum') Chapel containing the **tomb★** and gilded bronze effigy of Richard de Beauchamp, Earl of Warwick. The church tower offers spectacular views.

EXCURSIONS
Coventry

⏵12mi/19kn N of Warwick via the A 46.
🅘 Old Cathedral ruins, Priory Street. ✆024 7622 5616. www.visitcoventry andwarwickshire.co.uk.

Coventry is known for its magnificent modern cathedral and the legend of **Lady Godiva**.

In 1043, the city was so heavily taxed by Leofric, Earl of Mercia that his wife, Lady Godiva, repeatedly begged him to repeal the taxes. In the end he agreed to do so if she rode naked through the streets. In order not to embarrass the Lady, the people of Coventry cleared the route, everyone, that is, with the exception of a tailor, named Tom. On

©John Cave/iStockphoto.com

Coventry Cathedral by Sir Basil Spence, St Michael Defeating the Devil *by Jacob Epstein in the foreground*

seeing Godiva he was struck blind and so the name Peeping Tom was coined. A statue of Godiva graces Broadgate in the centre of town and behind, her ride is 're-enacted' by a small horse appearing from a clock each hour.

On 14 November 1940, the biggest bombing raid of its time destroyed most of the city, including the 13C church, which in 1918 had become a cathedral. The only remains of medieval Coventry are the timber-framed properties in **Spon Street (Y)**.

Cathedral★★

Fairfax Street. **New Cathedral**: open Mon–Sat 10am–5pm, Sun noon–4pm. **Old Cathedral ruins**: open 9am–5pm daily. **Tower climb**: open daily except during bell-ringing sessions. New cathedral £6, Old Cathedral and tower +£2.50. ✆024 7652 1200. www.coventrycathedral.org.uk.

The **New Cathedral**, by Sir Basil Spence, was one of the few post-war buildings to meet with the approval of the general public. The tower and spire, with restored bells, dominate the city centre of Coventry, which is known as the city of the three spires. Flanking the entrance steps is *St Michael Defeating the Devil* by **Jacob Epstein**. The majestic porch links the new cathedral with the ruins of the old as a symbol of resurrection. The overwhelming impression of the **interior** is of height, light and col-

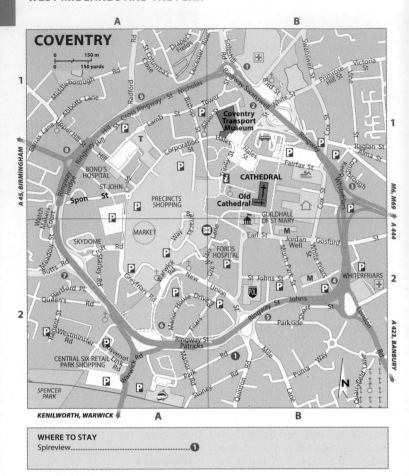

COVENTRY

our: height from the soaring slender nave pillars supporting the canopied roof; light from the great west screen, a wall of glass engraved with patriarchs, prophets, saints and angels by John Hutton; colour from the Baptistery window by John Piper.

The font is a great rough boulder from the hillside at Bethlehem. The whole is dominated by the huge tapestry, *Christ in Glory* designed by **Graham Sutherland**.

The ruined **Old Cathedral★** is late-13C with large-scale Decorated and Perpendicular additions. All that remains are the walls, the crypt and the tower (90m), and the spire, third highest in England. The east end is marked by a simple cross of charred timbers.

Set amid the ruins, the **Blitz Experience Museum** contains reconstructions of five rooms from the 1940s.

♣♣ Coventry Transport Museum★

Millennium Place, Hales Street. Open daily 10am–5pm. Closed 24–26 Dec and 1 Jan. ♿✕ ☎024 7623 4270. www.transport-museum.com.

This museum, featuring the world's largest road transport collection, is wholly appropriate for the city that was the birthplace of the British car industry and had nearly 600 companies making cycles, motorcars, commercial vehicles and motorcycles. Walk through time, from 19C boneshakers, via a land speed record simulator (£5) and into the future.

Worcestershire★

Best known for the tangy sauce that originated here, Worcestershire is busy in the north but elsewhere a mostly green and pleasant rural county, watered by the mighty rivers Severn and Avon.

WORCESTER★

Population: 99 600. ■ Guildhall, High Street. ℘01905 726 311. www.visitworcester.com.

The great red sandstone cathedral rising above the bend in the River Severn, the wealth of timber-framed buildings and the Georgian mansions make Worcester among the most English of cities. The city name is also synonymous with its Royal Worcester porcelain and Worcester(shire) sauce. Worcester was the site of the final battle of the Civil War, where Cromwell's 'New Model Army' defeated Charles I's Cavaliers.

Cathedral★★

Open daily 7.30am–6pm. Tower open Feb–Oct Sat–Sun and school holidays (full list of times on website). Tower £4; Guided tours (£5) Mar–Nov Mon–Sat 11am and 2.30pm; Dec–Feb Sat only. ♿✗ ℘01905 732 900. www.worcestercathedral.co.uk.

In the late-11C an earlier church was rebuilt by Wulfstan, the Saxon Bishop of Worcester, who thrived under his new Norman masters and was later canonised. His superb **crypt** survives but the greater part of his building, including the tower, was reconstructed in the 14C. The **choir** is an outstanding example of the Early English style. Monuments include **King John's tomb** in the choir, the **Beauchamp tomb** (14C) in the nave, and the alabaster effigy (c.1470) of the Virgin and Child in the southeast transept.

Prince Arthur's Chantry and its delicate tracery are late Perpendicular work. The Cloisters were rebuilt in 1374 with wonderful medieval bosses. The east walk leads to the **chapter house** (c.1150), with its shaft vaulting. The **Edgar Tower**, once the main entrance to the medieval monastery and fortified against anti-clerical rioters, now opens into the serene cathedral precincts.

Museum of Royal Worcester

Severn Street. Open Mon–Sat: Mar–Oct 10am–5pm; Nov–Feb 10am–4pm. £6. Closed 25–26 Dec. ♿🅿✗ ℘01905 21247. www.museumofroyalworcester. org. ♿ The museum will be closed until May 2018 for re-display, check website for latest details.

Founded in 1751, Royal Worcester's historical success was due to the use of Cornish soaprock to simulate Chinese porcelain and the ability to adapt to changing fashions (Chinoiserie, Classicism, Romanticism), all of which are displayed here. However, in 2006 tableware production ceased in Worcester and only a few talented artists continued to hand paint and gild bespoke items. The Worcester factory site closed in 2009.

MALVERN HILLS★★

■ ℘01684 892 289. www.visitthemalverns.org.

The Malverns boast some of the most spectacular views in the region, crisscrossed with 100mi/160km of bridleways and footpaths, with routes for both short strolls and long-distance walks.

The highest of the hills is **Worcestershire Beacon★** (425m), from which

---

Sidebar:

♿ **Michelin Map:** Michelin Atlas p27 or Map 503 N 27.

■ **Info:** Worcester Foregate Street railway station (Birmingham New Street, 41 mins) is 0.5mi/0.8km north of the centre. The bus station, to the rear of Crowngate shopping centre, is a little closer.

▶ **Location:** 28mi/45km southwest of Birmingham.

there is claimed to be a **view** of 15 counties and three cathedrals.

Sir Edward Elgar (1857–1934), that most 'English' of composers, helped put the Malverns on the map and his music evokes this countryside of broad, tranquil vales and soaring hills. A 40mi/64km circular tour, the **Elgar Route★**, signposted with violins, includes the **Elgar Birthplace Museum** (Crown East Lane, Lower Broadheath; 3mi/5km W of Worcester; closed until end of 2017 following transfer to the National Trust; www.nationaltrust.org.uk).

Great Malvern

◗ 8mi/13km S on the A 449.

In the late-18C, this small settlement, which had grown up round a priory, became fashionable owing to the medicinal properties of the local water. A Greek Revival-style **Pump Room** and Baths were built in 1819 and its popularity as a spa town grew in the Victorian era. You can no longer 'take the waters' here, but many of the impressive old spa buildings remain in public use. George Bernard Shaw and Edward Elgar brought Great Malvern into the 20C with their music and theatre festivals held in the Winter Gardens.

Herefordshire★

This quiet unspoiled sparsely populated agricultural county borders Powys and Monmouthshire in Wales and shares towns with both. It is notable for its 'black-and-white villages' (of half-timbered houses). The Wye valley is particularly beautiful.

HEREFORD★

Population: 58 896. 🄸 1 King Street, Hereford. ℘01432 268 430.
www.visitherefordshire.co.uk.

Seat of a bishop in 676, Hereford was a flourishing city and became capital of Saxon Mercia, with its own mint. In 1070, however, a new market was created where the roads converged north of the town. Today, Hereford is the prosperous centre for a rich agricultural region on the border with Wales. There are many outstanding half-timbered buildings preserved in the city. In the heart of the city, just north of the River Wye, is the **cathedral★★** (Cathedral: open daily 9.15am–5.30pm/Sun 3.30pm; **Guided tours** Mon, Wed–Sat, 11.15am, 12.15pm, 2.15pm; £5; **Tower tours** (218 steps) Wed–Thu and Sat during summer months only 11.30am, 12.30pm, 1.30pm, 2.30pm; £5; **Mappa Mundi and Chained Library**: open Mon–Sat 10am–5pm; £6;

◔ **Michelin Map:** Michelin Atlas p26 or Map 503 L 27.
◗ **Location:** 56mi/90km SW of Birmingham and 57mi/92km NE of Cardiff.

&✕; ℘01432 374 200; www.hereford-cathedral.org), a mainly 12C red sandstone building. The massive tower was added in the 14C. The chantry to John Stanbury, bishop in 1453–74, is a fine example of Perpendicular architecture. Among the treasures is the **Mappa Mundi★**, a map of the world with Jerusalem at its centre, made by Richard of Haldingham in Lincolnshire, c.1300. The **Chained Library**, one of the finest in the country, contains 1 400 books and over 200 manuscripts, dating from the 8C to the 15C, including the 'Cider Bible' (in which the 'strong drink' of the authorised version has been translated as 'cidir'). There is a small 13C Limoges enamel reliquary, which used to contain a relic of Thomas à Becket, whose murder is depicted on the side.

Head west from here towards Eign Street and turn left down Ryelands Street until you arrive at No. 21 and the **Cider Museum** (open Mon–Sat 10am–4.30pm £5.50; & 🄿 ✕; ℘01432 354 207; www.cidermuseum.co.uk). An old cider factory houses this museum, which tells the story of cider-making, particularly during its heyday in the 17C.

EXCURSIONS
Kilpeck church★
◑ 8mi/13km SW of Hereford via the A 465 and minor road (right). Open daily dawn–dusk. Contribution requested. 🅿 ✆01981 570 315.

The Church of St Mary and St David was built in 1135. Nowhere else in Britain has such rich Norman **carving** decoration survived. Only two of the 70 grotesques around the corbel have any religious significance. The gargoyle heads on the west wall are pure Viking and there is a notorious sheela-na-gig (carving of naked woman displaying an exaggerated vulva).

Hay-on-Wye★★
◑ 20mi west of Hereford.
🗎 ✆01497 820 144.
www.hay-on-wye.co.uk.
Set on the Welsh–English border in Powys (also claimed by Herefordshire), this likeable little town is Britain's most famous literary centre, world famous for its secondhand and antiquarian **book** shops. It is also renowned for its numerous festivals, of which the biggest is the **Hay Festival of Literature and the Arts** (www.hayfestival.com), when for 10 days, around 85 000 people visit.

Ross-on-Wye★
◑ 15mi southeast of Hereford.
🗎 ✆01989 562 768.
This pretty little market town owes its fame to the spectacular stretches of the **Wye Valley★** close by. In fact, it claims to be the birthplace of the British tourist industry, when in 1745, the local rector started taking friends on boat trips down the valley from Ross-on-Wye.

The valley's chief man-made attraction are the mighty remains of **Goodrich Castle** (open Apr–Sept daily 10am–6pm; Oct daily 10am–5pm; Nov–Mar Sat–Sun 10am–4pm (Feb holidays, daily 10am–4pm); £7.60; 🅿£1; ✆01600 890 538; www.english-heritage.org.uk) standing majestically on a wooded hill above the river in the picturesque valley known as **Symonds Yat.** Built in the 11C, the castle was destroyed in the English Civil War. **Symonds Yat Rock★**, a viewpoint towering some 120m above the river on the Gloucestershire side, provides a panoramic much-photographed viewpoint of the River Wye.

Shropshire★★

Despite its proximity to the industrial heartlands of the West Midlands, Shropshire is largely untouched by 20C industry, or major roads, and its patchwork fields hark back to days of pre-mechanised agriculture. Ironically this was the birthplace of the Industrial Revolution and Ironbridge Gorge, now a UNESCO World Heritage Site, is Britain's greatest industrial heritage site, with intelligent award-winning visitor attractions set in beautiful surroundings. The county town of Shrewsbury and smaller market towns also have much to offer while

🗎 **Info:** www.shropshire tourism.co.uk.
◗ **Location:** Shropshire borders Wales to the west. Trains Shrewsbury–Birmingham New Street 50 mins; Telford Central–Birmingham New Street 35 mins
😊 **Don't Miss:** Ironbridge Gorge; Weston Park; Ludlow.
👥 **Kids:** Blists Hill and Enginuity at Ironbridge Gorge.

Shropshire's 'blue-remembered hills' (Housman) are renowned for being wonderful walking territory.

IRONBRIDGE GORGE★★

The Gorge is on the River Severn, 5 mi
5mi/8km south of Telford.

The densely wooded, mineral-rich
Severn Gorge was the birthplace of the
Industrial Revolution. In 1708, Abraham
Darby (1678–1717) came to Coalbrookdale and revolutionised the industry by
using coke as a fuel for smelting iron,
replacing traditional charcoal.

His experiments made it possible to
use iron in transport, engineering and
construction (including the world's first
iron bridge. A number of sites along the
gorge now form the UK's most important, and most interesting, industrial
heritage complex. The Iron Bridge itself
is one of the great symbols of the Industrial Revolution.

Ironbridge Gorge Museums★★★

Coalbrookdale. The opening times of
the 10 museums are detailed on the
website. Passport ticket all sites £25,
child £15 (online discounts: prices for
individual museums below). The Gorge
Connect shuttle bus connects most sites
Apr–Oct Sat–Sun and bank holiday Mons
(charge). &♿🅿 (£1.50 or pay and display,

all sites). ✕ all sites. ✆01952 433 424.
www.ironbridge.org.uk.

Ironbridge Area

The **Iron Bridge★★** is the iconic landmark bridge across the Severn Gorge
at Coalbrookdale, erected to replace
the hazardous ferry crossing. It was
designed by Shrewsbury architect
Thomas Pritchard, and built over three
years by Abraham Darby III, opening
on New Year's Day 1781. The bridge's
single graceful span was a triumph of
the application of new technology to
the solution of a difficult problem. The
ironwork weighs over 378 tons.

The **Museum of the Gorge★** (£4.50)
houses the information centre, an exhibition and audio-visual introduction to
Ironbridge Gorge.

The **Jackfield Tile Museum** (£8.85) is
housed in an original gas-lit trade show-
room, where galleries and period room
settings show off the often magnificent
colourful wall and floor tiles once manufactured here in immense quantities.

Broseley Pipeworks (open late May–
late Sept daily 1–5pm; £5.15) **was once
the biggest clay tobacco pipe-maker
in Britain, exporting all over the world.**

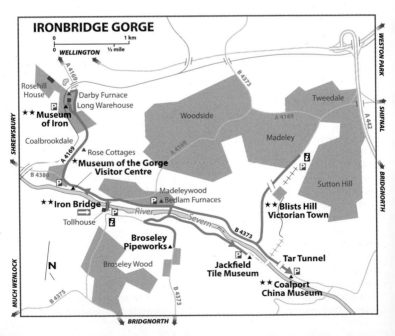

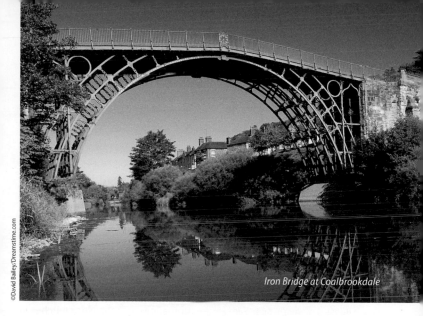

Iron Bridge at Coalbrookdale

It closed in the 1950s but remains preserved, as if in a time capsule.

Coalbrookdale Area

The **Museum of Iron★★** (£8.85) illustrates the history of iron-making and the story of the Coalbrookdale Company. It is housed in a huge warehouse, built in 1838, with cast-iron windows, sills and lintels. By the time of the Great Exhibition in 1851, the Coalbrookdale Company employed 4 000 men and boys and produced 2 000 tons of cast iron a week, for railway stations, bridges, fireplaces and a multitude of other uses.

Enginuity (£8.85, child £6.95) is a hands-on interactive exhibition designed to explain the principles of the manufacturing processes at Ironbridge in simple and fun terms.

The **Darby Houses** (£5.50, combined ticket with Museum of Iron £9.25) are where the Ironmasters lived; the rooms are packed with original furniture, costumes and mementoes.

Blists Hill area

The **Coalport China Museum★★** (£8.85) dates from 1792, and manufacturing continued here until 1926. The old works, including the interior kiln of a bottle oven, have been restored as a museum of china, showing techniques of manufacture and particularly the products of Coalport.

Nearby, you can walk through the **Tar Tunnel** (closed winter; £3.40), cut in 1786 to aid drainage from the Blists Hill Mine. It was found to ooze bitumen through the mortar of the brick lining (it still does) and this was turned into pitch, lamp-black and rheumatics remedies. Many visitors' favourite part of the whole Ironbridge area is **Blists Hill Victorian Town★★** (closes winter 4pm; £16.25, child £10.75), a delightful reconstruction of a Victorian community of the 1890s, including a bank, pub, butcher's shop, school, mason's yard, mine, miner's railway and candle factory, as well as the inclined plane which carried boats from Blists Hill to the Severn and Coalport. Many of the buildings have been brought from elsewhere and rebuilt on site.

SHREWSBURY★

14mi/22km northwest of Ironbridge.
Population: 71 715.
🛈 The Square. ✆01743 258 888.
www.shrewsburyguide.info.

Set at the very heart of Shropshire, the medieval border settlement of Shrewsbury grew up around its Norman castle, which commanded the loop in the Severn. The modern county town has elegant Queen Anne and Georgian buildings, a wealth of black-and-white houses and 'shuts' – medieval shortcuts and alleyways.

Shrewsbury Abbey★

Open Apr–Oct 10am–4pm; Nov–Mar 10.30am–3pm. & ✆01743 232 723. www.shrewsburyabbey.com.

The Benedictine abbey, founded in 1083, stands just outside the town, across the landmark **English Bridge**. The 14C tower has a statue of Edward III, in whose reign it was built, and there are Norman pillars in the nave dating from the 11C.

WESTON PARK★★

22mi/36km E of Shrewsbury via the A 5.
Open: **House:** Jun–Aug 1–5pm, Sun–Fri (free flow basis Fri, Sun–Mon, guided tours only Tue–Thu, £10; **Park and Gardens:** 10.30am–6pm, £7.70. & P ✆01952 852 100. www.weston-park.com.

This 17C house is unusual (for its time) in having been built by a woman, Lady Elizabeth Wilbraham. The splendidly furnished interior is remarkable for the quality of the portraits – from Holbein to Lely's likeness of Lady Wilbraham and a rare portrait by Constable.

Beyond the formal gardens is the park, designed by 'Capability' Brown, grazed by deer and rare breeds of sheep. It contains many family attractions – a miniature railway, pets corner and adventure playground. The converted **Granary**, built 1767, is the beautiful new home to an art gallery, farm shop and restaurant.

MUCH WENLOCK

12mi/20km SE via the A 458.
Population: 2 877. ☒ The Museum, High Street. ✆01952 727 679.
www.visitmuchwenlock.co.uk.

This pretty little market town boasts a wealth of historic buildings and its colourful small **museum** (open 10.30am–1pm and 1.30–4pm: Easter–Oct Tue–Sun; Nov–Easter Fri–Sun; ✆01952 727 679, http://shropshire.gov.uk/museums) tells the fascinating little-known story of the **Much Wenlock Olympic Games**,

initiated in 1850 by a local doctor. They inspired the modern Olympic movement (one of the mascots for the London 2012 games was named Wenlock) and are still held in the village even today. The village was a location for the 1986 British comedy film *Clockwise*, starring John Cleese.

A short walk away are the tranquil ruins of **Wenlock Priory★** (open Apr–Sept daily 10am–6pm; Oct 10am–5pm, rest of year Sat–Sun 10am–4pm except Feb half-term hol, daily 10am–4pm. £5.20; P £1; ✆01952 727 466; www.english-heritage.org.uk), set in beautiful landscaped grounds. The Cluniac priory was founded c.690, pillaged by the Danes and later refounded. The church, one of the longest monastic churches in England (the nave is 106m long), was built in the 1220s by Prior Humbert. The delicate interlaced arcading of the chapter house is the work of the Normans. So too is the **lavatorium** (1180), where the monks washed before meals.

Just southwest on the B 4378 is **Wenlock Edge★**, a massive limestone escarpment providing magnificent **views**.

CHURCH STRETTON

13.5mi/22km S via the A 49.
Population: 4 671. ☒ Library, Church Street. ✆01694 723 133.
www.churchstretton.co.uk.

This is the probably the most popular part of the whole county for **walking**, with the favourite starting point being the National Trust-owned Chalet Pavilion at **Carding Mill Valley** (just outside Church Stretton), which dispenses information alongside tea and coffee (open daily mid-Feb–Oct half-term holidays, weekends at other times).

There are walking trails for all comers and NT rangers also lead guided walks. A popular route is **The Port Way**, an ancient track which was used in prehistoric times by drovers and axe traders. It follows the crest of the **Long Mynd** (mynd is Welsh for mountain), which comprises some 4–5sq mi/10–13sq km of wild moorland plateau, its higher slopes covered with gorse and bracken, and Its eastern side intersected by many steep valleys. As well as walking it is renowned for gliding, hang gliding and paragliding.

The **village** of Church Stretton was a thriving health resort in Victorian times. Its fine church is part Norman, part 17C. Nearby at **Acton Scott Farm** (open: Sat– Wed 10am–4.30pm; £9; & ✗; ☎01694 781 307; www.actonscott.com), a star of several BBC TV programmes, you can watch traditional 19C farm life unfold daily.

STOKESAY CASTLE★

21mi/34km south.

Open Apr–Sept daily 10am–6pm; Oct daily 10am–5pm; Nov–Mar Sat Sun 10am–4pm (Feb half-term hol daily). Closed 1 Jan, 24–26 Dec. £7.60. & ▣£1. ☎01588 672 544.

www.english-heritage.org.uk.

Set alongside a picture-postcard yellow pastel-washed 16C gatehouse and a 17C church, Stokesay castle is part of a much-photographed grouping. Something of a misnomer, the 'castle' is the best preserved example in England of a 13C fortified manor house. The hall has a fine roof of shaped and tapered tree trunks. The solar (private apartment block) Is furnished with a notable stone fireplace, peepholes into the hall below and 17C fittings.

LUDLOW★

28mi/45km south. Population: 10 266.
🚹 Assembly Rooms, 1 Mill Street.
☎01584 875 053. www.ludlow.org.uk.
Set in the south of the rolling Shropshire Hills, close to the Welsh border, Ludlow is a Norman 'planned' town. Some-time seat of the powerful Mortimer family, the castle passed into royal ownership with the accession of Edward IV. The town prospered in the 16C and 17C in its role as seat of the Council for Wales and the Marches.

The centrepiece of the **Ludlow Fringe Festival** (last wk Jun–first wk Jul; www. ludlowfringe.co.uk) is a Shakespeare play performed in the inner bailey of the castle.

In recent years the town has also become one of Britain's **gastronomic capitals** with a famous **food and drink festival** each September.

Town

The picturesque ruin of **Ludlow Castle★** (open daily 10am–5pm; £5; & ✗; ☎01584 874 465; www.ludlow castle.com) stands on a fine defensive site protected by the River Teme and low limestone cliffs and dominates the view of the town. It was begun by Roger de Lacy shortly after the Domesday survey and built of locally quarried stone. It was from here that Roger Mortimer, the most powerful and perhaps the richest man in all England, virtually ruled the country, after using his power to topple Edward II in 1326. He completed the block of buildings containing the **Great Hall** and Solar, one of the leading palaces of the day. **Arthur, Prince of Wales** brought his young bride **Catherine of Aragon** to honeymoon in Ludlow in the winter of 1501 and it was here that Arthur died early the following year (to be succeeded by his brother and future king Henry VIII). The chapel with its richly ornamented west door is one of only five round chapel naves still standing in Britain.

Heading east from the castle towards Bull Ring/Old Street, take a left onto College Street to find **St Laurence's church★** (open daily 10am–5pm; £3 donation suggested; &; ☎01584 872 073; www.stlaurences.org.uk). The tower dominates the surrounding countryside and is mentioned in the locally famous collection of poems, *A Shropshire Lad* by **A E Housman** (1859–1936), whose ashes are buried in the churchyard.

Note the 28 outstanding **misericords★** in the choir stalls, dating from 1447.

On Bull Ring is the **Feathers Hotel★** (www.feathersatludlow.co.uk). The existing building was enlarged and re-fronted in 1619 to produce what Pevsner described as '...the prodigy of timber-framed houses'.

Birmingham★★

The 'Second City of the Kingdom' and one of the centres of the Industrial Revolution, Birmingham still produces a high proportion of Britain's manufactured exports. Tourism and culture are also very much a priority of the city these days, as exemplified by the City's new landmark Library.

A BIT OF HISTORY

Industry – Industrialisation began in the mid-16C, the city '...swarming with inhabitants and echoing with the noise of anvils' (William Camden). Its 18C growth, marked by the miles of canals radiating from the centre (Birmingham has more miles of canal than Venice), attracted **James Watt** (1736–1819), inventor of the double-action steam engine, **William Murdock** (1754–1839), inventor of coal-gas lighting, and **Matthew Boulton** (1728–1809), whose Soho factory was the first to be lit by gas.

The grim conditions caused by the city's phenomenal growth in the 19C stirred the philanthropic cocoa manufacturer, George Cadbury (1839–1922), to create one of the world's first garden suburbs, **Bournville**.

Modern city – Though much crass post-war development was demolished in the course of enthusiastic redevelopment, enough fine late-19C/early-20C buildings remain to evoke the atmosphere of the city's civic heyday.

The **Bull Ring**, a symbol of insensitive mid-20C architecture, became Europe's largest retail-led regeneration project, representing an investment of over £1 billion into a new shopping centre boasting spectacular designer buildings – most notably the astonishing landmark **Selfridges** department store, clad in 15 000 shiny aluminium discs, supposedly inspired by a sequinned dress. Today, Britain's second city is determined to acquire a new image as a **European business and cultural centre**. A superb symphony hall in the **International Convention Centre** is home to the internationally acclaimed City of Birmingham Symphony Orchestra (CBSO), while the refurbished Birmingham Hippodrome Theatre is the new headquarters for the equally renowned Birmingham Royal Ballet, formerly Sadler's Wells.

In the heart of town the **National Indoor Arena** (NIA) and, 14mi/23km west, the **National Exhibiton Centre** (NEC) host important exhibitions, concerts, shows and sporting events.

▸ **Population:** 1 101 000.

🚗 **Michelin Map:**
Michelin Atlas p27 or Maps 503 or 504 O 26.

🄸 **Info:** Baskerville House, Centenary Square, Broad Street. ℰ0121 202 5115. www.visitbirmingham.com. New Street Station ('Birmingham Gateway'), in the heart of the city, is where most train travellers arrive. The Digbeth bus station is a 10-minute walk from the centre.

▶ **Location:** Close to the geographical centre of England, 117mi/188km northwest of London.

😋 **Don't Miss:** Birmingham Library, Birmingham Museum & Art Gallery, (Pre-Raphaelite collection); Barber Institute of Fine Arts; Black Country Living Museum; Dudley.

🕐 **Timing:** Allow 2 days.

🅿 **Parking:** Avoid driving in the city centre.

👪 **Kids:** Cadbury World, Bournville; Thinktank; National Sea Life Centre; Black Country Living Museum.

🚶 **Tours:** The route marked on the map offers a pleasant stroll.

CITY CENTRE

Library of Birmingham★★

Centenary Square, Broad Street.
Open Mon–Tue 11am–7pm, Wed–Sat
11am–5pm. ♿✕ ✆0121 242 4242.
www.libraryofbirmingham.com.

Opened in 2013 and costing £189 million this stunning new cultural flagship building houses a collection of one million books, 200 public access computers, theatres, an exhibition gallery and music room. Despite its striking modern architecture, the Shakespeare Memorial Room, designed in 1882, has been recreated, to once again house one of the UK's most important Shakespeare collections. On top is a roof garden with a wild flower meadow.

Birmingham Museum and Art Gallery★★

Chamberlain Square. Open daily 10am (Fri 10.30am)–5pm. ♿✕ ✆0121 348 8038. www.bmag.org.uk.

Birmingham's municipal gallery is famed for its outstanding collection of **Pre-Raphaelite paintings**. The elaborate ironwork of the two-tiered Industrial Gallery is a late Victorian marvel, a fascinating setting for its ceramics and stained glass. Beyond is the spectacular **Edwardian Tea Room**.

Among the extensive holding of European paintings are outstanding works, like the *Madonna and Child* by Bellini, Claude's *Landscape near Rome* and a *Roman Beggar Woman* by Degas. At the heart of the collection are the Pre-Raphaelites: mostly key works like *The Last of England* by Ford Madox Brown, *The Blind Girl* by Millais, *Beata Beatrix* by Rossetti and *Two Gentlemen of Verona* by Hunt. Even this collection, however, has been eclipsed by the **Staffordshire Hoard**; (www.staffordshirehoard.org.uk) comprising over 3 500 items of gold and silver with precious stone decorations it is the largest hoard of Anglo-Saxon gold ever found.

Other rooms are devoted to local history, archaeology and natural history; there is a spectacular **fossilised skull** of a triceratops.

♿♟ Thinktank Birmingham Science Museum

Millennium Point, Curzon Street. Open 10am–5pm. Closed 24–26 Dec. £13.50, child (3–15) £9.75. Advance tickets online discount. ♿🅿(charge) ✕ ✆0121 348 8000. www.thinktank.ac.

Four floors of interactive galleries (the past, the present, the city, the future) chart both local and global scientific and technological invention. Testimonies account Birmingham's industrial progress, while the Giant (22m screen) cinema and planetarium (additional £1) add wow factor.

Gas Street Basin Canal Walk

The walk between Gas Street Basin and Newhall Street passes the canals, locks, bridges and buildings spawned by the city's 19C expansion.

The **Gas Street Basin** is surrounded by both new and restored 18C and 19C buildings. The painted narrowboats moored along the quay are typical of the craft that once plied the Midlands' canal network. Nearby, the **Water's Edge** and **Brindley Place** (Oozells Square) developments are full of lively wine bars, cafés, restaurants and traditional canalside pubs. The latter is also home to Birmingham's leading contemporary gallery, **Ikon Gallery of Contemporary Art** (open Tue–Sun 11am–5pm, ✆0121 248 0708, www.ikon-gallery.org).

BEYOND THE CITY CENTRE

Barber Institute of Fine Arts★★

University of Birmingham, Edgbaston. 2.5mi/4km S of the centre on the A 38. From the Bristol Road turn right up Edgbaston Park Road to the university south car park. Open Mon–Fri 10am–5pm, Sat–Sun 11am–5pm. Closed 1 Jan, Good Fri, 25–26 Dec. ♿🅿 ✆0121 414 7333 (enquiries). www.barber.org.uk.

This small but lovingly chosen collection was built up with the bequest of Lady M C H Barber (d.1933) and is displayed together with furniture and other *objets d'art*. Among the Italian Old Masters are several Venetians including Bellini, Cima and Guardi. Flemish painters include Brueghel the Younger

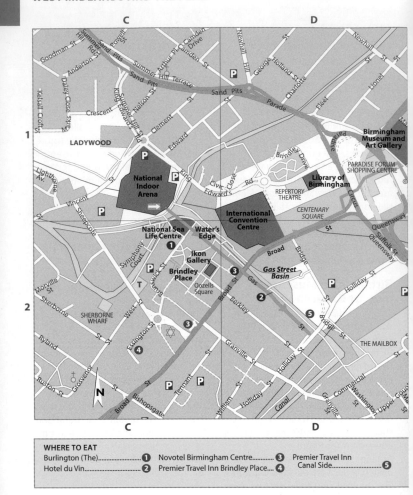

WHERE TO EAT

Burlington (The)........................ ❶ Novotel Birmingham Centre........... ❸ Premier Travel Inn
Hotel du Vin.............................. ❷ Premier Travel Inn Brindley Place.... ❹   Canal Side............................ ❺

and Rubens. The French school is well represented, with works by Poussin, Watteau, Delacroix, Ingres, Corot and Courbet and an outstanding group of Impressionists, post-impressionists, including Bonnard, Degas, Gauguin, Manet, Monet, Renoir, Vuillard and Van Gogh. English painters include Gainsborough, Turner and Whistler.

Aston Hall★★

2mi/3km N of the city centre on the A 38 (M). Open Tue–Sun 11am–4pm. Closed Aston Villa FC home matchdays; 23 Dec–2 Jan. £8. 🅿️ ✕ ✆0121 348 8100. www.birminghammuseums.org. uk/aston.

The '…*noble fabric which for beauty and state much exceedeth anything in these parts*' (William Dugdale, 1605–1686) was built 1618–35 by John Thorpe. The Jacobean **interior** is characterised by splendidly ornate ceilings and fireplaces.

Its most gorgeous rooms are the Long Gallery, with its strapwork ceiling, arcaded oak panelling and de la Planche tapestries of the *Acts of the Apostles*, and the Great Dining Room, with more extravagant strapwork and paintings by Romney and Gainsborough.

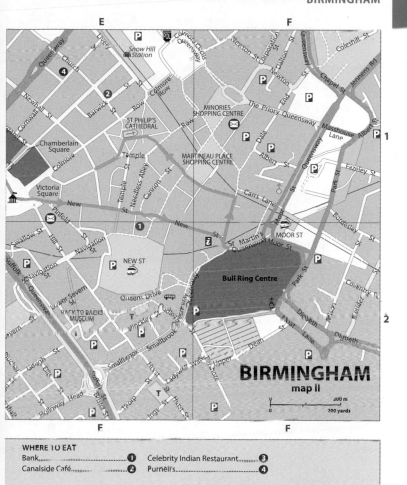

BIRMINGHAM
map ii

WHERE TO EAT

Bank.. ①   Celebrity Indian Restaurant........... ③
Canalside Café........................... ②   Purnell's................................... ④

Jewellery Quarter

Hockley. 1mi/1.6km NW.
Something of the atmosphere of early industrial Birmingham, with its countless workshops and specialist craftspeople, survives in this densely built-up area.
The **Museum of the Jewellery Quarter** (75–80 Vyse Street; open Tue–Sat 10.30am–5pm; closed 1 Jan, 24–26 and 31 Dec; &✗; £7; ✆0121 348 8140; www. birminghammuseums.org.uk/jewellery), set up in the former premises of a jewellery business, tells the story of the area as well as demonstrating traditional skills and techniques. A 10-minute walk away via Spencer Street and Caroline Street, the splendid Georgian **St Paul's**

Church forms the centrepiece of St Paul's Square, the only remaining 18C square in Birmingham.

♣♣ National Sea Life Centre

Brindley Place. Open Mon–Fri 10am–5pm, Sat–Sun and bank holidays 10am–6pm. Closed 25 Dec. Geneeral admission tickets from £12.75; but see website for packages and online discounts. &✗ ✆0871 423 2110. www.visitsealife.com.
While boasting the usual features of this nationwide group of marine life centres, this new-wave aquarium also concentrates on the specific story of the River Severn. A pathway climbs up through the displays of sea and freshwater fish

395

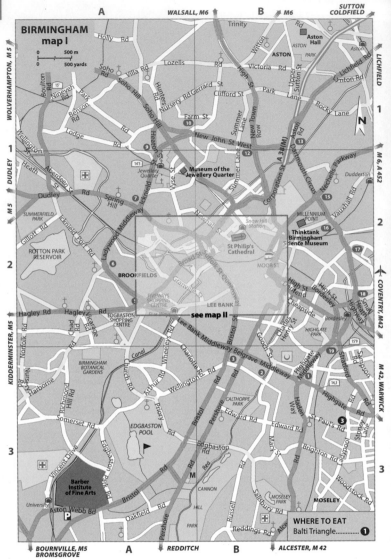

WALSALL, M6 • M6 • SUTTON COLDFIELD

**BIRMINGHAM
map I**

0 500 m
0 500 yards

Trinity
Aston Hall
ASTON
Lozells
Victoria
Soho Rd
Villa Rd
Soho Hill
Hunters Rd
Nursery Rd
Gerrard St
Clifford St
Farm St
New John St West
Summer Lane
New Town Row
Nineveh
Park
Benson Rd
Lodge Rd
Jewellery Quarter
Museum of the Jewellery Quarter
Vyse St
Heath
Aberdeen Rd
Dudley Rd
Spring Hill
Icknield St
Rocky Lane
Nechells Parkway
Duddeston
MILLENNIUM POINT
Thinktank Birmingham Science Museum
Snow Hill Station
St Philip's Cathedral
MOOR ST
BROOKFIELDS
Granville St
Broad St
Suffolk St Queensway
LEE BANK
see map II
FIVEWAYS SHOPPING CENTRE
HAGLEY RD
Hagley Rd
Vicarage Rd
Chad Rd
Norfolk
EDGBASTON SHOPPING CENTRE
Five Ways
Lee Bank Middleway
Belgrave Middleway
Bristol St
Gooch St
Cheapside
Bordesley
HIGHGATE PARK
High St
Bordesley
Stratford Rd
COVENTRY, M42
M 42, WARWICK
Canal
Wheeleys Rd
Charlotte Rd
Calthorpe Rd
BIRMINGHAM BOTANICAL GARDENS
Church Rd
Arthur Rd
Wellington Rd
Pershore Rd
Bristol Rd
Pecheore Rd
Edward Rd
Edward Rd
Mary St
Haden Way
Highgate Rd
St Paul's Rd
Stoney Lane
Brighton Rd
Woodstock Rd
Somerset Rd
Richmond Hill Rd
EDGBASTON POOL
Priory Rd
Edgbaston Rd
M
CANNON HILL PARK
Russell Rd
MOSELEY PARK
Salisbury Rd
MOSELEY
Vincent Drive
Barber Institute of Fine Arts
University
Aston Webb Bd
Oakfield Rd
Reddings Rd
Alce
WHERE TO EAT
Balti Triangle............... ❶

BOURNVILLE, M5 BROMSGROVE • REDDITCH • ALCESTER, M 42

WOLVERHAMPTON, M 5 • DUDLEY • M 5 • KIDDERMINSTER, M5 • LICHFIELD • M 6, A 452

---

as the landscape changes from the oceans to the estuary and upriver to its source. From the top, with a view over the canals below, a lift takes visitors down to the 'seabed' and an impressive transparent tunnel, to walk beneath rays and sharks. Also included in the ticket price is a **4-D movie** with special effects including wind, rain and snow supplementing the 3-D screen images. Dolphins, sea lions and other sea creatures leap from the screen as you feel the wind and salt spray on your face.

Bournville★

4mi/6km SW of the city centre on the A 38 and A 441.

In 1879, the Quaker Cadbury brothers moved their cocoa factory from the cramped conditions of the city centre to the rural surroundings of the Bournbrook estate. Cottages and community facilities for their workers were built around the Village Green, where the stone Rest House, presented to Mr and Mrs George Cadbury in 1914 as a silver wedding anniversary gift from

Cadbury employees worldwide, is now an information centre. To one side the Bournville School tower houses the **Bournville Carillon**, which rings out every Saturday at noon and 3pm.

Selly Manor

Maple Road, NW of the green. Open Tue–Fri 10am–5pm (plus Sat–Sun Easter–Sept 2–5pm) £4. ✆0121 472 0199. www.sellymanormuseum.org.uk. Selly Manor and Minworth Greaves are two of the city's oldest houses, rescued by George and Laurence Cadbury. Relocated and restored, they are now home to a fine collection of 13C–18C vernacular furniture. A Tudor-style garden has been re-created featuring plants that would have been planted in home gardens.

Cadbury World

S of the green. Open last wk Jan – Dec. Call or see website for times; pre-booking essential. Closed 23–26 Dec. £16.75, children £12.30 (discount online). ⚒🅿🍴✖ ✆0844 880 7667 (tickets and general enquiries). www.cadburyworld.co.uk

This is the visitor centre of the famous chocolate company, though it should be emphasised that the factory itself is *not* open to visitors. Instead this chocolate-flavoured mini theme-park (with animatronics, video presentations, multi-sensory cinema, interactive displays and activities) tells the story of the product, of the company, gives an insight into production and marketing, past and present, and tasting opportunities.

EXCURSIONS

The Black Country Living Museum★

⊙ Tipton Road, Dudley. 10mi/16km NW of Birmingham on the A 4123 or 3mi/5km from junction 2 on the M 5. Open Apr–early Nov daily 10am–5pm; rest of year 4pm. Closed 25–26 Dec, 1–mid-Jan. £17.50, child (5–16) £8.75 (discount online). ⚒🅿(£3). ✖ ✆0121 557 9643. www.bclm.co.uk. The sprawling landscape of the South Staffordshire coalfield may have given

rise to the name Black Country, which comprises Wolverhampton, Walsall, Dudley and Sandwell. Over 50 historic buildings from all around the area have been moved and authentically rebuilt to form this museum-village, which covers 11ha. Costumed actors present the rich industrial heritage and everyday life of the region. Coal mining is represented by a reconstructed pit-head and an impressive underground display of the conditions in a 'Thick Coal' mine in the 1850s. Nearby is a working replica of the world's first steam engine (1712). The heart of the display, reached by an electric tramway and flanked by two canal arms, is the village: houses, a grocery, hardware shop, baker's, chemist's, sweet shop, glasscutter's, chainmaker's, nail shop, rolling mill, anchor forge, boatdock, Methodist chapel and pub. Spectacular limestone caverns beneath the adjacent Castle Hill can be visited by canal boat.

Lichfield★

⊙ 17mi/27km north. Population: 32 219. 🅸 Market Square. ✆01543 412 112. www.visitlichfield.co.uk

This predominantly Georgian town lies just north of the Midlands industrial conurbation and is graced by its cathedral★★ (open Mon–Fri 7.30am–6.15pm, Sat 8am–6.15pm, Sun 7.30am–5pm; donation requested, ⚒✖; ✆01543 306 100; www.lichfield-cathedral.org.uk). the smallest in the country but also one of the most beautiful and most picturesquely sited.

The present building, which replaced an earlier Norman church, was begun in 1195 and is a fine synthesis of the Early English and Decorated styles. During the Civil War the cathedral was bombarded and the central spire collapsed in 1646. Repairs were made during the 1660s and the interior of the building was changed substantially by Wyatt in the 18C, but its medieval grandeur was restored by the sensitive work carried out by Sir George Gilbert Scott (1857–1901).

The three spires – unique among English cathedrals – are known as the **Three**

Sisters of the Vale. The perfectly pro-portioned nave, leads the eye past the Transitional crossing and western choir to the Lady Chapel and the fine 16C Flemish glass at the east end. Among the monuments are those to Samuel Johnson and David Garrick.

Samuel Johnson Birthplace Museum

Breadmarket Street. Open daily Mar–Oct 10.30am–4.30pm; Nov–Feb 11am–3.30pm. Closed 1 Jan, 25–26 Dec. ℘01543 264 972. www.samueljohnsonbirthplace.org.uk. Samuel Johnson (1709–84), the famous **lexicographer**, was born in this house, built by his father. The exhibits illustrate his life from childhood to marriage, his move to London, the English dictionary and his friendship with Boswell.

ADDRESSES

SHOPPING

Birmingham is the principal shopping centre for the Midlands with branches of famous London stores, such as Selfridges, in the Bull Ring Centre, and Harvey Nichols, in the designer mall, The Mailbox. Explore the Jewellery Quarter for shops selling handmade gold and silver jewellery.

ENTERTAINMENT

The City of Birmingham Symphony Orchestra (CBSO) and Birmingham Royal Ballet are internationally renowned. Pop and rock concerts and other events are staged in the National Indoor Area (NIA), part of the National Exhibition Centre (NEC). After dark, Broad Street, The Mailbox and the Water's Edge are hot-spots for drinking, dining and dancing.

Peak District★★

South Yorkshire, Derbyshire, Staffordshire

Bordering the teeming northern industrial areas of Sheffield, Manchester, the Potteries and West Yorkshire, lie the contrasting landscapes of the Peak District National Park. To the north, the sombre moorlands and gritstone outcrops of the Dark Peak culminate in Kinder Scout (636m), while to the south is more pastoral White Peak, a limestone plateau divided up by drystone walls and by spectacular steep-sided dales. It was on Kinder Scout, in 1932, that a mass trespass by ramblers, anxious to establish a permanent right of access to these wild spots, was organised. It resulted in imprisonment for five of their number. In the end, however, it was a catalyst in the establishment of national parks.

- **Michelin Map:** Atlas p35 or Map 502 O, P 23 and 24.
- **Info:** Visitor Centres: Bakewell, Castleton, Edale (good walking info), Bamford/Upper Derwent. Tourist Centres: Ashbourne, Buxton, Chesterfield, Derby, Holmfirth, Leek Saddleworth, Swadlincote. www.visitpeakdistrict.com.
- **Location:** Bounded by Holmfirth (north), Ashbourne (south), Sheffield (east) and Macclesfield (west).
- **Kids:** A cave visit; the Heights of Abraham; and Adventure Playground.

SIGHTS

Derwent Reservoirs

10mi/16 km W of Sheffield. Created to supply water to the nearby cities, **Derwent**, **Howden** and **Lady-bower reservoirs** are today a mini-'Lake District'.

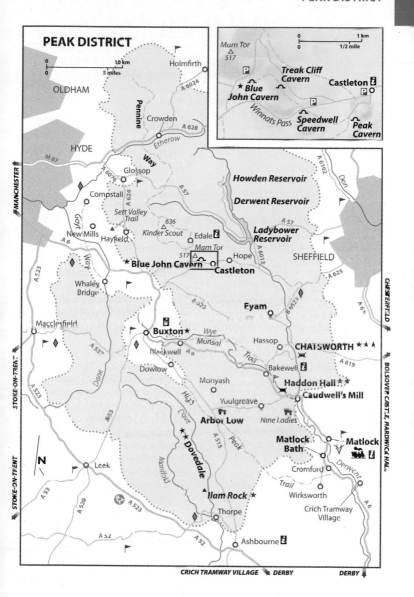

🏛 Castleton and Caves

17mi/27km W of Sheffield.

The village of Castleton is dominated by the ruined 12C keep of **Peveril Castle** (open daily Apr–Sept 10am–6pm; Oct 10am–5pm; Nov–Mar Sat–Sun (daily during Feb half-term hols) 10am–4pm; closed 1 Jan, 24–26 Dec; £5.60; ☎01433 620 613; www.english-heritage.org.uk), built soon after the Norman Conquest.

From the top are wonderful views over the Hope valley.

The local caves – lofty chambers with attractive mineral colourings and limestone formations – are natural cavities and/or lead-mining workings.

Peak Cavern/'The Devil's Arse' (off Goosehill; Apr–Oct daily 10am–5pm; Nov–Mar Sat–Sun 10am–5pm, and daily during school holidays; £10.75, child 5–15,

399

£8.75; joint ticket with Speedwell Cavern £18/£14.50; **P** (charge); ✖; ☏01433 620 285; www.peakcavern.co.uk) is entered at the foot of the hill below the castle. Near the impressive entrance of the cave the roof is still blackened by soot from the chimneys of a community of rope-makers, who built houses in the cave for 300 years until 1974.

Speedwell Cavern (Winnat's Pass, W on the B 6061; Apr–Oct daily 10am–5pm; Nov–Mar daily 10am–4pm; £11.50, child 5–15, £9.50; joint ticket with Peak Cavern £18/£14.50; **P** (charge); ✖; ☏01433 620 018; http://peakcavern.co.uk) is reached by boat along an underground canal.

Blue John Cavern★ (off the A 625; guided tour only, daily 9.30am–5.30pm/dusk, last tours 3.45–4.30pm; closed 25 Dec, 1 Jan; £12, child £6; ☏01433 620 638; www. bluejohn-cavern.co.uk) is the source of a purplish-blue form of fluorspar, called Blue John, a semi-precious mineral which is worked into jewellery and larger pieces. Blue John is also mined in **Treak Cliff Cavern** (Buxton Road; guided tours only, daily from 10am until 4.20pm/3.20pm in winter; closed 1 Jan, 24–26 Dec; £9.75, child (5–15) £5.20; **P**✖; ☏01433 620 571; www.bluejohnstone. com). In 1926, the skeletons of Bronze Age miners were found here.

Eyam

◯11mi/18km) southeast of Castleton. Eyam (pronounced 'eem') has been known as 'The Plague Village' since 1665, when in an act of altruistic self-sacrifice, the villagers, stricken by the disease, cut themselves off voluntarily from the outside world; only a quarter of them survived. Their heroic and fascinating story is told in the **Eyam Museum** (Hawkhill Road; open spring–summer Tue–Sun and bank holiday Mons 10am–4pm; £2.50; ☏01433 631 371; www.eyam-museum.org.uk).

Eyam Hall & Craft Centre (Hope valley; Hall and garden: open mid-Feb–early Nov Tue–Sun 10.30am–4.30pm; Dec 10.30am–4pm; Craft Centre: open daily 10.30am–4.30pm; £8.09; ♿✖; ☏01433 639 565; www.nationaltrust.org.uk/eyam) is a remarkably unspoilt example of a Jacobean manor house still owned by the Wright family, who built it in 1671. Rooms are furnished with portraits, costumes, silver and porcelain, and 15C and 16C tapestries. A craft centre has been added in the historic farmyard.

Buxton★

12.5mi/20km E of Macclesfield.
Population: 22 215.
🛈 Pavilion Gardens. ☏01298 25106.
Buxton is the Peak's spa town, set amid some of England's most beautiful scenery. The Romans discovered the warm springs and built baths here around the year 79. In the 16C, Mary Queen of Scots was occasionally permitted, during her long captivity at Sheffield Manor, to 'take the waters'. Buxton took on the aspect of a spa town in 1780 when John Carr of York built **The Crescent**, which, with the nearby **Opera House**, is still the centre.

Chatsworth★★★

◯ 10mi/16km west of Chesterfield.
Open daily: Apr–mid-Nov: **House:** 11am–5pm; **Gardens:** 11am–5.30pm; **Farmyard and playground:** 10.30am–5.30pm; Jun–Aug: **House:** 10.30am–5pm; **Gardens:** 10.30am–6pm; **Farmyard and playground:** 10.30am–5.30pm. Closed 24–26 Dec, 1 Jan.
Admission: House, garden, farmyard and playground £21.90, child £14; House and garden £20, child £11; Garden only £12.90, child £7; Farmyard and adventure playground £6 (all visitors). ♿**P** (£2–£3, free if any tickets booked online). ✖ ☏01246 565 300. www.chatsworth.org.
Set amid magnificent countryside, Chatsworth is one of the finest stately homes in the country with one of Europe's outstanding private art collections. The glorious verdant grounds are a delight. The original Chatsworth was begun in 1551 by Sir William Cavendish and Bess of Hardwick (ⓒsee Hardwick Hall, opposite), an indomitable woman who married four times and multiplied her wealth with each marriage. It was transformed 1686–1707 by the first Duke of Devonshire into a Baroque palace, and extended 1820–27.

House

The Painted Hall, by Laguerre, is unashamedly Baroque; the ceilings and walls are a soaring profusion of colours. Beneath the Great Stairs is the **grotto**, with superb stone carvings. The two coronation chairs in the lobby were used by William IV and Queen Adelaide in 1830. The long landscape by Gaspard Poussin is '...among the finest landscapes in the world' (Gustave Waagen). **The State Rooms** are characterised by unrestrained ceilings by Laguerre and Verrio and Louis XIV furniture; the gilt side tables in the Dining Room are by Kent; the Drawing Room tapestries (c.1635), based on Raphael, were woven at Mortlake; the violin on the inner door of the Music Room is a remarkable *trompe l'œil* by Jan van der Vaart.

The wrought iron panels on the landings of the West Stairs are by Jean Tijou. The ceiling depicting the Fall of Phaeton is an early work by Sir James Thornhill (1675–1734) and the painting of Samson and Delilah is by Tintoretto (1518–94). In the corridor are two Egyptian memorial tablets which are 3 800 years old. The chapel is unaltered since 1694 and includes a fine work by Verrio and a gloriously Baroque altarpiece by Cibber. A Veronese hangs in the passage.

The Library (28m) has some 17 000 books and a splendid gilded stucco ceiling by Edward Goudge (Wren's best pupil) framing Verrio's paintings.

The **Sculpture Gallery** houses an incomparable collection, including works by Antonio Canova. Hanging amid these is *King Uzziah* by Rembrandt.

👥 Park and Garden★★★

The genius of 'Capability' Brown made this one of the grandest of 18C parks. The garden's most majestic feature is the Cascade, designed in 1696, each step a different height that varies the sound of the falling water that disappears into pipes, to reappear out of the Seahorse Fountain on the south lawn. The garden as we see it today is mostly the creation of Joseph Paxton (1803–65). Modern family-friendly additions include a waterworks in which children

can freely splash around, a maze, the **farmyard** and a huge woodland adventure playground for children. There is also a sculpture garden.

Bolsover Castle ★

▶ 16mi/26km E of Matlock.
Open Apr–Sept daily 10am–5pm; Oct daily 10am–5pm; Nov–Apr Sat–Sun (daily during Feb half-term holidays) 10am–4pm. Closed 1 Jan, 24–26 Dec. £10.80. 👍🅿✕ ✆01246 822 844. www.english-heritage.org.uk.

This Gothic folly castle is perched on a hill above the coal mines and pit-heads. Completed in 1633, its interior is rich in carved Jacobean fireplaces, panelling, strapwork and ceiling paintings. It once boasted a famous riding school and every weekend (Apr–Sept excl bank hol Aug) riders in 17C costume give spectacular classical dressage performances.

Hardwick Hall★★

▶ 20mi/32km east of Matlock.
Hall: Open Apr–Nov daily 11am–5pm (house closed 2 wks in Nov); Dec (until Christmas) 11am–3pm.
Gardens: Open same days and times as house (daily during summer school holidays); . £6.88. 🅿(£4). ✕ ✆01246 850 430. www.nationaltrust.org.uk.

Directly after building Chatsworth and abandoning her husband (the Earl of Shrewsbury), **Bess of Hardwick** returned to the modest manor house where she was born, and rebuilt it. However, her descendants preferred to live at Chatsworth so Hardwick Old Hall fell into ruins and the new Hardwick Hall was left unoccupied, frozen in time, now one of the purest examples of 16C design and décor left in the country. The **interior** is famous for its Elizabethan fireplaces, friezes, tapestries and **embroideries**; one of these is by Mary Queen of Scots and three are by Bess. The house appeared in the last two *Harry Potter* films as Malfoy Manor.

Haddon Hall★★

◐2mi/3km S of Bakewell. Open 10.30am–5pm: early Apr–Sept daily; Oct Sat–Mon; 1–20 Dec 10.30am–4pm. Closed 19 Dec–Jan. £14.50. **P** (£2). ✗ ✆01629 812 855.
www.haddonhall.co.uk.
Overlooking the River Wye since the 12C, Haddon Hall is one of the finest fortified medieval manor houses in the country, continually enlarged until the early 17C. The rambling **interior**, like the exterior, is in a multitude of styles; the Hall (1370) is medieval, the Dining Room and Great Chamber are Tudor and the Long Gallery is Elizabethan. The rooms are matched in splendour by their Mortlake **tapestries**. The chapel boasts splendid **murals**.
The terraced **gardens** date from the 17C or earlier. Lavishly planted with roses they tumble prettily to the river with its venerable stone packhorse bridge.

Arbor Low

◐3mi/5km W of Youlgreave, 11mi/8km W of Matlock.
The best known of the Peak's prehistoric monuments, this circle of stones lies within a surrounding bank and ditch.

Matlock Bath and Matlock

◐17mi/27km N of Derby.
The cliffs and woods of the deep gorge carved by the River Derwent formed a picturesque setting for the Victorians

to develop spa facilities at **Matlock Bath** and with its riverside cliff setting, it resembles an inland seaside resort. The former Matlock Bath Hydro now houses a **freshwater aquarium** (110 North Parade; open Easter–Oct daily 10am–5.30pm, Nov–Easter Sat–Sun 10am–5pm; £3.30; ✆01629 583 624; www.matlockbathaquarium.co.uk) and various other exhibitions, including holograms.
The ancient Peak District industry of lead mining is celebrated in the fascinating **Peak District Mining Museum** (open Apr–early Sept daily 10am–5pm; early Sept–Oct 11am–4pm; Nov–Mar Sat–Sun 11am–4pm; museum £4, mine £4.50, both £7; **P**; ♿ museum only; ✗; ✆01629 583 834; www.peakdistrictlead-miningmuseum.co.uk), housed in the grand turn-of-the-20C Pavilion, once the centre of the town's social life. There is also a mine to visit.
A **cable car** ♟♙ runs from Matlock, 2mi/3km north of Matlock Bath, over the river gorge to the **Heights of Abraham**, where you can take **cave tours**, see exhibitions on the area, enjoy views from the Victorian Prospect Tower, and explore hilltop trails (open 10am–4.30pm: Feb holidays and Apr–early Nov daily; Mar Sat–Sun only; £16, child £11; ♿**P**✗; ✆01629 582 365; www.heightsofabraham.com).

Dovedale★★

◐Ilam Park Visitor Centre is 4.6mi/7.4km NW of Ashbourne. Visitor centre open dawn–dusk. **P** (charge). ✗ ✆01335 350 503. www.nationaltrust.org.uk/white-peak.
This dramatic gorge in the Derbyshire hills has been formed by the River Dove washing away the soft limestone, exposing cliffs, caves and crags. From its entrance between Thorpe Cloud (287m) and Bunster Hill (305m), it meanders for 2mi/3km below the rocky outcrops of Lovers' Leap, The Twelve Apostles and Ilam Rock★.

Derby★

and around

Derby is not one of England's most attractive county towns but it does provide a base for the Peak District and is surrounded by outstanding country houses. In 1756, the Derby porcelain industry began here, and in the early-20C it was the birthplace of Rolls-Royce.

▶ **Population:** 248 752.
Ⓖ **Michelin Map:** Michelin Atlas p35 or Map 502 P 25.
🅸 **Info:** Assembly Rooms, Market Place. ℘01332 643 411. www.visitderby.co.uk. The train station is 1mi/1.6km southeast of the centre; the bus station is a five minutes walk from town.
Ⓛ **Location:** 41mi/66km northeast of Birmingham.

CITY

At the heart of the city, west of the River Derwent on Queen Street is **Derby Cathedral** (open daily 8.30am–5.30pm; £5 contribution suggested, guided tours £4.50; Ⓖ; ℘01332 341 201; www.derby cathedral.org), a sublime blending of three eras – early-16C (the high tower), early-18C (James Gibbs' nave) and late 20C (retrochoir). The highlight is the magnificent Bakewell wrought-iron screen and gates, and the baldachin over the high altar. South of the chancel rests Bess of Hardwick (Ⓖ*Hardwick Hall, p401*).

Close by, on The Strand, is the **Derby Museum and Art Gallery★** (open Tue–Sat 10am–5pm, Sun noon–4pm; closed Christmas and New Year; Ⓖ; ℘01332 641 901; www.derbymuseums.org), home to two superb collections. The **Gallery of Ceramics** contains the world's largest collection of **Derby Porcelain★**, while the **Wright Gallery** holds many of the finest paintings and drawings of Joseph Wright of Derby (1734–97).

A 20-minute walk south of here, near the Derbyshire Royal Infirmary, is **Royal Crown Derby Porcelain★** (194 Osmaston Road; museum and exhibition: Mon–Sat 10am–3pm, £2; factory tours (booking essential) Tue–Thu at 1.30pm; £5; Ⓖ🅿✕; ℘01332 712 800; www.royalcrownderby. co.uk). A collection dating from 1756 to the present day is on display in the museum. In the **Raven Room** a priceless mint collection of Royal Crown Derby is displayed as it would have been in a Victorian house.

EXCURSIONS

Kedleston Hall★★

Ⓛ4mi/6km NW of Derby on Kedleston Road. **House:** Open late Feb–early Mar Sat–Wed noon–5pm, late Mar–early Nov daily noon–5pm. **Grounds and park:** Open daily mid-Feb–Oct 10am–6pm. £13.60 (park and pleasure grounds only, £6.80). Ⓖ🅿✕. ℘01332 842 191. www.nationaltrust.org.uk.

This Palladian mansion is the work of three architects: Matthew Brettingham, James Paine and Robert Adam; together they created one of the grandest 18C houses in England. The Curzon family have lived here since the 12C. The rooms centre on the **Marble Hall**. The **State Drawing Room** shows Adam at his most colourful; note the Cuyp landscape and the Veronese Achilles. The **Saloon** or **Rotunda** reaches to the coffered dome (19m). Adam's **Ante Room** and **Dressing Room** is graced by a Neoclassical screen with a segmental arch above the entablature, in a room hung with 17C and 18C Masters.

Sudbury Hall and the National Trust Museum of Childhood★★

Ⓛ15mi/24km W of Derby via the A 516 and A 50. **Hall:** open mid-Feb–early Nov Wed–Sun and Bank Holidays 1–5pm. **Museum:** open mid-Feb–late Apr Wed–Sun 11am–5pm; late Apr–early Nov daily 10.30am–5pm; early Nov–21 Dec Thu–Sun 11am–4pm.

Admission: Hall or museum £9.20 (child £4.60); Whole property £16.90.
&🅿✗ ✆01283 585 337.
www.nationaltrust.org.uk.
Although the **Jacobean exterior** (1660–1702) of this fine mansion is conservative, the **interior**, a radical combination of late Renaissance Classicism and Baroque, is exuberant. The hall, which is densely hung with 18C paintings, is beautified by the work of Grinling Gibbons, Edward Pierce and James Pettifer (all craftsmen who had worked with Wren on many of his London churches) and capped by Louis Laguerre's ceiling paintings. The **Staircase** was built by Pierce and the exquisite plasterwork above it is by Pettifer; note the superb **Long Gallery** ceiling.

The **Museum of Childhood** 👤👤 covers a variety of childhood experiences from the 19C to the present day, in eight new interactive galleries including outdoor adventures, stories and imagination.

Denby Pottery Visitor Centre

▶ Derby Road, Denby. 8mi/13km N of Derby. Visitor centre: Open daily Mon–Fri 9.30–5.30pm, Sat 9am–5.30pm, Sun 11am–5pm. Closed Easter Sun, 25 Dec.
&🅿✗ ✆01773 740 799.
www.denby.co.uk.
All aspects of the production of the famous Denby earthenware are demonstrated to visitors with opportunities to try making and decorating pieces, plus cookery demonstrations.

Stoke-on-Trent
and around

The potteries that this area is world famous for (and for which it is nicknamed) existed long before the time of England's most distinguished potter, Josiah Wedgwood (1730–95). Kilns date back to the early-14C, but it was the opening of Wedgwood's Etruria factory in 1769, the exploitation of Staffordshire's coalfields and the opening of the Trent–Mersey Canal that turned a local industry into a national one and an industry into an art. Most of the great brick kilns have now disappeared but a few monumental survivors remain, particularly in Longton.

▶ **Population:** 259 252.
🌀 **Michelin Map:** Michelin Atlas p35 or Map 503 N 24.
🛈 **Info:** Victoria Hall.
✆01782 236 000.
www.visitstoke.co.uk.
A car is best for getting around the 'Five Towns' that make up Stoke-on-Trent.
▶ **Location:** 43mi/69km north of Birmingham (train to Birmingham New Street, 48min).
👁 **Don't Miss:** Wedgwood; Little Moreton Hall.
🕐 **Timing:** Allow 1–2 days including an excursion.
👤👤 **Kids:** Alton; Trentham.

CITY MUSEUMS

Gladstone Pottery Museum★

Uttoxeter Road, Longton. Open Tue–Sat and bank holidays: Oct–Mar 10am–4pm; Apr–Sept 10am–5pm. £7.50.
&🅿✗ ✆01782 237 777.
www.stoke.gov.uk/museums.

This unique surviving pottery factory or 'potbank' retains its original workshops, cobbled yard and distinctive bottle ovens. It produced bone china from 1850 until the 1960s when it was converted into a museum of British pottery. Workshops show traditional skills.

Here, the history of all The Potteries are wrapped up in one museum.

The Potteries Museum and Art Gallery★

Bethesda Street, Hanley. Open Mon–Sat 10am–5pm, Sun 11am–4pm.
&.✕.☎01782 232 323.
www.stoke.gov.uk/museums.

The main city museum houses a superb ceramics collection from 14C English pottery right through to the modern studio movement, and current industrial production. There is a Second World War Spitfire, and major art exhibitions are regularly held. All have been upstaged recently, however, by the **Staffordshire Hoard** (www.staffordshirehoard.org.uk) comprising over 3 500 items of gold and silver with precious stone decorations. Discovered near Lichfield in 2009, it is the largest hoard of Anglo-Saxon gold ever found and part of it is now on permanent display here.

EXCURSIONS

♟ Alton Towers★★

◑12mi/19km E via the A 50, A 521 and B 5032. Open: check website for details. £55, child £48 (online discounts available). & ☐(£5) ✕ ☎0871 222 3330. www.alton-towers.co.uk.
Britain's most famous theme park still offers more thrills than the rest with a huge variety of spectacular rides, a waterpark, and a spa as well as tranquil gardens. It is set in the beautiful grounds of Alton Towers, a 19C Gothic Revival mansion, now in ruins.

Biddulph Grange Garden★

◑Grange Road, Biddulph. 7mi/11km N. Open daily early Nov–Feb 10am–3.30pm; mid-Mar–late Oct 10am–5.30pm; late Oct–early Nov 10am–4.30pm;. £9.05. ☐✕ ☎01782 517 999. www.nationaltrust.org.uk.
This unusual and exciting garden with themed sections devoted to different parts of the world was designed in the mid-19C by James Bateman to display specimens from his extensive plant collection.

Little Moreton Hall★★

◑Congleton 10mi/16km N. Open 11am–5pm (4pm in Dec), but see website for days and times, which vary. £10.20.
& ☐✕ ☎01260 272 018.
www.nationaltrust.org.uk.
This picture-postcard moated black-and-white half-timbered manor house is characterised by rich and intricate patterns on square panels, elaborate joinery and window tracery and 16C glass. It was begun in the 1440s with the building of the Great Hall and completed some 140 years later with the addition of John Moreton's Long Gallery.

Wedgwood Visitor Centre★

◑7mi/11km S on the A 500, A 34 and a minor road (left) to Barlaston. Open daily 10am–5pm. Closed 25–27 Dec, 1 Jan. Admission: Factory tour and museum, £15; factory tour only, £10; museum only, £7.50. &(not tours). ☐✕ ☎01782 282 986.
www.wedgwoodvisitorcentre.com.
Established in 1938 the Wedgwood Factory offers the perfect overview of the pottery-making process, with an excellent collection of Wedgwood ware, and Wedgwood portraits by Stubbs, Reynolds, Lawrence and Wright of Derby.

♟ Trentham Gardens★

◑5mi/8km south of Hanley.
Open Apr–Sept 9am–6pm/dusk (Jun–Jul 9pm, Aug 8pm). £11.25, child (5–15), £9.60 (online discounts). ☎01782 646 646. www.trenthamleisure.co.uk.
Britain's most spectacular Italian garden, designed by Capability Brown, covers 300ha. It has recently become the region's second-largest leisure centre, featuring a monkey forest, Aerial Extreme treetops walk, big wheel, garden centre, shopping and restaurants.

ADDRESSES

🏠 STAY

STRATFORD-UPON-AVON

⊖🍽🛏 **Mercure Shakespeare Hotel** – Chapel Street. ☎02477 092 802. www.mercure.com. 73 rooms. Housed in a charming 17C half-timbered building, this smart hotel stylishly combines old and new at reasonable prices.

⊖🍽🛏 **The Falcon Hotel** – Chapel Street. ☎01789 279953. www.falconstratford hotel.com. 83 rooms. In the centre of town, behind a half-timbered façade, this stylish hotel combines ancient and modern to good effect. Lovely courtyard garden in summer, log fires in winter.

⊖🍽🛏🛏 **The Arden Hotel** – 44 Waterside. ☎01789 298 682. www.theardenhotelstratford.com. 45 rooms. Opposite the Royal Shakespeare Theatre, the Arden is the smartest address in town. It boasts the chic Waterside Brasserie, a champagne bar, and rooms with river views.

COVENTRY

⊖🍽 **Spireview** – 36 Park Road. ☎024 7625 1602. Simple B&B accommodation.

WARWICK

⊖🍽🛏 **Lord Leycester Hotel** – 19 Jury Street. ☎01926 491 481. www.lord-leycester.co.uk. 40 rooms. This 600-year old place has historical charm, a brasserie and bar, and is 400m from the Castle.

WORCESTER

⊖🍽🛏 **Diglis House Hotel** – Severn Street. ☎01905 353 518. www.diglishouse hotel.co.uk. 28 rooms. This gracious 18C house enjoys a wonderful position on the banks of the Severn, just a short walk from the city centre. Accommodation is in a modern annex.

LUDLOW

⊖🍽🛏 **The Feathers Hotel** – Bull Ring. ☎01584 875 261. www.feathersatludlow. co.uk. 40 rooms. Set in a magnificent timber-framed building, and centrally located, the famous Feathers features spacious, elegantly decorated bedrooms, and a decent restaurant.

⊖🍽 **The Lion** – Leintwardine, Craven Arms. ☎01547 540 203. www.thelion leintwardine.co.uk. 8 rooms. Set in a picturesque village, this quiet country Inn has been beautifully modernised without losing its character. Excellent restaurant (⟳see opposite).

BIRMINGHAM

⊖🍽 **Premier Inn** – **Brindley Place**, 80 Broad Street. ☎0871 527 8076 and **Canal Side** 20 Bridge Street. ☎0871 527 8078. www.premierinn.com. These cheerful budget chain hotel branches offer simple comfortable modern accommodation in two excellent locations in and around Birmingham's buzzing canal area.

⊖🍽🛏 **Novotel Birmingham Centre** – 70 Broad Street. ☎0121 643 2000. www.accorhotels.com. 🅿. 148 rooms. Set in the centre of town there may be few surprises in this modern international-style chain hotel but it provides a very comfortable base.

⊖🍽🛏🛏 **The Burlington** – Burlington Arcade, off New Street. ☎0844 879 9019. www.macdonaldhotels.co.uk/burlington. 110 rooms. Polychrome marble, plush carpets and elegant décor give an inimitable Victorian atmosphere in this historic hotel, strong on design and modern art. VIPs stay here.

⊖🍽🛏🛏 **Hotel du Vin** – Church Street. ☎0121 200 0600. www.hotelduvin.com. 🅿. 66 rooms. Set in the revitalised Jewellery Quarter, this large ornate Victorian red-brick former hospital has been sympathetically converted to timelessly styled bedrooms and suites, set around a courtyard. There is also a spa, gym, billiards room, a bistro and lovely pub.

PEAK DISTRICT

⊖ **Fountain Villa** – 86 North Parade, Matlock Bath. ☎01629 56195. 🅿. 4 rooms. This elegant classic Georgian house is something of an Aladdin's cave inside with fussy but characterful rooms. Good value.

⊖🍽🛏 **Cavendish Hotel** – Chatsworth Estate, Baslow. ☎01246 582 311. www.cavendish-hotel.net. 🅿 23 rooms. Located on the Chatsworth House Estate, the Cavendish, originally the local inn, is steeped in history, with perfect views and peaceful surroundings. Open fires, oak beams and antique furnishings.

♀ EAT

STRATFORD-UPON-AVON

⊜☻ **Garrick Inn** – High Street. ☎01789 292 186. Atmospheric venerable pub (established in 1595), now also a restaurant serving upmarket pub grub.

⊜☻☻ **Lambs** – 12 Sheep Street. ☎01789 292 554. www.lambsrestaurant. co.uk. Closed lunch Mon– Tue. Hidden behind a 16C façade, this fashionable, stylish restaurant serves brasserie favourites in a modern way; one of the oldest buildings in Stratford.

WORCESTER

⊛ Try **Friars Street** for European and ethnic cuisines.

⊜☻ **Brown's @ the Quay Restaurant** South Quay. ☎01905 23800. www. brownsworcester.co.uk. A trendily coverted riverside building is the setting for this 'all-day, all-kinds-of-eating' (and drinking) wine bar/restuarant.

HEREFORD

⊜☻ **Butchers Arms** – Woolhope (7.5mi/13km). ☎01432 860 281. www. butchersarmswoolhope.com. Attractive, half-timbered 16C inn, with a pretty garden by a brook and a lively bar with low-slung beams and open fires. Daily changing menu of regional dishes; with local lamb and cheese the highlights.

LUDLOW

⊜–⊜☻ **Green Cafe** – Mill on the Green, Dinham Bridge. ☎01584 879 872. http:// thegreencafe.co.uk. Open 10am–4pm. Closed Mon. Part of a restored watermill complex, overlooking Dinham Weir, the café features seasonal cooking using local organic products. Michelin Bib Gourmand.

⊜☻ **The Lion** – Leintwardine, Craven Arms. ☎01547 520 203. www.thelion leintwardine.co.uk. Set on the riverside by a picturesque medieval bridge, this gastro pub serves beautifully presented seasonal dishes using only the finest local ingredients.

⊜☻☻☻ **La Bécasse** – 17 Corve Street. ☎01584 872 325. www.labecasse.co.uk. The characterful dining room of this

17C former coaching inn is split into three intimate areas, with linen-laid tables and wood panelling.

BIRMINGHAM

⊛ Visit the **Water's Edge** and **Brindley Place** developments in the Gas Street Basin area for lively wine bars, cafés, restaurants and pubs. Birmingham is famous for its Indian and Chinese restaurants and its Balti curry houses.

⊜ **Canalside Café** – 35 Regency Wharf, Gas Street Basin. ☎0121 248 7979. This tiny former cottage, built 1770, on the waterside, is now a café-cum pub serving real ales to wash down its home-cooked, good-quality food.

⊜☻ **Celebrity Indian Restaurant** – 44 Broad Street. ☎0121 643 8969. www.celebrityrestaurant.co.uk. Popular upmarket 'new wave' stylish Indian restaurant beside the canal, serving intriguing contemporary dishes alongside old favourites.

⊜☻☻ **Bank** – 4 Brindley Place ☎0121 633 4466. http://individualrestaurants. com/bank. This spacious airy modern brasserie has large glass walls which look onto its canalside terrace. Grills and shellfish are the specialities. Good lunchtime offers.

⊜☻☻☻ **Purnell's** – 55 Cornwall Street. ☎0121 212 9799. www.purnells restaurant.com. Closed Sun–Mon, and 1st fortnight Aug. Set in a Victorian red-brick-and-terracotta building, this chic 45-cover, contemporary fine-dining restaurant holds one Michelin-star.

PEAK DISTRICT

⊜☻☻ **Rowley's** – Church Lane, Baslow. ☎01246 583 880. www.rowleysrestaurant. co.uk. On the edge of the Chatsworth Estate (and under the same ownership as the one-star Michelin restaurant, Fisher's at Baslow Hall), this sturdy old stone-built pub offers excellent value Modern British cuisine.

⊜☻☻☻ **Fisher's at Baslow Hall** – Calver Road, Baslow. ☎01246 583 259. www.fischers-baslowhall.co.uk. Fine dining (Michelin 1-star) in a Grade 2 listed Edwardian stone-built manor house on the edge of Baslow; rooms, formal grounds and walled vegetable garden.

North West

Imperial War Museum North designed by Daniel Libeskind, Salford Quays, Manchester
© Grant Rooney/age fotostock

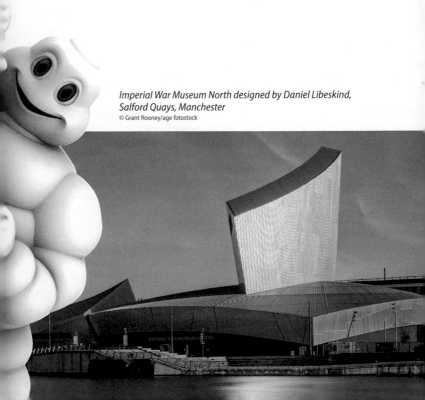

Introduction

Although the North-South divide has long gone, the North West still retains a fiercely independent spirit, not only regionally but in its own city loyalties. There is little love lost between Mancunians and Liverpudlians, with the rivalry, at its fiercest on the football pitch. For visitors, the good news is that there's a different kind of rivalry; that to offer the finest visitor attractions (drawing on a long and rich working-class heritage), and the finest shopping, eating, drinking and nightlife. As a result this region is one of the most exciting in the country.

Manchester

Today's visitors will find little trace of 'Cottonopolis' (the world's first industrial city) as Manchester was known in its first flush of fame. The present face of the city reflects both its Victorian wealth and its recent modern urban redesign. Salford Quays is the most stunning example of the latter but there are also many iconic new buildings popping up in the city centre. Manchester also hosts superb visitor attractions, but what makes the city special is its buzz: from its shops to its nightclubs; a dynamic art and student scene; a thriving gay community; great live music, from some of the finest rock bands to world-beating classical orchestras; and of course, two of the world's most famous football clubs.

Chester

By contrast with the two major cities of the North West, Chester is quiet and provincial, but for visitors more easily accessible in terms of size and layout. Its centre is a perfect little black-and-white half-timbered walled town – a repository of Britain's most important Roman heritage.

Liverpool

Liverpool is famous for its music, which dominated the world (thanks largely to The Beatles) in the 1960s, and its football teams, which did the same in the 1980s. The wry, often black humour of its (Scouse) inhabitants – their regional accent instantly recognisable – reflects the long vibrant history of living and working in a major port which has had its many ups and downs, particularly over the last half-century or so. At present, however, Liverpool is very much on the up, having reinvented itself to become European Capital of Culture in 2008, and revitalising its docks to house the

Highlights

1 Get hands on with industry at MOSI, **Manchester** (p411)

2 Delve into the Imperial War Museum and The Lowry, **Salford Quays** (p413)

3 Go shopping in another era at The Rows, **Chester** (p416)

4 Enjoy all things Liverpudlian at Albert Dock, **Liverpool** (p418)

5 Take in the view from the top of the Tower at **Blackpool** (p425)

best museums in the north of England. Like Manchester, it boasts a vibrant restaurant, nightlife and shopping scene.

Blackpool

England's most famous seaside town enjoyed its heyday in the 1950s and 60s before the advent of cheap foreign travel. Today it tends to polarise opinion, and while it is deeply unfashionable to many, the resort still attracts well over one million overnight visitors per annum. They come for the donkey rides, the long golden beaches, the famous promenade, the white-knuckle rides of Pleasure Beach theme park, the shows at the recently revitalised iconic Blackpool Tower, and seaside culture. Out of summer (Sept–Oct) they visit again to enjoy the town's famous Illuminations.

Isle of Man

To escape the crowds and experience a slower way of life (and some unusual and antique forms of transport), the Isle of Man can make a rewarding short break. Pack your walking boots.

Manchester★★

and around

Though the smoking chimneys of the cotton mills in this North West metropolis have long gone, Manchester retains many fine historic buildings erected by the Victorian successors to the city's hard-headed Georgian merchants. Today, it has developed into a major provincial centre of finance, and has recently added a number of high-profile visitor attractions. It has long been renowned for its nightlife, the local music scene and the most famous football club in the world.

A BIT OF HISTORY

Thanks to trade with the American colonies, Manchester became the centre of the rapidly expanding cotton industry. However, its principles of free trade led to tragedy on 16 August in 1819 when a crowd assembled on St Peter's Fields to demand Parliamentary reform and repeal of the Corn Laws; the cavalry were sent in to disperse them and, in what came to be known as the **Peterloo Massacre**, 11 died and many were injured. The **Free Trade Hall** (now a hotel) was constructed on the site of this outrage.

CASTLEFIELD★

South end of Deansgate.

Castlefield is the perfect place to trace the development of Manchester, from Roman times to the present day. In fact the remains of the **Roman fort** – 'the castle in the field' – and the north gate and part of the west wall have been reconstructed on their original site.

In 1761, Castlefield became the centre of Manchester's canal system, which started with the Duke of Bridgewater's canal. The towpath is open to pedestrians and a walkway (1mi/1.6km) beside the River Irwell links Castlefield with the Ship Canal and Salford Quays. Cruises are offered along the waterways that once carried goods across the Pennines

▶ **Population:** 530 300.
 Michelin Map: Michelin Atlas p39 or Map 502 N 23.
 Info: Piccadilly Gardens. ☎0871 222 8223. www.visitmanchester.com. Manchester's main train station is Piccadilly (London Euston 2h07, Birmingham New Street 1h25), a 10-minute walk east of the city centre. The two coach stations, Chorlton Street and Piccadilly Gardens, are close to each other, a 5-minute walk east. The city centre is compact. The **Metrolink tram** system (www.metrolink.co.uk), runs fast frequent services across the city and beyond. A £7 Travelcard will get you unlimited travel on all Metrolink tram services for 1 day. The **free Metroshuttle bus** service links the main rail stations, car parks, shopping areas and all main sights in the city centre.
 Location: Manchester is 6.3 km/35mi north-east of Liverpool and the same distance north-west of Sheffield.
 Don't Miss: MOSI; The Lowry; The Imperial War Museum North.
 Timing: Allow at least 2 days to explore Manchester.
 Kids: Get hands-on at MOSI; for football-mad kids, the National Football Museum and Manchester United's stadium tours.

by **Manchester Ship Canal Cruises** (☎0151 330 1003; www.merseyferries. co.uk), between Salford Quays and Liverpool (approx 6h, plus 1 h return by bus), and **Manchester River Cruises** (☎0843 208 0500; www.manchesterrivercruises.

com), along the Irwell and Ship Canal to Salford Quays. In 1830, the world's first passenger railway station was opened by the Liverpool and Manchester Railway. On its Liverpool Road site now stands the city's largest museum.

👥 Museum of Science and Industry (MOSI)★★

Open daily 10am–5pm. Closed 1 Jan, 24–26 Dec. Entry to the museum is free, but certain activities and some special exhibitions are chargeable; check website or call for details. ♿ ✖(Mon–Fri 8am–5pm, Sat–Sun 9am–5pm). ☎0161 832 2244. www.msimanchester.org.uk. Manchester's industrial heritage is presented in a series of lively exhibition galleries devoted to textiles, cameras, gas and electricity, working engines, locomotives, 'discoveries, inventions and innovations', the history of flight, a science centre, a walk-through Victorian sewer, an 1830s warehouse, and more. All have interactive features.

CITY CENTRE

National Football Museum★

Urbis Building, Cathedral Gardens. Open daily 10am–5pm. Admission free (voluntary donation suggested). Guided tours are available Mon–Fri between 10.30am and 3.30pm, weekends at 11am and 3pm. Closed 1 Jan, 24–26 Dec. ♿✖ ☎0161 605 8200. www.nationalfootballmuseum.com. Housed in a stunning glass building, the national museum of the national game is the world's biggest collection of its kind and covers six floors. It features internationally famous exhibits such as the 1966 World Cup Final ball and The Jules Rimet (World Cup) trophy, but also delves into the history of the game at all levels.

Manchester Cathedral★

Open Mon and Fri 8.30am–5.30pm, rest of week 8.30am–6.30pm. ♿✖ ☎0161 833 2220. www.manchestercathedral.org. The parish church of Manchester, built 1215, was refounded as a chantry college in 1421 and became the cathedral

in 1847. Six bays form the nave – the widest of any church in England – and six the **choir**, famed for its medieval carving. The **choir screen** is unique and in the choir itself, note the workmanship on the **stalls and canopies★**. The **misericords** (c.1500) are a comic depiction of medieval life.

Royal Exchange★

Manchester owes its prosperity to 'King Cotton'. Raw cotton imported via Liverpool and the canal network, pure water from the Pennines, a high degree of humidity, and a large available working population were the factors responsible for the rapid growth of the cotton and ancillary industries. English cotton was sold throughout the world and the Manchester cotton exchange was the nerve centre of this trade. Inside the exchange, the prices of cotton on the day the market last traded are still shown (on the board near the roof).

Today this hall is occupied by the 700 seat **Royal Exchange Theatre** (♿; ✖; ☎0161 833 9833; www.royalexchange. co.uk) a spectacular seven-sided, glass-walled capsule, suspended from huge marble pillars, providing theatre in the round.

People's History Museum

Left Bank, Spinningfields. Open daily 10am–5pm (2nd Thu of month 10am–8pm). Closed 24–26 Dec, 1 Jan. ♿✖ ☎0161 838 9190. www.phm.org.uk. Occupying its current striking premises since 2010, this is the national museum of the history of working people in Britain. Much of its content deals with social justice; the exhibition starts with the **Peterloo Massacre** of 1819 (*see opposite*) and ends in the present day.

John Rylands Library

Open Sun–Mon noon–5pm, Tue–Sat 10am–5pm. Introductory tours, Wed and Fri 3–3.30pm. ♿✖ ☎0161 306 0555. www.library.manchester.ac.uk. This beautiful library is one of the finest examples of modern Gothic architecture in Europe, designed by Basil Champneys, opened in 1900 and

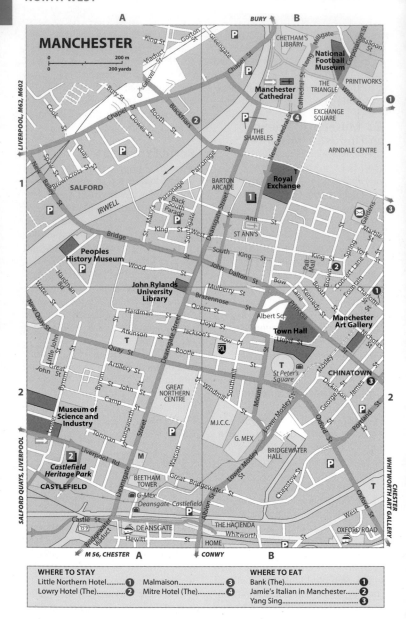

MANCHESTER

WHERE TO STAY		WHERE TO EAT	
Little Northern Hotel............ ❶	Malmaison............................ ❸	Bank (The)... ❶
Lowry Hotel (The)................ ❷	Mitre Hotel (The)................ ❹	Jamie's Italian in Manchester........ ❷
		Yang Sing... ❸

founded in memory of a successful textile manufacturer. The library possesses many early printed books, and rare and valuable manuscripts. Exhibitions and tours showcase many of these.

Town Hall★

Designed in Gothic style by Alfred Waterhouse and built in 1868–77,

the town hall is one of the greatest civic buildings of the Victorian era. Its tower with octagonal top stage rises 87m above the pedestrian area of Albert Square and guided tours take place regularly (see website; www.manchester.gov.uk/townhall). Two staircases lead from the low vaulted entrance hall to the **Great Hall**, with its hammerbeam roof and 12 Pre-Raphaelite-style murals by Ford Madox Brown 1876–88.

Manchester Art Gallery★

Mosley Street. Open daily 10am–5pm (9pm Thu). Closed 1 Jan, 24–26, 31 Dec. &✗ ℘0161 235 8888. http://manchesterartgallery.org.

Recently restored to its 19C glory, this acclaimed gallery boasts a fine Pre-Raphaelite collection, with works by Millais, Hunt and Rossetti, and Ford Madox Brown's *Work* (1852) illustrating the various classes of a developing industrial society. Note the works of Stubbs, Turner and Constable and the industrial landscapes of the North, captured by L S Lowry (*see below*).

SOUTHWEST CITY CENTRE

▲▲ The Lowry★

2.5mi/4km southwest of city centre. Pier 8, Salford Quays. Galleries open daily 11am (Sat 10am)–5pm. &✗ ℘0843 208 6000. www.thelowry.com.

This visually stunning arts and entertainment complex, opened in 2000 as one of Britain's flagship Millennium projects, gracing the regenerated docks of **Salford Quays**. It houses two theatres and studio space for performing arts, presenting drama, opera, ballet, dance, musicals, children's shows, popular music, jazz, folk and comedy. Its gallery space showcases the works of **L S Lowry** (1887–1976), a locally born painter, nationally famous for his childlike 'matchstick' figures and northern England street scenes, alongside contemporary exhibitions.

Imperial War Museum North★

2.7mi/4.3km SW of city centre. Salford Quays, Trafford Wharf. Open daily 10am–5pm. Closed 24–26 Dec. &🅿 (from £5). ✗ ℘0161 836 4000. http://north.iwm.org.uk.

Located in an astonishing award-winning building by international architect Daniel Libeskind, on the city's ship canal, this museum, like its London counterpart, takes a sober look at how 20C conflicts have affected both

ordinary combatants and the people at home. A highlight is the **Big Picture Show**, a 360° audio-visual show which immerses visitors into the IWM's world-renowned collections of war-related images and sound. Continually changing images are projected onto the gallery walls, floor and visitors themselves, accompanied by sounds and reminiscences from the oral history archives.

▲▲ Manchester United Museum and Stadium Tour

2.5mi/4km SW of city centre. Old Trafford, North Stand. Open (except match days): **Museum:** Mon–Sat 9.30am–5pm, Sun 10am–4pm. **Stadium tours:** 9.40am–4.30pm (70min) booking advisable. &🅿✗ ℘0161 826 1326. www.manutd.com.

Take a look behind the scenes to see what makes the world's most famous football club so successful.

Whitworth Art Gallery★

1.5mi/2.5km S. Whitworth Park, Denmark Road. Open daily 10am–5pm (Thu 10am–9pm). ℘0161 275 7450. www.whitworth.manchester.ac.uk.

Internationally famous for its collections of art and design, the Whitworth Gallery has recently undergone the biggest remodelling and refurbishment since it opened in 1889, and will reopen to the public in summer 2014. It is home to an impressive range of watercolours, prints, drawings, modern art and sculpture by Barbara Hepworth and Henry Moore. The Whitworth also features the largest collections of textiles and wallpapers outside London.

EXCURSIONS

Quarry Bank★

10mi/16km S. Quarry Bank Road, Styal. Open: **Mill and Apprentice House:** Jan–mid-Feb and early Nov–Dec Wed–Sun 10.30am–4pm; mid-Feb–early Nov daily 10.30am–5pm; **Garden:** mid-Feb–Dec daily 10.30am–4pm. Admission: Whole property: £18.15; &🅿✗ ℘01625 527 468; www.nationaltrust.org.uk.

In a wooded country park (284 acres/ 115ha) beside the fast-flowing River Bollin, stands a five-storey cotton mill, built in 1784, powered by the most powerful working waterwheel in Europe (50 tons), with two mill engines which help to bring the past to life.

The production of cloth, from the cotton plant to the bolt of calico on sale in the mill shop, is traced in a fascinating exhibition including live demonstrations of hand-spinning and loom weaving.

The Apprentice House (limited timed tickets only) shows the spartan lifestyle of the pauper children that worked here.

Jodrell Bank Discovery Centre

21mi/34km S Bomish Lane. Open daily 10am–5pm. Adult £7.30, child (4–16) £5.40 (online discounts). 🄿✕ ☎01477 571 766. www.jodrellbank.net.

Discover how the giant landmark Lovell Telescope works and explore the Universe with interactive exhibits at this small complex attached to Britain's most famous radio telescope. Features include the Planet Pavilion, the Space Pavilion, Star Pavilion, Gardens and Grounds, and café.

Chester★★

Cheshire

Set on the northeast border of Wales in green and prosperous Cheshire, Chester has been an important city since Roman times and retains many tangible reminders of this period. The lasting impression on most visitors is, however, its classic black-and-white half-timbered buildings, which feature prominently in this well-preserved historic walled city.

A BIT OF HISTORY

Deva (or Dewa), the Roman legionary fortress and naval base built on a loop of the River Dee, was one of the largest in Britain and home to the XX Valeria Victrix Legion for 200 years. The legionary headquarters stood at the junction on the site now occupied by St Peter's Church.

The port of Chester is known to have been used by seagoing vessels during the Roman occupation. The period of greatest prosperity was the 12C–14C; even until the end of the 16C, Chester regarded the Mersey as a 'creek of the Port of Chester'. But by the 15C, the Dee estuary was silting up and ships had to anchor some 12mi/19km downstream. The **Roodee** (Anglo-Saxon for 'Island of the Cross') is a tract of land between the

▶ **Population:** 118 200.
♿ **Michelin Map:** Michelin Atlas p34 or Map 403 L 24.
🄸 **Info:** Town Hall, Northgate Street. ☎0845 647 7868. www.visitchester.com.
The train station (Manchester Piccadilly 1h03) is on City Road, a 10–15min walk from the centre. Almost everything of interest is inside the old city walls. Take a walking tour (daily, from the information centre), or open-top bus tour: either hop-on hop-off with City Sightseeing (www.city-sightseeing.com), or a 30-min tour on a 1924 vintage bus with Chester Heritage Tours (☎0844 585 4144; www.chesterheritagetours.co.uk).
▶ **Location:** Chester lies on the River Dee, not far from the border with Wales.
🖐 **Don't Miss:** The Rows; historic racecourse (www.chester-races.co.uk).
🕐 **Timing:** At least a day.
👪 **Kids:** Chester Zoo; Dewa Roman Experience.

river and the city wall now occupied by Chester Racecourse. Horse races have been held here since 1540.

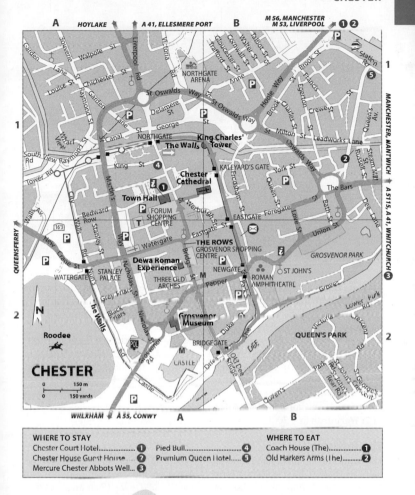

CHESTER

WHERE TO STAY		WHERE TO EAT	
Chester Court Hotel .... **①**	Pied Bull .... **④**	Coach House (The) .... **①**
Chester House Guest House ... **⑦**	Premium Queen Hotel ...... **⑤**	Old Harkers Arms (The) .... **②**
Mercure Chester Abbots Well ... **③**			

WALKING TOUR

City Walls★

No other city in Britain has preserved a continuous circuit of walls. From the Eastgate, by the Clock Tower, looking west to the spire of Holy Trinity Church (now the Guildhall) you can see the width of the Roman fortress.

Parts of the Roman wall are visible between the Northgate and **King Charles' Tower**.

Chester Cathedral★

Open Jan–Mar 9am–5pm; Apr–Dec 9am–6pm. £3 donation suggested. Guided tours Mon–Sat 11am, 1.30pm, 3pm (from West Steps of the cathedral).

Tower tours, check website for times (usually Sat at 11.30am) and charges. ⚫✗ ✆01244 324 756. www.chestercathedral.com.

The 14C gateway leads into Abbey Square, once the outer courtyard of the abbey; ahead are the cloisters. The Norman abbey church was replaced between 1250 and 1540 by the present magnificent red sandstone building. Many of the original abbey buildings stand round the 16C **cloisters**. The hammerbeam roof of the refectory has been superbly re-created. The Dean and Chapter still meet in the 13C **Chapter House** and the clergy and choir assemble in the vestibule before services. The north transept contains the old-

The Rows

© Robert Harding/hemis.fr

est part of the cathedral fabric, an 11C round-headed arch and arcade, and the oldest wooden ceiling, the **camber beam roof** (1518–24), which carries a splendid display of Tudor heraldry. The **stalls** and **misericords** in the choir date from 1390 and are among the finest in the country. The **Lady Chapel** has been restored to its 1250 appearance. Behind the High Altar is the 14C **shrine of St Werburgh** (d. c.700).

The Rows★★

The Rows are continuous half-timbered galleries, reached by steps, which form a second row of shops above those at street level. Unique in Britain, they probably originated in the 14C when merchants erected shops at street level against the lower courses of the Roman buildings that had lined the streets, or on top of the stone rubble, and made steps and walkways to link them. Upper storeys provided accommodation for the traders and their families.

Grosvenor Museum

27 Grosvenor Street. Open Mon–Sat 10.30am–5pm, Sun 1–4pm. ℘01244 972 197. www.grosvenormuseum.co.uk. This lively Chester history museum is particularly strong on the Roman period but all ages are covered. To the rear of the museum is a townhouse which recreates domestic life from the 17C to

the 1920s including a Victorian kitchen, Georgian drawing room, a nursery and a fully fitted Edwardian bathroom.

♣♣ Dewa Roman Experience

Pierpoint Lane. Open Feb–Nov Mon–Sat 9am–5pm, Sun 10am–5pm, Dec–Jan daily 10am–4pm. ♿. £5.50, child £3.95. Tours of Chester through the eyes of a Roman Soldier, £3.50, call for details. ℘01244 343 407. www.dewaromanexperience.co.uk. This walk-through experience moves from a Roman galley to a street scene, experiencing the sights, sounds and smells of Dewa (Roman Chester). There is an audio-visual presentation, archaeological excavations and lots of hands-on exhibits where you can try on Roman armour, fire a catapult, handle Roman-style artefacts and more.

EXCURSION

♣♣ Chester Zoo★

▶3mi/5km N on the A 5116. Upton-by-Chester. Open daily from 10am; closing times vary. Admission: £16.36–£23.63, child £13.18–£20. Book online to benefit from discounts. ♿🅿✕ ℘01244 380 280. www.chesterzoo.org. A splendid zoo where the 7 000 or so animals are housed in spacious enclosures, amid ward-winning gardens, separated from the public by moats and flower borders, rather than cages.

Liverpool★

and around

Though its days of mercantile splendour are long over, Liverpool remains an eminently handsome city, with some glorious architecture and fine civic buildings, reflecting the energy, taste and philanthropy of the Victorian age.

The city's most famous sons, The Beatles, gave the city a new reputation in the 1960s, and the Liverpool sound – the MerseyBeat – they helped create, their lives and their career are still celebrated throughout the city. During the 1980s, Liverpool Football Club dominated the football world and are still a major force today. In the 21C, leisure developments have led the way in the revival of Liverpool's fortunes, and it now includes more museums and galleries than anywhere outside London. In 2008, the city received the accolade of European Capital of Culture.

In 1999, the first **Liverpool Biennial** was held and has since grown to be the largest as well as one of the most exciting contemporary visual arts events in the UK; with around 1 million visits, it is one of the best-attended events of its kind in the world (www.biennial.com; mid-Jul–Oct).

▶ **Population:** 465 700.

◔ **Michelin Map:** Michelin Atlas p34 or Map 502 L 23.

▣ **Info:** Anchor Courtyard, Albert Dock. ℘0151 233 2008. www.visitliverpool.com. Lime Street Station (London Euston 2h08, Manchester Piccadilly 47 mins) links to a small underground network; the bus station is just around the corner on Norton Street. City Sightseeing hop-on hop-off open-top bus tours run every hour (www.city-sightseeing.com).

◑ **Location:** Liverpool is in northwest England, around 75mi/120km south of the Lake District and 34mi/55km west of Manchester.

⊚ **Don't Miss:** Walker Gallery; Liverpool Anglican Cathedral; Albert Dock museums.

◔ **Timing:** Allow at least 2 days (to include one excursion).

♟ **Kids:** Hands-on fun at World Museum; sharks at Blue Planet Aquarium; animals at Knowsley Safari Park; World of Glass.

⇜ **Walking Tours:** Daily in summer from the tourist office and Albert Dock.

A BIT OF HISTORY

On 28 August 1207, King John granted a charter for settlers to establish a port on the Mersey. Gradual silting up of the Dee estuary and the attendant abandonment of Chester, a port since Roman times, turned the new village of Liverpool into England's second port. It centred around seven streets, which still exist today – Castle and Old Hall, Water and Dale, Chapel and Tithebarn, up to Hatton Garden – and the 'Pool', an inlet following today's Canning and Paradise Streets and Whitechapel.

Liverpool started to expand when trade with the West Indies – sugar, rum, cotton and, until 1807, slaves – brought such prosperity that by 1800 there were more than 80 000 'Liverpudlians'. In the 19C, Liverpool, home to the Cunard and White Star liners, was Britain's gateway to the Empire and the world. The Mersey Docks and Harbour Company handled the cargo traffic, employing some 20 000 men in the immediate post-war period. Today, with container ships and mechanical handling, only around 2 500 men now work in the docks.

🐾 WATERFRONT WALK

Pier Head

The spirit of Liverpool and the Mersey is best appreciated by standing on the corner of Water Street and the Strand. The ferries on the Mersey have been part of the scene since the monks of Birkenhead Priory began rowing travellers across in about 1150. The green-domed **Port of Liverpool Building** (1907) and its neighbour, the **Cunard Building** (1913), reflect the city's maritime connections but the **Royal Liver Building** (1908), with its 'Liver Birds' (pronounced 'lie-ver') on the cupolas, is probably the best-known symbol of Liverpool. This ensemble is known locally as 'The Three Graces'.

Museum of Liverpool★

Pier Head. Open daily 10am–5pm. Closed 1 Jan, 24–26 and 31 Dec. ♿🅿✕ ☎0151 478 4545. www.liverpoolmuseums.org.uk.
Opened in 2011 as the largest newly built national museum in Britain for more than a century, this stunning new city flagship covers 800 years from medieval 'Lyverpoole' to 21C 'Liverpool'. It includes the following galleries: **Wondrous Place**, featuring Liverpool's sporting and cultural history with particular emphasis on The Beatles, and Liverpool and Everton football clubs; **Global City:** relating the story of how Liverpool became the second city of the British Empire; **The People's Republic**, about the experience of living in the city and what it means to be Liverpudlian; **Liverpool Overhead Railway**, telling the remarkable story of the first electric elevated railway in the world; **Little Liverpool**, a children's hands-on space; the **Skylight Gallery**, a dramatic space featuring changing art exhibitions.

Albert Dock★

Massive brick warehouses enclose a dock basin (3ha). Completed in 1846, finally closed in 1972, the complex has now been revitalised with shops, cafés and apartments, museums and the northern arm of the Tate Gallery.

Merseyside Maritime Museum★

Open daily, 10am–5pm. Closed 1 Jan, 24–26 and 31 Dec. ♿🅿✕ ☎0151 478 4499. www.liverpoolmuseums.org.uk.
Liverpool's rich seafaring heritage is presented through displays on the history of shipbuilding; the evolution of the port; **Liverpool and the American Civil War**; the **Battle of the Atlantic**, ship models and paintings; and much more… The museum's largest exhibit is the **Edmund Gardner**, a former pilot cutter now in dry dock. Visitors may also be able to also step aboard the three-masted schooner *De Wadden*. In the basement is **Seized!**, which charts the fight against smuggling over the centuries as well as modern detection methods.

International Slavery Museum★

All details as Merseyside Maritime Museum.
Sharing the same building as the Maritime Museum, this moving and unsettling collection is just yards away from the dry docks where 18C slave trading ships were repaired and fitted out. Its main permanent galleries and exhibitions are: Life in West Africa; **Enslavement and the Middle Passage** – the latter being the second leg of the triangular slave trade route; **Legacies of Slavery**; as well as (more upbeat) temporary exhibitions.

Tate Liverpool★

Open daily 10am–5pm. Closed 24–26 Dec. Charge for special exhibitions only. Guided free tour daily at noon, also 3pm Sat & Sun. ♿🅿✕ ☎0151 702 7400. www.tate.org.uk/liverpool.
The Tate family, who made their fortune from sugar before becoming synonymous with modern art in Britain, originated from Liverpool, so the choice of Liverpool to house part of their national collection of 20C art in this transformed warehouse was wholly appropriate.
The gallery is best known for hosting major touring exhibitions but it also boasts semi-permanent exhibitions from the Tate's primary collections of 20C art (presently the DLA Piper Series:

Constellations). These are displayed alongside Liverpool Biennial exhibits (👁see above).

The Beatles Story

Britannia Vaults, Albert Dock, and Mersey Ferries Terminal Building, Pier Head. Open Apr–Oct daily 9am–7pm. Nov–Mar 10am–6pm. Closed 25–26 Dec. £15.95, child (5–15) £9.50. ♿🅿(charge). ✆0151 709 1963. www.beatlesstory.com.

Relive or discover the decade of The Beatles, the 1960s, the new phenomena of rock'n'roll, teenagers, the MerseyBeat and, of course, Beatlemania.

For those few who don't know, The Beatles consisted of **John Lennon** (1940–1980), **Paul McCartney** (b.1942), **George Harrison** (1943–2001) and **Ringo Starr** (b.1940); their manager was Brian Epstein, the 'Fifth Beatle' (1934–67). The places (The Cavern, Strawberry Fields, Penny Lane, Hamburg) and the hits are presented in a lively and entertaining manner by a walk-through presentation.

The Pier Head part of the exhibition is housed in the striking new Mersey Ferries Terminal Building; it hosts special exhibitions and the **Fab 4D** cinema experience.

The **childhood homes** of Paul McCartney and John Lennon, are now owned by the National Trust and are open to the public by guided tour only (open late Feb–Nov Wed–Sun times and pick-up locations vary, check website or call for details, advance booking essential; £23, NT members £9.50; ✆0151 427 7231, booking, or ✆0844 800 4791 infoline; www.nationaltrust.org.uk/beatles). **20 Forthlin Road** was the home of McCartney and where The Beatles composed and rehearsed some of their earliest songs; **Mendips** is where Lennon grew up. The most popular Beatles tour in town however is the two-hour **Magical Mystery Tour** ending at the legendary **Cavern Club** (daily from Albert Dock; advance reservations recommended; closed I Jan, 25–26 Dec. ✆0151 703 9100, buy tickets online or from tourist office; www.cavernclub.org). The tour ticket also gives you free admission to the Cavern Club if you return in the evening.

Every August the city celebrates **International Beatle Week Festival** (www.cavernclub.org). Across the road, **The Wheel of Liverpool** (open Mon–Thu 10am–9pm, Fri 10am–11pm, Sat 9am–11pm, Sun 10am–9pm; £10, child £6.50; ♿; ✆0151 709 8651, www.freijwheels.com) is a 60-m high observation wheel.

CITY

Liverpool Anglican Cathedral★★

St James Mount. Open: **Cathedral:** daily 8am–6pm. Contributions welcome. **Tower:** Open Mon–Fri 10am–5pm, Sat 9am–5pm, Sun noon–4pm. £5.50. ♿✗ ✆0151 709 6271. www.liverpoolcathedral.org.uk.

This monumental edifice in red sandstone is the largest Anglican church in the world. Work began in 1904 and it took most of the century to build, a triumphant reinterpretation of the Gothic tradition by its architect **Sir Giles Gilbert Scott** (1880–1960).

Before entering the church visit the film theatre for the 10-minute panoramic HD **Great Space film** on a large screen that fills your field of vision.

On entering, the first impression is of vastness, strength and height. Scott's unusual design includes double transepts and the central '**Great Space**' (1 400sq m) under the tower, giving an uninterrupted view of altar and pulpit. The **tower** is 100m high but actually rises 153m above the Mersey and offers wonderful **views**. Reached by 2 lifts and 108 stairs, it extends across the full width of the building and houses the highest and heaviest (31-ton) peal of bells in the world. Entry to the tower lso includes the Elizabeth Hoare **Embroidery Gallery**, a unique collection of Victorian and Edwardian ecclesiastical embroidery. Set in the floor immediately below is the memorial to Scott, who is buried just outside the west door. The **Baptistery**, with its marble font and a baldachin and font cover, contains some of the finest woodcarving in the cathedral.

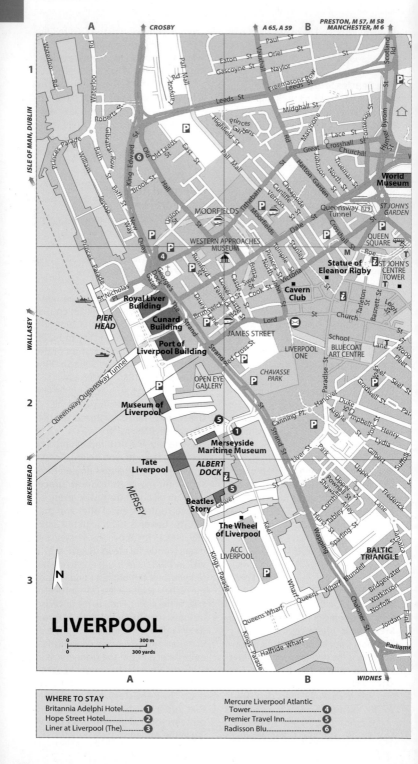

LIVERPOOL

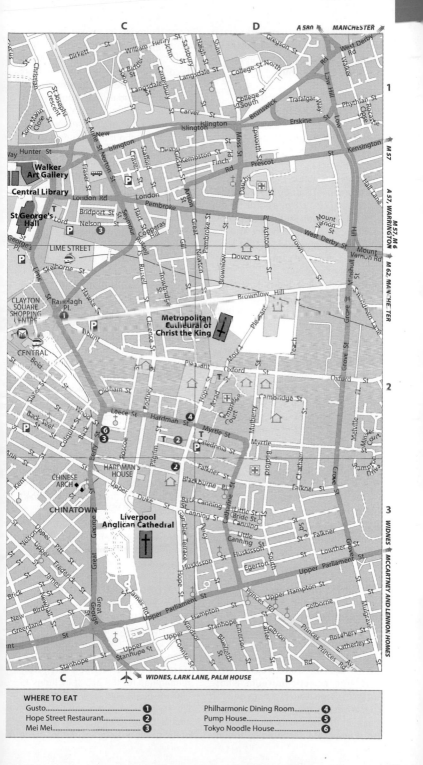

WIDNES, LARK LANE, PALM HOUSE

WHERE TO EAT

Gusto.................................. ❶	Philharmonic Dining Room.............. ❹
Hope Street Restaurant................... ❷	Pump House.................................... ❺
Mei Mei.. ❸	Tokyo Noodle House......................... ❻

In the **choir** there are liver birds on the steps leading into the stalls. Beyond is the **Lady Chapel★** with a notable reredos and a 15C Madonna.

Metropolitan Cathedral of Christ the King★★

Mount Pleasant. Open 7.30am–6pm. Contribution requested. Lutyens' crypt and treasury £3. ♿✗ 🅿(charge). ☎0151 709 9222. www.liverpoolmetrocathedral.org.uk.

The cathedral stands on Brownlow Hill, occupied 1771–1928 by a home for Liverpool's destitute. **Sir Edwin Lutyens** was chosen as the architect and the foundation stone was laid in 1933. However, the completed cathedral was not consecrated until 1967.

The distinctive **exterior** is an extraordinary buttressed circular concrete structure, culminating in the lantern (88m high) with its crown of pinnacles. From the inner porch the High Altar is immediately visible, at the centre of the circular nave (59m in diameter). The **tower**, its stained glass in the colours of the spectrum, rises above the **High Altar**, the architectural as well as liturgical focal point. The clever design of the baldachin candlesticks and crucifix ensure an uninterrupted view of the celebrant at the altar for every member of a full 2 300-strong congregation.

The massive brick-vaulted **crypt** includes the **treasury**, and the **Chapel of Relics**, burial place of the archbishops; its door is a six-ton marble disc, which rolls back as did the stone traditionally sealing the tomb of Christ.

👥 World Museum

William Brown Street. Open year-round daily 10am–5pm. Timed ticket to planetarium (£2.50, child £1.50) from information desk. Closed 1 Jan, 25–26 Dec. ♿✗ ☎0151 478 4393. www.liverpoolmuseums.org.uk.

This large, eclectic museum, whose subjects range from live bugs and fish to space exploration, combines historic treasures from across the globe with the latest interactive technology. Its internationally important collections include archaeology, ethnology and the natural and physical sciences. The oldest exhibits come from the collection of Joseph Mayer (a mid-19C local goldsmith and antiquarian) and include Anglo-Saxon treasures, mummies and Wedgwood china. The museum also features special events throughout the summer including dance workshops, musical performances and storytelling in a giant tent, and (year-round) boasts Britain's only free planetarium.

Walker Art Gallery★★

William Brown Street. Open daily 10am–5pm. Closed 1 Jan, 25–26 Dec. ♿✗ ☎0151 478 4199. www.liverpoolmuseums.org.uk/walker.

The Walker's collection of British and European paintings is among the best in the country. Numerous painters of the Italian school are represented, from the 14C to the Renaissance and beyond. The extensive holdings of northern European art include works by Rembrandt, Elsheimer and Cranach.

The range of British work is particularly complete, extending from Elizabethan and later portraits, to key works by Stubbs, Wright of Derby and Richard Wilson; there are typically uncanny works by Fuseli and many **Pre-Raphaelites**, including Millais and Ford Madox Brown. Narrative paintings include W R Yeames' famous masterpiece *And When Did You Last See Your Father?*

A small number of French Impressionists – Degas, Seurat and Monet – are juxtaposed with their British contemporaries like Sickert.

Liverpool Central Library★

William Brown Street. Open Mon–Fri 9am–8pm, Sat 9am–5pm, Sun 10am–5pm. ☎0151 233 3069. http://liverpool.gov.uk/libraries.

Reopened in 2013, this beautiful Victorian building has been splendidly reimagined for the 21C. It includes 15 000 rare books on display in the Hornby Library and Oak Room and the classic circular Picton Reading Room. The view of the newly redesigned interior dome spiralling upwards is stunning. There are also spectacular views from the roof terrace.

St George's Hall

Heritage Centre (entrance St John's Lane) open daily 10am–5pm. Closed 1 Jan, 25 Dec. ♿ ℘0151 233 3020. www.stgeorgesliverpool.co.uk.

'One of the finest neo Grecian buildings in the world' (Pevsner), St George's Hall was completed in 1854 and dominates the neighbouring neo-Classical civic buildings, which are a focal point of the city. it was a multipurpose community building where people could be tried for murder, attend a ball or listen to a concert – all under one roof. It fell into disrepair in the 1980s but was reopened in April 2007 and is now a focal point for cultural, community, civic, corporate and performing arts activities. It contains a circular Concert Room and a vast and opulent **Great Hall**.

A **Heritage Centre** features imaginative exhibitions, reconstructions and hands-on activities which bring the story of the Hall alive. It offers visitors opportunities to visit the cells used by prisoners awaiting trial and to see the newly refurbished Criminal Court and Judge's Robing Room.

Statue of Eleanor Rigby

Stanley Street.

The statue is the work of former pop singer Tommy Steele, a contemporary of The Beatles; a plaque behind the dedicates the statue 'To all the lonely people'. Around the corner in Mathew Street is the **Cavern Club**, where The Beatles and many other bands from the era performed.

Sefton Park Palm House

Sefton Park, South Liverpool. Open daily from 10am; Nov–Feb closes 4pm; Mar–Oct closes 5pm (later openings during summer months); check website. ♿ ℘0151 726 9304. www.palmhouse.org.uk. This magnificent tiered octagonal Grade II-listed Victorian glasshouse showcases the Liverpool Botanical Collection.

EXCURSIONS

Southport

➤20mi/32km N via the A 565.
Population: 90 336. 🅸 ℘01704 533 333. www.visitsouthport.com.

This elegant seaside resort is distinguished by its tree-lined streets, attractive flowerbeds and famous gardens (Flower Show held late Aug). Broad and spacious **Lord Street**, where the shops have wrought-iron and glass-roofed canopies extending over the pavements, is the epitome of a Victorian promenade. Families enjoy the long sandy beaches – **Crosby Beach** is famous for its haunting Antony Gormley figures staring out to sea – and amusement parks, while **Royal Birkdale** is the best of several local golf courses.

Rufford Old Hall★

➤20mi/32km N on the A 59, Liverpool Road. Open Mar–Oct Sat–Wed 11am–5pm (4pm Feb–early Mar). Open daily during Aug; Nov–mid-Dec Sat–Sun 11am–4pm. £9. ♿🅿✕℘01704 821 254. www.nationaltrust.org.uk.

This is one of the finest 15C houses in Lancashire. The **Great Hall★** has a magnificent **hammerbeam roof** and ornate carved screen. The Carolean wing was reconstructed in brick in 1662. There is much original furniture, arms and armour, and a folk museum.

Martin Mere Wildfowl and Wetlands Centre

➤20mi/32km N on the A 59 to Rufford and west on the B 5246. Open daily Oct–Mar 9.30–4.30pm (Mar–Oct 6pm). £10.62, child £5.06. ♿🅿✕℘01704 895 181. www.wwt.org.uk/martin-mere.

This wildfowl habitat (140ha) has hides and nature trails. The mere (lake) is home to over 100 species of rare and endangered ducks, geese, swans and flamingos, and offers a winter haven to thousands of pink-footed geese, Icelandic whooper swans, Bewick's swans from Russia. Hen harriers appear regularly, along with large numbers of teal and shelduck, and there is always the possibility of spotting a rarity. There are also beavers and otters here. The on-site restaurant/café helps make a great day at Martin Mere all the more agreeable.

🙎🙎 Knowsley Safari Park

⏵8mi/13km E by the A 5047 and the eastbound carriageway of the A 58 (Prescot bypass). Open daily 10am–4pm (last admission). Closed 24–25 and 31 Dec, 1 Jan. £17.50, child 3–16, £13.50 (book online for discount). ♿🅿✕ ℘0151 489 4827. www.knowsley.com.

It was in the menagerie, established at Knowsley in the 19C by the Earl of Derby, that **Edward Lear** made many of his animal drawings; the tales he told to Lord Derby's grandchildren became his *Book of Nonsense*. Today, visitors can drive **safari**-fashion along a 5mi/8km route, passing herds of antelopes, camels, buffalo and white rhino, plus tigers, monkeys, giraffes and more. There is also an elephant paddock, a sea lion show, a birds of prey display an **Aerial Extreme** tree-top walkway, and amusement rides (additional charges).

🙎🙎 The World of Glass

⏵12mi/19km east by the A 5047 and A 57 to St Helens. Open Mon (except Bank Holidays)–Sat: Mar–Oct 10am–5pm; Nov–Feb 10am–4pm. Closed 1 Jan, 25–26 Dec. £8, child (5–16), £6. ♿🅿✕ ℘01744 22766. www.worldofglass.com.

Visitors pass through a brick cone recalling the old furnaces into the modern building on the site of the pioneering Pilkington factory. There's live glass-blowing, a 3-D theatre and lots of interactive stations at this very family-friendly place.

Speke Hall, Garden and Estate★

⏵Near airport, 8mi/13km SE on the A 561.

Open mid-late Feb Wed–Sun 11am–4pm; 1st 2 wks of Mar and early Nov–mid Dec Sat–Sun 11am–4pm; late Mar–late Jul and Sept–Oct Wed–Sun 12.30pm–5pm; Aug Tue–Sun 10.30am–5pm. Entry to house before 12.30pm by guided tour only (places limited, call for details).

⊘ Access and closing times to the whole property are subject to change in February and March.

Admission: Whole property £11.70; Grounds only £8.10.
🅿✕ ℘0151 427 7231.
www.nationaltrust.org.uk.

This black-and-white Elizabethan manor house was built between 1490 and 1612 by successive generations of the Norris family. The **Great Hall** is the oldest part of the building; its panelling, including the Great Wainscot of 1564, is particularly fine. The many smaller rooms reflect the Victorian preference for privacy and comfort. In the courtyard two ancient yews possibly pre-date the house.

Port Sunlight

⏵ West-side of the Mersey, south of Birkenhead.

The model village was established in the late-19C by William Hesketh Lever for the workers of his soap factory, giving them a lifestyle very different from that of the crowded slums of the period. Lord Leverhulme's company became Unilever, one of the world's largest manufacturers of consumer goods.

The **Lady Lever Art Gallery** (open daily 10am–5pm; ♿🅿✕; ℘0151 478 4136; www.liverpoolmuseums.org.uk), also founded by Lord Leverhulme and opened in 1922, contains British paintings including Pre-Raphaelite works, period furniture, and a fine Wedgwood collection.

🙎🙎 Blue Planet Aquarium

⏵ Cheshire Oaks. M 6, then M56/M6 at junction 20, then the M 53 at junction 15. Open daily 10am–5pm/Sat–Sun 6pm. £17.75, child under 12, £12.75 – buy online for discount. ♿🅿✕ ℘0151 357 8804. www.blueplanetaquarium.co.uk.

This claims to be the largest aquarium adventure of its kind and has more types of shark (10 species) than anywhere else in Europe. Its shark-infested Aquatunnel is one of the longest in the world at 70m.

Blackpool★

and Lancaster

Since 1846 when the railway first made seaside holidays a possibility for the working classes, Blackpool has been one of the most popular and typical (in all except location) British seaside resorts. From the 1950s onwards, tens of thousands of holidaymakers from the industrial towns of the North and Midlands traditionally flocked here for their annual week or fortnight holiday. Today, short breaks are the norm and around a third of all visitors to Blackpool now come in autumn to see the celebrated Illuminations.

▶ **Population:** 142 065.

⚅ **Michelin Map:** Michelin Atlas p38 or Map 502 K 22.

🖪 **Info:** Festival House, Promenade. ℘01253 478 222. www.visitblackpool.com. The main train Station, Blackpool North (Liverpool Lime Street 1h24), is around 400m from the centre on Talbot Road. The bus station is on the same road, 45m away.

◖ **Location:** 55mi/88km due north of Liverpool.

☺ **Don't Miss:** A trip up Blackpool Tower; a ride on an old-fashioned tram.

🕐 **Timing:** One day minimum.

👪 **Kids:** The whole of Blackpool is geared to children.

RESORT

Blackpool Tower★

Open daily from 10am – check website for times of individual attractions.
Admission: Tower: £56.45, child £44 (£30 and £25.50 online); The Blackpool BIG ticket (7 attractions and valid 90 days): £89.45, child £71 (£45 and £32.50 online); Visit 3 attractions: £46.50, child £37.50 (£31 and £26.50 online); check website for individual attraction prices (up to 50% discount for online booking). ♿✖ ℘0871 222 9929 (booking); 01253 622 242 (general enquiries). www.theblackpooltower.com.

Inspired by the Eiffel Tower and opened in 1894, the 158m high tower Is Blackpool's trademark. It includes old favourites and brand new attractions. The **Circus** features shows most days *(see website)* while you can dance and/or take tea at the famous glittering **Tower Ballroom**. **Jungle Jim's** is a highly themed children's play area, while the **Blackpool Tower Dungeon** (www.thedungeons.com/blackpool) is a gory walk through experience with actors, special effects, bloody scenes, lots of laughs and a white-knuckle ride. **The Blackpool Tower Eye (Skywalk) with 4D Cinema Experience** is the Tower's new flagship attraction. Before ascending to the top level, you watch, hear, feel and smell a 4-D film about the tower and resort. You then progress to the **Skywalk**, a floor-to-ceiling glass observation platform which runs along an entire side of the Tower providing magnificent views out to the Irish Sea. Look down between your feet for a dizzying bird's-eye view of the famous Blackpool Promenade and coastline over 122m below.

Pleasure Beach

Open times vary throughout the year – see website for prices and opening hours; book online for major savings. ♿✖ ℘0871 222 1234. www.blackpoolpleasurebeach.com.

With over 6 million visitors a year, this huge theme park is Britain's biggest and most visited paid-entry tourist attraction, boasting state-of-the-art rides and sideshows.

For younger guests there is Nickleodeoen Land; for older, white-knuckle thrill seekers there are some of the fastest, highest, scariest rides in Europe. In between are family rides and no fewer than 15 shows: magic and variety, ice-skating shows, talent searches, and an adult-only circus.

Blackpool Illuminations

Blackpool Illuminations first appeared in 1879 (when they were described as 'Artificial Sunshine' attracting 100 000 visitors. Today, around 3 million come to town each year for 'the lights'. The 'Big Switch On' is in late August/early September and the light lasts for just over two months, closing down early November. The dazzling display stretches almost 6mi/10km along and around the seafront and comprise lasers, neon, fibre optics, searchlights and floodlighting, plus over 1 million conventional bulbs and around 500 scenic designs, tableaux and other features – www.blackpool-illuminations.net.

Also on the site is a small branch of **Ripley's Believe It or Not!** (open from 10am – see website for details; £6; ♿; ☎01253 341 033; www.ripleys.com/blackpool) boasting its usual offering of weird and wonderful artefacts from around the world.

The Great Promenade Show
South Promenade.
This is an outdoor exhibition of 10 sculptures by some of the UK's leading artists and designers celebrating the character of Blackpool; each exhibits takes a theme – the Illuminations, the Ballroom, the 'dirty weekend', the Circus, the freak shows of Victorian Blackpool.

Madame Tussauds
Open daily from 10am (excluding 25 Dec). Closing times vary throughout the season – check website for details. £16.50 (online discounts).
♿☎0871 282 9200.
www.madametussauds.com/blackpool.
The Tussaud's formula by the seaside, with five floors of famous (mostly British) music, TV, movie and sports personalities, as well as royalty, politicians and historical figures, all captured in wax.

Sea Life Blackpool
Open Mon–Fri 10am–5pm, Sat–Sun 10am–6pm. £17.50, child £14.50 (£13 and £10.50 online). ♿✕ ☎01253 621 258.
www.visitsealife.com/Blackpool.
The Blackpool branch of this successful aquarium chain features over 200 creatures from sharks, octopuses and rays to tiny seahorses, inhabiting over 50 displays including a coral reef, a rainforest and an underwater shark tunnel.

Grundy Art Gallery
Queen Street. Open Tue–Sat 10am–5pm. Closed between exhibitions.
♿🅿(charge). ✕ ☎01253 478 170.
www.grundyartgallery.com.
Blackpool's premier art gallery stages often challenging contemporary visual art exhibitions by established and emerging artists from the UK and abroad. Its permanent collection includes Victorian oils and watercolours, modern British paintings, contemporary prints, jewellery, ivories, ceramics, and interesting old souvenirs of Blackpool.

Stanley Park
This majestic 256-acre park is a green oasis 2mi/3km from the bustling seafront. It features display gardens, ornate fountains, woodlands, and a boating lake. Immediately west, in 2.5 acres/1ha of landscaped gardens, is **Blackpool Model Village & Gardens** open Apr–early Nov daily 9.30am–dusk, £6.95, child £5.75; ♿🅿✕; ☎01253 763 827; www.blackpoolmodelvillage.com).

EXCURSIONS
Lancaster Castle
▶25mi/40km NE. Open daily 9.30am–5pm. Closed Christmas/New Year holidays. £8. ☎01524 64998.
www.lancastercastle.com.
The Normans built the original castle and the oldest surviving part is the imposing mid-12C keep. It has been a court and prison for centuries and still functions as a crown court today, with only around a quarter of the complex open to visitors. Entertaining tours.

Isle of Man★

This mountainous island in the Irish Sea was settled by Celts, then by Norsemen, ruled by Scotland, then by England. Its own language, Manx, akin to Gaelic, is now largely extinct, though the famous tail-less cat survives. The island, a British dependency but not part of the United Kingdom or the EU, has its own laws, presented each year to an open-air parliament of the people; this 1 000-year-old descendant of the Norse *Thingvollr* ('assembly field') is held at a central point on the island, Tynwald Green, a site with prehistoric associations. The lowland pattern of unspoiled farmland, small fields bounded by stone walls or high hedgebanks, gives way as the land rises to wild open moorland, bright in late summer with gorse and heather. The highest summit is Snaefell (621m), from which England, Scotland, Ireland and Wales can be seen. Most of the coastline (100mi/160km) is untouched by modern intrusions. The island still attracts significant numbers of holidaymakers, mainly from the north of England. It is most famous for the Isle of Man TT (Tourist Trophy) motorcycle Races (www. iomtt.com) held late May–early June. The racecourse is one of the world's most dangerous.

Douglas

The great sweep of Victorian and Edwardian hotels facing promenades and the sandy bay give the island's capital an unmistakable identity.
The **Manx Museum** (open Mon–Sat 10am–5pm; closed 1 Jan, Tynwald Day, 25–26 Dec; P✕; ℘01624 648 000; www. manxnationalheritage.im), '...the treasure house of the island's story', displays good examples of early Christian sculpture; the Folk-Life Galleries include a reconstructed Manx farmhouse.
The island's halcyon days of mass tourism were the late-19C and early-20C and

- ▶ **Population:** 83 327.
- ⌖ **Michelin Map:** Michelin Atlas p42 or Map 402 G 21.
- ℹ **Info:** Sea Terminal, Douglas. ℘01624 686 801. www.gov.im/tourism.
- ◖ **Location:** The Isle of Man Steam Packet Company (www.steam-packet. com) runs ferries from Liverpool, Birkenhead, Heysham (Morecambe), Larne, Dublin and Belfast.

an extensive network of vintage transport remains. Horse trams – nicknamed 'toast racks' – ply the Douglas promenades, narrow-gauge steam railways serve the south and, most remarkable of all, double-track electric tramways lead from Douglas along the high cliffs to the northern resort of Ramsey and to the very summit of Snaefell.

Laxey Wheel★★

Take the Manx Electric Railway N along the coast. Walk up the valley (0.6mi/1km). Open Apr–early Nov daily 9.30am–5pm. £8. P ℘01624 648 000. This giant working waterwheel, the biggest in the world at over 22m high, is a splendid monument of the industrial age, built in 1854 when the Laxey valley was the scene of intense lead- and silver-mining activity. Part of the old mines may be visited.

Snaefell Mountain Railway★

Take the Manx Electric Railway via Laxey on the east coast. Operates (weather permitting) Laxey to summit Apr–Sept, see website or call for schedule and fare. P✕ ℘01624 662 525; https://manxelectricrailway.co.uk.
A vintage tramcar climbs up the side of the glen and on to the mountain slopes to the terminus at the café just below the summit (621m). On a clear day there are stupendous **views★★★** of the lands fringing the Irish Sea.

ADDRESSES

🏠 STAY

MANCHESTER

⌂ Little Northern Hotel –
67 Thomas Street. ℘0161 839 0213,
www.littlenorthernhotel.co.uk. ℗.
15 rooms. Busy central hotel in
Manchester's 'mini-Soho' with a good
pub attached. Entertainment 4 nights
per week.

⌂ Mitre Hotel – 1-3 Cathedral Gates.
℘0161 832 2400. http://the-mitre-hotel.
manchesterhoteltour.com. 32 rooms. Set
in a lovely old Victorian building next
to the cathedral, the Mitre offers simple
but up-to-date rooms. Good value.

⌂⊜⊜⊜ Malmaison – Piccadilly.
℘0161 641 1883. www.malmaison.com.
167 rooms. Set in an old warehouse, 'Mal
Manchester' is one of the most stylish
places in town, visited by pop stars
and celebrities for its quirky up-to-the-
minute 'Gothic-lite' fashion, with bold
colours, funky furnishings, spa and
buzzing music.

⌂⊜⊜⊜⊜ The Lowry Hotel – Chapel
Wharf, Salford. ℘0161 827 4000. www.
thelowryhotel.com. ℗. 165 rooms. This
boldly designed contemporary 5-star
hotel at the heart of the Quays is
Manchester's most fashionable; indoor
pool, spa and wellness facilities.

CHESTER

⊜⊜ Chester House Guest House –
44 Hoole Road. ℘01244 348 410. www.
chesterhouseguesthouse.co.uk. ℗.
8 rooms. A 15-min walk from the centre,
this modest Edwardian house has been
impeccably refurbished and offers a
warm welcome.

⊜⊜ Chester Court Hotel – 48 Hoole
Road. ℘01244 320 779. www.chestercourt
hotel.com. ℗. 20 rooms This characterful
Victorian house, a five-minute bus
journey from town, is a mix of old
and new styles, with some rooms in
an annex.

⊜⊜ Pied Bull – 57 Northgate Street.
℘01244 325 829. www.piedbull.co.uk. 12
rooms. Within the city walls, this friendly
historic 16C inn offers comfortable
characterful rooms, decent pub grub
and beer from its own micro-brewery.

**⊜⊜⊜ Mercure Chester Abbots
Well –** Whitchurch Road, Christleton.
℘0844 815 9001. www.mercurechester.
co.uk. ℗. 126 rooms. Two miles/3km
east of Chester in 0.8ha of grounds, this
modern, superior chain hotel boasts
a health club and spa. Rooms are very
comfortable. Very good deals online.

⊜⊜⊜ Premium Queen Hotel –
City Road. ℘01244 305 000 - www.
hallmarkhotels.co.uk. ℗. 218 rooms. Set
in an impressive Victorian building in
the heart of town, with a lovely terrace
and gardens, bedrooms boast every
facility and range from 'contemporary-
Victorian' to grand luxury antique-
carved four-posters.

LIVERPOOL

⊜ Premier Travel Inn – Albert Dock.
℘0871 527 8622 - www.premierinn.com.
℗. This highly popular hotel (part of
a budget chain) is set in a sensitively
converted 19C building with some
lovely bedrooms. Perfect location for a
short break and great-value.

⊜⊜ The Liner at Liverpool – Lord
Nelson Street ℘0151 709 7050. www.
theliner.co.uk. 6 rooms. A two-min walk
from Lime Street Station, this hotel is
themed to a classic cruise ship. It offers
nautical decor and cabin-style rooms
with marble bathrooms.

⊜⊜⊜ Britannia Adelphi Hotel –
Ranelagh Place. ℘0871 222 0029. www.
adelphi-hotel.co.uk. 402 rooms. Steeped
in the history of the city, the Adelphi
has played host to all kinds of VIPs,
including Roy Rogers and Clark Gable.
It is still very grand, including a lovely
indoor marble pool and new gym.
Prices vary, choose online.

**⊜⊜⊜ Mercure Liverpool Atlantic
Tower –** Chapel Street. ℘0871 376 9025.
www.atlantic-tower-thistle.hotel-rn.com.
226 rooms. Enjoy wonderful views over
the Mersey from the restaurant terrace
and upper floors of this large modern
ship-shape (in every sense) hotel. Smart
rooms. Great value online advance
saver offers.

⊜⊜⊜ Hope Street Hotel –
40 Hope Street. ℘0151 709 3000.
www.hopestreethotel.co.uk. 89 rooms.
This cosy boutique-design hotel, with
gorgeous contemporary rooms, is

housed in an 1860 Venetian-style building in a chic part of town.

Radisson Blu – 107 Old Hall Street. 0151 966 1500. www.radissonblu.co.uk/hotel-liverpool. 194 rooms. A stunning atrium welcomes guests to this contemporary hotel which enjoys magnificent views over the Mersey. Rooms are stylish and good value.

ISLE OF MAN

The River House – Ramsey. 01624 816 412. www.theriverhouse-iom.com. 3 rooms. This handsome 1820s country house enjoys a peaceful location, a 10-min walk from Ramsey, beside the river, in 1.2ha of mature gardens. Classic spacious chintzy bedrooms, each with a lovely outlook.

Ascot Hotel – 7 Empire Terrace, Douglas. 01624 675 081. www.ascothotel.im. This is a warm, friendly and contemporary Isle of Man hotel which enjoys a fantastic location just off Douglas Sea Front and Promenade. Free sea travel as foot passengers (subject to availability) for visitors staying a minimum of 5 nights.

Ⓨ EAT

MANCHESTER

Visit **Deansgate Locks** for pubs and bars, for Indian restaurants, **Rusholme**.

The Bank – 57 Mosley Street. 0161 228 7560. www.nicholsonspubs.co.uk. Superior pub food is served in the grand surrounding of an early 19C neo-Classical library hall.

Jamie's Italian in Manchester – 100 King Street. 0161 241 3901. www.jamieoliver.com. Set in a Grade II Listed former bank in which many of the original features have been kept.

Yang Sing – 34 Princess Street. 0161 236 2200. www.yang-sing.com. Open since 1977 and set on several floors in smart minimalist style, Yang Sing is one of the best Cantonese restaurants in the UK, but it can get very noisy at busy times.

CHESTER

The Coach House – 39 Northgate Street. 01244 351 900. www.coachhousechester.co.uk. This beautifully refurbished 19C coaching inn in the heart of town serves award winning gastropub food (and simple traditional pub meals) in attractive 'trad-contemporary' surroundings.

The Old Harkers Arms – 1 Russell Street. 01244 344 525. www.brunningandprice.co.uk/harkers. Set in the basement of an old warehouse that once fronted the canal, this beautifully furnished atmospheric post-industrial chic pub serves a broad menu of gastropub food and lighter bites.

LIVERPOOL

Albert Dock (www.albertdock.com/food-drink), Hope Street and Exchange Street are the main eating and drinking areas. Liverpool's Chinatown is around Nelson Street, Duke Street and Berry Street.

Mei Mei – 9 Berry Street. 0151 707 2888. According to many this is the best Chinese restaurant in town and certainly one of its most popular.

Pump House – The Colonnades, Albert Dock. 0151 709 2367. www.albertdock.com/the-pump-house. The Albert Dock's former pumphouse, built 1870, has been converted into an atmospheric cosy pub/bar with a waterside terrace; superior pub grub.

Tokyo Noodle Bar – 7 Berry Street. 0151 708 6286. Enjoy Cantonese, Thai and Japanese cuisine at this popular noodle bar in the heart of Chinatown.

Gusto – Edward Pavillion, Albert Dock. 0151 708 6969. www.gustorestaurants.uk.com. At the entrance to the docks, in an old warehouse, this classic buzzing atmospheric Italian ristorante has a stylish interior.

Philharmonic Dining Rooms – 36 Hope Street. 0151 707 2837. www.nicholsonspubs.co.uk. One of the most lavish pubs in the UK, the 'Phil' has dark wood-panelling with copper reliefs, Art Deco lighting and a beautiful mosaic floor and bar. Superior pub food.

Hope Street Restaurant – 60 Hope Street. 0151 707 6060. www.60hopestreet.com. This elegant family-owned/family-run restaurant covers three floors of a Georgian townhouse, serving a changing menu of seasonal Modern British food.

Cumbria and the Lakes

Carlisle castle © Wojtek Buss/AGF Foto/Photononstop

Introduction

The Lake District, since 2017 a World Heritage Site, is regarded by many as England's most beautiful landscape. It has inspired poets and writers for over 200 years and is still one of the most popular holiday regions in the UK. Its fells (mountains) can attract seemingly endless rain and extreme weather changes, adding atmosphere to an already emotive landscape. It is only the weather that stops the summertime crowds from moving in full time. Whatever the time of year, it is a magnificent place for enjoying the simple beauty of nature.

Lake District National Park

A combination of mountains and lakes, woodland and farmland, this is the largest of Britain's national parks, covering an area of 880sq mi/2 280sq km, of which a quarter is part of the National Trust. Appropriately it is home to Scafell Pike, England's highest mountain, and Wastwater, England's deepest lake.

Ice shaped the troughs and corries, while glacial rubble dammed the valleys and underlying rock dictated whether the hills were softly rounded, like Skiddaw, or wildly rugged, like Scafell Pike and Helvellyn.

The main activity in the Lake District – often shortened to 'the Lakes' – is walking, and there are trails for literally every age and ability. Climbing and fell-walking are other popular pastimes, and latterly windsurfing, mountain biking, daring treetop walks and even a Dolomites-style Via Ferrata have been established. For many visitors, however, simply the sight of the fells reflected in the deep blue waters of the lakes is enough. And if that is viewed from the side of a vintage steamboat, sailing across the lake, then so much the better!

Ironically, there is only one 'lake' in the Lake District – Bassenthwaite Lake; all the others are 'tarns', 'meres', or 'waters'.

Highlights

Windermere – This is the most famous, and busiest part of the Lakes, made so by eminent literary names such as Wordsworth, Ruskin and Beatrix Potter, all of whose former homes are open to the public. The little settlements of Hawkshead, Ambleside and Grasmere are delightful, particularly out of season.

Eskdale and the northern Llakes – If you want to escape the thick of the crowds and like your landscapes to be more robust, then the lesser-visited lakes of Buttermere

and Wast Water and the valleys of Eskdale, Langdale and Borrowdale will not disappoint. Keswick is an interesting old town to use as a break or a base.

Kendal, Furness and South Cumbria – On the southeast fringe of the national park, Kendal is a popular gateway to the region and its excellent museums are a good introduction to the Lakes. The South Cumbria coast may lack the drama and picture-postcard scenery of the national park but with the likeable town of Ulverston, Cartmel Priory and some fine historic houses, does not lack visitor interest.

Eden valley and Penrith – On the northeast edge of the park, the Eden valley is a continuation of the dramatic landscapes. The highlight is beautiful Ullswater lake, while the enjoyable small historic towns of Penrith, Appleby-in-Westmoreland and Alston all spring to life on market days.

Carlisle

The only city in the region, and an important border post between England and Scotland, Carlisle has been fought over for many centuries. Its rich history is well documented in its museum and the very fabric of its historic centre.

Lake District★★★

Cumbria

William Wordsworth said of the Lakes, 'I do not know of any tract of country in which, in so narrow a compass, may be found an equal variety in the influences of light and shadow upon the sublime and beautiful'. In 2017, the region was designated a UNESCO World Heritage Site.

LANDSCAPE

The region's name comes from the beautiful stretches of water that occupy many of the glaciated valleys radiating out from a high central core of volcanic rocks, presenting abrupt cliffs, crags and precipices. Among the many famous peaks is **Scafell Pike** (978m), the highest point in England. Elsewhere, much of the landscape has been formed by slate: to the north, in the gently-rounded but majestic heights of the Skiddaw group; to the south, in the more broken country reaching its highest point in the commanding presence of **The Old Man**, looming over Coniston Water. The most austere scenery is near the head of Wasdale, where awesome granite screes plunge to the shore of **Wastwater**, the deepest and most forbidding of the lakes.

The wild drama of the fells is set off by the gentler, pastoral character of the lowland, particularly in the park-like surroundings of Lake Windermere. Although the area generates its own micro-climate, overall it is not significantly different from the rest of northern Britain. The rocks are used in the man-made structures of the countryside: in ancient bridges; in the drystone walls which climb high into the fells; in the rough-hewn stone of sturdy vernacular barns, cottages and whitewashed farmhouses with massive roofs of slate. Even the towns are mostly built of stone and slate. Until well into the 20C, mining was an important activity in Cumbria; coal, iron-ore, lead, copper and graph-

- ⌖ **Michelin Map:** Michelin Atlas p44 or Map 502 K, L 20.
- ▶ **Location:** The Lake District is in the extreme north-west of England, roughly west of the A6/M6 corridor.
- ℹ **Info:** There are numerous visitor and information centres across the Lakes. A good starting point is the Brockhole Visitor Centre, near Windermere (℘015394 46601 www.brockhole.co.uk); see also www.golakes.co.uk; www.lakedistrict.gov.uk. Oxenholme Station, near Kendal, is the rail gateway to the Lakes (Manchester Piccadilly 1h16) with a branch line to Windermere. Ambleside and Windermere make good bases. Half-day and full-day guided tours in mini-coaches are available. Try Lakes Supertours (℘015394 42751; www.lakes-supertours.com) or Mountain Goat tours (℘015394 45161; www.mountain-goat.co.uk).
- ☺ **Warning:** In many places, mountain roads are very narrow with sharp bends and severe gradients.
- ⊙ **Timing:** At least 3 days.
- ♟ **Kids:** Hill Top (Beatrix Potter's cottage) for little ones; The Lakes Aquarium.
- 🐾 **Walking:** It is worth investing in only the most recent walking guides to the region from such publishers as Cicerone (www.cicerone.co.uk), and Crimson (www.crimsonpublishing.co.uk).
- 🚲 **Bicycle Trails:** Cycles are readily available for hire. Try Windermere Station.
- ⚓ **Sailing:** Lake Windermere has plenty of watersports. Or try Coniston Boating Centre (℘015394 41366; www.conistonboatingcentre.co.uk).

ite, some of which was transported to the coast by rail and made the coastal fishing villages thriving ports.

🚗 DRIVING TOURS

1 LAKELAND POETS TOUR
30mi/48km.

The more frequented area round Windermere evokes the memory of the Lakeland poets – **Wordsworth**, **Coleridge** and **Southey** – who were variously inspired by the landscape.

Lake Windermere★★
At 16km/10mi, Windermere is the longest lake in England, beautifully framed by wooded slopes and bare fells, and lively and popular for watersports.
The rail-town of **Windermere** was created during the 19C tourist boom, and a trip on the lake from nearby Bowness is still de rigueur. **Windermere Lake Cruises** (☎015394 43360, www.windermere-lakecruises.co.uk) offer a choice of cruises, from 45 minutes to a full-day combined with visits to local attractions.

Bowness-on-Windermere
Population: 3 814.
The ancient village is known for its promenade skirting the bay. A car and pedestrian **ferry**, with more than 500 years of history, crosses the lake from south of Bowness to Sawrey.
The main family visitor attraction is **The World Of Beatrix Potter** 🧒 (Crag Bow; open daily 10am–6.30pm; £7.50, child £3.95; ♿🅿🍴; ☎015394 88444; www.hop-skip-jump.com) where all 23 tales by Beatrix Potter are brought to life using the latest audio-visual and interactive techniques, complete with sights, sounds and smells.
Nearby, at Lakeside, the **Lakes Aquarium** 🧒 (Lakeside, Newby Bridge; open daily 9am/10am–4.30pm/6pm; closed 25 Dec; £6.95, child £4.95 (online booking discount); ♿🅿(charge); 🍴; ☎015395 30153; www.lakesaquarium.co.uk) reveals the aquatic and animal life of the riv-

ers, streams and lakes. There is a walk-through plexi-glass tunnel and displays on piranhas, otters and marmosets.

◐ Take the road running south from Bowness, and shortly turn right for the ferry across the lake (charge, paid on board). Take care driving the narrow, winding roads that follow.

🧒 Hill Top
Near Sawrey. Open: entry by timed ticket: mid-Feb–Oct Sat–Thu 10am–4.30pm (3.30pm Feb–Mar, late May–Aug 10am–5.30pm). Try to avoid peak periods, especially school holidays. £10.40, child £5.20. 🅿(very limited). ☎015394 36269. www.nationaltrust.org.uk/hilltop.
This tiny 17C house was the home of **Beatrix Potter**, who created Peter Rabbit, Benjamin Bunny, Jemima Puddle-Duck and many more favourite characters. Unchanged since her death in 1943, it now attracts thousands of visitors seeking the inspiration for their childhood delight. Inside are Beatrix Potter's watercolours, her dolls' house and mementoes.

Hawkshead★
Population: 519.
The narrow slate-walled lanes and paths of this traditional Lakeland village are bordered by flower-decked cottages. Wordsworth attended the local grammar school from 1779 to 1787. Enjoy views over the village from the nearby **Hawkshead and Claife Viewing Station** (www.nationaltrust.org.uk).
The **Beatrix Potter Gallery** (Main Street; open mid-Feb–late Mar Sat–Thu 10am–3.30pm; late Mar–Oct 10am–5pm, plus Fri Jun–Aug; entry by timed ticket in busy periods; £6.30, child £3.10; ♿; ☎015394 36355; www.nationaltrust.org.uk) covers her work as artist, author and local farmer, and displays a selection of her watercolours.

Coniston Water★
The road from Hawkshead to Coniston provides a fine view of the lake and the surrounding fells dominated by the bulk of **The Old Man of Coniston** (803m).

Grasmere lake and village from Loughrigg Fell

Coniston

Population: 928. 🈯 Ruskin Avenue.
☎015394 41533. www.conistontic.org.
The little slate-grey town is known for its associations with the author, artist and social reformer John Ruskin (1819–1900), who came to live at nearby Brantwood in 1872. He is buried in the churchyard, where a fine memorial marks the spot.

Nearby, the **Ruskin Museum** (open mid-Mar–mid-Nov daily 10am–5.30pm; mid-Nov–early Mar Wed–Sun 10.30am–3.30pm; £6; ♿; ☎015394 41164; www. ruskinmuseum.com) holds drawings, manuscripts and other mementoes. The museum's **Bluebird Wing** is dedicated to the world water-speed record-breaking boat *Bluebird*, and its driver, **Donald Campbell**, who set four successive records in the late 1950s on Coniston Water. He was killed when *Bluebird* crashed on Coniston in 1967, and his body, having been found only in 2001, is now buried in the Coniston graveyard. On the northeast shore of the lake is **Brantwood★** (open mid-Mar–Nov 10.30am–5pm; Dec–mid-Mar Wed–Sun 10.30am–4pm; closed 23–26 Dec,1 Jan; £7.70; ♿🅿✕; ☎015394 41396, www. brantwood.org.uk), '...the most beautifully situated house in the Lake District'. This was the home of **John Ruskin**, one of the greatest figures of the Victorian age. On the walls are exquisite watercol-

ours by himself and by Pre-Raphaelite contemporaries whom he championed. His study turret provides a splendid **view★** of Coniston in its attractive lakeside setting with the form of The Old Man to the left, perfectly mirrored in the tranquil waters of the lake.

▶ From Coniston take the A 593 northwards; at Skelwith Bridge turn left, and continue towards Elterwater village, to the north of which there is a prominent crossroads. Here, turn right, for Grasmere. *Do not take any earlier signed roads for Grasmere*. The road over the fells to Grasmere, via the area known as Red Bank, is one that passes through delightful scenery, but it is tortuous for the driver.

Grasmere

Population: 3 971.
This beautiful village is synonymous with **William Wordsworth** (1770–1850). The churchyard of 13C St Oswald's is where Wordsworth, members of the family, and Coleridge's son, David Hartley, are buried.
If the wind is blowing the right way, simply follow your nose to the **Grasmere Gingerbread Shop** (open daily; ☎015394 35428, www.grasmereginger-bread.co.uk), tucked away in the corner of the churchyard. A Lakes institution, the fabulous smell of Sarah Nelson's

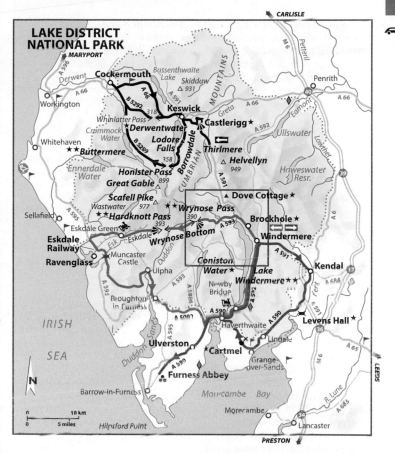

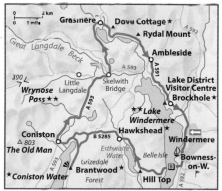

freshly baked gingerbread (sold only here) has been drawing customers to this delightful 17C house-cum-shop since the 1850s.

▶ Leave the village southwards to reach the main A 591. Go forward.

Dove Cottage and the Wordsworth Museum★

Town End, just off the A 591. Open daily: Mar–Oct 9.30am–5.30pm; Nov–Feb 10am–4.30pm. Dove Cottage closed 24 Dec–Jan (for conservation work). Cottage and Museum closed 24–26 Dec. £8.95. ℘01539 435 544. www.wordsworth.org.uk.

The home of William Wordsworth (1770–1850) and his sister Dorothy from 1799 to 1808, the cottage takes its name from being an early-17C inn (The Dove and Olive Bough) and became a magnet for early-19C literary Romantics such as

Coleridge, Southey and De Quincey. In the kitchen, where Dorothy cooked the inhabitants' two meals per day (both porridge), are three chairs embroidered by Dora Wordsworth (the poet's daughter), Sara Coleridge and Edith Southey. The room off it was first Dorothy's, then William's.

Upstairs is the sitting room, looking out over the waters of Grasmere, the main bedroom, the Newspaper Room (wallpapered in newspaper to keep it warm), and the pantry-cum-spare room. Behind is a museum containing manuscripts, memorabilia and Lakeland paintings, and the **Jerwood Centre** Reading Room, home to many rare first editions.

▷ Return to the A 591 and turn left.

Rydal Mount and Gardens

Windermere–Keswick Road. Open Mar–Oct daily 9.30am–5pm; Nov and Feb, Wed–Sun 11am–4pm. £7.50.
🅿✖ ☏015394 33002.
www.rydalmount.co.uk.

Overlooking Rydal Water, this 16C cottage, extended in the 18C into a farmhouse, became the home of William Wordsworth (1770–1850) from 1813 until his death in 1850.

Here he wrote his most financially successful book, *Guide to the Lakes*. Inside, his library now forms part of the drawing room, and the study ceiling is still painted with the Renaissance design he copied from a visit to Italy. Outside is a beautiful garden; inside, a pleasant café.

▷ Follow the A 591 S to Ambleside; use the main car park just before you enter Ambleside itself.

Ambleside

Population: 2 600.
🛈 ☏0844 225 0544.

This attractive and long-established little town makes a good touring base. The much-photographed 17C **Bridge House** is claimed to be one of the smallest houses in Britain. It was originally an apple store, then home to a family of eight, now a National Trust shop. Also worth a visit is the local museum,

The Armitt (Rydal Road; open Tue–Sat 10am–5pm; £5; ☏015394 31212; www.armitt.com), which also owns or has on loan many works by the German artist, Kurt Schwitters.

② ESKDALE VIA WRYNOSE PASS

50mi/80km.

This route leads to the less-frequented wilder and at times desolate expanses of Ulpha Fell and Furness Fell and goes over two high passes (*Beware very severe bends and steep gradients*). This is demanding driving, and must be tackled only in good conditions.

▷ From Windermere take the A 591 N for 3mi/5km.

Brockhole★

Get your bearings at the comprehensive and imaginative **Lake District Visitor Centre** (open daily 10am–6pm; ♿🅿(charge); ✖; ☏015394 46601; www.brockhole.co.uk), set in a fine country mansion, with large lawns, exhibitions, an indoor play space, adventure playground and Treetop Trek Aerial Adventure (☏015394 47186; www.treetoptrek.co.uk; from £22, child £18).

▷ S of Ambleside; take the A593 (signed for Coniston). Keep left at Skelwith Bridge towards Coniston, but soon turn acutely right, descending through a hairpin, and shortly turning left for Little Langdale. At first the road is enclosed by walls and then starts to climb the V-shaped valley between the bare grazing grounds for hill sheep to the top of the pass.

Wrynose Pass★★

From the pass (393m) there is a **view** back down to Little Langdale. The nearby Three Shire Stone (damaged in 2017), marks the location where the historic counties of Lancashire, Cumberland and Westmorland met.

Wrynose Bottom – The road runs parallel with the River Duddon along Wrynose Bottom through the wild splendour and gently rounded forms of the fells, which rarely exceed 1 000m but are scarred by steep scree slopes.

▶ At Cockley Beck, turn right over a bridge, to engage the Hardknott Pass, a series of tight zigzag bends both going up and down the other side.

Hardknott Pass★★

Near the top of the pass (393m), are the ruins of **Hardknott Fort**, a stone-built Roman auxiliary fort (2C).

Ravenglass and Eskdale Railway

Operates Apr–Oct daily, rest of year reduced service, see website for timetable. £8.20 one-way, £13.90 return. &🅿✕ ℘01229 71 71 71. www.ravenglass-railway.co.uk.
The narrow-gauge railway travels 7mi/11.3km from Ravenglass to Dalegarth. The line, laid in 1875 to carry iron ore and granite, now carries passengers in closed, semi-closed or open carriages drawn by either steam-powered or diesel engines. The line passes from the high fells and tributary waterfalls down the Esk valley, through the heather, bracken or tree-clad lower slopes to Ravenglass, where seabirds gather.

▶ Either return by the same route, or make a long but infinitely easier detour via Ulpha, Broughton-in-Furness and Coniston.

③ KESWICK AND NORTHERN LAKES

29ml/47km.

North of Dove Cottage the road runs up to Dunmail Raise before descending into the Thirlmere valley overshadowed by the western slopes of **Helvellyn** 949m). Wordsworth used to walk this route to visit Coleridge and Southey in Keswick.

Thirlmere – Originally two smaller water bodies, the lake (3.5mi/55km long, 1.2mi/2km wide), enclosed by mountains and forest, is a reservoir, surrounded by plantations.

Castlerigg Stone Circle★ – (signposts) The circle is older than Stonehenge and its purpose is unknown. It is set on a grassy outcrop offering far-flung **views** south towards Thirlmere and Helvellyn and west to Derwentwater and Keswick.

Keswick

Population: 4 821.
🅘 Moot Hall. ℘017687 72645.
Keswick, a lakeland town of medieval origin, claims the world's first pencil factory (1832), using graphite mined in Borrowdale as early as the mid-16C. The small **Pencil Museum** ♣♣ (open daily 9.30am–5pm, later at peak times; closed 1 Jan and 25–26 Dec; &🅿; ℘017687 73626; www.derwentart.com) celebrates the town's 175-plus years of pencil making. The local Keswick **Museum & Art Gallery** (Main Street; open daily 10am–4pm; £4.25; &; ℘01768 773 263; www.keswickmuseum.org.uk) is a real cabinet of curiosities including a 665-year-old cat, the remarkable Musical Stones 'pianola' played by Royal Command for Queen Victoria, Napoleon's teacup, the skin of Britain's rarest fish and manuscripts by both Wordsworth and Southey.

▶ From Keswick take the B 5289 S.

Derwentwater★

This lake is 3mi/5km long, 1mi/0.6km wide and flanked by granite crags. Southey thought it was the most beautiful of English lakes. Of the nearby **Lodore Falls**, he wrote that they came '...thundering and floundering, and thumping and plumping and bumping and jumping and whizzing and hissing and dripping and skipping and grumbling and rumbling and tumbling and falling and brawling and sprawling', which is about right.

Borrowdale

The attractive valley, where graphite was mined in the mid-16C, leads to the tiny hamlet of Rosthwaite set in a clearing in characteristic Lakeland scenery. The area around Rosthwaite is the site of pro-glacial lakes centred around a *roche moutonée* near the centre of the village.

Honister Pass

From Seathwaite, the road climbs over the pass (358m). To the south are two of the region's major summits – **Great Gable** (899m) and **Scafell Pike** (977m). On the pass, **Honister Slate Mine★** (open daily 9am–5pm; mine tours, Via Ferrata Classic and Extreme; pre-booking required on all tours – check website for all details including All-Day Passes; ✆017687 77230; http://honister.com) is the last of its kind in England and runs fascinating underground tours. Even more of a thrill is its **Via Ferrata** trail (the only one in the country) offering breathtaking views with only a wire between you and a drop of several hundred feet.

Beyond the pass, the road descends to **Buttermere★★**, which is separated by a glacial delta from Crummock Water, and continues to **Cockermouth**.

Wordsworth House and Garden

Cockermouth. Main Street. Open early Mar–Oct Sat–Thu 11am–5pm £7.90. ✗ ✆01900 820 884.
www.nationaltrust.org.uk.
Costumed servants welcome you to the elegant neo-Classical Georgian house (1745), in which **William Wordsworth** was born in 1770 and where he spent his early years. It is furnished with his own or contemporary furniture and exhibits some of his work, documents and the Wordsworth family tree.

◐ From Cockermouth return to Keswick on the A 66.

④ KENDAL AND FURNESS

40mi/64km.

◐ From Windermere take the A 591 east.

Kendal

Population: 28 586.
🄸 Town Hall. ✆01539 793 102.
The 'Auld Grey Town', built out of the local limestone, is a thriving regional centre. It was birthplace of Henry VIII's sixth wife, Katherine Parr, and before then was famous for its wool trade.
Kendal Museum (Station Road; open Tue–Thu 10am–4pm; closed one wk Xmas; £2; ✆01539 815 597; www.kendalmuseum.org.uk) features displays on the Lakes' natural history, archaeology, geology and changing exhibitions. **Abbot Hall★** is an 18C country house, home to a gallery and museum. Occupying the main house, the **Abbot Hall Art Gallery** (open Mon–Sat 10.30am–5pm (Nov–Feb 4pm), and Sun noon–4pm; in Jul–Aug; £7.70, gallery and museum £9.90; 🅿 (charge). ✆01539 722 464; www.abbothall.org.uk) features important changing exhibitions and works, paintings by George Romney (1734–1802). Set in the old stable block, the **Museum of Lakeland Life & Industry** (open as Abbot Hall; £5/£5.50; www.lakelandmuseum.org.uk) explores the story of the Lake District and its inhabitants before the arrival of the railway and motorcar, with re-created period rooms and workshops, and collections dealing with the Arts and Crafts movement, *Swallows and Amazons* author Arthur Ransome, and the Victorian period.

◐ Take the A 591 and then the A 590 S.

Levens Hall and Garden★

Open Apr–early Oct Sun–Thu gardens 10am–5pm, house noon–4pm. £13.50.
🅿✗ ✆01539 560 321.
www.levenshall.co.uk.
An Elizabethan manor has been added to a 13C pele tower to give the present graceful residence, notable for its outstanding carving and **plasterwork**. The dining room, covered in Cordova leather in 1692, has a magnificent set of Charles II walnut dining chairs. The picture-postcard **Topiary Gardens** are some of the oldest in the world, and unique in that the 1690 design has been preserved intact.

◐ Take the A 590 W to Lindale and then minor roads (signed) to Cartmel and Furness abbey (*⊙see South Cumbria Coast*).

South Cumbria Coast★

The Furness Peninsula and the Cartmel Peninsula ('the Lake District Peninsulas') jut into Morecambe Bay and are a quiet, largely rural area. Compared to the national park, the South Cumbria coast receives very few visitors.

CARTMEL PRIORY★

Cartmel. Open Mon–Sat 9am–5.30pm, Sun 9am–4.30pm (3.30pm in winter). No visits during services. Guided tours Apr–Oct Wed 11am and 2pm; Nov–Mar 11am Wed only. £4. & ✆015395 36261. www.cartmelpriory.org.uk.

Cartmel Priory survived the Dissolution of the Monasteries and is the grandest medieval building (mostly 12C) in the Lake District. It has a curious double tower, one set diagonally upon the other. Inside there is a fine east window and, above the droll misericords in the choir, a beautifully carved screen (1620). The **Priory Gatehouse** and the 17C and 18C houses give the market square an urbane air. The graveyard contains the bodies of numerous souls drowned while trying to cross Morecambe Bay. While here, visit the Cartmel Village Shop (www.cartmelvillageshop.co.uk), famous for its sticky toffee puddings, and the **Unsworths Yard** (micro) **Brewery** (tasting room and tours, call for times, ✆07966 681706; www.unsworthsyard-brewery.co.uk).

Also in the yard is the Cartmel Cheese shop (open daily 10am–4pm; www.cartmelcheeses.co.uk). Cartmel is also the base for the foodie empire of two Michelin-starred chef Simon Rogan: L'Enclume and Rogan & Co are neighbours, while the Pig & Whistle pub is just a short walk away.

HOLKER HALL & GARDENS★

Cark-in-Cartmel, 2 mi/3.2 km south. Open Apr–Oct Wed–Sun and bank holidays Mons 11am–4pm; gardens 10.30am–5pm. £12.50, Gardens only,

⏱ **Timing:** Allow a day.
👁 **Don't Miss:** Holker Hall gardens, or the Cartmel Sticky Toffee Pudding.

£8.50; Hall only, £8. & ☐✕ ✆015395 58328. www.holker.co.uk.

One of the finest country estates in Cumbria, Holker Hall lies in a glorious setting (on land once owned by Cartmel Priory) with gardens that merge into parkland, framed by the Lakeland Hills. The home of the Cavendish family for over 400 years, the present house was built in 1838–42 and according to Pevsner was '...the grandest of its date in Lancashire'. The award-winning gardens are a successful mix of formal and informal.

ULVERSTON

12 mi west of Cartmel.
Population: 11 678.
🛈 County Square. ✆01229 587 120.

This attractive old-fashioned market town of grey limestone cottages and cobbled lanes owes its wealth to the cotton, tanning and iron-ore industries which once flourished nearby. Stan Laurel (of Laurel and Hardy fame) was born here in 1890, and the town celebrates the duo in the enjoyable **Laurel and Hardy Museum** (Brogden Street; open Apr–Oct daily 10am–5pm; Nov–Mar Mon and Wed only; £5; ✆01229 582 292; www.laurel-and-hardy.co.uk).

FURNESS ABBEY

Barrow-in-Furness, 19mi southwest of Cartmel. Open Apr–Sept daily 10am–6pm; Oct daily 10am–5pm; Nov–Mar Sat–Sun 10am–4pm. Closed 1 Jan, 24–26 Dec. £5. ☐✕ ✆01229 823 420. www.english-heritage.org.uk.

The impressive remains of this abbey founded in 1123 by Stephen, Duke of Boulogne (later King of England), include much of the east end and west tower of the church, and the ornately decorated chapter house and cloister buildings.

Penrith and East Cumbria

The Eden valley divides the Pennines from the Lake District and is close both to the borders of Scotland and the Yorkshire Dales. It is an area of dramatic landscapes and interesting market towns.

PENRITH

Northeast of Lake District, beside M6. Population: 15 200.
🄸 Middlegate, Penrith. ℘01768 867466. www.visiteden.co.uk.

This distinctive red-sandstone market town is the regional centre for the Eden valley, at its most attractive in the old streets around the **Market Square**. In St Andrew's churchyard lies the **Giant's Grave**, the possible resting place of Owen, King of Cumbria in the 10C. It comprises two pre-Norman crosses and four Norse 'hogback' tombstones. You can learn more about this, the town and the region, at the **Penrith & Eden Museum** (Robinson's School, Middlegate; open Mon–Sat 10am–5pm, and Sun Apr–Oct 11am–4pm. ℘01768 865 105, www.eden.gov.uk/leisure-and-culture).

Dalemain Mansion and Historic Gardens (3mi/5km SW of Penrith; house open Apr–Oct 10.30am–5.30pm; Garden and museums 10am–4.30pm (4pm in Oct); Nov–20 Dec; Gardens and tearoom only Sun–Thu 11am–3pm; £11.50, gardens only £8.50; ✕; ℘01768 486 450; www.dalemain.com) is the area's finest country house. Home to the same family since 1679, it is an intriguing mix of Medieval, Georgian and Tudor buildings and styles.

ULLSWATER★

9.5mi SW of Penrith, in Lake District.
This is not only England's second-largest lake, but, in many people's eyes, also its most beautiful, twisting its way through spectacular scenery.
To one side are high fells, most notably, **Helvellyn**. To the other is a gently curving shoreline of green fields and woodlands, which provided the inspiration for Wordsworth's famous *Daffodils*.
Ullswater Steamers (℘017684 82229) www.ullswater-steamers.co.uk) offers cruises from 35 minutes (single journey £6.80) to round-the-lake day passes (£14.20), departing from Glenridding Pier at the lake's southern tip.

APPLEBY-IN-WESTMORELAND★

15.5mi southeast of Penrith.
Population: 3 048. 🄸 Moot Hall, Boroughgate. ℘017683 51177. www.applebytown.org.uk.

The former county town has a broad handsome main street, Boroughgate, shaded by ancient lime trees, which runs from High Cross to Low Cross. At the lower end of the street sits the **12C Church of St Lawrence** (rebuilt in the 17C), while the sturdy Norman keep of **Appleby Castle** (open for tours summer daily, contact tourist office for details and tickets) guards the top of the hill. Halfway along Boroughgate is a picturesque courtyard of **almshouses** built in 1651. In between, the street's architectural styles vary from Jacobean to Victorian. In the first week of June the **Appleby Horse Fair** is the UK's largest annual gathering of Gypsies and Travellers, attracting around 40 000 to the town.

ALSTON

20.8 mi northeast of Penrith. Population: 6 858. 🄸 Town Hall, Front Street. ℘01434 382 244.

The highest market town in England (although Buxton begs to differ), Alston sits at the junction of several trans-Pennine routes; its steep cobbled streets, hidden courtyards and quaint shops invite exploration. Although it's hard to imagine today, 250 years ago this was one of the richest lead mining areas in the country.

At the **Nenthead Mines Heritage Centre** (Nenthead, 4.5mi/7.2km E; open, see website for details; ℘07519 836 019; www.nentheadmines.com) you can see reminders of the area's halcyon days.

Carlisle★

The centre of Carlisle is marked by the Market Cross, which stands on the site of the Forum of Luguvalium, founded by the Romans, whose occupation lasted 400 years. The following 500 years of decline and border warfare did not encourage the inhabitants to build grandly or for posterity. The Guildhall (1407) is a rare timber-framed survivor.

▶ **Population:** 71 773.
⚹ **Michelin Map:** Michelin Atlas p44 or Map 502 L 19 – Local map Hadrian's Wall.
🗐 **Info:** Old Town Hall. ✆01228 598 596. www.discovercarlisle.co.uk. The compact town centre lies between Town Hall Square and the castle; get your bearings from the view from the ramparts.
◗ **Location:** 13mi/21km northeast of Calbeck, on the northwest tip of the Lake District and 10mi/16km south of the Scottish border.
☺ **Don't Miss:** The painted ceiling of the choir in the cathedral.

CITY

Cathedral★

Open daily 7.30am–6.15pm (Sun 5pm). Donation suggested. ♿🅿 ✗(Mon–Sat). ✆01228 548 151. www.carlislecathedral.org.uk.

Henry I created the See of Carlisle in 1133, though all that remains of the original Norman building is the truncated nave and the south transept. New work was begun in 1225 and includes the Decorated east window, a fine example of tracery, containing much original 14C glass, and the choir, with its set of sculptured capitals. In the choir, too, is a magnificent **painted ceiling★**, completed in 1360, featuring golden suns and stars on a blue ground. The 16C Brougham Triptych in the north transept is a masterpiece of Flemish craftsmanship.

Tullie House Museum and Art Gallery

Castle Street. Open Apr–Oct Mon–Sat 10am–5pm, Sun 11am–5pm; Nov–Mar Mon–Sat 10am–4pm, Sun noon–4pm. Closed 1 Jan, 25–26 Dec. £7.70. ♿✗ ✆01228 618 718. www.tulliehouse.co.uk.

The original house, which dates from 1689 and contains its original oak staircase, has been extended to house the local museum, which presents the long and often turbulent history of Carlisle through well-presented and lively displays, including Roman occupation, Hadrian's Wall, border *Reivers* (raiders) and the Civil War siege.

Carlisle Castle

Open Apr–Sept daily 10am–6pm; Oct daily 10am–5pm; Nov–Mar Sat–Sun 10am–4pm (daily Feb half-term hol). Closed 1 Jan, and 24–30 Dec. £6.80. ✆01228 591 922. www.english-heritage.org.uk.

Established by William II in 1092, the castle served to block the passage of Scots raiders. Opposite the entrance to the keep is the shell of the medieval hall, now home to the **Cumbria Military Museum**. All that remains of the original tower, in which Mary Queen of Scots was held in 1568, is the staircase to the east of the museum building.

Church of St Cuthbert with St Mary

Church: Open daily, dawn–dusk. Tithe barn: Open most mornings. ✆01228 521 982. www.stcuthbertscarlisle.org.uk.

The galleried church dates from 1779. Its unique moving pulpit was installed in 1905 to enable the preacher to speak to the galleries. The adjacent **tithe Barn★** (35m long) was built c.1480.

ADDRESSES

🏠 STAY

WINDERMERE

⊜🛏 **The Coach House** – Lake Road. ✆015394 44494. www.coachhouse windermere.co.uk. 🅿. 5 rooms. Unusual contemporary decor is the draw at this late–19C coachhouse cottage, a 10-min walk from Windermere and Bowness. A pretty patio looks onto woods.

⊜🛏 **The Ravensworth** – Ambleside Road. ✆015394 43747. www.theravensworth.com. 🅿. 11 rooms. A mile from the lake, this elegant, detached, 1850s-built Lakeland stone residence is a haven of tranquillity with smart modern rooms and a lovely garden terrace. Complimentary membership of local five-star spa and wellness included. Good value. No children.

BOWNESS-ON-WINDERMERE

⊜🛏💰 **Laurel Cottage** – St Martins Square, Kendal Road. ✆015394 45594. www.laurelcottage-bnb.co.uk. 🅿. 13 rooms. This charming 17C cottage in the heart of Bowness, is just a few yards from the lake.

CONISTON

⊜🛏 **Wheelgate Country Guest House** – Little Arrow. ✆015394 41418. www.wheelgate.co.uk. 🅿. 6 rooms. This charming 17C farmhouse cottage is surrounded by lovely gardens.

GRASMERE

⊜🛏💰 **Lake View Country House** – Lakeview Drive. ✆015394 35384. www. lakeview-grasmere.com. 🅿. 7 rooms. Perfectly located at the end of a private lane within an easy walk of the centre, Lake View sits in beautiful open gardens offering stylish traditional rooms.

⊜🛏💰💰 **Swan Hotel** – Keswick Road. ✆0344 879 9120. www.macdonaldhotels. co.uk/swan. 🅿. 38 rooms. Built in 1650 as a coaching inn, the Swan is one of the oldest hotels in the Lakes. Cosy, spacious traditional rooms. Access to spa and leisure facilities.

AMBLESIDE

⊜🛏💰 **The Old Vicarage** – Vicarage Road. ✆015394 33364. http://oldvicarage ambleside.co.uk. 🅿. 15 rooms. This beautiful Victorian vicararge, a two-minute walk from town, has its own swimming pool and hot tub, sauna, guest lounge and extensive terrace.

⊜🛏💰💰 **Drunken Duck Inn** – Barngates. ✆015394 36347. www.drunkenduckinn. co.uk. 🅿. 16 rooms. This splendid modernised family-owned, family-run pub, with an acclaimed restaurant and own micro-brewery, offers lovely trad-modern rooms, a glorious garden and full use of Langdale Spa and Leisure Club. Tariff incl. afternoon tea on arrival.

⊜🛏💰💰💰 **Linthwaite House** – Crook Road. ✆015394 88600. www. linthwaite.com. 🅿. 30 rooms. This late-19C romantic country house hotel with breathtaking views of Lake Windermere is one of the region's finest and most expensive places to stay. Its superior luxurious trad-modern rooms are full of character and boast superb bathrooms.

KESWICK

⊜🛏💰 **Highfield Hotel** – The Heads. ✆017687 72508. www.highfieldkeswick. co.uk. 🅿. 18 rooms. This splendid Victorian hotel is a local landmark with its towers, balconies and veranda. Rooms are large and traditional with modern styling; the gardens are glorious with wonderful views over the lakes and mountains.

WASDALE HEAD

⊜🛏💰 **Wasdale Head Inn** – Near Gosforth. ✆019467 26229. www.wasdale.com. 🅿. 12 rooms. This traditional old pub is a legend among local climbers ('the birthplace of British rock climbing') who come to ascend Scafell Pike, England's highest mountain. Traditionally decorated modest rooms and hearty dining await.

BUTTERMERE

⊜🛏💰 **Wood House** – ✆017687 70208. www.woodhousebuttermere.uk. 🅿. 3 rooms. The setting of this quiet tastefully traditional guesthouse may be unsurpassed in the Lakes, with fabulous views. Dinner also available on Tue, Thu and Sat on request in advance.

CARTMEL

⌣ 🍽🍽 Aynsome Manor Hotel –
📞015395 36653. www.aynsomemanor
hotel.co.uk. 🅿. 12 rooms. This charming
old manor house offers a warm
welcome, traditionally styled bedrooms
and serves excellent dinners.

GRANGE-OVER-SANDS

🍽🍽🍽 Netherwood Hotel and Spa –
Lindale Road. 📞015395 32552. www.
netherwood-hotel.co.uk. 🅿. 28 rooms.
Set in extensive grounds overlooking
Morecambe Bay, this large dramatic
stately 19C residence sits in beautiful
gardens. Traditional cosy rooms, most
with bay views. Its spa facilities are first
class.

ULLSWATER

🍽🍽🍽 Leeming House –
Watermillock. 📞0344 879 9142. www.
macdonaldhotels.co.uk/leeminghouse.
🅿. 40 rooms. Set in 9ha of grand
landscaped gardens (including a
croquet lawn) and woodland, this
200-year-old luxury country house hotel
boasts direct access to the shores of
Ullswater and private fishing.

🍽 EAT

WINDERMERE

🍽🍽 The Lighthouse – Main Road.
📞015394 88260. www.lighthouse
restaurantwindermere.co.uk. Set in a
handsome Victorian building with fine
views from its middle floor, and with
a pavement terrace below, this is an
attractive popular all-day eating place.

🍽🍽🍽 Miller Howe – Rayrigg Road.
📞015394 42536. www.millerhowe.com.
Gourmet cuisine served in a
magnificent setting with views
of the lakes and mountains.
15 rooms 🍽🍽🍽.

BOWNESS-ON-WINDERMERE

🍽🍽 Bodega Bar – Ash Street. 📞015394
46825. This cosy but stylish little place
features leather chairs and stripped
wooden floors serving tapas until
around 10pm.

🍽🍽 China Boat Restaurant –
Church Street. 📞015394 46326. Closed
Sun winter. This was the first Chinese
restaurant to open in the Lakes, in 1984,
and is still one of the very best.

HAWKSHEAD

🍽🍽🍽 Queen's Head Hotel –
Main Street. 📞015394 36271. www.
queensheadhawkshead.co.uk. This early-
17C flag-stone floored, oak-beamed inn
serves traditional and Modern British
dishes with an emphasis on locally
sourced ingredients.

GRASMERE

🍽🍽 The Traveller's Rest Inn –
Keswick Road. 📞015394 35604. www.
lakedistrictinns.co.uk. This traditional 16C
Lakeland inn is full of character with
oak beams and inglenooks, roaring log
fires in winter and beer gardens with
panoramic views in summer. Traditional
favourites and local specialities are on
the menu.

AMBLESIDE

🍽🍽 Jintana Thai Restaurant –
Compston Road. 📞015394 33394. www.
jintanathaicuisine.com. An excellent and
popular restaurant serving authentic
Thai cuisine; go early, or make a
reservation. Open all year.

🍽🍽🍽 The Old Stamp House
Restaurant – Church Street. 📞015394
32775. www.oldstamphouse.com. This
small fine-dining restaurant is located
in the former work place of William
Wordsworth, and produces dishes
inspired by the heritage, people and
landscapes of Cumbria

KESWICK

🍽 Lakeland Spice – 81 Main Street.
📞01768 780 005. This popular Indian
restaurant serves up some of the best
curries in the Lake District.

CARTMEL

🍽🍽🍽 L'Enclume – Cavendish Street.
📞015395 36362. www.lenclume.co.uk.
Closed Mon–Wed lunch. Two-star
Michelin nouvelle cuisine under the
supervision of chef Simon Rogan.
Reservation essential. Idyllic riverside
location in the most highly rated
restaurant in Cumbria.

ULLSWATER

🍽🍽 The Pooley Bridge – Pooley Bridge.
📞017684 86215. www.pooleybridgeinn.
co.uk. This fine old pub with a large
traditional bar and original timber
ceiling offers open fires in winter and
courtyard dining in summer.

Yorkshire

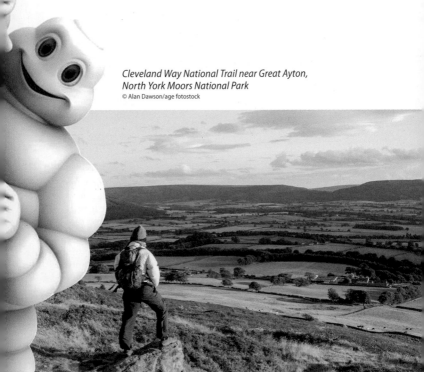

Cleveland Way National Trail near Great Ayton,
North York Moors National Park
© Alan Dawson/age fotostock

Introduction

The largest county in the UK, Yorkshire arouses fierce patriotism among its natives, who affectionately call it 'God's own country'. For walkers, the thought of the Dales and Moors is a heavenly, if often damp, prospect; fashionistas love Leeds; Goths flock to Whitby; lovers of film and curry beat a path to Bradford; while genteel tourists enjoy a cup of tea in Harrogate or Richmond. But no trip to the county is complete without York itself, where the glory of the minster is a tribute to the master builders of yesteryear.

South and West Yorkshire

This traditional coal, steel and textile manufacturing region has long ceased to be an industrial powerhouse and finished the 20C on a low note. However, within the last decade or so its three major cities, Sheffield, Leeds and Bradford, have successfully augmented and revitalised their museums and other visitor attractions, in addition to investing in other major leisure and retail facilities. Industrial heritage is of course key to many visitor attractions, with the UNESCO-listed Saltaire millworkers' village being the prime example. Art, literary and media history are also important. Sheffield and Leeds are particularly strong on 20C art and Bradford is the home of the National Media Museum. Nearby, the Brontë sisters shrine, Haworth, is an evergreen with visitors.

Yorkshire Dales

In terms of popular imagery, it is the Dales (valleys) of North Yorkshire that most visitors think of when the county's name is mentioned. This unspoilt region is famous for its glorious rolling countryside, perfect for walkers; its attractive patchwork of stone villages, home to local brewers and cheesemakers; its many romantic religious ruins such as Fountains Abbey (Yorkshire boasted more religious Pre-Reformation establishments than any other English county); charmingly old-fashioned market towns such as Ripon, Masham and Richmond, and the genteel spa of Harrogate. The stately homes of Harewood House, Newby Hall and grandiose romantic Castle Howard, reflect the historic wealth of the region.

York

The city of York is without doubt the county's main attraction. Once the second city of the kingdom, it boasts within its

Highlights

1 Choose your weapons at the **Royal Armouries**, Leeds (p447)

2 Combine art and history at atmospheric **Saltaire** (p451)

3 Picnic in the perfect setting of **Fountains Abbey** (p456)

4 Marvelling at the stained glass (and other treasures)in **York Minster** (p461)

5 Train spotting in the **National Railway Museum**, York (p465)

ancient compact centre a wealth of historical monuments, museums (particularly its magnificent Railway Museum) and superbly interpreted Roman, Viking and Georgian visitor attractions, that is unrivalled outside London.

North and East Yorkshire

By contrast with York, which in summer fairly teems with visitors, the North Yorkshire Moors and East Yorkshire are mostly unchartered territory. Like York, Beverley has a majestic soaring Minster and Hull boasts a world-class aquarium, while the main attraction of the Moors is its very wildness, punctuated only by long-deserted romantic ruins and villages offering shelter to walkers. The coast however has been popular, despite lack of clement weather, since Victorian times. And, while the fortunes of Scarborough and Bridlington have waned, visitors who make it to Whitby, in the far northeastern corner of the county, are rewarded by one of England's most intriguing resorts, rich in atmosphere and history. Close by, Robin Hood's Bay has retained its charm.

Sheffield

The fourth-largest provincial city in England, Sheffield has been known since the 14C for the production of steel and fine cutlery. Today it remains an important manufacturing centre and the commercial and cultural focus of a wide region, with revitalised art galleries, and excellent nightlife and shopping.

- **Population:** 575 400.
- **Michelin Map:** Michelin Atlas p35 or Map 502 P 23 – Local map Peak District.
- **Info:** Surrey Street. ℘0114 275 7754. www.welcometo sheffield.co.uk/visit.
- The train station is on Sheaf Street in the city centre (York, 53 min).
- **Location:** 54mi/86km S of York.
- **Kids:** Weston Park; Magna.

CITY

Millennium Gallery★

Arundel Gate. Open Mon–Sat 10am–5pm, Sun and bank holidays 11am–4pm. Charge for temporary exhibitions only. Closed 1 Jan, 24–26 Dec. ℘0114 278 2600. ♿✕ www.museums-sheffield.org.uk.

This is the cultural heart of the post-Millennium city, showcasing its heritage alongside contemporary art and design exhibitions. A light, spacious glass-and-white-concrete building is home to four galleries, featuring: craft and design; the Ruskin Gallery with over 900 paintings, watercolours and drawings; metalwork; and world-class touring exhibitions. Adjacent is the **Winter Garden★** (open Mon–Sat 8am–8pm, Sun 8am–6pm; ♿✕; www.sheffield.gov.uk), one of the largest temperate glasshouses to be built in the UK during the last century, 70m long and 22m high, it is home to 2 500 plants from around the world and is a stunning green oasis in the heart of the city. Nearby, the **Peace Gardens**, featuring eight water features, is an award-winning initiative.

Graves Gallery

Surrey Street. Open Tue–Sat 11am–4pm (Wed 1–6pm). Closed 1 Jan, 24–26 Dec and bank holidays. ℘0114 278 2600. ♿✕. www.museums-sheffield.org.uk.

This attractive suite of galleries features an acclaimed holding of 19C and 20C British and European art, including works by famous names, from Pablo Picasso and Pierre Bonnard to Stanley Spencer and Helen Chadwick.

Kelham Island Museum

Alma Street. Open Mon–Thu 10am–4pm, Sun 11am–4.45pm. £6. ℘0114 272 2106. ♿P✕. www.simt.co.uk.

Located in one of the city's oldest industrial districts, the museum stands on a 900-year-old man-made island and sets the tone by welcoming visitors with a giant Bessemer converter (used to make steel from iron). Interactive galleries tell the metalworking story of the city from the Industrial Revolution onwards.

Weston Park Museum

Western Bank. 1mi/1.6km from centre. Ooen Mon–Sat and bank holidays 10am–5pm, Sun 11am–4pm. ℘0114 278 2600. ♿✕ www.museums-sheffield.org.uk.

This eclectic gallery showcases the city's varied and unusual treasures in a lively populist style, with lots of hands-on exhibits, ranging from Egyptian Mummies to live ants and bees.

EXCURSION

Magna Science Adventure Centre

Sheffield Rd, Rotherham. 9mi/14km NE. Opening hours vary; check website for current details. £10.95, child £8.95. ♿P✕ ℘01709 720 002. www.visitmagna.co.uk.

Interactive discovery centre with atmospheric and multimedia effects used to evoke the old furnace environment. Exhibits are themed, and there are huge indoor and outdoor play areas.

Leeds★

and around

Set in the heart of northern England, Leeds is one of Britain's great Victorian cities; its population multiplied tenfold between 1800 and 1900 and its conurbation ranks third in size in England after London and Birmingham. Moreover, it is Britain's fastest-growing metropolis. Its docklands area, derelict less than two decades ago, is now thriving and home to a vast array of restaurants, pubs and shops. Heavy industry has been replaced by light engineering and offices, and clothing manufacture by retailers; the precincts and arcades attract shoppers from all over the North. The rich cultural life of this provincial capital ranges from acclaimed opera to the fashionable nightclubs, which bring in multitudes of weekend revellers.

ROYAL ARMOURIES MUSEUM★★★

Armouries Drive. Open daily 10am–5pm. Closed 24–26 Dec. Free, but charge for events. ℘0113 220 1999 (infoline). ♿✗ www.royalarmouries.org.

This purpose-built multi-million-pound citadel in glass, grey brick and marble was inaugurated in 1996 to provide a setting for more than 8 500 objects from the superlative collection of weaponry formerly housed in the Tower of London. The quality of the exhibits is matched by an array of advanced and imaginative display techniques that set the items in their context and encourage visitor participation: interactive computers and video screens chatter and hum, and live demonstrations provide movement and drama. A splendid central space, the **Street**, rises between the six floors of the main part of the building to the glazed roof. It terminates in a glazed keep, known as the **Hall of Steel** (over 30m high), its interior walls hung with a stunning assortment of weap-

> **Population:** 751 500.
> **Michelin Map:** Michelin Atlas p40 or Map 502 P 22.
> **Info:** The Headrow. ℘0113 378 6977. www.visitleeds.co.uk.
> The train (York, 23min) and bus stations are in the centre of town.
> **Location:** 25mi/40km southwest of York.
> **Kids:** Royal Armouries Museum. National Coal Mining Museum.

onry arranged in decorative patterns. Six spacious galleries are devoted to War (including Peace Farewell to Arms?), Hunting, the Tournament, Self Defence, Oriental Weaponry. The countless treasures include a grotesque grinning face-mask presented to Emperor Maximilian (the museum's emblem), gorgeously inlaid sporting guns, a set of Japanese armour presented to King James I in 1614 and a near-complete set of elephant armour. Among the curiosities is a tiny cyclist's revolver designed to discourage dogs and a monumentally unwieldy punt gun once used by wildfowlers to fell dozens of ducks at a single discharge.

The **Tiltyard**, the first to be built in Britain for hundreds of years, is the setting for thrilling performances of jousting and combat of all kinds.

👣 WALKING TOUR

Town Hall and Victoria Square

The town hall was the winning design in a competition in 1853. External Corinthian columns, the Baroque tower (69m) and the splendour of the interior made it a symbol of civic pride when opened by Queen Victoria in 1858.

On fine days, chess enthusiasts can be seen playing 'Giant Chess' on the boards marked out in Victoria Square.

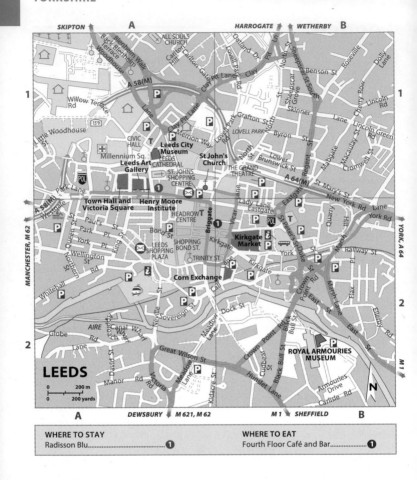

WHERE TO STAY	WHERE TO EAT
Radisson Blu.. ❶	Fourth Floor Café and Bar.................... ❶

Leeds Art Gallery★

The Headrow. Open daily except Mon 10am–5pm (Sun noon–4pm). ♿✖
☎0113 247 8256.
www.leeds.gov.uk/artgallery.

This is one of the best provincial galleries in Britain, with international-class permanent and temporary exhibitions. Its strength lies in its collection of **19C and 20C British art**, particularly of the early–mid-20C, with virtually all major artists of the period being represented. The dominance of British art is relieved by French paintings: a Courbet, several Impressionists and a brilliant Derain of 1905, *Barges on the Thames*.

The gallery's magnificent Victorian **Tiled Hall** restaurant, with its grand marble columns, ornate tiles, barrel-vaulted mosaic ceiling and original parquet flooring, is alone worth a visit. The greatest British sculptor of the 20C, **Henry Moore** (1898–1986), was a Yorkshireman; the range of his achievement, from exquisite small-scale studies to the *Reclining Figure* of 1929 and the powerful post-war *Meat Porters*, is shown in the gallery and at the neighbouring **Henry Moore Institute** (open Tue–Sun 11am–5.30pm (Wed 8pm); ☎0113 246 7467; www.henry-moore.org/hmi).

St John's church

Open Tue–Sat 9.30am–5.30pm.
☎0113 244 1689.
The oldest church in central Leeds. Sensitive restoration in 1868 revived its 1630s incarnation.

Leeds City Museum

Millennium Square. Open Tue–Fri and bank holiday Mons 10am–5pm, Sat–Sun 11am–5pm. Closed 1 Jan, 25–26 Dec. ♿✖ ☎0113 224 3732. www.leeds.gov.uk/citymuseum.

Occupying the beautiful old Civic Theatre building and established in 2008, this bright colourful eclectic museum has galleries devoted to World View, Life on Earth, Ancient Worlds, The Leeds Gallery and Leeds Collectors.

EXCURSIONS

Kirkstall Abbey and Abbey House Museum★

➲3.5mi/5.6km NW on the A 65. Open Tue–Sun and bank holiday Mons: Apr–Sept 10am–4.30pm, Oct–Mar 10am–4pm. ♿🅿✖ ☎0113 378 4079. www.leeds.gov.uk/kirkstallabbey

Kirkstall was a traditional Cistercian abbey, founded 1152. The austere ruins, which still stand almost to roof height, are dominated by the 16C crossing tower. Across the busy road, the former abbey gatehouse is now the **Abbey House Museum**, a lively interactive place that recreates the sights and sounds of life in Victorian Leeds in 1880.

Temple Newsam★

➲Temple Newsam Road. Near Whitkirk, 4mi/6km E on the A 63. Open: House: Tue–Sun 10.30am–5pm/4pm; Farm (summer) Tue–Sun 10am–5pm, (winter) 4pm. ♿🅿(charge). ✖ ☎0113 336 7460. www.leeds.gov.uk/templenewsam.

Set within over 600ha of parkland, woodland and farmland landscaped by 'Capability' Brown in the 18C, this magnificent Tudor–Jacobean mansion was the birthplace of Lord Darnley, husband of Mary Queen of Scots.

The brick house, begun in the late-15C and rebuilt in the first part of the 17C, is an attractive setting for a collection of English, European and Oriental **decorative arts★** and for many of the Old Master paintings owned by the City of Leeds.

The farm includes rare breeds and re-created workshops and exhibitions.

Nostell Priory★

➲Doncaster Road, Nostell, nr Wakefield, 18mi/29km SE by the A 61 and A 638. House: Open Mar–Oct Wed–Sun and bank holiday Mons 1–5pm; open first two weeks Dec Sat–Sun 10am–4pm. £11.55, garden only £7.20. ♿🅿(£4). ✖ ☎01924 863 892. www.nationaltrust.org.uk.

This Palladian mansion was begun in 1733 by James Paine, then only 19 years old. **Robert Adam** was commissioned in 1765 to complete the State Rooms and they are among his finest interiors. **Thomas Chippendale** was once an apprentice on the estate and the house contains the largest collection of Chippendale furniture in the world.

♿ National Coal Mining Museum for England★

➲ South of Leeds, 6mi/10km west of Wakefield on the A 642. Open daily 10am–5pm. Closed 1 Jan, 24–26 Dec. ♿🅿✖ ☎01924 848 806 www.ncm.org.uk.

Caphouse Colliery contributed significantly to Britain's industrial might until its closure in the 1980s. There are displays, exhibits and an array of old machinery around the pithead buildings, but the highlight of a visit is the donning of helmet and lamp, and the descent (140m) into the old workings in the company of a former miner.

Yorkshire Sculpture Park★

➲West Bretton. 20mi/32km S by the M 1 to junction 38 and 1mi/1.6km N off the A 637. Open daily: Ground and Centre 10am–6pm (5pm in winter); Underground gallery and chapel 10am–5pm (4pm in winter). Closed 24–25 Dec. ♿🅿(£3–£10). ✖ ☎01924 832 631. www.ysp.co.uk.

Amid lovely parkland lies an outstanding array of modern sculpture, including works by the two most famous British sculptors of the 20C, Henry Moore and Barbara Hepworth (both were born in Yorkshire and both attended Leeds School of Art). An indoor gallery and a fine café provide for wet days.

ADDRESSES

PUBS/RESTAURANTS

🔎 Leeds Waterfront, once derelict, is now home to a vast array of restaurants, pubs and shops. The **Exchange Quarter** along Call Lane and **Granary Wharf** are also good areas for fashionable cafés, bars and dining.

SHOPPING

Many of the main high street stores are to be found in **Briggate**, and the elegant **Victoria Quarter**, which boasted the first Harvey Nichols store outside London. For handmade goods head for **Granary Wharf**. For something special or eclectic pay a visit to the **Corn Exchange**, a striking building which has over 50 places to shop, eat and drink. Another splendid historic city centre showpiece building is **Kirkgate Market** (Leeds City Markets); with 800 stalls, it is said to be the largest covered market in Europe.

ENTERTAINMENT

🔎 Leeds is renowned for its vibrant club culture. If you are in search of more laid-back nightspots, try:

The Wardrobe (www.thewardrobe. co.uk) with an eclectic programme; the **Hi Fi Club** (www.thehificlub.co.uk), a subterranean bar/club close to Call Lane with DJs and live music nights. They also run a popular comedy night every Saturday.

The **City Varieties Music Hall** (www. cityvarieties.co.uk), the **West Yorkshire Playhouse** (www.wyp.org.uk) and the **Grand Theatre and Opera House** (www.leedsgrandtheatre.com) are the main performing arts venues. Outdoor opera, ballet, pop, jazz and classical music concerts are held in the summer. Leeds also hosts an **International Film Festival** (www.leeds film.com), an **International Concert Season** (www.leedsconcertseason. com) and an **International Pianoforte Competition** (www.leedspiano.com). For listings visit www.leedsguide.co.uk.

Bradford★

West Yorkshire

Bradford prospered through the wool trade and by 1500 it was a bustling market town '...which already standeth much by clothing'. By 1850 there were 120 mills and Bradford had become the world's capital for worsted (cloth). Among its famous sons are the author J B Priestley (1894–1984), composer Frederick Delius (1862–1934) and the contemporary painter David Hockney (b.1937). The Bradford of today is essentially a Victorian city, but also a UNESCO City of Film. It boasts a large South Asian population, and has become Britain's curry capital, famed for the quantity and quality of its restaurants. The Bradford Mela, now the city's principal festival, is a British-Asian cultural celebration, held in June.

▸ **Population:** 582 155.
🔎 **Michelin Map:** Michelin Atlas p39 or Map 402 O 22.
🔎 **Info:** Britannia House, Broadway. ☎01274 433 678. www.visitbradford.com.
🔎 Bradford Interchange just south of the centre, off Bridge Street, is the terminus for buses and trains (Manchester 58 mins).
🔎 **Location:** 9mi/14km west of Leeds.
🔎 **Timing:** Allow one day.
🔎 **Kids:** Media Museum.

CITY

🔎 National Science and Media Museum★

Prince's View. Open daily 10am–6pm. Cinemas open daily 10am–late.
🔎✖ ☎0844 856 3797.

www.nationalmediamuseum.org.uk.
Part of the same family as London's
Science Museum, this lively modern
museum is home to over 3.5 million
items of historical significance which
trace the history and practice of
photography, the cinema, television
and all new media. There is a huge
IMAX cinema and conventional
screenings showing arthouse and
fringe films; film festivals are also
staged, and at the BFI Mediatheque,
you can log on at your personal
viewing station, choose from over
2 500 TV and film titles.

Wool Exchange
Market Street.
Built 1867 in grand Italianate/Gothic
style, this was once the centre of the
world's wool trade. The statues at the
entrance are those of St Blaize, patron
saint of wool combers, and of Edward III,
who did much to encourage the wool
industry. It now houses shops and
offices. In Waterstone's you can see the
original splendid hammerbeam roof
and interior.

Bradford Cathedral
1 Stott Hill. Open Mon–Sat 9am–4.30pm.
Sun for services only. Closed bank
holidays. & ✆01274 777 720.
www.bradfordcathedral.co.uk.
The battlemented exterior does not
give the impression of a building which,
in parts, dates back to the 1440s; the
west tower with battlements and pinnacles dates from 1493. The chancel has
some fine stained glass, c.1862, by William Morris, Rossetti and Burne-Jones.

Little Germany
Near the cathedral.
This merchants' district, named after
the booming mid-19C trade links with
Germany, has been restored to show its
fine Victorian architecture (1830–99).

EXCURSION

Saltaire★
3mi/5km north.
With its cobbled streets and honey-
coloured stonework, Saltaire village

© Darrell Evans/Dreamstime.com

Salt's Mill by the River Aire, Saltaire

was built as a model village in the 19C
by mill owner and philanthropist Sir
Titus Salt for the spiritual, physical and
moral welfare of his workers. Thanks to
its outstanding state of preservation it
has been designated a **UNESCO World
Heritage Site**.
The vast imposing complex of **Salt's
Mill** (open Mon–Fri 10am–5.30pm, Sat–
Sun 10am–6pm, but different areas have
different opening times; see website for
details; closed 25–26 Dec, 1 Jan; & ☐ ✕;
✆01274 531 163; www.saltsmill.org.uk) is
still the key feature of the village. **The
1853 Gallery★** is a beautiful space,
showcasing the largest collection of art
in Europe by **David Hockney**. A major
contributor to Pop Art in the 1960s and
still active today (in his 70s), Hockney
was one of the most influential and is
still probably the best-known British
artist of his generation, contributing
his works to Salt's Mill, from canvasses
to iPad art.
There is a Saltaire history exhibition,
several arty shops, and the building also
makes a lovely setting for the Hockney
designed **Café Opera restaurant**.

Haworth

North Yorkshire

Haworth (pronounced "HA-wuth") is a Yorkshire hill village, its dark, gritstone cottages crowded together on the edge of the Pennine moors. The long, steep main street is lined with souvenir shops and tearooms, all enjoying the benefits of association with the Brontë sisters, who lived in the parsonage at the top of the hill and wrote most of their stories there.

VILLAGE

Brontë Parsonage Museum★

Church Street. Open Apr–Oct 10am–5.30pm; Nov–Mar 10am–5pm. £8.50. ℰ01535 642 323. www.bronte.org.uk.

▶ **Population:** 6 379.
  Michelin Map: Michelin Atlas p39 or Map 502 O 22.
  Info: 2–4 West Lane. ℰ01535 642 329. www.visitbradford.com.
▶ **Location:** 19mi/31km west of Leeds, 8mi/13km west of Bradford.

The parsonage where Patrick Brontë and his family lived conserves furniture, paintings and fascinating memorabilia, such as the children's drawings and home-made books. Here they conceived imaginary kingdoms (Angria and Gondal), wrote poetry and fiction, and here too their brother, Branwell, painted the three sisters. A gateway (marked by a stone) led from the parsonage garden

Brontë Country

The Brontë sisters drew on their local knowledge for descriptions of the places in their novels. Two houses which appear in *Shirley* under other names can be visited near Batley. In the 19C, the family of Mary Taylor, one of Charlotte's close friends, lived in an 18C red-brick house, more latterly the **Red House Museum** (now permanently closed); the house appears in *Shirley* as Briarmains. **Oakwell Hall** (Nutter Lane, Birstall, near Batley, on the A 638; open noon–4pm, Sat–Sun and Tue–Thu during school holidays; £2.50; ℰ01924 324 761; www.friendsofoakwellhall.org.uk) is a dark-stone Elizabethan manor, with impressive latticed windows, furnished as it was for the Batt family in the 1690s; it is surrounded by traces of a moat and a country park (Visitor Centre open daily 10am–5pm; the Countryside Centre is currently closed. ✖).

Patrick Brontë was born Patrick Brunty in Northern Ireland and studied for holy orders at St John's College in Cambridge. He came to Haworth as curate in 1820, bringing his wife, Maria and their six children. His wife, who was consumptive, died the following year. In 1825, the two eldest girls, Maria and Elizabeth, fell ill at boarding school in Cowan Bridge and died. In 1846, the first publication by the three surviving sisters appeared, a joint volume of poems by 'Currer, Ellis and Acton Bell', names chosen to preserve their initials but conceal that they were women. Next came *Wuthering Heights* (1847) by Emily and *The Tenant of Wildfell Hall* by Anne, who also drew on her experience as a governess for *Agnes Grey* (1847). Also in 1847 Charlotte wrote *Jane Eyre*. All died young: their brother, Branwell, aged 31 in September 1848, Emily (at 30) three months later and Anne (at 29) the following summer in Scarborough, where she is buried. Charlotte married her father's curate in 1854 and died in 1855, aged 39. Patrick Brontë died in 1861, in Haworth, having outlived his wife and all six children.

to the church, where five of the Brontë children and their mother are buried.

EXCURSION

Keighley and Worth Valley Railway

Oxenhope. 2mi/3km S on the A6033. Day Rover Ticket £16, child (5–15) £8; Full-line return (Haworth – Keighley – Oxenholme – Haworth) £11, child £5.50. Tickets can be purchased at booking offices of all six stations. It is not possible to book in advance and reservations are not required. See website for timetables. &🅿✗ 𝒫01535 645 214. www.kwvr.co.uk.

Steam and heritage diesel engines travel through moor scenery along a branch line linking Oxenhope with Haworth, Oakworth, Damems, Ingrow and Keighley. A re-created Edwardian station is this railway's terminus. At Ingrow is the **Museum of Rail Travel** (𝒫01535 680 425; www.vintagecarriage strust.org), which preserves traditional wooden rail carriages.

Yorkshire Dales★★

North Yorkshire

Northwest of the great manufacturing towns of Leeds and Bradford lie the Yorkshire Dales (valleys), featuring dramatic limestone scenery, crags, caves, and swallow holes in which streams disappear. In the broad dales such as Airedale, Wensleydale and Wharfedale the stone-built villages are set harmoniously in an ancient pattern of stone-walled fields. Most of the area lies within the protected national park, which in 2016 was extended as far as the Lune valley on the edge of the Lake District.

☙ WALKING

The Dales are a walker's delight, criss-crossed with paths and a specially designated cycleway. The four main routes are the **Nidderdale Way** (53mi/85km), starting and finishing in Pateley Bridge; the **Dales Way** (80mi/129km), from Ilkley to Bowness-on-Windermere (in the Lake District), via Wharfedale, Langstrothdale and Dentdale; the challenging **Yorkshire Three Peaks Way** (24.5mi/39km), taking in Pen-y-ghent, Whernside and Ingleborough; and the

ℹ **Michelin Map:** Michelin Atlas p39 or Map 502 N, O 21 and 22.

ℹ **Info:** www.yorkshiredales.org.uk; www.yorkshire.com.

👪 **Kids:** White Scar Caves; Falconry Centre.

Pennine Way, at 268mi/431km the ultimate long-distance route, passing through Airedale, Malhamdale and Three Peaks country.

SKIPTON

South Yorkshire Dales, beside the A59 and A65.
Population: 14 623. ℹ High Street.
𝒫01756 792 809.

This historic town is the Dales' southern gateway and a good base for exploring farther afield. Time your visit for bustling market day (*Mon, Wed, Fri, Sat*). At the top of the High Street is **Skipton castle★** (open Mon–Sat 10am–5pm (4pm in Oct–Mar), Sun open 11am; closed 23–25 Dec; £8.10; ✗; 𝒫01756 792 442; www.skiptoncastle.co.uk), one of the most complete and best-preserved medieval castles in England. Beautiful **Conduit Court** was built by the 10th Earl. Its present appearance owes much to mid-17C restoration.

Skipton sits halfway along the trans-Pennine **Leeds–Liverpool Canal** and 1-hour cruises with **Skipton Boat Trips** (Wharf Canal Basin, Coach Street; operate daily Easter–Oct; 01756 790 829; www.canaltrips.co.uk) depart regularly from the centre of town.

WHARFEDALE★

Wharfedale is one of the most popular dales, on account of its delightful limestone landscapes and riparian loveliness, that make it hugely popular with walkers and casual visitors alike. In Bolton Abbey village, **Bolton Priory** (9mi/14km S of Grassington; the Estate is open daily 9am–dusk; £10 per vehicle, varies seasonally; ; 01756 718 000, www.boltonabbey.com) was founded by the Augustinians c.1154, in a beautiful setting on a bend of the River Wharfe. Only partially destroyed at the Dissolution, it still functions as a parish church. The villages of Burnsall, Grassington and Kettlewell are especially pleasing with pubs and tea rooms galore, and, in the case of Grassington, souvenir and craft shops and the headquarters of the national park.

MALHAMDALE★

10.8mi northwest of skipton.
The tiny village of Malham is popular with walkers, who come to do the 8mi/13km 'Cove, Tarn and Scar Trail', although the Pennine Way passes through here also.
Malham Cove★ is a spectacular natural carboniferous limestone amphitheatre, around 80m high and 300m wide. At its summit (steep climb up steps), walkers are rewarded with great views and an unusual 'limestone pavement', deeply fissured and fretted by naturally eroded channels, which featured in the penultimate 'Harry Potter' film. If the climb to the top doesn't appeal, it's a fine walk from the village to the very base of the cove cliffs. Higher still, **Malham Tarn** is a natural upland lake set before Malham Tarn House, originally a hunting lodge, visited by Charles Kingsley author of *The Water Babies*; **Gordale Scar** is another

spectacular cliff formation, carved as a meltwater channel beneath the ice-sheet aeons ago.

RIBBLESDALE

16.5mi northwest of Skipton.
Town Hall, Market Place, Settle.
01729 825 192.
The main settlement in Ribblesdale is **Settle**, the starting point of the very picturesque 72mi/116km **Settle-Carlisle Railway★** (www.settle-carlisle.co.uk).
On the western edge of the national park, 12mi/19km north of Settle is **White Scar Cave** (1.3mi/2km E of Ingleton; guided tours from 10am, daily Feb–Oct, Sat–Sun only Nov–Jan: £9.95, child £6.50; ; 01524 241 244; www.whitescarcave.co.uk), a vast show-cave and the longest in England. It includes a massive ice-age cavern, underground waterfalls, and streams and stalactites galore.

WENSLEYDALE★

Along the A684 in the northern Dales.
Dales Countryside Museum.
01969 666 210.
The largest of the dales, Wensleydale is famous not only for its eponymous cheese, but as the setting for the *James Herriot* books and TV series which were filmed here, most notably in Askrigg. Fans of the local vet will enjoy a pint in the Kings Arms, which made many appearances as the Drover's Arms.

Hawes

Wensleydale's main town is at its best on market day *(Tue)* when it sells, among many other things, Wensleydale cheese, which has been made locally for centuries (*see p81*).
Around the marketplace are workshops, antiques and speciality shops.
Housed in the old railway station, the **Dales Countryside Museum** (open Feb–Oct daily 10am–5pm, and 10am–4.30 during Nov–Dec; closed 25–26 Dec; £4.80; charge; 01969 666 210, www.dalescountrysidemuseum.org.uk) looks at the Dales' domestic life, leisure and work over the centuries.

Aysgarth

🏠 Aysgarth Falls. ☎01969 662910.
The main attraction here, **Aysgarth Falls**, lies 0.5/1km out the village (waymarked trail from visitor centre). Another popular walk (*6mi/10km*) leads to **Bolton Castle★** 🚶🚶 (open Apr–Oct 10am–5pm; £8.50, child £7; 🅿✗; ☎01969 623 981, www.boltoncastle.co.uk). This classic sturdy four-square fortress is one of the country's best-preserved medieval castles with stunning views over the Dales. Its colourful history includes Mary Queen of Scots being imprisoned here, and its interiors, complete with sounds and smells, are very atmospheric. There is a bird of prey centre with daily flying displays.

Masham★

🏠 7 Little Market Place. ☎01765 600200.
Pronounced 'mass-em', this pretty little village boasts the largest **market square** in the county, holding a weekly market (Wed, Sat) since 1393.
Masham is famous for **beer** with two very traditional breweries open to the public. The original is the famous **Theakston's Brewery** (open 10.30am–4.30pm; guided tours at 11am, noon, 2pm and 3pm; £7.50; ☎01765 680 000, www.theakstons.co.uk), which has been here since 1827. Just a few minutes' walk away, the **Black Sheep Brewery** (visitor centre open Mon–Wed and Sun 10am–5pm, Thu–Sat 10am–11pm, call for tour times, booking advisable; ✗; ☎01765 680 101; www.blacksheep.co.uk) was established in Masham in 1992 by Paul Theakston, as a riposte to the takeover of his family's business by a multinational company. Black Sheep beers rapidly became a regional favourite and, thanks to its location in an old Victorian brewery, it has both heritage and atmosphere.

RICHMOND★

Northeast Dales, near the A1.
🏠 Friary Gardens, Victoria Road. ☎01748 828 742.
This attractive country market town enjoys a beautiful location set at the foot of Swaledale on the northeast edge of the Dales National Park.

Richmond Castle★

Open Apr–Sept 10am–6pm; Oct 10am–5pm, Nov–Mar Sat–Sun (Feb half-term hol daily) 10am–4pm. £5.70. ✗ ☎01748 822 493. www.english-heritage.org.uk.
This ruined castle, begun 1071, stands on a cliff edge high above the river. The **keep**, built of grey Norman masonry (30m), is stout enough to stand comparison with the White Tower in the Tower of London. An 11C arch leads into the courtyard. **Scolland's Hall**, built in 1080, is the second oldest such building in England. From the roof of the keep there is a splendid **view** across the cobbled marketplace and over the moors.

The Georgian Theatre Royal and Museum★

Victoria Road. Guided tours mid Feb–mid-Nov. ✗ ☎01748 825 252. www.georgiantheatreroyal.co.uk.
The only Georgian theatre in the country with its original form and features, it was opened in 1787 but fell "dark" in 1848 until being reopened in 1963.

THE BOWES MUSEUM★

15mi northwest of Richmond via A66. Barnard Castle. Open daily 10am–5pm. Closed 1 Jan and 25–26 Dec. £14. ♿🅿✗ ☎01833 690 606. www.bowesmuseum.org.uk.
A French-designed château, set in landscaped gardens (8ha), is an unexpected surprise in this area. It was built, from 1869 onwards, to house the extraordinary array of ceramics, pictures, tapestries, furniture and other *objets d'art* amassed by John Bowes and his French wife, Josephine.
Their treasures include novelties like an automated silver swan; its rippling neck, as it swoops to catch a wriggling fish in its beak, is remarkable. There are also paintings of the first rank: a magnificent St Peter by El Greco, part of an extensive collection of 15C–19C Spanish work; two Goyas, two Canalettos and works by Boudin and Courbet.

Ruins of Fontains abbey

© christopher smith/iStockphoto.com

Fountains Abbey and Studley Royal★★★

and around

⚬ **Michelin Map:** Michelin Atlas p39 or Map 502 P 21.
◐ **Location:** 27mi/43km northwest of York.
⊘ **Parking:** At Visitor Centre (free); at Deer park (charge).

Set in the wooded valley of the little River Skell amid glorious North Yorkshire countryside, these Cistercian ruins – the largest abbey ruins in England – are not only famously picturesque but also wonderfully evocative of monastic life. They are beautifully complemented by the spectacular Georgian water gardens of Studley Royal. The whole has been declared a World Heritage Site.

A BIT OF HISTORY

In 1132 a small band of Benedictine monks, revolting against the slack discipline at their abbey in York, were granted land in this '...place remote from all the world'. They set about transforming their wilderness into the flourishing and productive countryside characteristic of Cistercian endeavour and, within a century, Fountains abbey was the centre of an enormous enterprise, managing fish-farms and iron-workings, as well as forests and vast tracts of agricultural land, the profits from which paid for an ambitious building programme.

The complex fell into decay following the Dissolution, but in 1768 it was bought by the Aislabie family, who coveted it as the ultimate in picturesque ruins to complete their lavish landscaping of the adjacent Studley Royal estate.

VISIT

Open daily Feb–late Oct 10am–6pm (5pm in Feb–Mar); rest of year Sat–Thu 10am–5pm. £15 (NT and EH members free). ✗ ✆01765 608 888. www.fountainsabbey.org.uk; www.nationaltrust.org.uk.

Fountains Hall – Stone from the abbey was used to build the splendid five-storey Jacobean mansion (1598–1611). Behind the striking **façade★** with its Renaissance details, the interior is laid out to the conventional medieval plan.

Fountains Abbey – The grassy levels of Abbey Green extend to the west front of the roofless abbey church and the monastic buildings adjoining the south side. The scale and diversity of the monastic buildings suggest the varied activities of the great community of monks and lay brothers. The church's tall tower (c.1500) rises above the stately Norman nave. At the east end is the spectacular 13C **Chapel of the Nine Altars** with soaring arches and a huge Perpendicular window.

The most complete and beautiful remains are those of the buildings grouped round the cloister in accordance with the standard Cistercian plan: in the western range is the **Cellarium**, with its astounding 90m vaulted interior below the lay brothers' dormitory; in the south range is the **Great Refectory**. In the east range is the **Chapter House**, entered through three fine Norman arches

Studley Royal Water Garden – The gardens were designed to be visited starting from the Canal Gates. From 1720 until his death in 1742 John Aislabie, Chancellor of the Exchequer, devoted his vast personal fortune to create a garden at his Yorkshire estate. He remodelled the sinuous valley of the Skell into a spectacular landscape consisting of a series of formal water features and contrived views, embellished with garden buildings and flanked by woodland on the steeper slopes.

The canalised river, emerging from a dark grotto, is led past the **Moon Pond**, overlooked by a Classical **Temple of Piety**, and finally discharges into a lake over a grand cascade flanked by pavilions, known as fishing tabernacles. Along the east side of the valley is a high-level walk which passes through a twisting tunnel, past the **Gothic Tower** and the elegant **Temple of Fame** to **Anne Boleyn's Seat** and the surprise view of the east end of the abbey ruins. The **Seven Bridges Walk** follows the course of the Skell downstream from the lake, zigzagging from bank to bank. In the deer park stands **St Mary's Church**, a masterpiece of High Victorian Gothic by William Burges, on the axis of a long avenue which extends east to the

original entrance to the park from the village of **Studley Royal** and aligned on the twin towers of **Ripon cathedral**.

EXCURSIONS
Ripon★
▶ 3.7mi/6km N. Population: 16 702.
🚹 Market Place. ℰ01765 604 625.
www.discoverripon.org.
Ripon's cathedral qualifies its status as one of the smallest cities in England. This, and the large thriving market square (Thursday is the main market day) are the focus. Here, at nine o'clock every night, a horn is blown to 'set the watch', an ancient custom commemorating the responsibility of the medieval Wakeman for the safety of the citizens at night.

Ripon Cathedral★
Minster Road. Open daily 0.30am–6pm (5pm on Sun). Guided tours summer holidays (ask Guides/Welcomers in Cathedral). ♿🅿 ℰ01765 603 462. http://riponcathedral.info.
The cathedral was started in 1254 on the Saxon crypt of St Wilfrid's church (672). Pevsner called the imposing Early English west front '...the finest in England'. The medieval font stands near the west door in the south aisle. Above it are the remains of the great 14C **east** window shot out in 1643 by the Roundheads. The tiny **Saxon Crypt** (3.3m x 2.4m x 2.7m high) was built by St Wilfrid on his return from Rome. **Misericords** and exquisite **choir stalls** were carved at the end of the 15C. The **Chapel of the Holy Spirit** has a striking modern metal screen, symbolising the Pentecostal 'tongues of flame'. The **Treasury** displays silverware given to the cathedral, as well as the **Ripon Jewel**, a Saxon gold brooch set with amber and garnets.

Market Square
This is one of the largest squares (0.8ha) in the North. The **town hall**, built by Wyatt in 1801, has an Ionic portico and carries along its frieze the motto 'Except ye Lord Keep ye Cittie ye Wakeman Waketh in Vain'. The **Wake-**

man's House, a 14C two-storeyed, timber-framed house, was the home of the last incumbent, Hugh Ripley, who in 1604 became first Mayor of Ripon.

Yorkshire Law and Order Museums

Open mid-Feb–Nov daily 1–4pm (workhouse open 11am). School holidays open from 10am. Courthouse £4.50, Prison and Police £6.50, Workhouse £6.50, joint ticket £12. ℰ01765 690 799. www.riponmuseums.co.uk.

These three museums on the same theme sit in separate historic buildings in very close proximity to each other – the 1830 **Courthouse Museum** (Minster Road); the **Prison and Police Museum** (St Marygate), and the **Workhouse Museum** *(Allhallowgate)*. The Prison and Police Museum, housed in the old Ripon Liberty Prison, built 1816, contains cells, a pillory, a pair of stocks, a whipping post and an old blue police box. Saddest of all is the Workhouse, the present building dating from 1855. Together these collections provide a fascinating interwoven insight into law and order and the harsh conditions, for both felons and ordinary folk, in bygone days in this part of the world.

ஃ Lightwater Valley

❍ North Stainley, 8mi/13km N of Fountains Abbey, off the A 6108. Open Apr–Oct and Christmas for seasonal events, open from 10am, close from 4.30–6pm. Over 1m tall £20, under 1m £5. ♿🅿✕ ℰ01765 635 321. www.lightwatervalley.co.uk.

This is one of the biggest theme parks in the north of England, with over 40 rides and attractions for all ages. 'The Ultimate' is the longest roller coaster in Europe. Adjacent, but accessible without the admission fee, is **Lightwater Country Shopping Village** (open 10am–5pm; www.lightwatervalley.co.uk/shoppingvillage), a very popular complex of factory outlet **shops** and eating places, also home to a **Bird of Prey Centre** with over 50 birds of prey, plus a snake section.

The World of James Herriot

❍ 23 Kirkgate, Thirsk. 16mi/26km NE of Fountains Abbey via the A 61. Open Mar–Oct daily 10am–5pm; Nov–Feb daily 10am–4pm. £8.50. ♿🅿 ℰ01845 524 234. www.worldofjamesherriot.org.

A tour of the house and surgery gives a snapshot of life in the 1940s and reveals the dedication of Alf Wight, the vet-turned-author, who wrote under the pseudonym James Herriot. He went on to win international fame and gain the hearts of millions of viewers of the popular television series *All Creatures Great and Small*, based on his series of semi-autobiographical novels.

Newby Hall & Gardens★

❍ 7mi/11km E of Fountains Abbey. Open Apr–Sept Tue–Sun and bank holiday Mons, 11am–5.30pm (daily Jul–Aug). Access to the House is by guided tour only, booked at the Entrance Pavilion before you proceed to the House. **Tours:** Jul–Aug and all Sat–Sun and bank holidays, half hourly from 11.30am–3pm; Easter and half-term holidays (Mon–Fri), hourly noon–3pm; Apr–Jun and Sept (Mon–Fri) – noon and 2pm only. **Admission:** House and Gardens: £17 (garden only, £12). Discounts online, except House tickets; upgrade to House and Gardens and book house tour on arrival. ♿🅿✕ ℰ01423 322 583. www.newbyhall.com.

The original 17C mellow-brick mansion, designed by Sir Christopher Wren, and extended and remodelled during the 18C by John Carr and Robert Adam, is renowned for its Adam interiors, collection of Chippendale furniture, Gobelins **Tapestry Room★** and its gallery designed for a rare collection of Classical sculpture brought from Italy by William Weddell in 1765.

From the south front of the house, 10ha of award-winning **gardens**, including one of Europe's largest double herbaceous borders, descend to the River Ure. A miniature railway runs beside the river. There is also an Adventure Garden for children and a woodland walk.

Harrogate★

and around

Harrogate is a genteel little town. Its heyday as a famous 19C spa town has left a legacy of elegant buildings with fine shops and hotels, which make an excellent base for touring the Yorkshire Dales and Moors.

▶ **Population:** 75 950.
🅖 **Michelin Map:** Michelin Atlas p40 or Map 502 P 22.
🅗 **Info:** Royal Baths, Crescent Road. ☎01423 537300. www.visitharrogate.co.uk.
🅖 Both the bus and train stations are on Station Parade, in the town centre.
▶ **Location:** Harrogate is 21mi/34km west of York.
🅖🅖 **Kids:** Mother Shipton's Cave.

TOWN

The **Royal Pump Room**, built in 1842, and the **Royal Baths Assembly Rooms**, built in 1897, were the hub of this spa town at its height at the end of the 19C when some 60 000 people a year came to 'take the waters' bubbling up from 36 springs in the town centre. At the **Royal Pump Museum** (Crown Place, ☎01423 556 188; www.harrogate.gov.uk), you can taste the strongest sulphurous water in Europe (Mon–Sat at 11am, 2pm, 3pm, Sun 3pm only), wonder at the old spa treatments, discover how Harrogate became a spa town, its Victorian past and see treasures from ancient Egypt – the museum houses an internationally renowned collection of Egyptology, including a unique Anubis mask and a stunning mummy case. .

The Cyclists Touring Club of Great Britain was founded in Harrogate in 1878, and it was here that the Tour de France staged its Grand Départ in 2014.

EXCURSIONS

Harewood House★★

🅖8mi/13km S by the A 61. **House**: Open Apr–Oct daily. Gardens and grounds 10am–6pm, State Rooms, Below Stairs and Terrace Gallery 11am–3.30pm. Admission: Grounds and Below Stairs £12.50; all attractions £16.50. ♿🅿✕ ☎0113 218 1010. www.harewood.org.
Pronounced 'har-wood', this splendid pile, '...a St Petersburg palace on a Yorkshire hill', was begun in 1759 by Edwin Lascelles, and is an essay in Palladian architecture by John Carr of York; its interiors are Neoclassical, one of the greatest achievements of Robert

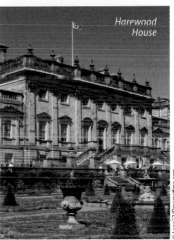

Harewood House

© Lana2/Dreamstime.com

Adam. **Thomas Chippendale**, born at nearby Otley, made the furniture and Lancelot 'Capability' Brown developed the grounds.

The **Entrance Hall** is the only room to retain its original form, complete with fine plaster-work ceiling. Old Master paintings are hung throughout; there is much rare Chinese porcelain, as well as Sèvres pieces collected at the beginning of the 19C. The **Gallery★** is perhaps the pinnacle of Adam's work at Harewood. The **Bird Garden** with over 90 species of threatened and exotic birds housed in sympathetic environments is one of England's most important avian collections. Family-friendly additions include a huge outdoor adventure playground and indoor play areas.

Knaresborough

▶2mi/3km E of Harrogate on the A 59. This small market town is set on the north bank of the River Nidd. **Knaresborough Castle** (Castle Yard; open Apr–mid-Sept daily 11am–4pm (5pm during Aug); £3.50; **P** (charge); ☎01423 556 188; www.harrogate.gov.uk/museums), now in ruins, was started in about 1130. After the murder of Thomas à Becket in Canterbury cathedral in December 1170, the four killers took refuge here. In addition to its underground sallyport it has a rare surviving Tudor courtroom, now a museum.

Beside the river is **Mother Shipton's Cave** ▲▲ (High Bridge; open Apr–Oct daily 10am–4.30pm (5.30pm during summer holidays); £7, child (3–15) £5; **P** (£2); ✕; ☎01423 864 600; www.mothershiptonscave.com), where Mother Shipton, England's most famous prophetess (b. c.1488) was reputed to have lived and made her predictions in poetry form. The grounds include the **Petrifying Well**, a geological phenomenon whose cascading waters seem to turn items into stone. In fact they are covering it with a stalactite deposit. It is said to be England's oldest visitor attraction, first opening its gates in 1630.

York★★★

and around

York first came to prominence as a Roman capital, later as capital of eastern England under the Danes, then as a wool trade hub. York is marked by many elegant Georgian buildings that reflect the wealth of those moving from the North into what had become an important centre of social and cultural life. It is the survival of these and many much older buildings that draws hundreds of thousands of visitors here every year and has established the city as the tourist capital of northeastern England. It is famous for its minster, its wonderful railway museum and its many ghost walks.

A BIT OF HISTORY

In 71, the Roman Ninth Legion built a fortress, **Eboracum**, later capital of the northern province, and here in 306 Constantine the Great was proclaimed emperor. After the departure of the Romans the Anglo-Saxons made **Eoforwic** the capital of their Kingdom of Northumbria. In 866, the Vikings captured the city and made it

▶ **Population:** 200 018.
◔ **Michelin Map:** Michelin Atlas p40 or Map 502 Q 22.
🛈 **Info:** 1 Museum Street. ☎01904 55 00 99. www.visityork.org.
🚃 The train station (Manchester Oxford Road, 1h22; London Kings Cross, 2h) is just outside the city walls. Buses call in the vicinity. Most attractions are within the old walls, easily explored on foot. Try a York City Sightseeing hop-on open-top bus tour (☎01904 633 990; www.city-sightseeing.com; from £13).
▶ **Location:** 84mi/135km south of Newcastle-upon-Tyne; 25mi/40km northeast of Leeds.
🚃 **Don't Miss:** The stained glass in York Minster; National Railway Museum; The Shambles; Castle Howard.
🕐 **Timing:** Two–three days.
▲▲ **Kids:** National Railway Museum; Jorvik; DIG, York Castle Museum.

York Minster

Jorvik, one of their chief trading bases. The prosperity of medieval York, a city of 10,000 people and 40 churches, was based on wool. York was once the richest city in the country after London. With the decline of the wool trade after the Wars of the Roses (1453–87) and following the Dissolution of the Monasteries (16C) the city's prosperity waned.

YORK MINSTER★★★

Open daily 9am (Sun 12.45pm)–5pm (last entry); Undercroft Mon–Sat 10am–5pm, Sun 1–5pm. All areas £15; Minster only £10. Guided tours Mon–Sat hourly 10am–3pm (free). &✕ ℘01904 557 200. www.yorkminster.org.

The minster is the largest Gothic church north of the Alps (163m long; 76m wide across the transepts; 27m from floor to vault; 60m to the tops of the towers). The nave, built 1291–1350, is in Decorated style; the transepts of the mid-13C are the oldest visible parts of the present building.

The **Chapter House★★**, octagonal with a magnificent wooden vaulted ceiling, is late-13C. The late-15C **Choir Screen★★** is by William Hyndeley. Its central doorway is flanked by statues of English kings from William the Conqueror onwards. The finest monument in the minster is the **tomb** (1) of the man who began the present building, **Archbishop Walter de Gray**.

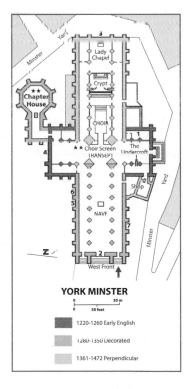

YORK MINSTER

0 _____ 30 m
0 _____ 50 feet

1220-1260 Early English
1280-1350 Decorated
1361-1472 Perpendicular

Minster Stained Glass★★★

The minster contains the largest single collection of medieval stained glass to have survived in England. The **West Window** (2) was painted in 1339 by Master Robert. It was the largest in the

461

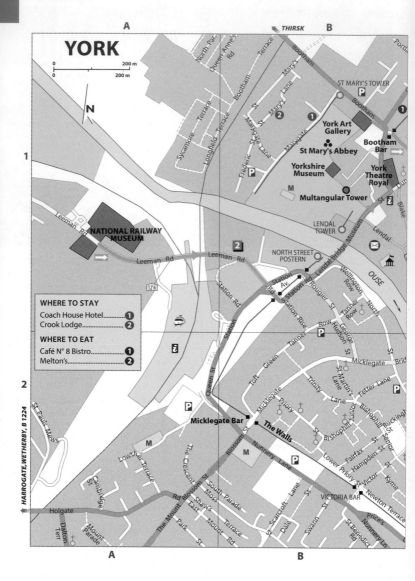

YORK

200 m

N

ST MARY'S TOWER

York Art Gallery

St Mary's Abbey

Bootham Bar

Yorkshire Museum

York Theatre Royal

Multangular Tower

LENDAL TOWER

NATIONAL RAILWAY MUSEUM

NORTH STREET POSTERN

WHERE TO STAY
Coach House Hotel..............❶
Crook Lodge........................❷

WHERE TO EAT
Café N° 8 Bistro..................❶
Melton's..............................❷

Micklegate Bar

The Walls

VICTORIA BAR

HARROGATE, WETHERBY, B 1224

THIRSK

OUSE

minster at the time but was surpassed by the **East Window** (3) in the Lady Chapel, painted by John Thornton of Coventry 1405–08. It is the largest expanse of medieval glass in the country and revitalised the York school of glass painting. The **Five Sisters Window** (4), lancets of grisaille glass from c.1250, is the oldest window still in its original place in the minster.

The **Pilgrimage Window** (5), c.1312, shows grotesques, a monkey's funeral

and scenes of hunting. Next to it is the **Bellfounders Window** (6), given by Richard Tunnoc, buried in the minster in 1330. He is depicted presenting his window to the archbishop, among scenes of casting and tuning a bell. The **Jesse Window** (7), depicting Jesus' family tree, dates from 1310.

An insight behind the scenes of maintaining and restoring the cathedral's windows is provided in the **Bedern Glaziers' Studio** (guided tour only, ask

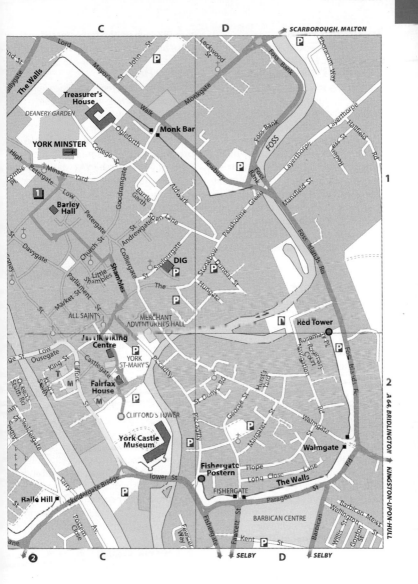

on arrival; &; &01904 557228, www. yorkglazierstrust.org), built in the 13C as the chapel of the College of Vicars Choral. This is now the workshop for the **York Minster Glaziers**, the team of craftspeople who are responsible for the preservation and conservation of the stained glass and go about their delicate work in full view of the public. Climbing the 275 steps to the top of the minster's central **tower** is an exhilarating experience. En-route you pass the medieval pinnacles and gargoyles and look over its rooftops. At the top is the best view in town of York's ancient streets.

Easier on the legs is the Cathedral's latest attraction, **Revealing York Minster.** This is a network of interactive galleries, housed in the **Undercroft** and Treasury, which tells the colourful story of York Minster, from the lives of the Roman garrison through to the 21C.

Treasurer's House

Minster Yard. Open daily mid-Feb–Oct
11am–4.30pm. £7.70. Ghost tours
of cellar daily £3 (also applies to NT
members). &X Ø01904 624 247.
www.nationaltrust.org.uk.

Rebuilt in the 17C and 18C, this fascinating property, renowned for its ghosts,
features a magnificent series of rooms
with furniture and pictures from many
periods. The **Great Hall** has had its false
ceiling removed, and has an unusual
staircase c.1700. The early 18C ceiling in
the **Dining Room** has decorated beams
and panels, and a fascinating collection
of 18C drinking vessels illustrates the
skill and ingenuity of the glass-maker.

WALLED TOWN

The City Walls★★

The walls (3mi/5km) embrace virtually the whole of medieval York. The
Multangular Tower, the western corner of the Roman fort, still stands in
the Yorkshire Museum gardens (*see
p465*). The 13C walls follow the course
of the Roman wall to the north of the
minster and are built atop the earthen
bank raised by the Anglo-Danish kings.
Where roads entered the city through
the earthen bank the Normans built
fortified gateways, now known as
'bars'. **Bootham Bar** is on the site of
the Roman gateway. The walls lead
around the Deanery garden to **Monk
Bar** and on to Aldgate; here a swampy
area and the River Foss constituted
the defences. Brick-built walls, c.1490,
run from **Red Tower**, pass **Walmgate**
around the south of York Castle to **Fishergate Postern**, built in 1505 on what
was then the riverbank. Here York castle
took up the defences.

Beyond Skeldergate Bridge and **Baile
Hill**, the walls resume to **Micklegate
Bar**, the traditional point of entry of
the monarch into York, and where the
severed heads of traitors were exposed
after execution. This is now a **museum**
(open daily Feb–Oct 10am–3pm; £3;
Ø01904 634 436, www.micklegatebar.
com). From here the walls turn northeast and lead to the North Street Pos-

tern (BY), where the ferry crossed the
Ouse before Lendal Bridge was built.

Barley Hall

2 Coffee Yard, off Stonegate. Open Apr–
Oct 10am–5pm; Nov–Mar 10am–4pm.
Closed 24–26 Dec. £6. & Ø01904 615
505. www.barleyhall.org.uk.

The oldest parts of this classic picturesque timber-framed hall, magnificently restored by **YAT**, date from
c.1360, when it was built as the York
townhouse of Nostell Priory (*see
Leeds, p447*). In the 15C it became the
home of William Snawsell goldsmith
and Lord Mayor of York.

The Shambles★

This is the most visited of the many
picturesque ancient streets of the
city, with overhanging timber-framed
houses. See also nearby **Pavement**, the
first street in medieval York to be paved.

≗ DIG

St Saviour's Church, St Saviourgate.
Open daily 10am–5pm. Tours are timed,
so book ahead at peak periods. Closed
24–26 Dec. £6.50, child (5–16), £6. &
Ø01904 615 505. http://digyork.com.

At this family-friendly simulated excavation site, a tour by a qualified archaeologist introduces you to excavation pits
filled with Roman, Viking, medieval and
Victorian finds; visitors then dig up clues
that show how people lived in these
times, with costumed staff (during
holiday periods) there to lend a hand.

≗ Jorvik Viking Centre★

15–17 Coppergate. Open Apr–Oct
10am–5pm; Nov–Mar 10am–4pm.
£10.25, child (5–16), £7.25.
Ø01904 615 505.
www.jorvik-viking-centre.co.uk.

During building work in Coppergate in
the late-1970s, ancient remains were
found. A major six-year-long archaeological project, known as the **Coppergate Dig**, went on to make the most
remarkable and revolutionary discoveries concerning Viking-age York, or
Jorvik. You can see an interpretation
of this dig beneath the **Discover Cop-**

pergate glass-floored gallery, installed in 2010. This includes 1 000-year-old timbers that once formed the wall of a Viking house, and hundreds of the most important objects discovered during the Coppergate excavations. To help interpret what otherwise may be a dry subject are seven lively state-of-the-art animatronics who interact with visitors in Old Norse (happily, also translated into English!). You then journey back into Jorvik, complete with sights, sounds and smells as they might have been on an October day in 948.

YAT (York Archaeological Trust), the team behind Jorvik, stage the **Jorvik Viking Festival** each February, with longship races, feasting and fireworks, and in August there is a **Medieval Festival** across town.

Until 2020, Jorvik is displaying Viking treasures loaned from the British Museum, including items from the Halton Moor Hoard, coins of Canute as king of both England and Denmark, and weaponry found near Windsor (from 10am daily).

Fairfax House★

Castlegate. Open early-Feb–Dec: Mon by guided tour only at 11am and 2pm; Tue–Sat and bank holiday Mons 10am–5pm; Sun 11am–4pm. Closed 24–26 Dec. £7.50. ✆01904 655 543. www.fairfaxhouse.co.uk.

Perhaps the finest Georgian town house in England, Fairfax House was built in 1755. It houses a collection of Georgian furniture, paintings, clocks and porcelain, and there are displays of eating and dining in 18C England.

York Castle Museum★

Open daily 9.30am–5pm. Closed 1 Jan, 25–26 Dec. £10, child under 16 free with paying adult. ✆01904 687 687. www.yorkcastlemuseum.org.uk.

In what was the **Debtors Prison** and the **Female Prison**, two striking buildings from 1705 and 1777 respectively, is now a superb museum of everyday life. The highlight is Kirkgate, a re-created **Victorian Street**, which combines real shop fittings and stock, with sound and light effects which evoke the period atmosphere.

There are costumes, period rooms, pubs and shops and as part of the entertaining new **York Castle Prison** exhibition area, the actual cell in which legendary highwayman Dick Turpin was held before execution in 1739 (you'll even get to see the virtual Turpin!). However, not all exhibits or collections are continuously available because of display rotation, which makes every visit a new surprise!

OUTSIDE THE WALLS

Immediately outside the line of the old walls, west of the minster next to the River Ouse, is **Museum Gardens**, home to the ruins of **St Mary's Abbey** and the 14C **Hospitium**. The latter is one of the oldest surviving half-timbered buildings in York, originally a guesthouse for the abbey. By contrast, a Classical 19C building houses the **Yorkshire Museum** (open daily 10am–5pm; closed 1 Jan, 25–26 Dec; £6.81; ✆01904 687 687; www.yorkshiremuseum.org.uk), which displays some of the city's finest Roman, Viking and medieval treasures.

York Art Gallery

Exhibition Square. Open daily 10am–5pm. £6.81, child under 16 free with paying adult. ✆01904 687 687. www.yorkartgallery.org.uk.

This extensive collection of paintings spans over 600 years and ranges from 14C Italian panels and 17C Dutch masterpieces to Victorian narrative paintings and 20C works by Lowry and Hockney. When it reopens in 2015 it will also house a British Studio Ceramics centre.

National Railway Museum★★★

Open daily 10am–6pm. Closed 24–26 Dec. 🅿 (charge). ✆08448 153 139. www.nrm.org.uk.

This magnificent collection, the largest railway museum in the world, presents the history of the railways in the country of their invention.

© Y. Kanazawa/MICHELIN

National Railway Museum

The **Great Hall**, a wonderfully spacious former locomotive shed, houses an array of locomotives from clunky early-19C machines to the sleek super-trains of the 21C.

The museum's brief extends beyond the glamour of machines like these, to the whole technology and culture of the railway, demonstrated by an extraordinarily rich and varied array of other related objects. The **South Hall** re-creates the atmosphere of a mid-20C mainline station, allowing close inspection of engine cabs, the interiors of coaches, both primitive and luxurious, dining and sleeping cars, goods wagons and road vehicles. Outside are more treasures undergoing or awaiting restoration, plus a mini ride-on railway.

EXCURSION
Castle Howard★★★

▶ 15mi/24km NE via the A 64.
Open: House: daily 10.30am–4pm (last entry); Grounds 10am–dusk; shops and cafés, open daily 10am–4pm/dusk.
£18.95. ♿🅿✕ ✆01653 648 333.
www.castlehoward.co.uk.

Remarkably Castle Howard, **Sir John Vanbrugh**'s tour de force, was the first building he had ever designed.

The landscaping of the surrounding **park★★★** is one of the most grandiose

landscaping projects ever; it consists of a series of compositions focused on some of the most ambitious and beautiful garden structures ever built, notably the **Temple of the Four Winds**, and, crowning a distant rise, a colossal colonnaded **Mausoleum** by Hawksmoor. The woodland garden presents rare trees, shrubs, rhododendrons and azaleas. There is also an adventure playground, and boat trips on the Great Lake.

The striking entrance to the house, topped by a painted and gilded dome (24m), is familiar to many as the castle was used as the principal location for the TV series *Brideshead Revisited*.

The **statuary** in the **Grand Entrance** is remarkable, particularly the **altar** from the Temple of Delphi.

The heart of the house is the **Great Hall**, which rises through two storeys into the painted dome. In the **Long Gallery** and its **Octagon** are pictures by Lely, Kneller and Van Dyck and two **Holbeins** – the portrait of **Henry VIII** shows a stricken monarch, painted in 1542, just after the execution of Catherine Howard. The magnificent stained-glass windows in the **Chapel** are by the 19C artist Sir Edward Burne-Jones. The **Stable Court** presents period costume (17C on).

East Yorkshire★

This is not only the least visited part of Yorkshire, but one of the least visited parts of the country by any domestic or foreign tourists. Don't let that deter you, however, as it's worth the detour just for Beverley Minster and The Deep at Hull.

HULL

Population: 260 200.

UK City of Culture in 2017, Kingston-upon-Hull (to give it its full name) was once an important centre for fishing – particularly for whaling – and is still a major seaport. Its famous modern landmark is the **Humber Bridge**, built 1972 81, as the longest single-span suspension bridge in the world, measuring 1 410m.

In the city centre on Queen Victoria Square is the **Hull Maritime Museum** (open Mon–Wed, Fri–Sat 10am–5pm, Thu 10am–7 30pm, Sun 11am–4.30pm; closed Good Fri, 1 Jan, 24–28 Dec; &; ℘01482 300 300; www.hullcc.gov.uk/museums), covering over seven centuries of maritime heritage with models, artefacts and paintings. Next door, the Ferens Art Gallery (same times as the Maritime Museum) traditionally holds the city art collection, ranging from European Old Masters to contemporary art, including works by such artists as Hals, Canaletto, David Hockney and Henry Moore.

A short walk away is the **old town**, retaining some of the narrow cobbled lanes and ancient inns of medieval and 17C Hull. On the High Street is the **Museums Quarter** with three adjacent collections (details as Maritime Museum. The **Wilberforce House Museum** commemorates the life and work of William Wilberforce (1758–1833), an instrumental player in the abolition of slavery. The highly popular **Streetlife Museum** shows two centuries of transport history and a re-creation of a 1940s high street. The **Hull & East Riding Museum** of archaeology depicts an Iron Age village, a Roman bathhouse with fine mosaics, and a Viking treasure hoard.

Close by is **The Deep**★★ 👥 (open daily 10am–6pm; closed 24–25 Dec; £12.50, child £10.50 (online discounts), &✕🅿£3; ℘01482 381 000, www.thedeep.co.uk). In a stunning building on the Humber estuary, designed by Sir Terry Farrell, this is one of the most spectacular aquaria in Europe, home to over 3 500 fish and Europe's deepest viewing tunnel. A visit culminates in a ride in the world's only underwater lift, face to face with sharks and rays.

BURTON CONSTABLE★

Skirlaugh Grounds 16mi/26km E. Open: Hall: Easter–Oct Sat–Thu 11am–5pm (daily in Jul–Aug); Grounds: mid-Mar 20 Dec daily 11am–5pm. £10.50, grounds and stables only £5.75. &🅿✕ ℘01964 562 400. www.burtonconstable.com.

The house was built c.1600 with a handsome **east front**, brick with mullion windows and projecting wings. The **Entrance Hall**, dates from 1760. In the **Muniment Room**, the remodelling of the house in Georgian times can be followed. The **Long Gallery**, of grand proportions and decoration, contains many family portraits.

BEVERLEY★

Georgian façades hide the ancient timber buildings of a town which in 1377 already boasted one of England's finest churches, a sizeable population of some 5 000 inhabitants, and which was the principal town of the area.

Flamborough Head

Beverley Minster★★

Open Sun all year noon–5pm; Apr–Oct Mon–Fri 9am–5.30pm' Nov–Mar Mon–Fri 9am–4pm. **Tours:** Ground floor: Wed 11.30am, £5; Roof: Sat 11am £10. &. ℘01482 868 540. www.beverleyminster.org.uk.

The present minster was begun c.1220 and at 101m long is of cathedral-like proportions. The **Great East Window**, a Perpendicular nine-lighted window containing all the fragments of medieval glass the minster once possessed, was bequeathed in 1416.

The **Percy Tomb** (1340–49) and its canopy, with angels, symbolic beasts and leaf carvings, is the most splendid of funerary monuments from the Decorated period. It probably commemorates Lady Eleanor Percy, who died in 1328. The early-16C **misericords** in the choir stalls are some of the finest in Britain.

St Mary's church★

Open Mon–Fri 11am–3pm, Sat 10am–3pm, Sun 7.30am–noon, 6–7.30pm. Donation requested. ℘01482 869 137. http://stmarysbeverley.org.

Founded c.1120, St Mary's was adopted by the wealthy trade guilds. The tiny (11m x 5.5m) Chapel of St Michael with its ingenious 'telescopic' **spiral staircase** is contemporary with the Percy Tomb in the Minster. The Perpendicular west front is comparable with King's

College Chapel in Cambridge. By 1524 the addition of the tower completed one of the finest parish churches in the north of England.Look for the extensive collection of **carvings of medieval musical instruments** shared between the minster and St Mary's at Beverley. All told there are 140, on pew ends, choir stalls, ceiling bosses and in the south porch. The chancel ceiling, painted in 1445, with its pictorial record of 40 English kings, is unique. Adorning the choir stalls are 23 **misericords** with extraordinary carvings of animals and men, including a 'Pilgrim Rabbit' carved c.1325.

THE COAST

Bridlington and **Filey** are the region's two resorts. The former is a typical British seaside family resort, albeit with a pleasant Georgian old town.

Filey is much quieter, retaining vestiges of its Edwardian and Victorian heyday. Both resorts have excellent sandy beaches, even if they rarely have the weather to match.

Flamborough Head★

A lighthouse marks the headland (66m), from which there are spectacular sea and coast **views**.

The Cleveland Way coastal footpath follows outstanding chalk-cliff scenery northwards near **Bempton** the cliffs soar to 130m.

North York Moors★★

The beauty of this expanse of open moorland lies in its wildness. The heather-covered high ground stretches southeast from industrial Middlesbrough to Whitby and Scarborough on the coast and to Pickering and Helmsley in the south. Much of the land is embraced by the **North York Moors National Park**.

🄸 **Info:** The Old Vicarage, Bondgate, Helmsley. ℘01439 772 700. www.northyorkmoors.org.uk.

😊 **Don't Miss:** Rievaulx Abbey; a ride on the North Yorkshire Moors Railway.

👪 **Kids:** The NYMR, Go Ape.

🐾 WALKING

Four regional walking routes have been designed by the National Park Authority with a short holiday/long weekend in mind, and are an easy and enjoyable way to explore the North York Moors National Park. These are the **Esk Valley Walk**, the **Tabular Hills Walk**, the **Hambleton Hillside Mosaic Walk** and the **Newtondale Horse Trail**. These avoid roads wherever possible and link with local services such as bus routes. Maps and specialist guidebooks are available from the park shop or online. You don't have to complete any of these, just dip in and out for as little or as long as you wish. Serious walkers may also like to consider the **Cleveland Way National Trail** (www.nationaltrail.co.uk/clevelandway) and the Yorkshire bit of the **North Sea Trail**.

HELMSLEY AREA

The southern gateway to the North York Moors, **Helmsley** is an attractive village boasting the impressive 12C–13C ruins of **Helmsley Castle** (open Apr–Sept daily 10am–6pm, Oct 10am–5pm, Nov–Mar Sat–Sun 10am–4pm (Feb half-term holidays open daily); £6.20; ♿🅿(charge); ℘01439 770 442; www.english-heritage.org.uk). Its visitor centre tells the story of how it evolved over the centuries, from a mighty medieval fortress to a luxurious Tudor mansion, to a Civil War stronghold and a romantic Victorian ruin. Below the castle, **Helmsley Walled Garden** (open Apr–Oct daily 10am–5pm; £7.50; ♿🅿✗; ℘01439 771

427; www.helmsleywalledgarden.org.uk), which dates from 1759, is a restored walled garden, conserving old, rare and endangered garden plants. It includes fruit trees, herbaceous borders, herb and ornamental gardens, glasshouses, ponds and fountains.

Neighbouring **Duncombe Park** (open: Parklands, Nature Reserve and Walks: Feb–24 Dec daily 10.30am–5pm; Gardens: mid-Apr–Aug Sun–Fri 10.30am–5pm; ♿🅿✗; ℘01439 770 213; www.duncombe park.com), was built as the seat of the Feversham family in 1713. The Classical landscaped grounds include Doric and Ionic temples, and there is a nature reserve where most of the trees are over 250 years old. Duncombe Park is also home to the **International Centre for Birds of Prey** (open daily Feb–24 Dec 10am–5.30pm/dusk; £9, ℘0844/ 422 035, www.ncbp.co.uk), boasting the largest collection of raptors in the north of England, with three flying demonstrations each day.

On the B 1257, 3mi/5km northwest of Helmsley, lie the majestic ruins of **Rievaulx Abbey★★** (open Apr–Sept daily 10am–6pm, Oct daily 10am–5pm, Nov–Mar Sat–Sun/Feb half-term wk daily 10am–4pm; £8.50; 🅿✗; ℘01439 798 228; www.english-heritage.org.uk), one of the most complete, and atmospheric, of England's abbey ruins, and one of the most popular visitor attractions in the North. Pronounced 'ree-voh', it was the first major monastery built by the Cistercians, founded c.1132 and completed in the late-12C. The ruins – infirmary, chapel, kitchens and a warming house – give an idea of the community's work and show how Rievaulx evolved into one of Britain's wealthiest monasteries. For many the abbey café and beautiful grounds are worth the trip alone.

Adjacent, but with no access from the abbey grounds, is **Rievaulx Terrace** (open daily mid-Feb–Oct 11am–5pm (Oct 4pm); £5.40; ☎01439 798 340, 01439 748 283 (winter); www.nationaltrust.org.uk), one of Yorkshire's finest 18C landscape gardens, featuring two Classical Georgian temples and a long curving grass terrace with fine views.

Some 12mi/19km east, sheep nibble the grass verges in the charming village of **Hutton-le-Hole**, which gets very busy with summer visitors. The **Ryedale Folk Museum** (open mid-Feb–Mar and Oct–early Dec daily 10am–4pm; Apr–Sept 10am–5pm; £7.50; ♿; ☎01751 417 367; www.ryedalefolkmuseum.co.uk) is a fascinating collection of local bygones housed in over 20 reconstructed buildings including a school classroom, a Witches' Hovel and an Iron Age dwelling made of mud, horse hair, wood and straw.

Some 4mi/6km northeast of the village, at the bottom of a very steep (1:3) slope, lie the fragmentary ruins of 12C **Rosedale Abbey**. From here there is a panoramic **view★** across the moors.

PICKERING AREA

The busy market town of Pickering, built on a limestone cliff at the southern edge of the national park, is the regional centre and 'Gateway to the Moors'.

High on a strategic site just north lie the ruins of **Pickering Castle** (open Apr–Sept daily 10am–6pm; Oct daily 10am–5pm; £4.90; ☎01751 474 989, www.english-heritage.org.uk). This motte-and-bailey castle was a favourite hunting lodge of English kings until the 15C.

In town, don't miss the 15C parish **Church of St Peter and St Paul** (Birdgate; www.pickeringchurch.com), famous for its vivid (restored) 15C frescoes. A walk along Birdgate, into Bridge Street, is the **Beck Isle Museum** (open mid-Feb-Nov 10am–5pm (Feb–Mar and Oct–Nov 4pm); £6.50; ☎01751 473 653, www.beck-islemuseum.org.uk), which records local rural life over the last two centuries.

Just around the corner from the museum is Pickering's main attraction, the lovingly preserved **North Yorkshire Moors Railway** ♨♨ (for fares and schedule, visit website; on certain days during the summer trains also run along a branch line the full length of the Esk valley for 24mi/39km. ☎01751 472 508, www.nymr.co.uk). Running for 18mi/29km between Pickering and Whitby, riding the line takes you back some 50 years to the romantic era of steam, complete with cosy wood-panelled carriages, beautifully tended rural stations and smartly uniformed staff. The train stops at **Levisham**, **Newton Dale**, **Goathland** and **Grosmont** before terminating beside the sea at **Whitby** (♨see opposite). The full journey takes 95 minutes but with a Day Rover ticket you're free to break your journey at no extra cost. A popular jumping-off point is the attractive village of **Goathland**. It was popularised as 'Aidensfield' in the BBC TV series *Heartbeat*, and the station was also the Hogsmeade stop in *Harry Potter* films. It does, however, boast the refurbished **Warehouse Tea Room** with authentic furniture and artefacts. From Goathland you can walk the signposted **Rail Trail** (3.5mi/5.6km) to **Grosmont**; it runs along the route of George Stephenson's original railway line of 1836.

Grosmont, restored to the British Railways' style of the 1960s, is the main depot for the NYMR and its gleaming locomotives can be seen at close quarters in the **Engine Sheds**.

The much-photographed village of **Thornton-le-Dale** lies 2mi/3km east of Pickering and from here minor roads head into the **Dalby Forest** (Mar–Oct £8 until 4pm, then £4, Nov–Feb £4 all day).

In Low Dalby is the Dalby Forest Visitor Centre (♿; ✗; ☎01751 460 295; www.forestry.gov.uk/dalbyforest), where you can pick up information, maps and booklets for various walking and cycling trails (bike hire available).

Near Low Dalby is the **Go Ape** ♨♨ treetop adventure (☎0333 920 6657; http://goape.co.uk).

North Yorkshire Coast

Given the nature of the weather here, it seems incongruous that this is where the first seaside resort in Britain sprang up; but Scarborough claims that very honour, with its entrepreneurial Victorian residents the first to successfully sell the benefits – proven or otherwise – of seaside breezes, sandy beaches and natural spa waters, well before other seaside towns. Yorkshire's other coastal towns soon followed suit.

Michelin Map: Michelin Atlas p47 or Map 502 S 21.

Info: ℊ01723 383 636. www.discoveryorkshirecoast.com.

SCARBOROUGH

1mi/66km NE of York. Population: 61 749.
Scarborough reached its fashionable zenith in the late 19C/early 20C, and despite, or perhaps lack of, recent developments, remains a fine place to savour the English Victorian seaside.

Along its **seafront** are promenades, cliff railways, bridges spanning deep denes, pavilions, cafés, chalets, pretty little shelters and the great bulk of the refurbished **Spa** (the waters were declared unfit to drink in the 1930s), now an entertainment and conference centre.

The elegant early-19C **Crescent** is home to **Scarborough Art Gallery**, (open Tue–Sun and bank holiday Mons 10am–5pm; £3; ℊ01723 374 753, http://scarboroughartgallery.co.uk). Just off North Bay Beach is **Scarborough Sea Life Sanctuary** (Scalby Mills Road; open daily 10am–4pm; from £9 online in advance; ℊ01723 373 414; www.visitsealife.com), an underwater safari plus a section on locally rescued animals.

ROBIN HOOD'S BAY★

16mi/26km north on the A 171, then a minor road to the right (signposted).
The little village in this picturesque bay was once the haunt of smugglers. It is the finishing (or starting) point of the hugely popular Coast-to-Coast Walk, linking this bay with St Bees Head in western Cumbria.

WHITBY

47mi/76km NE of York.
Population: 13 213. ℊ01723 383 636.
Once a centre for shipbuilding and whaling, Whitby is now a fishing port and holiday resort at the mouth of the River Esk. The east side is overlooked by the atmospheric abbey ruins on the headland; the first few chapters of **Bram Stoker**'s *Dracula* are set here and over the years a veritable industry in ghosts, vampires and Gothic related aspects has grown up in Whitby.

Whitby Abbey★

Open. Apr–Sept daily 10am–6pm; Oct daily 10am–5pm; Nov–Mar Sat–Sun 10am–4pm (Feb half-term holidays, daily). £7.60. ℊ01947 603 568. www.english-heritage.org.uk.

in 657, **St Hilda**, Abbess of Hartlepool, founded the first abbey and earned Whitby an outstanding reputation as a holy place. In 867, however, it was sacked by the Danes. Two centuries later it was re-founded by one of William the Conqueror's knights, Reinfrid, though the present ruins belong to a second rebuilding that took place between 1220 and 1320. It was finally suppressed by Henry VIII in 1539.

Captain Cook Memorial Museum

Grape Lane. Open mid-Feb–Mar 11am–3pm, Apr–early Nov 9.45–5pm. £5.70. ℊ01947 601 900. www.cookmuseumwhitby.co.uk.
The late-17C house of shipowner John Walker, where James Cook served as an apprentice, is now a museum celebrating the years Cook spent in Whitby and his achievements as one of the world's greatest navigators. The tour ends in the attic where Cook had his quarters.

ADDRESSES

🏠 STAY

SHEFFIELD

🛏🍴 **Quarry House** – Rivelin Valley Road, Rivelin Glen Quarry. ☏0114 234 0382. www.quarryhouse.org.uk. 3 rooms. This handsome sturdy stone country house, formerly the quarry master's home, is 10mi/16km south of Sheffield (also convenient for the Peak District). It has a bohemian air.

LEEDS

🛏🛏🍴🍴 **Radisson Blu (The Light) No 1 The Light** – The Headrow, ☏0113 236 6000, www.radissonblu.com/en. Art Deco style is given a modern twist in this splendid listed building in the centre of town. Rooms and public areas are contemporary, minimalist and very fashionable.

YORKSHIRE DALES

🛏🍴 **Beck Hall** – Malham. ☏01729 830 729. www.beckhallmalham.com. 18 rooms. Ancient and modern rooms in this rambling, rustic early-18C building by the river. Period features include four-posters, carved antique beds, mullion windows and panelling. Dog friendly.

🛏🍴 **Stow House Hotel** – Aysgarth, Leyburn. ☏01969 663 635, www.stowhouse.co.uk. 9 rooms. Set apart, over-looking lawns (croquet in summer) and with wonderful open views over Wensleydale, this comfortable characterful Victorian mansion is just five minutes' walk from Aysgarth Falls.

🛏🛏🍴 **Herriots Hotel** – Broughton Road, Skipton. ☏01756 792 781. www.herriotsforleisure.co.uk. This Victorian listed building is tastefully furnished. Special rooms include four-poster and spa rooms; some have French doors onto the canal. Rhubarb Modern British restaurant (🛏🍴🍴) on site.

🛏🍴–🛏🛏🍴 **Ripon Spa Hotel** – Park Street. ☏0800 158 5455. www.riponspa.com. 40 rooms. A five-minute walk from the cathedral, this elegant building sits in beautiful grounds with croquet lawns and terraces (though no spa!). Modern and traditional rooms.

🛏🛏🍴 **Devonshire Arms Hotel and Spa** – Bolton Abbey Estate, Skipton. ☏01756 710 441. http://thedevonshirearms.co.uk. Close by the River Wharfe, this luxurious hotel and spa is perfect as a base for a few days in and around Wharfedale. The rooms are comfortable and sumptuous, and the Burlington Restaurant provides a touch of fine-dining, set against the more relaxed atmosphere of the adjacent brasserie.

HARROGATE

🛏🍴 **The Bijou** – 17 Ripon Road. ☏07897 576 476. www.thebijou.co.uk. 10 rooms. Boutique-style accommodation in a bijou Victorian villa in the fashionable neighbourhood of Harrogate's Duchy Estate, a 5-minute walk from the centre.

YORK

🛏🍴 **Coach House Hotel** – Marygate, Bootham. ☏01904 652 780. 14 rooms. This 300-year-old stone walled oak-beamed hotel was once a coach-builder's house. It Is only 275m from the minster in a quiet road and has parking facilities. Full bar with beer on tap.

🛏🍴 **Crook Lodge** – 26 St Mary's, Bootham. ☏01904 655 614. www.crooklodge.co.uk. Stylish and pretty de-luxe bedrooms in an attractive Victorian house enjoying a quiet city centre location; private parking.

NORTH YORK MOORS

🛏🍴 **Cawthorne House** – 42 Eastgate, Pickering. ☏01751 477 364. www.cawthornehouse.com. 5 rooms. This handsome sturdy stone house, with a lovely terrace garden, is a 5-min walk from the town centre. Bedrooms are stylish, with a mixed traditional and modern feel. Very comfortable.

🛏🍴 **No 54** – 54 Bondgate, Helmsley. ☏01439 771 533. 3 rooms. This charming highly popular B&B, within walking distance of the centre, was built in the early-19C. It has cosy bedrooms, York flagstone floors, real fires in winter, superb food and a lovely courtyard garden for the summer.

🛏🛏🍴 **The Black Swan** – Market Place, Helmsley. ☏01439 634065. The Black Swan – an interesting mélange of architectural styles – has stood on the edge of the North York Moors for years. A sometime coaching inn, but now a boutique hotel, this stylish residence is well worth seeking out. A touch of fine dining in the integral Gallery Restaurant (👍 *see below*).

NORTH YORKSHIRE COAST

◔🛏 **Heathfield Guest House** – 22 Prospect Hill, Whitby. ℘01947 605 407. www.bedandbreakfast-whitby.co.uk. 3 rooms. Simple but stylish acclaimed small family-run B&B guesthouse a short walk from the town centre.

◔🛏🛏 **Royal Hotel** – St Nicholas Street, Scarborough. ℘01723 364 333. www. britanniahotels.com. 118 rooms. This classic grand old English seaside hotel (built 1830) overlooking South Bay has a spa and wellness facilities.

🍴/EAT

SHEFFIELD

◔🛏🛏 **Rafters** – 220 Oakbrook Road. ℘0114 230 4819. www.raftersrestaurant. co.uk. Situated in a leafy suburb 10 minutes from the centre, Rafters has been setting the standard for local and regional restaurants for many years. Special menus mean that this otherwise exclusive gastronomic experience is open to most wallets.

LEEDS

◔🛏🛏 **Fourth Floor Café and Bar** – Cross Arcade. ℘0113 204 8000. www. harveynichols.com. This chic space on the top floor of Harvey Nichols, with a spectacular view over the rooftops, is spacious, light and airy. By night expect subdued lighting and twinkling candles. Excellent Modern British cuisine.

BRADFORD

Bradford is renowned for the quality of its Indian and Pakistani restaurants.

◔ **Karachi** – 15-17 Neal Street, Bradford. ℘01274 732 015. A short walk from the city centre, the no-frills Karachi is one of the oldest restaurants from the Indian continent in town, and serves some unusual dishes Good value.

YORKSHIRE DALES

◔🛏 **Cross View Tea Rooms & Restaurant** – 38/39 Market Place, Richmond. ℘01748 825 897. www. crossviewtearooms.co.uk. These lovely traditional tearooms in a listed Georgian building overlook Richmond's historic

cobbled marketplace. Open for breakfast, good lunches and afternoon tea.

◔🛏🛏 **Lockwoods** – 83 North Street, Ripon. ℘01765 607 555. www.lockwoods restaurant.co.uk. Bright, cheerful, laid-back and very stylish, this multi-award-winning brasserie, café and restaurant successfully mixes traditional and contemporary in menu and artwork.

◔🛏🛏 **Angel Inn** – Hetton, nr Rylstone. 5mi/8km north of Skipton. ℘01756 730 263. www.angelhetton.co.uk. One of the country's longest-running gastropubs, serving locally sourced Modern British cuisine. Parts of the Angel date back 500 years.

YORK

Look along the Riverside (between Lendal Bridge and Ouse Bridge), Micklegate Bar, Stonegate Walk and Swinegate are also worth exploring.

◔🛏 **Café No. 8 Bistro** – 8 Gillygate. ℘01904 653 074. www.no8york.co.uk. Relaxed all-day eating, from full vegetarian breakfast to spicy Moroccan dishes for dinner. Outdoor seating.

◔🛏🛏 **Melton's** – 7 Scarcroft Road, ℘01904 634 341. www.meltonsrestaurant .co.uk. Closed Sun, Mon. Superb Modern British cooking from a husband-and-wife chef proprietors team, using the finest Yorkshire ingredients served in casual, stripped-down surroundings. For even better value (◔🛏), try its café-bistro offspring (25 Walmgate. ℘01904 629 222. www.walmgateale.co.uk).

HULL

Bars, cafés and pubs can be found mostly in and around Trinity Square.

NORTH YORK MOORS

◔🛏🛏 **White Swan** – Market Place, Pickering. ℘01751 472 288. www.white-swan.co.uk. Home-made locally sourced gastropub dining in a cosy characterful 16C coaching inn, on the main square.

◔🛏🛏 **The Gallery Restaurant** – The Black Swan Hotel, Market Place Helmsley, ℘01439 634 041. www. blackswan-helmsley.co.uk. Fine dining restaurant with a subtle, modern style, set within a 16C coaching inn recently converted to a boutique hotel. Its Cygnet Bar (◔🛏) offers more informal, relaxed dining.

North East

Alnwick castle   © Ethel Davies / age fotostock

Introduction

Like in Yorkshire and Liverpool, folk in the North East have a fierce sense of place and a dry self-deprecating humour, in part borne out of hardship. The region has suffered much in the late-20C declining from a major industrial powerhouse to little more than an historical footnote. Newcastle-upon-Tyne is the dynamic focus of the North East, an exciting city break and a good base to learn about its history and culture. Elsewhere much of this once violently disputed border region has returned to nature.

Durham and Tees valley

Durham is one of England's most perfectly sited towns. Its magnificent cathedral makes a picture-perfect composition that has graced a thousand travel posters. In contrast to today's genteel cathedral city, much of the coal that powered Britain was mined around here. The area's most enjoyable foray back in time is at family-friendly Beamish The Living Museum. A grittier perspective on the recent past can be had at Hartlepool, Middlesbrough and Darlington.

Newcastle-upon-Tyne

The regional capital is famous for its spectacular bridges, its black-and-white football team, and its raucous short-sleeved, high-heeled Toon ('town') nightlife. The town is solidly Victorian, though it also boasts much fine Georgian architecture. Its collection of museums and art galleries (all free of charge) are outstanding. The quayside, once a frenzy of industrial shipping activity, has been regenerated by new iconic landmarks such as the Sage and Baltic music and arts centres, its Millennium Bridge, and hip hotels such as Malmaison and Hotel du Vin. The biggest icon of all, The Angel of the North, with its giant outstretched wings, lies just outside the centre.

Hadrian's Wall Country

The North East has always been an important frontier region, from the Romans' Hadrian's Wall (built to keep out the Scots Picts), to the many wars and skirmishes between Scotland and England, from the 14C right through the 16C. Hadrian's Wall, now a World Heritage Site, is still partially intact and many of the most important places along its way feature excellent re-creations and interpretations of life on the Roman frontier. The surrounding area is a paradise for walkers and nature lovers.

Highlights

1 Become part of the picture at **Durham cathedral** (p476)
2 A family day out at **Beamish, The Living Museum** (p478)
3 Stroll the Quayside at **Newcastle** (p481)
4 Step back in time at Housesteads Fort on **Hadrian's Wall** (p484)
5 Have a wizard time at **Alnwick Castle** and **Garden** (p488)

Northumberland National Park

Remote from highways and towns, and free from holiday crowds and theme parks, this is (officially) one of England's most tranquil spots. Kielder Water and Forest Park is the favourite day out for walkers, mountain bikers and families who like to keep things natural.

For a little more excitement, Chillingham Castle provides a window on both a glorious and a grim past.

Northumberland Coast

The picturesque and very desirable market town of Alnwick boasts a splendid 'Harry Potter' castle, and the finest new garden in the country. Close by, Cragside, the former home of the industrialist who did more than anyone to put Newcastle on the map, the Holy Island of Lindisfarne, and the windswept Farne Islands, all make for fascinating and contrasting excursions. England's northernmost town is Berwick-upon-Tweed, fought over so many times between England and Scotland that even today Brits don't know to whom it belongs! It's worth the journey for its rampart views alone.

Durham★★★

and around

The quiet streets of the little medieval city with its castle are the perfect foil for the great sandstone mass of the Norman cathedral rising above the deep wooded gorge of the River Wear in a sublime fusion of architecture and landscape, in what is a truly remarkable setting★★★.

A BIT OF HISTORY

Christianity flourished early in the Saxon Kingdom of Northumbria but conditions were rarely stable in this border country with its coastline exposed to raiders from the east. In 875, the monks of Lindisfarne fled south from Danish attacks, carrying with them the body of **St Cuthbert** (d.687), but it was not until more than 100 years later that his much-venerated remains found their final resting place on easily defended bluffs carved out by the Wear. From the 1070s, the site's natural advantages were strengthened by the Normans, who built their castle to command the peninsula's narrow neck. In 1093, the cathedral's foundation stone was laid. Uniquely in England, Durham's bishop was not only spiritual leader but lay lord, the powerful Prince Palatine of a long-troubled province. The city has remained compact, physically unaffected by the once intense industrial activity all around it. Its scholarly character was confirmed with the foundation in 1832 of the university, after Oxford and Cambridge England's oldest. It is also the county town, an important administrative and shopping centre.

On the second Saturday in July, it is thronged with the thousands attending one of Britain's last great working-class festivals, the **Miners' Gala**.

CATHEDRAL★★★

Open Mon–Sat 9.30am–6pm, Sun 12.30–5.30pm. Donation requested. Open Treasure £7.50. Guided tours £5

▶ **Population:** 50 000.

Michelin Map: Michelin Atlas p46 or Map 501 P 19.

Info: Owengate. 03000 26 26 26. www.thisisdurham.com. The train station and bus station are almost opposite each other on North Road, 10 minutes from the centre. You can see this compact city on foot. Boat trips and rowing boats available.

Location: 18mi/29km south of Newcastle-upon-Tyne (13 mins by rail).

Don't Miss: Chapel of the Nine Altars; riverside views from or near Prebend's Bridge.

P **Parking:** Parking is difficult in the centre.

take place Mon–Sat 11am and 2pm (additional tour in summer at 10.30am). 0191 386 4266. www.durhamcathedral.co.uk.

Durham cathedral's beauty lies in its unity: its fabric was mostly completed in the short period between 1095 and 1133 and though added to since, it remains a supremely harmonious achievement of Norman architecture on the grandest possible scale. The cathedral and adjacent 11C castle were designated a World Heritage Site by UNESCO in 1986. The **Open Treasure** visitor experience gives visitors access to previously hidden spaces within the Cathedral's Claustral buildings, showcasing the Cathedral's collections (tickets available online and at the Visitor Desk).

Exterior

The usual entrance is the northwest portal, which has many arches and is embellished with the celebrated lion's head **Sanctuary Knocker★**, a 12C masterpiece of expressive stylisation. **Palace Green** is dominated by the cathedral.

© travellinglight/iStockphoto.com

Durham cathedral and the Old Fulling Mill viewed from the River Wear

Interior

In the **nave★★★** the first impression is one of overwhelming power. Huge deeply grooved columns alternate with massive many-shafted piers to form an arcade supporting a gallery and clerestory. The pointed ribs of the beautiful vault are an important technical and aesthetic innovation, heralding the lightness and grace of Gothic architecture. The great weight of masonry, its arches enriched with various zigzag patterning, is, however, so well proportioned that the final effect is one of repose, of great forces held in equilibrium. From the crossing there is a stupendous view up into the vault under the central tower, while in the south transept is an extraordinary brightly painted 16C clock. In the choir there are fine **stalls** and the splendidly vain **throne** and **tomb** of the 14C Bishop Hatfield. Beyond the 14C **Neville Screen** with its delicate stonework is the **Shrine of St Cuthbert**.

The 13C **Chapel of the Nine Altars ★★★**, an earlier example of which is to be found at Fountains Abbey, is an Early English addition to the cathedral. The sunken floor, designed to gain as much height as possible, and the extravagantly tall lancet windows, which are separated by columns of clustered shafts, reveal a new preoccupation with lightness and verticality.

The carved stonework of the bosses and capitals is extremely rich.

At the extreme western end of the building, perched on the very edge of the ravine, is the **Galilee Chapel** Twelve slender columns, their arches profusely decorated with zigzag carvings, subdivide the interior, which contains the tomb of the **Venerable Bede** (d.735), England's first historian. From the top of the cathedral's central tower *(a long climb of 325 steps: access from south transept)* spectacular **views★** reinforce the full drama of Durham's site.

Monastic Buildings

Around the much rebuilt cloisters are grouped the buildings of the former abbey. They include the monks' dormitory and the **Cathedral Treasury★**, with its collection of Anglo-Saxon embroideries, precious objects and manuscripts and, above all, the evocative relics associated with St Cuthbert – his tiny portable altar, his pectoral cross, fragments of his oak coffin… To the south is the tranquil precinct of the **college**, its mellow, mostly 18C buildings resting on medieval foundations.

CITY AND RIVERSIDE

From the **Market Place**, sited at the very neck of the peninsula, streets descend steeply to the sloping Elvet Bridge on the east and to **Framwellgate Bridge** on the west. From here there is a fine **view★★** upstream of the cathedral and the stern walls of the castle.

North Bailey and **South Bailey**, with their many pleasant 18C houses, follow the line of the town wall.

Nearby is the church of St Mary-le-Bow, now housing the **Durham Heritage Centre** (North Bailey; open Apr–May and Oct Sat–Sun 2–4.30pm; Jun daily 2–4.30pm; Jul–Sept daily 11am–4.30pm; ♿; ✆0191 384 5589; www.durhamheritagecentre.org.uk), telling the story of the city from medieval times to the present day. From here a lane leads downhill to Kingsgate footbridge of 1963, elegantly spanning the gorge to link the city with the uncompromisingly modern building of the University Students' Union, **Dunelm House**. South Bailey ends at the Watergate, from which a track leads down to **Prebend's Bridge**. From here, from the path on the far bank and from the riverside itself are those **views★★★** which have long captivated writers and artists; a perfect composition of water, trees and humble mill buildings.

Durham Castle★

Guided tours only (subject to events) daily at 1.15pm, 2.15pm, 3.15pm and 4.15pm (during University vacations, also at 10.15am, 11.15am, 12.15pm). £5. Closed Christmas holidays. ✆0191 334 2932. www.dur.ac.uk/durham.castle.

The present castle began in 1072 as a simple defensive mound commissioned by William the Conqueror. The Norman architecture of the castle was much modified by successive prince bishops. Today its Norman keep houses **University College** (or Castle as it is known), Durham University's oldest college, founded 1832.

From the courtyard, protected by the much rebuilt gatehouse and overlooked by the keep on its great earth mound, the tour proceeds via the 15C **kitchen** into the imposing **Great Hall**, then to galleries built around the original castle wall, whose fine arched doorway is still intact.

The upper floors are reached by the broad steps of the spectacular **Black Staircase** of 1662. There are two chapels, one of the 16C with humorous misericords including a bagpipe-playing pig and a nagging wife in a wheelbarrow. The **Norman chapel★**, deep below, dates from the castle's earliest days and evokes a more primitive world, with its capitals crudely ornamented with weird figures and savage faces.

Oriental Museum (Durham University)★★

Elvet Hill, off South Road. Take the A 1050 and A 167 S towards Darlington. Open Mon–Fri 10am–5pm, Sat–Sun and bank holidays noon–5pm. Closed 22 Dec –early Jan. £1.50. ♿ 🅿 ✗ ✆0191 334 5694. www.dur.ac.uk/oriental.museum. Changing displays range from Ancient Egypt via India and Southeast Asia to Japan; of outstanding interest are its ceramics, jade and other hardstone pieces, and an extraordinary roomlike bed, all from China. In 2013 a new Korean Gallery was added.

EXCURSIONS

👥 Beamish, The Living Museum★★

◆10mi/16km S by any of the river bridges and the A 692 towards Consett. Open Apr–Oct daily 10am–5pm; Nov–Mar daily 10am–4pm. Closed 25 Dec. £19, child (5–16), £11. 🅿 ✗ ✆0191 370 4000. www.beamish.org.uk.

This popular museum, in a lovely 120ha countryside setting, re-creates life in the north of England around the turn of the 20C and also evokes the environment of ordinary people at the start of the 19C, just as the full effect of the Industrial Revolution began to be felt in the region.

Preserved tramcars, supplemented by a pre-second World War motorbus, take visitors through the extensive site to the **town**, whose shops, houses, bank, working pub, sweet factory, newspaper office and printer's workshop, stocked and furnished authentically, and inhabited by costumed guides, evoke the urban scene of yesteryear. Visitors can also go underground into a real mine (summer only).

National Railway Museum Shildon (Locomotion)

➤ Shildon. 13mi/21km S of Durham. Open daily 10am–5pm. ♿🅿✕ ✆01904 685 780. www.nrm.org.uk.

This impressive outpost of York's famous National Railway Museum (✿ see York, p460) has a permanent display of over 70 railway heritage vehicles and a busy programme of events and rides on historic trains.

Raby Castle

➤ 19mi/31km SW of Durham. Open 12.30–4.30pm: mid-Apr–Jun and Sept Wed–Sun and bank holiday Mons; Jul–Aug Tue–Sun and bank holidays Mons; £12. 🅿✕ ✆01833 660 202. www.rabycastle.com.

Built for the powerful dynasty of the Nevills, this picturesque medieval lakeside castle exudes a powerful exterior of towers, turrets and fortifications dating back to the 11C. Its interiors range from Medieval to Victorian, and its treasures include Meissen porcelain, tapestries, furnishings and paintings.

Tees Valley

Iron and steel (in Middlesbrough), the railways (in Darlington) and shipbuilding (in Hartlepool) made Teesside one of the powerhouses of the UK in the late-19C. All these industries have now disappeared but can be traced in the burgeoning heritage attractions of the region.

🚹 **Info.** ✆01642 688 701; www.teesvalleytourism alliance.co.uk.

👥 **Kids:** Hartlepool's Maritime Experience.

Darlington

Population: 106 000.

🚹 13 Horsemarket. ✆01325 388 666. www.thisisdarlington.com.

Darlington's railway museum **Head of Steam** (North Road Station; open Apr–Sept Tue–Sun 10am–4pm, Oct–Mar Wed–Sun 11am–3.30pm; £4.95; ♿🅿✕; ✆01365 460 532, www.darlington.gov. uk/Leisure) gives pride of place to *Locomotion*, the first ever steam train to carry fare-paying passengers from Darlington (to Stockton-on-Tees) in 1825.

Middlesbrough

Population: 138 400.

🚹 www.lovemiddlesbrough.com.

Housed in a landmark 2007 building, the town's new pride and joy is **MIMA**, the Middlesbrough Institute of Modern Art (Centre Square; open Tue–Sat 10am–4.30pm/Thu 7pm, Sun noon–4.00pm; ♿🅿✕; ✆01642 931 232; www.visit-mima.com) with outstanding fine and applied art from 1900 to the present day, presented in rotating exhibitions. The town's most famous son, Captain James Cook, is commemorated in the **Captain Cook Birthplace Museum** (Stewart Park, Marton; open Jun–Oct Tue–Sun 10.30am–3.30pm; £4; ♿🅿✕; ✆01642 311 211, www.captcook-ne.co.uk).

Hartlepool

Population: 92 000. 🚹 Art Gallery, Church Square. ✆01429 869706. www.thisishartlepool.co.uk.

In the 19C this was England's third-largest port and its halcyon days are recalled at the lively **Hartlepool's Maritime Experience★** 👥 (Jackson Dock; open daily Apr–Oct 10am–5pm, Nov–Mar 11am–4pm; £10, child (5–15), £8; ♿🅿✕; ✆01429 860 077; www. hartlepoolsmaritimeexperience.com). This excellent award-winning re-creation of an 18C seaport is staffed by guides in authentic period dress and moored here is Britain's oldest warship still afloat, *HMS Trincomalee*, built 1817,.

Newcastle-upon-Tyne★★

and around

Newcastle is an important hub on the busy east-coast route to Scotland. Its dramatic site, rich history and the distinctive dialect spoken by its population of 'Geordies' give this undisputed capital of the North East an exceptionally strong identity. Despite recent decline, Newcastle retains great vigour as a commercial, educational, entertainment and cultural centre. The city centre shopping complex in Eldon Square was one of the most ambitious of its kind when built, while the gargantuan MetroCentre on the outskirts of Gateshead is billed as one of the largest shopping and leisure complexes in Europe. Post-Millennium, the BALTIC Centre for Contemporary Arts and The Sage music venue are powerful symbols of the city's new cultural ambitions.

A BIT OF HISTORY

The easily defended bridging point where the Tyne enters its gorge was exploited by the Roman founders of Pons Aelius, one post among many along Hadrian's Wall, then by the Normans, whose 'New Castle' dates from 1080. Later, abundant mineral resources, particularly coal, stimulated trade, manufacturing and engineering. The great railway inventor **George Stephenson** (1781–1848) was born nearby, as was his son Robert, and in the 19C Tyneside became one of the great centres of industrial Britain, dominated by figures like **William Armstrong**, later Lord Armstrong (1810–1900), whose engineering and armament works at Elswick helped equip the navies of the world.

GATESHEAD

The approach from the south through **Gateshead** reveals an astonishing

▶ **Population:** 295 200.

🜨 **Michelin Map:** Michelin Atlas p51 or Map 502 P 19.

▣ **Info:** Central Arcade, Market Street. ℘0191 277 8000. www.newcastle gateshead.com.

⊘ Newcastle Central Station (York 56min) is just that, with a Metro station attached. Haymarket Bus Station is north of the city centre, also linked to the Metro network, which offers fast, efficient travel around Newcastle and Tyneside. Newcastle-upon-Tyne is the city north of the river (where nearly all the major sites are found), while the separate town of Gateshead begins across any of the town-centre bridges. The city centre is best seen on foot.

▶ **Location:** 84mi/134km due north of York.

⊘ **Don't Miss:** The BALTIC Centre; views from the city bridges.

🕓 **Timing:** At least 2 days.

👥 **Kids:** Discovery Museum. Life (Science Centre).

urban panorama★★. The city of Newcastle has spread slowly from the north bank of the Tyne via steeply sloping streets and precipitous stairways up to the flatter land to the north. Buildings of all periods and materials are dominated by the castle and the cathedral tower.

BALTIC Centre★

Gateshead Quays. Open daily 10am (Tue 10.30am)–6pm. Closed 24–26 Dec, 1 Jan. ♿✕ ℘0191 478 1810. www.balticmill.com. Housed in a landmark former flour mill on the River Tyne in Gateshead, this is the biggest gallery of its kind in the world – presenting an ever-changing international programme of contemporary visual art.

River Tyne with Gateshead Millennium Bridge, The Sage and Tyne Bridge

The Sage★

South of the Tyne. Open 9am –closing times vary. ♿🅿✕ ☎0191 443 4661 (Ticket office); 0191 443 4666 (Welcome desk). www.thesagegateshead.org.

This amazing addition to the riverfront, likened to a giant stainless steel armadillo, was built 1994–2004, designed by Sir Norman Foster and Mott MacDonald, and has already become a city icon. It is home to the Northern Sinfonia but hosts all kinds of musical performances taking in every genre. It is home to a smart café and brasserie, four bars, and offers wonderful views.

◆◆WALKING TOUR

Quayside★

Newcastle and Gateshead are linked by seven bridges, which make an outstanding **composition★** extending upstream. The oldest is the unusual **High Level Bridge** (1848), designed by **Robert Stephenson** with railway tracks above and roadway below. The newest is the graceful **Gateshead Millennium Bridge★**, the world's first (and as yet, only) tilting bridge. The **Swing Bridge** (1876) designed by Lord Armstrong, brightly painted and nautical-looking, follows the alignment of the original crossing. The monumental stone piers of the great **Tyne Bridge** (1928) add drama while the riverside walkways, with sculpture, pubs, bars and hotels, are a popular place for a stroll.

Among the tightly packed Victorian commercial buildings off the Quayside are a few much older survivors: the 17C **Guildhall**, the 18C **All Saints Church★** and the remarkable timber-framed **Bessie Surtees House** (open Mon–Fri 10am–4pm; ☎0191 269 1255) two five-storey 16C and 17C merchants' houses which boast splendid period interiors.

Castle Keep★

Open daily 10am–5pm. Closed 1 Jan, 25, 26 Dec. £6.50. ☎0191 230 6300; www.newcastlecastle.co.uk.

PRACTICAL INFORMATION
PUBLIC TRANSPORT

The Tyne and Wear Metro runs 5.30am–11.30pm, linking Newcastle city with Tyneside and the coast. Trains run every seven minutes to the airport and the coast, and every three minutes at peak times within the city. For full details on bus and Metro travel contact Nexus (www.nexus.org.uk).

SIGHTSEEING

For sightseeing on the River Tyne, **River Escapes** (☎01670 785 666; www.riverescapes.co.uk) runs regular cruises from Newcastle Quayside, beside the Millennium Bridge, during the summer months, with three themes: the city, the countryside, out to sea.

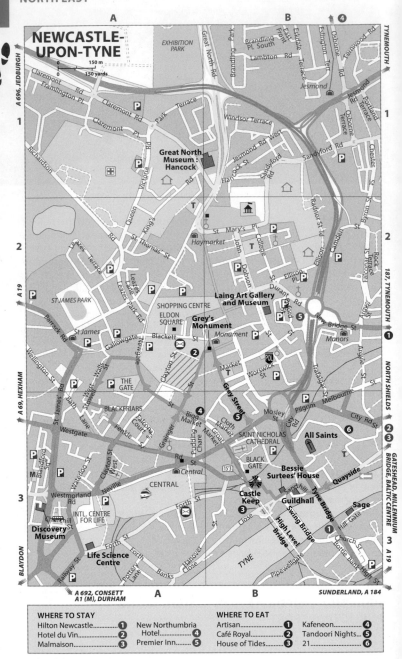

NEWCASTLE-UPON-TYNE

EXHIBITION PARK

Great North Museum: Hancock

Laing Art Gallery and Museum

SHOPPING CENTRE
ELDON SQUARE

Grey's Monument

Monument

ST JAMES PARK

St James

THE GATE

BLACKFRIARS

Grey Street

SAINT NICHOLAS CATHEDRAL

All Saints

BLACK GATE

Bessie Surtees' House

Castle Keep

Guildhall

Sage

Quayside

CENTRAL

INTL. CENTRE FOR LIFE

Discovery Museum

Life Science Centre

TYNE

WHERE TO STAY		WHERE TO EAT	
Hilton Newcastle............❶	New Northumbria Hotel............❹	Artisan.....................❶	Kafeneon................❹
Hotel du Vin.....................❷	Premier Inn.........❺	Café Royal.............❷	Tandoori Nights...❺
Malmaison.........................❸		House of Tides......❸	21.............................❻

The city took its name from the 'new castle' built by William the Conqueror's eldest son, Robert Curthose in 1080. The present keep is all that remains of its 12C successor and is a particularly good example of a Norman keep. From the roof of this massive stone edifice there is an all-embracing panorama of city, river and distant countryside.

City Centre★

Enlightened planning gave 19C New-castle a new centre of Classical dignity, comprising fine civic buildings, great covered markets and shopping arcades and spacious streets, of which the most splendid is **Grey Street★**, curving ele-gantly downhill from the high column of **Grey's Monument**, past the great portico of the Theatre Royal.

ADDITIONAL SIGHTS

♣♣ Discovery Museum

Blandford Square. Open Mon–Fri 10am–4pm, Sat–Sun 11am–4pm. Closed 1 Jan, 25–26 Dec. 🅿(charge). ♿✗ ℘0191 232 6789. www.discoverymuseum.org.uk. This entertaining, colourful museum, full of interactive displays, is the ideal starting point from which to find out all about life on Tyneside, from the domestic to heavy industry, and to inventions which changed the world, including the 35m long *Turbinia* which dominates the entrance. Invented on Tyneside, this was the first ship to be powered by a steam turbine and was once the fastest ship in the world.

♣♣ Life Science Centre

Times Square. Open Mon–Sat 10am–6pm, Sun 11am–6pm. £13, child (5–17), £7.50. ♿🅿(charge). ✗ ℘0191 243 8210. www.life.org.uk. This landmark Millennium project offers live science shows, a planetarium, an interactive theatre, all kinds of hands-on displays, a simulator ride and family-based laboratory workshops. Although it is child oriented it is the public face of a pioneering science village, where scientists, educationalists and business-people come together to promote life sciences.

Great North Museum: Hancock★

Barras Bridge. Open Mon–Fri 10am–4pm, Sat 10am–4pm, Sun 11am–4pm. Closed 1 Jan, 25–26 Dec. ℘0191 222 6765. www.greatnorthmuseum.org.uk. On the edge of the university campus, this important museum, boasting 3 500

natural history, archaeological and eth-nographical artefacts, has recently been extended and refurbished. Its remit is both global history and matters closer to home. Highlights of its 11 galleries include a large-scale, interactive model of Hadrian's Wall, the wonder and diver-sity of the animal kingdom (including a near complete life-size T-Rex dinosaur skeleton), life and death in Ancient Egypt, and spectacular objects from the Ancient Greeks. There is also a planetarium.

Laing Art Gallery★

New Bridge Street. Open Tue–Sat and bank holiday Mons 10am–5pm, Sun 2–5pm. Closed 1 Jan, 25–26 Dec. 🅿(charge). ♿✗ ℘0191 278 1611. www.laingartgallery.org.uk. This is the region's finest collection, renowned for its English watercolours the sculpture. It emphasises the 19C, with works by eminent Pre-Raphaelites, the apocalyptic works of the visionary **John Martin**.

EXCURSIONS

Angel of the North★

◗5mi/8km S. Between the the A 1 and A 167, Gateshead. Access off A 167. www.gateshead.gov.uk. Erected in 1998, Antony Gormley's majestic steel Angel, 20m high, with a wingspan of 54m and a weight of 208 tonnes, is not only Britain's larg-est sculpture, but its most iconic and best-loved statue of the 21C so far.

Segedunum

◗Buddle Street, Wallsend. 4mi/6.5km E. Open Jun–mid-Oct daily 10am–6pm. Closed 20 Dec–mid-Jan. £5.95. 🅿♿✗ ℘0191 278 4217. www.segedunumromanfort.org.uk. 'Segger-doon-um' means strong fort, and this is the nearest section of **Had-rian's Wall** (⟲see Hadrian's Wall, p484) to Newcastle. It features a reconstructed bath-house, a museum of artefacts and a replica full-size section of the wall which once stretched 73mi/117km west.

Hadrian's Wall★★

In 122, the Roman Emperor Hadrian visited Britain and ordered the building of a defensive wall across the northernmost boundary of the empire from Wallsend on the Tyne, to Bowness on the Solway Firth (73mi/117km). Although Hadrian's Wall has come to represent the frontier between England and Scotland, it is well south of the modern border. Parts of this wall can still be seen today and museums, camps and settlements give a picture of military and civilian life on Rome's 'Northwest Frontier'.

A BIT OF HISTORY

The wall – The wall was built by legionaries, citizens of Rome, and garrisoned by as many as 24 000 auxiliaries from conquered territories. It was defended by a ditch on the north side; on the south side it was paralleled by a military road and 'vallum', defining the military zone. The wall was built in stone and turf, with forts, turrets and milecastles (military bases) numbered, from east to west, from Wallsend (0) to Bowness (80). It follows the best strategic and geo-

Michelin Map: Michelin Atlas p50, p51, or Map 502 L 19, M, N and O 18.

Info: ☎0191 440 5720. www.visithadrianswall.co.uk.

Getting Around: The AD122 Hadrian's Wall Country Bus (operates Apr–Sept daily; ☎0871 200 22 33; http://hadrianswallcountry.co.uk/travel/bus) runs the length of the wall, stopping at all major points of interest.

graphical line and, at places such as Cawfields and at Walltown Crags, commands splendid **views**.

ALONG THE WALL

Follow the B 6318.
The main sites (listed below from east to west) all have car parks and are indicated by light brown signposts.

Corbridge Roman Town★

West of Corbridge. Open Apr–Sept daily 10am–6pm; Oct daily 10am–5pm; Nov–Mar Sat–Sun (daily half-term hols) 10am–4pm. Closed 1 Jan, 24–26 Dec. £5. ☎01434 632 349. www.english-heritage.org.uk.

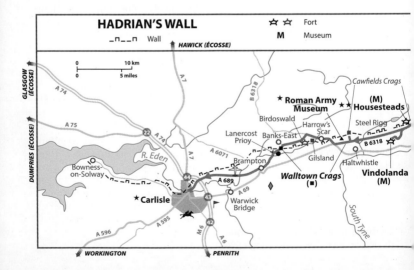

Ruins of the granaries, Corbridge Roman Town

This site was occupied for longer than any other on the wall. The **museum** of the Corbridge Roman Town presents the layout with its granaries, fountain, headquarters building and temples. From the elevated viewpoint there is a good overall **view** of the visible remains, which represent only a small part of the base and settlement.

Hexham Abbey★

Open daily 9.30am–5pm. Contribution requested. &.✕. ☎01434 602 031. www.hexhamabbey.org.uk.
Stones from the Roman settlement of Corbridge (Corstopitum) were used in the construction of Hexham abbey, which was founded in 674. All that remains of the original abbey is the **Saxon Crypt★★** (open twice daily when services permit).

The fine Early English choir with imposing transepts belongs to the later church (1180–1250). The stone staircase in the south transept was the Night Stair, which led to the canons' dormitory.

The **Leschman Chantry★** (1491) has amusing stone carvings on the base and delicate woodwork above.

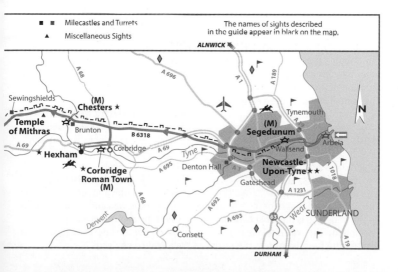

485

Hadrian's Wall at Walltown Crags

© Gannet77/iStockphoto.com

Chesters Roman Fort and Museum★

Near Chollerford. Times as Corbridge (👁*see opposite*). £6.60. ♿🅿(charge). ✕(summer). 📞01434 681 379. www.english-heritage.org.uk.

The best-preserved Roman cavalry fort in Britain lies just west of the point where the wall crossed the River Tyne and remains of the bridge can still be seen on the far bank. The four gateways, headquarters building and barrack blocks of this fort can be traced from their foundations. By the river are the remains of England's best-preserved Roman **bath-house★**.

Temple of Mithras

Carrawburgh.
5min walk from car park.

This is an unexpected find in such a desolate stretch of moorland. Inside the lobby is a statue of the mother goddess (the original is reconstructed in the Museum of Antiquities in Newcastle). The temple was destroyed early in the 4C, probably by the Christians.

Housesteads Roman Fort★★

Open times as Corbridge. £7.50. ♿🅿(charge). ✕ 📞01434 344 363. www.english-heritage.org.uk. www.nationaltrust.org.uk.

This large fort (2ha) is perched high on the ridge and is the most complete example on the wall. Still clearly visible are the foundations of the large courtyard house of the commandant, the granaries, barracks, headquarters building, the four main gateways, the **hospital** and 24-seater **latrine block** as well as part of the civilian settlement.

Vindolanda

Bardon Mill, Chesterholm. Open daily: Feb–Mar and Oct 10am–5pm; Apr–Sept 10am–6pm; Nov–1 Jan 10am–4pm. £7, child £4.25, combined ticket with Roman Army Museum £11/£6. ♿🅿✕ 📞01434 344 277. www.vindolanda.com.

The fort and civilian settlement on the Stanegate, south of the wall, date from the period before the building of the wall. Full-scale replicas have been built of a stretch of the wall with a stone turret, as well as of the turf wall, which was the earliest barrier, with a timber milecastle. The **Vindolanda Museum★** holds a unique collection of **writing tablets** (the oldest surviving handwritten documents in Britain), leather goods, textiles and wooden objects.

👥 Roman Army Museum★

Carvoran. Open times as Vindolanda. £5.75, child £3.25, combined ticket with Vindolanda £11/£6. ♿✕ 📞01697 747 485. www.vindolanda.com.

This is the largest and most modern of the wall museums and presents a lively picture of the wall and its garrison. To the east the quarry viewing-point overlooks one of the finest sections of the Wall, **Walltown Crags**.

Northumberland National Park★

Cheviot sheep graze the high open moorland that makes up a lot of this park, which is popular with walkers, mountain bikers, and for watersports. On the eastern outskirts lie two outstanding historic properties.

ℹ **Info: National Park:**
📞01434 605 555.
www.northumberland
nationalpark.org.uk.
Kielder: Tower
Knowe Visitor Centre:
📞01434 240 436.
Kielder Castle Visitor
Centre: 📞01431 250 209.
www.visitkielder.com.
👥 **Kids:** Birds of Prey Centre.

KIELDER WATER AND FOREST PARK

Not only is Kielder Forest the biggest working forest in England, covering 250sq mi/650sq km, Kielder Water is also the biggest man-made lake in northern Europe. Get your bearings at the **Tower Knowe Visitor Centre**, where you can jump aboard the *Osprey* for a cruise. It stops at **Leaplish Waterside Park**, where there are various facilities for family fun, including the **Kielder Water Birds of Prey Centre** 👥 (open daily Apr–mid-Oct 10.30am–4.30pm; mid-Oct–Mar 10.30am–3.30pm; £7, child £4.50; &; 📞01434 250 400, www.kwbopc.com).

Just north of the lake, **Kielder Castle Visitor Centre** 👥, formerly the hunting lodge for the Duke of Northumberland, is home to a variety of exhibitions, and is the hub for mountain biking. **Kielder Observatory** (📞0191 265 5510; www.kielderobservatory.org) 1.2mi/2km west, is housed in a striking modern wooden structure and enjoys some of the darkest night skies in England.

WALLINGTON

30mi (50km) west of Kielder Water, outside the National Park. Open mid-Feb–Oct, Wed–Mon noon–5pm. Gardens and grounds daily 10am–dusk. £12.40. &✕🅿 📞01670 773 600. www.nationaltrust.org.uk/wallington. Wallington is a monument to local industrial magnates, Sir Walter Blackett, who made his fortune from coal- and lead-mining and rebuilt the original late-17C house in the 1740s. It has a splendid interior and fine collections. The landscaped grounds and enchanting **walled garden** are even more impressive.

CHILLINGHAM CASTLE★

Northeast, between the national park and A1. Open Apr–Oct daily noon–5pm. £9.50. &✕🅿 📞01668 215 359. www.chillingham-castle.com.
This splendid medieval castle, with its original battlements, has been much augmented through the ages but retains a real sense of history, some of it very unpleasant. In the 13C, it was used as a base by Edward I for his raids on the Scots and its torture chamber contains horrific devices. Partly as a result of this period, it is widely regarded as one of the most haunted places in the country. The Elizabethans added Long Galleries, Capability Brown designed the park in 1752 and the Italian Garden was laid out in the 19C by Jeffrey Wyatville.

Adjacent, but with a separate entrance from the castle, in Chillingham Park, is **Chillingham Wild Cattle Park** (visit by guided tour only: Mon–Fri 10am, 11am, noon, 2pm, 3pm and 4pm, Sun 10am, 11am and noon; allow 2h for the tour; £16; 🅿. 📞01668 215 250, www.chillingham-wildcattle.com), featuring the last wild cattle in the world. Numbering around 93 strong, these potentially very dangerous creatures are the sole survivors of herds that once roamed the forests of Britain.

Northumberland Coast★

The charming town of Alnwick (pronounced 'ann-ick') is the jewel in the crown of this region. Its castle, like those at Warkworth, Dunstanburgh, and Bambrugh, and the tug-of-war town of Berwick-on-Tweed are reminders that this was once a fiercely disputed border region. More typical of this coast these days, however, is the peace and quiet on Holy Island and the Farne Islands.

Ⓖ **Michelin Map:** Michelin Atlas p51 or Map 502 O 16/17.

🛈 **Info: Alnwick:** The Shambles. ℘01670 622 152. **Berwick-upon-Tweed:** Walkergate. ℘01670 622 155. **Seahouses:** Seafield Road car park. ℘01670 625 593. www.visitnorthumberland.com.

👥 **Kids:** Alnwick Castle (exploring in the footsteps of Harry Potter); Alnwick Garden. The arms and armour at Bamburgh Castle.

😊 **Don't Miss:** Alnwick Castle; Alnwick Garden, Holy Island.

ALNWICK★

Population: 8 116.

This attractive grey-stone town grew up around the great medieval castle whose stern walls still seem to bar the route to and from Scotland. Though its streets were laid out in the Middle Ages, Alnwick's present sober and harmonious appearance dates from the 18C when much dignified rebuilding in stone took place. If possible visit on market day, Thursday and Saturday.

👥 Alnwick Castle★★

Open daily Apr–Oct 10am–5.30pm (State rooms 4.30pm). £15.50, child (5–16), £8 (combined ticket with Alnwick Garden £26.10, child £11.15 (discount online)). 🅿✕ ℘01665 511 100. www.alnwickcastle.com.

Among the many fortifications of this much-contested border country, Alnwick's castle is the most formidable. Begun in Norman times, it was acquired in 1309 by the **Percys**, the region's greatest family, and has remained in their hands ever since. Though much remodelled in the 19C, its basic features are all intact and, in an exquisite setting by the River Aln, it epitomises the romantic ideal of a mighty medieval fortress. It was featured in two *Harry Potter* films and stages various themed activities for children.

👥 Alnwick Garden

Denwick Lane. Open Apr–Oct daily 10am–5.50pm. £12.10, child £4.40 (combined ticket with Alnwick Castle £25.10, child £10.40). ♿🅿✕ ℘01665 511 350. www.alnwickgarden.com.

Part of the castle estate, this 5ha walled plot was rescued from dereliction in 2000 and has developed into one of the most exciting contemporary British gardens in modern times. It features a spectacular water Cascade, a rose garden holding over 3 000 specimens, a Poison Garden (where guides share tales of deadly plants) and a magnificently higgledy-piggledy **tree house**, which is one of the largest in the world; and hosts a restaurant (Ⓖ*see Addresses*). Alnwick is also unusual among British gardens for being very child-friendly with water features to get soaked by (on a hot day!), a bamboo labyrinth, and the tree house to explore, with its walkways in the sky and wobbly rope bridges for bouncing on.

WARKWORTH CASTLE AND HERMITAGE★

7.5mi/12km SE of Alnwick on the A 1068. Open: **Castle:** Apr–Aug daily 10am–6pm; Sept–Oct daily 10am–5pm; Nov–Mar Sat–Sun only 10am–4pm (Feb half-term holidays daily). **Hermitage:** Apr–Aug Sun, Mon and bank holidays 11am–4pm;

Sept–Oct 11am–4pm. Closed 1 Jan, 24–26 Dec. Castle £6.20, Hermitage £4.30. &P 01665 711 423. www.english-heritage.org.uk.

Perched high above the river, the castle dates from the 12C and since 1332 has belonged to the Percys. It fell into ruin in the late-16C, but has since been preserved. Its only furnished interiors are the **Duke's Rooms**. The general layout is best appreciated from the upper floor of the fine 13C **gatehouse**. The most prominent feature is the beautifully-restored **keep**, designed for comfort and convenience as much as for defence.

From the castle the single street of the little planned town runs steeply downhill to the Norman **church of St Lawrence** and to the river crossing with its rare medieval bridge tower.

Don't miss the **Hermitage** (half a mile upstream, accessible only by boat), in use between the 14C and the mid-16C.

CRAGSIDE ★

Rothbury. 12mi/19km SW of Alnwick via the B 6341. Open: House 11am–5pm; mid-Feb–mid-Apr Tue–Sun; mid-Apr–Oct daily: Gardens and woodland: mid-Feb–Oct daily 10am–6pm (mid-Feb–mid-Apr closed Mon); Nov–mid-Dec Fri–Sun 11am–4pm. £17 (winter £5.60), gardens and woodland only £11; Admission by cash only. PX 01669 620 333. www.nationaltrust.org.uk/cragside.

The stupendous success of his engineering and armament works at Newcastle enabled **Lord Armstrong** (1810–1900), one of the greatest Victorian inventor/industrialists, to build this extraordinary country house in which Old English and Germanic styles are romantically combined. It was regarded as a wonder of the age and was the first house in the world to be lit by hydroelectricity, of which Armstrong was a pioneer. The many rooms of its well-preserved **interior★** give a fascinating insight into the comforts and pretensions of late Victorian domestic life, as well as housing many of Armstrong's ingenious gadgets. This redoubtable man is also hailed as a landscaping genius and Cragside's gardens, laid out under his supervision, are home to the largest sandstone rock garden in Europe.

CRASTER

8mi/13km NE of Alnwick on the B 1340; after 3mi/5km turn right.

This dark-stone fishing village is famed for its **kippers** (cured herrings).

From the car park, it is well worth the windy walk (there is no vehicular access) around 1.5mi/2.4km to the skeletal ruin of **Dunstanburgh Castle★** (open Apr–Sept daily 10am–6pm; Oct daily 10am–4pm; Nov–Mar Sat–Sun 10am–4pm (Feb half-term holidays daily); £5; 01665 576 231; www.english-heritage.org.uk, www.nationaltrust.org.uk). Sitting on its lonely crag of volcanic rock this is one of the most stirring sights of the Northumbrian coast. From here there are searching **view** right up and down this wonderfully unspoiled coastline of rocky headlands and sweeping sandy bays backed by dunes.

FARNE ISLANDS ★

Seahouses. 15mi/24km S by the A 1 and B 1342/1340.

Inner Farne: daily: Apr and Aug–early Nov 10.30am–5.30pm; May–Jul 1.30–5.30pm; **Staple Island:** May–Jul 10.30am–1.30pm.

Admission: charges are per island and variable (£7–£9), and do not include boat charges (see below). Island tickets may be purchased at the National Trust trailer at the harbour. Boat tickets may be purchased in Seahouses harbour. 01665 721 099 (infoline). www.nationaltrust.org.uk.

Boat information: 01665 720 308; www.farne-islands.com.

Apr–Jul wear a wide-brimmed hat or baseball cap to protect against dive-bombing birds.

In the care of the National Trust, the Farne Islands number 15 to 28 in total, depending upon the tide, and lie between 2mi/3km and 5mi/8km off the coast. They provide nesting sites for 18 species of seabirds, and are home to the largest British colony of grey seals.

Bamburgh castle

© Edward Shaw/iStockphoto.com

The wildlife is generally very tame and it is possible to get very close-up views.

👥 BAMBURGH CASTLE★

7mi/27km north of Alnwick via the A 1 and B 1341. Open mid-Feb–Oct daily 10am–5pm (State rooms open 11am); Nov–mid-Feb Sat–Sun 11am–4.30pm. £10.85, child (5–16), £5.
🅿 (charge). ✖ 🕿01668 214 515. www.bamburghcastle.com.

Beautifully sited on a rocky plateau above a long sandy beach, its original **Norman keep** still dominant, Bamburgh is one of the largest inhabited castles in the country. It was restored in the Victorian era and bought by the redoubtable Lord Armstrong (ⓒ *see Cragside House, p489*) in 1894. It now houses a fine collection of arms and armour from the Tower of London, and Sèvres, Crown Derby, Worcester and Chelsea porcelain. There are exquisite small collections of vinaigrettes, Fabergé carvings and jade.

In Bamburgh village, two minutes by car, is the **Grace Darling Museum** (Radcliffe Road; open Easter–Sept daily 10am–5pm, Oct–Easter Tue–Sun and bank holidays 10am–4pm; closed 1 Jan, 24–26 Dec; ♿; 🕿01668 214 910, www.rnli.org/gracedarling), which celebrates the area's most famous person. The daughter of the Longstone lighthouse keeper, Grace was just 22 years old when she risked her life in an open boat with her father, to help save several survivors of the wrecked *SS Forfarshire* in September 1838. The **Longstone lighthouse** still stands and can be seen on boat trips to the Farne Islands (ⓒ *see above*).

HOLY ISLAND (LINDISFARNE)★

22mi/35km N of Alnwick to Beal via the A 1, then cross the causeway to Holy Island. This can be crossed only at low tide; timetables posted at either end of the causeway, but see also the Holy Island website (www.holy-island. info). Lindisfarne Centre open generally 10am–5pm (winter 4pm), according to tides, see website. £4, child (5–15), £2.
♿🕿01289 389 004.
www.lindisfarne-centre.com.

Here on this tiny island, the **Lindisfarne Gospels** were written and magnificently illuminated in the Celtic tradition. The original is kept at the British Museum but a (conventional) facsimile and an interactive turning page edition can be viewed here at the centre.

Lindisfarne Priory★

Open Apr–Sept daily 10am–6pm; Feb school half-term week and Oct, daily 10am–4pm; Nov–Mar Sat–Sun only, 10am–4pm. Closed 24–30 Dec, 1 Jan. £6.50. 🕿01289 389 200.
www.english-heritage.org.uk.

The ruins visible today are those of a Benedictine house, founded from Durham in 1093. The ruins are dominated by the 12C priory church, which itself is probably built on the site of an Anglo-Saxon church. A visitor centre interprets the ruins and stages occasional events.

Lindisfarne Castle★

Castle: Open early Feb–early Nov Tue–Sun (and Mon in Aug). Times vary according to the tide; either 10am–3pm,

or noon–5pm, £6.30 🅿 (charge).
♿ Limited toilet facilities at castle.
☎01289 389 244.
www.nationaltrust.org.uk.

Accessible via a 3mi/5km causeway at low tide only, this 16C castle was restored in 1902 by Edwin Lutyens as a holiday home for Edward Hudson, founder of *Country Life* magazine. The austere but beautiful interior is in inimitable 'Lutyens' style.

BERWICK-UPON-TWEED★

30mi/50km N of Alnwick via the A 1.

As a result of its location right on the border – facing northeast to the English, looking southwest to the Scots – the Georgian market and seaside town of Berwick (pronounced 'berrick') has been fought over many times, changing hands on no fewer than 14 occasions in the 12C alone.

Today, this is England's northernmost town, a fact unknown to many English folk outside the north, who would consider Berwick as Scottish. Their confusion is compounded by the town's football team, Berwick Rangers, who elect to play in the Scottish League. From 1558 onwards, the **walls★** were replaced with ramparts and bastions. The elegant 15-arch **Old Bridge**, built in 1611, is the fifth-known structure to have been built between Berwick and Tweedmouth. The castle has largely been demolished and the railway station was built on part of the site in the 19C.

Some of the stone was used for Holy Trinity Church (1651), one of the few to have been built during the Commonwealth, and the remainder was "quarried" in 1720 to build **Berwick Barracks**.

Berwick Barracks and Main Guard

The Parade, off Church Street. Barracks open Apr–Sept daily 10am–6pm; Oct Wed–Sun 10am–4pm. £4.90. ☎01289 304 493. www.english-heritage.org.uk.

Built in the early-18C, this complex is now home to the King's Own Scottish Borderers Museum, the Berwick Gymnasium Contemporary Art Gallery and the Berwick Borough Museum. The highlights are the excellently crafted pieces collected by the "magpie millionaire" **Sir William Durrell**, which include imari ware (Japanese porcelain), brassware, medieval religious art, Chinese bronzes and glassware.

ADDRESSES

🛏 **STAY**

DURHAM

🍴🍴 **Victoria Inn** – 86 Hallgarth Street. ☎0191 386 5269. www.victoriainn-durham city.co.uk. 🅿. 6 rooms. This family-run Grade II listed inn, a five-min walk from town, is a much-feted family-run classic Victorian pub with pleasant bedrooms.

🍴🍴 **Farnley Tower** – The Avenue. ☎0191 375 0011. www.farnley-tower.

Berwick-upon-Tweed

© Jose Antonio Moreno/Travel Pictures

co.uk. ▣ 13 rooms. This superb de-luxe guesthouse, a 10-min walk from town, dates from 1870 and is set in lovely grounds. Rooms are traditional-modern Victorian style; book a superior for views of the cathedral and castle. Excellent restaurant (*see opposite*).

▬▬ **Cathedral View Town House** – 212 Lower Gilesgate. ☎0191 386 9566. 6 rms. This former Georgian merchant's house dates from 1734 and has stylish modern bedrooms. A 10-min walk from town, it enjoys sweeping views over the cathedral, town and countryside.

▬▬▬ **Durham Marriott Hotel Royal County** – Old Elvet. ☎0191 386 6821. wwww.marriott.co.uk. ▣. 50 rooms. Situated on the banks of the Wear, this luxurious property, parts of which date back to the 17C, offers great views of castle and cathedral. Its leisure club includes an indoor pool.

NEWCASTLE

▬ **Premier Inn Newcastle Central** – New Bridge Street West. ☎0871 527 8802. www.premierinn.co.uk. Next to Eldon Square shopping centre in the heart of 'the toon', this is the best central no-frills hotel in Newcastle, with bright, modern rooms and king-size beds.

▬▬▬ **The New Northumbria Hotel** – 61/73 Osborne Road. ☎0191 281 4961. www.thenewnorthumbriahotel.co.uk. ▣ 55 rooms. This boutique hotel in Jesmond, a mile from Newcastle city centre, is almost a night out in its own right, including the buzzing Osborne's Bar, and the informal attractive Scalini's restaurant.

▬▬▬▬ **Hotel du Vin** – City Road. ☎0191 229 2200. www.hotelduvin.com/newcastle. ▣. 42 rooms. On the banks of the Tyne, with outstanding views of Quayside and bridges, the former Tyne Tees Steam Shipping Company HQ has been gloriously converted into timelessly styled bedrooms, a superb trademark bistro, courtyard for al fresco dining and an outstanding wine cellar.

▬▬▬▬ **Malmaison** – Quayside. ☎0191 389 8627. www.malmaison-newcastle.com. ▣. 20 rooms. Very chic designer hotel next to the Millennium Bridge with an excellent restaurant and superb bar.

▬▬▬▬ **Hilton Newcastle** – Bottle Bank. ☎0191 490 9700. www.hilton.co.uk/newcastlegateshead. ▣. 254 rooms and suites. The best river view in town, from the Gateshead side of the water, can be enjoyed from several of the Hilton's luxurious rooms and from its Windows on the Tyne Restaurant. Health club with swimming pool.

HADRIAN'S WALL

▬ – ▬▬ **Beggar Bog Farm** – Housesteads. ☎01434 344 652. www.beggarbog.co.uk. ▣. 3 rooms. Next to Housesteads Roman Fort, this tastefully renovated farmhouse features stripped-back wood-and-stone rooms. Dinner available, good local pubs. Excellent value.

▬▬ **Ashcroft Guest House** – Lanty's Lonnen. Haltwistle. ☎01434 320 213. www.ashcroftguesthouse.co.uk. ▣. 9 rooms. This elegant Victorian vicarage features spacious high-ceilinged guest rooms. It is located in lovely countryside, near the Wall, on the edge of Haltwhistle village, and stands in 0.8ha of award-winning gardens festooned with thousands of flowers in spring.

▬ – ▬▬ **Bush Nook Guest House** – Gilsland, Upper Denton. ☎016977 47194. www.bushnook.co.uk. ▣. 8 rooms. Overlooking Birdoswald Roman Fort and with panoramic countryside views, this old farmstead has been tastefully converted to a very high standard. Dinner available. Attentive friendly hosts. Excellent value.

▬▬▬ **Crown & Mitre Hotel** – English Street, Carlisle. ☎01228 525 491. http://www.peelhotels.co.uk. ▣. 94 rooms. This grand Edwardian landmark hotel has very comfortable trad-modern rooms, a splendid 'pubby' bar (serving food), a reasonably priced restaurant and a lovely indoor pool.

ALNWICK

▬▬ **Aln House** – South Road. ☎01665 602 265. www.alnhouse.co.uk. ▣. 7 rooms. This charming modern-styled Edwardian house with gardens is just a short stroll from town.

▬▬ **Greycroft** – Croft Street (via Prudhoe Street). ☎01665 602 127. www.greycroft.co.uk. 6 rooms. A short walk from the centre of town, this attractive and spacious Victorian house has been beautifully renovated in trad-modern style, and draws universally glowing reviews.

KIELDER FOREST

☺☻🍴 **The Pheasant Inn** – Stannersburn Nr Kielder Water, Falston. ✆01434 240 382. www.thepheasantinn.com. 8 rooms. Remote but ideal if you are exploring Kielder; a perfect family-run getaway with excellent bar food and restaurant dishes. Well worth tracking down, and staying for a few nights.

BERWICK-UPON-TWEED

☺☻🍴 **West Coates** – 30 Castle Terrace. ✆01289 309 666. www.westcoates.co.uk. 3 rooms. Large elegant Victorian mansion in 0.8ha of mature gardens on the edge of town with spacious comfortable traditional rooms. The owner runs cookery classes; dinner (☺☻🍴🍴) is available.

☺☻🍴🍴 **The Captains' Quarters** – 1 Sallyport, off Bridge Street. ✆01289 763 209. www.the-captainsquarters.co.uk. 📶. 5 rooms. Located in the heart of Berwick's old town, this super-stylish eclectic 'bar and brasserie with rooms', is widely acclaimed as one of the best new places to stay in the North .

🍴 EAT

DURHAM

☺ Good traditional pubs to try in Durham include the Market Tavern (Market Place) and the Victoria (Hallgarth Street).

☺☻🍴 **DH1** – The Avenue. ✆0191 384 6655. www.restaurantdh1.co.uk. Open Tue–Sat dinner. Serving modern cuisine, this is an intimate restaurant on the lower floor of a large Victorian house. There is a wide choice of dishes from a weekly market menu to a vegetarian tasting menu.

NEWCASTLE

☺ **Kafeneon** – 8 Bigg Market. ✆0191 260 2577. www.kafeneon.co.uk. The darling of Newcastle's café scene, this unpretentious well established little place is as good for a cup of real coffee as it is for authentic Greek and Mediterranean food at bargain prices.

☺ **Tandoori Nights** – 17 Grey Street. ✆0191 221 0312. Opposite the Theatre Royal, this stylish Indian restaurant specialises in Balti cuisine, vegetarian dishes and sharing *thali* plates.

☺☻ **Café Royal** – 8 Nelson Street. ✆0191 231 3000. Open 8am–6pm. Closed Sun. This attractive contemporary European café-bistro is as good for weary shoppers as it is for impressing a lunch date.

☺☻ **Artisan** – The Biscuit Factory, Stoddart Street. ✆0191 260 5411. www.artisannewcastle.com. Closed Mon–Tue. Bright and airy, set in the Biscuit Factory, the UK's largest art, craft and design gallery; the menu changes each monthly to make the most of seasonal produce.

☺☻ **21** – Trinity Gardens. ✆0191 222 0755. www.artisannewcastle.com. www.21newcastle.co.uk. Fresh ingredients, well prepared; the menus offer an array of confidently cooked classics. Try the dish of the day; great value.

☺☻🍴🍴 **House of Tides** – 28–30 The Close. ✆0191 230 3720. www.houseoftides.co.uk. Closed Sun. This Michelin-starred eatery is housed in a 16C merchant's house with original flagged floors, cast iron pillars and exposed bricks. The dishes are well balanced, perfectly presented and reflecting the locale in its choice of produce.

HADRIAN'S WALL

☺☻ **The Angel of Corbridge** – Main Street, Corbridge. ✆01434 632 119. www.theangelofcorbridge.com. This fine old 18C coaching inn has been handsomely restored and serves both traditional pub grub and gastropub fare.

☺☻ **Ristorante Adriano** – 1 Rickergate, Carlisle. ✆01228 599 007. http://ristorante adriano.co.uk. Carlisle's top Italian restaurant serves pizzas, pastas and a wide range of classic dishes.

ALNWICK

☺☻ **Tree House** – Alnwick Garden. ✆01665 511 852. www.alnwickgarden.com. Closed dinner Mon–Wed. Dine in magical surroundings with either a simple lunch or a special candlelit dinner, on locally sourced British cuisine.

Scotland

*Pipe band performing at The Muster, a regional gathering of
Lowland and Border Clans, Bowhill House, Scottish Borders*
© Loop Images/Photononstop

Introduction

There are few countries that offer so much instant popular imagery as Scotland: lochs and mountains, tweed and tartan, kilts and bagpipes, haggis and whisky. It may fuel the tourist trade, but this fiercely patriotic nation entered the 21C bearing a new identity, most vigorously represented by the new Scottish Parliament, a symbol of a modern country intent on self-rule. The old cultural trappings remain, but are now joined by many modern icons, and the country as a whole has become a fashionable destination for both short city breaks and get-away-from-it-all holidays, often in the great outdoors.

Southern Scotland

The romance of the gentle rolling **Scottish Borders** is encapsulated in the words of Walter Scott – whose Abbotsford home is a star attraction – and the many evocative ruins of abbeys and castles littering the landscape.

Robert Burns took his poetic inspiration from **Ayrshire**, **Dumfries and Galloway**, which remain largely unspoilt. Across the water from Ayr, the Isle of **Arran**, known as 'Scotland in miniature', is a tonic for the stresses of modern life. **Edinburgh** is a useful introduction to many aspects of Scottish history and culture. Not only is it the nation's most beautiful and sophisticated city, during Festival season is also the most exciting place in Britain. Its hinterland, the **Lothians** is home to some of Scotland's most famous sights, while across the Firth of Forth is the ancient kingdom of **Fife**, not only the ancestral home of Scottish monarchs, but, in St Andrews, also the cradle of golf. Due west of Edinburgh, the buzzing, sometimes gritty metropolis of **Glasgow** is a vibrant mix of year-round arts and culture, world-class museums, stylish places to eat and stay, and some of the best shopping in the UK.

Central Scotland

Heading north, **Stirling and Argyll** is the glorious Scotland of the popular imagination and stunning landscapes, home to Rob Roy, William ('Braveheart') Wallace, the Mull of Kintyre, Tobermory, and Loch Lomond, among many other national icons. **Dundee**, Scotland's fourth city, has recently spruced itself up for visitors. **Angus** is famous for Glamis Castle and its Pictish legacy. The picturesque central region of **Perthshire** was Scotland's ancient royal heartland; today it is one of the adventure-sports capitals

Highlights

1   Stroll **Edinburgh's** Royal Mile from castle to palace (p505)
2   Discover the secrets of the **Burrell Collection** (p519)
3   Ascend **Cairn Gorm** and walking or skiing its slopes (p538)
4   Cruise the bonny bonny banks of **Loch Lomond** (p527)
5   Take in the scenery, **Kyle of Lochalsh** to **Gairloch** (p547)

of Europe. The **Grampians** are famous for their turreted castles, malt whisky distilleries, dramatic mountains rugged coastlines, and Royal Deeside. Less traditionally known is Aberdeen, Scotland's third city, today grown wealthy and sophisticated on oil wealth.

Northern Scotland

Imagined Scotland comes to life in the **Highlands** with majestic scenery, awesome wilderness, towering mountains, and broad expanses of shimmering water, none more famous than Loch Ness. The west coast islands known as the **Western Isles**, or **Outer Hebrides**, have a magic and identity all their own, with elemental beauty and stern weather, well-known to walkers and nature watchers.

To the north, beyond the isolated edge of the wild mainland lie the remote archipelagos of the **Orkneys, Fair Isle** and **Shetland**; the latter feels almost Scandinavian. Both island groups have a deep sense of history and local culture, are surprisingly varied, and boast some of Europe's oldest prehistoric monuments.

Scottish Borders★★

The gentle rolling countryside of the Borders makes an easy transition from England, but its multitude of ruins and castles tell of a turbulent history. Ironically, these very places, where destruction and death were meted out, are now some of the region's favourite beauty spots.

◔ **Michelin Map:** Michelin Atlas p50 or Map 501.
🖹 **Info:** www.scot-borders.co.uk.

TWEED VALLEY★★

The River Tweed rises in the Tweedsmuir Hills to the west of the Borders and flows eastwards acting as the frontier with England for the latter part of its journey, ending at Berwick-upon-Tweed, 97mi/156km east. Allow three days.

The Tweed valley has long been a favoured area of settlement. Ancient forts and monastic houses are found all over the region. It was much fought over and the troubled times are remembered in many a Border ballad and poem. Today, the valley is primarily agricultural, though the traditional woollen and knitwear industries are the mainstay of the towns. On its long and beautiful course the Tweed flows past several famous landmarks – castles, abbeys and great houses – making the exploration of its banks a delight.

🚗 DRIVING TOUR

106mi/170km.

Moffat

At the head of the Annan valley, the small town of Moffat makes a good base from which to explore the area.

◖ Take the A 708 Selkirk road.

Grey Mare's Tail★★

At the head of Moffat Water valley is the Grey Mare's Tail, a spectacular hanging valley waterfall with a 60m drop. The road leads on up the now narrow

V-shaped valley to cross the pass and then descends the valley of the Little Yarrow Water. Here, by St Mary's Loch, is Tibbie Shiel's Inn (www.tibbieshiels.com), meeting place of **James Hogg** (1770–1835), 'the Ettrick Shepherd' and his friends.

◖ Half way along St Mary's Loch, take the road to the left (signed for Tweedsmuir,) soon passing Megget Reservoir and, later, Talla Reservoir. At Tweedsmuir, turn right onto the A 701 towards Broughton, but 2km before reaching Broughton turn right onto the B 712. At the junction with the A72, turn right towards Peebles.

One mile short of Peebles, on a rocky outcrop overlooking the river is **Neidpath Castle**, a 14C L-plan tower house, typical of the fortified dwellings needed in the days of border and clan warfare.

Peebles

The former spa town is a good centre from which to explore the Tweeddale countryside, or to fish for salmon.

It has a rich literary tradition. **Robert Louis Stevenson** lived here, while **William Chambers**, publisher of the famous dictionary, was born in Peebles and donated to the town the **Chambers Institution**, comprising a library, and a museum and art gallery. The latter also includes the **John Buchan Story Museum** (High Street; open Easter–Oct Mon–Sat 10am–4.30pm; £2; ✆01721 723525; www.johnbuchansociety.co.uk), a tribute to the author (1875–1940), best known for *The Thirty-Nine Steps*, who as Lord Tweedsmuir also became a famous statesman. Buchan grew up in this area. Another famous local is the explorer of West Africa, **Mungo Park** (1771–1806) who lived in Pebbles.

▶ Some 6mi/10km down river, by the A 72, cross the Tweed at Innerleithen

Traquair House★★

Open daily: Apr–Sept 11am–5pm; Oct 11am–4pm; Nov Sat–Sun only 11am–3pm. £8.80, grounds only, £4.50. ♿🅿✕ ✆01896 830 323. www.traquair.co.uk.

There was a royal hunting lodge here as early as 1107, which was transformed into a Border 'peel', or fortified tower house, during the Wars of Independence. The wings were added in the late-17C. This typical tower house has a wealth of relics, treasures and traditions and many Jacobite associations and personal belongings of Mary Queen of Scots. Also of interest are the **vaulted chamber** where cattle used to be herded in times of raids, a priest's room and a **brew-house** whose ale is highly regarded. In the grounds are a maze and craft workshops. The biennial **Traquair Fair**, held on the first weekend August, is a very popular family event.

▶ Return to the A 72 and turn right (east). At a junction, keep right onto the A 707, still following the course of the Tweed. After 4.3km/2.5mi turn onto the B 7060 to its junction with the A 7. Turn right, and having crossed the Tweed, left along the B 6360 to Abbotsford.

Abbotsford★★

Open Mar and Nov daily 10am–4pm; Apr–Oct 10am–5pm. £9.60, child under 17, £4.90. 🅿♿✕ ✆01896 752 043. www.scottsabbotsford.co.uk.

Abbotsford is typical of **Sir Walter Scott** (1771–1832), the man who did so much to romanticise and popularise all things Scottish. He bought the house in 1812 and transformed it into a Scottish baronial fantasy in stone. An extensive programme of refurbishment was completed in 2013, including a new **visitor centre** interpreting Scott's life and achievements.

In Abbotsford House is Scott's massive writing desk together with a collection of some 9 000 rare books, and many other items relating to Scotland and its history.

▶ Continue along the B-road to junction with A 6091, and turn right to Melrose.

Melrose★

The pleasant town, grouped around abbey ruins, is dominated by the **Eildon Hills**. Their triple summit – of volcanic origin – was believed to have been the work of Michael Scott, a 13C wizard, who is buried in the abbey.

David I founded **Melrose Abbey★★** (open daily: Apr–Sept 9.30am–5.30pm; Oct–Mar 4pm; £6; 🅿; ✆01896 822 562; www.historicenvironment.scot) in 1136. Once one of the richest abbeys in Scotland, the original buildings were damaged in the 14C, notably in 1322 by Edward II's retreating army. Robert the Bruce, whose heart is buried here, ensured their rebuilding. The ruins date from the late-14C to the early-16C and are distinguished by a profusion of **decorative sculpture★★★**: delicate tracery, canopied niches, intricate vaulting and ornate gables.

▶ Leave Melrose and join the A 6091 (heading east) to A 68, turn left. Once over the river, right onto a minor road to Leaderfoot and on to the junction with B 6365, then up Bemersyde Hill.

Scott's View★★

The magnificent viewpoint (181m) faces west across the winding Tweed to the three conical peaks of the Eildons.

▶ Local road to Dryburgh abbey.

Dryburgh Abbey★★

Open daily: Apr–Sept 9.30am–5.30pm; Oct–Mar 4pm; £6; 🅿 ✆01835 822 381. www.historicenvironment.scot.

One of the group of Border abbeys founded by David I, begun in 1150, Dryburgh was repeatedly attacked by the English in the 1300s and badly damaged when the town was razed in 1544. A sheltered meander of the Tweed provides a splendid **setting★★★** for the majestic ruins of the abbey in mellow red stone. Sir Walter Scott is buried in the east chapel.

▶ Return to the B 6356 and turn right; take the B 6404 to St Boswells; turn left on the A 699 by the Tweed.

Kelso★

Standing at the confluence of the Tweed and the Teviot, Kelso grew from a fording place into a thriving market town. Here again are the ruins of a fine **abbey**, founded 1128, but many times destroyed. The town has some remarkable Georgian architecture and the cobbled town **square★★** features an elegant 19C **town hall**. The graceful bridge was built in 1803 by John Rennie. On the outskirts of Kelso is **Floors Castle★** (open Easter and late-Apr–Sept daily 10.30am–5pm; Oct Sat–Sun only; £11.50; grounds only, £6.50; ♿️🅿️✗; ☎️01573 223 333; www.floorscastle.com). The distinctive pinnacled silhouette stands on a terraced site overlooking the Tweed. The main block, built to the designs of William Adam, was extended in the 19C when William Playfair added the wings. Many of the rooms were refurbished early this century to accommodate an outstanding collection of **tapestries** and **furniture**.

Mellerstain House & Gardens★★

6mi/10km NW of Kelso via the A 6089. Open Apr–Sept Fri–Mon 12.30–5pm; gardens 11am–5pm. £8.50. Gardens only, £5. ♿️🅿️✗ ☎️01573 410 225. www.mellerstain.com.
The glory of this 18C mansion is the delicacy of Robert Adam's interior. The **ceilings★★★** in delicate pastel colours are complemented by matching fireplaces, woodwork and furniture. The **Library★★★** is a masterpiece.

▶ Return to Kelso and continue NE on the A 698 to Coldstream.

Follow the A 698 to Cornhill-on-Tweed, then A 697 to Branxton.

Flodden Field

www.flodden1513.com.
A monument inscribed 'To the brave of both nations' marks Pipers Hill, the centre of the English positions. Here, on 9 September 1513, the English army, some 20 000 strong, slaughtered around 10 000 of their Scottish opponents who numbered 25 000. This included most of Scotland's nobility and their king, James IV, who had led them into battle in support of his recently renewed 'Auld Alliance' with the French. It is said that the English suffered between 1 000 and 4 000 dead.
An old red telephone box in the village has been converted into what is termed 'the smallest visitor centre in the world'.

Jedburgh★

10mi/16km N of the border.
The royal burgh of Jedburgh, spanning the Jed Water with a mid-12C triple-arched bridge, was once a much fought-over border post. Today it is a peaceful market town.

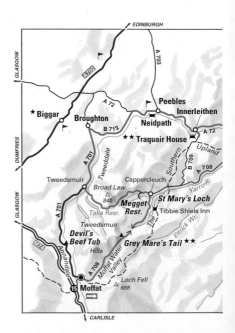

Jedburgh Town Walk

Begin at **Jedburgh Abbey★★** (open daily 9.30am–5.30pm/Oct–Mar 10am–4pm; £6; &▣; ℰ01835 863 925; www.historicenvironment.scot), founded in 1138 for the Augustinian order. This was one of the many Border abbeys founded by David I to spread monasticism in 12C Scotland and witnessed the coronation of Malcolm IV in the 12C. The abbey was often plundered and attacked before the final destructive raid in 1545.

Continue north on Abbey Bridge End and turn down High Street. On Queen Street is the **Mary Queen of Scots Visitor Centre★** (open Mar–Nov Mon–Sat 9.30am–4.30pm, Sun 10.30am–4pm; ℰ01835 863 331; www.scotborders.gov.uk/museums), a fine 16C tower house where Mary stayed in 1566. Engraved glass panels, paintings and documents relate the life of this tragic queen.

Jedburgh Castle Jail and Museum (open Easter–Oct Mon–Sat 10am–4.30pm; Sun 1–4pm; ℰ01835 864 750, www.scotborders.gov.uk/museums), built in 1823 on the site of the original castle, was one of the most modern jails of its day.

Bowhill★★

19mi/31km NW by the A 68, A 699, A 7 and A 708. **House**: visit by guided tours only; check website for relevant days. **Park**: Apr–Aug Mon–Fri 10am–4pm, Sat–Sun 10am–5pm and daily in Jul–Aug; Sept Fri–Mon. £10, Park only £4.50. ℰ01750 22204. www.bowhill.org.

Among the many treasures that grace Bowhill are fine pieces of French **furniture**, Mortlake tapestries, relics of the Duke of Monmouth and an important collection of paintings including works by Leonardo da Vinci, Canaletto, Claude, Wilkie *(George IV in Highland Dress)*, Reynolds *(Winter, The Pink Boy)*, Gainsborough and other masters.

Hermitage Castle★

26mi/42km SW on the B 6358 and A 698, B 6399. Open Apr–Sept daily 9.30am–5.30pm. £5 ▣ ℰ01387 376 222. www.historicenvironment.scot.

In its isolated moorland setting this massive 14C ruin has a history of torture, treason and romantic trysts and evokes the Borders' dark past. A strategic stronghold of the Wardens of the March, it guarded the old reivers' routes.

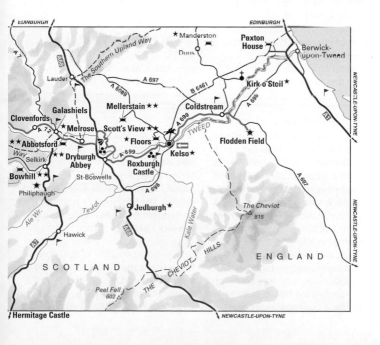

Beach at Lamlash, Isle of Arran

Ayrshire and Arran★★

Aside from Burns' pilgrims and keen seaside golfers, few visitors have Ayrshire as a 'must see' on their itinerary. Most of the visitors who come to the west coast are Irish (from just across the sea) though many American holidaymakers also make their first Scottish footfall just outside Ayr, at the confusingly named Glasgow Prestwick Airport. Most head east, to Edinburgh, but they could do worse than turn west, and cross the water to the Isle of Arran for an equally fine introduction to the country.

ISLE OF ARRAN★★

Arran is the largest of the islands in the Firth of Clyde, measuring some 20mi/32km long by 10mi/16km wide and with a population of just over 5 000. Cut in two by the Highland Boundary Fault, it is said to present 'Scotland in miniature'. A mountainous northern part (Goat Fell 874m) has deep valleys and moorlands, while the southern half consists of lowland scenery. Sheltered bays and sandy beaches, together with ample facilities for yachting, swimming, golf, sea-angling and fishing, make tourism the island's principal industry.

- ◔ **Michelin Map:** Michelin Atlas p48, p53 or Map 501 E 17.
- ▯ **Info:** The Pier, Brodick. 22 Sandgate, Ayr. ℘0845 225 5121 (both). www.ayrshire-arran.com.
- ☺ **Don't Miss:** Brodick Castle's rhododendron garden in bloom (late spring). Culzean Castle for its clifftop setting.

🚗 ISLAND TOUR

56mi/90km. Allow about half a day, not including visiting time. ☺ Make sure the fuel tank is full before setting out as there are few filling stations.

Mainly a coastal route, the road affords views of the diversity of scenery; but as well as the coast road, try the 10mi/16km String Road across the waist of the island, between Blackwaterfoot and Brodick. The first highlight is outside the port and bay from which it takes its name. **Brodick Castle★★** (currently closed to the public; grounds remain open; check website for details. ℘01770 302 202; www.nts.org.uk) is the historic stronghold of the Hamiltons, Earls of Arran. The 13C red sandstone castle was extended by Cromwell in 1652 and again in the

Baronial style in 1844. The Hamilton and Beckford treasures comprise a fine collection of silver, porcelain, furniture and family portraits as well as paintings by Watteau, Turner and Herring. The gilded heraldic ceiling is remarkable. The castle's 18C formal walled garden and 26ha **rhododendron garden**, one of the finest in Britain, benefit from the mild local climate.

Arran was on the main migration route for Neolithic agriculturalists up the western seaboard of Scotland and around 1.5mi/2.4km inland off the road north of Blackwaterfoot, lie the **Machrie Moor Stone Circles** (accessible at all times). Built about the same time as the later parts of Stonehenge, these remnants of five Bronze Age stone circles remains enjoy a powerful setting of moorland backed by mountains.

As the road swings round Arran's southern tip, the granite island of **Ailsa Craig** (300m high) can be seen to the south. The road from Lamlash Bay, sheltered by Holy Island, back to Brodick gives a spectacular view of its castle, dominated by Goat Fell.

SOUTH AYRSHIRE

Ayr is 36mi/58km SW of Glasgow. Ayr station is 1mi/1.6km from the town centre. The bus station is at Sandgate in the centre.

Ayr is a pleasant market town that has grown up around a medieval core. Today it is a thriving resort on Scotland's southwest coast with splendid sandy beaches as well as a famous racecourse and golf courses which host international competitions. It is most notable, however, as the hub of **Burns Country**.

Robert Burns Birthplace Museum★

Alloway 3mi/5km S of Ayr by the B 7024. Main entrance Murdoch's Lane. Open daily 10am–5.30pm. Closed 24 Dec–3 Jan. £9. ⊒✕ ☏01292 443 700. www.burnsmuseum.org.uk.

Alloway is famed as the birthplace of Robert Burns (1759–96), whose birthday on 25 January is celebrated throughout the world. At the entrance is an

A Moving Landmark

According to tradition, Ayr's Auld Brig (13C), a narrow cobbled bridge immortalised by the Scottish bard, Robert Burns, was financed by two sisters who lost their fiancés when they drowned trying to ford the river in spate.

excellent new visitor centre leading to an idyllically landscaped site where the story of Scotland's national poet is imaginatively followed. The spartan **Burns Cottage★** evokes his humble origins and displays an extensive collection of manuscripts and relics; the **Burns Monument** overlooks the River Doon and the 13C **Brig o'Doon**, while **Alloway Kirk** also has Burns associations.

Culzean Castle★

16mi/26km SW of Ayr by A 719.
Castle: open Apr–Oct daily 10.30am–5pm. **Country Park**: open all year daily 10am–3pm. Castle and country park £15.50 (country park only £10.50). ⎃⊒✕. ☏01655 884 455. www.nts.org.uk.

Culzean Castle ('cull-ean') enjoys a dramatic clifftop **setting★★★**. It was the work of **Robert Adam** (1728–92), who, although a Classicist, added arrow slits and battlements to complete the mock-medieval touch. The harmonious interior is enhanced by friezes, chimneypieces and delicately patterned ceilings. The elegant **Oval Staircase★★** and **Saloon** are good examples of the architect's original style. He also designed the splendid furnishings. American visitors may be interested in the castle's connection with former American president Eisenhower.

The grounds include a Victorian walled garden comprising the Pleasure Garden with extensive herbaceous borders, the restored Victorian Vinery and Peach House, a Fountain Court Garden, a herb garden, wildlife garden and an adventure playground.

Dumfries and Galloway

If Scotland has an unknown corner, then it is probably the western borders region of Dumfries ('dum-freece') and Galloway. It is less polished than its better-known neighbour, the Borders, due east, but has many of the same appealing ingredients, some truly wild areas, much fewer visitor numbers and a distinct lack of coach parties on the 'Shortbread and Tartan' heritage trail.

⚅ **Michelin Map:** Michelin Atlas p49 or Map 501 J 18.

⬛ **Info:** 64 Whitesands. ✆01387 253 862. www.visitdumfries andgalloway.co.uk.

⬤ Both the train station (Station Road, off English Street; Glasgow Central 1h44) and the bus station (Whitesands) are in the town centre.

◗ **Location:** Southwest Scotland, 33mi/53km northwest of Carlisle across the border.

◷ **Timing:** Allow 2 days.

DUMFRIES★

The 'Queen of the South', Dumfries is the chief town of Scotland's south-west, best known for its historical associations. **Robert the Bruce** (1306–29) started his long campaign to free Scotland from Edward I in Dumfries by killing John Comyn, one of the competitors for the crown, and having himself crowned at Scone in 1306. Eight years later, his victory at Bannockburn was key to achieving Scotland's independence. **Robert Burns** is Dumfries' most famous son.

Drumlanrig Castle★★

18mi/29km northwest of Dumfries on the A 76. Castle: open Easter, May bank holidays and Jul–Aug (tours start 11am); gardens Apr–Sept daily 10am–5pm. Castle £10. gardens only, £6. ♿🅿✕ ✆01848 331 555.
www.drumlanrigcastle.co.uk.
The castle was a 14C–18C Douglas stronghold and stands impressively with four square towers quartering the courtyard structure. Innovation comes with the main façade and its terraces, horseshoe staircase, dramatic turreted skyline and rich sculptural detail. The interior holds a superb collection of paintings (including a Holbein and a Rembrandt), fine furniture and clocks. In the oak-panelled Dining Room, carved panels attributed to Grinling Gibbons alternate with 17C silver sconces and family portraits.

New Abbey

8mi/13km southwest of Dumfries on the A 710.
This pretty little one-street village with ducks on the millpond grew up to service **Sweetheart Abbey★** (open Apr–Sept daily 9.30am–5.30pm; Oct–Mar daily except Thu–Fri 10am–4pm; £5; 🅿; ✆01387 850 397; www.historicenvironment.scot). Founded in 1273 by Lady Devorgilla of Galloway, in memory of her husband John Balliol, this was the last Cistercian abbey in Scotland. The name derives from the fact that the foundress was laid to rest together with a casket containing the embalmed heart of her husband. The beauty and charm of the ruins are enhanced by the contrast between warm red sandstone and the clipped green of surrounding lawns.

A short walk away is the **New Abbey Corn Mill** (open Apr–Sept daily 9.30am–5.30pm; Oct–Mar daily except Thu–Fri 10am–4pm; £4.50; 🅿; ✆01387 850 260; www.historicenvironment.scot), a fully restored water-powered corn mill built around the end of the 18C and in service unit just after the Second World War. Now a charming time capsule, it operates daily in summer.

Caerlaverock Castle★

9mi/15km southeast of Dumfries
on the B 725. Open daily: Apr–Sept
10am–4.30pm; Oct 10am–3.30pm;
Nov–Mar daily except Tue and Thu
10am–3.30pm. £5.50. ♿✗🅿 ✆01387
770 244. www.historic-scotland.gov.uk.
Overlooking the Solway Firth, this
imposing medieval castle is girt by a
moat and earthen ramparts. Its formidable exterior is in contrast to the harmonious **Renaissance courtyard façade★★**.
It suffered many border conflicts and it
was besieged by Edward I in 1300 (there
is a siege warfare exhibition in the castle
visitor centre). It was besieged again in
1640, and following its surrender to the
Covenanters was demolished.

Ruthwell Cross★

Ruthwell Parish Church, 8.5mi/13.5km
southeast of Dumfries. Open by
arrangement only. ✆01387 550 7612.
www.historic-scotland.gov.uk.
The late-7C Ruthwell Cross is regarded
as one of the major monuments of
early medieval Europe and depicts
the Life and Passion of Christ, complete with detailed tracery, animals
and birds, and runic inscriptions. It
is an outstanding example of **early
Christian art**. The cross was demolished in 1642 by the General Assembly; the pieces were re-assembled and
installed here in the church in 1887.

KIRKCUDBRIGHT★

26.5mi southwest of Dumfries.
Now promoted to visitors as an 'artist's
town', Kirkcudbright (pronounced 'cur-
coo-bree') has historically depended
on farming and fishing, and is the only
town in the region to retain its fishing
fleet. The attractive town centre dates
from the Georgian and Victorian periods and has several historic properties
open to visitors. The town's artistic
legacy (late-19C and the early-20C),
outlined in the **Tolbooth Art Centre**
(open Apr–Sept daily 10am–4pm; Oct–
Mar Mon–Sat 11am–4pm; ✆01557 331
556, www.dumgal.gov.uk).

Threave Estate★★

Castle Douglas, 17mi southwest of
Dumfries. Open **House:** Apr–late Oct,
Wed–Fri and Sun 11am and 3.30pm
guided tours only; Garden Jan–Feb
and Nov–23 Dec 11am–3pm, Mar–Oct
10am–5pm. £12.50; garden only, £7.50
✆01556 502575. www.nts.org.uk.
Best known for its magnificent display
of springtime daffodils, **Threave Garden**
is worth a visit in all seasons.
Highlights include the rose garden, the
herbaceous perennials, and the walled
garden with its outstanding temperate glasshouse collection. The principal
rooms of the Scottish Baronial Threave
House have been restored to the way
they were in the 1930s.

Robert Burns (1759–96)

The Bard lived and farmed in and around Dumfries and a statue stands at the
north end of the High Street. The **Robert Burns Centre Film Theatre** (Mill
Road; ♿🅿✗; ✆01387 264 808; www.rbcft.co.uk) is an excellent introduction.
Burns spent his final years just across the river, at **Burns House**, now a museum
(Burns Street; open Apr–Sept Mon–Sat 10am–5pm, Sun 2–5pm; Oct–Mar Tue–Sat
10am–1pm, 2–5pm; ✆01387 255 297; www.dumgal.gov.uk). He had moved here
after giving up his former home at **Ellisland Farm** (Hollywood Road; open early
Jan–Nov Mon–Sat 10am–1pm, 2–5pm, Sun 2–5pm; Oct–Mar closed Sun–Mon;
closed Dec–early Jan; £5; ✆01387 740 426; www.ellislandfarm.co.uk), just north
of Dumfries, in order to take up a post with the Excise. Back in town, a few
yards from Burns House, the churchyard of St Michael's is home to the **Burns
Mausoleum** where Burns, his wife (Jane Armour) and several of their children
are buried. **Alloway** *(3mi/5km S of Ayr)*, his birthplace, is also on the **Burns Trail**
(leaflets from tourist information centres).

Edinburgh★★★

City of Edinburgh

Edinburgh, capital of Scotland, lies on the Firth of Forth, a deep inlet gouged into the east coast. The city is located on a series of volcanic hills, each giving a different and often spectacular vantage point. Most famous of these is Arthur's Seat (251m), overlooking Holyrood Park. Edinburgh boasts a colourful history; the Old Town, huddled for years on the ridge running down from the Castle Rock, contrasts with the New Town, with its elegant Georgian streets and squares. Both are inscribed as World Heritage Sites.

A BIT OF HISTORY

The Castle Rock had been a secure refuge for generations when in the late-11C Malcolm Canmore and Queen Margaret chose the site for their residence. Their son, David I, favoured the site by founding the Abbey of the Holy Rood. During the reign of the early Stuarts Edinburgh gradually assumed the roles of royal residence, seat of government and capital of Scotland. With the Union of the Crowns (1603) and subsequent departure of James VI of Scotland and I of England for London, Edinburgh lost much of its pageantry and cultural activity. In 1707 self-rule came to an end with the Union of the Parliaments.

It was in the late-18C during the Enlightenment, a period of intellectual ferment, that plans were mooted for a civic project of boldness and imagination:

PUBLIC TRANSPORT

Bus services are frequent and usually run on time. A tram service in the city centre was installed in 2009. Visit the Tourist Information Centre for all transport enquiries.

▶ **Population:** 495 360.

🌐 **Michelin Map:** Michelin Atlas p56 or Map 501 K 16.

ℹ **Info:** 3 Princes Street. ℘0131 473 3868. www.visitscotland.com.

🚶 The city is compact. You can visit most of the centre on foot. Waverley Station, accommodates all main bus and train services (London Kings Cross 4h20, Glasgow Queen Street 49min). Haymarket Station is 2mi/3km west of the centre and also services Glasgow (42min), Fife and the Highlands.

▶ **Location:** Edinburgh lies 4km/2½mi inland of the Firth of Forth at Leith, and 42km/26mi from the east coast of Scotland.,

👁 **Don't Miss:** The Royal Mile; a ghost tour; the Scottish Parliament Building; the views Arthur's Seat; Charlotte Square; Royal Museum and Museum of Scotland; Royal Yacht *Britannia*; Forth Bridges view.

🕐 **Timing:** At least 3 days.

👪 **Kids:** Edinburgh Zoo; Our Dynamic Earth; Deep Sea World (North Queensferry).

🚶 **Walking Tours:** Edinburgh Literary Pub Tour (℘0131 226 6665; www.edinburgh literarypubtour.co.uk); Mercat Tours (℘0131 225 5445; www.mercattours. com); City of the Dead Tours (℘0131 225 9044; www.cityofthedeadtours. com – not for children). **Bus Tours:** City tours depart daily from Waverley Bridge (℘0131 220 0770; www. city-sightseeing.co.uk).

🅿 **Parking:** Difficult and expensive. Walk or use the bus and tram.

Military Tattoo at Edinburgh Castle

the creation of the Georgian New Town. The town has gained further status as the seat of the Scottish Assembly, which sits in the new Parliament building next to the Palace of Holyroodhouse.

OLD TOWN

1 THE ROYAL MILE★★★

The principal thoroughfare of Old Edinburgh runs from the castle down the ridge through Castle Hill, Lawnmarket, High Street and Canongate to the abbey and Palace of Holyroodhouse. For two centuries the city's Flodden Wall (16C) restricted the spread of Edinburgh, confining expansion to the 10- and 12-storey "tenements", with narrow wynds and closes, so typical of the Old Town. The few original buildings which remain can still today give the impression of what medieval and 17C Edinburgh must have looked like.

Castle★★

Open daily Apr–Sept 9.30am–6pm; Oct–Mar 9.30am–5pm (1 Jan 11am–5pm). Closed 25–26 Dec. £17. ⚐✕ ℘0131 225 9846. www.edinburghcastle.gov.uk.

The iconic silhouette of the castle on its strategic site atop **Castle Rock-★★★** is the best-known view of Edinburgh. Although a royal residence since the 11C, the castle and most of the buildings today are basically those resulting from its use as a military garrison over recent centuries. The esplanade, an 18C parade ground, is the setting for the Edinburgh Festival's most popular event, the Military Tattoo. The fortifications afford splendid **views** across Princes Street to the New Town. The **one o'clock salute** is fired from one of the batteries. The main points of interest are as follows: the **Honours of Scotland★★★** (the Scottish Crown Jewels), kept, along with the **Stone of Destiny**, in the Crown Room; **Mons Meg**, one of the oldest cannons in the world; the **National War Museum**; the

---

Edinburgh International Festival★★★

This prestigious festival held every August has provided a top-quality programme in all the art forms since 1947. The **Military Tattoo** presents a spectacle rich in colour, tradition, music and excitement, under the floodlights of the Castle Esplanade. **The Fringe** spills out onto the streets and squares of Edinburgh, with performers from all over the globe presenting over a thousand productions, often avant-garde, sometimes just plain eccentric. Also held during this period is the **International Book Festival**. Visit www.eif.co.uk for full details.

EDINBURGH

WHERE TO STAY

Glasshouse (The)...................... ❶

Prestonfield............................... ❷

Principal (The)........................... ❸

Scotsman (The)......................... ❹

WHERE TO EAT

Grain Store (The)....................... ❶

Le Café Saint-Honoré................. ❷

Tower Restaurant....................... ❸

Witchery by the Castle (The)...... ❹

Camera Obscura and
World of Illusions................... A

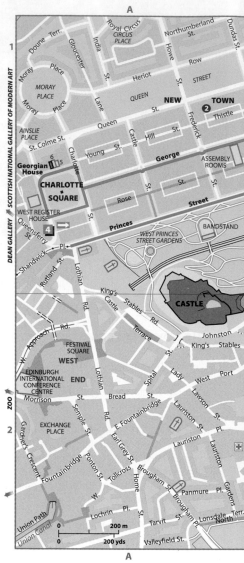

12C **St Margaret's chapel**, dedicated to Malcolm's queen and the panoramic **views**★★★ from its terrace; **Prisons of War**, an atmospheric re-creation of prison life in the late-18C; the **National War Memorial**; the 16C **Great Hall** with its hammerbeam roof★★, and its striking display of arms and armour; the **Royal Palace**, built in 1617 for James VI with outstanding plasterwork ceilings★★★.

Castle Hill

Just below the castle is the **Scotch Whisky Experience** (entry by tour only, Silver Tour daily Jan–Mar and Sept–Dec 10am–5pm; Apr–Jul 6pm; Aug Mon–Fri 10am–5pm, Sat–Sun 10am–5.40pm; closed 25 Dec; £15; ♿✕ ℘0131 220 0441; www.scotchwhiskyexperience.co.uk), with a ride through a replica distillery and various clever audio-visual exhibits on the art of whisky distilling.

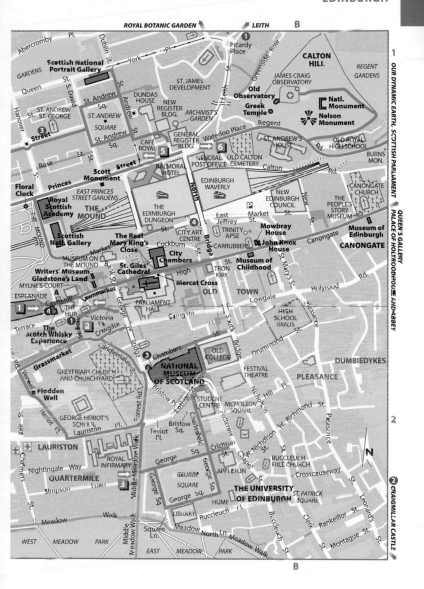

Opposite, stands the Outlook Tower housing Edinburgh's **Camera Obscura and World of Illusions** 👥👤 (open daily Apr–Jun and Sept–Oct 9.30am–7pm; Jul–Aug 9am–10pm; Nov–Mar 10am– 6pm; closed 25 Dec; £15, child 5–15, £11; &; ℘0131 226 3709; www.camera-obscura.co.uk), which affords a fascinating ever-changing live window on the city, as well as several galleries on illusions and magic.

Lawnmarket

Castle Hill leads into Lawnmarket. **Gladstone's Land**★ (open Apr–Oct daily 10am–5pm; £7; &; ℘0131 226 5856; www.nts.org.uk) is a typical narrow six-storey tenement erected within the city walls in the 17C; in 1617 it was acquired and extended by Thomas Gledstanes, a wealthy merchant.

The atmospheric restored premises comprise a shop with living quarters above, complete with original painted ceilings and furnishings.

A few strides downhill, along the narrow alleyway of Lady Stair's Close, **The Writers' Museum** (open Wed–Sat 10am–5pm, Sun noon–5pm; ℘0131 529 4901; www.edinburghmuseums.org.uk) showcases three of Scotland's greatest literary figures: Robert Burns (1759–96), Sir Walter Scott (1771–1832) and Robert Louis Stevenson (1850–94).

High Street

Lawnmarket leads into High Street and **St Giles' Cathedral★★** (open May–Sept Mon–Fri 9am–7pm, Sat 9am–5pm, Sun 1–5pm; Oct–Apr Mon–Sat 9am–5pm, Sun 1–5pm; contribution suggested; ✖; ℘0131 226 0674; www.stgilescathedral. org.uk). The present High Kirk of Edinburgh is probably the third church to occupy this site. Alterations and restorations have, however, drastically changed its character since its rebuilding in the 14C. The only original exterior feature is the crown **spire★★★** dating from 1495. Inside, it is the monuments and details that provide much of the interest.

Behind the cathedral on Parliament Square is the 17C **Parliament Hall** (open Mon–Fri 10am–4pm; closed bank holidays; ♿; ℘0131 225 2595), which was decreed by Charles I and in which the Scottish Parliament met from 1693 to 1707. It is now behind a Georgian façade. Its magnificent **hammerbeam roof** is an original feature. Nearby is a 17C equestrian statue of Charles II. At the east end of the square stands the **Mercat Cross**, formerly the hub of Edinburgh life, meeting place of traders and merchants and scene of royal proclamations, demonstrations and executions. Opposite the cathedral are the **City Chambers**, formerly the Royal Exchange built in 1753.

Adjacent, part of the same complex is the entrance to **The Real Mary King's Close** (Warriston's Close; open Apr–Oct daily 10am–9pm; Nov–Mar Sun–Thu 10am–5pm, Fri–Sat 10am–9pm; tours every 15 min from 10am; closed 25 Dec; £14.95; ✖; advance booking essential.

℘0131 225 0672. www.realmarykings close.com). Hidden beneath the Royal Mile lies a warren of 'closes' (narrow alleyways) where people lived, worked and died. As the Old Town expanded ever upwards, these closes became built over, or as legend has it, deliberately sealed up, inhabitants and all, whenever the dreaded plague visited (which it did frequently). For centuries they lay forgotten and abandoned, until the late-1990s when tours were licensed to reintroduce them to the general public. The Real Mary King's Close, complete with its many ghosts, is now the most popular of these.

Further down High Street is the picturesque **John Knox House** (open Mon–Sat 10am–6pm, Jul–Aug only Sun noon–6pm; £5; ♿✖; ℘0131 556 9579; www.tracscotland.org) built in about 1490, associated with both John Knox, the religious reformer, and with James Mossman, the goldsmith to Mary Queen of Scots. An exhibition incorporates details on both men and re-creates the atmosphere of 16C Edinburgh.

Next door is the early-17C **Mowbray House**, while across the road is the **Museum of Childhood ▲▲** (open Mon –Sat 10am–5pm, Sun noon–5pm; ♿; ℘0131 529 4142; www.edinburgh museums.org.uk), a fascinating collection devoted to anything and everything to do with local childhood.

Canongate

High Street leads into Canongate. Just before Canongate church stands the attractive 16C **Canongate Tolbooth★**, home to **The People's Story Museum** (open Wed–Sat 10am–5pm, Sun noon–5pm; ♿; ℘0131 529 4057; www.edin burghmuseums.org.uk). which uses oral history, reminiscence and written sources to tell the story of the lives, work and leisure of the ordinary people of Edinburgh, from the late-18C to the present day.

Opposite stand three 16C mansions known as Huntly House, occupied by the **Museum of Edinburgh** (open Mon and Thu–Sat 10am–5pm, Sun noon–5pm; ♿; ℘0131 529 4143) offering some fascinating local exhibits including the true story of the famously faithful dog, 'Greyfriars Bobby'.

Just before you arrive at the Scottish Parliament Building, turn right on Reid's Close to **Our Dynamic Earth** ♠♠ (open Apr-Oct daily 10am–5.30pm/Jul–Aug 6pm; Nov–Mar Wed–Sun 10am–5.30pm; £15; child 4–15, £9.50; ♠✕; ℘0131 550 7800; www.dynamicearth.co.uk). Occupying what appears to be a giant marquee just below the dramatic Salisbury Crags, Edinburgh's major Millennium visitor attraction gallops through the natural and geological history of the earth via a series of often spectacular exhibits, a 3-D and a 4-D film, and many hands-on displays.

At the end of Canongate is Britain's most controversial post-Millennium building, the **Scottish Parliament**★ (open Mon-Sat and public holidays 10am–5pm; Tue-Thu 9am–6.30pm – When Parliament is in recess (excluding February Recess and the Christmas break) the building is open from 10am until 5pm. ♠✕; ℘0131 348 5200; www.visitparliament.scot), where members of the public can attend debates, and visit both this remarkable building and exhibitions staged here. It was designed by Spanish architect Enric Miralles (1955–2000), who died before its completion in 2005, four years late and ten times over budget. Its unusual design and outlandish features make it not only a must-see for students of modern architecture, but also recommended viewing for anybody remotely interested in Scottish politics.

Palace of Holyroodhouse★★

Open Apr–Oct daily 9.30am–6pm; Nov–Mar daily 9.30am–4.30pm. £12.50 (joint ticket with Queen's Gallery £17.50). ♠ ℘0131 556 5100. www.royalcollection.org.uk.

At the east end of the Royal Mile, amid the green slopes of Holyrood Park, leading up to Arthur's Seat, stands the Palace of Holyrood, official residence of the monarch in Scotland.

The abbey was founded by David I, in 1128. James IV started to transform the guesthouse of the abbey into a royal palace but it was Charles II's architect Sir William Bruce who created a magnificent building in the Palladian style. On arrival you will find the **Queen's Gallery** (same hours as palace; £7, joint ticket with palace £17.50; ♠), which stages a programme of changing exhibitions of pieces from the Queen's private Royal Collection.

The inner court elevations are outstanding Renaissance work of the Stuart period and among Scotland's earliest examples. The decoration and craftsmanship in the **State Apartments** is outstanding, particularly the **plasterwork ceilings**★★★, the fruit of 10 years' labour by 'gentlemen modellers'.

The **Historic Apartments** in the 16C round tower have close associations with Mary Queen of Scots and contain tapestries from the Mortlake workshop founded by her son; the painted ceilings are magnificent. In the small room adjoining the bedchamber Mary's secretary, Rizzio, was murdered in 1566.

The roofless nave is all that is left of this once-great **abbey** (same opening times as the palace; guided tours in summer), dating from the late-12C and early-13C. Here lie David II, James II, James V and also Lord Darnley, father of James VI of Scotland, who united the crowns.

②/③ SOUTH OF THE MILE

Grassmarket was once one of Edinburgh's main markets, as well as the setting for public executions. Today it is a popular area for student accommodation and busy pubs and restaurants. Off here are the remains of the **Flodden Wall**, built following the disastrous battle in 1513 (see p498). Follow the route marked on the map to see **Edinburgh University**, laid out around George Square, before continuing to the National Museum of Scotland.

National Museum of Scotland★★★

Chambers Street. Open daily 10am–5pm (26 Dec and 1 Jan noon–5pm). Closed 25 Dec. Free, but donations welcome. ♠✕ ℘0131 247 4422. www.nms.ac.uk.

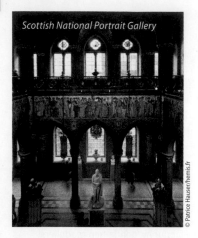

Scottish National Portrait Gallery

© Patrice Hauser/hemis.fr

The elaborate Venetian Renaissance-style façade of the main building contrasts with the interior. The spacious, well-lit Main Hall is a masterpiece of Victorian cast-iron and plate-glass construction. The museum, recently refurbished to great effect, has all-encompassing collections, devoted to the arts and sciences, from natural history to sculpture, and decorative arts from all over the world.

A sandstone drum tower highlights the innovative design of the **Scotland Galleries**, which traces the story of the country from 3 500 years ago to the present day with the unique collections placed in their historical perspective and with the help of an interactive computer system. The exhibits explain the natural landscape and geological foundation, the peopling of the country, the independent kingdom (1100–1707), the modern state and various other aspects of Scotland.

NEW TOWN★★★

When the decision had been taken to extend the Royalty of Edinburgh, the development was organised by a then unknown architect, James Craig, whose design had won the competition. The **North Bridge** was built across the valley and the New Town was laid out on a grid-iron pattern, with vistas and focal points. The wealthy soon took up residence in these splendid squares and elegant streets.

4 GEORGE STREET

The principal street of Craig's plan is closed at either end by Charlotte and St Andrew squares. From the street intersections there are good views away to the Forth or down to Princes Street Gardens with the castle as backdrop. George Street ends at St Andrew Square.

Head north from here on St Andrew Street to the **Scottish National Portrait Gallery★** (1 Queen Street; open daily 10am–5pm; closed 25–26 Dec; &✗; ✆0131 624 6200; www.nationalgalleries. org). Housed in a splendid Victorian building with wonderful mosaics at the entrance, it ...illustrates Scottish history by likeness of the chief actors in it'. This includes masterpieces of portraiture of royalty, statesmen, politicians, literary figures, sportsmen and musicians past and present, with some superbly innovative modern works.

In 1791, Robert Adam was commissioned to design **Charlotte Square★★★**, the New Town's most elegant ensemble. On the square, the National Trust for Scotland has magnificently refurbished No. 7, the **Georgian House★** (7 Charlotte Square; open daily Mar and 2 wks in Dec (Thu–Sun) 11am–4pm, Easter–Oct 10am–5pm, Nov 11am–4pm; £7.50; &; ✆0131 225 2160; www.nts.org.uk), is filled with Georgian treasures: furniture, silver, porcelain and fine paintings, while its lower floors give a good impression of domestic life in the period 1790–1810.

5 PRINCES STREET

Princes Street has grown from a totally residential street, looking out onto gardens in the newly filled-in Nor'Loch, into Edinburgh's prime shopping street. The gardens, famous for the **Floral Clock** composed of 20 000 annuals, opened to the public in 1876.

Following Sir Walter Scott's death in 1832, a public appeal was launched and the foundation stone of the **Scott Monument★** (Princes Street; open daily: Apr–Sept 10am–7pm; Oct–Mar daily

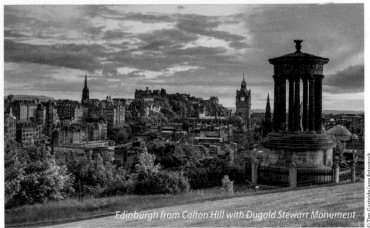

Edinburgh from Calton Hill with Dugald Stewart Monument

© Tim Gartside/age fotostock

10am–4pm; £5, ⬜cash only; ℘0131 529 4068; www.edinburghmuseums.org.uk) was laid in 1840. The 61m-tall Gothic spire shelters a marble statue of **Scott** and is surrounded by 64 characters from his novels and by the busts of 16 Scottish poets. A viewing platform (287 narrow stairs to the top) affords a magnificent **view★** over central Edinburgh. Dividing Princes Street Gardens into East and West are two imposing Classical buildings, the National Gallery and the Royal Scottish Academy.

The **Royal Scottish Academy** (entrance on Princes Street Gardens; open Mon–Sat 10am–5pm, Sun noon–5pm; closed in between exhibitions; &✖; ℘0131 225 3922, www.royalscottishacademy.org), stages temporary exhibitions of contemporary art.

Scottish National Gallery★★

The Mound. Open daily 10am–5pm (Thu 7pm). Closed 25–26 Dec. &✖ ℘0131 624 6200. www.nationalgalleries.org.
An imposing Classical building houses masterpieces of European art (15C–19C) by Raphael, Rembrandt, Vermeer, Poussin, Claude Lorrain, Boucher, Monet, Van Gogh and many more. The British tradition is represented by Turner, Gainsborough and Constable, among others. There is a fine collection of **Scottish paintings**, including Ramsay, Raeburn, McTaggart and the Glasgow school.

6 CALTON HILL

East of Princes Street, beyond elegant Waterloo Place, rises **Calton Hill** crowned by Classical monuments and follies which gave rise to the nickname 'Edinburgh's acropolis': the porticoed **National Monument**, a Greek temple and the 18C **Old Observatory**. There are wonderful views from here but for Edinburgh's best **panorama★★★** climb to the top of the **Nelson Monument**, a folly in the shape of an upturned telescope (open Apr–Sept Mon–Sat 10am–7pm, Sun noon–5pm; Oct–Mar Mon–Sat 10am–3pm; £5; ℘0131 556 2716; www.edinburghmuseums.org.uk). The harmonious sweep of **Regent**, **Calton** and **Royal terraces** (19C) is enhanced by its fine architectural and ironwork features.

OUTSKIRTS
Royal Botanic Garden★★★

1mi/1.6km from city centre by Broughton Street. Open daily Mar–Sept 10am–6pm; Feb and Oct 10am–5pm; Nov–Jan 10am–4pm. Garden free; glasshouses £6.50. &✖P. West Gate, Arboretum Road. ℘0131 552 7171. www.rbge.org.uk.
In 1670, when Edinburgh was emerging as a centre for medical studies, a physic garden was established by the university. The original plot was situated near Holyrood Abbey, but around 1820 it was moved to the present site. Today the

28ha of the Royal Botanic Garden are a refreshing haven from the city bustle. Highlights include the rhododendrons; the modernistic Exhibition Plant Houses (1967), which provide unimpeded interiors where winding paths lead through a series of landscaped presentations; the Exhibition Hall, devoted to changing displays and the Tropical (1834) and Temperate (1858) palm houses. Don't miss the view from the café terrace.

Scottish National Gallery of Modern Art★

West of the centre, on Belford Road beyond the Belford Bridge over the Water of Leith (signed footpath). Open daily 10am–5pm. Closed 25–26 Dec. &0131 624 6200. ⅂🅿✕ www.nationalgalleries.org.

In a garden setting with sculptures by Epstein, Hepworth and Moore, among others, the SNGMA is a treasure trove of 20C art. This ranges from Fauvism and Cubism, Dada and Surrealism (including works by Dalí, Miró, Ernst, Magritte and Picasso), to Russian Primitivism, Nouveau Réalisme, Pop Art and Scottish art, in particular by the Scottish Colourists and Edinburgh school.

While the main collection is now known as Modern One, immediately across the road is **Modern Two★** (same opening details and facilities as SNGMA), famous for its extensive collection of Dada and Surrealist art and work by Edinburgh-born Eduardo Paolozzi, among other works by him, and home to a changing programme of world-class exhibitions and displays drawn from the permanent collection.

Modern One is housed in a neo-Classical building, designed by William Burn in 1825. Modern Two was originally built in 1833 and later converted into a Gallery.

Royal Yacht Britannia★

Ocean Terminal Centre, Port of Leith. 2mi/3km N of city centre. Open daily Jan–Mar and Nov–Dec 10am–3.30pm; Apr–Sept 9.30am–4.30pm; Oct 9.30am–4pm. Closed 1 Jan and 25 Dec. £15.50, booking online (£1) advisable to avoid waiting in line at peak times.

Closed 1 Jan, 25 Dec. &🅿✕. &0131 555 5566. www.royalyachtbritannia.co.uk.

The Royal Yacht was launched from a Clydebank shipyard in 1953. By the time she was decommissioned in 1997 she had sailed more than a million miles on nearly one thousand official engagements, carrying Queen Elizabeth II and her family all over the world. Aboard visitors can see the royal apartments, crew's quarters, bridge and wheelhouse and engine room. A fascinating audio tour and visitor centre brings it all to life.

▲▲ Edinburgh Zoo★★

2mi/3km W on Corstorphine Road. Open daily 9am–6pm (Oct and Mar 5pm, Nov–Feb 4.30pm). £19, child (3–15), £14.50. &🅿 (£4); ✕ &0131 334 9171. www.edinburghzoo.org.uk.

One of Britain's finest and most successful zoo parks (in terms of breeding), Edinburgh is home to over 1 000 animals and is famous for the largest **penguin colony** in captivity. It is also home to the only **giant pandas** and koalas in the UK. The collection of big cats and the **Budongo Trail** – which allows visitors to see chimpanzees in, what is claimed to be, the world's most innovative, interactive chimpanzee enclosure – are other highlights.

Craigmillar Castle★

3mi/5km SE. Open Apr–Sept daily 9.30am–5.30pm; Oct–Mar Sat–Wed 10am–4pm. Closed 1–2 Jan, 25–26 Dec. £6. &0131 661 4445. www.historicenvironment.scot.

Even in ruins Craigmillar has an air of impregnability. The 14C tower house rises massively above two curtain walls. The outer wall encloses a courtyard in front and gardens on either side. The inner curtain built in 1427 is quartered with round towers, pierced by gunloops and topped by attractive oversailing machicolated parapets. The Great Hall, (at first floor level) is a grand apartment, where, it is said, Mary Queen of Scots sought refuge after the murder of Rizzio, and plotted the murder of Darnley. Climb to the top to appreciate the strategic excellence of the castle layout.

Vaulting, Rosslyn Chapel

Lothians★★

The Lothians is both a dormitory region and countryside playground for Edinburgh, with first-class beaches, golf links, coastal scenery and Scotland's sunniest weather.

Info: www.visiteastlothian.org;
www.visitmidlothian.org.uk;
www.visitwestlothian.co.uk.
Timing: Three days.
Kids: Deep Sea World, Falkirk Wheel, New Lanark.

MIDLOTHIAN
Forth Bridges★★

Best viewed from the esplanade at South Queensferry, 9mi/15km west of Edinburgh on the A 90 (www.forth-bridges.co.uk).

The first ferry across this point, the narrowest part of the Forth, was operated around 1070 by the monks of Dunfermline, for pilgrims travelling to the abbey. By the 17C it was the busiest ferry crossing in Scotland.

The **Forth [Rail] Bridge** (a World Heritage Site since 2015) was begun in 1883 and was opened in 1890. The **Road Bridge**, a slimline suspension bridge with its amazing curve, was built 1958–64. A new £1.35bn bridge, the Queensferry Crossing was opened in September 2017; it is Britain's tallest bridge, and the longest free-standing balanced cantilever bridge in the world. Just on the Fife side of the bridge stands **Deep Sea World** (open Mon–Fri 10am–4pm, Sat–Sun 6pm; £14, child £9.75; online discount, £1.50 transaction charge; &PX; 01383 411 880; www.deepseaworld.com), a spectacular aquarium boasting the longest underwater viewing tunnel in Britain. Fearless visitors can book a shark dive (additional charge).

Rosslyn Chapel★★

Roslin village (signposted). 7mi/11km S. Open Mon–Sat 9.30am–5pm, Sun noon–4.45pm (Jun–Aug Mon–Sat 9.30am–6pm, Sun noon–4.45pm). £9. &PX. Guided talks included in admission price. 0131 440 2159. www.rosslynchapel.org.uk.

One of the most mysterious and mythologised sites in Britain, famously starring in Dan Brown's *The Da Vinci Code*, Rosslyn Chapel stands on the edge of the Esk valley. A prime example of master craftsmanship, it was built by Sir William St Clair, third and last Prince of Orkney (1396–1484). Work lasted from 1446–86, just after his death. Among the intricate decoration, the best-known item is the **Apprentice Pillar★★★**.

Legend has it that while the master mason was abroad, his apprentice carved the pillar. On his return, seeing the quality of craftsmanship, the master killed his apprentice in a fit of jealousy.

Dalmeny★★
6mi/10km W by A 90.

The village is famous for its parish **Church of St Cuthbert★** (℘0131 331 1100, www.dalmeny.org), an exceptionally fine example of Norman architecture, with an intricately carved south doorway★★.

East of the village is **Dalmeny House★** (South Queensferry; guided tour only, Jun–Jul Sun–Wed, 2.15pm and 3.30pm; £10; ♿🅿✖; ℘0131 331 1888; www.dalmeny.co.uk), home of the Earls of Rosebery. Of particular interest are the Rothschild collection of 18C French furniture, porcelain and tapestries.

EAST LOTHIAN
Haddington★
18min/29km E.

This handsome market town grew up in the 12C around a royal palace and by the 16C was the fourth-largest town in Scotland. In the 18C, it entered a golden age based on agricultural wealth. Follow The Sands past the 16C **Nungate Bridge** with its pointed cutwaters up to the **High Street★** and its continuous line of frontages.

The historic house of **Lennoxlove★** (1mi/0.6km S on the B 6369; guided tours only, Easter–Oct, Wed–Thu and Sun hourly 12.30–3.30pm; £5.50; 🅿✖; ℘01620 828 605; www.lennoxlove.com) has strong associations with **Mary Queen of Scots**; it includes her death mask and other memorabilia, as well as boasting several fine **portraits** and **furniture**. The attentions of differing architects over the years have given the house its defining styles, including the earliest example of Palladianism in Scotland.

WEST LOTHIAN
Hopetoun House★★
South Queensferry. 1mi/18km W on the A 90 and A 904. Open mid-Apr–late Sept 10.30am–5pm. £9.85 (grounds only £4.55). ♿🅿✖ ℘01 31 331 2451.

www.hopetoun.co.uk.

A mansion of contrasts, set in beautiful landscaped grounds, the house (built 1699–1707) displays the mature Classicism of **Sir William Bruce**, its main staircase richly embellished with carving leading the eye upwards to the painted cupola. The flamboyant extensions and frontage (1721–67) are the work of William Adam, completed by his son John.

Linlithgow Palace★★
19mi/31km W by the A 8 and M 9. Open Apr–Sept 9.30am–5.30pm; Oct–Mar 10am–4pm. £5.50. 🅿✖ ℘01506 842 896. www.historicenvironment.scot.

The history of the town is that of its royal palace, around which it grew from the 12C. Following the rebuilding of the palace in 1424 it enjoyed over a century of grandeur as the centre of Scotland's court until the Union of the Crowns (1603). The roofless and forbidding foursquare ruin still shelters several delicate features, notably the 1530s **fountain★** in the courtyard and a superbly carved **fireplace**. Alongside the palace stands the 15C–16C late Gothic **St Michael's church★** (℘01506 842 188. www.stmichaelsparish.org.uk) with its modern spire (1964).

👥 Falkirk Wheel★★
28.5mi W. Tamfourhill. Open Mar–Oct 10am–5.30pm; late Nov–Feb Wed–Sun 11am–4pm. Closed Nov. Visitor centre free; boat trip £12.95, child £7.50 ♿🅿✖ ℘0870 050 0208.

www.thefalkirkwheel.co.uk.

The Falkirk Wheel is one of Scotland's most ingenious modern engineering achievements, designed to relink the Forth and Clyde Canal to the Union Canal. The problem was that the latter lay 35m above the level of the former. Historically, the two had been joined at Falkirk by a flight of 11 locks that stepped down across a distance of 0.9mi/1.5km, but these have been dismantled in 1933, thus breaking the link. The wheel, the world's first and only rotating boat lift, was thus created to lift a canal barge 35m from one canal to the other.

Glasgow★★★

Scotland's most populous city is both an important industrial centre and port, lying 44mi/74km west of Edinburgh. Many of Scotland's leading businesses make Glasgow their home. In recent years the city has had a cultural renaissance and in summer 2014 hosted the Commonwealth (athletics) Games. Glasgow is an experience you won't forget.

A BIT OF HISTORY

It was to this part of the embattled Kingdom of Strathclyde that **St Mungo** came in the mid-6C: he set up his wooden church on the banks of the Molendinar Burn, and became the first bishop of the city. In the 17C Glasgow became the centre of the Protestant cause. By the 18C the city was rich from trade in textiles, sugar and tobacco, her wealth increasing in the 19C through banking, shipbuilding and industry.

The arts prospered amid the wealth; neither the **Glasgow Boys** (W Y MacGregor, James Guthrie, George Henry and John Lavery, who advocated realism in an age of romanticism), nor the pioneer Modern movement led by **Charles Rennie Mackintosh**, could have so flourished in any other city.

The realist and radical traditions have been adopted by the Glasgow painters of the 1980s (Steven Campbell, Ken Currie, Peter Howson, Adrian Wisniewski and Stephen Conroy). Today Glasgow is the home of the Scottish Opera, Scottish Ballet and several notable **art collections**.

🐾 WALKING TOURS

1 CITY CENTRE

Gallery of Modern Art★

Royal Exchange Square. Open daily 10am (Fri and Sun 11am)–5pm (Thu 8pm). ♿✕ ☏0141 229 3050. www.glasgowlife.org.uk/museums.

▶ **Population:** 598 830.
◔ **Michelin Map:** Michelin Atlas p55 or Map 501 H 16.
ℹ **Info:** Gallery of Modern Art, Royal Exchange Square. ☏0845 8591006. www.peoplemakeglasgow.com.
🚉 Trains from England (London Euston 4h30) arrive at Central Station; from Edinburgh at nearby Queen Street Station (Edinburgh Haymarket 42min). Neighbouring Buchanan Street Bus Station is the terminus for regional, intercity and local buses. Underground stations are indicated on our map. Open-top hop on hop-off bus tours leave from George Square (☏0141 204 0444. www.citysightseeingglasgow.co.uk).
▶ **Location:** 46mi/74km west of Edinburgh via the M 8.
🏛 **Don't Miss:** The Burrell Collection; Glasgow Cathedral; Hunterian Art Gallery Mackintosh Wing; Museum of Transport; an excursion to New Lanark.
🕐 **Timing:** Allow at least 3 days in the city.
👪 **Kids:** Glasgow Science Centre; New Lanark.

This landmark 18C neo-Classical mansion houses a wide-ranging collection of contemporary art. It has a massive Corinthian portico and a magnificent main hall with a barrel-vaulted ceiling.

Glasgow School of Art★

167 Renfrew Street. Mackintosh Gallery.Open daily 10am–4.30pm. No photography. ♿✕ ☏0141 353 4500. www.gsa.ac.uk.

Charles Rennie Mackintosh designed this building, regarded as his masterpiece, in 1897–1909. It holds his acclaimed library with three-storey-high windows and suspended ceiling.

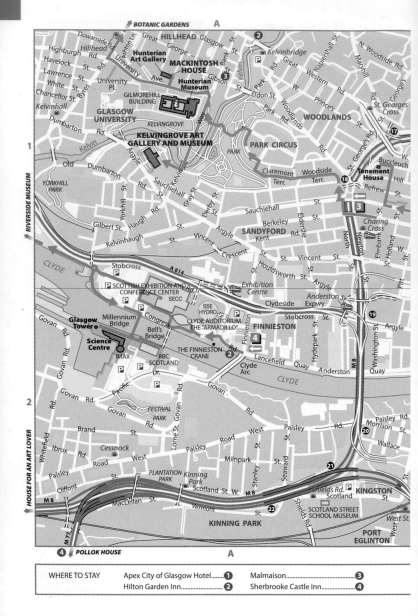

WHERE TO STAY	Apex City of Glasgow Hotel........**1**	Malmaison...**3**
	Hilton Garden Inn.....................**2**	Sherbrooke Castle Inn....................**4**

Tenement House

145 Buccleuch Street. Open Apr–Jun and Sept–Oct daily 1–5pm; Jul–Aug Mon–Sat 11am–5pm, Sun 1–5pm. £6.50. ☏0141 333 0183. www.nts.org.uk.

This two-room flat, with kitchen and bathroom, portrays turn-of-the-century tenement life and is a piece of important Glasgow social history.

2 CATHEDRAL– THE BARRAS

Begin your walk at **Glasgow Cathedral** ★★★ (open Apr–Sept Mon–Sat 9.30am–5.30pm, Sun 1–5pm; Oct–Mar Mon–Sat 10am–4pm, Sun 1–4pm; closed 1–2 Jan, 25–26 Dec; ☏0141 552 8198; www.glasgowcathedral.org.uk). This is the

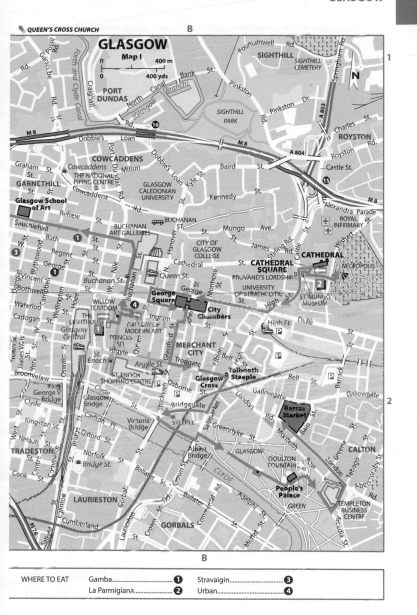

WHERE TO EAT	Gamba.....................................❶	Stravaigin..............................❸
	La Parmigiana.......................❷	Urban.....................................❹

fourth church on the site of St Mungo's original building, and best viewed from the heights of the nearby Necropolis. The cathedral is mostly 13C and 14C with 15C additions. The **nave** is late Gothic; its elevation of richly moulded and pointed arches, more numerous at each level, rises to the timber roof. Beyond the 15C stone screen is the **choir**, mid-13C in the finest early pointed style. Beyond the ambulatory, through one of the four chapels leading off from it, is the upper chapter room (rebuilt in the 15C) where the medieval university held its classes.

The lower church is another Gothic delight, where light and shade play effectively amid the piers enshrining

PUBLIC TRANSPORT

Buchanan Bus station (📞0141 332 3708) gives information on travel passes for the metro, bus and trains. The **SPT (Strathclyde Partnership for Transport)** range of travelcards and day tickets is worth checking before you travel. It includes the **Mackintosh Trail**, which gives one-day unlimited travel and free access to all Charles Rennie Mackintosh attractions in the city, plus the Hill House in Helensburgh.

SIGHTSEEING

Boat trips 'doon the watter' along the Firth of Clyde with **Clyde Cruises** (📞01475 721 281, www.clydecruises. com) are very popular.
Gift Experiences Scotland (📞0345 257 4375, www.gift experiencescotland.com) offers helicopter rides which afford spectacular views of the city and River Clyde.

the **tomb of St Mungo**, Glasgow's patron saint, whose legend is illustrated on the St Kentigern Tapestry (1979). The 15C **Blacader Aisle** is an extension by Glasgow's first archbishop with ribbed vaulting and carved bosses.

Follow the High Street, then Duke Street to reach **George Square**. Though started in 1782 George Square is magnificently Victorian. Of special interest are the 1869 **Merchants' House** and, opposite, the **City Chambers★**, where the grandeur and opulence of the loggia, council and banqueting halls are reminders that Glasgow was the second city of the Empire in Victorian times.

Follow the map route to **Glasgow Cross**. The heart of Glasgow until Victorian times, the **Tolbooth Steeple★** is the last reminder of its faded elegance.

Further along this walk you come to the **People's Palace and Winter Gardens★** (Glasgow Green; People's Palace: open Tue–Thu and Sat 10am–5pm, Fri and Sun 11am–5pm; &P✗; 📞0141 276 0788; www.glasgowlife.org.uk/museums). This social history museum, with exotic gardens attached, is sited on Glasgow Green, a place used for grazing, jousting, parades, public hangings and, above all, free speech.

From the gardens, follow the route marked on the map to see **The Barras**, a colourful centuries-old weekend street market.

3 KELVINGROVE/ WEST END

The area around Kelvingrove Park is home to two impressive museums and a park with a famous 1924 bandstand.

Hunterian Museum, Art Gallery and Mackintosh House★★★

Open Tue–Sat 10am–5pm, Sun 11am–4pm (Zoology Museum Mon–Fri 9am–5pm). &✗ 📞0141 330 4221 (Zoology Museum: 📞0141 330 4772). www.gla.ac.uk/hunterian.

These University of Glasgow museums offer fascinating free collections including medicine and anatomy, one of the world's great **coin** collections, Roman and Egyptian artefacts and a separate zoology museum. Free tours are also given to The **Mackintosh House★★★** – a reconstruction of the home of Charles Rennie Mackintosh.

The recently refurbished **art gallery★★** is home to the world's largest permanent display of works by **James McNeill Whistler★★★** (1843–1903), as well as portraits and 19C and 20C Scottish art.

Kelvingrove Art Gallery and Museum★★★

Open Mon–Thu and Sat 10am–5pm, Fri and Sun 11am–5pm. Closed 1–2 Jan, 25–26 Dec. &P✗ 📞0141 276 9599. www.glasgowlife.org.uk/museums.

Opened in 1902, financed by the 1888 Glasgow International Exhibition, the Kelvingrove houses one of Europe's great art collections.

The European art section includes one of the largest and finest collections of 17C Dutch and Flemish art and one of the most important collections of 19C century French oil paintings in the UK. The former includes works by Jordaens, Rubens, Brueghel the Elder and Rembrandt, as well as Ruisdael landscapes. French 19C and early-20C movements are represented by Millet, Fantin-Latour and Courbet; and the Impressionists by Monet, Pissarro, Renoir and Sisley. Van Gogh's 1887 portrait depicts the Glasgow art dealer, Alexander Reid, with whom he shared a flat in Paris. The most famous picture at Kelvingrove is Salvador Dali's *Christ of St John of the Cross*.

The British section includes portraits by Ramsey, Raeburn, Reynolds and Romney and the work of the Pre-Raphaelites. William McTaggart's outdoor scenes and the highly distinctive works of the Scottish Colourists are enjoying a growing reputation.

The **Charles Rennie Mackintosh and the Glasgow Style** gallery provides a permanent home for the city's extensive collection of Charles Rennie Mackintosh exhibits, including the spectacular interior of Kate Cranston's **Ingram Street Tea Rooms**.

4 CLYDE WATERFRONT

👤👤 Glasgow Science Centre★

50 Pacific Quay. Open daily 10am–5pm (winter 3pm Wed–Fri and closed Mon–Tue). £11, child £9. Planetarium or IMAX documentary add-on +£3 each; Glasgow Tower add-on +£3.50 each; Tower only £6.50; Planetarium only £5.50. ♿🅿(£3). ✕ ℘0141 420 5000. www.glasgowsciencecentre.org.

Housed in three stunning modern buildings, this state-of-the-art hands-on science centre contains hundreds of interactive exhibits plus a Science Show Theatre, a Climate Change Theatre, a planetarium and an IMAX cinema.

The rotating **Glasgow Tower**, at 127m high offers a splendid view of the city.

👤👤 The Riverside Museum★★

100 Pointhouse Place. Open Mon–Thu and Sat 10am–5pm, Fri and Sun 11am–5pm. Closed 1–2 Jan, 25–26 Dec. ♿✕ ℘0141 287 2720. www.glasgowlife.org.uk/museums. (Tall Ship open daily 10am–5pm (Nov–Jan 4pm). ℘0141 357 3699; www.thetallship.com)

Housed in a stunning new landmark building, and named European Museum of the Year for 2013, the hugely popular state-of-the-art interactive Riverside Museum incorporates the old much-loved **Museum of Transport.** Its vehicles collection features comprehensive displays of trams and trolleybuses (1872–1967) and vintage cars, with the emphasis on **Scottish-built cars★★**, as well as fire vehicles and bicycles.

The **Clyde Room of Model Ships★★★** displays the varied and impressive output of Scottish and Clydeside shipyards. There are also three streets with access to re-created shops dating 1895–1980s.

Moored alongside the museum, the **Tall Ship Glenlee** first sailed as a cargo carrier in 1896. She circumnavigated the globe four times and is one of only five Clyde-built sailing ships that remain afloat in the world.

POLLOK PARK

This 146-hectare country park is located in Pollok, just southwest of the Clyde Waterfront.

Burrell Collection★★★

3mi/5km SW on the M 77. Pollok Park. Closed until 2020 for refurbishment; check website or call for updates. ℘0141 287 2550. www.glasgowlife.org.uk/museums.

[*Original text*]: The mind-boggling collection of shipowner **Sir William Burrell** (1861–1958) is spaciously laid out in a custom-built gallery, surrounded by parkland. The **Ancient Civilisations** section includes items from Egypt, Mesopotamia, Italy and Greece. **Oriental Art** incorporates ceramics, bronzes and

Charles Rennie Mackintosh (1868–1928)

The city's famous architect, designer and artist developed his original style combining the Scottish vernacular tradition and Art Nouveau influences. Glasgow takes great pride in its legacy of fine buildings and interiors by Mackintosh: **Glasgow School of Art**, the **Mackintosh House**, **The Willow Rooms** *(217 Sauchiehall Street)*, **Queens Cross Church** *(270 Garscube Road)* and **Scotland Street School** *(225 Scotland Street)* as well as the offices of the *Daily Record (Renfield Lane)* and the **Glasgow Herald** *(Mitchell Steet)*. **Hill House** in Helensburgh is a must for fans of domestic architecture. An unusual recent addition is the **House for an Art Lover** *(Bellahouston Park)* built to Mackintosh's original design for a competition. See also the recently redesigned **Kelvingrove** collection.

jades from the third millennium BCE to the 19C, and features the enamelled Ming figure of a **lohan**, or disciple of Buddha, which is dated to 1484. Burrell's particular interest was in **Medieval** and **post-Medieval European Art** and there are some outstanding examples. Of the early works to be found in **Paintings**, **Drawings and Bronzes**, Bellini's *Virgin and Child* is notable. The **Hutton Castle Rooms** are complete with medieval and antique furnishings.

Pollok House★

Open daily 10am–5pm. Closed 1–2 Jan, 25–26 Dec. £6.50. &🅿✕ 𝒫0141 616 6410. www.nts.org.uk.
Set in the scenic surroundings of Pollok Country Park on the outskirts of Glasgow, the highlight of this mainly 18C example of Georgian grandeur is the collection of **Spanish paintings★★** acquired by Sir William Stirling Maxwell (1818–78). These include portraits by El Greco and etchings by Goya as well as works by Tristan, and Murillo.

EXCURSIONS
Hill House, Helensburgh★

◗ Upper Colquhoun Street. 21mi/34km NW via the A 82 and A 814. Open Apr–Oct 11.30am–5pm. £10.50. 𝒫01436 673 900. www.nts.org.uk.
Overlooking the Clyde, built 1902–04, this is the finest of Charles Rennie Mackintosh and his wife, the artist Margaret Macdonald's, domestic creations. The beautiful garden has been restored in line with some of the early designs.

New Lanark★★

◗ 20mi/32km SE via the M 74 and A 72. Visitor centre open daily Apr–Oct 10am–5pm; Nov–Mar 4pm. Closed 1 Jan, 25 Dec. £12.50, child (3–15), £9. Mill Ticket: £7.50 per person gives access to Annie McLeod Experience, Working Textile Machinery and Roof Garden only. &🅿✕ 𝒫01555 661 345. www.newlanark.org.
In the deep gorge of the River Clyde, an 18C planned industrial village comprising four cotton mills, housing and amenities for the workforce was the acclaimed achievement of the Glasgow manufacturer and banker David Dale and his son-in-law Robert Owen, a social reformer. The village, still partly residential, is a World Heritage Site.
Mill No. 3, which houses the **visitor centre**, including the Annie McLeod Experience Ride, is the most handsome of the four units. Other points of interest include the Nursery Buildings (for pauper apprentices), the village store, the counting house, Robert Owen's School for Children, Robert Owen's house, and a working textile machinery. There is also a beautiful **Roof Garden** to enjoy.
The riverside **Dyeworks** has displays on the wildlife of the **Falls of Clyde**, a beauty spot that has inspired painters (including Turner) and poets (such as Scott and Wordsworth) alike.

Angus and Dundee★

Dundee is Scotland's fourth largest city and trying hard to break into Scotland's tourist destination major league. It boasts first-class maritime and industrial heritage attractions, a splendid revitalised art gallery and museum, and a burgeoning cultural, restaurant and shopping scene. Predominantly agricultural, the most famous landmark in Angus is Glamis ('glaams') Castle, made famous by Shakespeare. The region is also famous for its Pictish remains, while on a sunny day, its glory is the beautiful gardens at Edzell castle.

⏱ **Michelin Map:** Michelin Atlas p62 or Map 501.

🏠 **Info:** 16, City Square, Dundee. ☎01382 527 527. www.angusanddundee.co.uk.

👥 **Kids:** Discovery Point; Sensation.

DUNDEE★

Dundee is a busy seaport, an educational centre and the capital of Tayside. The area has been continuously occupied since Mesolithic times. Traditional historic activities (such as whaling and jute milling) have given way to modern high-tech industries. The city centre blends fine Victorian buildings with modern shopping facilities.

The new V&A Museum of Design Dundee (www.vandadundee.org), to be open by 2018, will be the focal point of the city's new waterfront.

City Walk

Just east of the Tay Bridge in Victoria Dock is **HMS Unicorn★** (open Apr–Oct daily 10am–5pm; Nov–Mar Thu–Sun noon–4pm; closed 21 Dec–4 Jan; £5; ⚓✕; ☎01382 200 900; www.frigateunicorn.org), launched in 1824 as a 46-gun frigate for the Royal Navy. She is now the oldest British-built ship still afloat. Visitors can explore the main gun decks, with their 18-pounders, and the captain's and officers' quarters, and discover the flavour of life in the Royal Navy in the golden age of sail.

West of the Tay Bridge near the railway station is **Discovery Point★** 👥 (Discov

ery Quay, Craig Harbour; open Apr–Oct Mon–Sat 10am–6pm, Sun 11am–6pm; Nov–Mar Mon–Sat 10am–5pm, Sun 11am–5pm; closed 1–2 Jan, 25–26 Dec; £9.25, child £5.50, joint ticket with Verdant Works (⏱see below) £16, child £9; ⚓🅿✕; ☎01382 309 060; www.rrsdiscovery.com) and the pride of the city, the **RRS Discovery★**, which was custom built in Dundee in 1901 for scientific exploration. The ship forms the centrepiece of an exciting exhibition, with a spectacular audio-visual presentation devoted to Captain Scott's epic Antarctic Expedition (1901–04), including the vessel's dramatic rescue and other journeys and actual artefacts of the crew.

On the other side of the tracks, on Greenmarket, is **Dundee Science Centre** (👥; open 10am–5pm; £7.95, child £5.95; ⚓✕; ☎01382 228 800; www.dundeesciencecentre.org.uk), an award-winning hands-on experience with over 80 interactive stations, shows and exhibitions.

Just north of here is the University of Dundee and beyond, on West Henderson's Wynd, is the **Verdant Works★** (open Apr–Oct Mon–Sat 10am–6pm, Sun 11am–6pm; Nov–Mar Wed–Sat 10.30am–4.30pm, Sun 11am–4.30pm; admission as Discovery Point, ⏱see above. ⚓🅿✕; ☎01382 309 060; www.verdantworks.com), which tells, in lively fashion, the story of how the weaving of the natural fibre, jute, became a major industry in Dundee in the 19C. It features original working machinery alongside the latest hands-on exhibits.

Northwest of the Tay Bridge, a splendid recently refurbished Victorian Gothic building is home to **The McManus★** (Albert Square; open Mon–Sat 10am–

Glamis castle

5pm, Sun 12.30–4.30pm; ♿✖; ☎01382 307 200; www.mcmanus.co.uk), **Dundee's** principal art gallery and museum. Its galleries cover prehistory; Modern Dundee (from 1850 to date); Dundee and the World (housed in the stunning Albert Hall, with its magnificent wooden ceiling and spectacular stained glass); an authentic Victorian Art Gallery; contemporary art and the city's nationally significant collection of 20C art.

GLAMIS★

12mi/19km N of Dundee.

Set in the rich agricultural Angus Glens countryside, this picturesque small village (pronounced 'glaams') was made famous by Shakespeare, its castle the residence of Macbeth.

Glamis Castle★★

Dundee Road. Visit by guided tour only, Open daily Apr–Oct 10am–5.30pm (last tour 4.30pm). ▯✖ ☎01307 840 393. www.glamis-castle.co.uk.

Glamis is the archetypal Scottish castle; its massive sandstone pile bristles with towers, turrets, conical roofs and chimneys. It has a fascinating history including a ghost (Lady Glamis, burned as a witch), literary associations (Macbeth was Thane of Glamis) and Royal Family connections since the 14C; most recently it was the childhood home of the late Queen Mother.

Exterior – The 15C L-shaped core of the castle has been added to and altered, apparently at random through the cen-turies. Statues of James and his son, Charles I, flank the driveway. To the side is a beautiful Italian Garden.

Interior – Guided tours take visitors throughout the castle's 10 principal rooms. Jacobean armour and furniture, Mortlake tapestries and interiors of many periods are on display. The chapel has a series of paintings of the Apostles and scenes from the Bible by Jacob de Wet (1695–1754), a Dutch artist who also worked at Blair and Holyroodhouse. The splendid **Drawing Room** is adorned by a **plasterwork ceiling** (1621) and a magnificent fireplace.

EXCURSIONS

Aberlemno Pictish Stones★

▶ 12mi/19km NE via the A 94 and B 9134. Open Apr–Sept. ⊶The stones are boarded up from last working day Sept–first working day Apr. www.historicenvironment.scot.

These Pictish sculptured stones depict animal and abstract symbols, hunting and battle scenes and a cross with flanking angels. They stand at the roadside and in the churchyard.

Meigle Sculptured Stone Museum★★

▶ Meigle. 7mi/11km west by A 94. Open Apr–Sept daily 9.30am–5.30pm. £5. Closed Oct–Mar. ♿ ☎01828 640 612. www.historicenvironment.scot.

The former village school displays an outstanding collection of 26 early **Christian monuments★★** in the Pictish tradition, all found locally. The carving is full of vitality and shows a high degree of skill

Edzell Castle & Garden★

◑25mi/40km NE by the A 94 and B 966 to Edzell village. Open Apr–Sept daily 9.30am–5.30pm. £5.50. Closed Oct–Mar. ⚬The Tower House is closed until further notice for conservation work.♿🅿 ☎01356 648 631. www.historicenvironment.scot.

The ruined castle is an early-16C tower house but the highlight here is the formal walled garden known as **The Pleasance★★★**, which is without equal in Scotland. Sir David Lindsay (c.1550–1610) created this garden in 1604; it is a product of the Renaissance ideas he had absorbed on his wide travels. The blaze of summer colour against the rich red of the walls diverts attention from the rich heraldic and symbolic sculptures on the surrounding walls, but these, too, reward closer inspection.

Stirling and Argyll★★★

This is the most romanticised area of Scotland in both fact and fiction: 'the bonnie bonnie banks' of Loch Lomond, Rob Roy, Scott's 'Lady of the Lake', the Holy Isle of Iona, Bannockburn and – more recently – Mull of Kintyre, 'Balamory' (Tobermory on Mull) and 'Braveheart' William Wallace. Each characterisation has passed far beyond just national fame. The scenery is also familiar from chocolate boxes and jigsaws: the hills and glens of the Trossachs and the many glorious lochs make for unmissable quintessential Scottish viewing.

STIRLING★★

Controlling the route between Edinburgh (69mi/70km SE) and the Highlands, and the crossing of the Forth at its tidal limit, Stirling has been strategically important from time immemorial. Most of its long history has therefore been essentially that of the castle and former royal residence perched on its well-nigh impregnable crag. Today, it is an ideal touring centre.

🧭 **Michelin Map:** Michelin Atlas p54–55, p59–60 or Map 501.

🛈 **Info: Stirling:** Old Town Jail, St John Street. ☎01786 475 019. www.destinationstirling.com. **Callander:** 52-54 Main Street. ☎01877 330 342. www.incallander.co.uk. **Craignure (Mull):** The Pier. ☎01680 812 377. **Oban:** North Pier. ☎01631 563 122. www.oban.org.uk. www.visitscottishheartlands. com; www.lochlomond-trossachs.org. www.welcometoiona.com; www.inveraray-argyll.com.

👥 **Kids:** Loch Lomond Sea Life Centre, Loch Lomond Bird of Prey Centre.

From its redoubtable site Stirling has seen many battles, the most important being the two victories over the English at Stirling Bridge in 1297 and Bannockburn in 1314. Stirling became a permanent royal residence with the accession of the **Stewarts**, and its golden age came under **James IV**. After his death at

Stirling Castle

© X. Forés/age fotostock

Flodden Field, in 1513, his queen, Margaret, brought her son to Stirling, where he was crowned as James V. His daughter, **Mary Queen of Scots**, was crowned in the Chapel Royal, and her infant son, the future **James VI** of Scotland and I of England, was baptised here in 1566. It was with his departure to Whitehall that Stirling's role as a royal residence ended.

Stirling Castle★★

Open daily: Apr–Sept 9.30am–6pm; Oct–Mar 9.30am–5pm. £14. ⚐🅿 £4, max stay 4 hrs. ✗ ☎01786 450 000; www.historicenvironment.scot; www.stirlingcastle.gov.uk.
The approach is through the old town. A statue of Robert the Bruce stands guard on the esplanade.

Rob Roy MacGregor (1671–1734)

Much of the rugged terrain of the Trossachs is closely associated with the daring exploits of the outlawed clan leader and hero of Sir Walter Scott's novel *Rob Roy* (1818). Rob Roy McGregor (1671–1734) was a real person; Glen Gyle at the head of Loch Katrine was his birthplace and he and his wife and two of their sons lie in the churchyard of Balquihidder on Loch Voil.

Begun by James IV in 1496, the palace is a masterpiece of Renaissance ornamentation, completed by his son in 1540. Its outstanding feature is the elaborate design of the **external elevations★★★** – best admired from the Upper Square. The castle has recently undertaken major interpretive improvements including a new exhibition telling its story, in the Queen Anne **Casemates**. Beneath the palace lie the atmospheric medieval vaults, now home to a series of family-friendly interactive displays all about the lives of people at court such as jesters and musicians.

The façade of the **Great Hall** (1460–88) is lit by four pairs of embrasured windows; the noble interior is notable for its **hammerbeam oak roof**, minstrels' gallery and dais flanked by oriel windows. In contrast the **palace** itself (1496–1540) is decorated with original figure carvings in recessed arches and above the cornice. The **royal apartments**, recently returned to their mid-16C appearance following a major refurbishment, boast fine 16C oak medallions known as the **Stirling Heads★★**. The early Renaissance **Chapel** (1594) features round-headed windows framing the elaborate doorway and an ornate interior.

The 500-year-old King's Old Building houses the **Argyll and Sutherland Highlanders Regimental Museum★** (closes 45min before castle), presenting 200 years of regimental history.

Old Town

The medieval town, with its narrow wynds and steep streets, spills downhill from the castle. **Argyll's Lodging★** (closed until further notice for essential maintenance; check website for updates: www.historicenvironment.scot) was built in 1632 by Sir William Alexander, founder of Nova Scotia and contains wonderful examples of fine **Scottish Renaissance decoration★**.

In the **Church of the Holy Rude★** (✆01786 475 275; www.holyrude.org) the infant James VI was crowned, in 1567, with John Knox preaching the sermon. It retains its 15C oak **timberwork roof**. Beyond **Bothwell House** *(39 St John's Street)* with its projecting tower, stands the Victorian **Old Town Jail**, until recently a visitor attraction, now home to the tourist office.

At the bottom of Broad Street, formerly the centre of burgh life, with its mercat cross and tolbooth, is **Darnley's House**, a 16C townhouse (now a popular café) where Mary's husband, Lord Darnley, is said to have stayed.

EXCURSIONS

Dunblane★

❯6mi/10km N on the A 9.

Modern Dunblane gained tragic notoriety in 1996 when a gunman killed 16 of its schoolchildren. Its most famous son is tennis champion Andy Murray, who attended the same school in Dunblane where the massacre took place and was at school on that dreadful day.

The old town is grouped round its beautiful 13C Gothic **cathedral★★** (open Apr–Oct Mon–Sat 9.30am–5.30pm, Sun 2–5.30pm; Oct–Mar Mon–Sat 10am–4pm, Sun 2–4pm. ✆01786 823 388; www.historicenvironment.scot; www.dunblanecathedral.org.uk), which survived the Reformation intact. The vigorous carving of the canopied 15C **Chisholm stalls** and their misericords is remarkable. In the glorious **choir** is the ornate **Ochiltree stalls**.

The **Lady Chapel**, the oldest part of the building, has ribbed vaulting and carved bosses. Adjoining the south side of the nave is a 12C tower, and the magnificent **west front★★**, overlooking the Allan Water.

Doune Castle★

❯10mi/16km on the A 84. Open Apr–Sept daily 9.30am–5.30pm; Oct–Mar daily 10am–4pm. Closed 25–26 Dec. £5.50. 🅿 ✆01786 841 742. www.historicenvironment.scot.

This late-14C fortress with its 30m-high **keep-gatehouse** stands apart from the village. With elaborate accommodation on a semi-royal scale, it is an example of a truly self-contained, secure residence of its period.

Monty Python fans may be amused to hear that *Holy Grail* was filmed here, and can take an audio tour of the castle narrated by Terry Jones.

Battle of Bannockburn Visitor Centre

❯2mi/3km south on the A 9. Open: **Grounds:** daily until dusk; **Visitor Centre:** Mar–Oct daily 10am–5.30pm; Nov–Feb daily 10am–5pm. £11.50. ♿🅿✕ ✆01786 812 664. www.battleofbannockburn.com.

An equestrian statue of **Robert the Bruce** marks the king's command post on the eve of the battle. By 1313 Bruce had retaken most of the kingdom lost to Edward I, who had died in 1307. On 24 June 1314, he routed a numerically superior English army, ineptly led by Edward II. After Bannockburn, independence for Scotland was assured. Opened on 24 June 2014 to mark the 700th anniversary of the battle, the Visitor Centre is a world-class attraction, harnessing interactive state-of-the-art 3D simulation technology, so that visitors can experience brutal and bloody medieval combat like never before and learn about this crucial event in Scottish history.

National Wallace Monument★★

❯1mi/1.6km NE by the A 9 and B 998. Open daily: Nov–Feb 10.30am–4pm; Mar 10am–5pm; Apr–Jun and Sept–Oct 9.30am–5pm; Jul–Aug 9.30am–6pm. Closed 1 Jan, 25–26 Dec, 2 days Jan for maintenance. £9.99.

🅿 ✕ 🕾 01786 472 140.
www.nationalwallacemonument.com.
This towering 150-year-old five-storey landmark commemorates **William Wallace** (1270–1305) the national hero, mythologised in the epic film *Braveheart*, who rallied Scottish forces against English rule. He recaptured the castle from Edward I's forces after his victory at Stirling Bridge in 1297, but following the Scots' submission in 1304, Wallace was captured and died a traitor's death in London in 1305.

An audio-visual presentation depicts Wallace and his place in Scottish history. From the viewing platform (*246 steps*) atop Abbey Craig (110m) there is a **panorama**★★ of Stirling surroundings.

TROSSACHS★★★

NW of Stirling.

Occupying Scotland's midriff area, the Trossachs stretch between Loch Venachar in the east to the shores of Loch Lomond and take in some of Scotland's most famous scenery, with rugged mountains and wooded slopes reflected in the waters of many lochs. Sir Walter Scott's romantic poetry and novels did much to popularise the Trossachs, reinforced by Wordsworth and Coleridge, who followed in his footsteps in 1830.

Callander★

This busy summer tourist centre, 18mi/29km from Stirling, popular with visitors for over a century, is the main eastern gateway to the Trossachs. It became known to millions of British TV viewers in the 1960s as the Tannochbrae of *Dr Finlay's Casebook*.

Loch Venachar

The Trossachs road (*A 821*) skirts the lower slopes of **Ben Ledi** (879m) overlooking the banks of Loch Venachar, before reaching the scattered settlement of **Brig o'Turk**.

The village has artistic associations, favoured by Ruskin and Millais and, later, the **Glasgow Boys**.

Loch Katrine★★

The best way to see this lovely loch is to take a **boat trip** (operates from Trossachs Pier late May–early Nov daily, see website or call for times; scenic cruise £16.50; ♿; 🕾 01877 376 315; www.lochkatrine.com) on the SS *Sir Walter Scott* or SS *Lady of the Lake*. The loch isles, Ellen's Isle and Factor's Isle figure respectively in works by Sir Walter Scott's *The Lady of the Lake* and *Rob Roy*. To the south of Loch Katrine looms the twin-peaked form of **Ben Venue** (727m). Beyond, a hilltop viewpoint affords a magnificent **panorama**★★★ across the Trossachs.

Looking out across Loch Lomond and Trossachs National Park from Ben Vane

© Zoonar/Peter Chisholm/age fotostock

Aberfoyle

The attractive much visited village was where Rob Roy abducted Baillie Nicol Jarvie. A road leads west through the forest park to Loch Lomond.

Loch Lomond★★

The blue waters of this famous loch (200m deep) are flanked by rugged mountains in the north and pastoral woodlands in the south.

Loch Lomond Shores is the area's main visitor centre (open daily 9.30am–6.30pm; &🅿✕; ✆01389 751 031; www.lochlomondshores.com) with upmarket shops, a café and restaurant, and canoes, kayaks, segways and bikes for hire. It is also home to two wildlife attractions.

Loch Lomond Sea Life Centre ♣♣ (open daily 10am–5pm; tickets from £9.77; &; ✆01389 721 500; www.visitsealife.com/loch-lomond) features Scotland's only giant sea turtle, a shark tunnel, touch pool, otters, stingrays and more. There are spectacular views from its roof terrace.

The **Loch Lomond Bird of Prey Centre** ♣♣ (open daily May–Sept 10am–5.30pm; Nov–Jan 10am–4pm; Feb–Apr and Oct 10am–5pm; £8, child £4; ✆01389 729239, www.lochlomondbirdofpreycentre.co.uk) with guided tours and flying displays.

A short walk away, **Sweeney's Cruise** offers loch cruises (see website for cruise times and prices; &; ✆01389 752 376; www.sweeneyscruises.com) calling among other places, at the attractive village of **Luss★** with its mellow stone cottages.

The **West Highland Way**, bound for Fort William, follows the east shore northwards to Crianlarich passing on the way along the base of **Ben Lomond★★** (974m), the most southerly of the Highland 'Munros' (mountains over 3 000ft/914m).

MULL★

Caledonian MacBrayne ('CalMac') ferries (www.calmac.co.uk) connect Mull with Oban (40–45min), Iona, Kilchoan and Lochaline on the mainland.

This narrow island (26mi/42km across) sits at the mouth of Scotland's Great Glen. Although unseen from Oban, the island is dominated by the mountain Ben More (966m), and has a long deeply indented coastline, ranging from rocky cliffs to sandy beaches and superb sea views. Inland, pastoral crofting landscapes contrast with desolate moorlands. In addition to walking, wildlife is the main attraction here.

The colourful main town and ferry port, **Tobermory** (star of BBC children's TV as *Balamory*), fringes the yachting centre of Tobermory Bay, 22mi/35km north along the coast from Craignure, the island's main ferry terminal.

From Craignure follow the coast road 3mi/5km to **Duart Castle** (open Apr Sun–Thu 11am–4pm; May–mid-Oct daily 10.30am–5pm; £6.50; 🅿✕; ✆01680 812 309; www.duartcastle.com), home of the Chief of the **Clan MacLean**, perched on a rocky crag guarding the Sound of Mull, with magnificent views. The keep dates from c.1250 but the 13C castle was burned in the late-17C. Sir Fitzroy MacLean, the 26th Chief, restored the stronghold to its present appearance in 1911.

Staffa★★

Open daily. Ferries Apr–Oct from Iona, Fionnphort and Ulva, see website for operators ✆01681 700659. www.nts.org.uk.

This basaltic island, now a National Nature Reserve, is known for its amazing rock formations and spectacular caves; Mendelssohn's overture, *Fingal's Cave*, was composed following his visit in 1829. Its awesome beauty has inspired poets and painters alike.

Iona★

West coast, off southwesterly tip of the Isle of Mull. CalMac ferries (www.calmac.co.uk) operate between the islands. www.ionahistory.org.uk.

St Columba established his monastic settlement here 1 400 years ago, and even today it is one of the most venerated places in Scotland.

The saint's community flourished until brought to an end by the Norse raids of the 8C and 9C. Intricately carved crosses and grave slabs are a testament to its prior artistic accomplishments. A Benedictine monastery was re-established in the early-13C but disappeared at the Reformation. In 1938 a third religious brotherhood – now an ecumenical community – came to the isle and a major restoration programme was completed in 1966.

Iona Abbey (open daily Apr–Sept 9.30am–5.30pm; Oct–Mar 4pm; £7.10; ♿; ℘01681 700 512; www.historicenvironment.scot; www.ionahistory.org.uk), stands on the site of its Columban predecessor. To the north of the west front is St Columba's shrine. Beyond the abbey is the **Infirmary Museum★** (open daily 9am–5pm) with a collection of early Christian and medieval stonework including the ornate 8C **Cross of St John★** (restored), medieval effigies and grave slabs. The abbey today is a place of hospitality, reflection and worship, while a small community of around 270 crofters inhabits the fertile island.

🐾 Short walk

Take the road from the old Benedictine **nunnery** with its medieval church and conventual buildings. Go through the gate past the intricately carved 15C **Maclean's Cross★** and the early Christian burial ground, **Reilig Odhrain** (where Scotland's kings from Kenneth MacAlpine to Malcolm III were buried) to the 12C **St Oran's Chapel★**, the oldest building on the island, with a fine Norman west door. Walk down the **Street of the Dead**, where three **High Crosses** catch the eye (an 8C **Cross of St Martin★**, a 9C–10C truncated shaft of St Matthew and a replica of the 8C St John's Cross). On the other side of the Street of the Dead is St Columba's cell, Tor Abb.

Isle of Ulva ★★

£5 return ferry for foot passengers and cyclists. www.isleofulva.com.
Once inhabited by several hundred people, Ulva, the birthplace of the colonial administrator, Major General Lachlan Macquarie, is now almost deserted. A network of footpaths lead to abandoned villages and a variety of landscapes (basalt cliffs, moors, woods). By the ferry slipway **Sheila's Cottage** is a faithful reconstruction of a traditional thatched croft house which was last lived in early this century by Sheila MacFadyen. With an exhibition on island history, **The Boat House** (www.theboathouseulva.co.uk) is outstanding for a simple coffee break or as a lunchtime showcase for Ulva's seafood...and cakes...and more cakes!

INVERARAY★★

37mi/60km SE of Oban.
This delightful small Georgian whitewashed township lies halfway along Scotland's west coast on the shores of Loch Fyne, a short distance from its castle, the seat of the Clan Campbell.

Inveraray Castle★★

Open Apr–Oct daily 10am– 5.45pm. £11. 🅿✕ ℘01499 302 203. www.inveraray-castle.com.
The exterior is in Gothic Revival style. The 5th Duke refurbished the interiors in the neo-Classical style after the fashion of Carlton House in London. In particular, the **dining room** is a masterpiece of delicately detailed plasterwork and painting.
The Tapestry Drawing Room reveals an Adam-designed compartmental ceiling, decorative panels and overdoors by Girard. The **armoury hall** with its decorative display of pole-arms, Lochaber axes and broadswords is where the duke's personal piper plays a medley of Campbell tunes to awaken the household.

🚗 DRIVING TOUR

LOCH FYNE TO LOCH AWE

Loch Fyne★★ stretches from the heart of the Argyll mountains, down the arm of Loch Gilp, where it turns due south to reach the open sea. In the 19C this was a successful herring fishery and today Loch Fyne is famous for its oysters.
Some 6mi/10km south of Inveraray, on the A 83 is the **Auchindrain Museum★**

Buachaille Etive Mor, Glen Coe

(open Apr–Oct daily 10am–5pm, Nov–Mar open most weekdays, but call to confirm; £7.50; ▣✕; ℰ01499 500 235; www.auchindrain.org.uk), an open-air museum evoking life in the typical bygone communal-tenancy farms.

Follow the loch south and round the headland to Lochgilphead, then take the A 816 and B 841 to Crinan★, a delightful hamlet at the western end of the Crinan Canal. From Crinan, two picturesque roads, the A 819 north to Cladich and the lochside B 840, lead to scenic **Loch Awe★★**. This is Scotland's longest lake (over 25mi/40km long), the third-largest freshwater loch in Scotland, and the site of two hydroelectric projects. The loch is famous for trout fishing, while its islands include several ruined castles.

Kilchurn Castle juts out on the northern shore. This 15C stronghold was abandoned in the mid-18C.

Oban★

A busy tourist centre and service town for the hinterland and islands, Oban lies opposite the Isle of Mull at the southern end of the Great Glen. It owes its development to the railways and steamboats. The outstanding landmark is **McCaig's Tower** (1897), a replica of the Colosseum, begun as a job creation scheme, but never finished.

On the shores of picturesque Loch Creran, 12mi/19km north, the **Scottish Sea Life Sanctuary★** ▲▲ (Barcaldine; open Mar–Oct daily 10am–5pm, 11am–4pm in winter; closed 25 Dec; £13.40, child £11, discount online; ᪲▣✕; ℰ01631 720 386; www.sealsanctuary.co.uk) is a busy rescue and rehabilitation facility for both common seals and grey seals.

Glen Coe★★

The dramatic approach to Glen Coe (11mi/18km long) – the stark and grandiose setting where the infamous **Glen Coe massacre** occurred in 1692 – is heralded by two mighty hills with Glen Etive between them.

The flat-topped rock known as The Study pinpoints the head of Glen Coe. Beyond the waterfall rise the mighty rock-faces of the **Three Sisters**. These are the outliers of **Bidean nam Bian**, which soars to 1 141m one side; the serrated ridge of **Anoach Eagach** is to the other, while Loch Achtriochtan spreads out on the valley floor. **Glencoe Visitor Centre** (open Jan–Easter and Nov–mid-Dec Thu–Sun 10am–4pm; Easter–Oct daily 9.30am–5.30pm; £6.50; ᪲ℰ01855 811 307; www.nts.org.uk) interprets the massacre and provides information on local walks and climbs. The village of **Glencoe** itself sits on the shores of Loch Leven and is home to the charming **Glencoe and North Lorn Folk Museum** (open Easter–Oct Mon–Sat 10.30am–4.30pm; ᪲▣; ℰ01855 811 664, www.glencoemuseum.com), set in two 18C thatched croft houses and three other ancient buildings.

The picturesque road south (*A 82, A 828*) skirts the south shore of Loch Leven and descends along the east coast of **Loch Linnhe**, the largest sea-loch in Scotland, and cuts across to Loch Creran and back to Oban.

Kingdom of Fife★★

Fife's regal connections began with the 4C Kingdom of the Picts and ended with the Union of the Crowns in 1603. Ever since then the 'Kingdom of Fife' has been peripheral to the Scottish power hierarchy. However, with St Andrews' perennial golfing popularity, the stunning Forth bridges, and the naval dockyard at Rosyth, it is hardly a forgotten corner. Where Fife resonates with modern visitors is its well-kept memories of its halcyon royal and aristocratic days, at Dunfermline, Culross and Falkland Palace. Its quaint fishing villages are another big draw.

- **Michelin Map:** Michelin Atlas p56 or Map 501 L 14.
- **Info: St Andrews:** 70 Market Street. ✆01334 472 021. www.visitstandrews.com. **Dunfermline:** 1 High Street. ✆01383 720 999. www.visitdunfermline.com. www.visitfife.com.
- The nearest train station is 5mi/8km northwest at Leucars (Edinburgh 55min), linked to St Andrew by bus. Buses from Edinburgh and Dundee terminate at the central City Road bus station.
- **Location:** St Andrews is 54mi/87km northeast of Edinburgh.
- **Don't Miss:** Dunfermline Abbey; Culross.

ST ANDREWS★★

This Fife coast resort is most famous as the home of golf, but is also known for its long-established university with its strong recent links to the Royal Family. In the 12C a priory, and later a cathedral were established, leading to the foundation of the university. By 1472, St Andrews was the ecclesiastical capital of Scotland. Its importance declined in the 17C, owing to the switch in trade from the Baltic to the American colonies, and after the Act of Union in 1707. The 19C, however, saw St Andrews return to prominence as a tourist and golfing centre, an importance it has kept to this day.

St Andrews cathedral★

At the eastern end of St Andrews' two main streets. Open daily Apr–Sept 9.30am–5.30pm; Oct–Mar 10am–4pm. £5.50, combined ticket with castle £9. ✆01334 472 563. www.historicenvironment.scot.

Town and castle of St Andrews

© Christophe Boisvieux/hemis.fr

The imposing **St Regulus church**, with its lofty tower, was **built by** Robert of Scone, 1127–1144 and may have been originally intended to house the relics of St Andrew. The tower *(151 steps)* affords a magnificent **panorama**★★ across St Andrews and its main monuments. The church was replaced from 1160 by the later cathedral, the largest church ever built in Scotland. After the Reformation this once-noble building was used as a stone quarry, and reduced to the ruin on view today. Its **museum** has some fine early Christian sculptured stones. Now in ruins, the 13C **St Andrews Castle** (open same hours as cathedral; £5.50. ℘01334 477 196; www.historic-scotland. gov.uk), overlooking the foreshore, was once a part of the palace of the archbishop. Visitors can explore its mine and counter-mine – unique underground passages which give a palpable sense of the horrific nature of medieval siege warfare – and the Bottle Dungeon – one of the most infamous castle prisons in medieval Britain, cut out of the solid rock.

EXCURSIONS

Scotland's Secret Bunker

◖Crown Buildings, Troywood. 10mi/16km SE on the B 9131 and B 940. Open Mar–Oct daily 10am–6pm. £12, child (4–16) £8. 🅿️♿✕ ℘01333 310 301. www.secretbunker.co.uk.

Around 40m below the surface of Fife's farmlands, this now-not-so-secret bunker was built as an early warning radar station and later converted to a nuclear command centre. Protected by 3m of reinforced concrete, all stages of operational life are brought hauntingly to life with audio-visual displays, a large selection of military vehicles and even a Russian anti-aircraft missile evoking the menace of the Cold War era.

East Neuk★★

◖Crail is 10mi/16km SE of St Andrews on the A 917.

The East Neuk ('neuk' means corner) coastline is dotted with picturesque fishing villages, each clustered around its harbour and with a wealth of vernacular architecture.

Crail★★ is the most attractive village, particularly around the **old centre** sloping down to the harbour; don't miss the cottages (Nos. 22–28) on Shoregate; the three-storey Custom House (No. 35 Shoregate); and the charming buildings at 32 Castle Street and at 1 Rose Wynd. In **Anstruther** is the **Scottish Fisheries Museum**★★ (St Ayles Harborhead; open Apr–Sept Mon–Sat 10am–5.30pm, Sun 11am–5pm; Oct–Mar Mon–Sat 10am–4.30pm, Sun noon–4.30pm; £9; ♿🅿️✕; ℘01333 310 628; www.scotishmuseum. org). Don't be misled by its apparently small setting as behind the façade is a

Golf: A Royal and Ancient Game

Since the 15C St Andrews links – with its swards of springy turf and sand bunkers – has been a place for playing golf or at least the early ball and stick version of this sport. So popular was the game that by 1457 an Act of Scottish Parliament was passed requiring that 'futeball and the golfe be utterly cryit down' in favour of kirk attendance and archery practice. Mary Queen of Scots was an occasional player; her son James VI popularised the game in England. Founded in 1754, the Society of St Andrews Golfers had the title **Royal and Ancient** conferred on it by William IV in 1834. It is now recognised as the ruling body. To meet the increasing popularity of the sport, new courses were laid out supplementing the **Old Course**, established several centuries ago. By the beginning of the 20C St Andrews was firmly established as golf's heartland. The town now regularly hosts the British Open and Amateur Championships, Walker Cup Matches and other tournaments, bringing huge crowds. Visit the **British Golf Museum** (Bruce Embankment; open Mon–Sat 9.30am–5pm, Sun 10am–5pm; £8; ♿ ℘01334 460 046, www.britishgolfmuseum.co.uk).

The Saltire

The St Andrews cross (white on a blue ground) was adopted as the Scottish flag in the 13C. **St Andrew**, who was the patron saint of Angus, King of the Picts, later became the patron saint of Scotland. The cross with diagonal beams (saltire) recalls the saint's martyrdom in c.69: the saint thought himself unworthy of being crucified on an upright cross. According to legend the relics of St Andrew were brought to Scotland in the 8C by St Rule (St Regulus).

large courtyard full of buildings, including the 16C Abbot's Lodging, a fisherman's cottage, the Merchant House (1724) and a covered historic boatyard. Aside from its huge collection of smaller artefacts, there are 19 historic boats, some berthed in the harbour opposite. **Pittenweem** is the least picturesque of the East Neuk's three main fishing villages but is Fife's busiest fishing port and still has some fine old properties. Head north on Church Street for around 3mi/5km to **Kellie Castle and Garden★** (**Castle**: open Jun–Aug daily 11am–5pm; Apr–May and Sept Sat–Thu 11am–5pm; ; Oct Sat–Thu 11am–4pm; **Gardens and grounds**: open daily 9am–dusk; £10.50; &P(charge); ✗; ℘01333 720 271; www.nts.org.uk), a fine example of unspoiled 16C–17C traditional Scottish architecture featuring corbelled turrets with conical roofs, pedimented dormers, and crow-stepped gables. The 17C **plasterwork ceilings** are notable.

DUNFERMLINE★

36mi/58km SW of St Andrew's.
Dunfermline, the former capital of Scotland, lies immediately north of the present capital, Edinburgh, across the Firth of Forth. Its great abbey and royal palace figure frequently in Scottish history.
The town has long been a thriving industrial centre, with coal mining

and linen weaving, and new industries maintain this tradition today.
In 1066, **Malcolm III** (Canmore) sheltered the heir to the English throne, **Edgar Atheling** and his family, fleeing from William the Conqueror after defeat at Hastings, in his Dunfermline Tower. Edgar's sister **Margaret** married the Scots king in 1070. She was a devout Catholic and was largely responsible for introducing the ideas which gradually supplanted the rituals of the Celtic church. The Benedictine abbey was founded by **David I**, son of Queen Margaret. **Robert the Bruce** (1274–1329) helped with the reconstruction of the abbey in 1034 and is buried here. After the Reformation, King James VI (James I of England) had an impressive new **palace** built to the west of the old cloister. He gave the palace to his queen, Anne of Denmark, and Charles I was born here. There were fleeting royal visits thereafter, but following the Union of the Crowns in 1603, the palace was never again a regular royal residence.

Town Walk

Northwest of the train station is **Dunfermline Palace and Abbey★** (open Apr–Sept daily 9.30am–5.30pm; Oct–Mar Sat–Wed 10am–4pm; £5; P; ℘01383 739 026; www.historicenvironment.scot), an 11C Benedictine abbey founded on the site of a Celtic church. The Norman nave of the **abbey church★★** with its massive pillars and round-headed arches is one of the finest in Scotland. The east end (rebuilt in the early-19C) serves as the parish church; a memorial brass marks the tomb of Robert the Bruce. There are few remains of the great monastic ensemble.
Nearby, **Abbot House** (Maygate; open daily 9.30am–5pm; closed 1 Jan, 25–26 Dec; &PX; ℘01383 733 266) is now an attractive heritage centre. Head south from here on St Margaret Street, which leads to Moodie Street and the **Andrew Carnegie Birthplace** (open Mar–Nov Mon–Sat 10am–5pm, Sun 2–5pm; &PX; ℘01383 724 302; www.carnegiebirthplace.com). The self-made steel baron and great philanthropist, Andrew Carn-

Culross Palace with a view to the Forth estuary

egie (1835–1919) was born in this house before emigrating to America in 1848. An exhibition traces his life.

EXCURSIONS
Culross★★

13mi/21km E on the A 944 and B 9037.
According to legend, St Mungo, patron saint of Glasgow, was born in this small burgh (pronounced 'coo-ross') on the north shore of the Firth of Forth.

A Cistercian house was founded here in the 13C and trade with the Low Countries, salt panning and coal mining brought prosperity.

Today the 'Royal Burgh of Culross' is famous for its fine examples of Scottish vernacular architecture of the 16C and 17C in all its rich detail. The small buildings in the **village★★★** feature inscribed lintels, decorative finials, skewputts, crow-stepped gables, forestairs, harling and rubble stonework with door and window trims.

The **Town House** is a stone-and-slate building erected in 1625 in Flemish style; it contrasts with the white harling and red pantiles of the surrounding buildings. The Back Causeway, behind, has a central line of raised paving stones for the exclusive use of local notables. Opposite, the **Study★**, which has a 17C painted ceiling (restored) and original panelling, is the oldest house in Culross with a replica of the 1588 mercat cross in front of its gable end.

The **palace★★** (open Apr–May and Sept Sat–Mon 11am–5pm; Jun Wed–Mon 11am–5pm; Jul–Aug daily 11am–5pm; Oct Sat–Mon 11am–4pm; garden 10am–4pm (Sat–Sun during Apr–Oct 11am–5pm); £10.50; 🅿 ♿ ✗; ☎01383 880 359; www. nts.org.uk) a comfortable house built (1597–1611) by George Bruce, a rich merchant and coalmine owner, boasts pine-panelled rooms and 21 fireplaces which burned coal rather than logs. Dutch tiles carried as ballast in his ships were used for flooring and roofing.

Falkland Palace★

31mi/50km NE by the M90, A 91 and A 912. Open Mar–Oct daily 11am (Sun noon)–5pm. £12.50. ☎0133/857 397. www.nts.org.uk.

In 1425, this hunting-seat of the Earls of Fife passed to the crown and became one of the Stewarts' favourite royal palaces. The gatehouse and street façade built in Gothic style by James IV, a Renaissance monarch who entertained a splendid court, is in sharp contrast with the Renaissance ornament of the courtyard façade of the south range added by his son, James V. A tour of the interior includes the keeper's gatehouse apartments, adorned with royal portraits, coats of arms and elegant furnishings.

The lovely **gardens★** feature a large collection of scented early summer blooms and also boast the original Real (Royal) Tennis court. Built for James V in 1539, it is the world's oldest court.

Perthshire★★

Situated in the very heart of Scotland, Perthshire boasts some of the finest and most accessible scenery anywhere in the Scottish Highlands. It has long been a retreat for the royal and well-heeled – from ancient Scone Palace to modern Gleneagles – and nowadays is also a mecca for adventure sports.

PERTH★

42mi/67km due N of Edinburgh.
🚇 45 High Street. ✆01738 450 600.
This former Royal Burgh, situated on the River Tay, retains the atmosphere of a country town, with many fine examples of **Georgian architecture★** and is an ideal touring base. The Tay is famous for salmon fishing and for freshwater mussels which produce beautiful pearls. The 'Fair City' has played a prominent role in Scottish history and might well have become the capital had not James I been assassinated here in 1437. Other tumultuous events included the murderous Clan Combat of 1396 and the destruction of the monasteries following John Knox's heated sermon of 1559.

📍 **Michelin Map:** Michelin Atlas p62 or Map 501 J 14.
ℹ **Info:** www.perthshire.co.uk.

Black Watch Regimental Museum★

Balhousie Castle, Hay Street. Open daily: Apr–Oct 9.30am–4.30pm; Nov–Mar 10am–4pm. ♿🅿✕ £7.50, guided tour £12.50. ✆01738 638 152; www.theblackwatch.co.uk.
In the early-18C General Wade enlisted and armed independent companies of Highlanders which became known as the **Black Watch**, for the 'watch' they kept on the Highlands, and for their dark tartan. The museum, set in Balhousie Castle (1860), traces the often turbulent history of this elite regiment.

Perth Museum & Art Gallery★

78 George St. ♿ Open 10am–5pm: Tue–Sat (Sun Apr–Oct only). ✆01738 632 488. www.culturepk.org.uk.
Displays of local glass, silver and clock-making industries, and natural history. Work by Scottish artists predominates.

The Stone of Destiny

According to legend, the Stone of Destiny was Jacob's pillow, which eventually reached Ireland by way of Egypt and Spain and is believed to have served as a coronation stone for the High Kings at Tara. Kenneth MacAlpine was the first king to be crowned on the stone at Scone and it subsequently served for the coronation of all Scottish kings until 1296 when the Scots were defeated by Edward I. He carried off the stone, which was placed beneath the Coronation chair in Westminster Abbey, where for 700 years it played an integral part in the coronation rituals. It was stolen in 1950 but was later recovered in Arbroath Abbey. From early days controversy has raged about the authenticity of the stone. Some believe the original stone never left Scotland. In 1996, the people of Scotland greeted the return of the Stone of Destiny, which is the symbol of Scottish nationhood, with great emotion. It is now on display with the Honours of Scotland in Edinburgh Castle, but will be returned (temporarily) to Westminster Abbey for use in future coronations.

Fergusson Gallery

Marshall Place. &. Open as Perth Museum and Art Gallery. &01738 783 425; www.culturepk.org.uk.

This handsome circular building, formerly the city's waterworks, is home to a rotating exhibition of the works of J D Fergusson (1874–1961), foremost among the Scottish Colourists.

EXCURSIONS

Scone Palace★★

◗ 2mi/3km NE by the A 93. Open Apr and Oct daily 10am–4pm; May–Sept 9.30am–5pm. £11.50 & ☐ ✕ &01738 552 300. www.scone-palace.co.uk.

One of Scotland's most hallowed sites, Scone (pronounced 'scoon') was the centre of Kenneth MacAlpine's Scotto-Pictish kingdom from the mid-9C. **Moot Hill**, now occupied by a 19C chapel, was where Scottish kings were enthroned on the **Stone of Destiny** (also known as the Stone of Scone). Wrecked in the wave of destruction of 1559, the abbey became the seat of the Earls of Mansfield. The present Gothic Revival palace dates from 1808. Its richly furnished apartments contain a splendid array of porcelain and ivories, unusual timepieces, busts and portraits, and collection of papier mâché *objets d'art*.

Dunkeld★

◗ 14mi/23km north on the A 9.

Dunkeld was the site of a monastic establishment from 700 and later a majestic Gothic **cathedral** (Cathedral Street; open Apr–Sept 10am–6.30pm; Oct–Mar 10am–4pm; &01350 727 249; www.dunkeldcathedral.org.uk) set in an attractive riverside precinct.

Pitlochry★

◗ 26mi/42km north of Perth on the A 9.
🏠 22 Atholl Road. &01796 472 215. www.pitlochry.org.

This attractive town, set in the Tummel valley, makes a fine touring centre to enjoy the magnificent scenery of mountains, lochs and moors. It hosts a famous festival of drama, music and art in summer and in recent years has become the adventure-sports capital of Scotland with a wide range of activities.

EXCURSIONS

Queen's View★★

◗ 10mi/16km W by the B 8019.

This beauty spot was named after Queen Victoria's visit in 1866, and commands a fine view up Loch Tummel.

Blair Castle★★

◗ Blair Atholl. 7mi/11km N on the A 9. Open Apr–Oct daily 9.30am–5.30pm. £11. & ☐ ✕ &01796 481 207. www.blair-castle.co.uk.

Blair Castle was the centre of the ancient kingdom of Atholl and the home of the Duke of Atholl until the death of the last of the line in 1996. It is still home to the only private army left in the British Isles, the **Atholl Highlanders**, sole survivor of the clan system. A large part of the tower built here in 1269 still remains, and the castle with its turrets and parapets continues to command a strategic route into the Central Highlands.

The 18C interiors include sumptuous stucco ceilings, family **portraits** (by Lely, Jacob de Wet, Hoppner, Zoffany and Landseer), collections of armour and porcelain, Jacobite and other historic relics. The grounds include nature trails and a deer park.

Aberfeldy★

◗ 10mi/16km SW.
🏠 The Square. &01887 820 276. www.visitaberfeldy.co.uk.

Burns wrote: "*Come let us spend the … days, In the birks of Aberfeldy*" and the deep pools and majestic waterfalls of the birks (birch trees) remain one of Aberfeldy's most popular attractions. They also power the big overshot waterwheel in the **Water Mill** (open Mon–Sat 10am–5pm, Sun 11am–5pm. ✕ &01887 822 896, www.aberfeldywatermill.com).

This now houses the largest bookshop in the rural Highlands, a contemporary art gallery, shop and cafe, set in a 19C watermill.

Grampians★★★

Comprising the Cairngorms, Moray and Aberdeenshire, the Grampians are Britain's finest mountain scenery. As wild as the Arctic or as tame as a family railway ride, they are accessible to any visitor. The delights of Royal Deeside are well known, those of Aberdeen less so, and the Granite City is often the Grampians' surprise package; few tourists expect city-slick culture this far north of Edinburgh. Outside the city are some of Scotland's best castles, finest fishing villages and a tempting malt whisky trail.

ABERDEEN★★

126mi/203km NE of Edinburgh.

The dignified and prosperous 'Granite City' developed from two fishing villages on the Dee and the Don and also prospered from its rich agricultural hinterland. During the latter part of the 20C Aberdeen gained new riches thanks to its proximity to the North Sea oilfields and became the oil and gas capital of Europe. Today the oil is running out but the city is still a major offshore centre.

A Bit of History

An episcopal city by the 12C, Old Aberdeen had a large secular community outside its precincts; in the late-15C Bishop Elphinstone founded a university. A second distinct burgh grew around the king's castle and became an active trading centre. As the city expanded the streets were lined with impressive buildings in a dignified but simple style by the native architect Archibald Simpson (1790–1847), who gave Aberdeen its **Granite City** nickname and its distinctive character by his masterly use of the local stone. Aberdeen has a strong **maritime tradition** with its shipbuilding industry: vessels for whaling, the Clipper ships which gave Britain supremacy in the China tea trade, wooden sailing vessels and iron steamships. The North Sea has brought prosperity with the growth of fisheries

Michelin Map: Michelin Atlas p61–62, p67–69 or Map 501.

Info: Aberdeen: 23 Union St. ✆01224 269 180. www. aberdeen-grampian.com. **Braemar:** The Mews, Mar Road. ✆01339 741 600. www.braemarscotland.co.uk. **Grantown-on-Spey:** 54 High Street, ✆01479 872 242. www.visitgrantown.co.uk. www.visitcairngorms.com.

Don't Miss: The heraldic ceiling in St Machar's cathedral; Aberdeen Art Gallery; Pitmedden Gardens; Grampian castles; a Highland Games gathering; the view from Cairn Gorm on a clear day.

Kids: Cairngorm Reindeer Centre; Landmark Forest Adventure Park. Strathspey Steam Railway.

– whaling from the 1750s, the herring boom in the 1870s and white fishing in the present day.

More recently Aberdeen has become the 'offshore capital of Europe' for the North Sea oil industry and exploration and supply-base activities continue to play an important role.

Most visitor attractions are clustered in Old Aberdeen and the city centre.

WALKING TOURS

2 OLD ABERDEEN★★

Aberdeen's medieval streets capture the essence of the old town, which became a burgh of barony in 1489, a status retained until 1891. The North Sea provided growth in the 18C–19C in the form of fisheries.

Start at **King's College Chapel★** (entry in Quadrangle, 25 High Street; open Mon–Fri 10am–3.30pm; ✆01224 272 137; www. abdn.ac.uk), **the only original building**

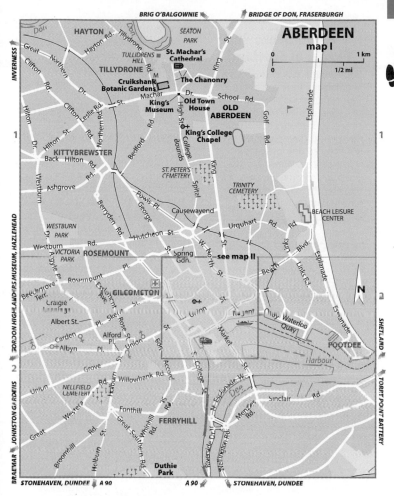

ABERDEEN
map I

left of Bishop Elphinstone's university in its campus setting. Outstanding features are a delicate Renaissance **crown spire★★★**, the tinctured arms on the west front buttresses (including those of James IV and his queen, Margaret Tudor) and rare, richly carved **medieval fittings★★★**.

At the crossroads stands the **Old Town House**, an attractive 18C Georgian house. Beyond is The Chanonry, a walled precinct for the residences of the bishop and other clerics.

From the chapel, walk up the High Street past the **Old Town House**, **Chanonry** and **Cruickshank Botanic Gardens** to get to **St Machar's cathedral★★** (The Chanonry; open daily Apr–Oct 9.30am–

4.30pm; Nov–Mar 10am–4pm; &; ✆01224 485 988; www.stmachar.com), whose twin spires have long been one of the landmarks of Old Aberdeen.

The cathedral, which dates from the 14C and 15C was built '...overlooking the crook of the Don' in compliance with instructions from St Columba. The impressive exterior is complemented by a splendid 16C **heraldic ceiling★★★**. The brightly coloured coats of arms present a vision of the European scene around 1520. The early-14C **Brig o'Balgownie★** *(approach via Don Street – V)*, with its pointed Gothic arch and a defensive kink at the south end, is one of Aberdeen's most important medieval structures.

Aberdeen, "Flower of Scotland"

Aberdeen's parks and gardens are justly famous. Try to see: **Union Terrace Gardens** (off Union Street) with their celebrated floral displays including Aberdeen's coat of arms; the splendid **Winter Gardens** in Duthie Park; the rose garden and maze at **Hazlehead** ♿; the delightful **Johnston Gardens** and the university's **Cruickshank Botanic Gardens**.

1 CITY CENTRE

Start at the **Maritime Museum★** (Provost Ross's House, Shiprow; open Mon–Sat 10am–5pm, Sun noon–3pm; ♿; ℘01224 337 700; www.aagm.co.uk). The museum is located in two 16C town houses bordering Shiprow, a medieval thoroughfare winding up from the harbour. Ship models, paintings, artefacts and interactive displays trace local maritime industries.

Follow Shiprow round to Union Street and turn right towards **Castlegate**. The medieval market place was situated here. Notable features are the Mannie Fountain (1706), a reminder of the city's first water supply, and the splendid **Mercat Cross★★** dating from 1686 and decorated with a unicorn, a frieze, and royal portrait medallions and coats of arms. It was the place for public punishment and proclamations.

Behind the 19C **Town House** on Castle Street rises the tower of the 17C **Tolbooth** (open Mon–Sat 10am–5pm, Sun noon–3pm; ♿; ℘01224 621 167; www.aagm.co.uk), now a museum housing exhibits on the history of crime and punishment within the city.

Handsome **Marischal Street** extends south from Castle Street. It was laid out in 1767–68 with houses built to a uniform three storeys and attic design. Return to Castle Street and turn left, then right on Broad Street for **Marischal College★**, founded in the 16C by and amalgamated with the older King's College to form Aberdeen University; it has a striking 20C granite façade. At the end of Broad Street turn left onto Upper Kirkgate for **Provost Skene's House★** (Guestrow, between Broad Street and Flourmill Lane; temporarily closed to the public; check website or call for updates; ℘01224 641 086; www.aagm.co.uk), a 17C townhouse containing tastefully furnished 17C, 18C and early-19C rooms with elaborate plasterwork ceilings and panelling.

Detail of A Ground Swell, Carradale, *(1883-1886) by William Mc Taggart, Aberdeen Art Gallery & Museums*

© The Print Collector/age fotostock

The chapel boasts an outstanding 17C painted **ceiling**★★ of New Testament scenes. Continue on Upper Kirkgate towards the **Aberdeen Art Gallery**★★ (closed for redevelopment – check website for updates. &03000 200 293; www.aagm.co.uk), whose permanent collection held a strong emphasis on contemporary art. Various works of art are displayed in its elegant marble-lined interior.

The **Scottish Collection** includes important works by local artists. The **Macdonald Collection**★★ of British artists' portraits is a survey of the art world in the 19C.

EXCURSIONS
Deeside★★
⊙50mi/80km W of Aberdeen on the A93. The splendid valley of the salmon-rich Dee flows from its source 1 219m high in the Cairngorms to the sea at Aberdeen.

Some 30mi/48km west of Aberdeen, the green at **Aboyne,** in the heart of Deeside forms the setting for the colourful **Highland Games** in August. Some 19mi/31km further west lies **Balmoral Castle** (open Apr–Jul daily 10am–5pm; £11.50; &🅿✗; &013397 42534; www.balmoralcastle.com). This has been the summer residence of the Royal Family since Queen Victoria's reign when Prince Albert bought it in 1852. It was then immediately demolished as it was too small for Albert and the present building was designed under the prince's supervision and completed in 1856. Victoria described Balmoral as '...my dear paradise in the Highlands', and the current Royal Family spend August, September and early October here. Before they arrive, however, the Ballroom (the largest room in the castle) its grounds and gardens, plus exhibitions, are open to the public.

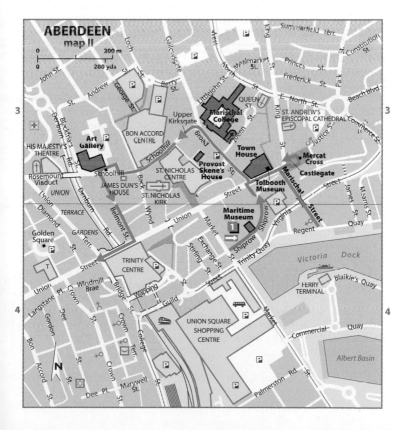

Red deer, Cairngorms National Park

© Nature in Stock/hemis.fr

Continue on the A 93 for 10mi/16km to **Braemar**. It too boasts a **castle** (open Apr–Jun and Sept–Oct Wed–Sun 10am–5pm; Jul–Aug daily 10am–5pm; £8; **P**; ℘013397 41219; www.braemar-castle.co.uk), albeit much humbler than its famous neighbour, and dates mostly from the 18C and 19C.

The village is best known for its **Highland Gathering**, held annually in September and normally attended by royalty. At the road's end is the famous beauty spot **Linn o'Dee**, where, in season, salmon may be seen leaping.

Pitmedden Garden★★

○ 14mi/23km N by the A 92. Open May–Sept daily 10am–5.30pm. £6.50. &**P**✗ ℘01651 842 352. www.nts.org.uk.

Sir Alexander Seton (c.1639–1719), possibly influenced by the Versailles designs of Le Nôtre, or the gardens of Sir William Bruce at Holyrood, laid out the original formal gardens. Honeysuckle, jasmine and roses create a succession of fragrances, while fountains, topiary, sundials, and a fascinating herb garden add to the sense of discovery around the walled garden.

The garden is seen at its best in July and August, from the Belvedere, when 30–40 000 annuals are in bloom. A Museum of Farming Life relives the agricultural past of the region.

THE CAIRNGORMS★★

Aviemore is 90mi/145km W of Aberdeen from the centre.

☻ The mountains are remote and are a treacherous place to all but well-equipped and experienced walkers and mountaineers.

This granitic range between the Spey valley and Braemar features some of Britain's wildest and most dramatic mountain scenery. Much of it lies close to or above 1 000m, with Ben Macdui (1 309m) as its highest point even though the region is named after the lower peak of Cairn Gorm (1 245m).

The **Cairngorms National Park** covers 26 000ha, making it the biggest national park in Britain, with the largest area of arctic mountain landscape in the UK at its heart.

The severe climate of the windswept summits allows only an Arctic-Alpine flora to flourish. The mountains are the home of the golden eagle, ptarmigan, snow bunting, dotterel and the rare osprey (RSPB observation hide at Loch Garten).

The only reindeer herd in Britain, numbering around 150, is to be found in the Glenmore Forest Park at the **Cairngorm Reindeer Centre** ♟♟ (&Paddocks: open daily 10am–5pm; £3.50, child £2.50; Hill trips daily Jan–early Feb 11am; May–Sept 11am and 2.30pm, Jul–Aug additional trip at 3.30pm Mon–Fri only; Hill trip £14, child £8; ☻ wear warm and waterproof clothing and sturdy footwear; ℘01479 861 228; www.cairngormreindeer.co.uk).

The centre has an Exhibition and Paddocks with a small number of deer, but most visitors make the short journey out into the wild to find the herd, which ranges freely in the open. The deer are very friendly and can be stroked and hand-fed.

Cairn Gorm★★★

Happily, for non-mountaineers, a modern **funicular railway** (operates daily from 10am, every 20min, last train 4pm depending on weather; £11.50; ♿✕; ☎01479 861 261; www.cairngormmountain.org) **provides an easy way of appreciating something of the magic and beauty of the mountains. The railway transports visitors to two levels. The first is Base Station, with a Mountain Garden. The Ptarmigan Top Station, nestled just below the summit of Cairn Gorm, includes a shop, bar, restaurant and exhibition.**
The already excellent view from the car park unfolds further as the train ascends. At the terminal, there is an extensive **view★★★** westwards of the Spey valley. A path leads up another 150m to the summit of Cairn Gorm (1 245m), which affords a wonderful **panorama★★★** in all directions, well beyond the Cairngorm mountains.
🙂 For conservation reasons, there is no exit out onto the mountain from the top station unless you are booked on a **Guided Walk** (May–Oct; www.cairngormmountain.org/guided-walks).
The northern and western slopes of Cairngorm are ideal for skiing, and the construction in the 1960s of the **Aviemore Centre** – a complex of shops, hotels and entertainment facilities with an après-ski flavour – transformed **Aviemore★** village into Britain's first winter-sports resort. There are ice-rinks for skating and curling, a dry-ski slope and a swimming pool.
The **Strathspey Railway** (♿; Dalfaber Road; daily service Apr–Sept, times vary rest of year; £14.25 return; ♿; 🅿; ✕ onboard train; ☎01479 810 725; www.strathspeyrailway.co.uk) **operates a steam service on a line 5mi/8km from Aviemore to Boat of Garten and Broomhill.**

Highland Wildlife Park★

Kincraig. 12mi/19km south of Aviemore. Open Apr–Oct daily 10am–5pm; Jul–Aug 10am–6pm; Nov–Mar 10am–4pm. £15.90, child (3–15), £12. ♿🅿✕ ☎01540 651 270. www.highlandwildlifepark.org. Home to Scottish wildlife as well as internationally endangered animals, this park is run by the Royal Zoological Society of Scotland and includes tigers, bison and the only polar bear living in a British zoo.

Highland Folk Museum

Newtonmore, Kingussie. 15.5mi/25km south of Aviemore. Open Apr–Aug daily 10.30am–5.30pm; Sept–Oct 11am–4.30pm. ♿🅿 ☎01540 673 551. www.highlandfolk.com.
This award-winning collection relates the life of the Highlanders (dress, musical instruments, farm implements, old crafts) and includes a 'black house' typical of the Western Isles, and a water-powered mill.

🚶 Landmark Forest Adventure Park

Landmark, Carrbridge. 6mi/10km N of Aviemore. Open daily 10am–5pm, peak periods 6pm/7pm. £20, child £17.95.50; winter £6.95, child £5.90. ♿🅿✕; ☎01479 841 613; www.landmarkpark.co.uk.
A favourite family day out with adventure climbs, watersplash rides, a mini-roller coaster, a high-wire challenge course and nature-themed activities.

ELGIN★

Elgin is 38mi/61km NE of Inverness.
Elgin stands on the banks of the Lossie just off the northeast coast. The original town plan has been well preserved, with the main street linking the two mainstays of any medieval burgh – the cathedral and the castle.

Elgin cathedral★

♿Open Apr–Sept daily 9.30am–5.30pm; Oct–Mar daily 10am– 4pm. Guided tours (free) Mon–Fri. £7.50. ♿ ☎01343 547 171. www.historicenvironment.scot.

The diocese dates back to 1120, but the ruins here are those of a cathedral built in 1270. In 1390, Alexander Stewart, the **Wolf of Badenoch**, second son of King Robert II, destroyed both cathedral and town. Both were repaired, and the 13C **chapter house★★** was reconstructed in the 15C. The cathedral suffered further deterioration after conservation was begun in the early-19C.

EXCURSIONS

Speyside

Dufftown is 18mi/29km S of Elgin.

A brown-and-white signposted **Malt Whisky Trail** (approx 70mi/112km; www.maltwhiskytrail.com) through the glens of Speyside, takes in eight famous distilleries and a cooperage, all of which offer a fascinating glimpse into the production of Scotland's 'sovereign liquor'. A basic distillery tour is often complimentary, with a charge for tasting tours where more than a wee dram or two is sampled. The trail centres on Dufftown and the following are essential stops: **Glenfiddich Distillery** (0.5mi/0.8km) north of Dufftown; open daily Apr–Oct 9.30am–4pm; Nov–Mar 11am–3pm; ♿ 🅿; ☎01340 820 373, www.glenfiddich.co.uk/distillery) is a perfect example of a working distillery, little changed since 1886.

Picturesque **Dallas Dhu Distillery** (1.2mi/2km S of Forres, 14mi/23km W of Elgin; open Apr–Sept daily 9.30am–5.30pm; Oct–Mar Sat–Wed 10am–4pm; £6; ♿ 🅿; ☎01309 676 548, www.historicenvironment.scot), dating from 1898, is no longer in production but is a fascinating time capsule.

Speyside Cooperage (Dufftown Road, Craigellachie, 4mi/6km N of Dufftown); open Mon–Fri 9am–5pm, last tour 3.30pm; £3.50; ♿ 🅿 ✕; ☎01340 871 108; www.speysidecooperage.co.uk) is the only working cooperage in the UK where you can witness the ancient craft of barrel making.

Sueno's Stone★★

13mi/21km west of Elgin. Just east of Forres off the A96.

This huge superbly carved Pictish sandstone slab (some 6m high) is unique in Britain. It is probably a funerary monument commemorating a battle. Three sides are decorative – one carved with a wheel cross. The fourth side, the most spectacular, shows horsemen, warriors and headless corpses.

Brodie Castle★

Brodie, near Forres. 16mi/26km W of Elgin. Open Apr and Sept daily 10.30am–4.30pm; May–Jun and Oct Fri–Tue 10.30am–4.30pm; Jul–Aug daily 10.30am–5pm. £10.50. ♿ 🅿 £2; ✕ ☎01309 641 371. www.nts.org.uk.

The seat of the Brodies since the 11C, the castle developed from a 16C tower-house to the present building. Interiors of various periods are the setting for a splendid collection of paintings, exquisite timepieces and French **furniture**. The ornate **plasterwork ceilings** date from the 17C.

BANFF★

40mi/64km N of Aberdeen.

This small royal burgh town, set on the coast at the mouth of the River Deveron, on Banff Bay, boasts many attractive 18C buildings, none more so than Duff House (*see below*). With magnificent views of cliffs and headlands all along this splendid coastline, Banff is an excellent base for excursions: west to the picturesque fishing villages of **Portsoy, Cullen** and **Buckie**; east to **Macduff, Gardenstown, Crovie** and **Pennan**.

Duff House★★

Overlooking the Duff House Royal Golf Club beside the River Deveron. Open Apr–Oct daily 11am–5pm; Nov–Mar Thu–Sun 11am–4pm. £7.50. ♿ 🅿 ✕ ☎01261 81 81 81. www.historicenvironment.scot.

This splendid Baroque mansion designed by William Adam has been restored to its former glory. A double curving staircase rises up to the great central block and Corinthian pilasters support a richly decorated pediment. Small intimate rooms surround the spacious vestibule dominated by a grandiose painting by William Etty, and the Great Drawing Room hung with Gobelins tapestries and pastoral paintings by Boucher.

GRAMPIAN CASTLES★★

Aberdeen's hinterland is rich in castles, both complete and ruined from the early Norman to the Scottish Baronial style; many of these characterise the golden age of castle-building, which occurred between the 16C and the 17C.

Haddo House★

26mi/42km N of Aberdeen by the A 92 and B 9005. Open by guided tour only at 11.30am, 12.30pm, 1.30pm, 2.30pm, 3.30pm. Apr–Oct and Sept Sat–Sun only; Jul–Aug Sat–Mon. £10.50. ♿🅿✕ ℰ01651 851 440. www.nts.org.uk.

The present house was designed by William Adam in 1469. George Hamilton Gordon (1784–1860), prime minister during the Crimean War, still found time to repair the house and to landscape the parkland. Its superb late Victorian interiors feature elegant rooms with coffered ceilings and wood panelling, a perfect setting for family portraits and mementoes. The country park offers splendid vistas.

Fyvie Castle★

26mi/42km north of Aberdeen on the A 947. Open Apr–May and Sept Sat–Wed 11am–5.15pm; Jun–Aug daily 11am–5.15pm; Oct Sat–Sun 11am–5pm. £12.50. ♿🅿✕ ℰ01651 891 266. www.nts.org.uk.

Alexander Seton, Lord Chancellor (c. 1639–1719), remodelled Fyvie creating the spectacular **south front** (46m long), an impressive example of 17C Baronial architecture, and the **wheel stair**. In the late-19C Fyvie was refurbished in opulent Edwardian style, decorated with portraits by the Scottish master of this art, **Henry Raeburn**.

Crathes Castle★★

15mi/24km SW of Aberdeen on the A 93. Open Jan–Mar and Nov–23 Dec Sat–Sun 11am–4pm, Apr–Oct daily 10.30am–5pm. £12.50. ♿🅿✕ ℰ01330 844525. www.nts.org.uk.

The wonderfully crowded and detailed skyline of this 16C tower house, including fairy-tale-like turrets and gargoyles of fantastic design, is a striking example of the inventive Baronial tradition.

The interiors include some fine early vernacular furniture as well as some outstanding examples of **painted ceilings**. Stone pendants and armorial paintings adorn the barrel-vaulted **High Hall**, where the **Horn of Leys** – the original token of tenure dating from 1322 –

Interior, Fyvie Castle

© Andrea Pistolesi/hemis.fr

Dunnottar Castle

© imageBROKER / hemis.fr

has pride of place above the fireplace. The oak-panelled roof decorated with armorial devices and the horn motif is a unique feature of the **Long Gallery**. The series of **separate gardens★★★** are a delight in the wealth and colour of the planting.

Castle Fraser★

15mi/24km west of Aberdeen via the A 944 and B 993 at Dunecht. Open Apr–Jun and Oct, Wed–Sun 10.30am–5pm; Jul–Sept daily 10.30am–5pm. £10.50. &⚿🅿✗ ℰ01330 833 463. www.nts.org.uk.
Castle Fraser, built 1575–1636, is a traditional tower house with highly individual decoration. The **exterior★★** is remarkable. The local style with its harmonious combination of traditional features – turrets, conical roofs, crow-stepped gables, chimney stacks, decorative dormers and gargoyles – was Scotland's unique contribution to Renaissance architecture. The **central block** of this Z-plan castle is distinguished by a magnificent heraldic achievement. The interiors bring to life the simple lifestyle of a 17C laird.

Dunnottar Castle★★

18mi/29km south of Aberdeen via the A 92. Open daily Apr–Sept 9am–5.30pm; Oct–Mar 10am–dusk/4.30pm. £7. ℰ01569 762 173. www.dunnottarcastle.co.uk.
Set on an almost inaccessible **promontory★★★** with sheer cliffs on three sides, the castle dates from the 14C and was the last castle remaining in Royalist hands during the Commonwealth. Here the Honours of Scotland (the royal regalia) were held during an eight-month siege by Cromwell's troops in 1651–52, before being finally smuggled out and hidden in a nearby church. The fortified **gatehouse** and **keep** contrast with the 17C **Waterton's Lodging** and the **16C–17C buildings** arranged around a quadrangle.

Tolquhon Castle★

17mi/27km N of Aberdeen via the B 999. Open Apr–Sept daily 9.30am–5.30pm. £5. ℰ01651 851 286. www.historicenvironment.scot.
Pronounced 'tol-hoon', this is one of the most picturesque castle ruins in the Grampians. The present structure dates from 1574. Its gatehouse is a gem, built not to deter, but to impress. The main house is a charming composition at the far end of the courtyard, with a good 'below stairs' and family rooms above to explore. In the laird's bedchamber on the second floor is a secret compartment below the floor where Sir William Forbes, the builder of the castle, hid his valuables.
In the nearby parish church in the village of Tarves, Sir William also built the **Tolquhon Tomb** burial vault. This is one of the best examples of Scotland's so-called 'Glorious Tombs' from the Jaco-bean age, finely decorated with beguil-ing stone effigies Forbes himself (d.1596) and his wife, Elizabeth Gordon.

Highlands and Western Isles★★★

If there were only one region that could fly the flag for Scotland abroad, then it would probably be the Highlands. It not only boasts Scotland's most awe-inspiring landscapes of dark lochs and snow-capped peaks, but also some of the most remote and extensive wilderness in Europe. There is island romance, on Skye and in the Hebrides, history aplenty (Glencoe, Bonnie Prince Charlie, standing stones), legends (Nessie, Macbeth), wildlife (dolphins, whales, eagles and deer), and a host of sporting opportunities in both summer and winter.

⚂ **Michelin Map:** Michelin Atlas p65–67, p74 or Map 501.

▓ **Info: Inverness:** 36 High Street. ☎01463 252 401. www.inverness-scotland.com.
Gairloch: The GALE Centre, Achtercairn. ☎01445 712 071. www.galeactionforum.co.uk.
Kyle of Lochalsh: Station Road. ☎01471 822716. www.lochalsh.co.uk.
Ullapool: 6 Argyle Street. ☎01854 612 486.
Isle of Skye: Bayfield House, Bayfield Road, Portree. ☎01478 612 992. www.skye.co.uk.
John o' Groats: County Road. ☎01955 611 373. www.visitjohnogroats.com www.visithighlands.com.

👥 **Kids:** Loch Ness Exhibition Centre at Drumnadrochit.

INVERNESS★

156mi/251km north of Edinburgh, 119mi/191km SW of John o' Groats. Standing at the northern end of the Great Glen, astride the River Ness (flowing from Loch Ness), Inverness is the traditional capital and hub of the Scottish Highlands. It services much of northern Scotland on a daily basis, while its legendary loch attracts many boating visitors.

☛ WALKING TOUR

Just east of the Young Street bridge on Castle Wynd is the **Inverness Museum and Art Gallery★** (open Apr–Oct Tue–Sat 10am–5pm; Nov–Mar Tue–Thu noon–4pm, Fri–Sat 11am–4pm; ☎01463 237 114; www.highlifehighland.com), an imaginative well-presented exhibition interpreting the region's rich heritage (and present day arts and crafts) including the Great Glen, the Picts, General Wade's roads and Telford's Caledonian Canal.

Immediately to the south on Castle Street, is 19C **Inverness Castle**, sitting on a low cliff, overlooking the River Ness and the cathedral on the opposite bank.

It now houses the Sheriff Court and is closed to the public, though a good **view** of the town and the River Ness may be enjoyed from its esplanade. Across the bridge, follow the road to Ardross Street and take a left for **St Andrew's cathedral** (open daily; ☎01463 237 503; www.inverness cathedral.com), a richly decorated neo-Gothic Revival church of 1866–69. Its nave piers are of polished Peterhead granite.

EXCURSIONS
Cawdor Castle★

13mi/21km NE on the A 96 and B 9090. Open May–early Oct daily 10am–5pm. £10.70. ▣✕ ☎01667 404 401. www.cawdorcastle.com.
Built in the late-14C by the Thanes of Cawdor (the title, meaning nobleman, Shakespeare's witches promised to Macbeth), the castle was added to in the 17C. Note the lovely 17C Flemish and English tapestries and, amid the many portraits, one of the 18C thane, splendidly dressed in an assortment of tar-

tans. Outside, there are three gardens to enjoy – the oldest being the Walled Garden, c.1600) – plus the Big Wood, a putting green and 9-hole golf course.

Fort George★

20mi/32km NE on the A 96 and B 9006. Open Apr–Sept daily 9.30am–5.30pm; Oct–Mar daily 10am–4pm. £9. ♿🅿✕ 𝒫01667 460 232. www.historicenvironment.scot.

Set on a peninsula jutting out into the Moray Firth, this is the most impressive artillery fortress in Britain, and was built between 1745 and 1746 on the orders of George II, to prevent his law and order from being disrupted by the Highland clans. Highlights include the historic barrack room, the grand magazine, the garrison chapel and the **Queen's Own Highlanders Regimental Museum** (closed weekends).

Cromarty★

26mi/42km NE via the A 9 and A 832. On the northern tip of the Black Isle, at the mouth of the Cromarty Firth, guarded by the Sutors Stacks, the tiny port of Cromarty has been aptly described as "the jewel in the crown of Scottish vernacular architecture". Learn more at the elegant 18C **Cromarty Courthouse Museum** (Church Street; open Easter–mid-Oct daily noon–4pm; 𝒫01381 600 418; www.cromarty-courthouse.org.uk).

Dornoch★

55mi/88km north east on the A 9. A scenic route cuts across the Black Isle, passes along the north bank of the Cromarty Firth, near the pretty little town of **Tain**, formerly an important pilgrimage centre, and crosses the Dornoch Firth to reach this charming burgh which boasts miles of sandy beaches and famous golf courses. The medieval cathedral dominates the town.

Culloden

6mi/10km east on the A 9 and B 9006. Visitor centre open daily: Feb–Mar and Nov–23 Dec 10am–4pm; Apr–May and Sept–Oct 9am–5.30pm; Jun–Jul daily 9am–6pm; Aug 9am–7pm. £11. Closed 24 Dec–31 Jan. Battlefield open daily all year. ♿🅿✕ 𝒫01463 796 090. www.nts.org.uk/Culloden.

Here, on 16 April 1746, the Jacobite army of Bonnie Prince Charlie was slaughtered by government troops under the command of George II's younger son 'Butcher Cumberland', finally ending the hopes of a Stuart restoration to the British throne.

An excellent **visitor centre** complete with a 360-degree film in the Battle immersion theatre relives the horror and helps interpret the battle.

🚗 DRIVING TOURS

1 GREAT GLEN★★

65mi/105km south west on the A 82.

The geological fault of the Great Glen cuts across the Highlands, linking the Atlantic Ocean with the North Sea through a series of narrow lochs joined together by part (22mi/35km) of Thomas Telford's **Caledonian Canal** (1803–22). The lochs and canals are now used principally for pleasure craft (operators offer 'Monster Hunting' trips on Loch Ness). At the southern end of the glen, **Fort William★** marks the northern tip of Loch Linnhe, sitting in the shadow of Britain's highest mountain, **Ben Nevis** (1 344m). The town makes an ideal touring centre.

Heading north from here on the A 82 you come to Torlundy, where cable cars (see website for times; 🅿♿✕; 𝒫01397 705 825. www.nevis-range.co.uk) **rise to** the **Nevis Range** ski resort with great **views★★** en route. From here the A 82 will take you past Loch Lochy and Loch Oich until you arrive at Loch Ness.

Loch Ness★★

The dark waters of this loch (230m deep) are renowned the world over as the home of the elusive 'monster', known as **Nessie**. First spied in the 8C by a local monk, Nessie has continued to captivate and mystify and, despite modern technology, remains an enigma.

From Fort Augustus and its canal lock, travel north on the west side of the loch on the A82 to see the much-photographed ruins of Urquhart Castle★ (open daily Apr–Sept 9.30am–6pm, Oct 9.30am–5pm, Nov–Mar 9.30am–4.30pm; £9; 🅿; ✆01456 450 551; www.historic-environment.scot), strategically set on a promontory jutting into the loch. This former stronghold was one of a chain of defences controlling this natural route. An exhibition and audio-visual display in the new visitor centre traces its history, including an outstanding array of medieval artefacts found at the castle. Next stop on the A 82 is the pretty little village of **Drumnadrochit**. Here you can satisfy your curiosity on all things Nessie at the **Loch Ness Exhibition Centre★** 👥 (open daily; Apr–Oct 9.30am–5pm/Jun–Aug 6pm, Nov–Mar 10am–3.30pm; £7.95, child (6–15) £4.95; ♿🅿✗; ✆01456 450 573; www.lochness.com).

② WESTER ROSS★★★

The main touring centres are Kyle of Lochalsh, Gairloch and Ullapool, respectively, 78ml/125km, 69mi/111km and 57mi/92km west of Inverness.

The Atlantic seaboard of Wester Ross is wild and dramatic, with magnificent mountains and placid lochs.

Eilean Donan Castle★

9mi/15km east of Kyle of Lochalsh by the A 87. Open Feb–Mar daily 10am–4pm; Apr–Oct 10am–6pm; Nov–Dec 10am–4pm. Closed 24–26 Dec, and at other times for private functions. £7.50. 🅿✗ ✆01599 555 202. www.eileandonancastle.com.

This much-photographed castle enjoys an idyllic **setting★★** on an island in the loch and is now linked to the shore by a bridge.

After two centuries of disuse, following a Jacobite raid in 1719, it was completely reconstructed 1911–31 according to its earlier layout. The ramparts afford **views** of three lochs.

Nessie

The initial sighting of a large snake-like, hump-backed monster with a long thin neck in Loch Ness was made in the 8C by a monk. Despite various expeditions, some highly equipped with submarines, helicopters and sonar electronic cameras, the loch has failed to reveal its secret. The tradition of the Loch Ness Monster however is not so surprising in a country where the kelpie or water-horse has been common in tales and legends over hundreds of years.

Kyle of Lochalsh to Gairloch★★★

120mi/193km Allow a whole day.
The route covers some of the finest scenery in Wester Ross – Loch Maree studded with islands, the Torridon area and the Applecross peninsula. Some of the roads will be busy in high season, but many stretches will allow the luxury of enjoying the scenery in solitude.

▷ Leave Kyle by the minor road along the coast to the north.

Plockton★

Once a refugee settlement at the time of the Highland Clearances, Plockton, with its palm-lined main street and sheltered bay, is a sailing centre.

▷ At Achmore, take the A 890 to the left, and at the junction with the A 896, go left again, towards Lochcarron. At Tornapress, you can elect to continue on the A 896 to Shieldaig, but the minor road across the peninsula, via Bealach-na Bo, well repays the effort. It has hairpin bends and 1:4 gradients, and is not recommended for caravans or inexperienced or nervous drivers.

Bealach-na-Bà

On the way up to the pass (626m) the hanging valley frames spectacular vistas of lochs and mountains, while from

Loch Maree with a view to Slioch

© David Woods/iStockphoto.com

the summit car park, the **views★★★** westward, of Skye and its fringing islands, are superb.

◐ Either continue north along the coast, via Applecross and Fearnmore, to Torridon (arduous), or the return to Tornapress, for Torridon by the A 896.

Torridon Countryside Centre

♿Open Apr–Sept, Sun–Fri 10am–5pm: Estate, Deer Enclosure and Deer Museum, all year, daily. 🅿 ✆01445 791221. www.nts.org.uk.
The centre interprets the area's spectacular geology and nature and includes a deer enclosure and deer museum. Information is available on walking and climbing.

◐ At Kinlochewe, take the A 832 to the left.

Loch Maree★★★

Loch Maree epitomises the scenic beauty and grandeur of the west coast. It lies between Beinn Eighe and the towering **Ben Slioch** (980m) to the north. To the north is the **Letterewe Estate**, one of Scotland's great deer forests.

Victoria Falls★

A platform and the riverside path give good views of these falls, named after Queen Victoria's visit in 1877.

Gairloch

The ideal centre for touring the Torridon area, exploring the hills and enjoying the sandy beaches of this part of the west coast, and admiring the splendid views of the Hebridean Islands. The pier at the head of the loch still has all the bustle of a fishing port.

Gairloch to Ullapool★★

56mi/90km. Allow 4hrs.
This route runs along the coastline with its bays, beaches and headlands and a backdrop of breathtaking mountains.

◐ Take the A 832 across the Rubha Reidh peninsula.

Stop before descending to the River Ewe and look back from the roadside **viewpoint★★★** at the superb view of Loch Maree with its forested islands.

Inverewe Garden★★★

Garden and visitor centre open daily: Apr 10.30am–5pm; May–Aug 9.30am–5.30pm; Sept 10am–5pm; Oct 10.30am–4pm: Garden only daily Jan–mid-Dec 10.30am–4pm. £10.50. ♿🅿(£2). ✗ ✆01445 712 952. www.nts.org.uk.
These outstanding 20ha gardens enjoy a magnificent coastal setting on the same latitude as Leningrad. Their profusion so far north is made possible by the influence of the Gulf Stream. Colour is found at most seasons, from azaleas and rhododendrons in May to heathers and maples in the autumn.

◐ Continue on A 832; until you can turn left onto the A 835 towards Ullapool.

Falls of Measach★★

The waters of the River Droma make a spectacular sight as they drop over 45m in the wooded cleft of the **Corrieshalloch Gorge★**. The road follows the north shore of **Loch Broom★★** in a particularly attractive setting.

◔ Continue northwest on the A 835.

Ullapool★

The village was laid out in the 18C and flourished during the herring boom. Fishing still plays an important part in the local economy. Ullapool is an ideal touring centre; the car ferry terminal for Stornoway, a haven for yachtsmen and an unrivalled centre for sea angling. Various boats sail to the **Summer Isles** to watch seals and sea birds.

▣ ISLE OF SKYE▲▲

Skye is joined to the mainland by the Skye Bridge at Kyle of Lochalsh and has two mainland ferry connections: from Mallaig to Armadale (www.calmac.co.uk), and Glenelg to Kylerhea (www.skyeferry.co.uk).

In Norse and Gaelic tales, Skye is known as the 'Winged Isle'. Mystery and enchantment still lie heavily here. Skye is the largest of the Inner Hebrides group, just off the northwest mainland. Crofting, tourism and forestry are the principal occupations of the 10 000 or so islanders. Gaelic is still spoken on the island.

The Cuillin★★★

The scenic splendour of the Cuillin – not Cuillins, or Coolins, nor Cuillin Hills – makes these peaks the isle's most famous feature. The **Black Cuillin** form a 6mi/10km arc of sharp peaks, encircle Loch Coruisk; many of these peaks are over 3 000ft (914m) in height, with Sgurr Alasdair (993m) the highest. On the other side of Glen Sligachan the softly rounded forms of the pink granite **Red Cuillin** contrast with their neighbours.

Portree★

Skye's pleasant little capital, arranged around a sheltered bay, is the main tourist centre on the island.

Kilmuir

The town stands on the north coast of the Trotternish peninsula▲▲, the most northerly of Skye's peninsulas, with lovely seascapes and a basalt rock pinnacle.
The small churchyard has a monument to **Flora MacDonald** (1722–90), known for her part in the escape of Bonnie prince Charlie after the collapse of the Jacobite cause at Culloden.

Skye Museum of Island Life★

Open Easter–Oct Mon–Sat 9.30am–5pm. £2.50. ♿▣ ✆01470 552 206. www.skyemuseum.co.uk.
The Skye Museum is a collection of thatched cottages – a crofter's house, a weaver's house, a smithy and a *ceilidh*

Water pool in rocks, Black Cuillin

house – depicting, as closely as possible, the conditions of a small township at the close of the 19C.

Dunvegan Castle

Open Apr–mid-Oct daily 10am–5.30pm. £13. &🅿✕ 🕾01470 521 206. www.dunvegancastle.com.

This Hebridean fortress, seat of the MacLeods, is set on a rocky platform overlooking Loch Dunvegan, and until 1748 the only entrance was by a sea gate. Most notable of the treasures kept here is the fragment of silk, known as the **Fairy Flag**. Legend has it that the flag, given to the 4th Chief by his fairy wife, has the power to ward off disaster to the clan, and has twice been invoked.

4 NORTHERN SCOTLAND
John o' Groats

19mi/31km north on the A 9.

Traditionally this is the northeastern-most point in mainland Britain, some 876mi/1 410km from the southeastern-most point, Land's End. The settlement takes its name from a Dutchman, Jan de Groot, who started a ferry service to the Orkneys in the 16C.

Duncansby Head★

2mi/3.2km east of John o' Groats.

The northeastern headland of mainland Scotland, Duncansby Head, overlooks the treacherous waters of the Pentland Firth. The **scenery** is spectacular. Standing just offshore, the **Stacks of Duncansby★★**, pointed sea stacks, rise 64m up from the water.

5 WESTERN ISLES

The chain of islands known as the Western Isles extends around 130mi/210km north–south.
Traditional activities include peat working and the weaving of Harris tweed. Buffeted by Atlantic waves, the islands are treeless and windswept, but rejoice in glistening *lochans* (small lochs), sandy beaches, and crystal-clear waters.
Mods (special events and festivals of Gaelic art and music), *ceilidhs* (gatherings often with music and dancing), concerts, Highland Games and agricultural shows are staged year-round. And, of course, Gaelic is still widely spoken.

Isle of Lewis
Stornoway

Stornoway, the capital and only sizeable town, is the base for excursions inland where hotels (and petrol) are scarce. The land-locked harbour is overlooked by a 19C castle. Eye peninsula to the north has some fine sandy beaches.

Callanish (Calanais) Standing Stones★★

6mi/26km west of Stornoway, signposted off A 858. The stones are free to visit all year round. Visitor Centre: call for opening times. &🅿✕ 🕾01851 621 422.
www.callanishvisitorcentre.co.uk.
www.historicenvironment.scot.
Over 4 000 years old and contemporary with Stonehenge, the stones, of Lewisian gneiss, form a circle, while approach avenues form the points of the compass. It is assumed that they were used for astronomical observations.
At the community run **Calanais Visitor Centre** you can learn more in the Story of the Stones exhibition.

Carloway Broch (Dun Carloway)★

5mi/8km beyond Callanish Standing Stones, signposted off A 858.
This is an incomplete example of a broch (small fortified farm c.500 BCE), though enough remains of the galleried walls and entrance chamber for the builders' skill to be admired.

Arnol Black House

6mi/10km beyond Carloway, signposted off the A 858. &Open Apr–Sept daily 9.30am–5.30pm; Oct–Mar daily except Wed and Sun 10am–4pm. £5. 🕾01851 710 395. www.historicenvironment.scot.
This typical basic dwelling has been preserved as a reminder of ancient island life as it was until half a century ago. This traditional, fully furnished thatched house was once shelter for a family and its animals...under the one roof.

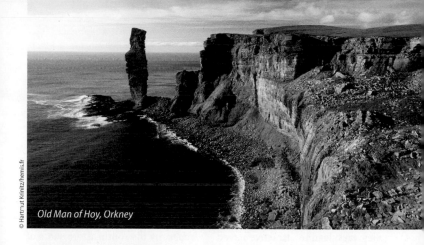

© Hartmut Krinitz/hemis.fr

Old Man of Hoy, Orkney

Orkney and Shetland★★

The archipelago of Orkney is is located off the northeast tip of Scotland – the nearest island is just 6mi/10km offshore – where the North Sea and the Atlantic Ocean meet. The largest island, known as 'Mainland', is home to most of the population. The islands are mainly low lying, with a gently rolling landscape of green fields, heather moorland heaths and lochs. Battered by sea and wind, the Shetland coastline is wildly indented with a savage beauty; in places rugged and rocky, elsewhere sandy and smooth. Here on the very edge of the British Isles you will find remains of the earliest human settlements and a Viking heritage that is still alive today. The islands are closer to the Arctic Circle than to Manchester, closer to Bergen in Norway than to Edinburgh, and many aspects of the local culture feel more Scandinavian than Scottish.

ORKNEY★★

The main island of Orkney is divided into the Eastern Mainland and the Western Mainland. Several British airports service Orkney and mainland ferries run here from Aberdeen and Scrabster (www.northlinkferries.co.uk),

- **Michelin Map:** Michelin Atlas p74-75 or Map 501.
- **Info: Orkney:** West Castle Street, Kirkwall. ℘01856 230 300. www.visitorkney.com. **Shetland:** Market Cross, Lerwick ℘01595 693434 www.shetland.org.
- **Don't Miss: Orkney:** St Magnus cathedral, Kirkwall; Skara Brae: **Shetland:** Sumburgh Head, Jarlshof.

Gills Bay (www.pentlandferries.co.uk) and John o' Groats (www.jogferry.co.uk). Orkney Ferries (℘01856 872 044, www.orkneyferries.co.uk) and Loganair (℘01856 873 457, www.loganair.co.uk) service the other islands.

Lying off the northeast tip of mainland Scotland, the Orkney archipelago comprises 67 islands of which fewer than 30 are inhabited. The cliffs are home to countless seabirds, and seals and otters are common. The first Neolithic settlers came in the 4th millennium BCE. Some of their dwellings remain and their fine stone tombs can be seen throughout the islands. From the early Iron Age – around the 5C BCE – fortified villages grew up round the massive stone buildings known as brochs. The Vikings came to Orkney from the late-8C, sweeping away the culture of the

Pictish Orcadians. Orkney's culture still has Scandinavian elements, though the islands were pawned to King James III of Scotland in 1468, as part of the dowry of his Danish bride.

Kirkwall★★

A capital since Viking days, Kirkwall stands on the isthmus separating the eastern and western parts of the island. Handsome townhouses (now shops), some emblazoned, line the stone-flagged main street and pends (alleyways) lead to attractive paved courtyards.

St Magnus cathedral★★ dominates the skyline of Kirkwall (open Apr–Sept daily 9am–5pm; Oct–Mar Mon–Fri 9am–5pm; &🅿; ✆01856 874 894, www.stmagnus.org). Built by Earl Rognvald, 1137–1152, and dedicated to his murdered uncle, Earl Magnus, the cathedral is an outstanding example of Norman architecture. The red stone exterior is severe and plain. The three west front **doorways** added later show confident originality in their combination of red and yellow sandstone.

Inside carefully controlled proportions create a sense of vastness belying the building's modest dimensions. The square pillars on either side of the organ screen enshrine the relics of St Magnus *(right)* and Earl Rognvald *(left)*.

Opposite on Broad Street in the fine 16C townhouse of Tankerness House is **The Orkney Museum★** (open May–Sept Mon–Sat 10.30am–5pm; Oct–Apr Mon–Sat 10.30am–12.30pm, 1.30pm–5pm; ✆01856 873 191; www.orkney.gov.uk), with excellent displays on the islands' prehistory.

Walk south from here on Broad Street and go left on Palace Road for **Earl's Palace★** (&open Apr–Sept daily 9.30am–5.30pm; £5; ✆01856 721 205; www.historic-scotland.gov.uk). The remains of this early Renaissance palace have splendid corbelling on the windows, chimney breast and corbel course, and sculptured panels above the main entrance and oriel windows. It was built c.1600–07 by **Earl Patrick Stewart**. The vaulted chambers on the ground floor

hold exhibitions of Orkney history from the early Middle Ages to the present, while the grand staircase leads to the Great Hall and apartments.

🚗DRIVING TOUR

Western Mainland★★

Leave Kirkwall west by the A 965 for the **Rennibister Earth House** *(behind the farmhouse, access by trapdoor and ladder)*, by the southeastern shore of Bay o' Firth. The oval chamber has five wall recesses and an entrance passage. Human bones were found in it, though its purpose remains uncertain.

Further west, approximately 500m from the southeastern shore of the Harray loch is **Maeshowe★★** (admission by guided tour only; access via a shuttle bus service from Skara Brae. There are 3 tours operating per day at 10am, 12pm and 2pm; £6; 🅿✕; ✆01856 761 606; www.historic-scotland.gov.uk). This Neolithic burial cairn, or chamber, dates from pre-2700 BCE and was covered by a mound (8m high and 35m wide). The cairn was broken into in the 12C by Norsemen, who left runic marks.

Maeshowe is part of the Heart of Neolithic Orkney World Heritage Site. West of Maeshowe, the **Stones of Stenness** sit at the base of a neck of land separating the lochs of Stenness and Harray. The **Ring of Brodgar** Stone Age circle stands on this neck. It still has 27 of its original 60 stones standing. Two entrance causeways interrupt the encircling ditch. West of the Stones of Stenness is a promontory jutting into the loch is **Unstan Cairn**, a Stone Age chambered tomb from the mid-4th millennium.

Further west on the A 965 is **Stromness★**, the second-largest town and principal port. Stromness grew from its original Norse settlement to become a whaling station in the 18C and the last port of call for the Hudson Bay Company ships sailing to Canada. The **Pier Arts Centre** (Victoria Street; & Open Tue–Sat 10.30am–

5pm/mid-Jun-mid-Sept Mon-Sat; 𝒞01856 850 209; www.pierartscentre. com) has a permanent collection of abstract art based on the work of the St Ives artists, Ben Nicholson and Barbara Hepworth. Aspects of Orkney's natural and maritime history are presented in the **Stromness Museum** (52 Alfred Street; &open Apr-Sept daily 10am-5pm; Oct-Mar Mon-Sat, 11am-3.30pm; £5; 🅿; 𝒞01856 850 025; http://stromness-museum.business.site).

North of Stromness on the A967 is **Skara Brae★★** (&open Apr-Sept daily 9.30am-5.30pm; Oct-Mar 10am-4pm; £7.10, winter £6.10; 🅿✕; 𝒞01856 841 815; www.historicenvironment.scot) on the southern shore of the Bay o' Skaill. This 5 000-year old settlement was buried in sand for a long period. The seven best preserved Stone Age dwellings are rectangular with coursed flagstone walls and a hearth in the middle, and are connected by a subterranean sewer system. A visitor centre interprets the site. Further north, separated from the mainland by the waters of Brough Sound is the **Brough of Birsay★** (access on foot across causeway at low tide; open mid-Jun-Sept daily 9.30am-5.30pm, when tides permit; £5; 𝒞01856 841 815; www.historicenvironment.scot). The earliest remains are Pictish. In the 10C, Norse farmers occupied the island and Earl Thorfinn the Mighty (c.1009-65) built a church after a pilgrimage to Rome. It became a cathedral and was the initial resting place of St Magnus before the construction of Kirkwall cathedral. Excavations show a small oblong nave, short narrow choir and rounded apse, surrounded by a Norse graveyard. A little to the southwest is a collection of stone-and-turf **Norse long houses**.

▶ Return to Kirkwall

About 10mi/16km south by the A 961, past St Mary's, is **Scapa Flow**. From the **Churchill Barriers**, built in the Second World War by Italian prisoners of war to link the four islands with the mainland, there is a good view of the naval base where the German Grand Fleet

scuttled itself in 1919. Beyond the first barrier is the **Italian Chapel★** (open Apr and Oct Mon-Sat 10am-4, Sun 10am-3pm; Jun-Aug daily 9am-6.30pm; May and Sept daily 9am-5pm; Nov-Mar daily 10am-1pm; £3; 𝒞01856 872 856; www.orkneycommunities.co.uk/italianchapel) a unique and moving testament to faith in adversity, built by the same prisoners inside two Nissen (prefabricated corrugated iron) huts.

Pentland Firth Crossing

The crossing (a frequently choppy 90min car ferry journey operating between Stromness and Scrabster) is an ideal way of seeing the outstanding cliff scenery of Hoy. The name means high island and its highlights are the sheer cliffs of St John's Head (347m) and the famous **Old Man of Hoy★★★**, a breathtaking red sandstone sea stack (137m) rising sheer out of the turbulent waters. It is the domain of myriad screeching and hovering seabirds.

SHETLAND ★★

Daily sailings from Aberdeen to Lerwick and regular flights from Aberdeen, Edinburgh, Glasgow, Inverness and London to Sumburgh. The capital, Lerwick, is on the east coast of Mainland, which is 50mi/81km long north to south, and 20mi/32km across at its widest.

There are 100 or so Shetland islands but fewer than 20 are inhabited. Shetland is hilly and has many inlets (voes), the most famous of which, **Sullom Voe**, is home to Europe's largest oil and gas terminal. Nonetheless, the oil industry still takes second place to fishing in importance, while the area directly affected by oil and gas exploration is bordered by beautiful, wild spaces. The islands also hold important evidence of early human settlement.

Lerwick★★

The Shetlands' capital sits in a natural harbour sheltered by the Island of Bressay. Local attractions include the ruined **Clickhimin Broch★** and the **Shetland Museum and Archives** (Hay's Dock; &open Mon-Sat 10am-4pm, Sun

Up Helly Aa★★★

This colourful and rousing fire festival is the most spectacular reminder of the Viking heritage. Explanations for the pageant held on the last Tuesday in January are various, from spring rites to placating the Norse gods, or up-ending of the holy days. The principal figure, the **Guizer Jarl** (earl) and his warriors, all clad in the finery of Viking war dress, head the great torchlit procession in their Viking longship. A thundering rendering of the *Galley Song* precedes the burning of the galley and the final song, *The Norseman's Home*. Celebrations continue throughout the night.

© Adam Woolfitt / age fotostock

---

noon–5pm; ✕; ℘01595 695 057; www. shetlandmuseumandarchives.org.uk). This modern waterfront centre is the perfect starting point to learn about Shetlands heritage and culture. As well as museum displays there is a lively programme of events, including storytelling, a popular islands' tradition.

Jarlshof★★

25mi/40km south of Lerwick on the A 970. Open daily Apr–Sept 9.30am–5.30pm; Oct–Mar restricted hours, call for details. Tickets from Sumburgh Hotel in winter. £5.50. **P** ℘01856 841 815. www.historicenvironment.scot. The site of Jarlshof has been occupied from the middle of the 2nd millennium BCE until the 17C. There are six Bronze Age houses, and a late Iron Age broch with other dwellings clustered around it. Numerous Viking longhouses tell of several centuries of occupation. There was a farmstead here in the 13C; the New Hall was built in the 16C.

Mousa Broch★★★

Mousa Island. Motor boat (15min) from Sandsayre Pier. Sailings Apr–mid/late Sept. Mousa Boat trips: www.mousa. co.uk. ℘07901 872 339. www.historicenvironment.scot. Small fortified farms, brochs, were peculiar to Scotland, the culmination of a tradition stretching back to 500 BCE. Most have crumbled, but Mousa, probably dating from the 1st or 2nd century AD, still stands to a height of over 13.3m and is the finest surviving Iron Age broch tower. A staircase, chambers and galleries were built into the thickness of the walls of this imposing kiln-shaped **tower**, which is more than 12ft across at its base. In the courtyard are a hearth and lean-to structures.

ADDRESSES

For a more extensive choice of accommodation and restaurants, consult the Michelin Green Guide to Scotland.

🛏 STAY

BORDERS

⊜⊜⊜ **Fauhope Country House** – Gattonside, Melrose. ℘01896 823 184. www.fauhopehouse.com. 3 rooms. Melrose Abbey is just visible from this stylish and charming 19C Arts-and-Crafts–type house with antiques and fine furniture. Massage room.

⊜⊜⊜ **Edenwater House** – Off Stichill Road, Ednam. ℘01573 224 070. www. edenwaterhouse.co.uk. 4 rooms and 1 self-catering apartment. This charming house enjoys an idyllic rural location next to a 17C kirk, 2mi/3km north of Kelso. Bedrooms and lounges boast antique furniture. Modern Scottish cuisine is served in an elegant **dining room** (🍽🍽🍽).

🛏🍽🍽🍽 **Cringletie House** – Edinburgh Road, Peebles. ☎01721 725750. www.cringletie.com. 12 rooms and 1 self-catering cottage in the grounds. This former baronial castle, just north of Peebles, is a perfect base for exploration and to visit Edinburgh. Superb grounds in which to walk; excellent afternoon tea, and a touch of fine dining in the restaurant (🍽🍽🍽). Walled garden, reputed to be the oldest in Scotland.

DUMFRIES & GALLOWAY

🛏🍽 **Baytree House** – 110 High Street, Kirkcudbright. ☎01557 330 824. www.baytreekirkcudbright.co.uk. 5 rooms. This elegant Georgian house, surrounded by a beautiful garden, is five minutes from the centre of town in the historic harbour conservation area.

🛏🍽🍽 **Rivendell** – 105 Edinburgh Road, Dumfries. ☎01387 252 251. www.rivendellbnb.co.uk. 10 rooms. Attractive Charles Rennie Mackintosh-style villa with parquet floors, distinctive woodwork and brass fittings. The comfortable bedrooms have views over a large garden.

EDINBURGH

🛏🍽🍽🍽 **Principal** – 19–21 George Street. ☎0131 225 1251. www.principal-hayley.com. Beautifully appointed Classic New Town hotel with Robert Adams 18C design. Its **Printing Press Bar & Kitchen** (🍽🍽–🍽🍽🍽) sits beneath a magnificent glass dome and ornate ceiling.

🛏🍽🍽🍽 **The Glasshouse** – 2 Greenside Place. ☎0131 525 8200. www.theglasshousehotel.co.uk. 77 rooms. This unusual trendy boutique hotel mixes ultra-modern styling (glass themes with great views onto park and city) and all the latest gadgets behind a 19C church façade.

🛏🍽🍽🍽 **Prestonfield** – Priestfield Road. ☎0131 225 7800. www.prestonfield.com. 23 rooms. This superbly restored 17C country house on the edge of Holyrood Park offers luxurious rooms and a gourmet restaurant, **Rhubarb** (🍽🍽🍽🍽☎0131 225 1333).

🛏🍽🍽🍽 **The Scotsman** – 20 North Bridge Street. ☎0131 556 5565. https://scotsmanhotel.co.uk. The grand marble offices of Edinburgh's principal newspaper now host this stunning modern hotel.

GLASGOW

🛏🍽🍽 **Apex City of Glasgow Hotel** – 110 Bath Street. ☎0141 375 3333. www.apexhotels.co.uk. The attractive rooms in this trendy 103-bedroom hotel (with a stunning penthouse) can be excellent value.

🛏🍽🍽 **Hilton Garden Inn** – Finnieston Quay. ☎0141 240 1002. http://hiltongardeninn3.hilton.com. Wide range of prices and good-value deals available in this super-smart functional contemporary-styled hotel with excellent café-bar-restaurant.

🛏🍽🍽🍽 **Sherbrooke Castle Hotel** – 11 Sherbrooke Avenue, Pollokshields. ☎0141 427 4227. www.sherbrookecastlehotel.com. A splendid celebration of late 19C Baronial style with romantic and rich furnishings, country house refinement and panelled dining room, 5-min from the city centre.

🛏🍽🍽🍽 **Malmaison** – 278 West George Street. ☎0141 378 0384. www.malmaison.com. Striking former Masonic chapel with ultra-stylish rooms in bold patterns and colours. Superb **Brasserie** (🍽🍽🍽).

ANGUS AND DUNDEE

🛏🍽 **Shaftesbury Lodge** – 1 Hyndford Street, Dundee. ☎01382 669 216. www.shaftesburyhotel.co.uk. 6 rooms. In a quiet street with views over the Tay and park, set in a fine old Baronial-style Victorian house, the Shaftesbury offers spacious attractive trad-contemporary rooms.

STIRLING AND ARGYLL

🛏 **Number 10** – Gladstone Place, Stirling. ☎01786 472 681. www.cameron-10.co.uk. 3 rooms. Set in a pleasant suburb within walking distance of the old town, this 19C terrace house is deceptively spacious and offers modern-traditional bedrooms.

🛏🍽 **Lomond View** – Tarbet. ☎01301 702 477. www.lomondview.co.uk. 3 rooms. Spacious light airy bedrooms tastefully decorated in tartan, with pine furniture and panoramic loch views.

⊖⊜ **The Park Lodge Hotel** – 32 Park Terrace, Stirling. ✆01786 474 862. www.parklodge.net. 9 rooms. This charming Georgian house, with splendid castle views, was built in 1825. Its bedrooms (some with four-posters) have style and period furnishings. There is also a lovely walled garden. Good value. **Restaurant** (⊖⊜) recommended.

FIFE

⊖⊜⊜ **The Russell Hotel** – 26 The Scores, St Andrews. ✆01334 473 447. www.russellhotelstandrews.co.uk. 10 rooms. This charming small Victorian terraced seaside townhouse hotel has rooms with sea views and a cosy **restaurant** (⊖⊜) serving Modern Scottish cuisine.

PERTHSHIRE

⊖–⊖⊜ **Dunmurray Lodge** – 72 Bonnethill Road, Pitlochry. ✆0778 346 2625. www.dunmurray.co.uk. 4 rooms. This charming immaculately kept 19C cottage has a homely sitting room and cosy cream-shaded bedrooms.

⊖⊜ **Taythorpe** – Isla Road, Perth. ✆01738 447 994. www.taythorpe.co.uk. 3 rooms. An immaculately kept modern guesthouse, a short walk from the city centre and close to Scone Palace, with cosy bedrooms, an inviting lounge and communal breakfasts.

⊖⊜⊜⊜ **Parklands Hotel** – 2 St Leonard's Bank, Perth. ✆01738 622 451. www.theparklandshotel.com. 14 rooms. Near the station, this hotel has contemporary accommodation, with every mod con, a fine-dining **restaurant** (63@ **Parklands** ⊖⊜⊜), and an excellent **bistro**, **No 1 Bank** (⊖⊜).

GRAMPIANS

⊖⊜⊜ **Atholl Hotel** – 54 King's Gate. ✆01224 323 505. www.atholl-aberdeen.co.uk. 34 rooms. This Baronial-style hotel is set in the leafy West End, close to the city centre. Rooms are light and airy with Tartan décor. Its popular restaurant serves fresh local produce and the bar has a wide selection of malt whiskies. Restaurant ⊖⊜⊜.

⊖⊜–⊖⊜⊜ **Highland Hotel** – 91–95 Crown Street, Aberdeen. ✆01224 583 685. www.highlandhotel.net. 50 rooms. Charming and very comfortable family-run hotel a short walk from the city centre.

⊖⊜⊜⊜ **Pittodrie House** – Chapel of Garioch, Inverurie. ✆0344 879 9066. www.macdonaldhotels.co.uk/pittodrie. 27 rooms. Set within its own ancient 810ha estate extending as far as the eye can see, this luxury hotel offers a tranquil retreat with romantic Scots Baronial turrets, mysterious passageways and stone spiral staircases. **Mither Tap Restaurant** (⊖⊜⊜⊜).

⊖⊜⊜⊜ **Raemoir House Hotel** – Raemoir, 12mi/3km from Banchory. ✆01330 824 884. www.raemoir.com. 18 rooms in main house and 2 rooms plus 2 suites in annex. Built in 1750 and converted into a hotel in 1943, the house stands in a beautiful 4ha park. Antique furnishings adorn the traditionally decorated bedrooms. **Modern British restaurant** (⊖⊜⊜⊜).

HIGHLANDS AND WESTERN ISLES
Inverness

⊖⊜ **MacDonald Guest House** – 1 Ardross Terrace, Inverness. ✆01463 232 878. www.macdonaldhouse.net. 6 rooms. This family owned B&B enjoys a superb situation in a picturesque areas of Inverness, on the River Ness opposite the cathedral.

⊖⊜–⊖⊜⊜ **Glen Mhor Hotel** – Ness Bank, Inverness. ✆01463 234 308. www.theinvernesshotel.co.uk. 75 rooms. Beneath the castle, on the river, this very smart hotel comprises six Victorian townhouses and offers a range of trad-contemporary rooms, each with their own character and varying prices. It has a particularly good bar and excellent **Nicky Tam's Restaurant and Bar** (⊖⊜). No lift.

Isle of Skye

⊖⊜ **Blà Bheinn B&B** – Crossal, Carbost, Isle of Skye. ✆01478 640 269. www.blabheinn.scot. 2 rooms. Open Apr–Oct. Award-winning B&B not far from Sligachan, with fine views of the Red Cuillin and the northern edge of the Black Cuillin. Highly recommended. 2 nights minimum stay.

⊖⊜⊜ **Sligachan Hotel** – Sligachan, Isle of Skye. ✆01478 650 204. www.sligachan.co.uk. 21 rooms. Perfectly situated on the main road across Skye, and with a stunning view of the Red and Black

Cuillin and Glen Sligachan. Serving mountaineers, walkers and lovers of wild scenery since 1830, and very much a part of Skye history. Self-catering cottages also available, along with bunkhouse for budget travellers, while Seamus' Bar offers a bewildering display of whiskies and hearty menus...not to mention a lively atmosphere.

Isle of Mull

⊖⊜⧈ **Tobermory Hotel** – 53 Main Street, Tobermory, Isle of Mull. ☎01688 302 091. www.thetobermoryhotel.com. This amalgamation of 200-yer-old fishermen's cottages has an idiosyncratic ambiance, small rooms, most with harbour view, but not all have a shower and bath (check on reserving). This is a boutique-style, family-run hostelry in a hugely popular location. Integral bar and restaurant (⊖⊜ *reservations advised*) serving mainly seafood dishes.

Isle of Lewis

⊖⊜ **Calaidh Inn** – 11 James Street, Stornoway. ☎01851 702 740. www.caladhinn.co.uk. 68 rooms. Just 300m from the centre of town, and an economical base from which to explore the northern part of Lewis. Integral Eleven Restaurant and Bar with contemporary carvery and buffet restaurant.

⊖⊜⧈ **Caberfeidh Hotel** – Manor Park, Perceval Road South, Stornoway ☎01851 702 604. www.cabarfeidh-hotel.co.uk. 46 rooms. Less than a mile from the centre of Stornoway, with spacious rooms, gardens, fitness suite and adjacent golf course. Peaceful location. The **Solas Restaurant** (⊖⊜⧈) serves a fusion of traditional Scottish recipes, French classic cuisine and world specialities.

North Uist

⊖⊜⧈⧈ **Langass Lodge** – Locheport, Isle of North Uist . ☎01876 580 285. www.langasslodge.co.uk. 12 suites. A breathtaking place; set on the edge of Loch Eport, this former shooting lodge is today a comfy updated small hotel. The restaurant (⊖⊜⧈) has an enviable reputation in spite of its comparative remoteness with the emphasis on seafood and game. Reservations needed for the restaurant.

SHETLAND

⊖⊜⧈ **Busta House Hotel** – Busta. ☎01806 522 506. www.bustahouse.com. 22 rooms. Close to the geographical centre of Shetland and dating mostly from the 18C, this characterful friendly place is the best hotel on the archipelago. Try the fresh local food on offer (⊖⊜⧈), along with some of its 160 malt whiskies.

⊖⊜⧈ **Lerwick Hotel** – 15 South Rd, Lerwick. ☎01595 692 166. On the southern edge of Lerwick overlooking Berwick Bay. 10 minute drive from the ferry port, and a 10 minute walk into the town centre. Integral restaurant (⊖⊜) serves traditional Scottish dishes and seasonal seafood.

ORKNEY

⊖⊖ **The Sands** – Burray. ☎01856 731 298. www.thesandshotel.co.uk. 6 rooms. A former fishing store, totally modernised with stylish rooms (all with sea view), a popular bar and spacious dining room also with views of the bay.

⊖⊜⧈ **Orkney Hotel** – 40 Victoria Street, Kirkwall. ☎01856 873 477. http://www.orkneyhotel.co.uk. 30 rooms. Tucked away in a side street behind the cathedral, this 17C lodging is convenient if using Kirkwall as a base. A bit awkward to find.

ⵘ EAT

In addition to the establishments listed below we also recommend places to eat in the *STAY* section (🕭*see above*).

BORDERS

⊖⊖ **Oscar's** – 35–37 Horse Market, Kelso. ☎01573 224 008. www.oscars-kelso.com. Open from 6pm Closed Tue and Sun. This stylish wine bar and restaurant successfully combines Scottish and Mediterranean flavours.

⊖⊖ **The Hoebridge** – Gattonside, Melrose. ☎01896 823 082. www.the hoebridge. com. This charming rustic converted 19C bobbin mill serves top-class traditional Scottish fare with a modern twist.

⊖⊜⧈ **Osso** – Innerleithen Road, Peebles. ☎01721 724 477. www.ossorestaurant.com. Open 10am–4.30pm All Week; 6–9pm Tue–Sat. Very much a great find, and a place to discover exciting food, deep flavours, reasonable prices and happy customers.

Sensibly priced wine list. Cakes, coffee, lunch and dinner.

DUMFRIES AND GALLOWAY

⊖⊜⊜ **Bruno's Italian Restaurant** – 3 Balmoral Road, Dumfries. ✆01387 255 757. www.brunosrestaurant.co.uk. Open dinner only. Closed Tue. Bruno's is the town's original and authentic Italian restaurant, serving traditional freshly prepared dishes, run by the same family for over 40 years and still getting rave reviews.

EDINBURGH

⊖⊜⊜ **The Tower** – National Museum of Scotland, Chambers Street. ✆0131 225 3003. www.tower-restaurant.com. Expect top-class game, grills and seafood at this stylish contemporary restaurant on the top floor of the museum; stunning views from window tables and terrace.

⊖⊜⊜ **The Witchery by the Castle** – 325 Castlehill, The Royal Mile. ✆0131 225 5613. www.thewitchery.com. Next door to the castle, Edinburgh's most atmospheric and spectacular dining destination occupies a 16C merchant's house, re-created to appear as it was 500 years ago. Theatre suppers and lunch menus put it within most budgets.

⊖⊜⊜ **The Grain Store** – 30 Victoria Street. ✆0131 225 7635. www.grainstore-restaurant.co.uk. On Edinburgh's prettiest street, diners sit beneath the cosy rustic stone vaulting and archways of the original storerooms. Authentic Scottish cuisine using local produce is served.

⊖⊜⊜ **Le Café Saint-Honoré** – 34 North West Thistle Street Lane. ✆0131 226 2211. www.cafesthonore.com. A bustling atmospheric, typical and authentic French bistro, celebrating the Auld Alliance. Booking essential.

GLASGOW

⊖⊜ **Stravaigin** – 28 Gibson Street Kelvinbridge. ✆0141 334 2665. www.stravaigin.co.uk. 'Think Global Eat Local' is the message of this long-established trend-setting unfussy bistro; its contemporary menu offers an eclectic range of original affordable dishes.

⊖⊜⊜ **Urban** – 23–25 St Vincent Place. ✆0141 248 5636. www.urbanbrasserie.co.uk. This stunning Grand Café-brasserie is set in the former Bank of England's Scottish HQ, serving Modern British cuisine.

⊖⊜⊜ **La Parmigiana** – 447 Great Western Road, Kelvinbridge. ✆0141 334 0686. http://lalanternawestend.co.uk. Compact traditional establishment serving the best Italian food in Glasgow.

⊖⊜⊜⊜ **Gamba** – 225a West George Street. ✆0141 572 0899. www.gamba.co.uk. Long established but very stylish modern restaurant, possibly the best seafood restaurant in Glasgow.

ANGUS AND DUNDEE

⊖⊜⊜ **Metro Bar and Brasserie** – Apex City Quay Hotel, Dundee. ✆0800 049 8000. www.apexhotels.co.uk. This contemporary brasserie, right on the city quay, offers a International cuisine.

STIRLING AND ARGYLL

⊖⊜ **The River House** – Castle Business Park, Craigforth, Stirling. ✆01786 465 577. www.riverhouse-restaurant.co.uk. Based on the design of a traditional Scottish *crannog* (ancient loch-dwelling), this stunning traditional-modern restaurant is set on a loch at the foot of the castle and offers great value with its excellent Scottish-Mediterranean dishes.

⊖⊜ **Callander Meadows** – 24 Main Street. Callander. ✆01877 330 181. www.callandermeadows.co.uk. Closed Tue–Wed. This lovely early-19C townhouse restaurant with rooms (⊖⊜), also has charm and character serves high-quality bistro-style dishes with fresh, seasonal food, sourced locally.

⊖⊜ **Lade Inn** – Kilmahog, E of Callander. ✆01877 330 152. www.theladeinn.com. Bright lively attractive traditional modern brew pub cooking modern variations on pub classics.

⊖⊜⊜⊜ **Highland Cottage** – Raeric Road (by Back Brae), Tobermory. Closed late Oct–late-Mar. ✆01688 302 030. www.highlandcottage.co.uk. This modern small luxury hotel by the harbour features a pretty dining room with an excellent locally sourced menu. It also has 6 lovely individually styled **rooms** (⊖⊜⊜⊜).

FIFE

⊖⊜ **The Vine Leaf** – 131 South Street, St Andrews. Closed Sun–Mon. ✆01334 477 497. www.vineleafstandrews.co.uk. Owned and managed by the same husband-and-wife team since 1987, the Vine Leaf serves probably the best Scottish food in town and has a top wine list.

⊖⊖⊖⊜ **The Seafood Restaurant** –
Bruce Embankment, St Andrews. ☎01334
479 475. www.theseafoodrestaurant.com.
Floor-to-ceiling glass on all four sides
of this spectacular award-winning
restaurant ensures a sea view for all.
Excellent service and changing
seafood menus.

PERTHSHIRE

⊖⊖⊜ **Deans** – 77–79 Kinnoull St., Perth.
☎01738 643 377. www.letseatperth.co.uk.
Closed Sun–Mon. Vibrant award-winning
Modern Scottish cuisine with a firm
focus on flavour and seasonability in a
relaxed contemporary setting, a short
walk from the centre.

GRAMPIANS

⊖⊜ **La Lombarda** – 2–8 King Street,
Aberdeen. ☎01224 640 916. www.la
lombarda.co.uk. Claimed to be the oldest
Italian restaurant in the UK (est. 1922),
Lombarda serves classic Italian dishes,
pasta, pizzas, meat and seafood dishes,
mainly sourced from local suppliers, in a
friendly, traditional atmosphere.

HIGHLANDS AND WESTERN ISLES

Strathcarron

⊖⊖ **Applecross Walled Garden
Café and Restaurant** – Applecross,
Strathcarron. ☎01520 744 440. www.
applecrossgarden.co.uk. Open daily
10am–8.30pm late Mar–Oct. This
delightful, quirky place on the beautiful
Applecross Peninsula is one of the best
(and very best value) places to eat in the
Highlands. Fresh seafood is their forte
and nearly everything is homegrown.

Fort William

⊖⊖⊜ **Crannog** – The Underwater
Centre, An Aird, Fort William. ☎01397
705 589. www.crannog.net. This lakeside
seafood restaurant was converted from
a bait store by its former fisherman
owner and enjoys wonderful loch views.

Isle of Mull

⊖⊖⊜ **MishDish** – Mishnish Hotel , Main
Street, Tobermory, Isle of Mull. ☎01688
302 500. www.themishnish.co.uk. The
MishDish is the restaurant adjacent to
the bar in the Mishnish Hotel. There
are 12 rooms (⊖⊖⊜) in the hotel,
hearty food in the bar, the MishDish is a
seafood restaurant, while the first-floor
Amaretto restaurant serves Italian food.

Isle of Skye

⊖⊖⊜⊜ **Three Chimneys** – Colbost,
Dunvegan, Isle of Skye. ☎01470 511
258. www.threechimneys.co.uk. This
renowned restaurant is set in an
atmospheric crofter's cottage on the
shore of Loch Dunvegan. It serves
accomplished seafood dishes and
Highland-sourced meat. It also has
6 beautiful **rooms** (⊖⊖⊜⊜), with
spectacular sea views.

SHETLAND

⊖ **Toll Clock Shopping Centre** –
26 North Road, Lerwick. www.
tollclockshetland.co.uk. For something
tasty and quick try the two eateries
in this comprehensive and compact
shopping centre: the **Skipidock Inn**
(☎01595 696 865), licensed restaurant
and cafeteria, and the **Olive Tree Deli**
(☎01595 697 222) for sandwiches
soups and home-made cakes.

⊖⊜ **Hay's Dock Cafe Restaurant** –
Shetland Museum building, Hays Dock,
Lerwick. ☎01595 741 569. www.haysdock.
co.uk. Closed Sun. Bright, modern, colourful
café/restaurant within the museum
building, serving Shetland produce, well
cooked and presented. A great find, it
would be wise to make a reservation.

⊖⊜ **Frankie's Fish and Chips** – Brae,
Shetland. ☎01806 522 700. www.
frankiesfishandchips.com. You would be
well-advised to book at table before
setting out for Brae, and the UK's
most northerly fish and chip shop and
takeaway. The food is excellent, the
chippie very popular, and the scenery
well worth the drive.

ORKNEY

⊖⊜ **Skerries Bistro** – St Margaret's Hope.
Open daily Apr–Sept. ☎01856 831 605.
www.vineleafstandrews.co.uk. Skerries
Bistro is a bespoke glass building
located 80 metres from the cliff with
stunning views across the Pentland
Firth. A bit of a trek, but well worth it,
whether for lunch or dinner. Unique
dining pod serving Seafood Tasting
Menu is a great idea.

⊖⊖⊜ **The Foveran** – Kirkwall. ☎01856
872 389. This restaurant-with-rooms
(8 rooms) is headed by one of Orkney's
top chefs, making the msot of local
produce.

Wales

Caernarfon Castle
© Ivan Vdovin/age fotostock

Introduction

There are many traditional Welsh icons: male voice choirs, rugby, coal pits, slate mines, medieval castles, Snowdon (Yr Wyddfa) and, of course, sheep, which still outnumber people. In recent times, many new icons have added to and updated Wales' offering to the world: outstanding national museums in stunning new buildings that interpret past industries; the striking new Welsh Senned (parliament) building and redevelopment of Cardiff's docks; pioneering coastal adventure activities such as coasteering and RIBs (rigid inflatable boats) in Pembrokeshire; Cardiff's Millennium Stadium and Snowdon's 21C visitor centre. Add to this near-deserted roads, wild walks, charming seaside towns, some of Britain's most beautiful beaches, and it's easy to see why Wales is back on the tourist map.

South Wales

South Wales is where Welsh industry began and 'The Valleys' have entered not only into national lore, but have become symbolic of a way of life and Welshness far beyond. After many lean years, national pride has returned to the region with Cardiff in the vanguard of the Welsh renaissance.

Pembrokeshire

The lovely golden beaches of the Pembokeshire Peninsula are just about as far as you can get from the cities of north and central England, and with no motorways, it is perhaps no surprise that crowds are rare in this lovely part of the world. It boasts a wonderful variety of beaches, some delightful seaside towns, and a cliffline that is often spectacular.

Mid-Wales

In the 19C English travel writers coined the term, the 'Green Desert' to describe Mid-Wales, on account of its lack of infrastructure. It still is the most deserted part of the Principality, though there's enough life in the delightful little border towns and the main settlements which serve the hills of the Brecon Beacons, famous among walkers.

North Wales

Dominated by Snowdonia and its surrounding hills, pastoral North Wales is very much a place for walking and the Great Outdoors. For sightseeing however its castles are legendary and it has a rich, industrial heritage which can be explored at some of the finest visitor attractions in the Principality. One of Wales' best-kept secrets is the beautiful seaside holiday coastline stretching along the Lleyn peninsula.

Highlights

1　Brave the miners' underground tour at **Big Pit Museum** (p565)

2　Chill out on glorious **Gower Peninsula** beaches (p568)

3　Climb the walls of mighty **Caernarfon Castle** (p578)

4　Ascend **Snowdon** (p584) – by whichever means suit you best!

5　Explore the ultimate folly, **Portmeirion** (p585).

National Parks

Snowdonia – Around half a million people reach Snowdon's summit each year and only a quarter of them admit to using the railway! The Aran Mountains in the south and the rugged Rhynogydd are less crowded.

Pembrokeshire Coast – For much of its length this narrow park is less than three miles wide. Steep cliffs display spectacularly folded and twisted rock formations; sheltered bays invite bathing and scuba-diving. Offshore islands such as Skomer and Skokholm support huge colonies of seabirds.

Brecon Beacons – High red sandstone mountains divide the ancient rocks of mid-Wales from the coalfields and industrialisation farther south. Along the southern edge of the park, a limestone belt provides a dramatic change in scenery and there are hundreds of sink-holes and cave systems.

South Wales★★

The south is the heartland of Welsh industry with 'The Valleys', just north of Cardiff, traditionally providing coal to Britain and the world, and the iron and steel works of Port Talbot, adjacent to Swansea, powering British Imperialism and industrialisation from the 1830s until around 50 years ago.

Today, where there was once over 600 mines burrowing deep into the earth, a mere handful of small drift mines pick over the pieces.

The history and sacrifices of the miners is recalled at the evocative Big Pit (the industrial landscape around here has been designated as a World Heritage Site) and at the Rhondda Heritage Park.

By contrast, the port cities that grew rich on coal and metal, are enjoying something of a renaissance. Cardiff – 'Europe's newest capital' (since 1955) – boasts cultural attractions, shopping, entertainment, restaurants and nightlife, particularly around Cardiff Bay, commensurate with that status. Swansea too has revitalised its moribund docks; its Maritime Quarter is home to all kinds of new places to eat, drink and visit, including the splendid new National Waterfront Museum. Its revitalised promenade leads west to Swansea's seaside resort, The Mumbles, and out to the glorious landscapes of the Gower peninsula with its beautiful golden sands.

CARDIFF★

On the Severn estuary opposite Weston-super-Mare. High-speed InterCity trains (London 2h) link most cities with Cardiff. The train and bus station are on and just off Central Square.

Sights are spread out; use the City Sightseeing hop-on hop-off bus tour to get around (daily; ℰ07808 713 928; www.city-sightseeing.com).

○ **Michelin Map:** Michelin Atlas p16 or Map 503 K 29.

🖪 Wales Millennium Centre, Cardiff Bay. ℰ029 2087 7927. www.visitcardiff.com.

◈ **Don't Miss:** National Museum Cardiff; the exotic interiors at Castell Coch and/or Cardiff Castle; Big Pit; St Fagans; Caerphilly Castle; Swansea's Maritime Quarter and the Gower peninsula beaches.

🕓 **Timing:** Allow a couple of days for Cardiff and a day for Swansea.

🎟 **Kids:** The National Museum Cardiff; Techniquest; Dan yr Ogof showcaves; the Dr Who Experience; the beaches of the Gower peninsula.

☍ **Tours:** The route marked on the Cardiff map offers a pleasant stroll.

Cardiff, capital of Wales, arose around the Roman fort guarding the crossing of the Taff, on the road between Caerleon and Carmarthen. By the start of the 20C it was the world's principal coal port and much of its appearance today can be directly attributed to this era. At the end of the 20C a series of major projects – most notably the Welsh National Assembly Building, the redevelopment of the Cardiff Bay dockside, and the magnificent **Millennium Stadium** – have helped revitalise the city.

🎟 National Museum of Wales (Cardiff)★

Museum Avenue, Cathays Park. Open Tue–Sun 10am–5pm. ♿ 🅿 (£5), ✕ ℰ0300 111 2 333. https://museum.wales.

The magnificently headquarters of the National Museum and Gallery of Wales is situated in **Cathays Park**, the spacious early-20C civic centre, which is the outstanding example in Britain of Beaux-Arts planning and architecture. There are impeccably arranged displays of archaeology, glass, silver and porcelain; the picture galleries and the natural history collections are among the finest in the UK. Outstanding works in the **picture galleries★★**, include masterpieces by Manet, Renoir, Monet, Cézanne and Van Gogh; European painting and sculpture from the Renaissance onwards, with fine works by Italian masters; works by Claude and Poussin; and by modern greats such as Oskar Kokoschka and Max Ernst. However, the great strengths of the gallery lie in its collections of **British art** and in works by the **French Impressionists** and **post-impressionists**.

Other galleries include the archaeology section, **Origins: in search of early Wales**; **The Evolution of Wales, from the Big Bang to dinosaurs;** and the popular hands-on **Clore Discovery Centre**.

Cardiff Castle★

Kingsway. Open daily: Mar–Oct 9am–6pm; Nov–Feb 9am–5pm. Closed 1 Jan, 25–26 Dec. £12.50. child (5–16), £9; House Tour +£3.25. ✕ ℘029 2087 8100. www.cardiffcastle.com.

The first known fortifications at Cardiff Castle were built by the Romans during 1C. After Hastings (1066), William the Conqueror gave Robert Fitzhamon a free hand in the southern borderlands, and he built a timber motte-and-bailey castle here within the ruins. The 12-sided stone keep is 12C. It was the 3rd **Marquess of Bute** (1847–1900), reputedly the richest man in Britain at the time, who in 1868 commissioned the architect **William Burges** (1827–81); his romantic imagination was given free rein in an extraordinary series of exotic **interiors** – Arab, Gothic and Greek – to create the unique monument to the Victorian age we see today.

An **interpretation centre** explains the history of the castle with a film presentation. From its open-air roof terrace, there are fine views of the castle and city skyline. Also in the grounds are the **Welch Regiment Museum** and the **Queen's Dragoon Guards Museum**.

Cardiff Bay★

South of the castle, the decline of Cardiff's extensive docklands, once the outlet for much of the coal dug from the South Wales valleys, has been largely reversed by an ambitious programme of conservation and restoration and by the creation of major new cultural and recreational facilities. Today, it is Europe's largest waterfront development. The project's keystone is the barrage constructed across the estuary of the Taff to create a freshwater lake with an 8mi/13km waterfront.

Butetown, named after the first promoter of the docks (the 2nd Marquess of Bute) was the core of the harbour area; its buildings, slowly being rescued from dilapidation, include the huge Renaissance Revival pile of the **Coal Exchange**, completed in 1888, now used as a concert and entertainment venue. By way of total contrast is the contemporary white tube-like building, home to the **Cardiff Bay Visitor Centre**, where you will find the tourist office.

Pride of place bayside goes to the stunning construction of timber, steel, slate and glass that is the **National Assembly (Senedd)** building, opened in 2006. This is the Welsh Government's debating chamber and commitee rooms (open to the public to see debates – see website for details, booking ahead advisable as there are only 120 seats; ♿✕ ℘0300 200 6565; www.assembly.wales).

Next door is the historic strident red brick-and-terracotta **Pierhead Building** of 1896 (open Mon–Fri 9.30am–4.30pm, Sat–Sun and bank holidays 10.30am–4.30pm; ♿; ℘0300 200 6565; www.pierhead.org), which hosts lively exhibitions, interactive displays and special events highlighting issues of national concern to Wales, from the past, present and future.

👥 Doctor Who Experience★

Open: outside of school holidays the Doctor Who Experience is open 10am to 5pm but opening days can vary – check website for details. £14, child (5–16), £9.75. ♿✕ ℘0208 433 3162. www.doctorwhoexperience.com.

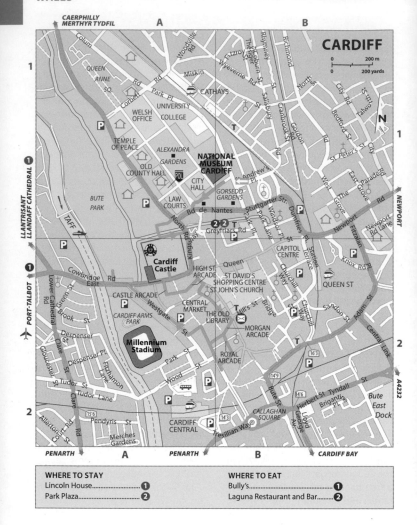

This interactive special-effects laden journey takes visitors alongside the Doctor on a 'spectacular adventure through time and space'. Of course it involves the TARDIS and the classic Dr Who villains (Daleks, Cybermen, Sontarans…) and exclusive filmed sequences with Matt Smith, the eleventh incarnation of the Doctor. Afterwards you can browse the world's most extensive collection of original Doctor Who props and artefacts, including every one of the Doctors' costumes from 1963 to the present day. There's the David Tennant TARDIS set and more of the Doctor's arch foes; if you like, you'll even be taught how to walk like a Cyberman!

👥 Techniquest★

Stuart Street. Open school term Tue–Fri 9.30am–4.30pm; School hols Mon–Fri 10am–5pm; Sat–Sun year-round and bank holidays 10am–5pm. Closed 24–26 Dec, 1 Jan. £7.20, child (4–15), £5.90. ♿✕ ✆029 2047 5475. www.techniquest.org. Overlooking the old dry docks, this ultra-modern structure in steel and glass houses a compelling array of over 150 hands-on exhibits plus a science theatre with shows and a planetarium.

Llandaff cathedral★

7mi/11km W Cardiff Castle by A 4119, across the River Taff. Open Mon–Sat 9am–6.30/7pm, Sun 7am–6.30pm. & ℘029 2056 4554.
www.llandaffcathedral.org.uk.

Tradition has it that St Teilo founded a community here in about 560, naming his church *(Llan)* after the Taff River nearby. The cathedral was built between 1120 and 1280 but fell into decay after the Reformation and it was not until the 18C that John Wood was chosen to restore the cathedral.

Almost the whole of his work was destroyed by a land-mine which fell to the south of the cathedral on 2 January 1941. The chancel is now divided from the nave by a concrete arch embellished with some of the 19C figures from the choir stalls and by a huge aluminium *Christ in Majesty* by Epstein. In the Memorial Chapel of the Welch Regiment is Rosetti's *The Seed of David*.

EXCURSIONS

South Wales valleys

Immediately to the north of Cardiff and the other ports of South Wales lie **The Valleys**, once one of Britain's greatest coalfields. The whole area is rich in the relics of an industrial age but the essence of 'The Valleys' is particularly concentrated in the Rhondda area.

Near Pontypridd, the **Rhondda Heritage Park★** ♣♟ (Lewis Merthyr Colliery; open Tue–Sat 9am–4.30pm; £5.95, child £4.75; & ☐ ✗; ℘01443 682 036; www.rhonddaheritagepark.com), developed around the old Lewis Merthyr mine, tells the fascinating and often poignant story of coal mining in these valleys and includes an 'underground' visit (part simulated). Retired miners act as genial guides – as they also do in the far east of the coalfield, at **Blaenafon** *(28mi/45km NE by the M 4, A 4042 and A 4043)*, a town that played a vital part in the Industrial Revolution and has been awarded UNESCO World Heritage Status.

The centre of activities today is **Big Pit National Coal Museum★** ♣♟ (Torfaen: open daily 9.30am–5pm; underground tours 10am 3.30pm; ☐(£3), ✗, ℘0300 111 2 333; https://museum.wales/bigpit). Mining may have ceased in 1980 but the former pitmen still descend deep underground (90m below the surface), accompanied (free of charge) by fascinated visitors. In the old pithead buildings are displays and galleries recalling the harsh realities and dangers of this ancient industry.

St Fagans National History Museum★★

◗ St Fagans. 4mi/6km W of Cardiff. Open daily 10am–5pm. Closed 24–26 Dec. & ☐(£5) ✗ ℘0300 111 2 333. https://museum.wales/stfagans.

One of the finest collections of vernacular buildings in Britain stands in the parkland of St Fagans castle, an Elizabethan mansion. There are over 40 re-erected buildings from all over Wales, including cottages, farmhouses, a chapel, bakehouse, school, corn mill, woollen mill, tannery, a village store and, more unusually, a toll house and a cockpit. A unique collection of coracles, a working farmstead and an award-winning terrace of miners' cottages add to the variety of the exhibits, while a number of traditional craftsmen demonstrate their skills in their craft workshops. Modern galleries present the traditional domestic, social and cultural life and there are displays on costume and agriculture.

St Fagans castle itself was built c. 1580 on the site of an earlier castle. It has been restored to its 19C appearance and furnishings. Its fine formal gardens include a mulberry grove and there are fishponds, stocked as in the 17C.

Caerphilly Castle★★

◗ 7mi/11km north of Cardiff via the A 470 and A 469. Open Mar–Jun and Sept–Oct daily 9.30am–5pm; Jul–Aug daily 9.30am–6pm; Nov–Feb Mon–Sat 10am–4pm, Sun 11am–4pm. £7.95. ℘029 2088 3143.
http://cadw.gov.wales.

This massive stronghold, the largest in Wales, sits behind its extensive water defences, reducing the busy town gath-

Caerphilly Castle

ered round the outer limits of its vast site to relative insignificance. Begun in 1268 by the powerful baron Gilbert de Clare, the castle was the first in Britain to be built from new on a regular concentric plan; the design of its walls, towers and gateways embodied many innovative features too and it served as a model for the castles of Edward I shortly to be built in North Wales.

The castle's decay was accelerated in the Civil War by deliberate destruction, of which the half-ruined 'leaning tower' in the southeast corner of the main ward is a poignant reminder. The present state of the impressive complex is largely due to the general restoration carried out in the 19C and 20C.

The approach to the castle is via the great gatehouse; this is set in the immensely long **East Barbican**, a fortified dam separating the outer moat from the inner moat and its flanking lakes to north and south. Behind these defences is the castle's core, an outer ward with semi-circular bastions and an inner ward with drum towers, mighty gatehouses and the **Great Hall**, the last rebuilt c.317. Protecting the western gatehouse, the original entrance, is an extensive western outwork and beyond this, the 17C redoubt on the site of a Roman fort.

The castle recently had a starring role in the popular BBC TV series *Merlin*.

Castell Coch★★

▶ 5mi/8km N on the A 470.
Open as Caerphilly Castle (◐see above).
£6.50. ℰ029 2081 0101.
http://cadw.gov.wales.

A pseudo-medieval stronghold, Castell Coch ('Red Castle') was created, like Cardiff Castle, by the wealth of the Marquess of Bute and the imagination of William Burges, who in 1875 started to build a fantasy 13C castle, with turrets inspired by Chillon and Carcassonne in France, complete with drawbridge, portcullis and 'murder holes'. French, Gothic and Moorish influences combine in the fantastic interior decorations.

CAERLEON★

12mi/19km north east on the M 4 to junction 25, then follow signs.

Caerleon ('City of the Legions' in Welsh), was home to between 5 000 and 6 000 men of the Legio II Augusta, from 75 until 300.

At the **Caerleon Amphitheatre, Roman Fortress & Baths★★** (open daily Apr–Oct 9.30am–5pm; Nov–Mar Mon–Sat 9.30am–5pm, Sun 11am–4pm; ℰ01633 422 518; http://cadw.gov.wales) you can see the remains of the enormous **Fortress Baths★**, now roofed over and filled with water.

On the High Street in the **National Roman Legion Museum★** (open daily 10am (2pm Sun)–5pm; closed 1 Jan,

24–26, 31 Dec; ♿; ℘0300 111 2 333; https://museum.wales/roman) are the remains of the fortress, which includes the most complete **amphitheatre★** in Britain and the only remains of a Roman Legionary barracks on view anywhere in Europe. The amphitheatre, just outside the fortress walls, was built about the year 90. The **barrack buildings** are in pairs, with verandas onto a central street, accommodating eight men to a room, with the centurion at the end of the block.

Tredegar House★★

11mi/18km east of Cardiff via the M 4. Open second wk Feb–Mar daily 11am–4pm; Apr–early Nov daily 11am–5pm; late Nov–17 Dec Sat–Sun 10.30am–5pm. £9.40. ♿🅿✕ ℘01633 815 880. www.nationaltrust.org.uk.

One of the finest houses to be built in England or Wales in the expansive years following the Civil War, this great mansion of 1664–72 was the residence of the fabulous wealthy Morgan family – landowners, entrepreneurs and the developers in the 19C of the docks in Newport. Many of the interiors have been refurnished, in part with original pieces; among the most striking are the Brown Room with its exuberant carving, the Gilt Room and the Cedar Closet with its scented panelling. The **grounds★** retain something of their original formal layout, with superb ironwork gates and geometric parterres.

SWANSEA★

Swansea is 40mi/64km W of Cardiff. Frequent trains run direct from London Paddington (3h), Bristol, Manchester and Cardiff (52min). The train station is a 10-min walk north, the bus station is in the centre by the Quadrant Shopping Centre. 🛈 Plymouth Street. ℘01792 468 321. www.visitswanseabay.com.

Swansea is the lively urban centre for southwest Wales and, after Cardiff, is the country's second city. Three centuries of industrial activity in the **Lower Swansea Valley** resulted in one of Britain's most spectacularly derelict landscapes. Since the late-1960s, however, a programme of reclamation has succeeded in transforming the area, which now comprises parkland, light industry, and commercial and retail developments, with few traces left of its industrial past. Over the next decade, Swansea city centre is also undergoing major restoration.

Maritime Quarter★

The recent developments, along and behind Swansea's 5mi/8km bayside promenade, are recognised as one of the top three waterside developments in Europe.

The mid-19C South Dock has been renovated as a 600-berth marina, the centrepiece of a new 'inner-city village' of nightclubs, bars, pubs, restaurants, spruce apartments, public squares and quayside walks.

The **Dylan Thomas Theatre** (and statue) commemorates poet **Dylan Thomas** (1914–53). Fans of Thomas may like to visit **Number 5 Cwmdonkin Drive, Birthplace of Dylan Thomas** (guided tour only, daily 10.30am–4.30pm; £8; ℘01792 472 555, www.dylanthomas-birthplace.com). The jewel in the crown of the Maritime Quarter is the **National Waterfront Museum★** (Oystermouth Road; open daily 10am–5pm; Closed 1 Jan, 25–26 Dec; ♿✕; ℘0300 111 2 333; https://museum.wales/swansea) housed in a magnificent building that elegantly combines old and new architecture. Its varied exhibits include a complete, re-erected woollen mill; several retired vessels, among them a lightship, are moored at the quayside, and historic vehicles of the Mumbles Tramway can be seen in the tramshed. The museum also explores the way of life for ordinary people at the time of the Industrial Revolution in Wales.

Adjacent the **LC** leisure centre (www.thelcswansea.com) is home to Wales' largest waterpark, a four-storey aquatic-themed play-area for young adventurers, a 9m climbing wall, and one of the largest exercise and wellness arenas in the Principality.

Rhossili Bay, Gower Peninsula

© David Chapman/age fotostock

Glynn Vivian Art Gallery★

Alexandra Road. Open Tue–Sun and
bank holiday Mons 10am–5pm. &
℘01792 516 900.
www.swansea.gov.uk/glynnvivian.
Built on the fortune made from copper-
smelting, this acclaimed gallery is one
of the best places in the country to see
a wide variety of Welsh art, from 1700
to the present day. It also boasts a fine
collection of Swansea pottery.

GOWER PENINSULA★★

Heading west from Swansea, a chain
of superb beaches and magnificent
cliffs extend along the south coast of
the peninsula (14mi/23km), Britain's
first designated Area of Outstanding
Natural Beauty.
The Mumbles, Swansea's very own
seaside resort, is overlooked by the spectacular shell of **Oystermouth Castle**
(open Apr–Sept daily 11am–5pm; £3.50;
℘01792 369 233, www.swansea.gov.uk).
The resort's many outdoor activities
include sailing, surfing, waterskiing and
parascending.
The approach to the tiny village of
Rhossili★★ in the far southwestern corner of the peninsula hardly prepares the
visitor for the breathtaking **views** which
open up from the coastguard cottages
housing the **Rhossili and South Gower
Coast Visitor Centre** (℘01792 390 707,
www.nationaltrust.org.uk).

The cliffs fall dramatically away to the
great arc (3mi/5km) of **Rhossili Bay**
with the surf crashing on its wonderful sandy beach. High above is Rhossili
Down (193m); to the south is **Worms
Head**, 1mi-/1.6km-long sea-serpent-
shaped rock, accessible only at low tide.

ABERDULAIS TIN WORKS AND WATERFALL★

1mi/17km NE of Swansea by the
A 483, A 48 and A 465. Open late Feb–
early Nov daily 11am–4pm (Apr–Aug
10.30am–5pm); mid-Nov–mid-Dec
Fri–Sun 11am–4pm; early Jan–mid-Feb
Sat–Sun 11am–4pm. £5.
&⊓X ℘01639 636 674.
www.nationaltrust.org.uk/aberdulais.
In a pretty wooded gorge, the waters
of the River Dulais crash down among
huge boulders and past the remains of
the works of the Aberdulais Tinplate Co.,
founded 1830.
The site's industrial history goes back
to 1584, when copper smelting began,
and a new exhibition and interpretation
project shows how the falls played an
important role in the industrialisation
of South Wales. It was also frequented
by artists (including Turner) who found
it an appropriately picturesque subject.
Today the waters of the Dulais are used
to make Aberdulais self-sufficient in
environmentally friendly energy, with
its waterwheel – the largest in Europe

– generating electricity. Lifts enable visitors to access the upper levels for excellent views of the falls and to see the waterwheel and turbine in action.

KIDWELLY (CYDWELI)★

21mi/34km NW of Swansea via the A 483, A 4070 and A 484. Open Mar–Oct daily 9.30am–5pm (6pm Jul–Aug); 10am Nov–Feb (11am Sun)–4pm. Closed 1 Jan, and 24–26 Dec. £4. &P 01554 890 104. http://cadw.gov.wales.

Kidwelly Castle ruins date from the 1280s. The walls enclosed the Norman town to form a 'bastide', as also found in North Wales at Conwy and Caernarfon. In town, **St Mary's church**, built c.1320, in Decorated style, originally served a Benedictine monastery.

NATIONAL BOTANIC GARDEN OF WALES★

20mi (32km) north of Swansea via the M4, then the A48. Open daily Apr–Oct 10am–6pm; Nov–Mar 10am–4.30pm. Closed 24–25 Dec. £10.50, child (5–16), £4.95. &PX 01558 667 149. https://botanicgarden.wales.

The gardens opened in May 2000, on the site of Middleton Hall and its historic parkland, dating back some 400 years Its centrepiece is the **Great Glasshouse**, the largest single-span glasshouse in the world. The 10 000 or so plants here (representing around 1 000 species) come from California, Australia, the Canary Islands, Chile, South Africa, the Mediterranean Basin; and the Great Glasshouse is zoned to reflect this. The surrounding grounds originally laid out in the Regency period include five lakes, herbaceous borders and a double-walled garden.

BRECON BEACONS★★

The main centres in the Brecon Beacons are Aberdare, Abergavenny, Brecon, Crickhowell and Hay-on-Wye.

For outdoor types the best starting point is the National Park Mountain Centre at Libanus, 5mi/8km SW of Brecon (01874 623 366; www.beacons-npa. gov.uk). Not without good reason are these mountains used for training elite military troops, so don't be fooled by their shapely domes.

Market Street, Brecon 01874 622 485. www.breconbeacons.org.

These red sandstone mountains culminate in a spectacular north-facing escarpment overlooking the lesser uplands of Mid-Wales. South from this great barrier (highest point Pen-y-Fan, 886m) extend high rolling moorlands cut by lush valleys, the broadest of them formed by the River Usk.

Downstream from Brecon, centrally placed for exploring the Brecon Beacons National Park, the river is accompanied by the delightful Monmouthshire and Brecon Canal.

Stream in Brecon Beacons

© tirc83/iStockphoto.com

Black Mountains

To the east the **Black Mountains** form a natural border with Herefordshire. **Hay-on-Wye** (*see Herefordshire*), at the northern end of the range, is famous for its numerous bookshops.

South is **Hay Bluff**★★ (4mi/6km by the B 4423 and a single-track road), an escarpment offering incomparable **views** over the Wye valley and far into central Wales. Some 8mi/13km south of Hay-on-Wye is **Llanthony Priory**★★ (open daily 10am–4pm; ℘01873 890487, http://cadw.gov.wales). The ruins of this late-12C Augustinian priory stand in the Vale of Ewyas beside the River Honddu. Eight splendid arches, topped by the ruined triforium, still stand beside the remains of the crossing tower and the east end of the church.

Llanthony Priory

© Sebastian Wasek/age fotostock

Central Beacons

The **Central Beacons** dominate the skyline south of **Brecon** (Aberhonddu), rising to 886m at Pen y Fan, the highest point in southern Britain. The Normans constructed a castle at Brecon, the ruins of which overlook the meeting of the rivers Honddu and Usk; they also built a priory whose church is now the cathedral.

The stone-built former county town has kept its intricate medieval street pattern and numerous dignified 18C houses.

Fforest Fawr Geopark

Continuing west is the sandstone massif of **Fforest Fawr** (www.fforestfawrgeopark.org.uk) – meaning Great Forest in English – and its hills, which are known as 'Fans' (Fan Fawr is 734m). Water run-off from these hills formed steep river valleys with spectacular waterfalls, including the 27m **Henrhyd Waterfall** and the falls at **Ystradfellte**★, and its caves, such as **Ogof Ffynnon Ddu**.

The **Black Mountain**, Y Mynydd Du (not to be confused with the Black Mountains, *see above*), is the most westerly peak, culminating in the summit of **Fan Brycheiniog** at 802m and the glacial lakes of **Llyn y Fan Fach** and **Llyn y Fan Fawr**.

♣ National Showcaves Centre for Wales/Dan-Yr-Ogof★

19mi/31km SW of Brecon via the A 40 and A 4067. Open Apr–early Nov daily 10am–3pm. £15, child (3–16) £11. ▣✗ ℘01639 730 284. www.showcaves.co.uk. Only the first section of the cave system is open to the public.

This 11mi-/17km-long underground complex includes the largest as well as the longest single-chamber cave open to visitors in Britain. Bones of humans and animals have been found in nearby chambers and human occupation of the caves dates back to the Bronze Age. They were formed in the permeable limestone which underlies this southern part of the Beacons, and include swallow-holes and underground rivers, examples of which can be seen in the 'waterfall country'' around the village of **Ystradfellte**★. There are archaeological displays, an interpretive exhibition and several areas themed for children, including a dinosaur park.

© Gail Johnson/Dreamstime.com

St David's Cathedral

Pembrokeshire★★★

Travelling the inland roads of the westernmost part of the Principality, even in high summer, can feel like a step back to a quieter time. And in the lonelier places dolmens, megaliths and Celtic crosses remain. But it is the Pembrokeshire Coast that attracts most visitors. The shoreline changes quickly from ragged rocks to glorious beaches with a rich bird- and animal life including puffins, seals, whales and dolphins. Tiny St David's is not only home to Wales' finest church, but in and around here a number of young adventure tour operators are bringing a whole new, and very different, set of pilgrims to this part of the world, pioneering coasteering and thrilling offshore white-water RIB (rigid inflatable boat) rides.

Beautifully located, historic Tenby is Pembrokeshire's established and deserved favourite resort with families seeking classic bucket-and-spade holidays, but is just one of many beaches to choose from on this stretch of coast. The Pembrokeshire peninsula, the most western part of Wales and part of the old Kingdom of Dyfed, abounds not only in the dolmens and megaliths of prehistory but also in

◔ **Michelin Map:** Michelin Atlas p14 or Map 503 E, F 27, 28 and 29.
🗎 **Info: Haverfordwest:** Off Dew Street. ✆01437 775 244. **Fishguard:** Town Hall. ✆01437 776 636. **Pembroke:** Commons Road (by castle). ✆01437 776 499. **Tenby:** Upper Park Road ✆01437 775 603. **St David's:** Oriel y Parc, Landscape Gallery. ✆01437 720 392. www.visitpembrokeshire.com; www.pembrokeshire coast.org.uk.
☺ **Don't Miss:** The Cathedral in St David's; an excursion aboard a RIB.

the splendid stone crosses of Celtic Christianity. In 1952 the coastline was designated the Pembrokeshire Coast National Park, the smallest of the national parks of Wales and England; its wonderful variety of beaches is backed by cliffs revealing a complex, spectacular geology and harbouring rich birdlife.

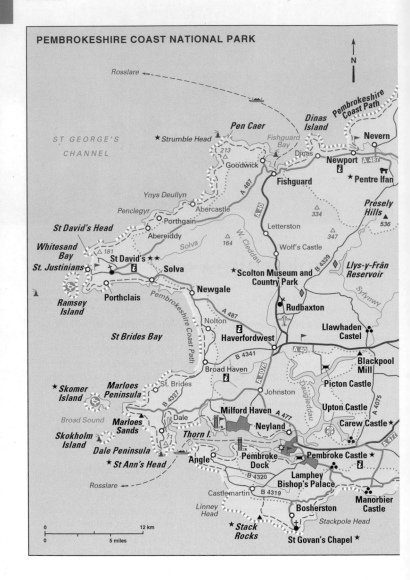

PEMBROKESHIRE COAST NATIONAL PARK

Rosslare

ST GEORGE'S CHANNEL

★ Strumble Head
Pen Caer
213

Dinas Island
Pembrokeshire Coast Path

Fishguard Bay
Djuas
Goodwick
Nevern
Newport
★ Pentre Ifan

Ynys Deullyn

Fishguard

Penclegyr
Abercastle
A 40
A 487
Presely Hills
536

St David's Head
Porthgain
Abereiddy
W. Cleddau
Solva
164
Letterston
334
347
Wolf's Castle
A 4329
Llys-y-Frân Reservoir
Syfynwy

Whitesand Bay
St. Justinians
△ 181
St David's ★★
Solva
★ Scolton Museum and Country Park

Ramsey Island
Porthclais
Pembrokeshire Coast Path
Newgale
Nolton
Rudbaxton

St Brides Bay
Haverfordwest
A 487
Llawhaden Castel
A 40

Broad Haven
B 4341
A 4076
Blackpool Mill

★ Skomer Island
Marloes Peninsula
St. Brides
B 4327
Johnston
Daigleddau
Picton Castle
Upton Castle
A 4075

Broad Sound
Marloes Sands
Dale
Milford Haven
A 477
Neyland
Carew Castle ★

Skokholm Island
Dale Peninsula
Thorn I.
A 477

★ St Ann's Head
Angle
Pembroke Dock
Pembroke Castle ★

Rosslare
Castlemartin
B 4320
Lamphey Bishop's Palace
B 4319
Manorbier Castle

Linney Head
Bosherston
Stackpole Head

0 — 12 km
0 — 5 miles
★ Stack Rocks
St Govan's Chapel ★

SOUTH COAST★★
(85mi/137km)

Tenby★★
53mi/85km W of Swansea.

This little medieval town on its rocky promontory, near the country's south-westernmost point, combines all the ingredients of a popular seaside resort in a compact attractive centre.

During the Victorian era Tenby was eagerly visited for its 'restorative quali-ties' and walkways were built here for seaside strolls.

Harbour and seafront★★ – This is a perfect composition of jetty, massive retaining walls, Fishermen's Chapel and rugged warehouses, backed by pretty Georgian and Regency houses, crowd-ing together and rising to crown the low cliff. Superb sandy beaches extend north and south. On Castle Hill is **Tenby Museum and Art Gallery** (open daily 10am–5pm (winter Tue–Sat only); ✘;

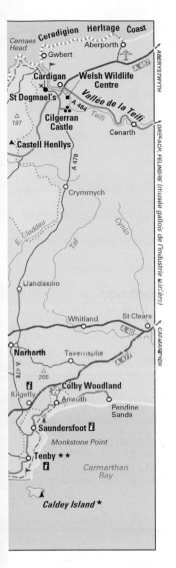

Map labels:
Ceredigion Heritage Coast · Cemaes Head · Gwbert · Aberporth · Cardigan · Welsh Wildlife Centre · St Dogmael's · Vallée de la Teifi · Cilgerran Castle · Cenarth · Castell Henllys · ABERYSTWYTH · A 487 · A 484 · Teifi · △ 197 · DREFACH FELINDRE (musée gallois de l'industrie lainière) · Crymmych · E. Cloddau · Taf · Cynin · Llandissilio · Whitland · St Clears · A 40 · CAERFYRDDIN/CARMARTHEN · Narberth · Tavernspite · △ 205 · A 477 · A 478 · Colby Woodland · Kilgetty · Amroth · Pendine Sands · Saundersfoot · Monkstone Point · Tenby ★★ · Carmarthen Bay · Caldey Island ★

Offshore Exploration

A boat trip, watching seals, dolphins and (hopefully) whales, is an essential part of exploring the Pembrokeshire Coast. There are several boat excursions that depart from St Justinian, a few minutes' drive from St David's, in search of marine wildlife. Choose from a conventional boat or a jet-powered rigid inflatable boat (RIB), which can be bumpy but is a real thrill: **Thousand Islands Expeditions** (Cross Square, St David's; ☎01437 721 721; www.thousandislands. co.uk); Voyages of Discovery (1 High Street, St David's; ☎01437 721 911; www.ramseyisland.co.uk).

Apr–late Jul and Sept–Oct Wed–Mon 11am–5pm, late Jul–Aug daily 11am–5pm; £5.25; ☎01834 842 279; www.national trust.org.uk) is a late-15C town dwelling, virtually unchanged externally and well preserved inside, with period furniture.

Manorbier (Maenorbyr)

'The most delectable spot in Wales', according to Giraldus Cambrensis, the traveller and historian born here c.1146. When seen from the bay, the mighty walls of **Manorbier Castle** (open daily 10am–5pm; £5.50; ♿ ℗; ☎01834 870 081; www.manorbiercastle.co.uk), recall the great Crusader strongholds of the Levant.

The spectacular stretch of coastline between St Govan's Head and Linney Head features high cliffs, arches (including the **Green Bridge of Wales**), sea-caves, blow-holes and stacks, including two impressive pillars, **Stacks Rocks★** (Elegug Stacks). Near Bosherston, the **chapel★** first established as a hermit's cell by St Govan in the 6C seems almost a part of the cliffface (☺ Note: this area

closed Christmas period; £4.95; ☎01834 842 809; www.tenbymuseum.org.uk), with paintings by Augustus and Gwen John and other Tenby artists.

Town – A good stretch of the **town walls** encloses a characteristically intricate web of medieval streets, widening out at **St Mary's** (☎01834 842 068), one of Wales' most substantial parish churches, with a spire over 45m tall. The **Tudor Merchant's House** (open daily mid-end Feb 11am–3pm; Mar and early Nov–24 Dec Sat–Sun 11am–3pm;

is part of the Castlemartin artillery range; enquire locally or visit http://nt.pcnpa.org.uk, for accessibility information).

Carew Castle and Tidal Mill★

Open Apr–Oct daily 10am–5pm, rest of year see website. £5.50. ⌖ ✆01646 651 782. www.carewcastle.com.

Much of what still stands today dates from the late-13C–early-14C. The magnificent Elizabethan architecture, with rows of tall mullioned windows reflected in the mill pool, recaptures some of the elegance of the period.

The **tidal mill**, the only one of its kind remaining in Wales, is a restored late-18C building and an audio-visual presentation explains its workings.

The heavily ornamented **Celtic cross** near the entrance to the castle is one of the earliest Christian monuments in Wales, erected shortly after 1035.

St Govan's Chapel

This tiny medieval cell, measuring 5.5m by 3.6m, occupies a delightful hidden spot and has many legends attached. The most common story is that St Govan (a contemporary of St David) was an Irish Christian who found refuge from pirates in the cleft which opened miraculously in the rock. Here he spent the rest of his life.

Pembroke Castle★

Open daily: Jan–Feb and Nov–Dec 10am–4pm; Mar and Sept–Oct 10am–5pm; Apr–Aug 9.30am–5.30pm. Closed 1 Jan, 3 days in mid-Jul, 24–26 Dec. £6. ⌖ ✕(summer only). ✆01646 684 585. www.pembrokecastle.co.uk.

This powerful ancient castle has for centuries guarded the strategically sited town of Pembroke and its safe anchorage. Soon after the Battle of Hastings in 1066 the Normans looked to Wales, but not until 1093 did Earl Roger of Montgomery build the first Pembroke Castle. The castle we see today was built in the 1190s and enlarged a century later.

The massive **keep**, 21m high with walls 6m thick at the base, is the crowning glory of the castle. The **Wogan Cavern**, below the Norman Hall, is unparalleled in British castles; a natural vaulted cavern, 18m by 24m, probably used as a store and boathouse.

Marloes Sands

This broad sandy beach separates the Dale and Marloes Peninsulas. On the beach, note the **Three Chimneys**, Silurian rocks up ended by powerful earth movements.

Visits can be made to the bird sanctuary islands of **Skomer★**, **Skokholm** and Grassholm, with their colonies of seabirds, including the charming puffin, the National Park emblem. **Pembrokeshire Island Boat Trips** (✆01646 603 123, www.pembrokeshire-islands.co.uk) depart from Martin's Haven.

Haverfordwest (Hwlffordd)

The former county town with its hill-top castle ruin is the regional urban centre.

Newgale

One of several holiday villages on this coast, its splendid 2mi/3km stretch of sand, backed by a storm ridge of shingle, makes this a family favourite.

Solva (Solvach)

The picturesque harbour at Lower Solva was built to be out of sight of sea-raiders. Today it shelters pleasure boats as well as fishing craft.

NORTH COAST★★

(55mi/88km)

St David's (Tyddewi)★★

Were it not for its splendid cathedral, St David's would rank as a mere village. Instead it is famous as Britain's tiniest city and a thriving tourist-oriented community, at the westernmost point of the **Pembrokeshire Coast Path**. There has been a Christian community and daily worship on this site for more than 14 centuries and in the 12C Pope Callixtus II decreed that two pilgrimages to St David's were the equivalent of one to Rome – a privilege shared only with Santiago de Compostela.

Cathedral★★

Open daily, 7.30am (12.45pm Sun)–6pm.
£5 donation requested. Guided tours
Aug Mon 11.30am, Fri 2.30pm. &.PX
𝄞01437 720 202.
www.stdavidscathedral.org.uk.

Wales' greatest church, built in lichen-
encrusted purple stone, sits in a
secludedhollow, revealing itself with
dramatic suddenness as you pass
through the gatehouse into the precinct
containing both cathedral and Bishop's
Palace.

The present building was started
in 1180 by Peter de Leia (1176–98),
a Florentine monk and the third
Norman bishop. Up to the wall behind
the high altar, what we see today is
substantially his cathedral. The whole
building slopes upwards from west
to east (approx 4m) and presents a
unique and striking impression to a
visitor entering the south porch, at
the western end of the nave. The late-
15C **nave roof** is a magnificent piece
of work, in Irish oak, incorporating the
dragon of Wales on the pendants. In
the south choir aisle is the tomb of the
historian **Gerald of Wales** (1146–1223).
Before the high altar is the table tomb of
Edmund Tudor, grandfather of Henry
VIII, who ordered it to be moved here
from Greyfriars at Carmarthen after the
Dissolution. The remains of St David's
shrine, built in 1275, are on the north
side of the presbytery.

Bishop's Palace★

Open daily: Mar–Jun and Sept–Oct
9.30am–5pm; Jul–Aug 9.30am–6pm;
Nov–Feb Mon–Sat 10am–4pm, Sun
11am–4pm. Closed 1 Jan, 24–26 Dec. £4.
𝄞01437 720 517.
http://cadw.gov.wales.

This mighty ruin comprises three buildings, surrounding a courtyard. The
Bishop's Hall and **Solar**, with kitchen
and chapel, appear to have been the
main residence; the **Great Hall** to the
south, with its elaborate porch and
stairs from the courtyard, was reserved
for entertaining important guests. The
main buildings date chiefly from the
13C and 14C and are the work of Bishop
Thomas Bek (1280–93) and Bishop
Henry de Gower (1328–47). Open-air
theatre performances are occasionally
staged here.

Fishguard (Abergwaun)

The lower town offers a pretty haven for
pleasure craft. Brunel planned to make
Fishguard a trans-Atlantic port to rival
Liverpool and for a brief period great
liners like the *Mauretania* berthed here.
Today the only significant traffic are the
ferries to and from Rosslare (Ireland).

Newport (Trefdraeth)

Trefdraeth means town by the beach in
Welsh and Newport is locally famous for
its golden sands, protected by craggy
headlands. Quiet and pretty with a
small ruined Norman castle and church
the village is a good base for walkers.

Nevern (Nanhyfer)

Among the yews in the churchyard of St
Brynach's Church stands a splendid 11C
Celtic wheelhead **cross** (4m high), richly
carved in interlacing patterns.

Pentre Ifan★

This massive *cromlech* (dolmen), overlooking Newport Bay, consists of four
great upright stones, three of which
support a massive capstone.

It stands on the lower slopes of the
rounded, heather-clad **Presely Hills**
(Mynydd Preseli), from whose eastern
crests came the bluestones of Stonehenge, probably transported across
from Newport Bay.

Castell Henllys

Meline. Open Apr–Oct daily 10am–5pm;
rest of year Mon–Fri 11am–3pm. Closed
around 20 Dec–2 Jan. £5.50, winter
£4.50. 𝄞01239 891 319.
www.castellhenllys.com.

This hilltop fort (its name means Castle of the Old Court) is the setting for a
partial re-creation of an Iron Age community with storage pit, cultivated
areas and three picturesque Hobbit-
like conical thatched huts with smoky
interiors. Inside you can grind flour and
make bread just like the Celts used to.

Mid-Wales★★

The area now known as Mid-Wales approximates to the old kingdom of Powys (by far the largest county in Wales) and occupies the mid-eastern part of the Principality, butting up to the English border. There are, of course, many well-trodden ways, but off the beaten track, you're more likely to meet sheep, or the odd mountain pony, than fellow humans. Attractive little towns near the English border, and (further afield) the magnificent gardens of Powis Castle offer other distractions. On the west coast of Mid-Wales, Aberystwyth is the Principality's most agreeable summer holiday resort, maintaining an elegant and unspoiled air.

MID-WALES, NORTH

Powis Castle and Garden★★

Welshpool. 68mi/109km N of Brecon. Open daily: Jan–Dec 11am–4pm (Apr–Sept 11am–5pm). Castle only £6.35; Garden only £9.21; Whole property: £12.50. &♿☐✗ ℘01938 551 944. www.nationaltrust.org.uk/powis.

The town of Welshpool (Y Trallwng) lies at the northern end of the ridge on which Powis Castle is built. The massive twin towers of the gateway date from the late-13C. Highlights include the Long Gallery, with its mid-17C *trompe l'œil* panelling; the Dining Room and Oak Drawing Room were remodelled in the early-20C. The castle houses the collections of Clive of India (1725–74) and many fine paintings.

The much acclaimed gardens, overhung with clipped yews, shelters rare and tender plants. Laid out under the influence of Italian and French styles it was created towards the end of the 17C, has not been remodelled and is one of the rare remaining masterpieces of the period.

MID-WALES, WEST

Aberystwyth★★

121mi/195km due W of Birmingham. The railway station (Birmingham 3h direct) and bus station are a 10min walk from the centre of town.

Set roughly halfway along the west coast, Aberystwyth successfully combines the difficult balancing act of being the liveliest seaside resort in the Principality with being a prestigious university town and maintaining its unspoiled Victorian appearance.

The unofficial capital of Mid-Wales, this is an historic market town and administrative centre, locally known simply as 'Aber' – although there is another 'Aber' on the North Wales coast, just to confuse things. Historically, Aberystwyth was part of the defunct county of Cardiganshire, and has been a key educational centre since the late 19C, when the university college was established in 1872.

Vale of Rheidol Light Railway★

Open: Mar–Oct most days, see website for schedule; closed Jan; ☐✗; ℘01970 625 819; www.rheidolrailway.co.uk.

The railway was built in 1902 to service the lead mines in the valley, shares the mainline station with National Rail services. The narrow–gauge steam train runs from Aberystwyth through the lovely wooded Vale of Rheidol to the waterfalls at **Devil's Bridge★**. The journey (12mi/19km) takes an hour as the train climbs slowly up to the terminus (195m). The engines and rolling stock are all original.

Terrace Road leads from the railway station to the seafront via the **Ceredigion Museum** (open Apr–Sept Mon–Sat 10am–

ℹ **Info: Aberystwyth:** Lisburne House, Terrace Road. ℘01970 612 125; www.discoverceredigion.co.uk

☺ **Don't Miss:** Powis Castle; in Aberystwyth, the Light Railway to Devil's Bridge Falls.

🕓 **Timing:** Two or three days to explore Aberystwyth, and do some coastal walking.

5pm; Oct–Mar noon–4.30; &; &01970 633 088, www.ceredigionmuseum.wales), next to the tourist office. The restored Edwardian Coliseum Theatre is now one of the most unusual and striking museum interiors in Britain. Objects of all ages are on display with the focus on the Victorian period and later.

Continuing on to the **seafront★**, you will find few modern intrusions to mar the Victorian harmony of Marine Terrace. To the north, the **Cliff Railway** of 1896 (Cliff Terrace; operates daily Apr–Oct 10am–5pm; out of season, the trains run to a limited timetable;, check website or call for details; £4 return; ✖; &01970 61/ 642; www.aberystwyth cliffrailway.co.uk), which operated on a water balance system until electrification in 1921, scales the heights of Constitution Hill, home to the world's largest **Camera Obscura** (open Apr–Oct, daily 11am–4pm, &01970 61/ 642).

Aberystwyth castle

On the promontory beyond the pier is the ruin of the castle begun in 1277 by Edward I. Today, it is a Gradel Listed Building.

It was built In response to the so-called First Welsh War in the 13C, and replaces an earlier fortress on the same site. During the uprising instigated by Owain Glyndŵr, the Welsh captured the castle, although, four years later in 1408, it was recaptured by cannon by the English. In 1637, it became the royal mint of Charles I.

National Library of Wales

(Reading Room: open Mon–Fri 9am–6pm, Sat 9.30am–5pm; guided tours (£5) Mon at 11am, and Wed at 2.15pm; & P (charge); ✖; &01970 632 800; www.llgc.org.uk).

Set on top of Penglais Hill with a magnificent **view★** across town, this is one of the UK's most important libraries. Its **permanent collection★** is priceless. This is the national legal deposit office for Wales and holds over 6.5 milliom books and periodicals, as well as large collections of archives, portraits, maps and photographic images.

© GordonBellPhotography/iStockphoto.com

Aberystwyth

Elan Valley★★

34mi/55km E of Aberystwyth via the A 44 to Rhayader; circuit of lakes 25mi/40km.

Reservoirs were built in the Elan valley, 1892–1904, to supply water to Birmingham. The Claerwen Dam, built to increase the supply, was opened in 1952. The **Elan Valley Visitor Centre** (Rhayader; open daily 9.30am–5pm; & P (£2); ✖; &01597 810 880 (winter); www.elan-valley.org.uk) at the foot of the Caban-coch dam, has displays explaining the construction and operation of this great engineering feat, as well as the ecology of the surrounding woods and high moorlands, habitat of the rare red kite. The reservoirs have created a landscape of great beauty. The dams are best seen in flood conditions.

Cardigan (Aberteifi)

38.5mi/62km SW of Aberystwyth via the A 487.

Tucked into the southwest corner of Mid-Wales, bordering Pembrokeshire, Cardigan is an excellent place for nature lovers. Its bay is home to Europe's largest population of bottlenose **dolphins** and various boat trips depart daily. The area is also excellent for birdwatching, particularly at the **Welsh Wildlife Centre** (Teifi Marshes, Cilgerran; (open Apr–22 Dec daily 10am–5pm; & P (charge); ✖ &01239 621 212, www.welshwildlife.org). Its visitor centre is a spectacular wood-and-glass construction offering panoramic views.

North Wales★★★

North Wales is a land of fortresses: Harlech, Conwy, Beaumaris, and, in particular, mighty Caernarfon Castle. Built by Edward I in the 13C, they may resemble giant rough hewn children's sandcastles, but this deadly serious 'Iron Ring' was constructed to intimidate the locals, to prevent and crush rebellion in the region. Collectively they have been designated as a World Heritage Site.

Towering above all is Snowdon (Yr Wyddfa), the highest point in England and Wales, and kingpin of an area unequalled in Britain for its majestic scenery. Snowdonia is not only a magnet for walkers; its railway and the small-gauge railways of Ffestiniog are evergreen attractions. Nearby, Portmeirion is the most extravagant folly village in Britain, an architectural Disneyland in the best possible taste. Moving west the (relatively) remote golden sands and unspoiled villages and resorts of the Lleyn peninsula have a real Welsh charm. Inland, Llangollen is world famous for its summer Eisteddfod, when Welsh music and voices ring out most proudly, but is worth a visit at any time of year for its stunning Pont Cysyllte 'waterway in the sky' aqueduct.

The north coast resort of Llandudno has been a family favourite since Victorian times. Heading out to the Principality's northwest extremity, the Isle of Anglesey is mostly pastoral and peaceful.

Last-stop west, before Ireland, is Holy Island's spectacular coast.

CAERNARFON★★

On the NW tip of mainland Wales.
Climb the castle walls and battlements to get your bearings across town.

The strategic importance of Caernarfon (Welsh for 'fort on the shore') has

⊘ **Don't Miss:** The view of Caernarfon Castle from the water; Beaumaris Castle; Plas Newydd; Conwy Castle; Penrhyn Castle; the ascent of Great Orme; Bodelwyddan Castle; Snowdon Mountain Railway and the view from the summit; Llechwedd Slate Caverns; Centre for Alternative Technology; the beaches of the Lleyn peninsula; Harlech Castle.

🕐 **Timing:** Allow two hours for Caernarfon, two full days for Anglesey, a minimum three days for Snowdonia.

long been appreciated. It was the most westerly position of the Roman Empire in Wales, who built their fort of Segontium nearby. The Normans chose the castle's present site, overlooking the Menai Strait, for their wooden stronghold. It was probably replaced by a stone castle even before Edward I began his mighty structure, bristling with towers and turrets, designed as a seat of power whose walls imitated those of mighty Constantinople.

The town today, still watched over by the castle and partly encircled within its walls, is a centre for visitors to Snowdonia and for yachtsmen eager to make use of its proximity to the waters of the strait and Caernarfon Bay. There are good beaches nearby.

Caernarfon Castle★★★

Open Mar–Oct daily 9.30am–5pm (Jul-Aug 6pm); Nov–Feb daily 10am (Sun 11am)–4pm. Closed 1 Jan, 24–26 Dec. £8.95. ✆01286 677 617. http://cadw.gov.wales.

Building work on this impressive structure started in 1283 under Master James of St George (c.1235–1308), who built for his royal patron a castle with walls decorated with bands of coloured stone and polygonal towers like those of Constantinople. Grandiose in design, it was to

Beaumaris Castle, with the Carneddau of Snowdonia in the background

serve as the seat of English government in the Principality. The appearance of the castle today is due to the vision of the constable in the 1840s, **Sir Llewelyn Turner** (1823–1903), who cleared, restored, re-roofed and renewed, in the teeth of local opposition. Massive curtain walls link the towers to form a figure of eight with the lower bailey to the right and the upper to the left. The great twin-towered gatehouse, **King's Gate**, was defended by five doors and six portcullises.

The **Eagle Tower**, crowned by triple turrets, each, as in Constantinople crested with an eagle, had accommodation on a grand scale. It now houses exhibitions. It was at the castle that the first English Prince of Wales – Edward of Caernarfon, later Edward II – was born in April 1284, and in 1969 the castle hosted the investiture of **Charles, Prince of Wales**.

The **Queen's Tower** houses the Regimental Museum of the Royal Welch Fusiliers. In **Castle Square** is the statue of the legendary Welsh politician **David Lloyd George** (1863–1945), Liberal MP for Caernarfon for 55 years and prime minister 1916–22.

Old Town

The old town hugs close to Edward I's castle, occupying the land just north. The circuit of the **town walls** and towers encircling the medieval town was built as a single operation at the same time as the castle. The walls are punctuated at regular intervals by eight towers and two twin-towered gates. On St Helen's Road is the station for the **Welsh Highland Railway★** (operates Apr–Oct daily, see website for full schedule and fares; ♿🅿✕; ✆01766 516 000; www.festrail. co.uk), the starting point for a spectacular 25mi/40km journey, hauled by the world's most powerful narrow-gauge steam locomotives. These climb from sea level to over 200m on the foothills of Snowdon, before zigzagging dramatically down the steep hillside to reach Beddgelert, then through the magnificent Aberglaslyn Pass and on to Porthmadog.

Beddgelert

Three valleys meet here and the village looks south to the Pass of Aberglaslyn. The dramatic scenery is enough to attract the tourist, but in the 18C the local innkeeper, anxious to encourage trade, embroidered an old legend, and created 'Gelert's Grave'.

The tale has it that Llywelyn the Great had a hound called Gelert. He left Gelert guarding his baby son and returned to find the child missing and the dog covered in blood. Llywelyn, believing Gelert had killed his son, slew the poor beast before he discovered that it had in fact saved the boy from a wolf, whose body was discovered nearby.

SEGONTIUM ROMAN FORT

SE of Caernarfon on the A 487.
Beddgelert Road. Open: for details of
opening arrangements, please contact
Cadw on 01443 336105. Closed 1 Jan,
24–26 Dec. ♿ 🅿 ✆01286 675 625.
http://cadw.gov.wales.

The scant remains of the Roman auxiliary fort of Segontium overlooks Caernarfon. Finds excavated are now in the
National Museum Cardiff.

ANGLESEY★★

Across the Menai Strait from Bangor.
Bangor and Holyhead are on the main
rail route with connections and services
from most parts of the UK.
✆01407 762 622.
www.visitanglesey.co.uk.

Anglesey is separated from the northwest tip of mainland Wales by the
Menai Strait. Its landscape of low
undulating hills, rich in prehistoric
remains, makes it popular with walkers as with yachtsmen.

Thomas Telford (1757–1834) built the
Menai Suspension Bridge (A 5) to
carry his road to Holyhead. The Admi-
ralty insisted upon a clearance of 30m
between water and roadway, and the
bridge, with its span of 176m between
towers, was the longest iron bridge in
the world when it was opened in 1826.
It gives its name to the small town on
the other side. Modern traffic also flows
to the island over the Britannia Bridge
(A 55).

Head 4mi/6km northeast from Menai
Bridge on the A 545 to **Beaumaris★★**.
One of the fortress towns founded in
the late-13C by Edward I, Beaumaris
is now a peaceful little resort, with a
wonderful prospect across the Menai
Strait to Snowdonia. **Beaumaris
Castle★** (open Mar–Oct daily 9.30am–
5pm/Jul-Aug 6pm; Nov–Feb daily 10am/
Sun 11am–4pm; closed 1 Jan, 24–26 Dec;
£5.25; ✆01248 810 361; http://cadw.gov.
wales) was the last and the largest of
Edward's Welsh strongholds. Though
never finished, Beaumaris is the finest
example in Britain of a concentric castle.
A moat surrounds it and there was once
a defended dock, capable of taking

ships of up to 40 tons. The Great Hall,
impressive enough today, was once
twice its present height.

Heading southwest from Menai
Bridge on the A 5, turn left in **Pentre
Uchaf** onto the A 4080 and continue
for 1.5mi/2.4km to **Plas Newydd★★**
(House open mid-Feb–early Nov daily
11am–4.30pm. Garden: 7 Jan–mid-Feb
Sat–Sun 11am–3pm; mid-Feb–early
Nov daily 10.30am–5pm; early Nov–
Dec daily 11am–3pm; £11, garden only,
£8.65; ♿🅿✗; ✆01248 714 795; www.
nationaltrust.org.uk/plasnewydd). This
magnificently sited late-18C mansion
in extensive parkland and gardens
(68ha), once home to the Marquess of
Anglesey, looks over the Strait to the
mountains of Snowdonia. In 1936, the
artist **Rex Whistler** decorated the long
dining room with a whimsical masterpiece of *trompe l'œil*.

Head west from Menai Bridge on the
B 5420 to Llangefni and turn right onto
the B 5111 for Rhosmeirch and **Oriel
Ynys Môn★** (open daily 10.30am–5pm;
♿; ✗; ✆01248 724 444; www.kyffinwil-
liams.info). This modern museum and
gallery succeeds admirably in explaining the island's special identity. Imaginative displays evoke Anglesey's rich
past as well as current issues and there
is a reconstruction of the studio of
Charles Tunnicliffe (1901–79), one of
the very finest British wildlife painters
of the 20C.

Penrhyn Castle★★

Bangor. 11mi/18km NE of Caernarfon via
the A 487 and A 55. Open Mar–early Nov
daily noon–5pm; 2–mid-Dec Sat–Sun
11am–4pm. £11.80, garden only £7.90.
🅿✗ ✆01248 353 084.
www.nationaltrust.org.uk.

This extraordinary evocation of the
Middle Ages was built in the 1820s and
30s for George Dawkins Pennant, heir
to the enormous wealth produced by
the Penrhyn slate quarries. Its mighty
keep (38m high) gives it the very image
of an impregnable Norman fortress,
but in fact it was a country home of
the utmost luxury, providing hospitality to the members of the Anglo-Irish

Conwy Castle

© Traci1002/Dreamstime.com

Ascendancy on their way to and from the port of Holyhead.

The décor of the interior is a *tour-de-force* of traditional craftsmanship, filled with furniture of an opulence seldom seen since. The paintings on show in the Dining Room include an array of Old Masters (Rembrandt, Canaletto, Jan Steen, Van der Velde…) unparalleled in North Wales. Its grandiose outbuildings house a fascinating industrial railway museum, a model railway museum, a dolls museum and large restored Victorian kitchens.

The extensive parklands include a walled garden with many unusual plants.

CONWY★★

23mi/37km NE of Caernarfon, via the A 487 and A 55. ℘01492 577 577. www.visitconwy.org.uk.

Viewed from the east bank, the walled town and massive castle, bristling with towers, make a breathtaking sight against the mountain background. Astride the River Conwy is the famous Conwy Suspension Bridge, designed and built by Thomas Telford in 1826, fitting seamlessly into the defensive ensemble.

Town

The 13C **town walls★★** (11m high and 2m thick) girdle the town on three sides, and were built at the same time as the castle. The circuit is defended by 22 towers and three gateways and provides a good wall-walk between Upper Church Gate and Berry Street.

The original founder of Conwy, Llywelyn the Great, dominates all from his column in Lancaster Square.

Farther down the High Street at the corner of Crown Lane is **Plas Mawr★★** (open Apr–Sept daily 9.30am–5pm, Oct 9.30am–4pm; £5.75; &; ℘01443 336 000; http://cadw.gov.wales), a mansion built in 1577 by Robert Wynne, a true Elizabethan adventurer. Its rooms still evoke the more gracious moments of that age. At the junction with Berry and Castle streets is **Aberconwy House** (open Mar–Nov daily 11am–5pm/Jul–Aug 10am–5pm, Nov–28 Dec Sat–Sun noon–3pm; £5.50; ℘01492 592 246; www. nationaltrust.org.uk), a remarkable surviving medieval timber townhouse, c.1300.

Conwy Castle★★

Open Mar–Oct daily 9.30am–5pm (Jul–Aug 6pm); Nov–Feb 10am (Sun 11am)–4pm. £8.95. ℘01492 592 358. http://cadw.gov.wales.

This masterpiece of medieval architecture (1283–87) was supplied from the sea, as were Edward I's other Welsh castles. Eight massive drum towers with pinnacled battlements protect the two wards of the castle, set on its rocky ridge. The inner ward with the royal apartments was approached by water and the large outer ward from the town.

Bodnant Garden★★

8mi/13km south of Conwy via the A 470. Open Jan–23 Dec daily 10am–4pm (May–Jun 9am–5pm). £12. &🅿❌ ✆01492 650 460. www.nationaltrust.org.uk/bodnant-garden.

The garden (40ha), laid out largely in the late-19C and early-20C, comprises formal terraces around the house and The Dell, an area for woodland walks. Noted for rhododendrons, camellias and magonlias, it is also justly famed for its golden Laburnum Arch, which flowers in late spring.

LLANDUDNO★

4.5mi/7.2km N of Conwy. To get your bearings take a ride on the tramway, or for a bird's-eye view jump aboard the Llandudno cable car. ✆01492 577 577. www.visitllandudno.org.uk.

Safe sandy blue-flag beaches with views of Snowdonia, Punch and Judy shows, a Victorian pier and other traditional British seaside trappings make Llandudno an evergreen family summer holiday resort. The Victorian **pier**★ of 1875, a delicious confection in Anglo-Indian style, is, unlike many contemporary structures of its kind, splendidly shipshape.

The family of Alice Liddell, inspiration for Lewis Carroll's immortal *Alice in Wonderland*, spent most of their holidays in Llandudno and a delightful statue of the White Rabbit stands on the West Shore. The hill above town, known as the **Great Orme** (207m), can be reached either by the 1903-vintage cable-hauled **Great Orme Tramway**★ (Victoria Station, Church Walks; operates late Mar–late Oct daily 10am–6pm, Mar and Oct 5pm; £7.50 return; ✆01492 577 877; www.greatormetramway.co.uk); by the **Llandudno Cable Car**★ (Happy Valley; operates Apr –Oct daily 10am–5pm; £10 return 🚠; ✆01492 877 205; www.visitllandudno.org.uk); or by road. It offers superb views across the water, town and Snowdonia. Far underground are the caves and passageways of the **Great Orme Ancient**

Copper Mines (open mid-Mar–Oct daily 9.30am–4.30pm (last entry); £7; 🅿; ✆01492 870 447, www.greatormemines.info), first worked by Bronze Age miners.

BODELWYDDAN CASTLE★★

Bodelwyddan. 11mi/18km E of Llandudno on the A 470 and A 55. Open Apr–Oct daily except Mon and Fri 11am–4pm (Parkland 10.30am–5pm). Closed 2 wks over Christmas. £7.50. &🅿❌ ✆01745 584 060. www.bodelwyddan-castle.co.uk.

Transformed in the course of the 19C to resemble a medieval stronghold, Bodelwyddan Castle has become a superb setting for a magnificent selection of **Victorian portraits** from London's **National Portrait Gallery**. The paintings are hung in rooms whose fittings and furniture have been carefully and entertainingly chosen and arranged to evoke various themes. The gardens have been restored to their Edwardian character.

RHUDDLAN CASTLE★★

6mi/26km E of Llandudno by A 470, A 5 and A 547. Castle Street. Open Apr–early Nov daily 10am–5pm. £4. ✆01745 590 777. http://cadw.gov.wales.

Diggers from the Fens (ℹ*see East Anglia and East Midlands*) and elsewhere laboured for three years during the war of 1277 to divert the River Clwyd, so that a castle which could be supplied from the sea could be built. A town grew up which, in the war of 1282, replaced Chester as the main base of operations against the Welsh in Snowdonia. In 1284 the 'Statute of Wales' was issued here, '...securing to the Principality of Wales its judicial rights and independence'. The castle was partly demolished after the Civil War. Entry to the remains is by the **west gatehouse**, the best-surviving feature.

First and second floors provided comfortable apartments with fireplaces. Similar suites must have existed in the east gatehouse. The concentric plan of the castle within its wide dry moat, with lower walls to the outer ward and

© esentunar/iStockphoto.com

View eastwards from near the summit of Snowdon

a defended river wall and dock, can still be traced on the ground.

ST ASAPH CATHEDRAL ★

15mi/24km E of Llandudno on the B 5155 and A 55. High Street. Open Mon–Sat 9am–6.30pm, Sun 7.30am–4pm. ♿ 🅿 (charge). 📞 01745 583 429. http://stasaph.churchinwales.org.uk.
This is the second-smallest cathedral city in the country, after St David's. St Kentigern founded a monastic community here in the 560. The present cathedral, mainly 13C, houses the Bible used at Prince Charles' investiture in 1969.

SNOWDONIA ★★★

Betws-y-Coed, Beddgelert, Blaenau Ffestiniog and Llanberis all make good bases. 📞 01766 770274 (National Park office). www.eryri-npa.gov.uk.
Snowdonia National Park covers about 840sq mi/2 180sq km of wild beauty among the scenic mountains of North Wales. Snowdon (Yr Wyddfa), at 1 085m, is the highest mountain in England and Wales, dominating the north. Cader Idris (Pen y Gadair) at 893m looms over the southern part of the National Park.

Betws-y-Coed ★

Beautifully set amid tree-clad slopes at the junction of the rivers Conwy and Llugwy, Betws-y-Coed (Chapel in the Woods) is the gateway to Snowdonia. A sturdy stone bridge, Pont y Pair, spans the Llugwy downstream from its romantically wooded ravine, where cascades form the famous **Swallow Falls**. Note Telford's ornate cast-iron bridge over the Conwy, built in 1815.

Llanberis ★

The starting point for the **Snowdon Mountain Railway** (*see below*), this little slate quarrying town is also home to the excellent **Welsh Slate Museum ★** (open Easter–Oct daily 10am–5pm; Nov–Easter Sun–Fri 10am–4pm; ♿🅿✖️ 📞029 2057 3700, https://museum.wales/slate), housed in the engineering workshops of the great Dinorwig Quarry.
In fact you can penetrate far into the depths of the mountain itself at the **Electric Mountain Visitor Centre** (tours daily, advance booking essential; 'sensible' footwear required on underground tours; £8.50; ♿🅿✖️; 📞01286 870 636; www.electricmountain.co.uk) to see where the turbines of the **Dinorwig Power Station** are housed in great man-made caverns.

Snowdon (Yr Wyddfa) ★★★

The easiest ascent is from Llanberis aboard the **Snowdon Mountain Railway ★★** (operates, weather permitting, mid-Mar–Oct, 9am–5pm every 30min; summit trains early May onwards; return £29; ♿ 🅿 (charge); ✖️ 📞01286 870 223; www.snowdonrailway.co.uk), a rack-and-pinion steam-powered line built in 1896 and the only one of its type in Britain. Principal footpaths are fully described in the leaflets and maps published by the Park Authority. The most straight-

Snowdon Mountain Railway

forward path follows the ridge used by the railway, while the most scenic begins at the Pen-y-Pass car park on Llanberis Pass.

For experienced walkers, the scramble along the knife-edge of Crib Goch is an exhilarating experience. In fine weather, the **panorama★★★** from the summit of Snowdon takes in Anglesey, the Isle of Man, and the Wicklow Mountains in Ireland. Take it all in from the comfort of Hafod Eyri, the striking £8.3million **Snowdon Summit Visitor Centre**, completed in 2009.

Blaenau Ffestiniog★

Slate is still quarried here albeit on a lesser scale than in the past. In the **Llechwedd Slate Caverns★★** 👤👤 (Opening times vary for specific parts of the attraction but the whole site will always be open daily 9.30am–5.30pm; closed 1 Jan, 25–26 Dec; £20; 🅿️✖; ☎01766 830 306; www.llechwedd-slate-caverns.co.uk) the story of Welsh slate is told on film and visitors are carried by train through two individual sets of caverns, where tableaux depict working conditions. Above ground, a working pub, shops, a workshop and house replicate Victorian and early-20C village life.

Blaenau Ffestiniog is linked to Porthmadog on the coast by the **Ffestiniog Railway★★** (operates Apr–Oct daily 9am–5pm; Nov–Mar certain days only, see website for full schedules and fares; ♿🅿️✖; ☎01766 516 024; www.festrail.

co.uk), built in 1836 to haul slate from quarry to port. The traditional narrow-gauge line (13mi/21km) now takes tourists through the splendidly wooded scenery of the Vale of Ffestiniog, past lakes and waterfalls, to the 'city of slate' among the mountains.

👤👤 Centre for Alternative Technology★★

3mi/5km N of Machynlleth on the A 487. Open daily Apr–early Nov 10am–5pm; early Nov–Mar 10am–4pm. £8.50 (£6.50 in winter), child (4–16), £4. ♿🅿️✖ ☎01654 705 950. http://visit.cat.org.uk. Pioneers in inventing and promoting ecological systems since 1973, there are working examples of environmentally responsible buildings, renewable energy generation, sustainability in the home, organic growing, composting, waste management, and a host of other 'green initiatives' on display at this family-friendly place. Interactive displays for kids and grown-ups make it fun as well as educational.

PORTMEIRION★★★

20mi/32km S of Snowdon. Open daily 9.30am–7.30pm. www.portmeirion-village.com. Built on a wooded peninsula, with wonderful views over the shining waters and sweeping estuary sandbanks, and with the mountains of Snowdonia (some 20mi/32km distant) as a backdrop, this fantasy village was created by the architect and pioneer preservationist Sir Clough Williams-Ellis (1893–1978). Many films and TV programmes have been shot here, the most famous being the cult-hit series *The Prisoner* (1966–67). 'The Village' is an extraordinary mixture of fantasy, theatrical effects and visual tricks; Sir Clough claimed that it was to serve '...no useful purpose save that of looking both handsome and jolly', sufficient incentive to attract the large number of visitors who come for the day, or those who stay longer, either in the hotel, or in one of the other many delightful Baroque-, Rococo- or Mediterranean-influenced buildings.

Archways lead to **Battery Square** with some of Portmeirion's earliest buildings, while the Citadel area is dominated by the **Campanile**, which looks much taller than its actual height (21m) because of Sir Clough's mastery of illusionism. In the valley leading down to the shoreline is the **Piazza**, the green heart of the village, with shops and restaurants and views to the **Pantheon** and the **Bristol Colonnade**, rescued from demolition and re-erected here.

HARLECH CASTLE★★

18mi/29km east of Portmeirion by the A 487 to Maentwrog then south on the 496. Open Mar–Oct 9.30am–5pm (Jul–Aug 6pm); Nov–Feb daily 10am (11am Sun)–4pm. £6.50. ☎01766 780 552. http://cadw.gov.wales.

Harlech Castle was built 1283–89, during Edward I's second campaign in Wales. Its impressive outline rises on a rocky crag, 60m above the plain; with panoramic views to Snowdonia, across the Lleyn peninsula and out to the open sea. Pause to look at the massive east front with its daunting **gatehouse**, and solid drum towers, which confronted would-be attackers. Enter by the modern wooden stairs, at the spot where a second, inner drawbridge pivoted to come down. Once inside, the strength and importance of the gatehouse soon becomes apparent.

LLEYN (LLYN) PENINSULA★★

West of Portmeirion via the A 487 and A 497.

Geologically a continuation of the mountains of Snowdonia, this remote peninsula with its wild scenery and splendid coastline is one of the strongholds of Welshness.

At the base of the peninsula is the charming Victorian seaside resort of **Criccieth** with the ruins of 13C **Criccieth Castle** (open Apr–early Nov daily 10am–5pm; early Nov–Mar Fri–Sat 9.30am (11am Sun)–4pm; £5; ☎01766 522 227; http://cadw.gov.wales), and the nearby resort of **Pwllheli**. Near the end of the peninsula, at Rhiw, sheltered from the winds among the trees of the west

Portmeirion Village

© tugdual/iStockphoto.com

585

ernmost woodland, are the gardens of **Plas-yn-Rhiw★** (open 11am–5pm: late Mar–late May Wed–Mon; late May–late Sept daily; Oct Thu–Sun 11am–4pm; closed some Tue, check website; £5.20; ⚫🅿; ✆01758 780 219; www.national-trust.org.uk), an endearing little country house, part Tudor, part Georgian, with spectacular bay views.

The other attractions of the peninsula are mostly natural, particularly its wonderful golden sandy **beaches**. Most beautiful is **Porthor** ('Whistling Sands') on the northern side; other good beaches include, Porth Nefyn; Porth Ceiriad, picture-postcard Portdinllaen, The Warren at Abersoch, backed by huge dunes with wonderful mountain views. It is nearly always warmer and more sheltered on the southern side of the peninsula.

Near the tip, by the attractive seaside fishing village of **Aberdaron**, the rugged hill of **Mynydd Mawr** overlooks the pilgrims' island of **Bardsey★**.

Visitors to the island can see the remains of the 13C abbey of the Augustinians, who took over from the ancient Celtic foundation of the 6C; legend has it that 20 000 saints are buried on Bardsey. Today it is renowned for its flora and seabirds including the rare Manx Shearwater.

Day-trip cruises, lasting around four hours, are run by Bardsey Boat Trips (see website for schedule; £30 includes a talk on history and wildlife; ✆07971 769 895, www.bardseyboattrips.com) from Porth Meudwy.

LLANGOLLEN★

12mi/19km south of Wrexham.

The verdant Vale of Llangollen and the valley of the Dee have long formed a convenient route for travellers from England on their way to North Wales.

This little market town, dominated by the dramatically sited ruins of the 12C Castle Dinas Brân, is still a popular stopping place. Llangollen hosts the **International Eisteddfod** (Festival) and many other events in and around the spectacular tent-like structure of the **Royal International Pavilion**.

Plas Newydd★ (10min on foot from the town centre, Hill Street; open 10.30am–5pm: Apr–Sept daily except Tue/Jun–Aug daily; £6; ⚫🅿✗; ✆01978 862 834; www.denbighshire.gov.uk) was the home of '**The Ladies of Llangollen**' from 1780 when they arrived from Ireland and set up house together. The lesbian relationship of Lady Eleanor Butler and Miss Sarah Ponsonby caused considerable comment in Regency Britain's high society, though they entertained a constant stream of distinguished visitors at their home. They began the transformation of a humble cottage into the eccentric 'black-and-white' building it is today. They are buried together in nearby St Collen's Church.

Llangollen Railway

Operates most days Apr–Sept and weekends and bank holidays throughout the year, see website for schedule. Standard return £15, child £8; All Day rover ticket £17, child £10. ⚫🅿✗ ✆01978 860 979 (enquiries). www.llangollen-railway.co.uk.

This is the only standard-gauge preserved steam railway in Wales, exploring the Vale of Llangollen upstream for 7.5mi/12km as far as Corwen Town. The line follows the River Dee, classed as a Site of Special Scientific Interest (SSSI), for its entire length.

Llangollen Wharf

Llangollen Wharf. Operates daily mid-Mar/Easter–Oct. Call for times. Horse-drawn barge trip 45min £7, child £3.50; 2 hrs £12.50. child £8. Aqueduct trip (2h) , booking required; £14, child £12. ⚫🅿✗ ✆01978 860 702. www.horsedrawnboats.co.uk.

Probably the most relaxing way of enjoying the scenery around Llangollen is to take a ride on a **horse-drawn barge**, on the winding Llangollen branch of the Shropshire Union Canal built by Thomas Telford. The towpaths follows the narrowing canal westward to join the Dee at Telford's **Horseshoe Falls**, a curving elegant weir in a romantic setting. You can also take motorised **aqueduct cruises**

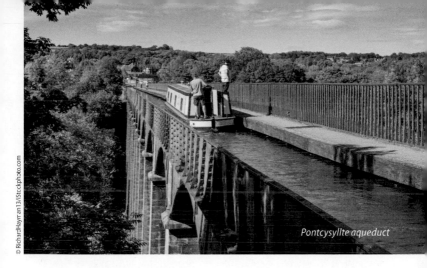

Pontcysyllte aqueduct

from here to cross the spectacular **Pont Cysyllte★★** 'stream in the sky' (⊙*see below*), or if you're in a group, hire your own barge to cross the bridge.

ERDDIG▲▲

2mi/3km S of Wrexham, off the A 525. **House**: open daily: mid-Feb–Dec 11.30am–2.30pm (late Mar–Oct 12.30–3.30pm); £11.80. **Garden**: open 11am–4pm (late Mar–Oct 10am–5pm); garden and outbuildings (summer), £7.60. ㅤㅤ℗✗ ✆01978 355 314. www.nationaltrust.org.uk/erddig.

This late-17C house was rescued in 1973 from dereliction due to mining subsidence. It contains much furniture of outstanding quality, supplied for it in the 1720s, as well as magnificent porcelain, tapestries and paintings. There is also a unique collection of portraits, photographs and poetic descriptions of staff. The restored joiner's shop, sawpit, laundry, bakehouse, kitchen and servants' hall all furnish an insight into the complex running of a country estate. The **State Bedroom** with 18C Chinese wallpaper contains a magnificently restored bed from 1720. The early-18C formal garden survives, at least in outline, and has now been restored.

CHIRK CASTLE★★

7mi/11km east of Llangollen on the A 5. Open Mar–Oct usually from noon–4pm/5pm in Apr–Sept, but check website for all other details. State Rooms by guided tour only (places limited).

Estate open all year daily 7am–7pm. £12.20, off-peak £6.10. ㅤ℗✗ ✆01691 777 701. www.nationaltrust.org.uk/chirk. Chirk Castle, or Castell y Waun, was built to a similar design to Beaumaris (⊙*see p500*), and started the same year, 1295. It has been in continuous occupation from then until the present day and shows the adaptation of a great fortress to the changing needs of later times. The **State Rooms** in the north wing are the great glory of Chirk.

The castle stands in a landscaped park of great splendour and extent, in part laid out in the late-18C by William Emes, a follower of 'Capability' Brown. Close to the house, topiary and hedging recall the formal gardens swept away by Emes, but the most distinctive feature of the grounds are the **wrought-iron gates★**, a Baroque masterpiece made at the nearby Bersham Ironworks.

PONT CYSYLLTE★★

4mi/6km east of Llangollen on the A 539.

One of the great monuments of the industrial age, this magnificent aqueduct (pronounced 'pont cuh-sull-ty') was built 1795–1810 by the great engineer Thomas Telford to carry the Ellesmere Canal over the River Dee. It is now on the UNESCO World Heritage List. Throughout its length (307m) it is accompanied by a towpath protected from the drop (37m) by iron railing. You can cross the bridge by barge.

ADDRESSES

🏠 STAY

CARDIFF

Lincoln House – 118 Cathedral Road. ☎029 2039 5558. www.lincoln-hotel.co.uk. Beautifully renovated and sympathetically furnished 23-bedroom Victorian house in an ideal central location. Friendly owners, good service.

Park Plaza – Greyfriars Road. ☎02920 111 111. www.parkplazacardiff.com. 129 rooms. Contemporary four-star city centre hotel with stunning spa (including pool), designer rooms with boutique-style trimmings and an excellent **Laguna restaurant** (*see opposite*).

SWANSEA

Morgans Hotel – Somerset Place. ☎01792 484848. www.morgans hotel.co.uk. 42 rooms. This striking luxury boutique hotel is set in a historic building previously home to the port authority, in the Maritime Quarter. The food is fashionable, served in a choice of rooms or alfresco, in sleek but casual surroundings.

PEMBROKESHIRE

The Esplanade – 1 Esplanade, Tenby. ☎01834 842 760. www.esplanade tenby.co.uk. A little old-fashioned but very comfortable rooms in a traditional family-run seaside hotel with great sea views directly over the main town beach.

St Brides Spa Hotel – St Brides Hill, Saundersfoot. ☎01834 812 304. www.stbridesspahotel.com. Contemporary luxury spa hotel, located on a headland overlooking the harbour with fabulous views (and infinity pool) over Carmarthen Bay. At The **Cliff Restaurant** sea views accompany contemporary dining.

BRECON BEACONS

Old Black Lion – Lion Street, Hay-on-Wye. ☎01497 820 841. www.oldblacklion.co.uk. 10 rooms. Parts of this 17C inn date back to the 1300s with original exposed timbers. The menu uses the best of British produce including locally reared meat.

Plough Inn – Rhosmaen, Llandeilo. ☎01558 823 431. www.plough rhosmaen.com. 23 rooms. This charming ex-farmhouse four-star boutique hotel and **restaurant** offers a gym, a sauna and panoramic countryside views.

ABERYSTWYTH

Gwesty Cymru – 19 Marine Terrace. ☎01970 612 252. www.gwesty cymru.com. 8 rooms. Enjoy breathtaking views of Cardigan Bay while enjoying a seasonal selection of contemporary Welsh food and drink in the beautiful rustic restaurant of this charming small boutique hotel.

CAERNARFON

Celtic Royal Hotel – Bangor Street. ☎01286 674 477. www.celtic-royal.co.uk. 110 rooms. The best hotel in town, very highly rated by its guests, tastefully decorated in trad-modern style with a chic Art Deco bar and leisure club (incl. 16m pool).

ANGLESEY

Ye Olde Bulls Head Inn – Castle Street, Beuamaris. ☎01248 810 329. www.bullsheadinn.co.uk. A characterful former coaching inn, dating from the 1670s. Separated into main house and town-house boasting a boutique collection of vivid, colour inspired bedrooms of matching five star quality. Award-winning **Loft Restaurant** (*see opposite*), and brasserie.

CONWY

Castle Hotel – High Street, Conwy. ☎01492 582 800. www.castlewales.co.uk. 27 rooms. This part 15C coaching inn with its unusual brick façade is one of Conwy's most-photographed buildings. The interior is elegant and contemporary; its dining room, **Dawson's** offers locally inspired brasserie classics.

SNOWDONIA

Tan y Foel – Capel Garmon. 1.6mi/2.5km from Betws-y-Coed. ☎01690 710 507. www.tyfhotel.co.uk. Dating in part from the 16C, this five-star country guesthouse has been sympathetically refurbished and styled.

HARLECH

⊖🍵🍵 – ⊖🍵🍵🍵 **Castle Cottage** – Pen Lech, Harlech. ☎01766 780 479. www.castlecottageharlech.co.uk. 7 rooms. Attractive cottage behind Harlech Castle, with cosy contemporary luxury interior. Bedrooms are spacious and comfy; some have stunning castle/ mountain views. Excellent **restaurant** (⊖🍵🍵), local produce and creative modern touches.

♀/EAT

CARDIFF

⊖🍵 **Laguna Restaurant and Bar** – Park Plaza Hotel, Greyfriars Road. ☎02920 111 111. www.parkplazacardiff.com. Smart modern restaurant serving interesting Modern (local) British dishes.

⊖🍵 **Bully's** – 5 Romilly Crescent. ☎029 2022 1905. www.bullysrestaurant.co.uk Modern French bistro dishes are served in a simply furnished interior.

SWANSEA

⊖🍵🍵 **Didier & Stephanie's** – 56 St Helens Road. ☎01792 655 603. http:// didierstephanies.restaurantwebx.com. Closed Sun–Mon. Cosy, neighbourhood styled restaurant in the Maritime Quarter with a strong Gallic influence. Welcoming owners provide tasty, good-value, seasonally changing menus with lots of French ingredients.

PEMBROKESHIRE

⊖ – ⊖🍵 **The Shed Fish and Chip Bistro** – The Quay, Porthgain (halfway between Fishguard and St David's). ☎01348 831 518. www.theshedporthgain.co.uk. At the tip of the harbour in a charming spot, this locally renowned rustic 'chippie bistro' with harbour sea views started life as a lobster pot store and now serves simply prepared, tasty seafood dishes.

⊖🍵🍵 **Cwtch** – 22 High Street, St David's. ☎01437 720 491. www.cwtchrestaurant.co.uk. Closed Sun, and Mon in winter. Pronounced 'cutsh', this friendly rustic-style restaurant features hearty portions of honest British classics, served with large sides of vegetable, followed by old-school desserts.

⊖🍵🍵🍵 **The Grove** – Molleston, Narberth. 10mi/16km N of Tenby. ☎01834 860 915. www.thegrove-narberth.co.uk.

This multi-award-winning restaurant in a charming boutique country house hotel serves gourmet Modern British food using locally sourced ingredients.

BRECON BEACONS

⊖🍵 **Nantyffin Cider Mill Inn** – Brecon Road West, Crickhowell. ☎01873 810 775. www.cidermill.co.uk. Originally a drovers' inn dating to the 16C and then a cider mill during the 19C, the building has been stunningly restored and serves Modern British cooking.

ANGLESEY

⊖🍵 **Loft Restaurant** – Ye Olde Bull's Head Inn, Castle Street. Beaumaris. ☎01248 810 329. www.bullsheadinn. co.uk/Eat. Closed Sun–Tue. Imaginative Modern British cooking supported by an excellent wine list, all set in a 17C coaching inn (&*see opposite*).

⊖🍵 **The Oyster Catcher** – Maelog Lake, Rhosneigr. ☎01407 812 829. www. oystercatcheranglesey.co.uk. Hugely popular eatery in the centre of Anglesey, in the former Maelog Lake Hotel. Well worth finding, but booking strongly advised.

⊖🍵 **Marram Grass** – White Lodge, Newborough. ☎01248 440 077. www. themarramgrass.com. Closed Mon–Wed. Developing from a simple all-day-breakfast eatery to a bistro with attitude, making the most of local produce and a creative imagination. The chef featured on the BBC programme the *Great British Menu*, so you may want to make a reservation rather than leave things to chance.

SNOWDONIA/CONWY

⊖🍵🍵 **Castle Deudraeth Brasserie** – Portmeirion Village. ☎01766 772 400. www.portmeirion-village.com. Expect locally sourced seafood, fish and lamb, classic gastropub puddings and unusual beers in this most unusual setting. Garden terrace. Free entry to the Village with two-course lunch.

⊖🍵🍵 **The Groes Inn** – 3mi/5km south of Conwy. ☎01492 650 545. www.groes inn.com. Beautifully refurbished multi-award-winning 16C hotel inn serving locally sourced Modern British cuisine and superior pub food.

INDEX

INDEX

C

M

INDEX

🛏 STAY

Ⓨ/EAT

Thematic Maps

Maps and Plans

MAP LEGEND

Highly Recommended	★★★
Recommended	★★
Interesting	★

Tourism

Sightseeing route with departure point indicated	**AZ B**	Map co-ordinates locating sights
Ecclesiastical building		Tourist information
Synagogue – Mosque		Historic house, castle – Ruins
Building (with main entrance)		Dam – Factory or power station
Statue, small building		Fort – Cave
Wayside cross		Prehistoric site
Fountain		Viewing table – View
Fortified walls – Tower – Gate		Miscellaneous sight

Recreation

Racecourse		Waymarked footpath
Skating rink		Outdoor leisure park/centre
Outdoor, indoor swimming pool		Theme/Amusement park
Marina, moorings		Wildlife/Safari park, zoo
Mountain refuge hut		Gardens, park, arboretum
Overhead cable-car		Aviary, bird sanctuary
Tourist or steam railway		

Additional symbols

Motorway (unclassified)		Post office - Telephone centre
Junction: complete, limited		Covered market
Pedestrian street		Barracks
Unsuitable for traffic, street subject to restrictions		Swing bridge
Steps - Footpath		Quarry - Mine
Railway - Coach station		Ferry (river and lake crossings)
Funicular - Rock-railway		Ferry services: Passengers and cars
Tram - Metro, underground		Foot passengers only
Bert (R.)…		Access route number common to MICHELIN maps and town plans

Abbreviations and special symbols

C	County council offices		**T**	Theatre
H	Town hall		**U**	University
J	Law courts			Park and Ride
M	Museum		**M 3**	Motorway
POL.	Police		**A 2**	Primary route

travelguide.michelin.com
www.viamichelin.com

Maps of Great Britain

Michelin maps 501, 502, 503, 504 –
Scotland; Northern England, The Midlands;
Wales, The Midlands, South West England;
South East England, The Midlands, East
Anglia (Scale 1: 400 000 -1cm = 4km - 1in:
6.30miles) cover the main regions of the
country, the network of motorways and
major roads and some secondary roads.
they provide information on shipping
routes, distances in miles and kilometres,
major town plans, services, sporting
and tourist attractions and an index of
places; the key and text are printed in
four languages.

Country Maps

The Michelin Tourist and Motoring Atlas
Great Britain & Ireland (Scale 1: 300 000 -
1cm – 3km - 1in: 4.75 miles) covers the
whole of the United Kingdom and
the Republic of Ireland, the national
networks of motorways and major
roads. It provides information on route
planning, shipping routes, distances
in miles and kilometres, over 60 town
plans, services, sporting and tourist
attractions and an index of places; the
key and text are printed in six languages.

Internet

Michelin is pleased to offer a route-
planning service on the Internet:
travelguide.michelin.com
www.viamichelin.com

Choose the shortest route,
a route without tolls, or the Michelin
recommended route to your
destination; you can also access
information about hotels and
restaurants from The Red Guide, and
tourist sites from The Green Guide.

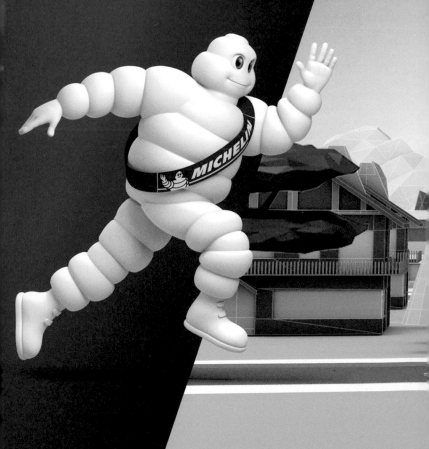

MICHELIN IS CONTINUALLY INNOVATING FOR SAFER, CLEANER, MORE ECONOMICAL, MORE CONNECTED... BETTER ALL-ROUND MOBILITY.

Tyres wear more quickly on short urban journeys.

?

TRUE!

You tend to accelerate and brake more often when driving around town so your tyres work harder!
If you are stuck in traffic, keep calm and drive slowly.

Tyre pressure only affects your car's safety.

?

FALSE!

Driving with underinflated tyres (0.5 bar below recommended pressure) doesn't just impact handling and fuel consumption, it will shave 8,000 km off tyre lifespan.
Make sure you check tyre pressure about once a month and before you go on holiday or a long journey.

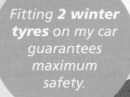

Fitting **2 winter tyres** on my car guarantees maximum safety.

FALSE!

In the winter, especially when temperatures drop below 7°C, to ensure better road holding, all four tyres should be identical and fitted at the same time.

2 WINTER TYRES ONLY – risk of compromised road holding.

4 WINTER TYRES = **safer handling** when cornering, driving downhill and braking.

If you regularly encounter rain, snow or black ice, choose a **MICHELIN Alpin tyre**. This range offers you sharp handling plus a comfortable ride to safely face the challenge of winter driving.

MICHELIN IS COMMITTED

▶ MICHELIN IS **GLOBAL LEADER IN FUEL-EFFICIENT TYRES** FOR LIGHT VEHICLES.

▶ **EDUCATING OF YOUNGSTERS IN ROAD SAFETY,** NOT FORGETTING TWO-WHEELERS. LOCAL ROAD SAFETY CAMPAIGNS WERE RUN IN **16 COUNTRIES** IN 2015.

QUIZ

1 TYRES ARE BLACK SO WHY IS THE MICHELIN MAN WHITE?

Back in 1898 when the Michelin Man was first created from a stack of tyres, they were made of natural rubber, cotton and sulphur and were therefore light-coloured. The composition of tyres did not change until after the First World War when carbon black was introduced. But the Michelin Man kept his colour!

2 FOR HOW LONG HAS MICHELIN BEEN GUIDING TRAVELLERS?

Since 1900. When the MICHELIN guide was published at the turn of the century, it was claimed that it would last for a hundred years. It's still around today and remains a reference with new editions and online restaurant listings in a number of countries.

3 WHEN WAS THE "BIB GOURMAND" INTRODUCED IN THE MICHELIN GUIDE?

The symbol was created in 1997 but as early as 1954 the MICHELIN guide was recommending "exceptional good food at moderate prices". Today, it features on the MICHELIN Restaurants website and app.

If you want to enjoy a fun day out and find out more about Michelin, why not visit the l'Aventure Michelin museum and shop in Clermont-Ferrand, France:
www.laventuremichelin.com

Reg. user No. 00/0000/P

Version A ATOC 10.15

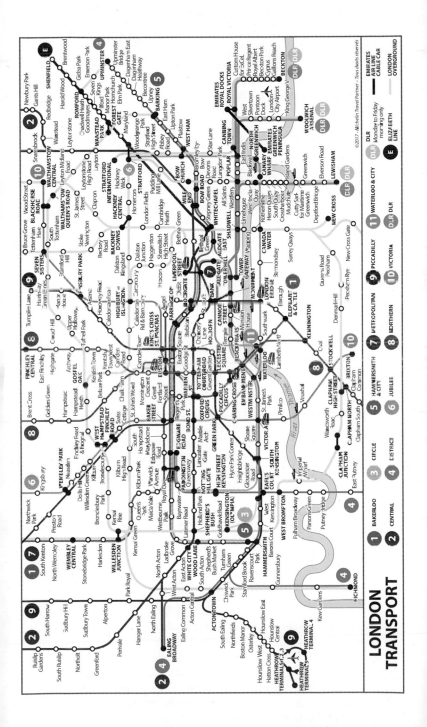

LONDON
TRANSPORT

THEGREENGUIDE **GREAT BRITAIN**

Editorial Director	Cynthia Clayton Ochterbeck
Editor	Sophie Friedman
Principal Writer	Terry Marsh
Production Manager	Natasha George
Cartography	Peter Wrenn
Photo Editor	Yoshimi Kanazawa
Interior Design	Natasha George, Jonathan P. Gilbert
Cover Design	Chris Bell, Christelle Le Déan
Layout	Natasha George

Contact Us

Michelin Travel and Lifestyle North America
One Parkway South
Greenville, SC 29615
USA
travel.lifestyle@us.michelin.com

Michelin Travel Partner
Hannay House
39 Clarendon Road
Watford, Herts WD17 1JA
UK
℘01923 205240
travelpubsales@uk.michelin.com
www.viamichelin.co.uk

Special Sales

For information regarding bulk sales,
customized editions and premium sales,
please contact us at:
travel.lifestyle@us.michelin.com